Ezra

A Critical Commentary

Ezra

A Commentary

Lisbeth S. Fried

Sheffield Phoenix Press
2017

First published in hardback, 2015.
First published in paperback, 2017.
Published by Sheffield Phoenix Press
Department of Biblical Studies, University of Sheffield
45 Victoria Street, Sheffield S3 7QB

www.sheffieldphoenix.com

A CIP catalogue record for this book
is available from the British Library

Typeset by the HK Scriptorium
Printed by Lightning Source

ISBN 978-1-909697-75-1 (hardback)
ISBN 978-1-910928-26-4 (paperback)

Contents

List of Maps

ABBREVIATIONS

AASOR	*Annual of the American Schools of Oriental Research*
AB	Anchor Bible
ABC	A.K. Grayson, *Assyrian and Babylonian Chronicles* (Winona Lake, IN: Eisenbrauns, 2000)
ABD	*Anchor Bible Dictionary*
ADAB	*Aramaic Documents from Ancient Bactria*
AEL	M. Lichtheim, *Ancient Egyptian Literature: A Book of Readings* (Berkeley, CA: University of California Press, 1980)
AJS Review	*Association for Jewish Studies Review*
AMI	*Archäologische Mitteilungen aus Iran*
ANET	*Ancient Near Eastern Texts Relating to the Old Testament with Supplement*
Ant.	Flavius Josephus, *Antiquities of the Jews*
AOAT	Alter Orient und Altes Testament
ARAB	D.D. Luckenbill, *Ancient Records of Assyria and Babylonia* (Chicago: University of Chicago Press, 1927)
BA	*Biblical Archaeologist*
BAR	*Biblical Archaeology Review*
BBSt	Babylonian Boundary Stones
BGU	Berliner griechische Urkunden
BHQ	Biblia hebraica quinta
BIFAO	*Bulletin de l'Institut français d'archéologie orientale*
BJSUCSD	Bibilical and Judaic Studies from the University of California, San Diego
BM	Tablet in the British Museum
BWANT	Beiträge zur Wissenschaft vom Alten und Neuen Testament
BZAW	Beihefte zur Zeitschrift für die alttestamentliche Wissenschaft
CAD	*The Assyrian Dictionary of the Oriental Institute of the University of Chicago*
CAL	Comprehensive Aramaic Lexicon
CBQ	*Catholic Biblical Quarterly*
CRAIBL	Comptes rendus des séances de l'Académie des inscriptions et belles-lettres

DB	Darius Behistun Inscription
DNa	Darius, Naqash-i-Rustam A
DNb	Darius, Naqash-i-Rustam B
EI	*Eretz Israel*
EPE	*Elephantine Papyri in English* (Porten)
FRLANT	Forschungen zur Religion und Literatur des Alten und Neuen Testaments
GKC	Gesenius' Hebrew Grammar
HALOT	*The Hebrew and Aramaic Lexicon of the Old Testament*
HdO	Handbook of Oriental Studies/Handbuch der Orientalistik
HL	Hittite Laws (Roth)
HUCA	*Hebrew Union College Annual*
HTR	*Harvard Theological Review*
IBHS	Bruce K. Waltke and M. O'Connor, *An Introduction to Biblical Hebrew Syntax* (Winona Lake, IN: Eisenbrauns 1990)
IEJ	*Israel Exploration Journal*
JANES	*Journal of Ancient Near Eastern Studies*
JAOS	*Journal of the American Oriental Society*
JBL	*Journal of Biblical Literature*
JHS	*Journal of Hellenic Studies*
JNES	*Journal of Near Eastern Studies*
JNSL	*Journal of Northwest Semitic Languages*
JQR	*Jewish Quarterly Review*
JSOT	*Journal for the Study of the Old Testament*
JSOTSup	*Journal for the Study of the Old Testament* Supplement Series
JSS	*Journal of Semitic Studies*
JTS	*Journal of Theological Studies*
KAI	*Kanaanäische und aramäische Inschriften*
KAJ	Keilschrifttexte aus Assur juristischen Inhalts
L&S	Liddell & Scott Greek–English Lexicon
MDAIK	*Mitteilungen des deutschen archäologischen Instituts—Abteillung Kairo*
MNDPV	*Mitteilungen und Nachrichten des deutschen Palästina-Vereins*
NABU	*Nouvelles assyriologiques breves et utilitaires*
NEAEHL	*The New Encyclopedia of Archaeological Excavations in the Holy Land*
NICOT	New International Commentary on the Old Testament
NS	New Series
OEANE	*The Oxford Encyclopedia of Archaeology in the Near East*

OLA	Orientalia lovaniensia analecta
PEFQS	*Palestine Exploration Fund, Quarterly Statement*
PEQ	*Palestine Exploration Quarterly*
PF	Persepolis Fortification Tablets (Hallock 1969)
PIHANS	Publications de l'Institut historique-archaéologique néerlandais de Stanboul
PT	Persepolis Tablets (Cameron)
RB	*Revue biblique*
RLA	*Reallexikon der Assyriologie*
SAA	State Archives of Assyria
SBL	Society of Biblical Literature
SHANE	Studies in the History of the Ancient Near East
TAD	B. Porten and A. Yardeni, *Textbook of Aramaic Documents from Ancient Egypt: Volumes A–D Newly Copied, Edited and Translated into Hebrew and English* (Winona Lake, IN: Eisenbrauns, 1986–1999)
UF	*Ugarit-Forschungen*
UT	C.H. Gordon, *Ugaritic Textbook* (Analecta orientalia, 38; Rome: Pontifical Biblical Institute Press, 1965)
VT	*Vetus Testamentum*
VTSup	Supplements to *Vetus Testamentum*
YOS	Yale Oriental Series, Texts
ZABR	*Zeitschrift für altorientalische und biblische Rechtsgeschichte*
ZAW	*Zeitschrift für die alttestamentliche Wissenschaft*
ZDPV	*Zeitschrift des deutschen Palästina-Vereins*

Preface and Acknowledgements

Ezra–Nehemiah is the only book of the Bible that portrays the period of the Judeans' return to Judah after the Babylonian Exile. In 586 BCE, Judah was conquered by Nebuchadnezzar, king of Babylon. In the process, the temple in Jerusalem was destroyed; the bulk of the population fled, was deported to Babylon, or died—either in the ensuing battles or by starvation and disease during the sieges of the cities. Forty-eight years later, in October of 539 BCE, Cyrus the Great of Persia conquered Babylon, and that summer, in 538 BCE, permitted the Judeans to return home to Judah and to rebuild their cities and their temple. The book Ezra–Nehemiah tells the story of the Judeans' return to Judah and their rebuilding their temple and city. If it were not for this book, we would know next to nothing about this important period of history.

A commentary on an ancient text must enable the modern reader to reach out across the chasms of space and time, language and custom, to touch the life of the ancient writer. It must enable the reader to understand the writer's historical context as well as his goals, objectives, preconceptions and world view. In an ancient text like that of Ezra–Nehemiah, the difficulties for the reader are numerous. To begin with, there were many authors, and they wrote over a long period of time. Moreover, they disagreed. They disagreed on the chronology of the events, on the persons of Ezra and Nehemiah, on the nature and date of their activities and on their roles in the Persian province of Yehud. I have tried to make all these various points of view, and the historical context in which they were embedded, clear and transparent to the reader. I hope I succeeded. This volume focuses on Ezra 1–10; volume II is forthcoming and will focus on Nehemiah 1–13.

Work on this commentary began almost ten years ago, when David Noel Freedman asked me to write a commentary on Ezra–Nehemiah for his new commentary series to be published by Eerdmans, to be known as the Eerdmans Critical Commentary Series. I began work very enthusiastically, but I had not progressed very far when Noel unexpected died in the spring of 2008, and Eerdmans terminated the series. The work languished until 2012, when Tamara Eskenazi suggested I write to David J.A. Clines to see if he would be interested in publishing my commentary on Ezra–Nehemiah for Sheffield Phoenix Press. He was! I began work on it again in earnest.

I would like to thank David Clines for accepting this commentary for publication and Tamara Eskenazi for suggesting it. I would also like to thank the many who read parts or even all of the previous drafts and made many helpful suggestions. (If I didn't always follow them, please forgive me.) These are David Noel Freedman ז״ל, Mark Boda, Baruch A. Levine, Marvin Lloyd Miller, Edward Jay Mills, Bezalel Porten, Philip Schmitz, Carla Salzbach, and Hugh Williamson. Thank you, thank you. All errors are my own. I also thank Gary Beckman and the Department of Near Eastern Studies at the University of Michigan for their unflagging support and encouragement of my work. I thank Karl Longstreth of the University of Michigan Map Library for his patience in drawing and redrawing the maps for this volume. I thank my daughter Carrie Fried Thorpe for being available to answer grammar questions and for her suggestion on formatting the volume. I also want to thank the terrific people at Sheffield Phoenix Press, particularly Ailsa Parkin and Paul Kobelski, for their painstaking work in editing my manuscript and for turning all my errant 'whiches' into 'thats', and to thank Duncan Burns of Forthcoming Publications for the reference index. Primarily I offer thanks to my wonderful husband for creating the bibliography, the list of abbreviations, his humor, his companionship, and his love during fifty years of marriage. Thank you.

Ann Arbor
June 9, 2015
Sivan 22, 5775

Introduction to the Books Ezra–Nehemiah

Ezra and Nehemiah are the two narrative books of the Bible that portray the period of the Judeans' return to Judah after the Babylonian Exile. In 586 BCE, Judah was conquered by Nebuchadnezzar, king of Babylon (see Comment C of Ezra 1). In the process, the temple in Jerusalem was destroyed, and the bulk of the population fled, was deported to Babylon, or killed—either in the ensuing battles or by starvation and disease during the sieges of the cities (Faust 2011). Forty-eight years later, in October of 539 BCE, Cyrus the Great of Persia conquered Babylon, and according to the biblical text (Ezra 1.1-4), that summer, in 538 BCE, he issued an edict permitting the Judeans to return home to Judah and to rebuild their cities and their temple (see Comment A of Ezra 1). The books of Ezra and Nehemiah tell the story of the Judeans' return to Judah and the rebuilding of their temple and city. If it were not for these two books, we would know next to nothing about this important period of history.

The purpose of Ezra–Nehemiah is to tell the story of the return to Judah, but more importantly it is to tell of the enduring faithfulness of Israel's god, Yhwh, who resurrected Israel from the dead and returned her to life in her new land (Ezra 3.11; cf. Ezek. 37.1-13; Holmgren 1987). Ezra 1–6 tells the story of how God led the Judeans back to resettle Judah and to rebuild their temple in Jerusalem after nearly fifty years of exile in Babylon. Ezra 1 begins with the statement that Yhwh 'stirred up the spirit of Cyrus' and commanded Cyrus to build him a temple in Jerusalem (Ezra 1.1, 2). Ezra 6 concludes with a celebration of the temple's dedication in the sixth year of Darius (Ezra 6.15-18).

In Ezra 7 a shift begins in the narrative from rebuilding the temple and reestablishing its sacrifices to installing torah law in Judah (Rothenbusch 2012: 47). Ezra, described as a priest and scribe of the law of Moses, arrives in Jerusalem in the seventh year of Artaxerxes with a desire to teach torah law in Judah (Ezra 7.10). As part of his effort, he brings about a mass divorce of the people from their foreign wives and so purifies them from all foreign influences (Ezra 9–10).

The book of Nehemiah, which follows Ezra in the biblical canon, tells the story of Nehemiah's arrival in Jerusalem as the Persian governor of Judah in the twentieth year of King Artaxerxes of Persia. Nehemiah rebuilds and rededicates the city walls and establishes the now-purified population within them (Nehemiah 1–6, 11–12). The climax of Ezra–Nehemiah is the so-called covenant renewal ceremony (Nehemiah 8–10) in which Ezra reads the law of Moses (the torah) to the assembled populace in Jerusalem. The people respond by affirming their allegiance to their torah, their temple, and their god. Nehemiah 13 can be viewed as a coda that ends Ezra–Nehemiah (Eskenazi 1988: 6). This chapter looks back on the main body of the work and recapitulates the various themes in the two books.

Throughout Ezra–Nehemiah, the major story is that of Yhwh's restoring his people to their homeland. Those who had been taken into captivity into Babylon in 586 BCE by the Babylonians had neither been forsaken nor forgotten. God remembered them and enabled them to leave the place where they had been strangers and to return home. Not only had God not forsaken them, but they had not forsaken God. They returned to Judah as soon as they were able, and once there they rushed to rebuild the altar and resume the sacrifices as they had done before the exile. They rebuilt the temple and Jerusalem's city wall, each in the place where it had stood, and they settled within the rebuilt city walls a population newly dedicated to the law of God as taught by Ezra. The people's dedication to the temple and the law reaffirmed the covenant between God and his people Israel. As in the story of the exodus, God again brought his people to their land, and the people again affirmed their allegiance and their dependence on him.

The Original Form of the Book

Is Ezra–Nehemiah One Book or Two?

Earliest evidence points to Ezra–Nehemiah's acceptance as one book, called simply Ezra. The Septuagint (LXX) includes Ezra and Nehemiah as one book labeled Esdras β, or 2 Esdras. Dated by scholars to the second / first century BCE (Z. Talshir 1999, 2001), it is a literal Greek translation of both Ezra and Nehemiah. Chapters 1–10 translate canonical Ezra, and chaps. 11–23 translate canonical Nehemiah. The Talmud (*Baba Bathra* 14b and 15a) counts Ezra and Nehemiah as a single book, and the Masoretes total the words of both Ezra and Nehemiah together (685), counting the middle of the text at Neh. 3.32, not at the end of Ezra.

Although, according to earliest tradition, Ezra and Nehemiah formed one book called Ezra, scholars have questioned whether these texts were written originally as one book or as two. Several ancient authors mention Nehemiah, but do not appear to know Ezra (i.e. Sir. 49.12-13; 2 Macc. 1.18, 20-36); and 1 Esdras knows Ezra, but does not seem to know about Nehemiah. Further, Josephus's story of Ezra (*Ant.* 11.1-158) is based on 1 Esdras, and he does not begin his story of Nehemiah until he has narrated Ezra's death (*Ant.* 11.158).

The current story of Ezra–Nehemiah must be seen as one book however. Ezra arrives in Jerusalem in order to teach statute and ordinance in Israel (Ezra 7.10). Yet the story of Ezra's teaching the law to the assembled populace is not told until chap. 8 of Nehemiah. Moreover, the book of Nehemiah begins, 'The [following are the] words of Nehemiah son of Hacaliah: "In the month of Chislev, in the twentieth year, while I was in Susa the capital, one of my brothers came [to me]"' (Neh. 1.1-2). The twentieth year refers to the twentieth year of the reign of a king, but we are not told which king. The reader does not need to be told this, since it would be assumed that the same king, Artaxerxes, who was the king in the previous four chapters, that is, in Ezra 7–10, is meant (Min 2004: 25-26). Although the final product must be read as one book (*pace* VanderKam 1992; Kraemer 1993; Becking 1998), it includes the work of several independent authors and editors, whose writings have now been completely intertwined.

Are Chronicles and Ezra–Nehemiah One Book, Two, or Three?

Many commentators beginning with Zunz (1832) have concluded that Ezra–Nehemiah is a continuation of the books of Chronicles and was written by the same author, the Chronicler (e.g. Batten 1913; Rudolph 1949; Freedman 1961; Haran 1986; Blenkinsopp 1988; Z. Talshir 1986; 1999: 22-36; D. Talshir 1988). They base this on the fact that the last few verses of 2 Chronicles are duplicated in the first verses of Ezra. They also point to the Greek apocryphal book 1 Esdras, which begins with all of chaps. 35–36 of 2 Chronicles, and continues directly to the story of Ezra with no break and no repetition of the verses. Torrey deviates from this view slightly in that he suggests that the Chronicler wrote Chronicles and continued with 1 Esdras, ending with Ezra's reading the law, and so did not write Nehemiah (Torrey 1970 [1910]). Besides the repetition of the verses, these scholars also maintain that Chronicles and Ezra–Nehemiah should be considered as one book because of the many linguistic features (140!) that the two books share (Torrey 1896; Driver 1913: 535-40; Curtis and Madsen 1910: 27-36). However, these similarities can be attributed to the nature of the language stratum—late Biblical Hebrew—and not to the identity of the author(s) (Williamson 1977: 37-59). Japhet has shown, more importantly, that the linguistic forms that the Chronicler has rigidly altered in his sources (i.e. in Samuel and Kings) remain unaffected in the Nehemiah memoir, thus demonstrating that the Chronicler could not have been the one who incorporated Nehemiah's memoir into the book of Ezra–Nehemiah (Japhet 1968).

What Was the Original Form of the Book?

Ezra–Nehemiah should be considered one book—the themes begun in Ezra are not completed until the end of Nehemiah. This does not address the composition process. Were they composed originally as one book or two?

One key to understanding Ezra–Nehemiah's transmission history lies in the lists of returnees in Ezra 2 and Nehemiah 7 (Williamson 1983; 1985: xxxiii-xxxv; Gunneweg 1985: 53; Pakkala 2004: 137-44). Not only are these lists identical (except for errors of transmission), but they conclude with a similar narrative verse: the notice that, when the seventh month arrived and the people Israel were settled in their towns, they gathered as one man in Jerusalem:

> When the seventh month arrived—the Israelites being in their towns—the entire people assembled as one man in Jerusalem (Ezra 3.1).

> When the seventh month arrived—the Israelites being in their towns—the entire people assembled as one man in the square before the Water Gate (Neh. 7.72–8.1).

The intent of this narrative verse is to link the population as a whole (as one) to what follows, but Ezra 3 continues with an account of Zerubbabel and his kin and Jeshua and his fellow priests setting up the temple's sacrificial altar sometime in the reign of Darius—between 520 and 516 BCE (see the discussion at Ezra 2.2 and at 3.2, 3), whereas Nehemiah 8 continues its narrative with the story of Ezra reading the law to the gathered populace in the time of Nehemiah and King Artaxerxes (445 BCE). Since only the story of the reading of the law in Nehemiah 8 actually involves the entire population, the narrative linking verse must be original to Nehemiah 8, not to Ezra 3 (Fried 2008).

This suggests that there must have been at least two authors: an earlier one who compiled Ezra 7–Nehemiah 13 and a later one who added Ezra 2, if not all of Ezra 1–6, copying Ezra 2 from Nehemiah 7. The earlier author created his story from Nehemiah's original memoir and from an early version of Ezra's story. The later author then prefaced the story of Ezra–Nehemiah that he received with an account of the return to Judah, and the rebuilding and dedication of the temple. This later writer, who created the final form of the text, was likely a priest. He interpreted the construction of the city wall and the people's recommitment to the torah as a consequence of the rebuilt House of God.

When Was Ezra–Nehemiah Written?

The dates of the individual components of Ezra–Nehemiah (e.g. the letters, Nehemiah's memoir) will be discussed *ad loc.* Determining the date of the final redaction of Ezra–Nehemiah, however, comes down to one verse, Neh. 12.22, and one name in the verse, 'Yaddua'. The verse lists the last four priests of the Persian Empire, up to 'Darius the Persian', that is, Darius III (up to 331 BCE), as Eliyashib, Yoiada (Yehoiada), Yoḥanan (Yehoḥanan), and Yaddua. The list of priests in Neh. 12.22 is complete to Darius III (Fried

2003a; VanderKam 2004: 44-99). Ezra–Nehemiah therefore must have been finalized during the Hellenistic period, that is, after the conquest of Alexander (330–323 BCE), perhaps in the early Ptolemaic period. Constituent elements would be earlier.

Location of Ezra–Nehemiah in the Canon

In the LXX and Vulgate, Ezra–Nehemiah follows Chronicles immediately, reflecting an early Babylonian Talmudic tradition that the former is a direct continuation of the latter. (This is also the order followed in most Christian Bibles.) In the Hebrew Bible, however, the books are not always together. The Aleppo and Leningrad Codices, for example, follow the Palestinian tradition in which Chronicles is placed first among the Writings and Ezra–Nehemiah last in that section and last in the Bible, in what D.N. Freedman calls an 'envelope construction'. Freedman suggests that the repetition of the end of Chronicles at the beginning of Ezra acts as an *inclusio*, indicating that the intervening books are to be read as a unit (personal communication). However, in the Babylonian Talmud's list of the order of the biblical books (*B. Bat.* 14b), the books are placed next to each other, with Ezra–Nehemiah unexpectedly preceding Chronicles, setting Chronicles as the last book in the Hebrew Bible. (This is the order followed in most Hebrew Bibles today). Placing Chronicles last allows the Bible to end with Cyrus's command to the Talmud's post-70 readers to go up to Jerusalem and rebuild their temple (2 Chron. 36.23).

Ancient Witnesses to the Text

The text of Ezra–Nehemiah employed in this commentary is the Masoretic Text (MT) as presented in the *Biblia hebraica quinta* (BHQ). The MT is defined as the agreement between three Tiberian manuscripts: the Leningrad Codex, manuscript EPB, I B 19a of the Russian National Library, St Petersburg, dated to 1008 CE; a tenth-century manuscript, Sassoon 1053, housed in the National Library of Israel; and manuscript 1753 of the Cambridge University Library (Marcus 2006: x, 8*). This last manuscript is Yemenite, but is very close to the Leningrad Codex. In fact, the three manuscripts differ only slightly, and only orthographically. Unfortunately, about one-third of Ezra–Nehemiah in the Sassoon manuscript is lost, and parts of the existing text are damaged and difficult to read (Marcus 2006: 8*). All three manuscripts place Ezra–Nehemiah last among the biblical books, and all three are preceded by Daniel, not Chronicles. This resulting eclectic text of Ezra–Nehemiah is the text presented in *BHQ, although the order of the books in these codices has been abandoned.

Prior to 1947 there were no Hebrew manuscripts earlier than these from the medieval period. In 1947, however, manuscripts were found in the caves above the Dead Sea (i.e. the so-called Dead Sea Scrolls), the oldest of which date to the second century BCE. Other manuscripts were found in the ruins of the Herodian fortress on Masada (which date to before 73 CE) and in other caves of the Judean desert (copied before 135 CE). Among the fragments at Qumran were several of Ezra (Ulrich 1992; Z. Talshir 2003) and one of Nehemiah (Charlesworth, in press). These are Ezra 4.2-6 (= 1 Esd. 5.66-70), Ezra 4.9-11 (no 1 Esdras parallel), and Ezra 5.17–6.5 (=1 Esd. 6.20-25), and Neh. 3.14-15. Except for orthographic differences, the manuscripts found at Qumran and in the Judean desert differ little from one another or from the consonantal text of the Leningrad Codex. In spite of the care with which these texts were preserved and copied, however, the Masoretes record 53 *kethib–qere* differences in Ezra–Nehemiah. That is, the Masoretes note that what is written in the body of the text (i.e. the *kethib*) is not to be read, but rather the *qere*, which they have written in the margin, is to be read instead. These differences note very early textual variants or scribal corrections that have been maintained over the millennia. These will be discussed in the course of the commentary as they occur.

Other witnesses to the Hebrew text are the two translations into Greek included in the Septuagint (LXX). One, called Esdras β or 2 Esdras, is a literal translation of the canonical Ezra–Nehemiah of MT (Marcus 2006: 9*). 2 Esdras is so-called because it is preceded in the LXX by an apocryphal version of Ezra, called Esdras α or 1 Esdras (Z. Talshir 1999). The basic texts of both these Greek versions are those prepared by Robert Hanhart, which primarily follow the text of MS Vaticanus (Hanhart 1974, 1993). There are major differences between the two versions of Ezra (i.e. between the MT of Ezra and 2 Esdras on the one hand, and 1 Esdras on the other). For example, both Ezra and 2 Esdras begin with the last two verses of Chronicles, whereas 1 Esdras includes Chronicles' entire last two chapters at its beginning. Second, the story of Zerubbabel's return to Judah and the chapters containing the correspondence with King Artaxerxes have exchanged positions in the two versions. Third, 1 Esdras contains a story of King Darius and his three bodyguards that is not present in MT Ezra or 2 Esdras; and finally, MT Ezra–Nehemiah and 2 Esdras contain the story of Nehemiah, which is omitted from 1 Esdras. Both versions include the story of Ezra. (For discussions of the different views of the relative priority of MT Ezra and 1 Esdras, see the articles in Fried 2011.)

In addition to the two Greek versions of Ezra, the Peshitta (Leiden Peshitta Project, CAL on-line version) is a translation into Syriac of the MT Ezra–Nehemiah that was maintained by the Syrian church. Although its origin is not known, the initial translation was likely completed in the first or second centuries CE essentially as a literal translation of the Hebrew. The earliest extant manuscripts are from the seventh and eighth centuries CE.

There are also two Latin translations—the Old Latin (derived from the apparatus of Hanhart 1993) and the Vulgate (Gasquet 1926–1987). Both are extremely literal translations of the Hebrew (Marcus 2006: 11*). The Latin editions label canonical Ezra as 1 Esdras, canonical Nehemiah as 2 Esdras, and the Greek 1 Esdras as 3 Esdras. The separation of Ezra and Nehemiah into two books is based on the Vulgate.

Since the manuscripts of these translations are older than the medieval copies we possess of the Hebrew (but not older than the fragments from the Judean Desert or the Dead Sea), it is possible to use them to reconstruct a putative original Hebrew text that lay behind them—that is, the texts' *Vorlage*. The assumption is that if the content of an ancient translation is the same as the Masoretic, then the translation's Hebrew *Vorlage* was indeed the Masoretic text. If not, it may suggest a version closer to the original than the present medieval text from which we are working.

Where Was Ezra–Nehemiah Written?

Jerusalem

Ezra–Nehemiah was finalized most likely in the Ptolemaic province of Yehud (Judah), in its capital, the city of Jerusalem, during the last quarter of the fourth century at the earliest. Archaeology shows that even in the late-fourth century Jerusalem continued to be small and thinly populated (Faust 2012a: 125; Finkelstein 2008a). It seems to have been inhabited only by temple personnel before Nehemiah built its walls and forcibly brought people into it (Neh. 3; 11.1; Lipschits 2001a; *pace* Finkelstein 2008a), but even after that effort, the built-up area of Jerusalem and its population was still no more than several hundred inhabitants (Finkelstein 2008a). The historicity of Nehemiah and his wall will be discussed further in the comment to Nehemiah 3.

Yehud

It is not likely that Yehud's provincial boundaries changed with the Macedonian conquest and the beginning of Ptolemaic rule at the end of the fourth century (Lipschits 2005: 146-49; Kasher 1990: 14-26). Therefore, we may use evidence from both the Achaemenid and early Hellenistic periods to determine Yehud's boundaries. The city lists in Ezra 2/Nehemiah 7, Nehemiah 3, and Neh. 11.25-36 have often been used to determine the boundaries of Yehud, yet use of these lists is problematic since there is very little overlap among them. One would expect, for example, that the list of cities in Nehemiah 3 would comprise the area over which Nehemiah held jurisdiction as governor of Yehud. Of the cities listed there, only two—Jericho

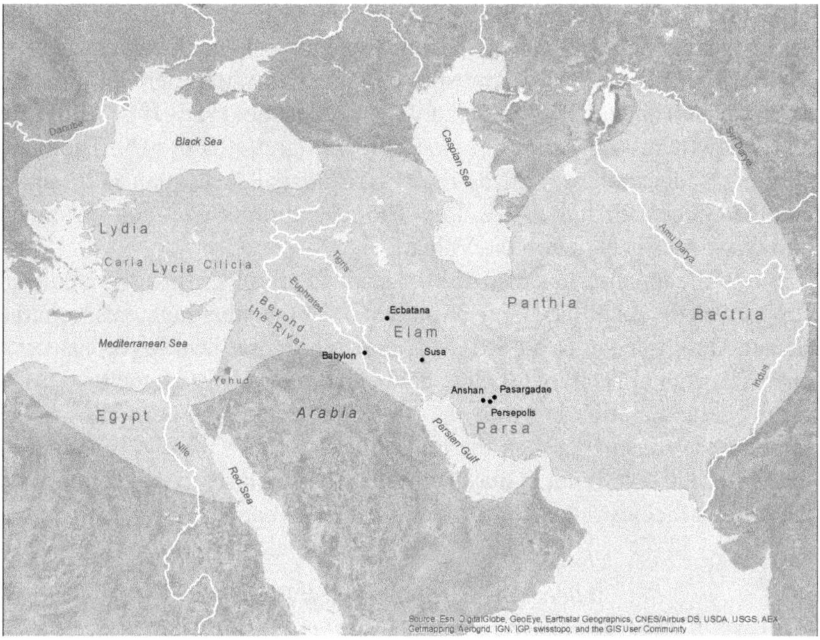

The Persian Empire at its Greatest Extent. Map courtesy of Karl Longstreth of the University of Michigan Map Library.

and Gibeon (Gibbar in Ezra 2)—are also listed in Ezra 2. Jerusalem itself is not mentioned in Ezra 2/Nehemiah 7.

The distribution of seal impressions on jars with the name Yehud, as well as the distribution of Yehud coins from the Persian and Ptolemaic periods, provides a way to determine the boundaries of the province of Yehud independent of the biblical lists. The distribution of these coins and impressions must be used cautiously, however, since the presence of a seal impression or a coin may result from travelers and may not indicate actual provincial boundaries (Lemaire 1990: 36; Carter 1999: 89-90). Seal impressions on sherds of pottery written in both Aramaic and Hebrew with the name Yehud (spelled *yhd* or *yhwd*) have been found in several Judean sites, with over half of them from Ramat Raḥel (307 sherds). The other sites are Jerusalem/City of David (136); Jerusalem/Western Hill and vicinity (27); Tell en-Naṣbeh (19); Jericho (18); Nebi Samuel (16); En-Gedi (10); Gezer (8); Rogem Gannim (7) plus 21 from other sites, and 13 with no known provenance (Stern 2001: 548; Lipschits and Vanderhooft 2011: 10-22).

Yehud's Southern Border. The most southerly point from which Persian Yehud stamp impressions or coins were found is Beth-Zur (Khirbet

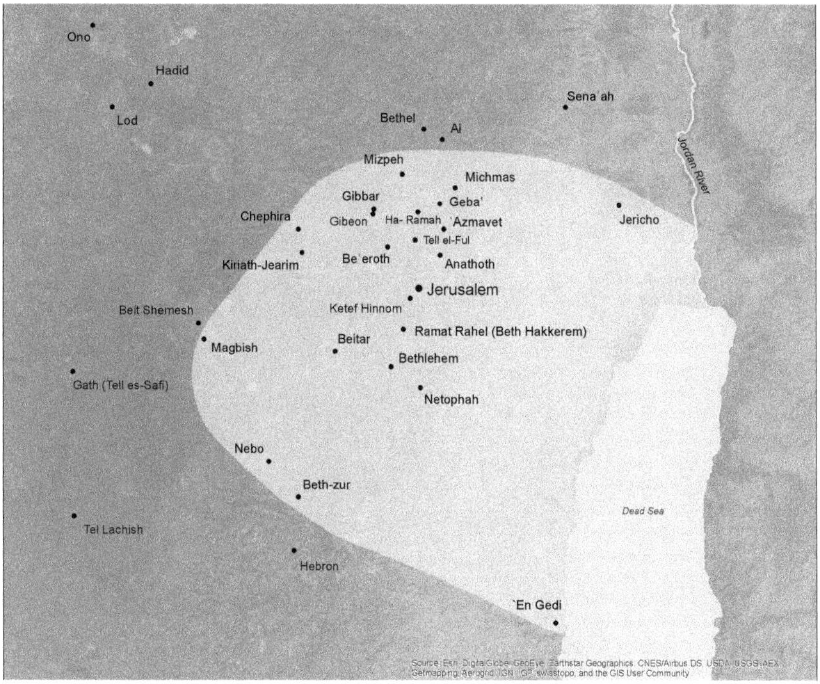

The Province of Yehud. Map courtesy of Karl Longstreth of the University of Michigan Map Library.

et-Tubeiqah), about 30 km. S of Jerusalem and 6 km. N of Hebron (Funk 1993: 259). After a long gap in settlement during the Babylonian period, sparse occupation resumed with the Persians in the mid-fifth century (Funk 1993: 261; Carter 1999: 153). The excavator noted clear traces of the Persian period, including seven jars that were found *in situ* beneath a pavement containing Hellenistic pottery. One jar contained an Attic tetradrachma, which is dated to the year 450 BCE (Stern 1982: 36). A study of the finds shows additional pottery and other objects from the Persian period. Aside from the tetradrachma found in the sealed Persian period context, six more coins from Athens, plus coins from Gaza, Sidon and Tyre, were found on the site, all dated to the fifth and fourth centuries. Most striking, a coin inscribed 'Yeḥizqiyah the governor' in Hebrew (*yḥzqyh hpḥh*) was found in a reservoir along with Persian period pottery (Stern 1982: 36). Such coins date to the last half-century of the Persian period (370–330 BCE; Fried 2003a). The complete absence of *yhd/yhwd* seal impressions has led some archaeologists to conclude that although Beth Zur was inhabited in the Persian period, it was not part of Yehud, and that Ramat Raḥel formed the southern boundary (e.g. Finkelstein 2010). Others maintain, conversely,

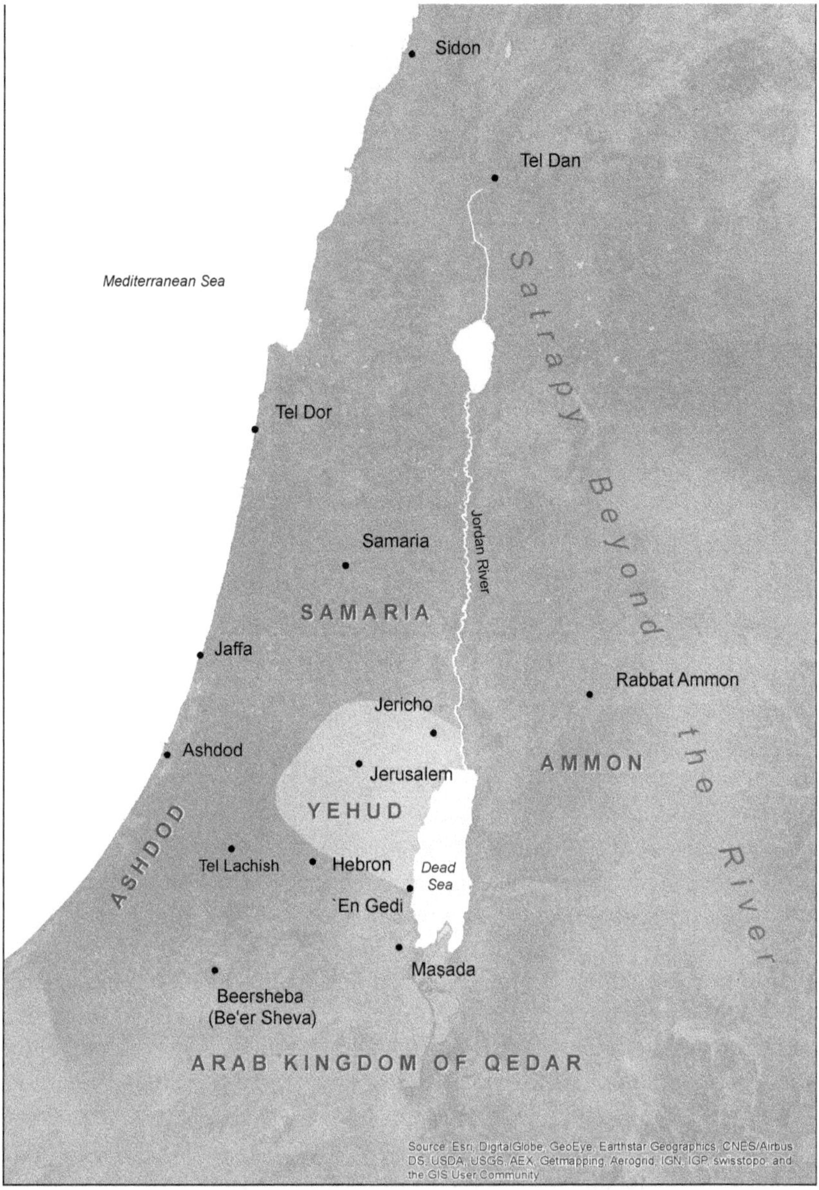

The Satrapy of Beyond-the-River. Map courtesy of Karl Longstreth of the University of Michigan Map Library.

that the absence of seal impressions at Beth Zur indicates that the distribution of seal impressions cannot delineate the full extent of the borders of the province (Lipschits 2005: 146-49; Lipschits and Vanderhooft 2011: 25). These scholars maintain that, since Beth Zur formed the southern boundary of Judah prior to the Maccabee expansions (1 Macc. 4.60), it would have formed the southern boundary of Judah as well (Lemaire 1990; Lipschits 2005: 140).

Drawing Yehud's southern border may depend on understanding the purpose of the jar seals. These were most likely stamped on jars used to collect taxes paid in kind in the form of wine and oil, probably to pay gubernatorial officials first and satrapal officials second. It would have been too costly to ship these commodities overland all the way to Susa. To pay the imperial taxes, commodities like oil and wine would have had to have been converted into silver ingots or coins. Indeed, market quotations from Babylonian diaries reveal that prices of all sorts of commodities decreased greatly during the Achaemenid and Seleucid empires as the great kings hoarded silver (Slotsky 1997). Since only major cities could provide the markets in which goods were exchanged for silver, it is possible that even if Beth Zur housed a Persian citadel and was a collection point for taxes paid in kind, the jars would not have remained there but would have been sent to Jerusalem (or Ramat Raḥel) for both the payment of salaries and to be exchanged into silver. With caution we may suppose that Beth Zur stood on the southern boundary of Yehud.

En-Gedi (Tel Goren), 800 m W of the Dead Sea and 41 km. SE of Jerusalem, is the primary southern site where jar handles were found stamped with *yh, yhd* and *yhwd* seals, and so may also have been a collection site for provincial taxes. Small amounts of Persian period pottery were also found. A significant amount of Attic pottery enables the site to be dated positively to the fifth and fourth centuries, when it was abandoned (Carter 1999: 158-89; *pace* Faust 2012a: 27).

Based on seals and coins, the southern border of Yehud may be estimated by a line extending from Beth-Zur down to En-Gedi on the Dead Sea (Lipschits 2005: 140; *pace* Lemaire 1990: 41, who does not include En-Gedi). This means that important pre-exilic cities such as Hebron and Lachish, as well as all the cities in the Negev (e.g. Arad and Beersheba), were not included in Persian period Yehud.

None of the cities listed in Ezra 2/Nehemiah 7 is south of the Beth-Zur—En-Gedi border. The list of towns named in Ezra 2/Nehemiah 7 can be supplemented by the home towns of the builders listed in Nehemiah 3. The southern towns cited there (Tekoa‘, Zanoah, Beth-Hakkerem [which might be Ramat Raḥel], and Beth-Zur) are all on or north of the Beth-Zur—En-Gedi southern border proposed here.

The Arab Kingdom of Qedar. South of Persian Yehud lay the Arab kingdom of Qedar. According to Herodotus (3.5-7),

> The road [to Egypt] runs from Phoenicia as far as the borders of the city of Cadytis [Gaza], which belongs to the Syrians of Palestine, as it is called. From Cadytis (which, as I judge, is a city not much smaller than Sardis) to the city of Ienysus the seaports belong to the Arabians.

The city of Ienysus has not been identified, but both Khan Yunis (Avi-Yonah 1961: 44; Katzenstein 1989: 70-71) and Tell er-Ruqeish (Lemaire 1994: 25) have been suggested. A twenty-mile coastal area south of Gaza thus belonged to Arabia, as well as 'a wide territory for as much as three day's journey, wondrous waterless' (Herod. 3.5). This seems to include the Sinai, the Negev, and the Arabah south to the Gulf of Aqaba/Eilat (Lemaire 1994). Under the Ptolemies the area was the kingdom of Idumea, ruled by the Edomites, with its capital at Maresha.

Among the Arab tribes were the North Arab Qedarites mentioned numerous times in the Bible (see esp. Jer. 49.28-33). During the time of Nehemiah, its king was Geshem or Gashmu (Neh. 2.19; 4.1; 6.1-9; see further discussion *ad loc.*). and its capital was at Lachish (Lemaire 1994). The area of Qedar extended south from the southern border of Yehud all the way to the Nile Valley, west to the Mediterranean south of Gaza, and east at least to Dedan (see also Graf 1990; Kloner and Stern 2007: 139).

Yehud's Northern Border. Excavations at Jericho reveal Persian period strata, including wedge- and reed-decorated pottery and Attic vessels dated to the fifth and fourth centuries BCE. Seal impressions with *yhwd* and with the name Uriahu Yehud (*'uryhw/yhwd)* were uncovered there, but in an unstratified location (Carter 1999: 162). It was certainly part of the province of Yehud.

On a line with Jericho is Tel en-Naṣbeh, biblical Mizpeh, 12 km. N of Jerusalem. Mizpeh and Jericho are the northernmost cities in which Persian period *yh(w)d* stamp seals were found. Accordingly, the line from Mizpeh to Jericho appears to have been the northern border of the province. This excludes both Bethel and Ai.

Samaria. On Judah's northern border was the province of Samaria, called Shomron in Hebrew and Aramaic. This area is attested as an Assyrian province from 722 BCE when the northern kingdom of Israel fell to the Assyrians (Stern 2001: 49-51). Its capital was the city of Samaria/Sebaste. The province of Samaria/Shomron continued into the Hellenistic period.

Yehud's Eastern and Western Borders. The easternmost point of Yehud, based on stamp seal impressions, was the city of Jericho. The eastern border of the province continued south to Netophah, to Tekoa, and as far as En-Gedi. Beyond these towns was the desert fringe, which sloped down to the Jordan River. Across the river from Jericho was Ammon, the northern area of present-day Jordan. Excavations in Jordan reveal that the Ammonites continued in Ammon after the destruction of Jerusalem and into the Persian period (Herr 1993, 1999; Lipschits 2004). It does not appear that they were deported. Seals have been found written in the Ammonite language, but using Aramaic letters. These seals, dated to the end of the sixth or the beginning of the fifth century BCE, bear the inscription Shuba' Ammon (*šb' 'mn*), indicating that Ammon, like Yehud, was a province of the satrapy Beyond-the-River from the beginning of the Persian period. Shuba' was likely the then governor of the Persian province of Ammon. Herr (1993) notes that prior to the mid-sixth century BCE, seals were written in Ammonite, but afterward in Aramaic, the language of the Persian Empire, indicating a loss of independence. South of Ammon was the Arab kingdom of Qedar.

Yehud's western border should be determined in the same manner as its northern and southern borders—by the distribution of Yehud coins and seal impressions. Beth Zur has not revealed seal impressions, but a rare Yehud coin was found there. Drawing a line from Beth-Zur northward to Mizpeh includes all the sites listed in Ezra 2 except for Ono, Lod and Hadid. These towns in the Shephelah very likely belonged to Phoenicia at the time, even though three Judean seal impressions dating to this period were found there (two to the late-sixth or fifth century and one to the fourth or third century; Lipschits and Vanderhooft 2011: 30). The funerary inscription of the Sidonian king Eshmun'azor II (mid-fifth century) states that he received from the king of Persia:

> Dor and Jaffa, the mighty lands of Dagon, which are in the Plain of Sharon, in accordance with the important deeds which I did. And we added them to the borders of the country, so that they would belong to Sidon forever (ll. 19-20, *ANET*^{3} 662).

The mention of Dor and Jaffa indicates that the entire northern coastal plain was placed under Sidonian, that is Phoenician, control, and was outside the jurisdiction of Yehud. Moreover, the fact that Sanballat and Geshem the Arab sent to Nehemiah suggesting they meet in one of the villages in the plain of Ono (Neh. 6.2) implies that Ono was neutral territory for all three governors and so outside of the jurisdictions of Judah, Samaria and the Arab kingdom of Qedar. It was likely under Phoenician control, a control that continued into Hellenistic times.

South of Phoenicia lay the coastal cities of Philistia. Four of the five cities of biblical Philistia were also prominent in the Persian period—Ashdod, Ashkelon, Gath (probably Tell eṣ-Safi), and Gaza—all Phoenician at this time. Ekron was not resettled in the Babylonian and Persian periods after its destruction by the Babylonians in 604 BCE, but was apparently ceded to Jonathan the Maccabee in 147 BCE, extending the western border of Judah (1 Macc. 10.89; Lipschits 2005: 148). A major Persian period occupation level was unearthed at Ashdod, and just north of it a Persian period fortress was discovered (Stern 2001: 407). Other Persian period cities dotted the coast; it seems that the whole coast was heavily populated. Like other coastal cities, Ashkelon was destroyed by the Babylonians in 603 BCE but recovered in the Persian period. Recent excavations reveal the Persian period stratum at Ashkelon to be one of the richest at the site (Stern 2001: 409). Persian period remains, dated from the end of the sixth or the beginning of the fifth century BCE, were found built directly over the destroyed seventh-century stratum. They were dated by the presence of Greek Attic ware, as well as by Corinthian and Ionian deposits. Other imports arrived from Egypt, Cyprus, Italy and Persia. The predominant form of the material culture in all these former Philistine sites was Phoenician. In addition to the pottery, Phoenician personal names on the seals, ostraca and inscriptions confirm a Phoenician identity. Moreover, an ostracon found at Nebi-Yunis near Ashdod is dedicated to the 'Lord of Tyre', and emblems of the Phoenician goddess Tanit-Pane-Ba'al were recovered at Ashdod-Yam and Ashkelon. Favissae, or deposits of cult objects, belonging to Persian period temples located at former Philistine cities reveal Phoenician cult objects, not Philistine.

Conclusions

The boundaries outlined here (Beth Zur to Mizpah to Jericho to En-Gedi) delimit a very small Yehud, 1,318 sq. km. (521 sq. miles, one-third the size of Rhode Island), surrounded on all sides by competitive and sometimes hostile neighbors—Samaritans, Ammonites, Idumeans, Arabs and Phoenicians.

The Political Status of Persian Yehud at the Time of the Return

Alt (1953) argued that when Judah fell to the Babylonians, the latter appointed Gedaliah in charge of Judah, but under Samaria's supervision—a status it retained under the first Persian emperors. Nehemiah's visit marked a change in Achaemenid policy; only then did Judah achieve provincial status with its own governor. This renewal of Judean independence was what caused the conflict between Judah and her neighbors, especially Samaria, because it meant a real diminution of Samaritan power.

Alt based his theory on a misunderstanding of the political situation revealed in Ezra 4–6. According to Ezra 4.7-9, high officials in the satrapy of Beyond-the-River wrote an accusation against the Judeans to King Artaxerxes urging him to order the rebuilding of Jerusalem's city walls to be stopped. Artaxerxes assented, commanding those officials to stop Jerusalem's reconstruction (Ezra 4.21). Soldiers hurried to Jerusalem and by force of arms made the Judeans cease wall-building (Ezra 4.23). Because Reḥum, the official corresponding with Artaxerxes, had his seat of office in Samaria (Ezra 4.17), Alt naturally assumed that Judah was under the jurisdiction of Samaria and was not originally a separate province. Alt misunderstood Reḥum's title of *be'ēl ṭe'ēm,* translated 'hyparch' or 'viceroy', in this commentary. This Aramaic title is well known; the letters of Arsames, satrap of Egypt during the reign of Darius II (423–405), refer to 'Anani, probably a Babylonian of Judean descent, who was the *be'ēl ṭe'ēm* of the satrapy of Egypt under Arsames. He was the vice-satrap, equivalent to the Greek hyparch, viceroy (Herodotus, *Histories* 5.27; 7.106, 194), second in command and in charge of the Egyptian satrapy while Arsames was away in Susa (*TAD* A 6.2:23). The Greek title hyparch is also found on an inscription memorializing the gift of a statue by Droaphernes, hyparch of Lydia in the 39th year of Artaxerxes II (Fried 2004: 129-37). Further confirmation of the title comes from a Babylonian legal text, BM 74554, dated to 486 BCE, the last year of Darius I (Stolper 1989a; Heltzer 1992). The tablet begins thus:

> On the instructions of Ḫuta- . . . , son of Pagakanna, the governor (*paḫat*) of Babylon and Beyond-the-River, and of Libluṭ, the brother of Adad-ibni, scribe (*si-pir-ri*) [and] hyparch (*bēl ṭè-e-mu)* and of Gedalyahu, son of Banna-Ea, scribe (*si-pir-ri*) [and] hyparch (*bēl ṭè-e-mu*). . . .

The tablet confirms that Ḫuta- . . . , son of Pagakanna, was the satrap of the combined satrapy Babylon and Beyond-the-River and that under him were at least two officials each called scribe, *sipiru*, and hyparch, *b^{e}'ēl ṭ^{e}'ēm*. The hyparch served directly under the satrap. It may be that Lubluṭ was in charge of Babylon under the satrap while Gedalyahu (a Babylonian of Judean descent?) had jurisdiction over Beyond-the-River. The tablet also demonstrates that it was usual for a person to be both scribe and hyparch, as was also the case with 'Anani in Egypt. The Babylonian Judean Reḥum was evidently the hyparch of Beyond-the-River serving under the satrap of Beyond-the- River. Although he had his own secretary, he served the same functions as 'Anani did in Egypt and as Libluṭ and Gedalyahu did in Babylon and Beyond-the-River in the time of Darius I. Reḥum's seat of office was in Samaria (Ezra 4.17, 21, 23).

The role of the hyparch, the second in command, is described by Xenophon: In the satrap's absence, the hyparch filled the satrap's role—'to govern the people, to receive the tribute, to pay the militia, and to attend to any other business that needs attention' (*Cyrop.* 8.3). When the satrap was at home, the hyparch served as garrison commander at the citadel in the satrapal capital (Herodotus, *Histories* 5.27; 7.106, 194). The hyparch also had a second role. According to Xenophon (*Cyrop.* 8.6.1),

> When [Cyrus the Great] arrived in Babylon, he decided to send out satraps to govern the nations he had subdued. But the commanders of the garrisons in the citadels and the colonels in command of the guards throughout the country he wished to be responsible to no one but himself. This provision he made with the purpose that if any of the satraps, on the strength of the wealth or the men at their command, should break out into open insolence or attempt to refuse obedience, they might at once find opposition in their province.

The hyparch was thus also to serve as one of the ‘eyes and ears’ of the king. He, like the provincial governors in the provinces (see comment at Neh. 2.9), had a garrison under his control, and this would have included cavalry (Fried 2002c).

Reḥum, then, was one such hyparch, *b*^{e}*‘ēl ṭ*^{e}*‘ēm,* vice-satrap, with his seat of office at Samaria (Ezra 4.17, 21, 23), serving under the satrap of Beyond-the-River, whose office was likely in Damascus. As such, he had authority not only over Judah but over all the provinces in the satrapy, including the province of Samaria—but always under the satrap. The recognition that officials living in the city of Samaria held jurisdiction over Judah led scholars (e.g. Alt 1953; Würthwein 1936) to conclude that Judah was not a separate province from the time of Cyrus. These scholars did not consider that there were political jurisdictions between the satrapal and provincial levels. There is no reason then to doubt that Judah was a separate province from the time of Cyrus or to doubt Nehemiah’s assertion that the former governors who were before him laid heavy burdens on the people (Neh. 5.15). Two of those governors were Sheshbazzar (Ezra 5.14) and Zerubbabel (Hag. 1.1).

The Plan of This Commentary

This commentary views Ezra–Nehemiah as one book. It will be divided into units for ease of discussion, the first two being the story of the Return (Ezra 1–6) and the story of Ezra’s Arrival and Work in Jerusalem (Ezra 7–10). These two units will be discussed in Volume 1 of the commentary. The story of Nehemiah’s Arrival and Construction of the City Wall (Nehemiah 1–6) is Unit 3; the Covenant Renewal Ceremony and the City’s Dedication (Nehemiah 7–12) form Unit 4, and Nehemiah 13, the Coda, is discussed in Unit 5. Units 3–5 form Volume 2 of this commentary.

Why Another Commentary?

Although the literature on Ezra–Nehemiah and on the Persian period in general has skyrocked in the last several decades, the last full-length commentary on Ezra–Nehemiah was that of Joseph Blenkinsopp in 1988. That was preceded by the commentaries of Antonius Gunneweg on Ezra and

Nehemiah in 1985 and 1987 respectively, and that of Hugh Williamson in 1985. There has not been a full-length commentary since. This fills that gap. While building on these previous works, this commentary intends to take advantage of all the new information, both archaeological and textual, that has come to light in recent decades.

My point of view differs from most others who work on these books, however. Along with previous commentators, I consider Ezra and Nehemiah to be historical characters; yet in contrast to previous commentators, I consider them to be Persian rather than Jewish. That is, although they are both certainly of Judean descent and worship Yhwh, the Judean god, they are, nevertheless, Persian officials, and therefore they operate with the goal of benefitting not Judah or the Judeans but the Persian king who sent them. This commentary thus reflects a paradigm shift. From the point of view of the local Judean hierarchy, the local Judean priesthood, for example, Ezra and Nehemiah represent the occupying powers—the enemy. This point of view is explained and elaborated upon throughout the commentary. It must be remembered, however, that the book Ezra–Nehemiah was not written by Ezra and Nehemiah themselves but by Judeans writing in the early Hellenistic period. The book as a whole reflects the views of these native Judean (Jewish) authors, and it is their views and opinions that I seek to explicate. I try to understand their words within the historical context that elicted them. I hear their voices speaking across a chasm of 2,300 years of history, and I try to interpret them.

Ezra 1–6

INTRODUCTION TO PART I:
THE STORY OF THE RETURN TO JUDAH AND OF BUILDING AND DEDICATING THE TEMPLE

Historical Background to Ezra 1–6

The historical validity of the various events portrayed in these chapters will be discussed *ad loc.*; here I summarize briefly what can be known of the period portrayed here (for a full treatment, see Briant 2002). In 552 BCE, the father of Cyrus II, the Great, died, leaving Cyrus ruler of Anshan, a small province of the Median Empire. Shortly thereafter he gathered an army and rebelled against Astyages, his maternal grandfather and the king of Media, and by 549 had conquered it. This necessitated a battle with Croesus, king of Lydia, brother-in-law and ally of Astyages, and his own great-uncle. Conquest of the Lydian Empire was completed by 542, at which point Cyrus turned his attention to Babylon. That empire was finally subdued in the fall of 539 after a series of battles. Cyrus ascended the throne of Babylon in the spring of 538 along with his son, Cambyses. It was probably sometime in the summer of 538 that Cyrus appointed Sheshbazzar as governor of Judah and allowed him to take the sacred vessels of the god Yhwh that Nebuchadnezzar had confiscated and deposited in the Esagila, the temple of Marduk in Babylon, and to lead a few Judeans back to Judah to rebuild Yhwh's temple there (Ezra 5.14-16). This he did. The temple was begun probably in the spring of 537, the second year of their return (Ezra 3.8), and was 'under the scaffolding' until 516, the sixth year of Darius I (Ezra 6.15).

A Temple Building Story: Ezra 1–6

Chapters 1–6 of Ezra comprise the first unit for the study of the Ezra–Nehemiah corpus. It begins with Cyrus the Great's decision to rebuild the temple of Yhwh in Jerusalem in 538 BCE, the first year of his reign over Babylon, and ends with the temple's completion and dedication twenty-two years later, in 516 BCE, the sixth year of Darius I (the Great). As described, it is a temple-rebuilding story, a story of rebuilding a temple after foreign conquest and destruction. This is a genre of literature typical of the ancient

Near East, where temples were routinely destroyed in battle and rebuilt (Hurowitz 1992; Boda and Novotny 2010). These temple rebuilding stories exhibit a common pattern, based on a common template (Younger 1990; Fried 2003b). This template, or typology, reveals not only the way in which temple restoration was described in ancient Near Eastern historiography, but also the ideology by which a particular temple-rebuilding project was understood. The story of the Judeans' return to Judah and of the temple's rebuilding as told in Ezra 1–6 assumes this common ideology of ancient Near Eastern temple rebuilding.

The Typology of Ancient Near Eastern Temple-Building Inscriptions
Ancient Near Eastern temple-rebuilding inscriptions are composed of nine fixed components (Ellis 1968; Hurowitz 1992; Fried 2003b; Boda and Novotny 2010). These components are as follows:

A. A brief history of the temple—why it was in ruins.
B. The decision to build: The king receives a divine command from the god to rebuild his temple, usually in the king's first year. Temples that had been destroyed through conquest could not be rebuilt without this ingredient.
   Additional aspects may be included:
   a. The god is reconciled to his city or temple.
   b. A specified pre-ordained period of time is concluded.
   c. The king clarifies the divine will—through extispicy, divination, prophetic visions, etc. Rarely, the initiative comes from the king himself, in which case this last step is doubly important.
C. The acquisition and preparation of building materials.
   a. Building materials are brought from the ends of the earth. Foreign peoples contribute involuntarily during the Assyrian period, voluntarily in the Persian period.
   b. Wood is brought from Lebanon and floated down to the building site.
D. Laying the foundations and preparation of the site
   a. The ruler participates in the foundation rites, and they are often performed according to the prescription of a diviner or prophet.
   b. If a new temple is built near the site of an old one, lamentations are sung by lamentation priests to placate the gods and bridge the gap between the old temple and the new. A stone taken from the old temple is placed in the new one during construction. Lamentations are made for the old temple until the new one is completed.
E. A ceremony for later building stages (e.g. the anointing of doors and sockets in preparation for the god's entrance).

F. A description of the completed temple and its furnishings.
   a. A description of the temple.
   b. A statement that the king has built the temple as he was commanded.
G. The dedication ceremony of the finished building.
H. The god is installed in the temple and takes up residence.
   a. Celebration.
   b. Presentation of gifts and appointment of temple personnel.
I. Prayer for the safety of the temple or curses upon anyone who would destroy it.

Hellenistic Additions

Although it includes many of these basic elements, Ezra 1–6 does not consist only of a building story. These chapters are a hodge-podge: they are written in both Hebrew (Ezra 1.1–4.6; 6.19-22) and Aramaic (Ezra 4.7–6.18); they include lists (Ezra 1.9-11; 2.2-70); letters to and from a series of different Persian kings in no chronological order (4.6-22; 5.6-17; 6.2-12); and a narrative segment about conflict between various groups of residents (4.1-5). These additions to the ancient temple-building account reflect Hellenistic, even Aristotelian, rules of historiography.

The Hellenistic writer is concerned to write tragedy, defined as a story about people who are to be taken seriously and whose actions have serious if not tragic consequences (Aristotle, *Poetics* 38b20-30). In writing tragedy, the author's goal is to arouse pity and fear in the reader, that is, to create a catharsis, an emotional response in him (Else 1967: 6-7). This is the reason for the addition of conflict to the basic temple-building story in Ezra. The Hellenistic writer also strives to be persuasive, to convince the reader of the validity of his statements. This is the art of rhetoric (Aristotle, *Rhetoric* 1354a1-10). To do this he must create trust in the reader and convince him that he knows his subject and has access to reliable sources (*Rhetoric* 1356a1-5; Garver 2005: 105). This is the reason for the letters and the lists. Thus Ezra 1–6 includes plot and drama but also letters and lists. The rhetorical force of each of these will be discussed as they occur, but none belongs to the genre of an ancient Near East temple-rebuilding story.

The plot of Ezra 1–6 follows Aristotelian rules of plot construction. According to Aristotle, an epic must have a prologue, which sets the stage—providing the time and place of the action, introducing the protagonists, and revealing their great good fortune. This is completed in Ezra 1–3. A reversal of fortune from good fortune to bad must then occur, a reversal that results from an ordinary decision by the protagonists. This is the tragic element and is portrayed in Ezra 4. A reversal back from bad fortune to good may occur as a result of the intervening of the gods, and this we see in the unexpected prophesying of Haggai and Zecharia (the *deus ex machina*), so that the reader may be left in a positive mood (Ezra 5 and 6). In spite of this Hellenistic organization of the plot, the underlying scaffolding upon which it rests is the typical ancient Near Eastern temple-rebuilding account, perhaps written for the temple's rededication under Darius I in 516 (to be discussed further below).

The Role of the Temple in Ancient Near Eastern Ideology

As said, the scaffolding upon which Ezra 1–6 rests is an ancient Near Eastern temple-rebuilding story. It is the story of the Judeans' return from Babylon, where they had been deported by Nebuchadnezzar, in order to rebuild their temple. Why did it need to be rebuilt, and why in Jerusalem?

Clines asks how should one understand the phrase 'the temple of Yhwh' (Clines 1994: 60). It may simply mean a building 'owned by Yhwh', but did Yhwh need to own a building? Did he need a temple? Was a temple necessary for people to establish a relationship with him? It is clear that even before the temple was rebuilt Yhwh was already 'with' the people of Judah (Hag. 1.13; 2.5); so why a temple?

Temples that had been destroyed were believed to be temples that the god had abandoned (Albrektson 1967; Cogan 1974: 10-21; Holloway 1992: 342-49; Hurowitz 1992: 268; Fried 2003b; Younger 1990: 72-79). This common ideology is emphasized in Ezekiel's writings (Kutsko 2000: 108; Zimmerli 1979: 251-254).

In the ancient Near East, people did not sacrifice at temples that the god had abandoned. According to the Nabonidus Verse Account (Col. VI.12-15):

> [The gods of Babyl]onia, male and female, he (Cyrus) returned to their cellas. [The gods . . . who] had abandoned their [cha]pels he returned to their mansions. [Their wrath] he appeased, their mind he put at rest. [Those whose power was] at a low point he brought back to life [because] their food is (now) served (to them) [regular]ly (*ANET* 315).

While the gods were in Babylon to escape the advancing Persian army, sacrifices were not conducted at their original locale, and being deprived of their regular meals, the power of the gods was at an ebb. It was only when Cyrus returned them to their usual abodes that sacrifices were resumed (i.e. their food was served them). This was true everywhere. While the Lady of Uruk (i.e. the cult statue of the goddess Ishtar, whose temple was at Uruk) was in Babylon (ahead of the advancing Persian army), barley and other items were sent from Uruk to Babylon for the regular offerings to the goddess (YOS 19.94; Beaulieu 1993). Sacrifices were not conducted for her at her temple in Uruk since she was not there; they were sent on to Babylon.

Babylonian Boundary Stone 36 is a record of Nabû-apla-iddina's (890 BCE?–851 BCE?) endowment of the temple of Shamash at Sippar (Hurowitz 2003). According to the inscription, during the reign of Adad-aplu-iddina

(1068 BCE–1047 BCE) the Sutû had overthrown the Ebabbar temple and destroyed the images of Shamash, the resident deity (1.8-9). The figure and the insignia of Shamash were gone (1.10-11). A later king, Simbar-šipak (1025 BCE–1008 BCE), looked for the statue of the god, but Shamash would not reveal himself to him. Nevertheless, Simbar-šipak built a sun-disk, suspended it from the temple ceiling, and established regular offerings to it. In the previous twenty years, no offerings had ever taken place. Sacrifices were resumed at Ebabbar only after the sun-disk had been set up and a manifestation of the god was again present in the temple.

In all these cases sacrifices to the god were withheld so long as the god was not there to receive them, and if a temple had been destroyed, then the god must have abandoned it, it could not have been destroyed otherwise. This ideology was ubiquitous in the ancient Near East, and did not depend on the existence of a cult statue. It was also held by the Judeans at Elephantine, who had no cult statue to their god. They too could not sacrifice at a destroyed temple:

> from the month of Tammuz, year 14 of King Darius [when the temple was destroyed] and until this day [the 20th of Marḥešvan, year 17 of King Darius] we have been wearing sackcloth and fasting; our wives are made as widow(s); (we) do not anoint (ourselves) with oil and do not drink wine. Moreover, from that (time) and until this day they did not make meal-offering or incense nor whole burnt offering in that temple (*TAD* A 4.7).

For at least three years, the temple of Yhw in Elephantine lay in ruins. Sacrifices ceased, not just animal sacrifices, but even meal and incense offerings, in spite of the fact that priests were present to perform the rites on the ruined site. There was no point in carrying out the sacrifices since the god who had been living in the temple was gone. For at least three years, the temple of Yhw in Elephantine lay in ruins. During that time the Judeans of Elephantine were in mourning, sitting in sackcloth and ashes. They were in mourning for their god, in the same way that the Israelites mourned after Yhwh when the ark was held at Kiriath-Jearim:

> From the day that the ark was lodged at Kiriath-Jearim, a long time passed, some twenty years, and all the house of Israel mourned after Yhwh (1 Sam. 7.2).

The Judeans at Elephantine continued to pray to Yhw (*TAD* A 4.8:14), but they could not sacrifice to him or worship him properly since he wasn't there. They requested permission to rebuild their temple at Elephantine only so that they could carry out the sacrifices again. If they did not need the temple, they would have simply requested permission to resume the sacrifices on the former site, without the expense and trouble of rebuilding. They did not do this because sacrifices could not be conducted without a temple and the god present in it. (Ezra 3.1-8 describes the returnees setting up an altar and sacrificing on it 'day and night' even before the foundations of the temple were laid. This is not likely, and will be thoroughly discussed *ad loc.*)

Hurowitz (2003: 584) states

> any study which asks 'why was the Temple rebuilt' must answer immediately with the obvious point that God needed a home or a locus of presence, and without a temple there could be no immanent divine presence and God could not be worshipped properly.

In the ancient Near East and Egypt the temples were the fixed homes of the gods, where the gods lived, and where their daily life was carried out. There they were washed, clothed, and fed their two meals daily (morning and evening) by the priests who comprised their household staff (Oppenheim 1977: 188; Anderson 1987: 15; Margueron 1997: 165). It is exactly this view of the temple and of the god that is reflected in Ezra–Nehemiah and in the priestly portions of the biblical text. Like their counterparts throughout the ancient Near East, the priestly writers saw Yhwh as inhabiting the tabernacle: 'Moses was not able to enter the tent of meeting because the cloud settled upon it, and Yhwh's glory filled the tabernacle' (Exod. 40.35); and the temple: 'And when the priests came out of the holy place, a cloud filled the house of Yhwh, so that the priests could not stand to minister because of the cloud; for Yhwh's glory filled Yhwh's house' (1 Kgs 8.10-11). The cloud was the physical manifestation of Yhwh's presence.

As was routine in the ancient Near East, the sacrifices were the god's daily meals. So also in the priestly portions of the biblical text (commonly dated to the Persian period), we read that the daily morning and evening temple sacrifices comprised Yhwh's food ration (Anderson 1987: 15). In the ancient Near East the gods were depicted receiving their meals (i.e. the sacrifices) in their homes (i.e. the temples) at fixed times, twice a day, a morning and evening meal, as was customary in antiquity. This was also the case in Judah and Israel:

> Command the Israelites, and say to them: My offering, my food, for my fire, my offerings of pleasing odor, you shall take care to offer to me at its appointed time. . . . two male lambs a year old without blemish, daily, as a regular offering. One lamb you shall offer in the morning, and the other lamb you shall offer at twilight (Num. 28.2-4).

This view of a god who partakes of the sacrifies as his daily meals is evident in Persian-period biblical texts. We read in Malachi (1.6-8) that Yhwh complains that the people are offering him polluted food.

> A son honors his father, and servants their master. If then I am a father, where is the honor due me? And if I am a master, where is the respect due me? says Yhwh of hosts to you, O priests, who despise my name. You say, 'How have we despised your name?'

> By offering polluted food on my altar, is that not wrong? And when you offer those that are lame or sick, is that not wrong? Try presenting that to your governor; will he be pleased with you or show you favor?' says Yhwh of hosts.

Yhwh compares himself to the Persian governor. As you would not offer polluted meat to your governor, how can you offer it to your god? The parallel is informative. Food for the governor is equated with food for the god. This worldview that we see expressed in the ritual and legal texts of the Hebrew Bible is very ancient, but it also continued into the Persian period.

The Role of the Local God in his Temple's Destruction

Central to ancient Near Eastern conquest accounts is the complicity of the god whose temple was destroyed (Albrektson 1967: Chapters 1, 2 and 6; Cogan 1974: 10-21; Fried 2003b; Holloway 1992: 342-49; Hurowitz 1992: 268; Kutsko 2000: 101-23, 157-69; Younger 1990: 72-79). It was the anger of the local god toward his people that caused him to abandon his temple and his city and to invite in a conquering army. The god's rejection is confirmed by his physical transfer (i.e. of its cult image) to the city and to the temple of the god of the conquerors. The transfer of foreign gods to Assyrian temples is a common theme in ancient Near East conquest accounts and is interpreted by both conquered and conquerors as the wish of the conquered god.

This ideology of the god's complicity in the conquest of his own temple was shared by the biblical writers. The entire text of Lamentations affirms that it was Yhwh who brought about the destruction of Jerusalem and the temple: 'Yhwh has scorned his altar, disowned his sanctuary; he has delivered into the hand of the enemy the walls of her palaces' (Lam. 2.7). Ezekiel 10–11 describes Yhwh's abandonment of his temple because of his displeasure with his people (Kutsko 2000: 108; Zimmerli 1979: 251-54; Hurowitz 1992: 268). In his vision, Ezekiel sees the Presence of Yhwh leave his usual seat on the Kerubim throne in the inner sanctum of the temple (9.3l; 10.4), move up to the threshold of the temple's east gate (9.3; 10.4), and from there out of the temple (10.18), out of the city, toward the mountains east of it, and then on to Chaldea (10.19-22). Ezekiel understood that Yhwh had voluntarily left his temple, had abandoned Jerusalem to the invaders (9.10), and had come to Babylon. In reality, Nebuchadnezzar had confiscated Yhwh's temple vessels as the prize of war.

> They took away the pots, the shovels, the snuffers, the dishes for incense, and all the bronze vessels used in the temple service. The captain of the guard took the firepans and the sprinkling bowls, those of gold and of silver (2 Kgs 25.14-15).

He very likely deposited them in the Esagila, the temple of Marduk in Babylon. The vessels had been brought to the הֵיכְלָא דִּי בָבֶל, *hêkᵉlāʾ dî bābel,* ‘the palace of Babylon’ (Ezra 5.14), which always refers to the Esagila (Hurowitz, personal communication, *CAD* 4, p. 55, entry 7′ of Ekallu). Moreover, we know from Nebuchadnezzar’s own inscriptions that he deposited booty from all the areas that he conquered into the temples of his gods. The following text is representative of Nebuchadnezzar’s inscriptions:

> Gold, silver, exceedingly valuable gemstones, thick cedars, heavy tribute, expensive presents, the produce of all countries, goods from all inhabited regions, before Marduk the great lord, the god who created me, and Nabû his lofty heir who loves my kingship, I transported and brought into Esagila and Ezida (*apud* Vanderhooft 1999: 46).

Lamentation rituals may have continued for a while at the ruined temple in Jerusalem (Jer. 41.5), but even this is doubtful. As will be discussed further in the comment to Ezra 3, lamentation rituals for ruined temples commence at the time of rebuilding, not before. Sacrifices, even incense sacrifices, are not performed at ruined temples. Lipschits (2001a: 129-42) points out the tendentious quality of this verse in Jeremiah. Samaria, Shechem and Shiloh were places where well-known cult sites had stood. Jeremiah had prophesied (Jer. 7.12; cf. 26.6) that the temple in Jerusalem would become like the temple in Shiloh that Yhwh had overthrown. He had also prophesied (Jer. 31.8, 9) that men would come from the northland, ‘they shall come with weeping and supplications’. Rather than being historical, Jer. 41.5 may have been intended to show that Jeremiah’s prophecies had been fulfilled.

Although, sacrifices could not be conducted at the ruins of a temple, this does not imply that the Judeans could not pray. In the above letter from Elephantine (*TAD* A 4.7:14), the Judeans state that ‘from the time this had been done to us (i.e. from the time of the destruction of their temple), we with our wives and our children have been wearing sackcloth, fasting, and praying to Yhw’. Prayers can be said; the god is still ‘with them’ in that sense, but now it is a transcendent, remote and angry god, not one immanent, accessible and favorable.

Why Persian Involvement?

Ezra 1 begins with a statement that Yhwh ‘god of heaven’ commanded Cyrus to build him a temple in Jerusalem; it was not Cyrus’s own idea. Ezekiel’s vision of Yhwh leaving his temple and going to Babylon reveals that the Judeans shared the common ancient Near Eastern ideology of conquest. They also shared the common ancient Near Eastern ideology of temple restoration after conquest. According to this ideology, a destroyed shrine can be restored only if there is evidence that the god who abandoned it has reconciled with his people and is willing to move back home, back into his temple again. This usually means that the cult statue has been returned. Only then can the temple be rebuilt. Kings of the conquering nation took pride in their ability to return the conquered gods to their original sites and to rebuild their temples for them (Cogan 1974: 29-31 nn. 44 and 54). Esarhaddon says, '(I am he who) returned the pillaged gods from Assyria and Elam to their shrines, and who let them stay in comfortable quarters until their temples could be completed for them'. Sargon says, 'I returned the pillaged gods to their cult centers and restored their interrupted regular offerings'.

According to an eighth-century text of Ninurta-kudurro-uṣur, governor of Suhu and Mari, the people of a city named Anat, in rebellion against the Suhu, hired Assyrians to desecrate the temple of the goddess Anat and make her dwell in a secret place (*puzru*) (Hurowitz 1993: 40-42). Ninurta-kudurro-uṣur brought her back, restored her temple and regalia, reinstituted her in her restored temple, and reestablished her ancient rites. The temple was restored only upon the return of the god. The pseudepigraphic inscription of the Kassite king Agum-Kakrime states that after many years in exile Marduk decided to return home to Babylon (Hurowitz 1993: 40-42). The god was then housed in temporary quarters in Babylon until the Esagila could be restored. This literary text illustrates the ideology of temple restoration: temple restoration is begun only when the god has indicated his willingness to return home.

Sometimes temple restoration must be delayed even after the god's return, and the god has to remain in temporary quarters until rebuilding is complete. The Stele of Nabonidus (IV.1-34) reports that

> (As to) the goddess Anunitum (now) residing in Sippar, whose residence in old time a (victorious) enemy had removed to Arrapha and whose sanctuary the Gutians had destroyed, and whose cult Neriglissar had renewed and whose (image) he had clad with an attire befitting her godhead, [Neriglissar] made her stay (provisionally)—her own temple being in ruins—in a chapel in Sippar-Amnanu arranging for her *nidbû* offerings [to be sent to her] (*ANET* 309).

The goddess resided in temporary quarters until her own residence could be rebuilt. There was no attempt to rebuild the temple until she had returned from her exile. This is also true of the temple Eḫulḫul in Harran, dedicated to Sin, the moon-god. According to the Nabonidus Stele (X.12-23), it lay in ruins fifty-four years until Sin was appeased and agreed to return to it:

> As to the temple É.ḫul.ḫul in Harran which was in ruins for 54 years—through a devastation by the Manda-hordes these sanctuaries were laid waste—the time (predestined) by the gods, the moment for the appeasement (to wit) 54 years, had come near, when Sin . . . returned to his place (*ANET* 311).

Finally, the Cyrus Cylinder has Cyrus say, 'I returned to (these) sacred cities . . . , the sanctuaries of which have been in ruins a long time, the gods who (used) to live therein, and I established for them permanent sanctuaries' (ll 30-33, *ANET* 316).

These texts make clear that the god's return is an absolutely necessary precondition for rebuilding a sanctuary devastated by foreign conquest. The return of the image implies the god's reconciliation with his people and his willingness to return to the temple dedicated to him. In reality, it is not the god who decides if he is willing to return. The decision to return the cult statue is that of the king of the conquering nation who possesses it. Whenever that king decides to return the statue is when the god relinquishes his anger with his people and returns home.

In fact, many temples were never rebuilt (Fried 2002a). Shrines in the Levant, peripheral to the great empires of Egypt and Assyria, were seldom restored after conquest; indeed, the temple in Jerusalem is a striking exception. The great Bronze Age Migdal or Fortress Temple at Shechem, a second large temple there, and another small sanctuary at the site were all destroyed in a twelfth-century conflagration, which the excavators attribute to Abimelech (Judges 9). None of these temples were rebuilt. A Bronze Age cult site at Lachish (Level V) and another at Ekron were destroyed by Pharaoh Sheshonq. Neither was rebuilt. The great Bronze Age temples in Megiddo were destroyed in an enemy onslaught; they were not rebuilt. The cult site at Ta'anach was destroyed in a conflagration attributed to Pharaoh Sheshonq. It was not rebuilt. Two cult sites at Tel 'Amal were destroyed in a conflagration dated to the end of the tenth century. They were not rebuilt. The cult site at Kedesh was destroyed in a violent conflagration attributed to Tiglath-Pileser III. It was not rebuilt. Eighth-century cult sites at Lachish, Beersheba and Tel Ḥalif continued in use until their destruction by Sennacherib in 701. None was rebuilt. The towns were rebuilt, but not the cult site.

Hamath, a city on the Orontes River, suffered heavy destruction in 720 BCE. The reliefs in Room V of Sargon II's palace at Dur-Sharrukin exhibit the destruction of this city, which included the removal both of its inhabitants and the statues of its gods (Na'aman 1999: 391-415). The city was not reoccupied until the Hellenistic period; the cult site was never rebuilt (Hawkins 1972–75: 69-70).

The temple to Ishtar in 'Ain Dara in northern Syria is a primary example of the situation of conquered temples in cities on the periphery of empire (Abu Assaf 1993: 155-71). Built in three stages, the temple was in continuous operation for five hundred years. First erected in the thirteenth century, it was renovated or rebuilt approximately around 1000 BCE; and later, sometime between 900 and 740, a walkway and decorative orthostats were added to the exterior. The temple was apparently destroyed by Tiglath-Pileser III between 742 and 740 BCE. It was not rebuilt. After its destruction it lay exposed for half a century, while its stones were robbed and plundered. Domestic buildings were finally built above it in the seventh century BCE. The excavator wonders why the temple was not rebuilt after its eighth-century destruction. The answer is clear. If conquerors do not return gods or cult objects to cities on the periphery of empire, then the ideological requirements for temple rebuilding after conquest cannot be met. The return of the cult statue means that the god has returned, has reconciled with his people, and has agreed to inhabit the temple again. The return of the cult statue is mandatory for the rebuilding of a temple after its destruction by foreign conquest.

Role of the Temple Vessels

If the proof of the god's reconciliation with his people is the return of his cult statue, what could be the proof when, as in the case of Yhwh, there was no cult statue? Evidence suggests that the temple vessels served this role. In 701 BCE, the Assyrian king Sennacherib conquered Lachish, the most important city in Judah next to Jerusalem. The conquest is depicted in a series of reliefs on the walls of Sennacherib's palace in Nineveh (Ussishkin 1982). In one scene (Segment IV) Assyrian soldiers are shown carrying away booty from the burning city. The first and second soldiers are carrying away large incense burners. The third is carrying a throne-like chair, with armrests. The fourth and fifth soldiers are pulling a ceremonial chariot. The last three are carrying weapons—spears, shields and swords. These are the three types of objects mentioned in the booty lists of Assyrian royal inscriptions: spoils of the temple, the palace, and the army, respectively (Na'aman 1999: 404). Instead of a statue of the god, since there was none, the Assyrian soldiers are shown carrying out the most impressive cult objects they could find—the large bronze incense burners. It is apparent from the relief that the incense burners functioned theologically in the same way that cult statues did. They represented the presence of the god, even an aniconic god, because they indicated where he determined to live. This ideology is also exhibited in ninth-century Moab. In the Moabite stele, King Mesha memorializes his victory over the trans-Jordan towns belonging to the Israelite tribe of Gad. In it King Mesha brags that he removed the 'altar-hearths of Yhwh' and 'dragged them before Kemosh', his god (lines 17-18). These 'altar-hearths' were similar to the incense burners shown in the Lachish reliefs. Thus, the aniconic god is represented in reliefs and in inscriptions by his cultic paraphernalia. In both cases, they are treated exactly as a cult statue would have been. They are taken out and placed in the temple of the god of the conqueror. This usage tells against the assumption that the temple vessels would have been melted down (so also Cogan and Tadmor 1988: 316; cf. Gesenius 123e; *pace* Ackroyd 1987: 45-60; Grabbe 2004: 277).

The importance of Yhwh's temple vessels in his return to Judah is emphasized by the prophet known as Deutero-Isaiah. This prophet asserts that Cyrus's primary task was to rebuild the temple (Isa. 44.27, 28) and to set the exiles free (Isa. 45.13). Deutero-Isaiah stresses that the Judeans had completed their punishment, that their penalty had been paid (Isa. 40.1, 2), and that Yhwh had reconciled with his people and was returning to Judah and Jerusalem. Thus the people must build a highway for him.

> A voice cries out: 'In the desert prepare the way for Yhwh, make straight in the Arabah a highway for our god. Every valley shall be lifted up, and every mountain and hill be made low; the uneven ground shall become level, and the rough places a plain. Then Yhwh's glory shall be revealed. All flesh shall see it together, for the mouth of Yhwh has spoken' (Isa. 40.3-5).

This passage is properly understood only when it is realized that Yhwh is assumed by the author to be in Babylon. The Arabah is the desert of Moab (Jordan), stretching between Babylon and Judah (Num. 22.1). The proof that Yhwh is in Babylon is the fact that his vessels were in the Esagila. Yhwh's return to Judah was a physical return on a physical highway across a very real desert. It was a journey visible to the flesh (Isa. 40.5). It was a physical event, not a metaphysical or eschatological one (*pace* Merendino 1981: 32; Blenkinsopp 2000: 181; Barstad 1996: 38). Yhwh's return to Judah was visible to the eye because it was accompanied by the physical return of Yhwh's vessels. To the biblical writer, the return of the vessels was nothing less than the return of God himself to Judah and to his temple in Jerusalem (Isa. 52.8):

> For eye to eye, they will see
> Yhwh's return to Zion.

That event is fully realized as the passage continues (52.11-12).

> Depart! Depart! Go out from there!
> Touch nothing unclean.
> Go out from the midst of it,
> Purify yourselves, you who carry Yhwh's vessels.
> You shall not go out in haste
> And you shall not go out in flight
> For Yhwh shall walk before you
> The god of Israel shall be your rear guard.

The first to return, the ones who return most dramatically, are those who carry Yhwh's vessels—the temple vessels (Isa. 52.11). The way of Yhwh's return to Judah was not a ladder connecting Heaven and Earth, but a real path across a real desert (40.3-5). Commentators have noticed the relationship between the way prepared for Yhwh in Isaiah 40 and the way prepared for the processions of the gods in Mesopotamia (e.g. North 1964; Westermann 1969). Nevertheless, they prefer to stress the differences, arguing that this is a return of Yhwh's glory, his *kābōd,* and should not be taken as a physical return. Yet, the biblical writer emphasizes that this is something the eye will see, meaning it must be interpreted physically. If the ancient audience did not see the return of the god himself, they did see his physical manifestation—they saw it in the return of his vessels.

The instantiation of the return of the god through the return of the temple vessels implies that only the Persian king could authorize the temple's rebuilding. Only he had the power to order the return of the vessels, the physical proof of Yhwh's presence. The relationship between temple and vessels, and the purpose of the temple as the resting place of the vessels, is reiterated by the Chronicler (1 Chron. 22.19). This is his interpretation of David's command to the leaders of Israel during the reign of his son Solomon:

> Now dedicate your hearts and your lives to seeking Yhwh your god. Rise and build the temple of Yhwh the god so that the ark of the covenant of Yhwh and the holy vessels of God may be brought into a house built for the name of Yhwh.

At the time of the Chronicler there was no longer an ark, so he included the holy vessels, allowing them to participate in the aura of the ark. The intent is clear. The house that is built for the name Yhwh is built in order to give the holy vessels a place of rest:

> Then King David rose to his feet and said: 'Hear me, my brothers and my people. I had planned to build a house of rest for the ark of the covenant of Yhwh, for the footstool of our god' (1 Chron. 28.2).

The concept of the sanctuary as a place of rest is especially important at the time of the Chronicler after the peregrinations of the vessels to Babylon and back.

The Role of the Persians

But would the Persians have really built the temple? Would they have cared whether a temple in Jerusalem was constructed? Would Cyrus have ordered Sheshbazzar to take Yhwh's vessels and some Judeans to Jerusalem to rebuild the temple of Yhwh there (Ezra 5.15)? Would Cyrus or Darius have ordered that the cost for rebuilding be paid out of the royal revenues (Ezra 6.4, 8)? In fact, the existence of the second temple itself demonstrates Persian approval. There could not have been a temple anywhere in the empire if the Persians had not supported it (Briant 2002; Fried 2004).

Though the Persians destroyed many temples, they did support some. Udjaḫorresnet's inscription states that Darius ordered Udjaḫorresnet to restore the temple of Neith in Sais, Egypt, after it had decayed (lines 43-44;

Lichtheim 1980: 36-41). Although the text does not say that Darius allocated funds for the restoration, it does say that he commanded Udjaḫorresnet to furnish the House of Life with 'every good thing, in order that they might carry out all their crafts', and that Udjaḫorresnet restored them 'as they had been before' (line 45). Darius could not have ordered Udjaḫorresnet to furnish the temple without supplying funds for it. If Udjaḫorresnet could have restored the temple himself, he would have done so rather than let it fall into decay. The Udjaḫorresnet inscription suggests that under special circumstances the Achaemenid rulers did support local temples.

An example of Persian support for newly built temples in out-of-the-way places is the temple to Osiris and Isis at the southern end of the Kharga oasis in Egypt, 120 km. from the modern town of Kharga (Wuttmann *et al.* 1996: 385-451; 1998: 367-462; 2000). The site was occupied from the end of the Paleolithic period, but at the end of the third millennium the springs dried up, and it was abandoned. In the middle of the fifth century BCE, during the reign of Artaxerxes I, a network of tunnels (*qanats*) was built which allowed an underground water reservoir to be tapped. Settlement continued as long as the water lasted, until the first decades of the fourth century CE, but the temple was abandoned in the Roman period. The excavators suppose that it must have taken at least five years to build one tunnel. The means necessary to build them and to establish a viable settlement in what had been an arid desert zone would have had to come from the satrap, if not from the king himself. The local community could not have built it by themselves. The temple at the Kharga oasis illustrates Persian establishment of important temples in out-of-the-way places. No reason is given for the creation of a temple at the oasis. Perhaps Xenophon (*Oecon.* 4.8) is correct in his assessment that the Persian emperor would not tolerate uncultivated land:

> As for the country (χώρα), he (the emperor) personally examines so much of it as he sees in the course of his progress through it; and he receives reports from his trusted agents on the territories that he does not see for himself. To those governors who are able to show him that their country is densely populated and that the land is in cultivation and well stocked with the trees of the district and with the crops, he assigns more territory and gives presents and rewards them with seats of honor. Those whose territory he finds uncultivated and thinly populated either through harsh administration or through contempt or through carelessness, he punishes, and appoints others to take their office.

If the Achaemenids were interested in cultivating barren land and in developing population and resources throughout the empire, as Xenophon maintains, then that would have been a good reason for the Persians to have built temples of local gods in out-of-the-way places. No one would move into an area that did not contain a temple to the local god, so the Persians built a temple to Osiris and Isis to enable people to move in. This could also explain why the Persians would build and support a temple in Jerusalem—they wanted Judah populated. There could not have been a return to Zion without the temple's rebuilding.

Exile and Return: Archaeological Evidence

Was there an exile? Was there a return? According to Grabbe (2008) we should 'now acknowledge that most Judeans were not deported from Palestine to Mesopotamia. There was thus no exile in the conventional sense' and so no return. This is quite a surprising statement. Is it true? Grabbe bases his opinion on the statement that after the destruction of Jerusalem 'Nebuzaradan the captain of the guard left some of the poorest people of the land to be vinedressers and tillers of the soil' (Jer. 52.16 = 2 Kgs 25.12). He asserts that 'probably only a minority of the people were taken away, with the *tens of thousands* still left. These people continued to live in Judah, work the land, raise families, carry on the daily life. Presumably they would have quietly taken over any land abandoned because the owners had been killed in fighting or deported to Babylonia' (Grabbe 1998: 138, emphasis added). Is this so? Rather than relying on the biblical text or on conjecture, we may answer the question by a study of the archaeological finds of Jerusalem, Judah, Benjamin, and by the data from Babylon itself.

The archaeology of Judah reveals Babylonian destruction levels in all its key cities followed by a collapse of the economic and administrative infrastructure in all of Judah accompanied by general desolation in both Judah and Benjamin. A gradual recovery was begun under the Persians, but the population did not reach its predestruction levels until the Hellenistic period.

Jerusalem

Archaeological evidence from excavations in Jerusalem and the City of David (the city's southern spur) shows that the Babylonian destruction of the city in 586 was complete and devastating (Lipschits 2001a; 2003; 2005: 210-18; 2011: 57; Stern 2001: 323-24; Finkelstein 2008a; 2008b; Faust 2012a: 23-24). Destruction at the end of the Iron Age has been found in every part of the city (Lipschits 2005: 211). There is no doubt that the temple in Jerusalem was destroyed, its vessels carried off to Babylon, its priests put to death or deported, and—one month later—the city razed to the ground (Lipschits 2006). The decline in Jerusalem's population was not entirely due to death in battle or exile, however. Many fled; others who survived the battle and subsequent deportation died from famine and disease (Faust 2011; 2012a: 140-43). Devastation persisted until the mid-Persian period. There is no evidence of occupation in Jerusalem or the City of David between the destruction in 586 and the beginning of Persian rule at the end of the sixth century. Archaeology testifies to a settlement gap in Jerusalem of over fifty years.

Archaeology also reveals that Jerusalem was reestablished at the very beginning of the Persian period. At this time settlement was limited to the area around the Temple Mount and the narrow ridge of the City of David (Lipschits 2003: 330; 2005: 213; 2006; Finkelstein 2008a; 2008b; 2009). It appears that under the Persians the inhabited area did not exceed fifteen acres and covered only the City of David (Ussishkin 2006; Stern 1982: 34; Lipschits 2003: 330; 2005: 210-18). It may not even have exceeded six acres (Finkelstein 2008b: 8). This is consistent with Nehemiah's memoir. Nehemiah describes the city in the mid-fifth century as 'wide on both sides and large, but the people within it are few and no houses built' (Neh. 7.4). Lipschits (2005: 213; cf. Lipschits 2003: 330; and Ussishkin 2006: 162) describes the city prior to Nehemiah's arrival as 'a temple, alongside of which there was a settlement both for those who served in the temple and for a small number of additional residents'. Just outside of the City of David, a small number of new farmsteads appeared at the beginning of the Persian period, each containing from a single building to three or four (Lipschits 2003: 331). The archaeology of Jerusalem thus demonstrates a complete destruction with the deportation, death, or flight of the populace at the beginning of the sixth century, and a small return to the city at its end.

The Cities of the Judean Hills

The picture emerging from the Judean Hills is the same, that of almost complete destruction, followed by collapse. Stern (2001: 324-26; cf., Lipschits 2005: 218-23; Faust 2012a: 28-30) provides a long list of excavated cities of the Judean hill country that were destroyed or abandoned as a result of the Babylonian onslaught and that recovered only in the Persian or Hellenistic period, if at all. Ein Gedi in the east was leveled in a major conflagration in the early-sixth century that destroyed the city (Stern 2007: 362; Mazar 1993: 402; Finkelstein 2010: 43; Faust 2012: 26). The city was rebuilt in the Persian period after a settlement gap. Jericho had been extensively settled in the seventh century, and habitation continued until the beginning of the sixth century (Lipschits 2005: 232-33; Kenyon 1993: 680-81; Faust 2012a: 26). Occupation resumed again only in the fifth century under the Persians after a settlement gap (Kenyon 1993: 681; Stern 2001: 324). Occupation at Beth Zur ended at the beginning of the sixth century and resumed only in the fourth century, as is witnessed by a very late-fourth-century Judean coin *yḥzqyw hpḥh*, Hezekiah the Governor (Funk 1993: 260-61; Fried 2003a; Finkelstein 2010: 41; Faust 2012: 25). Occupation at Hebron continued until the early-sixth century (Chadwick 2005: 70) and was followed by a settlement gap that continued throughout the Persian period (Faust 2012a: 25).

The southern Judean Hills and the Shephelah suffered a similar fate and were almost completely deserted (Lipschits 1998). Lachish, the second largest city in monarchic Judah at the time of Hezekiah was completely destroyed by the Assyrians in 701. After a period of abandonment, it was rebuilt under Josiah. This Stratum II city was poorer, less densely inhabited, with weaker fortifications. It was completely devastated by a raging fire during the Babylonian conquest. There is evidence of breaches in the city wall, and Babylonian arrowheads (Tufnell 1953: 56-58; Ussishkin 1993: 909; Lipschits 2005: 219). Among the so-called Lachish letters is one referring to the fall of Azekah (4.12-13, Tur-Sinai 1987: 106). Lachish was rebuilt in the fifth century, when it became a Persian administrative center (Fantalkin and Tal 2006).

Ramat Raḥel (probably Beth-Hakkerim) was an active administration site in the Assyrian period, and appears to have gone out of use in the late-seventh century BCE (the reign of Josiah?) until the beginning of the Persian period, when occupation resumed again as an administrative center (Lipschits *et al.* 2011: 34). There is no destruction level at the site.

Renewed excavations at Beit Shemesh indicate that it too was destroyed by the Babylonians (Fantalkin 2004; *pace* Bunimovitz and Lederman 2003). It did not recover in subsequent periods (Faust 2012a: 29). This story is repeated in all the cities of the Shephelah: Azekah, Tel Goded (Tell Judeideh), Tel Maresha, Tell Beit Mirsim, Tel Batash (Timnah) were all destroyed by the Babylonians in the beginning of the sixth century and recovered only slowly in the Persian period after a long settlement gap (Faust 2012a: 28-30; Lipschits 2005: 218-223).

The Cities of the Negev

This same is true of the southern part of Judah, all the way to the Beer-Sheba valley. Excavations reveal cities utterly destroyed or abandoned, with settlement not renewed until the mid-fourth century, if at all. In the Negev, the Judean city of Arad was settled in the late-twelfth or early-eleventh century. During the seventh and early-sixth centuries it blossomed and expanded to a considerable extent beyond its eighth-century perimeter (Amiran and Herzog 1997: 239). Indeed, this seems to have been true of all the cities of the Negev (Amiran and Herzog 1997: 239). This flowering was cut short abruptly with the Babylonian conquest at the beginning of the sixth century when all the Judean sites of the Beer-Sheba valley were destroyed (Amiran and Herzog 1997: 242). They remained in ruins for the next 150 years, until their partial recovery during the Persian period.

The Rural Areas

Many scholars assume that although the cities were destroyed that life in the rural sector continued as before (e.g. Lipschits 2005: 368). Archaeology shows this not the case (Faust 2003; 2004; 2006; 2012: 33-72). Of twenty-two rural sites in the area of Jerusalem that were excavated, only two exhibit any continuity between the monarchic and Persian periods (an additional one shows occupation in both the Persian and the monarchic periods, but not continuity). Data from these excavations are supplemented by data from surveys. They too reveal hundreds of late Iron Age rural sites throughout Judah, but none from the Neo-Babylonian period (the mid- to late-sixth century), and a mere fifteen from the Persian period, which indicates only modest recovery of rural sites in the Persian period after a settlement gap.

The same is true of Benjamin. Of four rural sites excavated in the Benjamin area, three ended in the Iron Age and did not continue; one location was occupied in both the Iron Age and the Persian period, but with no continuity between the two periods. Rural structures in northern Judah exhibit the same pattern. Of eleven sites excavated in northern Judah, only one shows habitation in both the Iron Age and Persian period. Of the several rural sites that existed in eastern Judah and in the Judean desert during the monarchic period, none continued past the late Iron Age. Of five rural sites excavated in the Negev, none showed later habitation.

Rural settlement in both Judah and Benjamin came to a virtual halt at the end of the Iron Age and picked up again only minimally during the Persian period. It must be concluded that rural areas were also decimated as a result of the Babylonian destruction.

The Area of Benjamin

Many scholars who admit that Judah and Jerusalem had been destroyed and depopulated argue that the area of Benjamin continued unscathed under the Babylonians (Barstad 1996; Stern 2001: 321; Lipschits 1999; 2005: 237-49). The theory that the area of Benjamin was spared may go back to an influential article by Malamat (1950). Malamat proposed that contrary to the conclusions of Tell en-Naṣbeh's (biblical Miṣpah's) own excavators, the town was not destroyed by the Babylonians. Malamat argued that the territory of Benjamin surrendered to the Babylonian army after the invasion and so was spared. Malamat relied solely on biblical evidence, particularly Ezra 2 (Nehemiah 7). Since most of the cities listed there are in Benjamin, Malamat reasoned that if they were able to return to these cities, they must not have been destroyed.

The list of Ezra 2 cannot be a list of cities to which exiles returned during the Persian period, however (Finkelstein 2008b: 13). Of the sixteen cities listed in Ezra 2 (Nehemiah 7), four show no evidence of Persian-period occupation. Moreover, cities in Judah that do show evidence of strong occupation during the Persian period—Mizpah, En Gedi, Beth-haccherem (probably Ramat Raḥel), Nevi Samuel—do not appear in the lists. Finkelstein suggests the list was composed during the Hellenistic period when all the listed cities were occupied. On the other hand, because all the cities listed also had strong occupation in the Iron Age, it may rather be a list of cities from which the exiles had fled or from which they had been deported.

Like Judah, the land of Benjamin has been extensively studied archaeologically. Magen and Finkelstein (1993) find no Iron Age sites inhabited in Benjamin after 586; all were abandoned. Persian-period sites that developed later were few and small. Lipschits argues against this that Magen and Finkelstein lumped pottery from the sixth century BCE with the rest of the Iron Age material, so that they would not have realized that it was only after the sixth century, during the Persian period, that the sites were deserted (Lipschits 2005: 246). According to Magen and Finkelstein (1993: 27), however, a severe crisis beset settlement in the Benjamin region at the time of the fall of Jerusalem, the picture being even more grim than their survey reflects. Recovery occurred only in the fifth and fourth centuries.

The conclusion of some that Benjamin was occupied and that it even prospered throughout the sixth century during the Babylonian occupation is based on four sites in Benjamin: Tell el-Fûl, Tell en-Naṣbeh, Tell el-Jib (Gibeon) and Beitin (Bethel), plus En-Gedi and the Judean tombs at Ketef Hinom, Mamila and 'Ain Shems in Judah (Barstad 1996: 47-50; Lipschits 2005: 203-206). Accordingly each of these sites will be discussed in turn.

Beitin. Beitin is commonly recognized as the biblical city of Bethel. Relying on the report of Kelso and Albright (1968), it is argued that Bethel was occupied throughout the Babylonian period and into the Persian (Lipschits 2005: 204 n. 77). Conclusions based on the material from Bethel is complicated by the fact that it was neither stratigraphically dug nor published. Kelso used the same loci numbers all the way down from Iron II to MBII. Loci were defined two-dimensionally, but not for the crucial third dimension. This dimension was not recorded and is not retrievable (Dever 1971: 459-71; see also Finkelstein 2008b: 9; Finkelstein and Singer-Avitz 2009). An examination of the pottery provides no evidence to show that Bethel was occupied between 587 and the Hellenistic period (Dever 1971: 469; de Groot 2001: 79; Köhlmoos 2006: 76-77; Koenen 2003: 59-64). Indeed, pottery assigned to the mid-sixth century belongs in fact to the eighth (Finkelstein and Singer-Avitz 2009: 42).

Gibeon (el-Jib). Gibeon is listed in Neh. 7.25 as well as in the list of wall builders (3.7). It is probably also the site called Gibbar in Ezra 2.20. Evaluation of the finds at Gibeon are controversial. The town served as a major center for the production and export of wine in the eighth and seventh centuries and reached its peak of prosperity in this period (Pritchard 1962; 1993). Pritchard found only scant evidence of occupation from the end of the seventh century to the beginning of the Roman period (Pritchard 1993: 513). The absence of a destruction layer between the Iron Age and the Persian period has indicated to some continuous occupation across the Babylonian period and into the Persian (Lipschits 1999; 2005: 243-45).

Burial caves outside of Gibeon are dated to the Roman period and to the late Iron Age, however (Eshel 1987). There is nothing in-between. There are no Babylonian- or Persian-period tombs here, implying no Babylonian- or Persian-period occupations.

The dates of the various inscriptions on decanter handles found at the site is disputed, as is the date of the MṢH stamp seal impressions found there. Since none of these were found in a secure stratigraphic location, the dating must rely on the typology of the jars and the paleography of the inscriptions. Regarding the typology of the jars, the closest parallel is from Tel Batash (Timnah), where they are clearly dated to the late-seventh century (Faust 2012a: 220-22; Mazar and Kelm 1993: 152-57). Regarding the paleography, the jars were inscribed with the name of the town and then one of three personal names, that is, *gb'n gdr* (Gib'on, the town), and the name Ḥannaniyahu, Azariayahu, or Amariyahu. According to Avigad (1959: 132) the inscriptions exhibit 'a remarkable paleographical homogeneity, and all of them can be placed within a short period, around 700 B.C.' In view of the clear typology of the handles, however, they must now be dated to the late-seventh century.

Four MṢH stamp seal impressions were also found at Gibeon (Zorn *et al.* 1994; Lipschits 2005: 150). Forty-two of this type of seal impression have been found in Judah and Benjamin, the bulk of them (thirty) in Tell en-Naṣbeh. Four have been found in Jerusalem, four in Gibeon, two in Jericho, and one each in Ramat-Raḥel and Belmont. The fact that these seal impressions were found primarily in the area of Benjamin does not make them Neo-Babylonian however (*pace* Zorn *et al.* 1994). Cross, Wright, and Albright each dates them to the end of the sixth century and the beginning of the Persian period (Stern 1982: 32-33, 208). Naveh dates them to the fourth century and Avigad to the late-fifth to early-fourth century (Stern 1982: 208). The MṢH stamp seal impressions will be discussed further below, but they are undoubtedly early Persian, suggesting Persian-period occupation at Gibeon, not sixth century.

Tell el-Fûl. Tell el-Fûl has been identified with Gibeah of Saul, the center of the tribal territory of Benjamin. This identification is contested in particular because the site is so small, 4 dunams, implying a settlement of only eighty people (Finkelstein 2011). Stratum III B at Tell el-Fûl has been dated to the sixth century and the Babylonian period (P. Lapp 1965; N. Lapp 1981, 1993, 1997) and is the primary site upon which the pottery of the sixth century is based.

Because Tell el-Fûl is built on bedrock, there is no clear stratigraphy, and no complete vessels were found since in order to build for later occupation, earlier levels had to be completely cleared away. Even so, there is evidence for three major periods of activity: Iron I, late Iron II, and Hellenistic (Finkelstein 2011: 4). The Iron I period at the site ended in c. 900 BCE without a destruction layer and appears to have been abandoned. Following the abandonment, the site was deserted for about two-and-one-half centuries (Finkelstein 2011: 6).

Again, because earlier occupation levels were cleared away rather than built on top of earlier ones, most of the buildings on the site date to the Hellenistic period, although some had a thin Iron II C phase beneath their floor (Finkelstein 2011: 6). The pottery from this stage dates to the seventh and early-sixth centuries BCE. There is no destruction layer found at this Iron II settlement; the conjecture is that it was too small and unimportant to have been destroyed by Nebuchadnezzar. One structure on the site resembles an Assyrian-style watchtower overlooking the northern approach to Jerusalem, so it may have been an Assyrian fort and administrative center in the seventh century.

Based on the lack of destruction over the entire site, the Lapps concluded that the fortress there was destroyed in 587 by Nebuchadnezzar, but that occupation continued afterward in the unwalled city, probably to the end of the sixth century, in spite of the lack of any evidence of occupation at this level on the tell. They label this occupation period Period III B. They date this so-called occupation level by the large number of sherds found in a cistern with YHD stamp impressions. These confirmed for the excavator settlement on the site in the Persian period (P. Lapp 1965). Lapp surmised, therefore, that pottery from the bottom of the cistern under the YHD stamp impressions must date earlier than this, and so he estimated a post-587, that is, a mid-sixth-century date for Period III B. It is only the pottery from this cistern and comparable pottery from an area of 'crushed pottery' just outside the cistern that has given rise to the notion of 'significant occupation' in the Babylonian period at Tell el-Fûl, and consequently in all the rest of Benjamin (Lipschits 2005: 204 n. 74). The pottery outside the cistern was found under a late-Hellenistic fence (P. Lapp 1965). It was probably spillage from the cistern.

The pottery labeled Period III B at Tell el-Fûl (i.e. the pottery from the bottom of the cistern) is scant, however, and difficult (Finkelstein 2011: 8). N. Lapp dated it to the Neo-Babylonian period, both because it was under the Persian-period pottery in the cistern, but also because it was comparable to pottery labeled exilic at Bethel, and at tombs from ʿAin Shems and from Lachish (Lapp 1981: 84). The comparable pottery at Bethel is no longer assigned to the Babylonian period, however, but is now known to be pre-exilic (see above). The material in Tomb 14 at ʿAin Shems is more likely Persian (see below in the discussion on the tombs). The comparable material from the tombs at Lachish (Lapp 1981: 86) is also pre-exilic (see further below). The Lapps also found III B pottery similar to that from cistern 166 at Tell en-Naṣbeh, which they regarded as sixth century (Lapp 1981: 86), but it too is more likely eighth century and pre-exilic (see below). They also found their Period III B pottery comparable to the wine bottles at Gibeon, which Wright had dated to the second half of the sixth century (Lapp 1981: 85). These wine bottles are now securely dated to the seventh century, however (see above).

Finkelstein (2011: 8) states that Tell el-Fûl produced a limited quantity of sixth-century finds, most of which were found in the bottom of the cistern. He refers to vessels with reed impressions and to elongated juglets as being the sixth-century items. N. Lapp refers to the vessels with reed impressions as having a 'chevron design' (N. Lapp 1981: 94). If these are the same type of wedge-decorated bowls that Zertal finds all over the area of Manasseh, then they seem to be seventh century BCE (Zertal 1990). Zertal considers them to have been brought in by newcomers deported into Samaria by the Assyrians, and Lapp agrees that they may be imported (N. Lapp 1981: 94). Regarding the elongated juglets, Lapp notes these juglets have parallels in En-Gedi IV (N. Lapp 1981: 99), a level which according to Lipschits is 'clearly dated to the Persian period' (Lipschits 2005: 194). Lapp also finds these juglets to be similar to those from Gibeon, Jerusalem, Taanach and Lachish, none of which had Babylonian-period occupations.

The material at the bottom of the cistern and under the Hellenistic fence appears to be largely pre-exilic, with perhaps a mixture of early Persian forms. The Lapps' Period III B does not exist. It is a will-o'-the-wisp.

Tell en-Naṣbeh. Scholars have included Tell en-Naṣbeh among the sites with sixth-century occupation. Because the stratification is unclear, this identification is based on the pottery found in pits and granaries on the site, even though these contained mixed pottery from both the Iron Age and the Persian period (Lipschits 2005: 204 n. 76). Lipschits relies on pit #166 for a sixth-century date however because of the bronze circlet with cuneiform characters inscribed on it that was found there. The excavator considers the jar handles with Iron Age *lmlk* seal impressions in the pit to be of greater significance for dating the material, however, not the circlet that he labels an intrusion (McCown *et al.* 1947: 130-31). Indeed, the cuneiform signs on the piece continued unchanged into the Persian period and cannot be used to date occupation at the site to the sixth century (Vanderhooft and Horowitz 2002). Lipschits also refers to pit #183 as sixth century (Lipschits 2005: 204 n. 76), a pit that McCown considers to hold two separate groups of pottery, one probably from 650 to 586 and the other from the late-sixth to the early-fourth century (McCown *et al.* 1947: 132). Lipschits's confidence in an exilic dating of some of the material in this pit, in contrast to McCown's own conclusions, is based on comparisons with the so-called Period III B assemblages from Tell el-Fûl (Lipschits 2005: 204 n. 76.). Since the material dated sixth century at Tell el-Fûl seems actually to be a mixture of pre-exilic and Persian forms, and since the material in pit #183 at Tell en-Naṣbeh matches that of Tell el-Fûl, those finds in this pit are also likely to be a mixture of Persian and pre-exilic forms, as McCown maintains. This material cannot be used to argue for Babylonian habitation at Tell en-Naṣbeh.

The lack of clear stratigraphy and definite sixth-century remains at Tell en-Naṣbeh forces Zorn and his colleagues to rely on the Aramaic *m(w)ṣh* seal impressions to argue for Babylonian period occupation (Zorn *et al.* 1994). These were found all over the tell, but not *in situ.* (Indeed, nothing was found *in situ* except three large pithoi dated by the excavator to the eighth–seventh centuries.) Of the forty-two such *m(w)ṣh* impressions presently known, thirty come from Tell en Naṣbeh. The rest are from Jericho (2), Gibeon (4), Ramat Raḥel (1), Jerusalem (4), and from the Belmont Crusader Castle (1), thus primarily in the area of Benjamin. Although Zorn *et al.* argue for a Babylonian date, scholars have dated these Aramaic seals to the early Persian period based on the paleography (538–500; Avigad 1958: 113-19; Naveh 1970: 58-62). Two stamp impressions were found in pit #361 at Tell en-Naṣbeh. This pit contained pottery of the Persian period, including a sherd of a Greek black-figure oinochoe, definitely dated to c. 500 (Stern 1982: 208-209). This Greek vessel confirms an early Persian date for the seal impressions, not a Neo-Babylonian one, and ought to define the beginning of Stratum II at the site (de Groot 2001: 79). Six seal impressions were found in the northeastern edge of the tell in areas built on top of the great inner–outer gate complex, the complex that defines Stratum II. The major cluster of the seal impressions (15) came from a 15 m radius in the southwestern corner of the site, also a clear Stratum 2 context. The remaining impressions were scattered over the tell. These find spots correspond to those of the Greek pottery and the Persian-period *yh(w)d* seal impressions which were also in abundance on the site. These *m(w)ṣh* seal impressions are therefore early Persian, not Babylonian.

Find spots outside of Mizpah corroborate this early Persian date for the *m(w)ṣh* seal impressions. The four found in Jerusalem's City of David were found in Stratum 9, the stratum of Persian-period occupation (Finkelstein 2008b: 8). Of these, one was taken from a Persian fill above an Iron Age floor, requiring an early-Persian-period date. In fact, the recognized lack of habitation in Jerusalem during the Babylonian period precludes a Babylonian date for these seal impressions. A seal impression from Jericho was found in a thick silt level above the collapse of a late Iron Age building, also implying the end of the sixth century, not its beginning (Zorn *et al.* 1994: 113). The finds from Gibeon, Ramat Raḥel and a Crusader castle were not sufficiently stratified to suggest a context more than from late-sixth century through the Persian period. Thus, the combined stratigraphic evidence for these Aramaic seal impressions places them at the beginning of the Persian period. They are not Babylonian and cannot be used to argue for occupation at Tell en-Naṣbeh under the Babylonians after the fall of Gedaliah. The numerous Yehud seals testify instead to strong Persian-period occupation on the site.

En-Gedi. En-Gedi, a perennial spring, forms an oasis on the western shore of the Dead Sea (Mazar 1993: 399-405). Excavations there have concentrated on Tel Goren, the most prominent site on the oasis. Stratum V is the earliest settlement of Tel Goren. The abundant pottery vessels there are all characteristic of the second half of the seventh century and the beginning of the sixth. The buildings on the mound also date to this period. Several inscriptions in Hebrew and Aramaic have been found, one reads לאריהו עזריהו ('belonging to Uriyahu [son of] 'Azaryahu'). Numerous rosette stamps were also discovered, plus one jar handle bearing a double-winged *lamelekh* seal impression. Other finds include stone weights marked with the shekel sign. In a building on the northern slope, a pot containing a hoard of silver ingots plus silver jewelry was found. The Stratum V site was destroyed in a conflagration, dated by the excavators to the beginning of the sixth century.

Although Barstad labels Stratum IV as evincing occupation in the Babylonian period, it is 'clearly dated to the Persian period' (Lipschits 2005: 194). The buildings from this stratum are impressive in size and strength. One covers about 550 sq. m and contains about twenty-three rooms, enclosed courtyards and storerooms. The pottery is characteristic of the Persian period and similar to that of Lachish Stratum I (Lipschits 2005: 194). The date is confirmed by numerous Aramaic יהוד (*yhwd*), יהד (*yhd*) and יה (*yh*) seal impressions. Based on the pottery, the excavator (Mazar 1993) estimates that the large building was erected in the first half of the fifth century and destroyed at about 400. There is no evidence of Babylonian occupation at the site. An imported conical chalcedony seal of the type common in Babylonia from the seventh to the fifth century cannot imply Babylonian-period occupation (*pace* Barstad 1996: 49). Mazar labels it 'a Babylonian seal from the Persian period'.

Tombs in Benjamin and Judah. Barkay's well-known conclusions that the tombs at Ketef Hinnom were used during the Babylonian period have had a great influence on subsequent research (Barkay 1985). Unfortunately they rely heavily on comparisons with the pottery labeled Period III B at Tell el-Fûl. Besides the pottery, the rich assemblage of finds in the tomb includes jewelry and imported Attic ware, all dated to the Achaemenid period. A Greek heirloom coin from the island of Kos dated to 570 cannot serve to date the tomb to the Babylonian period; it simply provides a *terminus post quem* for the time of the coin's burial. Nor can the presence of the bathtub-shaped coffins there indicate a sixth-century date, since these Assyrian-type coffins were in use as early as the seventh century and continued into the Persian period.

Lipschits (2005: 206) suggests that Tomb 5 at Mamilah has parallels with the finds in the tomb at Ketef Hinnom. According to the excavator, however, use of Tomb 5 began in the eighth century and stopped in the course of the seventh century BCE. After a gap of some years, the tomb began to be used again toward the latter half of the sixth or the beginning of the fifth century and continued into the Persian period (Reich 1993: 106-107). The parallels with the finds at Ketef Hinnom are also most likely mixed pre-exilic and Persian period.

Tomb 14 at ‘Ain Shems (Beth Shemesh) has also been used as evidence of sixth-century occupation (Lipschits 2005: 206). According to the excavator, Stratum II at Beth-Shemesh was destroyed in 586 by Nebuchadnezzar and the city was never rebuilt (Grant and Wright 1939: 13). Stratum II is that Iron II city. Stratum I is the modern surface of the tell, covered by erosion and, in the 1930s, by local agricultural endeavors. In spite of the excavators' conclusion that the city was never rebuilt, coins from the Hellenistic period were scattered all over the tell, and coin hoards were found buried in jars there (Grant and Wright 1939: 85). Additional Hellenistic jars and lamps were found near a cistern. The excavators concluded that Tomb 14 belonged to Stratum II, that it was the latest of the Stratum II tombs, and that it was in use during the sixth century. They based their conclusions on the fact that the pottery in the tomb was later than the Stratum II pottery on the tell; and since they found no later occupation level, the tomb had to have been associated with Stratum II. They supposed that it was exilic and that it was the family tomb of an exile who returned to it to bury his dead (Grant and Wright 1939: 78). In spite of their own conclusions about the exilic date of Tomb 14, they describe the pottery in it as Persian. I quote the excavator. I omit the references to plate numbers.

> One of the major problems in Stratum II is the date of Tomb 14. The latest pottery from the surface of the tell resembles that from Tell Beit Mirsim A so closely that there can be little doubt that Beth-Shemesh fell with the invasion of the Chaldeans in the early part of the 6th century.

Recent ceramic and epigraphic studies confirm, however, that Tell Beit Mirsim was destroyed by Sennacherib in 701 and did not recover (Greenberg 1993: 180). The resemblance of the pottery on the surface of the tell to that from Beit Mirsim indicates that it too was destroyed in the Assyrian invasion, although this is disputed (Bunimovitz and Lederman 2003; Fantalkin 2004). According to the excavators, the pottery in Tomb 14 is much later than that of the final stratum on the tell.

> On the other hand, the pottery of Tomb 14 appears, as a whole, to be much later than that of Stratum IIC [the latest stratum identified on the site]. It has previously been indicated that the dipper juglet, the water decanters, and one of the lamps, though descended from Iron II forms, really resem-

> ble vases of the Persian period. . . . Bronze bowls in the tomb and the bronze strainer handle belong to types which were common in deposits throughout the Mediterranean world between the sixth and fourth centuries B.C. . . . Another form which belongs to the same period and not earlier is the juglet with the long body. . . . Several of these juglets have been found in Palestine all dating between the sixth and fourth centuries, and the type can be traced as far as Rhodes and Mesopotamia. . . . Further, are sherds which do not resemble Iron II wares, either in shape or thickness of section. The side-walls are much thinner, and are closer to Persian period pottery (Grant and Wright 1939: 144-45).

After this long discussion explaining how the pottery in the tomb appears Persian (late-sixth to fourth century), the excavators conclude by dating the tomb to the mid-sixth century and the Babylonian period! Excavators elsewhere have been repeating this conclusion, while forgetting the Persian-period data upon which it is based. The Persian-period objects in Tomb 14 suggest Persian-period occupation on the site, not Babylonian, even though modern agriculture and erosion has obliterated all traces of Persian-period dwellings.

Tombs 106, 109 and 114 at Lachish have also been used to identify sixth-century pottery. Scholars have argued that pottery that is later than Stratum II (destroyed in 586) but earlier than Stratum I (Persian) has been uncovered in the tombs (Lipschits 2005: 206). According to the excavator, however, 'there is no pottery which suggests that burials other than those of the Byzantine period were made in Tomb 106 after the destruction of Level II (destroyed in 586)' (Tufnell 1953: 180). Tombs 109 and 114 had been disturbed and did not have the rich assembly that was available in Tomb 106, but what was there was comparable to the finds in Tomb 106. In Tufnell's chronological charts of the various pottery forms, pottery from the three tombs is grouped with Level II, and is even placed earlier in the chart than the pottery from the Level II houses (Tufnell 1953: 325-30). Pottery from Tombs 109 and 114 is listed as later than the pottery from Tomb 106, not because Tombs 109 and 114 date to the Babylonian period but because use of Tomb 106 seems to have begun at the end of the eighth century, just before the Level III destruction in 701—thus beginning earlier than the other two tombs.

In spite of all this, Tufnell dates Tombs 109 and 114 to between 600 and 550 (Tufnell 1953: 188). This late date is nowhere explained. Perhaps Tufnell was unwilling to date the end point of the pottery in the tomb precisely to 586, and so gave round numbers of 600–550. This does not mean that the pottery in the tombs postdates the pottery in the houses when the tell was destroyed. That was not the conclusions of the excavators. Tufnell states emphatically that 'the desertion of the site after the destruction of Level II [586] is reflected in the lack of material [i.e. in either the houses or the tombs] to fill the gap between the end of Level II and the contents of the administrative buildings of Level I [Persian]' (Tufnell 1953: 259). A comparison of the pottery in Tombs 109 and 114 with the pottery in the houses and in Tomb 106 reveals that with only one exception every item in Tombs 109 and 114 has a parallel with pottery in the houses from Levels II and III and with Tomb 106. The lone exception appears to be a dipper in Tomb 109, which elsewhere appears only in tombs from the earlier Levels V and IV. Evidence suggests, therefore, that all three tombs went out of use in 586 with the destruction of the city, and not later.

Conclusion

It must be concluded that the fall of Judah to the Babylonians in 586 was catastrophic and devastating and that a pronounced population dearth ensued in both Judah and Benjamin as a result, a dearth that lasted throughout the Babylonian period (586–538 BCE). Recovery began only very gradually with the return of Judeans to Jerusalem and elsewhere in Judah and Benjamin at the end of the sixth and in the early decades of the fifth century. It was not until the Hellenistic period that Jerusalem and Judah reached the level of development and population that they had at the end of the monarchy. During the Babylonian period the land of Judah and Benjamin was virtually empty, with slow and gradual growth beginning only with the return of Judeans to Judah under Persian occupation.

Evidence from Babylon for the Exile of Judeans to Babylon

Not only does the archaeology evince the complete devastation wreaked on Judah and Benjamin by the Babylonians, but cuneiform tablets from Babylon reveal the presence of exiled Judeans living there from the time of the fall of Jerusalem (Joannès and Lemaire 1999; Pearce 2006, 2011; Pearce and Wunsch 2014; Wunsch and Pearce forthcoming). One tablet, dated to the seventh year of Cyrus (532 BCE), and drawn up in the town of Našar, reveals that a certain Abdayahu ('Servant of Yhwh'), son of Barakahyahu ('Yhwh blessed'), has conveyed a tax payment from a widow to the local governor (Joannès and Lemaire 1999: 27-30). A second tablet, a sale of a steer, was written in the city āl-Yāhūdu, 'the city of the Judeans', in the 24th year of Darius I (498 BCE) (Joannès and Lemaire 1999: 17-27). The purchaser is Nêriyahu, or Neriah, 'Yhwh is my light', a name already known from the biblical text as the father of Jeremiah's scribe, from several ostraca, and from the texts at Elephantine. Witnesses to the sale also include those with Yahwistic names: Yahuazari ('Yhwh helped me'), Abduyahu ('Servant of Yhwh'), Shamahyahu ('Yhwh heard'). The place where the sale was written up, āl-Yāhūdu, indicates a city of deportees from Judah living in Babylon. In addition to these tablets, there is a corpus of over one hundred other tablets from these two cities and from other nearby locations near the city of Borsippa in Babylon (Pearce 2006; Pearce and Wunsch 2014). The earliest text in the corpus that refers to 'Judah-ville', āl-Yāhūdu, is dated to the 33rd year of Nebuchadnezzar (572 BCE), only fourteen years after the fall of Jerusalem in 586 (Pearce 2006: 402). The Judeans in the corpus are shown participating actively in the economic life of the area and are recorded as both debtors and creditors. Primarily, however, these data show that in contrast to the Assyrian deportees, the Judean exiles were resettled in their own cities in Babylon. The fact that they continued to name their children Yahwistic names (for the most part) suggests that they maintained their ancestral customs as well. The existence of 'Judahville' into the reign of Darius also shows that not all of the exiles returned to Judah at the beginning of the reign of Cyrus.

Evidence from Syria

The Judeans were not the only community to have been exiled to Babylon and to return under the Persians. The 1926–27 excavations at Neirab, Syria, revealed clay tablets from the reign of Nebuchadnezzar to the early years of Darius I (Eph'al 1978). The transactions described on the tablets refer to a people named the Neirabians, that is, the people who lived in the city where the archive was found. Yet the places where the transactions occurred were all in the vicinity of Nippur in Babylon. A community of Syrians who had been exiled to Nippur under Nebuchadnezzar had evidently been released to their own city in the beginning of Darius's reign.

Conclusions

Rather than base our understanding of the history of sixth-century Judah on an exaggeration of Jer. 52.16 (= 2 Kgs 25.12), in which 'some of the poorest' becomes 'tens of thousands', why not base it on Jer. 44.1-2?

> The word that came to Jeremiah for all the Judeans [who had fled to] the land of Egypt and were living at Migdol, at Tahpanhes, at Memphis, and in the land of Pathros,
>
> Thus says Yhwh of hosts, the god of Israel: You yourselves have seen all the disaster that I have brought on Jerusalem and on all the towns of Judah. Look at them; today they are a desolation, without an inhabitant in them.

Ezra 1

Prologue: The Return Home under Cyrus

In January of 588 BCE Nebuchadnezzar, king of Babylon, laid siege against Jerusalem; and after two-and-one-half years, in the summer of 586, the Babylonians had breached the city walls, destroyed both temple and city, and exiled much of the populace to Babylon (see Introduction to Ezra 1–6). Those of the populace who had not been deported and who had not been killed in battle either died from starvation or illness during the siege or fled to neighboring states such as Egypt and Ammon.

Thirty years later, in 559 BCE, Cyrus II, called 'the Great', became king of Fars (Parsa), a small province of the kingdom of Media on the Persian Gulf in what is now modern Iran. We know of Cyrus from the writings of the Greek historians, primarily Herodotus and Xenophon, from Babylonian texts such as the Nabonidus Chronicle and the Cyrus Cylinder, and from a few Persian inscriptions. In 559 BCE, Cyrus came to rule Parsa. His father was Cambyses I, son of Cyrus I, king of Anshan, a small Elamite kingdom centered at the city of Anshan in Parsa on the Persian Gulf. His mother was Mandane, daughter of Astyages, king of Media, and Aryenis, half-sister of Croesus, king of Lydia. In 553 he rebelled against his maternal grandfather, the king of Media, and by 550 had conquered the Median Empire. He then marched eastward and by 546 had conquered all of Asia Minor, including Lydia on the Aegean Sea. He soon turned his attention to Babylon, and after seven years of fighting, walked into the capital city of that same name. It was October 29, 539, and he had been at war for twenty years (Briant 2002: 13-49).

In conquering Babylon, Cyrus inherited all of its vassal states, including Judah. According to the biblical text (Ezra 1.1-4), one of his first acts upon ascending the Babylonian throne in the spring of 538 was to issue a decree allowing the exiled Judeans to return home to Judah and to rebuild their temple in Jerusalem. They were also permitted to bring with them the temple vessels that Nebuchadnezzar had taken when he destroyed the temple (Ezra 1.7, 8; 5.15; cf. 2 Kings 24–25; 2 Chronicles 36). The first four verses of Ezra 1 (Ezra 1.1-4) purport to present the decree of Cyrus that allowed the exiled Judeans to return home and to rebuild their temple. Theologically speaking, these first four verses form the beginning of a salvation history. They describe a return to God's favor after exile (Gunneweg 1985: 41).

Ezra 1.1

Setting the Stage for Cyrus's Edict

The first verse sets the stage for the decree that allowed the Judeans to return to their land. It provides the date, the name of the person authorizing the return, that is Cyrus the Great, king of Persia, and it provides Cyrus's motivation for doing so.

Translation

1. *And*[a] *in the first year of Cyrus, King of Persia,*[b] *at the fulfillment of the word of Yhwh from the mouth of Jeremiah,*[c] *Yhwh stirred up the spirit of Cyrus*[d] *King of Persia who sent out*[e] *a herald*[f] *throughout*[g] *all his kingdom—and also by writing—saying:*

Textual Notes

a. **1.1** *And.* This first word is not present in every version. It is present in the LXX of Ezra and in the Hebrew of 2 Chron. 36.22, but it is absent in the LXX of the Chronicles' verse. It is also absent from 1 Esdras, from the Vulgate, and from the Peshitta, but *lectio difficilior potior*, the more difficult reading is preferred. That means that the 'and' should be retained.

b. *Persia.* Greek Ezra reads 'of the Persians'.

c. *Jeremiah.* Syriac adds 'the prophet', thus providing an explanation of who this Jeremiah is.

d. *Cyrus.* Syriac omits 'Cyrus' here.

e. *Sent out a herald.* Greek Ezra reads παρήγγειλεν φωνήν, 'instruct, order a voice', a literal translation. First Esdras reads ἐκήρυξεν, 'proclaim', indicating that the translator sees an imperial edict in these verses.

f. *Herald.* Literally, a 'voice'.

g. *Throughout.* Literally, 'in'.

Notes

1.1 ***And.*** This passage, and so the book, begins oddly with a conjunction. It is true that 1 Kings also begins this way, but 1 Kings is really a continuation of 2 Samuel. In the Greek Bible, for example, 1 and 2 Samuel and 1 and

2 Kings are together known simply as 1–4 Kings. They are really all one book. The only other book to begin with a conjunction that is not the first letter of ויהי ('and it came to pass') is Exodus ('And these are the names'), and some commentators (e.g. Propp 1998) doubt that it is original there since it is missing in some of the versions. Thus, the conjunction is anomalous here. Medieval rabbinic commentators explain the 'and' by assuming that Ezra is a continuation of the book of Daniel. Modern scholars rule this out, since they date the book of Daniel to the period of the Maccabees (164 BCE), several centuries after Ezra–Nehemiah's writing.

Rather than a continuation of Daniel, many modern scholars note that nearly the identical wording of Ezra 1.1 is found in 2 Chron. 36.22 and conclude therefore that Ezra–Nehemiah is a continuation of the books of Chronicles.

Most scholars reject this idea however (see discussion in Introduction to Ezra–Nehemiah), but this leaves the 'and' and the repetition of the verses unexplained. If the two books had two separate authors, then three possibilities exist for the repetition. Either the author of Ezra–Nehemiah copied from Chronicles (Redditt 2008: 229-31; Knoppers 2003b: 77; Klein 2012: 545) or the Chronicler (or a later copyist) copied the lines from Ezra 1 (Freedman 1961; Williamson 1977: 9; 1987b: 57; Japhet 1993: 1076), or they each copied from a third source. If from a third source, it may have been the second temple's actual building inscription (Fried 2003b, 2010a). The type of statement included in vv. 1-4 of Ezra 1 is exactly the sort of component that would appear in ancient Near Eastern temple-building inscriptions. It would usually appear second, however; the first component would be the history of the temple and the reason for its destruction (see Introduction to Ezra 1–6). If these four verses were the second component of such a building inscription, then the 'and' would be understandable. Component A, the history of the temple and why it was destroyed, may have been omitted from Ezra when it was included in the Bible, since the story is told in Chronicles. It is also included in Tattenai's letter to Darius, Ezra 5.12. This is discussed further in Comment B, below.

In the first year of Cyrus King of Persia. This is Cyrus II, called 'the Great'. We must be cautious in accepting the historicity of this date for the initial return of the Judeans to Judah however. If these verses form the beginning of a typical ancient Near Eastern temple-building story, as I suspect, then citing the king's first year would be mandatory. Temple building in the ancient Near East is traditionally placed to the first year of a king's reign, whenever it may have actually occurred (see Hurowitz 1992; Boda and Novotny 2010, for examples and data). If the date is authentic, then it is 538 BCE, the year when Cyrus II became king of Babylon and the first time he would have been in a position to release the Judeans and allow them to return home. It would not refer to his accession to the throne of Persia, about twenty years earlier.

At the fulfillment of the word of Yhwh. Literally, 'at the completion'. The prophetic word is only the beginning of the prophetic act. The act is not completed until it is fulfilled. The return of the exiles to Judah is seen as the fulfillment of Jeremiah's prophecy and as proof that Yhwh is reliable and that he keeps his word as given by the prophets.

From the mouth of Jeremiah. When did the prophet Jeremiah mention Cyrus? Commentators have traditionally read this verse in the light of the parallel at the end of 2 Chronicles. Second Chronicles ends with two verses (2 Chron. 36.22-23) that are identical to Ezra 1.1-2. These last two verses of 2 Chronicles are preceded by two other verses that refer to Jeremiah:

> [Nebuchadnezzar] took into exile into Babylon those who had escaped from the sword, and they became servants to him and to his sons until the establishment of the kingdom of Persia, to fulfill the word of Yhwh by the mouth of Jeremiah, until the land had made up for its Sabbaths. All the days that it lay desolate it kept the Sabbath, to fulfill seventy years (2 Chron. 36.21-22).

This reference to seventy years in Chronicles may refer to the following statement of Jeremiah:

> I am going to send for all the tribes of the north, says Yhwh, even for King Nebuchadrezzar of Babylon, my servant, and I will bring them against this land and its inhabitants, and against all the nations round-about; I will utterly destroy them, and make them an object of horror and of hissing, and an everlasting disgrace. And I will banish from them the sound of mirth and the sound of gladness, the voice of the bridegroom and the voice of the bride, the sound of the millstones and the light of the lamp. This whole land shall become a ruin and a waste, and these nations shall serve the king of Babylon seventy years. Then after seventy years are completed, I will punish the king of Babylon and that nation, the land of the Chaldeans, for their iniquity, says Yhwh, making their land an everlasting waste (Jer. 25.9-12).

This implies that the seventy years before the return were predicted by Jeremiah to be a period when Judah was to lie fallow and desolate. Jeremiah refers to seventy years a second time:

> For thus says Yhwh: Only when Babylon's seventy years are completed will I visit you, and I will fulfill to you my promise and bring you back to this place (Jer. 29.10).

This prediction implies a seventy-year period of exile in Babylon. No matter which citation is used, however, scholars have been hard pressed to determine the beginning and end of these seventy years. If the return to Judah occurred in 538 BCE (the first year of Cyrus), then seventy years before that is 608 BCE, probably the first year of Jehoiakim and the time when Judah first became a vassal to Babylon. In this case, the seventy years would be the time that Judah was under Babylonian domination. This seems to have been Josephus's interpretation (*Ant.* 11.1-2; followed by Briend 1996: 37, who suggests that 'without doubt' this is the date that is meant).

However, this does not comport with the plain meaning of the text of Jer. 25.11, in which it is stated that Judah was to lie desolate for seventy years. If the prophecy refers to the exile, a period in which the land of Judah was to be a 'waste and a ruin', then that period was only forty-eight years, from 586 to 538 BCE. It has been suggested therefore that the period of desolation refers to the seventy years in which the temple lay in ruins, the seventy years of emotional desolation and mourning for Yhwh, when Yhwh could not inhabit his temple—from 586 BCE (the year of its destruction) to 516 BCE (the year of its rededication, Ezra 6.15; see Whitley 1954; Fried 2003b). This is the period of Yhwh's exile from his temple.

Alternatively, it could have been a real prediction that Jeremiah simply got wrong, and it was only forty-eight years of desolation, not seventy (D.N. Freedman, personal communication). Or, it is possible that the phrase 'seventy years' was not intended to be a real number but only 'a long time'. Destructions and desolations of cities were often predicted to last seventy years in the ancient world. Isaiah predicted that Tyre would lie destroyed for seventy years (Isa. 23.14-18) and a seventy-year period of desolation was predicted for Babylon after its destruction by Sennacherib (Luckenbill 1925; Borger 1959). If seventy is a round number (Rudolph 1949: 3), it may refer to the length of time of a man's life (Isa. 23.15; Ps. 90.10).

It may be, however, that Jeremiah's prophecy is referred to here in Ezra not because he predicted a seventy-year period of exile but because he predicted an end to Babylonian domination and a return of the exiles to Judah, which did occur (Jeremiah 32). This reference to the prophet Jeremiah then provides divine authority for the return itself, rather than for the exile. (See the following note.)

Yhwh stirred up the spirit of Cyrus King of Persia. In contrast to the reference to Jeremiah's prophecy in Chronicles (which is clearly to a seventy-year period), the reference to Jeremiah in Ezra refers not to a seventy-year period of exile but rather to Jeremiah's prediction that the Medes (i.e. the Persians) will destroy Babylon (Williamson 1985: 10). This is clear from Ezra's repetition of Jeremiah's phrase 'stir up the spirit'.

> For I am going to *stir up* and bring against Babylon a company of great nations from the land of the north; and they shall array themselves against her; from there she shall be taken. Their arrows are like the arrows of a skilled warrior who does not return empty-handed (Jer. 50.9).

> Sharpen the arrows! Fill the quivers! Yhwh has *stirred up the spirit* of the kings of the Medes, because his purpose concerning Babylon is to destroy it, for that is Yhwh's vengeance, vengeance for his temple (Jer. 51.11).

The reference to Jeremiah's prophecy and its fulfillment demonstrates Yhwh's continual relationship with his people, that his anger does not last forever, and that he can be relied upon to avenge his temple, his city and his people.

who sent out a herald throughout all his kingdom. This is the way edicts were promulgated in preliterate societies. (See the next note.)

—and also by writing—. The heralds read the edicts that they called out. A text (KAJ 310: 20 [MA] cited in *CAD* Š, vol. 17, pt. 2, p. 167) affirms that proclamations are physical tablets read aloud by the herald. The text refers to a chest in which such proclamations were stored:

> 1 quppu ša sasu nagirī ša bītāti ša Assur
>
> 1 chest containing the proclamations of heralds concerning the (purchase of) houses in the city of Assur.

Heralds did not rely on memory but were required to read their proclamations. The proclamations were evidently stored in a chest; they were not handed out on the street. Thus, if a proclamation had gone forth throughout the empire, the Judeans would not necessarily have retained a copy of it and would not have been able to prove their right to build the temple. That they did not have a copy of it is evident from Tattenai's letter to Darius (Ezra 5.6-17). (See Comment A below on the historicity of the decree.)

Ezra 1.2-4

The Edict of Cyrus

Verses 2-4 have been termed the Cyrus Edict, implying that these are the actual words that Cyrus proclaimed when he permitted the Judeans to return to their homeland and to rebuild their temple. The book of Ezra presents two versions of Cyrus's command concerning the return of Judeans from captivity, one in Hebrew (Ezra 1.2-4) and another in Aramaic (Ezra 6.3-5; Bickerman 1946: 249). The differences between these two texts have implied to scholars that they cannot both be authentic. Bickerman maintains, however, that these are two independent records of the same pronouncement, and that therefore they do not need to agree in wording. The Aramaic version is a memorandum of an official decision, and as such it was not made public but filed away. According to Bickerman, the Hebrew version presented here is a translation of an original Aramaic. (See Comment A below for further discussion.)

Translation

2. *'Thus says Cyrus, King of Persia: "All the kingdoms of the earth*[a] *Yhwh*[b] *god of heaven*[c] *has given me, and he has appointed me to build him a temple*[d] *in Jerusalem*[e] *which is in Judah.* 3. *Whoever among you of all his people*[f] *— may his god be with him*[g] *— let him go up*[h] *to Jerusalem which is in Judah and let him build the temple of Yhwh*[i] *the god of Israel (He is God!) which is in Jerusalem.*[j] 4. *And all who remain*[k] *in any of the places where he had resided,*[l] *let them — that is, the inhabitants of his place*[m] *— support him by means of silver and gold,*[n] *goods,*[o] *and animals,*[p] *and with free-will offerings*[q] *for the temple of the god which is in Jerusalem"'.*

Textual Notes

a. **1.2** *Kingdoms of the earth.* The Syriac reads 'the rule of the earth' rather than 'all the kingdoms of the earth', seeing *malkût* ('rule') rather than *malkôt* ('kingdoms') and omitting 'all'.

b. *Yhwh.* First Esdras reads 'the Lord of Israel' rather than simply 'the Lord', as is customary in Greek translations. This may be an attempt to clarify that the god is the god of Israel. This is unclear in the Greek since Yhwh's name is not used.

c. *God of heaven.* Rather than 'god of heaven', 1 Esdras reads 'Lord Most High'.

d. *Temple.* The Hebrew is literally 'house'; but the 'house of a god' is called a 'temple' in English, and this is how it will be translated in this commentary.

e. *Jerusalem.* Syriac adds 'the city' as an explanation.

f. **1.3** *Whoever among you of all his people.* Greek Ezra reads this as a question: 'Who is there among all his people?' as does the Vulgate: 'Who is among you of all his people?' 1 Esdras is closer to the MT in not seeing a question here. It reads, 'If anyone of you is from his people, may his Lord be with him, let him go up'. The Syriac reads 'all *the* people' rather than 'all *his* people'.

g. *May his god be with him.* 2 Chron. 36.23 reads, 'May Yhwh his god be with him', and likewise 1 Esdras reads, 'may his Lord be with him'. The name seems to have become corrupted in Ezra. Ezra reads יְהִי, 'may' or 'let', but probably God's name is intended, יהוה.

h. *Let him go up.* At this point the book of Chronicles ends.

i. *The temple of Yhwh the god of Israel.* Greek Ezra reads 'let him build the temple of the god of Israel'. First Esdras reads 'the temple of the Lord of Israel'. The Syriac reads 'a temple to the LORD, the god of Israel'.

j. *Which is in Jerusalem.* First Esdras reads 'the temple of the Lord—he is the Lord *who* dwells in Jerusalem'.

k. **1.4** *All who remain.* First Esdras omits 'all who remain' but the result is no clearer than the Hebrew. First Esdras reads, 'All who live throughout the(ir?) places shall help him, the men of his place. . . .' For a parallel expression to 'all who remain', see Isa. 4.3.

l. *In any of the places where he had resided.* Resided, that is, as an alien. The same Hebrew expression is used in Deut. 18.6. The verb *gār,* 'resided', can be a past tense, but also a present participle—the form of this verb is the same. The versions employ the participle. It is translated literally by Greek Ezra as παροικεῖ, 'to live as a stranger'. 1 Esdras reads οἰκοῦσιν, 'where they live'.

m. *The inhabitants of his place.* This is the subject of the verb 'support'.

n. *Silver and gold.* First Esdras reads 'gold and silver', which is the more common order in late Biblical Hebrew (Talshir 2001: 94). The present order may reflect Exod. 11.2.

o. *Goods.* That is, movable property. First Esdras reads 'gifts', δόσεσιν, which may reflect the מִגְדָּנוֹת, the 'precious gifts' of 1.6 (Talshir 2001: 95).

p. *Animals.* First Esdras reads 'with horses and pack animals', suggesting רכש, 'steed', rather than רכוש, 'movable property', that is, 'small animals'.

q. *Free-will offerings.* First Esdras reads 'the other things added to it as vows'. The translator of 1 Esdras must have read נדר, votive offering' (i.e. an offering made in fulfillment of a vow), rather than נדב, 'free-will offering'. Talshir suggests that the phrase כל הנשאר, 'all who remain', may have been moved to the end of the verse and translated as τοῖς κατ' εὐχὰς προστεθειμένοις, 'the other things added to it as vows'.

Notes

1.2 ***Thus says Cyrus.*** Literally, 'Thus said' in the past tense. This phrase routinely introduces direct discourse, not only in the Hebrew Bible (where it occurs 463 times, and is always translated 'Thus says'), but it is also a frequent occurrence in Achaemenid inscriptions, beginning with the reign of Darius. It does not appear earlier, nor does it appear in any of the numerous Akkadian royal inscriptions, including the royal inscriptions of Nabonidus (the last king of Babylon). Nor does it appear in the genuine inscriptions of Cyrus. (The phrase occurs in the inscription of Ariaramnes, Darius's great-grandfather, and in that of Arsames, Darius's grandfather, but these all turn out to be forgeries, composed in the reign of Darius I (Waters 2004). The Cyrus inscription at Pasargadae that includes this phrase is also known to have been written by Darius (Stronach 1978: 95-103; 1997:49).

As can be seen, the phrase occurs repeatedly throughout Darius's Behistun inscription and is formulaic in the inscriptions of every Achaemenid ruler after him; for example,

> I am Darius the Great King, King of Kings, King of Persia, King of countries, son of Hystaspes, grandson of Arsames, an Achaemenid.
>
> Thus says Darius the King: . . .

In contrast, the relevant portion of the Cyrus Cylinder reads:

> I am Cyrus, king of the world, great king, legitimate king, king of Babylon, king of Sumer and Akkad, king of the four rims (of the earth), son of Cambyses, great king, king of Anshan, grandson of Cyrus, great king, king of Anshan, descendant of Teispes, great king, king of Anshan, of a family which always (exercised) kingship; whose rule Bel and Nebo love, whom they want as king to please their hearts.
>
> When I entered Babylon . . . (Oppenheimer, ll. 20-22, *ANET*[3] 316).

There is no phrase in Cyrus's inscription introducing direct speech. Direct speech begins immediately. The phrase 'thus says' does not belong to any Persian proclamation dating to the time of Cyrus. It cannot be earlier than Darius I.

King of Persia. Cyrus's titulary, King of Persia, is another indication that these verses do not stem from Cyrus's own ministers (Wilson 1917; Bedford 2001: 120-22) but from the pen of the Judeans. At the time of Cyrus, the title 'King of Persia' appears only in texts written by non-Persians. Cyrus, King of Persia (Par-su-maš), probably Cyrus I, is mentioned by Assyrians, for example, in annals from the 640s as paying tribute to Ashurbanipal (668–630 BCE; Borger 1996: 191-92). Cyrus II is also called King of Persia in the Nabonidus Chronicle, a text written by Babylonian scribes in the ninth year of Nabonidus (546 BCE). Even so, this title is never used for Cyrus in any of the over eight hundred extant Babylonian legal, economic, or administrative documents dating from either his reign or that of his son Cambyses II; nor is it ever used in any of Cyrus's own royal inscriptions. The title is common for Achaemenid kings only beginning with Darius I.

Cyrus's own inscriptions always refer to him as 'King of Anshan' (Galling 1964: 69; Waters 2004). This is further evidence that the phrasing of this so-called Cyrus Edict dates at least to the time of Darius I.

The titles of the kings varied depending on location: in Egypt, Darius was given typical Egyptian titles (Bickerman 1946: 254-56). Rather than being called 'King of Persia', as in the Behistun inscription, he was called 'King of Upper and Lower Egypt, Lord of the Two Lands'; and in Babylonian documents he was given the typical Babylonian title 'King of Lands'. If so, then the appropriate Hebrew analogy would imply that he should be titled 'King of Judah' or 'Yhwh's Anointed', which does not occur (except in Isa. 45.1; see Fried 2002b for a discussion of this title applied to Cyrus). Bickerman suggests that Cyrus may have been known in the West by the title 'Cyrus, King of Persia' (Bickerman 1946: 256). Even if true, we do not have words from Cyrus's court but an appellation according to how he was known in the West.

All the kingdoms of the earth Yhwh, god of heaven, has given me. Yhwh, the name of the local Judean god, appears here in the mouth of Cyrus, as Cyrus, the Persian king, claims that Yhwh has given him all the kingdoms of the earth. This type of exuberant claim in the name of the god of the conquered people was common in the ancient Near East (Fried 2002b). The Babylonian Cyrus Cylinder has Cyrus, the foreign Persian conqueror, say that 'Marduk [the god of Babylon], the great lord, induced the inhabitants of Babylon to love me' (ll. 22-24, *ANET*^{3} 315-16; Schaudig 2001: 550-56).

The Cyrus Cylinder is a barrel-shaped clay cylinder 23 cm long and 11 cm wide. It was found in 1879 by Hormuzd Rassam in Babylon, and now belongs to the British Museum. It commemorates Cyrus's rebuilding both the city of Babylon and Marduk's temple, the Esagila (after he destroyed both of them!). Written after the Persian conquest, the cylinder intends to demonstrate to subsequent generations (and to the gods) that Cyrus the Persian king is the legitimate ruler of Babylon. He alone was chosen by Marduk, Babylon's god, to conquer Babylon and to rebuild Marduk's temple (Kuhrt 1983: 88-89; Fried 2002b).

An Egyptian inscription, the inscription of Udjaḥorresnet, is similar (Lichtheim 1980: 36-41). Found in the temple of Neith in Sais, in lower Egypt, it is also a building inscription, and it serves a similar purpose. It describes the restoration of the temple of the goddess Neith, begun under Cambyses, Cyrus's son (after he had destroyed it during his conquest of Egypt!), and completed under Darius. It too stresses that the Persian kings recognized and paid homage to Neith, the mother of the sun-god Re, and that Neith approved the Persian conquest of Egypt. It was thus common in the early years of the Persian empire for local priesthoods to state that their local gods supported the Persian kings and the Persian conquest (Fried 2002b). In return for local priesthoods in Babylon and Egypt handing over to the Persian conquerors the titulary and accolades of their local kings, the Persians aided them in rebuilding their destroyed temples. This was the case in Jerusalem as well.

According to the biblical writer, Cyrus could not have conquered Babylon on his own, but he was given all the countries of the earth by Yhwh only in order to enable the Judeans to return home and to rebuild their temple in Jerusalem. In the same way the priests of Marduk believed that Marduk called Cyrus to conquer Babylon and the priest of Neith believed that the goddess called Cambyses to conquer Egypt. The fact that it happened proves that their god commanded it. It could not have happened otherwise.

God of heaven. Literally, 'god of the skies'. This phrase is appended to God's name not only here but also in a letter (*TAD* A 4.7, 8) sent in 407 BCE from a group of Judeans garrisoned on the Nile island of Elephantine in southern Egypt. The letter was sent to Bagavahya, the Persian governor of Judah, from the Judean priests of the temple of Yhw at Elephantine. (Yhw is the spelling at Elephantine of the name of the Judean god, which is spelled Yhwh in the Hebrew Bible.) In the letter, the writers explain that since the time that their temple at Elephantine had been destroyed (three years before) they have been fasting and praying to 'Yhw Lord of Heaven'. They state further that if the temple is rebuilt, Bagavahya will have great merit before 'Yhw, god of heaven'. Bagavahya responds that the Judean priests may say to the satrap of Egypt that the temple of the god of heaven which is in Elephantine should be rebuilt as it was formerly (*TAD* A 4.9).

By using this title for their god, the Judeans at Elephantine may have been trying to affirm that Yhw was the local manifestation at Elephantine of the Persian imperial god of heaven, that is, the Persian supreme god, Ahuramazda (Bolin 1995). However, Ahuramazda was never known to the Persians as the god of heaven. Ahuramazda is not called such in any Persian inscription (Andrews 1964). The name Ahuramazda literally means 'Lord of Wisdom', not 'Lord of Heaven', although it is true that Ahuramazda is said to be 'clothed in the sky as a garment' (Yasna 30.5; Boyce 1982: 179-80). Nevertheless, the correspondence between the Judeans at Elephantine and the Persian officials in Judah demonstrates that the terms 'god of heaven' and 'Lord of Heaven' were titles that Judeans applied to their god when communicating with non-Judeans and which were also used by non-Judeans to refer to Yhwh in return. (This is nicely illustrated in Jon. 1.9, where Jonah explains to non-Judeans that he is 'a Hebrew', who worships 'Yhwh, the god of heaven, who made the sea and the dry land'.) The title 'god of heaven' was sometimes used among Judeans themselves as well. An Elephantine letter (*TAD* A 4.3) to Jedaniah, the priest of Yhw at the temple in Elephantine, from Mauziah son of Nathan (a Judean) stresses the hope that Jedaniah will continue 'in favor before the god of heaven', presumably Yhw. Both this and the previous letters are dated to the end of the fifth century BCE. Whether the title was also applied to Yhwh or Yhw in the time of Cyrus or Darius I, at the end of the sixth century, is not known—but is likely.

To complicate matters further, a separate god, Ba'al Shamem, literally, Lord of Heaven, or Lord of the Sky, appears at the head of the Phoenician pantheon in both tenth- and seventh-century BCE Phoenician inscriptions (*KAI* 4, 26; SAA 2, 5 IV: 10; Röllig 1999). By the Hellenistic period the Phoenician Lord of Heaven was assumed to be that god who was called Zeus among the Greeks (Eusebius, *Praep. evang.* 1.10.7) and Yhwh among the Judeans (Röllig 1999).

All the kingdoms of the earth Yhwh god of heaven has given me. This language is similar to that in one of Cyrus's inscriptions found on a stamped brick from Ur in southern Babylon (Schaudig 2001: 549). That brick reads, 'The great gods [of Babylon] have put all the lands into my hands'. In other words, it is a statement of the Babylonians written in Cyrus's name that their own Babylonian gods, not the Persian gods, had put Babylon into the hands of the Persian conqueror. It also gives recognition to the Babylonian gods themselves. The commonality of this type of language illustrates the global culture in which the Judeans lived and wrote.

And he has appointed me to build him a temple in Jerusalem. Cyrus states that it was Yhwh who ordered him to build a temple in Jerusalem. Cyrus has here stepped into the role of the Judean temple builder, a role that previously belonged only to David and Solomon. This phrase is a primary component of ancient temple-building inscriptions, however. The decision to build a temple must be made by the god whose temple it is; otherwise the temple will not stand (Hurowitz 1992; Fried 2003b; Boda and Novotny 2010), and the god's decision must be conveyed to the individual who has the actual power to build it—the king, in this case Cyrus.

A temple in Jerusalem which is in Judah. This is the type of description used in contemporary letters from Elephantine. The reference in those letters is to 'the temple of Yhw the god which (or who) is in Elephantine' (e.g. *TAD* A 4.7, 8).

1.3 ***Whoever among you of all his people.*** That is, among Yhwh's people, the people who worship Yhwh wherever they may be scattered, in Babylon, Assyria, or Egypt. The Hebrew of this verse is ambiguous. It can mean 'whoever among you of all his (Yhwh's) people [who wants to go up], may his god be with him, let him go up'. Or it can mean, 'whoever among all of you various peoples is of his (Yhwh's) people, then may his god be with him, let him go up (or even, "he shall go up")'. The announcement addresses a subset of a whole. Is it the subset of all the peoples of the world who are followers of Yhwh, or is it the subset of the followers of Yhwh who want to go up? The versions prefer the former. (See note on v. 5 below.)

May his god be with him. That is, may his god, Yhwh, accompany the Judean on his journey from Babylon to Jerusalem. There is a strong presumption, visible in the texts of the exilic prophets Ezekiel (esp. chaps. 1, 10 and 11) and of Deutero-Isaiah (esp. chaps. 40 and 52) that Yhwh was no longer living in Jerusalem but had gone to Babylon with the exiles. As the exiles travel back from Babylon to Jerusalem to rebuild their temple, Cyrus wishes that their god may go with them—that is, that he may literally, physically, accompany them on their journey to Judah. The fact that the temple vessels are traveling with the returnees from Babylon to Jerusalem (1.8) is tangible evidence that Yhwh is indeed accompanying them. See Isa. 52.1-12 and the discussion below on the temple vessels.

Let him go up to Jerusalem. This is the statement that permits the Judeans to return to Judah and Jerusalem. The verb 'to go up', used here, expresses a specifically Judean perspective in which going to Jerusalem, from any direction, is always going up. These would not be the literal words of Cyrus but would have been the appropriate Judean phrasing for a Hebrew temple-building inscription.

And let him build the temple of Yhwh in Jerusalem. This is the key provision, that the temple of Yhwh may be rebuilt in Jerusalem. There were temples to Yhwh elsewhere during the Persian period, most noticeably on Har Gerizim in Samaria (Magen 2000; 2007; Stern and Magen 2000, 2002), but also on the Nile island of Elephantine in Egypt (Porten 1968) and in Maqqedah, modern Khirbet el-Kôm, about 15 miles W of Hebron, in what was then Idumea (Lemaire 2001, 2004, 2006). Nevertheless, Jerusalem was central; this is Yhwh's primary dwelling, where he lived, for whereas everywhere else animal sacrifice was eventually curtailed in favor of incense altars, animal sacrifice continued unabated at the Jerusalem temple until its final destruction under the Romans (Knowles 2006). To Babylonian expatriates, moreover, Jerusalem was not just the central place; it was the only place to worship Yhwh, and rebuilding the temple there was their long-held hope (Ezekiel 40–43; Isa. 40.1-11; 44.26–45.1). To them, this was the reason to return.

Yhwh the god of Israel. Why is Yhwh called the god of Israel and not of Judah? Why is Israel mentioned here? In 721 BCE Sargon captured Samaria, the capital of Israel, the northern kingdom. After that, Israel ceased to exist as an independent political entity until 1948 CE when it was reestablished. After the Assyrian conquest in 721 BCE, the northern kingdom was absorbed into the Assyrian Empire as the province of Shomron (Samerina in Akkadian). This name continued as the title of the province in the Persian period. Coins testify to the Persian province of Shomron—not to Israel. Nor does the word 'Israel' appear on Judean coins from the Persian period. On those coins we have either YHD or YHWD (Judah, *Yehud,* spelled with or without the waw, the *W*). Moreover, neither the phrase 'god of Israel' nor the word 'Israel' ever appears on the documents found at Elephantine.

Besides signifying a political entity in the monarchic period, the term 'Israel' also had a theological connotation. The eighth-century prophet Isaiah may have created Yhwh's title as 'the Holy One of Israel', giving the term 'Israel' a theological import even when the word also denoted a political reality (Williamson 1994: 41-45). The god of Israel was the god who addressed not only those of the northern kingdom, the kingdom named 'Israel', but also those who lived in the southern kingdom, the Judeans living in Judah. The prophet continued to use the appellation 'Yhwh god of Israel' even after the northern kingdom ceased to exist (Isa. 37.21 = 2 Kgs 19.20). After the northern kingdom's destruction, Jeremiah says that 'Yhwh the god of Israel' speaks to the people of Judah and Jerusalem (Jer. 11.1-4). The title 'Yhwh god of Israel' occurs only once in the latter part of the book of Isaiah, and that is to name the god who calls Cyrus and makes himself known to him (Isa. 45.3). Ezekiel uses the full title 'Yhwh god of Israel' only once as well, and that is to name the god who will enter and inhabit the rebuilt temple (Ezek. 44.2).

To Jeremiah, the entire people Israel went out of Egypt during the exodus (e.g. Jer. 2.1-6), and the Judeans are the remnant of that people Israel. Deutero-Isaiah and Ezekiel refer to the Judean exiles as the people 'Israel', and as the 'House of Israel', suggesting that the Judean exiles continued to apply the label 'Israel' to themselves while in Babylon (e.g. Isa. 43.14, 15; Ezek. 2.3; 3.1; Bedford 2001: 116).

Would Cyrus have used the term 'god of Israel' in an authentic edict, however? Although Cyrus would not have known the term, scholars often assume that the edict is a response to the exiles' request to return to Judah and rebuild the temple, and that Cyrus simply repeats the phraseology of the request to which he responds (e.g. Williamson 1985: 11). As evidence for the probability of this hypothesis, Williamson cites the Elephantine memorandum (*TAD* A 4.9), which is 'a memorandum of what Bagavahya (then governor of Yehud) and Delaiah (governor of Samaria) said to me', that is, to Jedaniah, the priest of the temple of Yhw at Elephantine. The memorandum was in response to a letter in which Jedaniah requests that the temple at Elephantine be rebuilt. It repeats the words of Jedaniah's letter that he sent to Bagavahya, a copy of which (*TAD* A. 4.7, 8) was found in Jedaniah's archive.

The memorandum is not a written response from Bagavahya and Delaiah to Jedaniah, however, as Williamson supposes. It is simply a memorandum of the correspondence or perhaps of a meeting, but it is a note that Jedaniah wrote to himself. As such, it would be only natural for him to repeat the words of the letter that he himself had sent. The memorandum cannot be presumed to include Bagavahya's actual words. It is only Jedaniah's interpretation of what Bagavahya and Delaiah said to him. This memorandum cannot provide evidence that Ezra 1.2-4 are the actual words of Cyrus or even a replication of the words of a letter sent to him by the Judeans. What we have here may be a memorandum, however, as Williamson suggests, reflecting a memory of what Cyrus said, or perhaps more accurately, a memory of what he 'must have said', but not his actual words.

The temple of Yhwh the god of Israel (He is God!) which is in Jerusalem. Literally: 'He is *the* god', or perhaps 'He is the *only* god'. This expression occurs frequently in the Hebrew Bible in Persian-period texts, for example, Isa. 45.18, where it also appears as a parenthetic expression.

One could also translate the second half-verse as a new sentence: 'He is the god *who* is in Jerusalem'. The translation of the MT proposed here follows Porten (*TAD* A 4.7,8), who translates the Aramaic line אגורא זי יהו אלהא זי ביב בירתא as 'the temple of Yhw the god *which* is in Elephantine the fortress', rather than as 'the temple of Yhw the god *who* is in Elephantine the fortress', which is equally possible. Both Hebrew and Aramaic have only one relative pronoun, and it can stand for both animate and inanimate subjects (or objects) of clauses. Thus, the Aramaic of the Elephantine letter, like the Hebrew here, is ambiguous. By using the relative pronoun 'which' rather than 'who', Porten implies it is the temple rather than the god that is in Elephantine. The various ancient versions of Ezra 1.3 (Greek Ezra, 1 Esdras, the Vulgate) are all clear, however, that the reference is to that god *who* lives/dwells in Jerusalem, not to the building. I translate the ambiguous relative pronoun to refer to the temple and not to the god to allow for the possibility that Yhwh had gone to live with the exiles in Babylon. If the verse had been copied from the second temple's actual building inscription, however, then it would refer to the time when the building was already completed and dedicated, and Yhwh was inhabiting it once more. In that case it should be translated, 'He is the god *who* is in Jerusalem'. In any case, we do not have here a concept of a god who is omnipresent. That Greek, Platonic notion was not yet prevalent in Judah.

1.4 ***And all who remain.*** That is, all who remain behind, who do not go up to Jerusalem.

Of any of the places where he had resided. Resided, that is, as a resident alien, noncitizen. This notion of living in an area not as a citizen but as a foreigner, a resident alien, bespeaks a Judean viewpoint, not a Mesopotamian one. A great deal is known about the status of foreigners, including Judeans, in Mesopotamia (Cardasçia 1958; Oded 1979, 1995; Pearce 2006; Pearce and Wunsch 2014; Poo 2005; Younger 2003). Foreigners, even deportees from conquered nations, did not constitute a separate social or judicial category in the Mesopotamian states. The stereotyped phrase used by Assyrian kings, at least prior to Sennacherib, is 'I have counted them with the people of the land of Assyria' (*itti niše* ^{kur}*Aššur amnūšunūti*), that is, 'I have counted them as Assyrians'. Although originally settled with their families on lands from which they could not leave, eventually the deported had all the rights of free persons. Examination of the Assyrian onomostica shows that foreigners were well integrated into the life of the empire. They are seen owning and inheriting property, buying and selling real estate, acting as creditors and debtors, engaging in litigation and approaching the court. They engage in commerce and business, witness contracts and suits, all the while maintaining their ancestral traditions. Non-Assyrians, perhaps even deportees or their descendants, served as officials in the royal court, both in the capital in Assyria proper and in the provinces; many district governors bore non-Akkadian names. This was also true under the Babylonians. Deportees were assigned crown land, first as tenant farmers, but later this land became their heritage, passing from father to son. As Cardasçia concludes:

> In a world without a civil state, without an identity card, without a passport, the quality of being a foreigner is a fact, and purely a fact. One may attach juridical consequences, but these consequences disappear with the fact itself. As soon as the foreigner absorbs the language, the national customs, and this will often be the case for his descendants, the law ceases to consider him a foreigner (Cardasçia 1958: 114).

The designation of the exiles as resident aliens indicates Judean sensibilities and would not be original to Cyrus. (For further discussion with references, see Fried 2007a).

Let them—that is, the inhabitants of his place—. That is, the inhabitants of all those places that the Judean now leaves. Are these inhabitants other Judeans or are they Babylonians? The same phrase is used in Gen. 38.21 to refer to the (apparently non-Judean) residents of the town where Tamar the daughter-in-law of Judah lives, so that the author likely has non-Judeans in mind.

Support him. The verse is ambiguous because of the several pronouns without clear antecedents. Who is being supported? Who is doing the supporting? Rashi supposes that the ones left behind are Judeans who could otherwise not afford the journey up to Jerusalem and who were to be supported in their attempt to go up by Babylonians living in their towns. Ginsberg (1960) argues that this is, in fact, the only possible reading (so also Bickerman 1946: 259-60; and quite emphatically Williamson 1985). Batten admits this is the plain meaning of the text (Batten 1913: 59), but he emends it to follow 1 Esdras, which he believes makes more sense. According to his reading of 1 Esdras, those Judeans who are not going up to Jerusalem should lend support to those Judeans who are going. Batten surmises that the wealthiest would be loath to go, and also more willing to help out.

Gunneweg thinks that those who remain designates the entire community of exiles (Gunneweg 1985: 44). All the exiles are to be helped to go to Jerusalem by the men of their place, that is, by the Babylonians. To Gunneweg (and many other scholars, e.g., Rudolph 1949; Galling 1964; Clines 1984; Blenkinsopp 1988), the biblical writer presents the return as another exodus. In the story of the exodus, the Egyptians supported the fleeing Israelites (albeit not voluntarily) with gold and other valuables; so now, according to Ezra, the native inhabitants of Babylon are urged by Cyrus to pay tribute, even free-will gifts for the Jerusalem temple. Gunneweg argues that v. 6 makes it clear that it is the non-Judean neighbors who are to support the Judeans who leave.

The reader should perhaps hold both interpretations in mind simultaneously. The more likely interpretation from a historical perspective is that the Judeans who did not participate in this first return—and from the archaeology this would actually be most of them—would have helped out those who wanted to go up but were unable to pay the cost of the trip. Reading from a literary and theological perspective, however, it may be that the writer intended to present the return as a second exodus and therefore would have had non-Judean Babylonian neighbors in mind.

And with free-will offerings for the temple of the god, which is in Jerusalem. If Judeans are intended here as the ones remaining behind, it would be a rare opportunity for them to support not only those who are making the arduous journey up to Jerusalem but also to make a donation to the temple of the god of their ancestors.

Comments: The Edict of Cyrus

A. Does Ezra 1.2-4 Translate a Genuine Cyrus Edict?

Verses 2-4 of the first chapter of the book of Ezra contain what is usually termed the Cyrus Edict, an edict that allowed the exiled Judeans to leave Babylon, to return to their homeland in Judah, and to rebuild their temple. The question that has plagued researchers since the beginning of biblical criticism is whether or not the passage contains a Hebrew translation of Cyrus's genuine words or if they are just the words of the biblical author of Ezra or Chronicles (since they also appear there). Complicating the picture is that other words also representing Cyrus's edict appear in Ezra 6.3-5, and a memory of such an edict is reported in Ezra 5.13-15. While the edict repeated in Ezra 6 and the memory of it recorded in Ezra 5 agree with each other, they do not agree with what is written in Ezra 1.2-4. Although some scholars (e.g. Williamson 1985: xxiv) view the Cyrus decree as one of the sources available to the biblical author, the lack of agreement between Ezra 1.2-4 and Ezra 6.3-5 has led others to doubt the authenticity of the decree as recorded here and to interpret it as a free composition of the author (e.g. Torrey 1970 [1910]: 116; Rudolph 1949: 2; Clines 1984: 36; Blenkinsopp 1988: 74).

The reader should not expect the Hebrew words reported in Ezra 1.2-4 to be a direct translation of the Aramaic recorded in Ezra 5 and 6, however. The Aramaic and the Greek portions of a 338 BCE satrapal decree recorded on the trilingual Xanthus inscription of Lycia are not translations of one another (see, e.g., Fried 2004: 140-54). If we had only the Greek, we would not suppose that an Aramaic version existed, and vice versa. The Greek is not 'translation Greek', and it is not a translation of the Aramaic; they are independent renditions of the same edict created according to the needs of the different implied readers. Given that there was in fact only one edict, neither face of the inscription records it; they are both historiography, not history.

This point is brought out clearly by Habicht's study of a Greek inscription (Habicht 1961; cf. Jameson 1960). The inscription purports to record the exact words of Themistocles' decree of 480 BCE, although it was inscribed much later, probably during the time of Alexander (330 BCE). Habicht has shown that the text could not represent the actual decree and so cannot be used as a historical source. According to the inscription, only Athenians with legitimate children could serve as trierarches in the navy. Prior to Pericles' law, however, every child of an Athenian was automatically legitimate. After passage of the law in 451 BCE, both parents had to be Athenian in order for the child to be considered legitimate. This statement in the supposed edict thus has meaning only after 451 BCE, not in 480 BCE, its putative date. Habicht argues further that the allocation of a ship to a trierarch by lot, as provided for in the inscription, was a development of the democratic ideal, an ideal that belongs to the fourth century BCE, not the fifth. These and other anachronisms (e.g. the list of gods) date the text to the mid-fourth century BCE. Yet, Habicht does not suggest that the document is fictive. Rather, it is a fourth-century reconstruction of a genuine fifth-century decree. It describes the decree as it 'must have been'.

This is likely the situation of the so-called Cyrus Edict in Ezra 1.2-4. Rather than Cyrus's actual words, they are recorded as they 'must have been'. They seem to be the beginning of a temple-building story. They contain the requisite ingredients: they name the king; they state his year in office (the appropriate first year); they name the god whose temple it is; and most importantly they state that the impetus for the temple building came by a divine command from the god to the king. These are all required statements in a temple-building inscription (Hurowitz 1992; Fried 2003b; Boda and Novotny 2010), and record the decree 'as it must have been'.

Is there any historical validity to the verses? Scholars have argued that Cyrus would have been too worried about running the empire to concern himself with a temple in an out-of-the-way place like Jerusalem in the first year of his reign (e.g. Grabbe 2004: 273, and references cited there). While it is unlikely that a building story would assign a temple's founding to any other year than the first, Tattenai's letter to Darius, which may be a historical source, does state that permission for a temple was granted in Cyrus's first year (Ezra 5.13; see comment at Ezra 5 on the genuineness of the letter). The letter suggests that Cyrus did allow Judeans to return to Judah early in his reign. This is supported by notices in the Babylonian Chronicle (Grayson 2000: 110) and in the Cyrus Cylinder (Schaudig 2001: 552) that early in his reign Cyrus restored to their respective cellas the gods that Nabonidus had ordered to Babylon. Presumably he would have done the same for Yhwh (although no gods beyond Babylon's borders are actually mentioned in the Cyrus Cylinder; Kuhrt 1983) and would have permitted some priests and their attendants (i.e. some Levites) to escort Yhwh up to Judah (see Isa. 52.7-12).

Scholars object that the language of the decree in Ezra 1.2-4 is not authentic because it is Hebrew, whereas Cyrus would have issued an empire-wide decree in Aramaic, the official language of the empire (e.g. Clines 1984: 36; Grabbe 2004: 273). The language and the idioms, such as the phrases 'god of Israel' and 'let him go up', are indeed strange if interpreted as the authentic words of Cyrus (or even if interpreted as Cyrus's response to an official Judean request). They are expected, however, if a Judean wrote it for a building inscription, say, for the Judean temple of Yhwh in Jerusalem at the time of the temple's dedication in 516 BCE (Ezra 6.16) when the title 'King of Persia' first began to be used. Such an inscription would have been written by and for Judeans (see note at Ezra 1.2). Building inscriptions of local temples did not use the language or idioms of the Achaemenid bureaucracy. They used the local language and local idioms. Kuhrt (1983) has shown that the Cyrus Cylinder, for example, is a foundation document, a building inscription, for the restoration of the Esagila, the temple of Marduk in Babylon. It is not in Aramaic, the language of the Persian bureaucracy; rather it employs the Babylonian language and the idioms of the Babylonian priesthood who wrote it. The temple of Neith in Sais, Egypt, as another example, was restored by funds from the Persian kings Cambyses and Darius I (Lichtheim 1980: 36-41). Nevertheless, its building inscription was written by Egyptian priests completely in hieroglyphs, using expressions and idioms peculiar to Egyptian culture and, while naming the Persian emperors, gives due credit to Neith, the mother of Re. The genre of our biblical text is similar; it expresses the genre of a building inscription for the temple of the Judean god, Yhwh.

Halpern (1990) objects that there is no narrative statement in these two verses that the exiles have actually decided to build the temple. This is true, and conforms completely to the building-story genre. According to the ideology of temple building, it is not the people who can make the decision to build. That decision can come only from the god to the king who has the power to build his temple, and that is Cyrus. (See Hurowitz 1992; Fried 2003b; Boda and Novotny 2010.)

Others have noted that there is no mention in the so-called decree that Cyrus agreed to pay the building expenses (Ezra 6.4), but rather the emphasis is placed on the contributions of the 'inhabitants of his place' (Ezra 1.4; e.g. Blenkinsopp 1988: 94-95). This is not a 'conscious correction' of the Cyrus memorandum (*pace* Rothenbusch 2012: 109) but conforms to the temple-building inscription genre, in which it is stressed that donations come from all over the world. Although the king certainly paid for every temple built anywhere in antiquity, that fact is never stated in the building inscriptions (Hurowitz 1992; Boda and Novotny 2010).

Some commentators argue that all of Ezra 1 is a free creation of the biblical writer. They point to the numerous discrepancies between it and Cyrus's command to Sheshbazzar described in Tattenai's letter to Darius (Ezra 6.3-5; for reviews see Bedford 2001; Rothenbusch 2012: 109). If entirely a free composition of the historian, however, it is odd that the king named is no native ruler, neither Sheshbazzar nor Zerubbabel, but the Persian emperor. Naming Cyrus as the king to whom Yhwh gives his command is recognition that he, not the Davidic heir, is Yhwh's choice as interlocutor, and that it is Cyrus, not the Davidic heir, who controls the decision to rebuild. This speaks against the likelihood that the Cyrus Edict is a complete fiction. It is not based on a Persian document but rather on the building inscription of the second temple of Yhwh in Jerusalem—written by Judeans for Judeans in the sixth year of Darius I.

Was there an empire-wide proclamation? According to Ezra 1.1, a herald announced Cyrus's decision to rebuild Yhwh's temple in Jerusalem throughout his kingdom. There was also a written document—this last is stated almost as an afterthought. As stated in the Notes on 1.1, it is not likely that a herald was sent throughout the empire without a written edict. As was true through history, and as one of the letters in the archive of Arsames, the fifth-century Persian satrap of Egypt, makes clear (*TAD* A 6.1), heralds were high court officials who read the edicts they proclaimed; they did not recite official proclamations from memory.

The historical situation was likely as described in Tattenai's letter to Darius. Cyrus gave an order to Sheshbazzar, whom he had appointed governor of the Persian province of Yehud, to take Yhwh's vessels from the Esagila to Jerusalem, to rebuild the temple there, and to install Yhwh's vessels in it (5.15). That is all. Presumably Sheshbazzar did not go alone but brought with him a contingent of Judeans, probably priests and other temple personnel. The phrase שָׂם טְעֵם, *śām ṭeʿēm,* 'he issued an order', in Tattenai's letter (5.13) is used throughout the letters of Arsames, satrap of Egypt, during the fifth century BCE (*TAD* A 6.1, A 6.3, A 6.7, etc.) to indicate a simple command to a subordinate. There is no mention in either Tattenai's letter to Darius or in Darius's response to him of an order to anyone but Sheshbazzar.

The language of these two verses fits the language of a building story written during the reign of Darius I by Judeans who had returned from

Babylon. They fit the language of a temple-building inscription; they do not fit the language or idioms of an official Persian proclamation.

B. The Similarity between Ezra 1.1-4 and 2 Chronicles 36.22-23

Although the relationship of Ezra to Chronicles is discussed in the Introduction, further discussion here seems warranted. This commentary proposes that the second temple's actual building inscription provided a major source to the author of Ezra 1–6 (see Introduction to Ezra 1–6). The biblical writer likely had other sources at his disposal as well, such as the books of Chronicles. Indeed, Ezra 1.1-3a may have borrowed from 2 Chron. 36.22-23. It is unlikely that Chronicles has the original ending of a decree, however, since it does not include the command or the permission to those going up to rebuild the temple (*pace* Redditt 2008: 230; Klein 2012: 545).

Most commentators assume the reverse, however, that the Chronicler borrowed from Ezra. Japhet (1993: 1076) points out that the phrase 'god of heaven' occurs numerous times in Ezra–Nehemiah, but only this once in Chronicles. Kalimi (2005: 143-44) observes that since Ezra contains the longer, more complete form of the Cyrus Edict, and Chronicles only contains part of it, that Chronicles must have been drawn from Ezra. Ezra 1.1-4 must have been taken from a source, however, for otherwise the initial 'and' is unexplained (see note on 1.1). Further, the reference to 'the mouth of Jeremiah' assumes knowledge of this person on the part of the reader. This background is supplied in 2 Chronicles 35 and 36, where he appears four times (Knoppers 2003b: 76-77; Redditt 2008: 229-31). Jeremiah appears lamenting Josiah (2 Chron. 35.25), chastising Zedekiah who did not humble himself before Jeremiah who spoke from the mouth of Yhwh (2 Chron. 36.12), and Chronicles reiterates Jeremiah's prediction of seventy years of exile (2 Chron. 36.21). Except for this one verse, there is no other reference to Jeremiah in all of Ezra. The general lack of references to prophets in Ezra–Nehemiah (see notes and comments at Ezra 5.1 and 6.14) make it likely that the reference to Jeremiah is not original with Ezra and was borrowed.

Kratz (2005: 52-62) proposes that rather than from Chronicles, Ezra 1 is based on the Aramaic correspondence with the Persian authorities in Ezra 5–6, an independent source. It is obvious that the author of Ezra 1–6 had those letters before him, since he included them in his text. Nevertheless, it does not seem that Ezra 1 was composed by borrowing from the letter. As has long been discussed by commentators (e.g. Bickerman 1946; de Vaux 1937), the wording in the Aramaic form of Cyrus's decree differs considerably from that in the Hebrew of Ezra 1. There is no mention in Ezra 1 of the temple being a place of burnt offering or sacrifices (cf. Ezra 6.3), no mention of the dimensions of the building (cf. Ezra 6.3, 4), not even any mention of the cost being defrayed from the royal treasury (cf. Ezra 6.4b).

It is unlikely that these would have been omitted if the Hebrew passage had indeed been based on these letters. Ezra 1.1-4 is a borrowing from someplace certainly, perhaps from the actual building inscription of the second temple. If so, the inscription would have contained the usual explanation of how the temple came to be in ruins so that Ezra 1.1 would not have been the first verse in the inscription.

C. The Date of the Babylonian Conquest

The date of the conquest has been much discussed, the issue being whether the city fell in 587 or 586 BCE.[1] The answer depends on whether the reigns of the last kings of Judah were counted according to the Babylonian calendar, which began on Nisan 1, in the spring, or whether they were counted according to the Judean calendar (in use by Jews today), which begins on Tishri 1, in the fall. According to the Babylonian Chronicles, Nebuchadnezzar captured Jerusalem on the second of Adar, at the end of his seventh year (*ABC* 5.11-13), that is, March 16, 597 BCE (Parker and Dubberstein 1956: 27). At that time he took the young king Jehoiachin and his family into captivity and appointed Zedekiah, his uncle, as king in his place (2 Kgs 24.11-17). If Zedekiah counted his regnal years from the first month, Nisan, as the Babylonians did, then his reign would have begun the next month, on April 13, 597. If he counted from the seventh month, Tishri, then the first year of his reign would not have begun until October 9, 597, with the preceding months counted as an accession year. Unfortunately, there are no Babylonian Chronicles for the years of the final destruction of Jerusalem, but according to the biblical text, Nebuchadnezzar began his final siege of Jerusalem in the ninth year of King Zedekiah's reign, in the tenth month, on the tenth day of the month (2 Kgs 25.1). This would have been January 15, 588, and the sixteenth year of Nebuchadnezzar, no matter whether Zedekiah counted his regnal years from Nisan or Tishri. We read that the city was besieged until the eleventh year of Zedekiah (2 Kgs 25.2) and that in the fifth month, on the seventh day of the month, in the nineteenth year of King Nebuchadnezzar the temple was burnt and the walls of Jerusalem destroyed (2 Kgs 25.8; Jer. 52.12). If it was in the nineteenth year of Nebuchadnezzar, then it had to be August 15, 586 BCE (Parker and Dubberstein 1956: 28).[2]

In order for the fifth month (August) to fall both in the nineteenth year of Nebuchadnezzar and in the eleventh year of Zedekiah, Zedekiah had to

1. Hughes (1990: 159–82, 229–32) favors 587; while Galil (1996: 108-26) and Cazelles (1983) favor 586. See references cited therein for the numerous discussions.

2. The year is labeled the eighteenth year of Nebuchadnezzar in Jer. 52.29. This verse is not included in the Greek version and was likely added later as a correction by someone who did not understand how Zedekiah's eleventh year could fall in Nebuchadnezzar's nineteenth year, and not his eighteenth.

have been counting his regnal years from the seventh month, Tishri, the fall, and not from the first month, Nisan, as Nebuchadnezzar did. (Months were always counted and named starting with Nisan, the first month, which begins around April, no matter when the regnal years began.) Zedekiah was set on the throne at the beginning of Nebuchadnezzar's eighth year, in the first month (April) of 597 BCE. If the numbering of his regnal years did not begin until the seventh month, and the first six months counted as an accession year, then his eleventh year would not have begun until October 18, 587 BCE (*after* August, the fifth month of Nebuchadnezzar's eighteenth year). It would have continued until the next October 586, if fate had not intervened. The fifth month of Zedekiah's eleventh year then came in August of Nebuchadnezzar's nineteenth year August of 586 (as is reported, 2 Kgs 25.8).

If Zedekiah had counted his regnal years from the spring, April, then his eleventh year would have begun on April 23 of 587, and the temple would have fallen on the fifth month, August, of that year, 587. August of 587 falls in Nebuchadnezzar's eighteenth year, however, not his nineteenth. In order for the month of August to fall both in the eleventh year of Zedekiah and in the nineteenth year of Nebuchadnezzar, as reported by the biblical text, Zedekiah had to start his regnal years seven months after Nebuchadnezzar, in the fall, in the month of Tishri, as Jews do today.

Reflections

The wonder of the return to Judah and of this new change in the fortunes of the Judeans is aptly reflected by the psalmist as he records the joy they felt in their return to Judah. He also records their prayer that others may return as well, that all those who went out from Zion carrying their seed shall return carrying their sheaves. This refers not only to grain but to their offspring as well. This psalm also was in line to become the national anthem of Israel, the new Judean state, at the time of the return in 1948.

> A Song of Ascents
>
> When Yhwh restored the captives of Zion, we were like dreamers.
> 2 Then our mouth was filled with laughter, and our tongue with shouts of joy; then it was said among the nations, 'Yhwh has done great things for them'.
> 3 Yhwh has done great things for us! and we rejoiced.
> 4 Restore our captives, O Yhwh, like the watercourses in the Negev.
> 5 May those who sow in tears reap with shouts of joy.
> 6 Those who go out weeping, bearing the seed for sowing, shall come home with shouts of joy, carrying their sheaves (Psalm 126).

Ezra 1.5-11

THE PEOPLE RETURN HOME

This section presents the third component of a Persian-period temple-building inscription. The decree is implemented in great detail, and people from all over the world and from every walk of life contribute to its glorification.

Translation

1.5. *So*[a] *the heads of the fathers' [houses]*[b] *of [the tribes of] Judah and Benjamin, the priests and the Levites, that is,*[c] *everyone whose*[d] *spirit the god*[e] *awakened, rose to go up to build the temple of Yhwh which*[f] *is in Jerusalem.* 6. *And all those around them encouraged them*[g] *with objects of*[h] *silver and gold, with goods*[i] *and with cattle, and with choice gifts in abundance,*[j] *over and above all that was freely given.*[k]

7. *Now King Cyrus had [ordered] Yhwh's temple utensils*[l] *which Nebuchadnezzar*[m] *brought out*[n] *from Jerusalem and had put into the temple of his god brought out.*[o] 8. *Indeed, Cyrus, King of Persia, had Mithradates*[p] *the treasurer*[q] *bring them out and count them out*[r] *to Sheshbazzar,*[s] *the ruler over Judah.*

9. *These are their accountings:*[t]
Jugs[u] *of gold 1,000*[v]
Jugs of silver 1,000
Slaughtering knives[w] *29*
10. *Bowls*[x] *of gold 30*
Bowls of silver 2,410[y]
Other vessels 1,000
11. *All the vessels of gold and silver 5,469*[z]
Sheshbazzar brought everything up from Babylon to Jerusalem together with those who went up of the exiles.

Textual Notes

a. **1.5** *So.* First Esdras adds, 'So, taking charge (καταστάντες), the tribal leaders . . .'

b. *Heads of fathers'* [*houses*]. The word 'houses' is not here but is implied. First Esdras reads, 'The tribal leaders of the fathers of the tribes'. It makes explicit that Judah and Benjamin are tribes (φυλή) but does not seem to understand that 'fathers' [houses]' is shorthand for 'tribes' or 'families'.

c. *That is*. The lamedh, ל, is not used as a preposition here but an emphasizing particle or perhaps a partitive particle meaning 'with respect to' or 'that is' (see GKC 143e). The versions simply have either 'and all' or 'all'.

d. *Whose*. The Greek versions have this relative pronoun in the plural, since there it refers back to 'all'. The Hebrew and the Syriac have the pronoun in the singular.

e. *The god.* First Esdras reads 'the Lord'.

f. *The temple of Yhwh which.* Or *who.* Hebrew does not distinguish. First Esdras reads 'the temple for the Lord in Jerusalem'. In Greek Ezra also the relative pronoun refers to the temple.

g. **1.6** *Encouraged them.* Literally, 'Strengthened their hands', חִזְּקוּ בִידֵיהֶם. Greek Ezra translates, 'and all about them grew strong in their hands', which attempts a literal translation. First Esdras reads, 'And all around them helped in everything'. The Syriac, however, reads 'seized by their hands', a literal translation that misunderstands the text.

h. *With objects of.* בִּכְלֵי. Commentators often emend this phrase to בכל, 'in every way', with 1 Esdras. The MT is supported by Greek Ezra and the Syriac, however.

i. *Goods.* Again, 1 Esdras has 'with horses'. See textual note at 1.4.

j. *In abundance.* Emending לבד, 'apart from', to לרב, 'in abundance', with 1 Esdras and the Syriac. Every occurrence of לבד meaning 'apart from' is followed by מן, 'from'. Since מן, 'from', does not appear here, לבד is probably a metathesis for לרב, with ר/ד confusion.

k. *All that was freely given.* The infinitive construct התנדב is used here as a definite noun, an indirect (dative) object of 'strengthen the hands' (see *IBHS* 602). Instead of this final phrase, 1 Esdras reads, 'From the many whose heart [lit. mind, νοῦς] was stirred', which reflects the previous verse. The Syriac reads, 'and valuable gifts which pleased them'.

l. **1.7** *The utensils.* First Esdras adds the adjective ἱερά, 'holy'.

m. *Nebuchadnezzar.* The Syriac adds 'king of Babylon'.

n. *Had brought out.* The MT employs the same word, הוֹצִיא, in both occurrences of 'brought out' in the verse, whereas the LXX, the Vulgate, and 1 Esdras all use different words. Probably the second occurrence should be replaced by הביא, also meaning 'brought out'.

o. *The temple of his god.* First Esdras has ἐν τῷ ἑαυτοῦ εἰδωλίῳ, 'into his own idol-temple'. The writer adds 'holy' to refer to Yhwh's vessels and the word 'idol' to refer to Nebuchadnezzar's god and 'idol-temple' to refer to the temple in Babylon, in order to emphasize the differences between the two belief systems.

p. **1.8** *Had Mithradates.* Literally, עַל־יַד, 'by the hand of' Mithradates, that is, under the direction of Mithradates. Mithradates is a good Persian name, meaning 'gift of Mithra'. First Esdras reads, 'When King Cyrus of the Persians brought these out, he gave them to Mithradates, his treasurer'. This is a misinterpretation of the text. Cyrus did not personally bring them out but rather had his treasurer do it, or had his treasurer see to it.

q. *Treasurer.* גִּזְבָּר, *gizbar*. This is from the Persian word for 'treasurer', *ganzabara,* but in our text the *n* has been assimilated to the following consonant, a common occurrence. The assimilation of the *n* also occurs in this word in an early-fifth-century text from Bactria (*ADAB* B10, Naveh and Shaked 2012). The LXX does not understand the Persian term and translates as 'Mithradates son of Gazabara'.

r. *Count them out.* First Esdras reads 'hand over'.

s. *Sheshbazzar.* For this name, see notes below.

t. **1.9** *These are their accountings.* The Hebrew of the following list contains words that appear only here, and the total given does not add up to the sum of the separate amounts. The list has become corrupt in transmission.

u. *Jugs.* אֲגַרְטְלֵי *ʾagarṭlê.* The word is not Hebrew but a loan whose etymology has thus far escaped detection. Greek Ezra has ψυκτῆρες, 'wine cooler', but 1 Esdras translates by σπονδεῖα, meaning 'cup' or 'bowl', which is also the interpretation of the Syriac. The word *agartel* may be a corruption of the Persian *batugara,* 'drinking cups', with the initial *b* omitted by confusion with the initial preposition, 'in' (ב). If so, the corruption would involve g/t metathesis and r/l confusion.

v. *1,000.* The MT actually has 30, as do the LXX and the Syriac; but 1 Esdras has 1,000, perhaps the original; it would bring the total more into line with the number given in v. 11.

w. *Slaughtering knives.* מַחֲלָפִים, *maḥălāpîm.* This is another word of uncertain meaning, but *ḥalāpîm* are the slaughtering knives used in the temple and may be what is meant here. Greek Ezra translates it as παρηλλαγμένα, 'assorted items'. First Esdras reads θυίσκαι, which may be a pan for holding incense (L&S). The Syriac translates it as 'stoles', that is, 'outer garments'. The root *ḥlp* suggests an exchange, which in turn may suggest a change of clothes. (Clothes are listed among the gifts in Ezra 2.69.) On the other hand, the root *ḥlp* may simply be the result of a marginal note in which a copyist suggests that the text needs changing.

x. **1.10** *Bowls.* כְּפוֹר, *kᵉpôr.* The word occurs only here and in 1 Chron. 28.17. It too may be of foreign origin. The translator of Greek Ezra did not know the word and simply transliterated it into Greek, κεφφουρη. First Esdras has φιάλαι, 'bowls'. The Syriac has transposed the silver and gold items.

y. *2,410.* The Hebrew reads 'bowls of silver—second, or duplicates—410', as does the Syriac, which seems to have been corrupted. First Esdras reads 2,410, which is probably correct. The Hebrew כֶּסֶף מִשְׁנִים אַרְבַּע מֵאוֹת וַעֲשָׂרָה ('duplicate silver [bowls]—410') may have originally been כסף [אלפי]ם שנים אַרְבַּע מֵאוֹת וַעֲשָׂרָה, 2,410, with אלפי, 'thousands', having dropped out inadvertently.

z. **1.11** *5,469.* The Hebrew reads 5,400. First Esdras reads 5,469, the actual sum of the numbers reported here. The total may be original, the number 69 having dropped out of the text.

Notes

1.5 *So the heads of the fathers' [houses].* The head of the family, or 'father's house', was a prominent position in the society of the ancient Near East. He was in charge of managing the family estate and acted as their representative in business dealings such as purchasing or leasing real estate or movable property, and in other financial deals (Joannès 2004: 150). He also had responsibility for arranging matrimonial alliances. In addition, he was in charge of keeping the family archives and of handing them down to the next generation.

The returnees are stated here to be organized by ancestral houses, or clans, *bêt ʾābôt,* although the text omits the word 'houses' and reads literally 'heads of the fathers'. The phrase 'heads of fathers', or 'leaders of fathers', appears numerous times in Chronicles, Ezra and Nehemiah (and elsewhere: Exod. 6.25; Num. 31.26; 32.28; 36.1; Josh. 14.1; 19.51; 21.1; and 1 Kgs 8.1) as a shorthand for 'clans'. While indicating some form of family structure, the precise meaning of the term eludes understanding. It is usually defined as an extended family, including all the descendants and dependents of a single living man, excluding married daughters who have joined the *bêt 'āb* of their husbands (Wright 1992: 762). Weinberg has argued that this phrase, which appears throughout the Hebrew Bible, changes meaning between what he considers to be the pre-exilic and postexilic portions of the Bible (Weinberg 1992: 49-61). Whereas passages in Joshua–Kings (which he considers pre-exilic) refer to a *bêt 'āb* ('house of the father'), Ezra–Nehemiah and Chronicles (which are postexilic) tend to use *bêt 'ābôt* ('house of the father*s*'), or just *'ābôt* ('fathers'), as here in Ezra 1.5. The expected plural 'house*s* of the father or fathers' never occurs.

The division Weinberg finds between pre- and postexilic texts does not exist, however, since we have in the same verse both *bêt 'āb* and *bêt 'ābôt:*

> וַעֲשָׂרָה נְשִׂאִים עִמּוֹ נָשִׂיא אֶחָד נָשִׂיא אֶחָד **לְבֵית אָב** לְכֹל מַטּוֹת יִשְׂרָאֵל וְאִישׁ רֹאשׁ **בֵּית־**
> **אֲבוֹתָם** הֵמָּה לְאַלְפֵי יִשְׂרָאֵל׃
>
> And ten chiefs were with him, one from each *bêt 'āb* from all the tribes of Israel, each the head of their *bêt 'ābôt* among the divisions of Israel (Josh. 22.14).
>
> דַּבֵּר אֶל־בְּנֵי יִשְׂרָאֵל וְקַח מֵאִתָּם מַטֶּה מַטֶּה **לְבֵית אָב** מֵאֵת כָּל־נְשִׂיאֵהֶם **לְבֵית אֲבֹתָם** שְׁנֵים
> עָשָׂר מַטּוֹת אִישׁ אֶת־שְׁמוֹ תִּכְתֹּב עַל־מַטֵּהוּ׃
>
> Speak to the Israelites, and take from them a staff, a staff for each *bêt 'āb* from all the leaders of their *bêt 'ābôt,* twelve staves and each shall write his name on his staff (Num. 17.17).

The difference in usage that Weinberg notes seems rather to be one of meaning. When speaking about a particular family it is always *bêt 'āb*:

> וְעַתָּה הִשָּׁבְעוּ־נָא לִי בַּיהוָה כִּי־עָשִׂיתִי עִמָּכֶם חָסֶד וַעֲשִׂיתֶם גַּם־אַתֶּם עִם־**בֵּית אָבִי** חֶסֶד
> וּנְתַתֶּם לִי אוֹת אֱמֶת׃
>
> Now then, since I have dealt kindly with you, swear to me by Yhwh that you in turn will deal kindly with my *bêt 'āb* (*bêt 'ābî*). Give me a sign of good faith (Josh. 2.12).

Whereas when speaking about families in general, it is always *bêt 'ābôt,* or just *'ābôt:*

> וְאֵלֶּה אֲשֶׁר־נָחֲלוּ בְנֵי־יִשְׂרָאֵל בְּאֶרֶץ כְּנָעַן אֲשֶׁר נִחֲלוּ אוֹתָם אֶלְעָזָר הַכֹּהֵן וִיהוֹשֻׁעַ בִּן־נוּן
> **וְרָאשֵׁי אֲבוֹת** הַמַּטּוֹת לִבְנֵי יִשְׂרָאֵל׃
>
> These are the inheritances that the Israelites received in the land of Canaan, which the priest Eleazar, and Joshua son of Nun, and the heads of the *'ābôt* of the tribes of the Israelites distributed to them (Josh. 14.1).

It just happens that the stories in Genesis, Joshua–Kings (which Weinberg considers pre-exilic) often refer to individual families, whereas the stories in Exodus–Numbers, as well as in Ezra, Nehemiah and Chronicles (which Weinberg considers postexilic), usually refer to families or clans in general. In fact, this distinction in meaning also occurs within Chronicles, as in the texts here:

אֵלֶּה בְנֵי־לֵוִי **לְבֵית אֲבֹתֵיהֶם רָאשֵׁי הָאָבוֹת** לִפְקוּדֵיהֶם בְּמִסְפַּר שֵׁמוֹת לְגֻלְגְּלֹתָם עֹשֵׂה
הַמְּלָאכָה לַעֲבֹדַת בֵּית יְהוָה מִבֶּן עֶשְׂרִים שָׁנָה וָמָעְלָה׃

These were the sons of Levi by their *bêt 'ābôt*, the heads of *'ābôt* according to their accounting by the number of the names of the individuals from twenty years old and upward who were to do the work for the service of the house Yhwh (1 Chron. 23.24).

וַיְהִי־יַחַת הָרֹאשׁ וְזִיזָה הַשֵּׁנִי וִיעוּשׁ וּבְרִיעָה לֹא־הִרְבּוּ בָנִים וַיִּהְיוּ **לְבֵית אָב**
לִפְקֻדָּה אֶחָת׃

Jahath was the head, and Zizah the second; but Jeush and Beriah did not have many sons, so they were enrolled as a single *bêt 'āb* (1 Chron. 23.11).

Weinberg states that the Chronicler uses *bêt 'āb* only when quoting Samuel or Kings (Weinberg 1992: 49), but the statement just quoted (1 Chron. 23.11) does not appear in those sources.

Further, Esther, which is also postexilic, reads:

כִּי אִם־הַחֲרֵשׁ תַּחֲרִישִׁי בָּעֵת הַזֹּאת רֶוַח וְהַצָּלָה יַעֲמוֹד לַיְּהוּדִים מִמָּקוֹם אַחֵר וְאַתְּ **וּבֵית־אָבִיךְ**
תֹּאבֵדוּ

For if you keep silence at such a time as this, relief and deliverance will rise for the Judeans from another quarter, but you and your *bêt 'āb* will perish (Est. 4.14).

This is an interesting verse because although the phrase literally means 'the house of your father', we know that Esther's father and mother are dead, that she has been orphaned (Est. 2.7), and that Mordechai, the speaker in this verse, has adopted and raised her. So what is referred to here? Perhaps to Esther's own descendants who will be reckoned to the house of her father (cf. Ruth 4.11).

The *bêt 'āb* may have been the basic unit of land tenure, each *bêt 'āb* having its own inheritance of land (Wright 1992: 763). Most of the population lived in rural areas, farmsteads and small villages, in contrast to urban sites. Houses in these rural areas, which were often more than twice the size of those in urban ones, were divided into as many as eight rooms, twice as many as the average urban dwelling. In contrast to urban dwellings, these could easily house an extended family of three generations or more as well as other unmarried relatives, that is, house a *bêt 'āb* (Faust 2012a: 160). If so, it suggests that these *rā'šê 'ābôt,* 'heads of fathers' [houses]', who rose to go up to Judah and Benjamin may have each received a parcel of land for his *bêt 'āb*.

Some scholars have suggested that larger compounds of attached buildings were also used in cities for extended families. David Schloen has argued that in Bronze Age Ugarit, for example, each of the several nuclear families had its own house, but the houses of an extended family were joined by a common courtyard, a common oven or ovens in that courtyard, and a common entrance from the courtyard onto the city street (Schloen 2001).

Such compounds of attached houses with a single wall separating them have been found in urban sites throughout Judah and Samaria and could well house from fifty to one hundred persons. It has been customary to assume that these attached houses (even those with separate entrances onto the street) belonged to extended families. Analysis of Babylonian cities in which texts were found in neighboring houses reveals, however, that neighboring families were not related by blood (van de Mieroop 1997: 108), and this was likely the case in Judean and Samarian cities as well.

The few houses from the Persian period that have been excavated tended to be of the Assyrian court style rather than the typical Israelite four-room house, and consisted of a large open courtyard with rooms on all sides (Stern 1982: 54). The houses ran along a street and shared a common partition wall (Stern 1982: 57). The prevalence of this type of architecture cannot be known for certain, since Persian-period sites in the Levant have left very scanty remains (Stern 1982: 47; Lipschits 2001b; 2006). Persian-period sites that continued into the Hellenistic and Roman periods suffered extensive damage from later building activities so that Persian-period remains were often obliterated. Those sites that were not inhabited later, whose latest stratum was from the Persian period, became exposed to the elements, and subsequently denuded of all architectural structures. In spite of the dearth of archaeological remains, however, it may be that these large court-room buildings housed extended families, the *bêt 'āb*.

The text refers only to the heads of the *'ābôt*, that is, the *pater familias,* who alone was moved to go up. As was the custom everywhere in the ancient world, he alone had the power to make the decision and could make it for his wife or wives, his married sons and their families, his unmarried daughters, plus any slaves, servants, aunts, uncles, cousins, widows, orphans, etc., who might be living with them. All these are part of the *bêt 'āb*, the father's house, of which he was the head (King and Stager 2001: 40). When he decides to go up, everyone goes up.

Judah and Benjamin. The families from the tribes of Judah and Benjamin comprise the laity. The priests and Levites, who were scattered across both the northern and the southern kingdoms before the exile, were of the tribe of Levi. Benjamin remained with Judah during the revolt of the northern kingdom after the death of Solomon (1 Kgs 12.21-23), and with Judah after the fall of the northern kingdom to Assyria as well. Both Benjaminites and Judeans were exiled to Babylon at the time of the Babylonian conquest, and members of both tribes returned, along with some priests and Levites, to Judah and Jerusalem, during the period of Persian domination.

According to the book of Jeremiah (chaps. 40–42), after the Babylonian conquest, Judeans who had not been deported (and who remained alive) fled to the area of Benjamin (among other places) and to its capital, Mizpah. After Gedaliah's assassination, many then fled to Egypt, and so would not have been taken to Babylon. If the book of Ezra is correct, however, Benjaminites were also deported to Babylon, not just Judeans. This may have been during the third deportation, in the twenty-third year of Nebuchadnezzar, in response to the assassination of Gedaliah (Jer. 52.30).

Not included in the tribes of Judah and Benjamin were the so-called ten 'lost' tribes. These were residents of the northern kingdom who had been exiled to Assyria during the Assyrian conquests and were scattered throughout that kingdom. They are commonly viewed as having lost their national identity and as having assimilated into the local population there. This may not be the case, however. Archaeology reveals that a temple to Yhwh, the national god of Israel, was built on Mt Gerizim (near Shechem in the area of Manasseh) in the early- to mid-fifth century, at the beginning of the Persian period (Magen 2000; 2007; Stern and Magen 2000; 2002). No cult sites have been found in the cities of Samaria that existed during the Assyrian or Babylonian periods (Fried 2002a). Only under the Persians was a cult site permitted, and this was to Yhwh, the native god of Israel. The Israelites who had been deported by the Assyrians may have returned to the land of their fathers at the same time that the Judeans did. They concentrated in the north, near Shechem, where they built their temple at Har Gerizim.

Be that as it may, those who returned from Babylon to the southern kingdom, to the Persian province of Yehud, were members of the tribes of Judah, Benjamin and Levi. If northerners from the so-called ten lost tribes also returned, they returned to the Persian province of Shomron, Samaria. As will become clear in the rest of the commentary, the authors of Ezra–Nehemiah assumed that no one else of the people Israel returned, and, in fact, that no one else of the people Israel existed. Those of Judah, Benjamin and Levi comprised the remnant who survived of the original twelve tribes. The people living in the area of the former northern kingdom, the Samaritans, were assumed to be those brought there by the Assyrian kings (2 Kings 17) and were therefore not the descendants of the original people Israel. This attitude that the Samaritans were not part of the people Israel was prevalent throughout the entire second temple period, as is reflected in the words of Jesus:

> Τούτους τοὺς δώδεκα ἀπέστειλεν ὁ Ἰησοῦς παραγγείλας αὐτοῖς λέγων· εἰς ὁδὸν ἐθνῶν μὴ ἀπέλθητε καὶ εἰς πόλιν Σαμαριτῶν μὴ εἰσέλθητε· πορεύεσθε δὲ μᾶλλον πρὸς τὰ πρόβατα τὰ ἀπολωλότα οἴκου Ἰσραήλ (Matt 10.5-6).
>
> These twelve Jesus sent out with the following instructions: 'Go nowhere among the Gentiles, and enter no town of the Samaritans, but go rather to the lost sheep of the house of Israel'.

Priests and Levites. These comprise the cult personnel, traditionally not of the tribes of Judah or Benjamin, but of the tribe of Levi. The priests were the ones who manipulated the blood (e.g. Lev. 1.5); the Levites included every other temple official. They were divided into gatekeepers, who managed the finances and accounted for all temple property, everything that went in and out of the temple (1 Chron. 9, cf. Lev. 1.50); and singers, those who performed all the rites of the temple service, accompanying themselves on musical instruments (1 Kgs 10.12; 1 Chron. 15.16).

That is, everyone whose spirit the god awakened. Literally, 'stirred up', repeating the verb from 1.1. Certainly not everyone went up to Judah but only those whose spirit God awakened in them; that is, it was not the decree of Cyrus nor the exhortations of a prophet that inspired each person to go up, but it was God himself (Schneider 1959: 90). This passage makes clear that not everyone moved to Jerusalem. Josephus explains that 'many remained in Babylon, being unwilling to leave their possessions' (*Ant.* 11.8). Ezra 7 describes another return under Ezra. The archaeology of Judah reveals a gradual rebuilding of the area throughout the entire Persian period and later (Faust 2012a).

Rose to go up. Prepared to go up (Batten 1913: 65).

To build the temple of Yhwh. The purpose of the trip back to Jerusalem was not simply to return to one's homeland but to rebuild the temple. An immediate and enthusiastic response of all the exiles is not described. Only those who were moved to go up went.

1.6 ***All those around them.*** As discussed in the note to v. 4, it is not clear whether this phrase refers to the Judeans or their non-Judean neighbors. The reader ought to hold both possibilities open simultaneously, the more historically likely (that it refers to Judeans only) and the more theologically and literarily likely, that the author wants the reader to have the Exodus and the non-Judean neighbor in mind. The author does not call those who helped them 'their brothers' or 'their king' but simply 'all those around them' (Galling 1964: 76).

Encouraged them. Literally, 'Strengthened their hands', חִזְּקוּ בִידֵיהֶם. The Hebrew expression 'to strengthen the hands' is common in the Hebrew Bible, but the phrase 'their hands' is always in the accusative, never in the dative as here, preceded by the preposition ב. Here the sense could be 'they strengthened by means of their hands', which is possible, but unlikely.

Batten (1913: 67) suggests that it literally means 'put strength in their hands', referring to the physical objects put in their hands. More likely the preposition ב is simply an error, influenced by the many nouns preceded by the preposition ב in the rest of the verse (Rudolph 1949: 4).

With objects of silver and with gold. The intent of v. 6 is to show that Cyrus's command (v. 4) has been carried out in every way. The items and their order is the same in both verses. Since there is no reference to objects of silver and gold (but just the silver and gold itself in v. 4), many commentators assume that the word 'objects', *kly* כלי, is not original here, and they emend the verse from 'objects' to 'every', כל, to more closely conform to v. 4. They assume that the reference to objects of silver and gold was added secondarily to further the allusion to the Exodus (cf. Exod. 3.22; 11.2; 12.35; e.g., Rudolph 1949: 4; Williamson 1985: 5). The reference to objects, particularly temple vessels, agrees with the items in the list in vv. 9-11 below, however, so these would need to be included among the items brought back from Babylon. (For the use of gold and silver vessels as gifts and as a medium of exchange, see the note on Ezra 2.68 below.)

In her discussion of 1 Chron. 28.17, Japhet (1993) points out that except for these two late (i.e. late Persian or early Hellenistic) passages (Ezra 1 and 1 Chron. 28) there is no mention of objects of silver in use either in the tabernacle or in the temple. In both the tabernacle (Exod. 27.3; 30.18; 37.16, 17; 38.3) and the temple (1 Kgs 7.15-50) the vessels were all of either pure gold or of bronze, not of silver. Although it is not mentioned in the present verse that these objects would be for the temple rather than for the returnees themselves, it is assumed so based on v. 4.

All that was freely given. Commentators explain this 'despoliation of the neighbors' as the historian's direct concern to present the return as a second exodus (Williamson 1985: 16; Gunneweg 1985: 46). It may point instead to the existence of Persian-period embellishments in the exodus story. A common component of Persian-period temple-building stories is that men and kings come from all over the world to contribute their wealth to the new temple (see Introduction). If those in this passage described as 'left behind' are considered to be non-Judeans making free-will donations to the Judeans who return, then this is not only reminiscent of the exodus story but also of other Persian-period building inscriptions. At that time the description of voluntary donations from foreign nations to various building projects was common (Root 1979). As Hurowitz (1992: 208-10) notes, this motif is quite different from that of Assyrian and Neo-Babylonian building accounts in which materials are also brought from all over the world. Those were portrayed as from vassals subject to the Assyrian and Babylonian kings and forced (by the mighty power of the god Assur) to contribute; they were not portrayed as free-will offerings.

On the other hand, if here in Ezra the neighbors roundabout are not Babylonian Gentiles but Judeans who could not make the journey, then the theme expressed here may not be one of 'despoiling the neighbors' but rather one of Yhwh's people making free-will offerings to contribute to his temple. This theme is seen in both the books of Exodus and Chronicles (both usually attributed to the Persian period). For example, Exod. 35.21-22 reads,

> And they came, everyone whose heart was stirred, and everyone whose spirit was willing, and brought Yhwh's offering to be used for the tent of meeting, and for all its service, and for the sacred vestments. So they came, both men and women; all who were of a willing heart brought brooches and earrings and signet rings and pendants, all sorts of gold objects, everyone bringing an offering of gold to Yhwh.

And in 1 Chron. 29.6-7 we read of the people's donations for the house that Solomon built:

> Then the leaders of ancestral houses made their free-will offerings, as did also the leaders of the tribes, the commanders of the thousands and of the hundreds, and the officers over the king's work. They gave for the service of the temple of God five thousand talents and ten thousand darics of gold, ten thousand talents of silver, eighteen thousand talents of bronze, and one hundred thousand talents of iron.

This image of the largess in voluntary contributions from either Judeans or from their non-Judean neighbors is part of the genre of Persian-period building inscriptions (see Introduction) and is not to be taken as historic (although Judean neighbors who did not return may certainly have helped those who did). The image projected here of the great wealth pouring into the hands of the returnees conflicts with the poverty of the early returnees revealed in the book of Haggai (Gunneweg 1985: 46). It also conflicts with the archaeological record of Jerusalem in the early days of the return.

1.7 ***Now King Cyrus had brought out.*** Literally, 'had ordered be brought out'. The use of the word order subject–verb–object here indicates that the passage must be translated into the pluperfect (Batten 1913: 66; cf. Rashi's commentary on Gen. 1.2). It is action that takes place prior to the main action, suggesting that even before he had made his decree or at least before the heads of fathers' houses prepared to go up, he had already ordered that the temple vessels be taken out of the Esagila.

Vessels of the temple of Yhwh. The importance of these vessels being the very ones that had been taken by Nebuchadnezzar from the temple of Yhwh in Jerusalem is discussed in the Introduction to Ezra 1–6. (See also Ackroyd 1987.) The Chronicler stresses that the Judeans have the true sons of Aaron as priests and Levites among them, as well as the true temple sacrificial implements, and these are what insures that Yhwh is with them alone:

> But as for us, Yhwh is our god, and we have not abandoned him. We have priests ministering to Yhwh who are descendants of Aaron, and Levites for the work [on the house of God].
>
> They offer to Yhwh every morning and every evening burnt offerings and fragrant incense, set out the rows of bread on the table of pure gold, and care for the golden lampstand so that its lamps may burn every evening; for we keep the service of Yhwh our god, but you have abandoned him (2 Chron. 13.10-11).

This is why the vessels must be returned to Jerusalem along with the priests and Levites, for without them there is no assurance that Yhwh will take up residence in his temple again.

Commentators have questioned, however, whether this could be a list of actual vessels from the first temple, since one reading of 2 Kgs 25.14-15 implies that the Babylonians melted down the items and took them in the form of gold, of silver, and of bronze, or even that the conflagration in the temple had melted the items. The following is a common translation:

> They took away the pots, the shovels, the snuffers, the dishes for incense, and all the bronze vessels used in the temple service, as well as the firepans and the basins. *What was made of gold the captain of the guard took away for the gold, and what was made of silver, for the silver* (2 Kgs 25.14-15 NRSV).

However, it is also possible to translate it as Cogan and Tadmor do:

> They took the pots, the shovels, the snuffers, the spoons, all the bronze vessels used in the service. The captain of the guard (lit. the chief cook) took the firepans and the sprinkling bowls, *those of gold and of silver* (Cogan and Tadmor 1988: 316).

The Hebrew actually says nothing about melting down the items. It reads literally: אֲשֶׁר זָהָב זָהָב וַאֲשֶׁר־כֶּסֶף כָּסֶף, 'Those of gold, gold; and those of silver, silver'. This is simply the repetition of intensification, meaning 'those of gold, were really pure gold; those of silver, were really pure silver' (Gesenius §123e). According to Jeremiah, moreover, the vessels of the first temple were going to be returned, and perhaps they were.

> Thus says Yhwh of hosts, the god of Israel, concerning the vessels remaining (both) in the house of Yhwh, and in the house of the king of Judah, and in Jerusalem: They shall be carried to Babylon, and there they shall stay, until the day when I give attention to them, says Yhwh. Then I will bring them up and restore them to this place (Jer. 27.21-22).

The temple of his god. We are not told what temple it is, only that it is the 'palace of his (i.e. Nebuchadnezzar's) god'. As indicated in the Introduction to Ezra 1–6, this would have been the Esagila, the temple of Marduk in Babylon.

1.8 *Cyrus... had Mithradates.* Nebuchadnezzar had evidently deposited Yhwh's vessels in the temple of Marduk in Babylon, the Esagila (see Introduction to Ezra 1–6). At Cyrus's command, Mithradates, the Persian imperial treasurer, retrieved them from the Babylonian temple and presented them to Sheshbazzar. The priests of the Esagila had nothing to say about the disposition of the items donated to it. They had no possibility to protest that the items now belonged to Marduk and could not be removed. There was no private ownership. Everything in the empire was the emperor's; it all lay at Cyrus's disposal. (For the relationship between the Persian emperor and the local priesthoods, see Fried 2004.)

The description here is consistent with what we read in Tattenai's letter to Darius (Ezra 5.13-16). Indeed, Kratz (2005: 52-58) has argued that the present chapter (Ezra 1) is based on that letter. I have been suggesting that these chapters are based on the second temple's actual building inscription, but there is no disagreement, the building inscription may also have been based on those letters. The description of Cyrus, the king of Persia, voluntarily contributing to the largess of items flowing into Yhwh's temple is consistent with temple-building narratives of the Persian period and conforms to Component C of a temple-building narrative. This does not make it fact, but neither does it make it fiction.

Mithradates. The name means 'gift of Mithra', a very popular Zoroastrian god whose popularity increased throughout the Persian, Hellenistic and Roman periods. Mithradates was a very common Zoroastrian name.

Treasurer. The word for 'treasurer', *gizbar,* is a Persian loan word, from the Persian word גנז, *ganaz*, 'treasury' (found in Est. 3.9 and 4.7 to refer to the treasury of the king) and '*bara*' meaning 'to bear', 'carry', 'have responsibility for'. The Persian word *ganzabara* occurs numerous times in the Achaemenid texts from Persepolis, one of the capitals of the Persian empire (Hallock 1969; Stolper 2000). The motifs and inscriptions on the seals of treasurers at Persepolis, which sometimes stayed with the office when it changed hands, reveal the high administrative and social rank associated with the office. The term also occurs on an Aramaic ostracon excavated at Arad, in southern Judah, assigned on paleographic grounds to the mid-fourth century BCE. The seal records a treasurer's (*gnzbr*) order for the disbursal of supplies (Aharoni 1981: 166 #37; Stern 1982: 44-45; Stolper 2000).

Sheshbazzar. Very little is known about this person. As Japhet points out, we do not even know his father's name (Japhet 1982). We know the names of the fathers of Zerubbabel, Joshua and Nehemiah, but not his. All we know about him is from Tattenai's report to Darius (Ezra 5.14). There it is said that Cyrus had appointed Sheshbazzar פֶּחָה, *peḥāh,* governor over the Persian province of Yehud (Judah). We also know from that same letter that Sheshbazzar brought back to Jerusalem the vessels that Nebuchadnezzar had taken from the temple there, and that he was the one who laid the foundations of the rebuilt temple.

The rabbis sought an identity for him. Rashi (*ad loc.)* suggests he was Daniel. Ibn Ezra and Ralbag write that this was Zerubbabel since both are claimed to be in charge when the foundations of the temple were laid (Ezra 3.10; cf. Ezra 5.16). Modern exegetes speculate that Sheshbazzar is the same person who is listed in the genealogies as Shenazzar, the fourth son of Jehoiachin, the exiled Judean king (1 Chron. 3.18; e.g. E. Meyer 1965 [1896]: 76-77). The Chronicler lists seven sons for Jehoaichin, and this is verified by Babylonian administrative texts from the year 592, which list rations for Jehoiachin, 'King of the land of Judah', and for the five sons whom he had at that time. If Sheshbazzar was Shenazzar, then he would be the uncle of Zerubbabel (1 Chron. 3.19), and it would be natural for Zerubbabel to follow his uncle as governor of Judah.

Shenazzar is a Babylonian name reflecting something like Sîn-uṣur, 'May Sîn [the moon-god] protect (him)'. Sheshbazzar, on the other hand, may be a corruption of Šamaš-ab- uṣur, 'May Shamash [the sun god] protect the father', so that Sheshbazzar and Shenazzar are quite different names and cannot refer to the same person (Berger 1971; Dion 1983). Cross disagrees, arguing that the *m* in Shamash, the well-known sun god, would not be lost yielding 'Sheshbazzar' (Cross 1998: 179-80). The Greek transcriptions of Sheshbazzar do not supply an *m.* The Greek of Ezra reads Σασαβασαρ, Sasabasar, and 1 Esdras reads Σαναβάσσαρος, Sanabassaros, rendering either Sanabassar or Shenabassar (Greek has no 'sh' sound). Both of these may have been influenced by Shenazzar of Chronicles, so that if the Greek form is based on an original Hebrew, then it is possible that both Sheshbazzar and Shenazzar are corruptions of Shenabassar, and both names would mean 'May Sîn protect the father' (so Cross 1998: 179-80). The similarity of the names, together with Sheshbazzar's title *nāśî,* the facts that he is given responsibility for the temple vessels (Ezra 1.8; 5.14), that he is Judah's first governor (Ezra 5.14), and that he laid the foundations of the temple (Ezra 5.16), all increase the likelihood that Sheshbazzar is Shenazzar, the fourth son of Jehoiachin (Japhet 2006: 877-83).

In spite of all these positive indications, to suggest that Sheshbazzar was the Davidic heir goes against the grain of the text. In Tattenai's letter, he is referred to as 'one by the name of Sheshbazzar'. An odd referent, if the letter writer knew anything about him beyond what he wrote in the letter. Josephus refers to him as the *eparch* of Syria and Phoenicia, but shows no knowledge of his being the Davidic heir. On the other hand, Ezra tells us nothing about Zerubbabel either, other than the name of his father. Cross (1998: 180 n. 21) maintains that 'the practice of the Persian administration to appoint governors from local royal or noble houses is well-known', so this assumption may be what convinces him that Sheshbazzar is Shenazzar.

Cross does not supply evidence for this 'well-known' practice, however; but probably he refers to Herodotus 2.15, who states that even if the native kings revolt, the Persians give to their sons their inherited sovereign power. Herodotus refers here to the sons of Inaros and Amyrtaeus, who revolted against Persian rule in 465 BCE. Inaros was the son of Psammetichus, the last indigenous king, and Amyrtaeus was also a descendant of Saite kings. Hearing of Xerxes' assassination in 465 BCE, they rebelled against the new ruler, Artaxerxes I, and, aided by the Greeks, succeeded in gaining control of the delta up to Memphis, killing the Persian satrap, Achaemenes, in the process (Grimal 1993: 370-71). The Persians eventually succeeded in ousting the Greeks and in executing Inaros. Arsames, the new satrap of Egypt, allowed Inaros's sons to maintain their rule in the delta, trying to avoid revolutionary fervor. This does not imply a normal practice, however. The only other case I know of is that of the family of Mausoleus, which was left in charge of Caria in Asia Minor under the Persians. In all other cases, the men put in charge of either satrapies or provinces were Persians or their Babylonian subjects (including Babylonians of Judean descent). Indeed, part of what it meant to change from an independent (even vassal) state to a province of the Persian Empire was to change from rule by a member of the indigenous royal family to rule by a Persian official. (For a discussion of Achaemenid imperial practices see Briant 2002; Fried 2004; 2013c; 2015c; in press a.) So while it is possible that Sheshbazzar was Shenazzar, the fourth son of Jehoiachin, it is more likely that he was simply a Babylonian.

Indeed, Babylonians were prominent among the administrators of the Persian Empire, and among them were Babylonians of Judean descent. Besides Zerubbabel, Ezra, and Nehemiah were 'Anani, vice-satrap of Egypt under Arsames (*TAD* A 6.2:23) and Gedalyahu, vice-satrap and secretary of the combined satrapy of Babylon and Beyond-the-River, under Darius (Stolper 1989a). In addition to these, two governors of Persian Yehud are known from seal impressions stamped on jar handles: 'Aḥiāb the governor (late-sixth or early-fifth century; Lipschits and Vanderhooft 2011: 83-106) and Yehô'ezer the governor (fifth century; Lipschits and Vanderhooft 2011: 192-201); and a third is known from several miniature coins—Yeḥizqiya (last half of the fourth century; Fried 2004: 185-87). These three are also likely to have been from Babylon and of Judean ancestry. Another governor of Yehud, the one who immediately followed Nehemiah, is Bagavahya, known from the Elephantine papyri (*TAD* A 4.7, 8). He bears a Persian name ('Better by means of Baga, God', Tavernier 2007: 141), but he may also have been from Babylon and have been of Judean descent. None of these governors except for Zerubbabel would necessarily have been descendants of the Davidic royal dynasty.

The ruler. Others read 'prince'. Greek Ezra reads ἄρχων, 'ruler, leader'; 1 Esdras reads προστάτης, 'the one who stands before', that is, 'the chief', 'the leader'; and the Syriac reads רבא, 'leader', 'great one'. The Hebrew MT has נָשִׂיא, *nāśî'*, a term that is used throughout the torah to denote the head of a tribe. It is also used to refer to King Solomon in 1 Kgs 11.34 in a prophecy foretelling that the northern kingdom will split off from Judah and that Solomon's descendants will be reduced to ruling over only one tribe. Ezekiel uses the title to refer both to the kings of pre-exilic Judah as well as to Judah's expected future ruler. That future ruler will have greatly diminished powers, however. The use of the term נָשִׂיא, *nāśî'*, may be a deliberate attempt on the part of the writer of Ezra to state that Ezekiel's vision has been fulfilled.

The title *nāśî'* is appropriate for the one in charge of bringing up the temple vessels and other donations for the temple. We read in Numbers 7 about the donations that the *nāśî'îm* of each tribe gave at the dedication of the altar for the wilderness sanctuary. We also read of the role of the *nāśî'îm* when the ark and the temple vessels were brought into Solomon's temple after it was constructed:

> Then Solomon assembled the elders of Israel and all the heads of the tribes, the *nāśî'îm* of the ancestral houses of the people of Israel, in Jerusalem, to bring up the ark of the covenant of Yhwh out of the city of David, which is Zion. So they brought up the ark, the tent of meeting, and all the holy vessels that were in the tent; the priests and the Levites carried them up (1 Kgs 8.1-4 = 2 Chron. 5.2, 5).

It may be in this spirit that our author labels Sheshbazzar a *nāśî'*— he was charged with bringing the temple vessels up to the temple in Jerusalem. The title *nāśî'*, moreover, connotes someone selected by the Judeans themselves, whereas the title פחה, 'governor', his actual title, connotes one selected by the king.

1.9-10 ***These are their accountings.*** For a discussion of the utensils, see the textual notes, *ad loc.* The list of vessels would not likely have been included in the second temple's original building inscription. It is an addition added by the biblical writer in the Hellenistic period to conform to Hellenistic rules of historiography. (See comment below.)

1.11b ***Sheshbazzar brought everything up.*** This phrase summarizes vv. 5-11a, and by itself satisfies Component C of the typical ancient Near East temple-building story: Foreign peoples freely contribute to the building and sustenance of the temple for the glory of the temple's god.

Comment: The List of Temple Vessels

A list of donations to a temple is not typical of ancient Near Eastern building inscriptions, but lists of all sorts are prominent in Hellenistic historiography (Honigman 2003), even to the point of using spurious lists to gain credibility. Lists, whether genuine or fictive, were a favorite device used by Greek historians to bolster the credibility of their history. Ctesias (late-fifth century BCE), for example, presents his readers with a spurious list of Assyrian kings, which he claims to derive from Persian royal archives.[1] He created the list to increase his credibility. The fictive list of translators in the *Letter of Aristeas* (47-50) is another example of including lists to increase the credibility of the text and to display the writer's knowledge of his subject (Honigman 2003: 72). Herodotus's provision of the minutest details of the peoples, places and events that he describes are also likely intended to persuade the reader of his access to the sources rather than to provide historical facts, since his statements and the facts often conflict (West 1985).

This does not imply that the list is spurious, however. Porten and Yardeni have published the large number of lists and accounts found on the Egyptian island of Elephantine dated to the Persian period (*TAD* C). One, dated to after 411 BCE (*TAD* C 3.13), concerns vessels contributed to the temple of Yhw at Elephantine. It reads in part:

> Memorandum (זכרן): cups of bronze which
> Ḥanan son of Haggai gav[e] (in)to the hand of Jedaniah son of [PN]
> Cups of bronze, 21
> Silver cup, 1
> *tlpḥ[n],* 4
> [r]ods, [x]; rod [o]f [. . .]
> SPRINKLER[s], 4 [+1] +2 (= 7), to pour *libations*[. . .

As can be seen, this is a receipt, a memorandum (זכרן), of the vessels that Ḥanan bar Haggai donated to the temple and placed into the hands of the chief priest, Jedaniah. There are several of these lists at Elephantine recording goods donated to the temple and their donors. The form of the list is the same as in the list of temple vessels in our chapter—the item and then the amount. Further, many of the words on the lists from Elephantine are untranslatable at this time. This lends support to the theory that the list of temple vessels turned over to the temple of Yhwh in Jerusalem may also be genuine. Even if a genuine list of temple vessels, however, it may not actually be a list of those retrieved from the first temple and deposited in the second temple at the time of its building (Ackroyd 1973: 216); yet it must represent something. It is manifestly obvious that the second temple would have contained a great many implements with which to carry out the sacrificial cult. The author of our text, who lived during the period of the second temple, could have known their names. Thus, we ought to assume a genuine list of temple vessels even if not specifically a list of those taken from the first one.

1. His list of kings is quoted in Eusebius's *Chronici canones* and preserved in Migne 1892: 325-28.

The author's goal of convincing his readers of the validity of the list seems to have succeeded. Even modern commentators who argue that the Cyrus Edict and the response to it were created by the biblical author conclude that the list of vessels is genuine (e.g. Rudolph 1949: 7; Schneider 1959: 91; Gunneweg 1985: 47; Williamson 1985: xxiv; Blenkinsopp 1988: 78). Even Torrey, who argues that most of Ezra is a free creation of the Chronicler, assumes the list to be genuine (Torrey 1970 [1910]: 138-39). Ackroyd, who insists that all the temple vessels had been destroyed in the conflagration that destroyed the temple, gets around the issue by suggesting that the Chronicler had an 'actually existing inventory of vessels available to him, though this does not mean that it necessarily applied to this situation' (Ackroyd 1973: 216).

If the Greek authors from whom we receive our translations of the names of these objects are correct, however, then the returned vessels are only bowls, jugs and knives. We are missing the large bronze hearth altars that served as booty for both Mesha and Sennacherib (See Introduction, The Role of the Temple Vessels). Perhaps they had been melted down, or perhaps they are listed here and we have misunderstood the text, or perhaps they were not returned, and, representing the god, they continued to be held hostage in Babylon.

If the author is following Hellenistic rules of rhetoric, then he would have inserted this list to display his detailed knowledge of the subject under discussion, whether or not it was a genuine list of temple vessels. The list would have been added, not because the author had it at hand but to increase the reader's confidence in the historical reliability of the text and of the author's access to privileged sources. Most curious, however, is that we are not told what happened to these vessels. It is never stated that they were installed into the rebuilt temple, nor is it ever said what was done with them while the temple was being built.

Reflections

The paltry list of vessels here is a far cry from the list of the Tabernacle's furnishings (Exodus 36–39), or from those of Solomon's Temple (1 Kings 7). Indeed, according to the rabbis (*b. Yoma* 21b), five things were missing from the second temple—the ark, the fire, the spirit of prophecy, the *urim* and *thummim*, and the Shekinnah, the indwelling presence of God himself. That is, the rabbis assumed that God was absent from the second temple. Can this have been believed at the time, or did the rabbis assume that God did not dwell in it because it could not have been destroyed by Rome if God had dwelt in it?

The *urim* and *thummim* as well as the spirit of prophecy were present in the second temple, however (see below at 2.63; and Fried 2007c), but what about the indwelling presence of God himself? There was no ark to represent him, nor were there apparently the great incense altars, and there certainly was no statue. What might have represented his presence? At some point during the second temple period there seems to have been a gradual acceptance of the torah scroll as the instantiation of God's actuality on earth, his hypostasis, as it were. Ezra, priest and scribe of the law of God, is introduced to us as one who has "set his heart to seek an oracle (לדרוש) from the *torah* of Yhwh (Ezra 7.10); and, much later, we are told that Judas Maccabee opens the book of the law, the torah, to inquire into those matters about which the nations consult the likenesses of their gods (1 Macc. 3.48). In bringing God's torah into the temple, Ezra ushers in God himself. (See comment at Ezra 7.)

Ezra 2

The Prologue (Continued): The List of Returnees

The location of this list of returnees in the book of Ezra implies a return under Cyrus (538 BCE). The same list appears in 1 Esdras, where it is presented in the context of a return under Darius (520 BCE; 1 Esdras 5). The list is repeated nearly verbatim again in Nehemiah 7, where no king is named at all. Nehemiah 7.5 simply states that Nehemiah found a 'book of the genealogy of those who came up at the beginning'. The problem of the identical list appearing in both Ezra and Nehemiah is discussed in the Introduction. The literary function of the list at this point in the book, as well as the list's original purpose and date, are discussed in Comments A and B to this chapter.

Translation

1. *And these are the members of the province, the ones coming up from the captivity of the exile whom Nebuchadnezzar, King of Babylon, had exiled to Babylon. They returned to Jerusalem and to Judah, each to his own city.* 2. *[They are the ones] who had come with Zerubbabel, Jeshua, Nehemiah, Seraiah, Re'eliah, [Naḥamani], Mordechai, Bilshan, Mispar, Bigavahya, Reḥum, [and] Ba'anah.*

*The number (*mispar*) of the men of the people Israel:*

3.	*The family of Par'osh*	*2,172*
4.	*The family of Shephatiah*	*372*
5.	*The family of Araḥ*	*775*
6.	*The family of Paḥat-Moab of the family of Jeshua [and] Joab*	*2,812*
7.	*The family of Elam*	*1,254*
8.	*The family of Zattu*	*945*
9.	*The family of Zaccai*	*760*
10.	*The family of Bani*	*642*
11.	*The family of Bebai*	*623*
12.	*The family of Azgad*	*1,222*
13.	*The family of Adonikam*	*666*

14.	*The family of Bagavahya*	*2,056*
15.	*The family of Adin*	*454*
16.	*The family of Aṭer*	
	of Hezekiah	*98*
	[The family of Kilan and Azetas,	*67*
	The family of Azzur	*432*
	The family of Hodiah	*101]*
17.	*The family of Beṣai*	*323*
18.	*The family of Jorah*	*112*
19.	*The family of Hashum*	*223*
20.	*The family of Gibbar*	*95*
21.	*The family of Bethlehem*	*123*
22.	*The men of Netophah*	*56*
23.	*The men of 'Anathoth*	*128*
24.	*The family of 'Azmaveth*	*42*
25.	*The family of Kiriath-'Arim,*	
	Chephirah, and Beeroth	*743*
26.	*The family of Ha-Ramah*	
	and Geba	*621*
27.	*The men of Michmas*	*122*
28.	*The men of Beth-El*	
	and Ai	*223*
29.	*The family of Nebo*	*52*
30.	*The family of Magbish*	*156*
31.	*The family of the other 'Elam*	*1,254*
32.	*The family of Ḥarim*	*320*
33.	*The family of Lod, Ḥadid,*	
	and Ono	*725*
34.	*The family of Jericho*	*345*
35.	*The family of Sena'ah*	*3,630*
36.	*The priests:*	
	The family of Jedaiah	
	of the house of Jeshua	*973*
37.	*The family of Immer*	*1,052*
38.	*The family of Pashḥur*	*1,247*
39.	*The family of Ḥarim*	*1,017*
40.	*The Levites:*	
	The families of Jeshua and Kadmiel	
	of the family of Hodaviah	*74*
41.	*The singers:*	
	The family of Asaph	*128*
42.	*The families of the gatekeepers:*	
	The family of Shallum,	

the family of 'Aṭer, the family of Ṭalmon,
the family of 'Aqqub, the family of Ḥaṭiṭa',
the family of Shobai—
All of them *139*
43. *The temple servants:*
The family of Ṣiḥa',
the family of Ḥaśupha', the family of Ṭabba'ot,
44. *the family of Qeros, the family of Si'aha',*
the family of Padon,
45. *the family of Levanah, the family of Ḥagabah,*
the family of 'Aqub,
46. *the family of Ḥagab, the family of Shalmai,*
the family of Ḥanan,
47. *the family of Giddel, the family of Gaḥar,*
the sons of Re'aiah
48. *the family of Reṣin, the family of Neqoda',*
the family of Gazzam,
49. *the family of 'Uzza', the family of Paseaḥ,*
the family of Beṣai,
50. *the family of 'Asnah, the family of Me'ûnîm,*
the family of Nephisîm,
51. *the family of Baqbuq, the family of Ḥaqufa',*
the family of Ḥarḥur,
52. *the family of Baṣlut, the family of Meḥida',*
the family of Ḥarsha',
53. *the family of Barqos, the family of Sisera,*
the sons of Tamaḥ,
54. *the family of Neṣiaḥ, the family of Ḥatifa'.*
55. *The family of Solomon's servants:*
The family of Sotai, the family of Hassopheret,
the family of Peruda',
56. *the family of Ya'elah, the family of Darqon,*
the family of Giddel,
57. *the family of Shephatiah, the family of Ḥattil,*
the family of Pocheret-Hazzevaim,
the family of 'Ami.
58. *All the temple servants and*
the family of Solomon's servants *392*
[Those who could not prove their genealogy:]
59. *The following are those who came up from Tel-*
Melach, Tel Ḥarsha', Cherub, 'Addan, 'Immer
and could not name the house of their fathers or
their genealogy or whether they were from Israel:

60. *The family of Delaiah, the family of Ṭobiah,*
the sons of Neqoda' *652*
61. *as well as the family of the priests,*
the family of Ḥavaiah, the family of Haqqoṣ,
the family of Barzillai who married one
of the daughters of Barzillai the Gileadite
and was called by their name.
62. *These sought the registry of their genealogies but they could not be found and therefore they were [considered] unfit for the priesthood,*
63. *so the tirshata' said to them that they should not eat from the most sanctified food [lit. 'holy of holies'] until a priest appears*
to administer the urim *and* thummim.

[Summary:]

64. *The whole community together is* *42,360*
65. *besides their man-servants and*
maid-servants, these were *7,337*
and their male and female singers *200*
66. *Their horses were* *736,*
their mules *245,*
67. *their camels* *435,*
their donkeys *6,720.*

68. *From among the leaders of the patriarchal families at the time of their coming to the temple of Yhwh which is in Jerusalem, they made free-will offerings to the temple of the god to erect it on its site.*

69. *They gave to the maintenance fund according to their ability.*
Gold: *61,000 drachmas*
Silver: *5,000 minas*
Priestly robes: *100.*

70. *The priests, the Levites, and some from among the people settled [in Jerusalem and its vicinity], and the singers, the gatekeepers, the temple servants, and all Israel settled in their [own] towns.*

Notes

2.1 ***And.*** The use of the conjunction here as the first word in the heading of the list (it is not present in the parallel version in Neh. 7.6, although it is in 1 Esdras) implies that the entire list is to be construed as directly following the previous chapter, that is, that it is a list of those who returned under Cyrus. The difficulty with this idea is that Sheshbazzar's name is conspicuously absent. The author may have purposely omitted his name from the heading because even though he was given the Judean title *nāśî'* he was not Judean and the intention was to emphasize the Judean rather than the

Persian role in rebuilding and resettlement. (See note to Ezra 1.8 and Comments A and B below for the purpose and the date of the list.)

Members. Literally, 'sons of'. First Esdras 5.4 reads, 'These are the names of the men'. It is curious, as Batten (1913: 74) points out, that there are few individual names in the list that follows, only names of clans or towns. This is discussed in Comment A below.

The province. The Hebrew term *mᵉdînāh* denotes a political jurisdiction of the Persian Empire. Greek Ezra, in contrast, reads χώρα, meaning 'area', 'region' or 'countryside', that is, not necessarily a political unit. The MT is to be preferred. The Persian Empire was divided into satrapies, each headed by a satrap. Satrapies were in turn subdivided into provinces, *mᵉdinôt*, each headed by a governor, *peḥāh*. There were also areas of jurisdiction between the satrapy and the province. These were governed by men referred to as the viceroy, that is, as the *hyparch* (ὕπαρχος) in the Greek cities of Asia Minor (e.g. Droaphernes was hyparch of Lydia under the satrap Autophradates in the 39th year of Artaxerxes II; see Fried 2004: 129-37); and as the *bᵉʿēl ṭᵉʿēm* בְּעֵל־טְעֵם in the Hebrew Bible (Ezra 4.8), in Aramaic texts from Elephantine (*TAD* A 4.1), and in Akkadian texts from Babylon (Stolper 1989a).

Although not named, the province is Judah, or Yehud as it is termed on Persian-period seals and coins. This is more explicit in the parallel passage in 1 Esdras (5.7, 8): 'These are the ones of the Judeans who came up out of their captivity'. (For a discussion of the relevance of 1 Esdras and of the various translations in general, see the Introduction.) These were Judeans who had been deported into Babylon by Nebuchadnezzar and were now returning to the land from which they had been driven, that is, to Judah.

To Babylon. Nehemiah 7 lacks 'to Babylon', reading instead 'to exile'. There were at least three deportations from Judah to Babylon by Nebuchadnezzar (Jer. 52.28-30). The first two were in 597 BCE (2 Kgs 24.10-17) and 586 BCE (2 Kgs 25.1-21). It was in 586 BCE that the temple, the city of Jerusalem, and most of Judah were destroyed. In 582 BCE there was a third and final deportation of those who had fled from Judah and Jerusalem to the area of Benjamin. This deportion seems to have followed the assassination of Gedaliah, whom Nebuchadnezzar had installed as governor in Mizpah of Benjamin (Jer. 41; 52.30).

Each to his own city. Archives from ancient Nippur in Babylon reveal that communities of conquered nations had been exiled to Babylon from all over the Babylonian Empire and had maintained their ethnic identities there for hundreds of years (Cardasçia 1951, 1958; Stolper 1985; Eph'al 1978; Pearce 2006, 2011; Pearce and Wunsch 2014; Wunsch and Pearce forthcoming). Communities from Miletus, Sardis, Tyre, Hamath (Syria), Ashkelon, Gaza, Egypt, Arabia, Qedar, as well as Judah, continued to exist in Babylon as communities of deportees. They maintained their ethnic cohesion through local community assemblies. (See further in the Introduction.)

2.2 *[These are the ones] who came up with Zerubbabel.* Rather than a list of actual leaders of a return under Cyrus and Sheshbazzar (whose name is not mentioned), the following group of twelve names is more likely a list of twelve leaders of the Judeans from the entire Persian period who were known to the biblical author. Sheshbazzar may have been intentionally omitted because he was not ethnically Judean. (For a discussion of the purpose and date of the list, see Comments A and B below.)

Zerubbabel and Jeshua. These two men are also mentioned in Ezra 3.2, 8; 4.2, 3; and 5.2. For some reason, no titles are ever applied to them in the book of Ezra (Japhet 1982; Gunneweg 1985: 72), whereas in 1 Esdras (5.5) they are given their full pedigree: Zerubbabel was the descendant of David, the king of Judah and Israel, and Jeshua was the descendant of Aaron, the first high priest. Of the books in the MT, only in the book of Haggai (dated to the second year of Darius I, that is, 521–520; *pace* Edelman 2005) do we learn that Zerubbabel son of Shealtiel was governor of Judah, and that Jeshua (Jehoshua) son of Jehozadak was high priest (Hag. 1.1). According to 1 Chron. 3.17-19, Zerubbabel was the son of Pedaiah, Shealtiel's brother, not of Shealtiel, but either way, Zerubbabel was the grandson of Jehoiachin, the king of Judah who was taken captive to Babylon by Nebuchadnezzar in 597 BCE (2 Kgs 24.12). As his name implies (Zerubbabel = seed of Babylon), Zerubbabel was born (i.e. 'conceived', the result of insemnation) during the captivity in Babylon. As the Davidic heir, he became the focus of messianic aspirations (Hag. 2.23). It was likely his arrival in Judah that prompted a renewed fervor in temple building, so that we may date his arrival to the time of Haggai in the second year of Darius (Bedford 2001). This does not preclude an earlier group of returnees under Cyrus.

Jeshua (yešûaʿ). Jeshua, called Joshua (*yᵉhôšûaʿ*) in Haggai and Zechariah, means 'Yhwh is my deliverance' (Zadok 1988: 48). Jeshua was the son of Jehozadak, the son of Seraiah, the last high priest of Judah (1 Chron. 5.40, 41 [ET 6.14, 15]). Seraiah was killed by Nebuchadnezzar (2 Kgs 25.18-21), but Jehozadak, his son, remained alive and was taken into captivity to Babylon (1 Chron. 5.41 [ET 6.15]). Zerubbabel and Jeshua are thus the same generation, grandsons of the last Davidic king and the last high priest respectively.

Nehemiah. Nehemiah means 'Yhwh comforted'. The root נחם, *nḥm*, means 'to comfort'. The name was common. Besides Nehemiah, the governor of Judah in the mid-fifth century BCE, a Nehemiah is included among the wall builders (445 BCE; Neh. 3.16;); a Neḥemiyahu ben-Yehoʿaz is listed among seventh-century BCE recipients of wheat at Arad (Aharoni 1981: #31); an unknown ben-Neḥemiyahu is listed on a Stratum VII, seventh-century BCE ostracon from Arad (Aharoni 1981: #36); and a letter from another Neḥemiyahu (son of Malkiyahu?) was found in a Stratum VIII locus at Arad, dated to early-seventh century BCE (Aharoni 1981: #40). A slave named Nehemiah (*nḥmyh*) is listed among the slaves in the Wadi ed-Dâliyeh papyri (375–334 BCE; Cross 1963). A seal 'belonging to Neḥemyahu ben-Mikayahu' (Avigad and Sass 1997, #265) was purchased on the antiquities market in 1880. A second seal, inscribed 'belonging to 'Adayahu ben-Neḥemyahu' (Avigad and Sass 1997, #295), and a third, inscribed 'belonging to Ḥananyahu either ben-Naḥum or ben-Neḥemyahu' (Avigad and Sass 1997, #506), were also purchased on the antiquities market. It cannot always be ascertained, however, whether seals purchased on the antiquities market are genuine or forged.

Although the name was common, the Nehemiah named here in Ezra 2.2 most likely refers to the fifth-century governor of Judah for whom the biblical book is named. The biblical writer has included in the heading to this list every Persian-period Judean leader that he knew. In this way he implies that they all returned to Judah at the very first possible moment under Cyrus. (See Comment D below on the chronology of the Persian period assumed by the author of Ezra.)

***Śeraiah* שְׂרָיָה.** Seraiah appears here in Ezra 2, although the name 'Azariah, עֲזַרְיָה, appears in the identical position in this list in Nehemiah 7. The equivalent list in 1 Esdras 5 reads Ζεραιου, Zariah, supporting Nehemiah's 'Azariah. As can be seen from comparing the two words in the Hebrew script, when the initial ayin of 'Azariah touches the zayin next to it, it looks like the Hebrew letter sin, the first letter in Seraiah. The name 'Azariah is likely original and is the full form of the name Ezra, meaning 'Yhwh helped'; indeed it may refer to the same Ezra for whom this book is named. The name 'Azariah is very common. There may be as many as eight separate men by that name in the Elephantine documents alone. Nehemiah 12 contains another list of priests and Levites who came up with Zerubbabel and Jeshua to Judah. There both Seraiah and Ezra are included among the priests who returned (Neh. 12.1-7). The list there may be a combination of the lists of Ezra 2 and Nehemiah 7. A priest Seraiah is also included among the signatories of the Amanah (*'ᵃmānâ*) (Neh. 10.3). (See discussion at Nehemiah 10, or Fried 2005).

Seraiah is the name of Ezra's father (Ezra 7.1) and also the name of the high priest of Judah who was taken captive by the Babylonians and killed at Riblah (2 Kgs 25.18-21). His son Jehozadaq was deported to Babylon (1 Chron. 5.41 [ET 6.15]), where he fathered Jeshua, the high priest of the return. According to Ezra's genealogy (Ezra 7.1-5), Ezra and Jehozadaq share the same lineage and are brothers (cf. 1 Chron. 5.27-41). This is impossible historically, since the historical Ezra must be placed to the time of Artaxerxes II (398 BCE, or at least to 458 BCE and the reign of Artaxerxes I; see Fried 2014: 8-27 and discussion at Ezra 7), and Jeshua, his supposed nephew, to the time of Darius I (520 BCE). Yet, the view of the author of Ezra–Nehemiah is that Ezra and Jeshua are uncle and nephew and both returned at the first available opportunity, that is, under Cyrus in 538. (For a discussion of the chronology of the author of Ezra–Nehemiah as compared to the actual chronology, see Comment D below.) Although the death of the last high priest is described in 2 Kings, it is not mentioned in Chronicles. It is possible that the author of Ezra–Nehemiah did not know that he was killed.

The name Seraiah (Serayahu, 'Yhwh ruled') is common on seals sold on the antiquities market, but it is not known if they are genuine. A Seraiah, the brother of Baruch ben-Neriah, Jeremiah's scribe (Jer. 51.59), was sent from King Zedekiah to bring tribute to Babylon in Zedekiah's fourth year (594 BCE; Jer. 51.59-64), and a seal inscribed 'belonging to Serayahu ben-Neriyahu' may be his seal, if genuine (Avigad and Sass 1997, #390). It was available on the antiquities market in 1974, but its present location is not known. Two women named Seraiah are known at Elephantine: On an ostracon bearing a list of names is 'Seraiah daughter of (. . .)' (*TAD* D 9.14: 5) and a Seraiah daughter of Hosea son of Ḥarman is listed as contributing two shekels of silver to the house of Yhw at Elephantine on June 1, 400 BCE (*TAD* C 3.15:4).

Re'elaiah **רְעֵלָיָה**. Re'elaiah means 'friend of Yhwh'. Nehemiah 7.7 reads רַעַמְיָה Ra'amiah, 'Yhwh has thundered', instead of Re'elaiah, and 1 Esdras reads Ρησαιου, Resaiah. None of these three names is attested anywhere else to my knowledge. Rudolph (1949: 6) suggests that the name Ra'amiah may refer to an event that happened at the birth of the child, that is, a thunderstorm. The Persian name Ramiyauka, meaning in Persian 'you who are at peace' or 'may you be at peace', is known among the Persepolis Fortification Tablets (PF 1823). This could become Ra'amiah, 'may Yhwh bring peace'.

[Naḥamani]. The name is restored from Neh. 7.7. The name means 'he comforted me', and is based on the same root as the name Nehemiah, *nḥm*. (See note on Nehemiah above.) This is a hypocoristic, that is, a nickname formed by leaving out the theophoric, the element with the divine name. This name may have been inadvertently dropped from the list when copied. First Esdras has Ενηνιος, Eneneus, reflecting Naḥamani. This name would bring the total up to twelve, the total in both Neh. 7.7 and 1 Esd. 5.8. The total of twelve names may be intended to convey the impression that these are the leaders of all twelve tribes and that all twelve tribes participated in the return, as Ezekiel predicted (37.19-21).

Mordechai. This Babylonian name is based on the theophoric Marduk, the high god of Babylon. Names composed with this theophoric were common there and in Persia. Mordechai is likely a Hebraized form of the common Marduka (Moore 1971: 19). A Marduka is mentioned twice in the

Persepolis Treasury Tablets (Moore 1971: L; Cameron 1948: 84, Tablets 1 and 84). A Babylonian official in charge of one of the estates of Arsames, satrap of Egypt under Darius II, was named Marduk (*TAD* A 6.9). Moreover, the name Marduk-ʻidri (ʻMarduk is my help') is included in a list of names from Elephantine dated to the middle of the fifth century BCE. It is an Aramaic version of ʻAzariah with Marduk as the name's divine element instead of Yhwh. Lastly, a memorandum from Elephantine, dated to 471 BCE, refers to a Marduk-šar-uṣer ('May Marduk protect the king', *TAD* C 3.8 (IIIB):36). Although the name is not uncommon, the author may actually have had Queen Esther's famous cousin, the hero of the biblical book Esther, in mind. (See Comment D below on the chronology of the Persian period assumed by the biblical writer versus the conventional chronology.)

Bilshan. This name may refer to Bēlšunu, satrap of the satrapy Beyond-the-River between 407 and 401 BCE, and perhaps as early as 429 BCE (Stolper 1989a). If he was also satrap in 398, he would have been the satrap when Ezra arrived in Judah. (See Comment A to Ezra 7 for discussion of the date of Ezra.) The name Bēlšunu also appears in the Persepolis Fortification Tablets (PF 2018.21).

Mispar. The word מִסְפָּר is not a proper name but simply the normal Hebrew word for 'number'. It may have been erroneously copied from the end of the verse where the total number of the Israelite people is given. Nehemiah 7 has Mispereth, מִסְפֶּרֶת, and 1 Esdras has Ασφαρασυς, Aspharasus, both perhaps reflecting *haśoferet,* that is, 'the scribe' (Talshir 2001: 256). (See below at 2.55.) It may be that *mispār*, מספר, is a corruption of Esther, אסתר, however, and that the scribe dropped his eyes inadvertently from the similar אסתר to the word מספר that concludes the list and wrote *mispar* by dittography. On the other hand, the masculine Persian name Mishparra is known from the Persepolis Fortifications Tablets (PF 1638.3) and from the Elamite version of the Behistun inscription (DB 4.83), so that may be the correct reading.

Bagavahya. This Persian name, spelled בִּגְוַי, and vocalized Bigvai in Ezra and Nehemiah, was more likely pronounced Bagavahya (Baga = god, vahya = very good, so meaning '[worshiper of] Baga, the good; the corresponding name in Hebrew would be Tobiah, '[worshiper of] Yhwh, the good' (Porten and Lund 2002: 330; S. Shaked, personal communication). Bagavahya was the governor of Judah immediately following Nehemiah (*TAD* A 4.7; Fried 2003c; 2004: 185). First Esdras has Boroliou, Βορολιου, which, as Talshir (2001: 257) points out, is only vaguely reminiscent of either Bigvai or Bagavahya.

Reḥum. The name means 'compassionate', and may be a hypocoristic, that is, the name of the compassionate god is missing. Although Nehemiah has Neḥum (Naḥum?), 1 Esdras confirms a reading of Reḥum with Ροΐμου, Roimou or Roimos. This name may refer to Reḥum, the viceroy or vice-satrap, בְּעֵל־טְעֵם (*b*e*ʿēl t*e*ʿēm*; Ezra 4.9), of the satrapy Beyond-the-River during the reign of Artaxerxes I (see below at 4.9 for a discussion of the role). Reḥum may have been a Babylonian of Judean descent; a Raḥim son of Baniah ('Yhwh has built') is listed in an Akkadian tablet from Babylon dated to 423 BCE (Zadok 1988: 309: Ra-ḫi-im son of Ba-na-ia-a-ma). Coincidentally, a Reḥum son of Bani appears in the list of Nehemiah's wall builders (Neh. 3.17).

***Ba'anāh* בַּעֲנָה.** Ba'anāh, בַּעֲנָה, is listed in Neh. 10.27 as one of the 'leaders of the descendants' who signed the Amanah (*'ᵃmānâ*). (See the discussion at Nehemiah 10.) A Ba'anah is named as one of the commanders of Ishba'al son of Saul (2 Sam. 4). The name Ba'ani, בעני, a hypocoristic of Ba'aniah, is known from a seal impression 'Ba'ani ben-'Adayahu' (Deutsch and Lemaire 2000, #41).

The number of the men of the people Israel. This is the title for the section detailing the return of the laity. First Esdras adds the phrase τῶν προηγουμένων αὐτῶν, 'their leaders', here in 1 Esd. 5.8 and again in 5.9. Talshir (2001: 257) suggests, plausibly, that the word 'leaders' was written in the margin of the Hebrew causing it to be added twice to 1 Esdras and to be accordingly dropped from Ezra. The phrase does not appear in Nehemiah 7.

First Esdras is missing the term 'Israel', and thus is missing the distinction between the cultic officials and the laity. The word Israel is present in all the other versions, however.

2.3 *The family of.* Literally: 'the sons of'. The people Israel are grouped in this part of the list according to families or paternal lines. Beginning with Ezra 2.20, they are grouped by settlements. Commentators have suggested that these may have stemmed from two separate lists constructed for different purposes, but see Comment A.

Par'osh. Par'osh, פַּרְעֹשׁ, means 'flea' in Hebrew and Aramaic (1 Sam. 24.15; 26.20; Zadok 1988: 154). Even so, it is a common Phoenician–Punic name, and is also found at Ugarit (*Prǵṯ*; Zadok 1988: 154). It is known in Akkadian (*pir-ša-ḫu-um*) and in the common Palestinian Arabic surname *al-Barǵūṯi* (Zadok 1988: 154). A Zechariah with 150 of the family of Par'osh also apparently returned with Ezra in the reign of Artaxerxes II (Ezra 8.3), and several of this family are included among those who divorced their foreign wives in the time of Ezra (Ezra 10.25). A Pedaiah son of Par'osh worked on the city wall in the time of Nehemiah (Artaxerxes I); and finally a Par'osh is listed among the signers of the Amanah (Neh. 10.15). Avigad and Sass (1997, #334) report a seal 'formerly in the possession of W. Von Landau' but whose present location is unknown that bears the single name *Pr'š*.

2.4 *Shephatiah.* Shephatiah, 'Yhwh has judged'. The name appears on a number of stamp seals (Avigad and Sass 1997: 538; Deutsch and Lemaire

2000, #89), but does not appear at Elephantine. Though present on all three lists (Ezra 2; Nehemiah 7; and 1 Esdras 5), Shephatiah is not listed as a signatory to the Amanah of Nehemiah 10. Shephatiah was also the name of King David's fifth son born at Hebron.

2.5 *'Araḥ.* An 'Araḥ is listed among the men of the tribe of Asher (1 Chron. 7.39). The name, meaning 'way' or 'path', may be hypocoristic, that is, a shortened form with the theophoric (divine name) dropped off. 'Araḥiah, for example, would mean 'way of Yhwh'. According to Neh. 6.18, Tobiah, the governor of Amman, is the son-in-law of Shecaniah son of 'Araḥ. According to the Behistun inscription, an Arḫa, an Armenian, son of Haldita, rose up against Darius, claiming to be Nebuchadrezzar son of Nabonidus (DB 3.78). It may thus be an Armenian or Babylonian name. No 'Araḥ is listed as a signatory to the Amanah in Nehemiah 10.

775. The number of family members differs in the lists. Nehemiah reads 652 and 1 Esdras, 756.

2.6 *Pahat-Moab.* This name means 'governor of Moab'. Williamson (1985: 25) suggests that it goes back to a family name created under the monarchy when Judah controlled Moab and that it was originally Ba'al Moab (lord of Moab). It was changed to the present form to avoid the connection with the god Ba'al. This is an interesting speculation. Porten thinks it is simply a title which then became a personal name, and that these are descendants of a (former?) governor of Moab (personal communication). The family is also included among those who returned with Ezra (Ezra 8.4) and among those who had taken foreign wives (Ezra 10.30). A son of Paḥat-Moab is also listed as helping to build the wall around Jerusalem (Neh. 3.11), and a Paḥat-Moab is listed as one of the signatories of the Amanah (Neh. 10.14). Both Greek Ezra and 1 Esdras treat it as one word and so as a personal name not a title.

Of the family of Jeshua. *Yešua'* in Hebrew. Paḥat-Moab is apparently of the family of both Jeshua and Joab since only one number is given for all three names. The name Jeshua is common, and this lay person is to be distinguished from both the high priest and the Levite of the same name. This form of the name (Jeshua rather than Joshua = Yehošua), is limited to Ezra–Nehemiah, where even Joshua son of Nun is referred to as Jeshua (Yešua'; Neh. 8.17).

[and]. The conjunction (only one letter in Hebrew) is absent here in Ezra, but is present in Nehemiah 7, in 1 Esdras, and in the Peshitta. It likely fell out through haplography.

Joab. Yo'ab (Yeho'ab = 'Yhwh is [my] father') was also the name of David's nephew and head of his army. An unprovenanced seal now in the Israel Museum bears the legend 'belonging to 'Amaryahu ben Yeho'ab' (Avigad and Sass 1997, #449).

2,812. Nehemiah reads 2,818, but 1 Esdras agrees with Ezra. There is no way to understand how these differences occur.

2.7 *'Elam.* Although used here as a family name, it is an area in Iran, on the Persian Gulf and the lower Tigris River. Its language, Elamite, is a major language of the Persepolis tablets. The capital of Elam was Susa (Shushan in Neh. 1.1 and Esther), one of the four capitals of the Persian Empire (the other three being Ecbatana, Babylon and Persepolis), and Elam was an important province of the empire. The name is used as a geographical entity in Ezra 2.31/Neh. 7.34 where it is called 'the other Elam'. Members of the Elam family are listed among those who returned with Ezra (8.7) and among those who divorced their foreign wives (Ezra 10.26). An 'Elam is listed as one of the signatories of the Amanah in Neh. 10.14. Zadok (1988: 3) suggests that these are all really gentilics because the word does not appear as a personal name outside of these passages in Ezra–Nehemiah.

2.8 *Zattu.* The family of Zattu is listed in Ezra 10.27 as having members who divorced their foreign wives. As an individual, he is listed as a signer of the Amanah in Neh. 10.15. The name may be Persian (Zadok 1988: 176). A Persian Zatuvahyah (זתוהי) is known at Elephantine (*TAD* A 6.9: 1) and a Zattukka appears on one of the Persepolis Fortification Tablets (PF 1957.22).

2.9 *Zaccai.* *Zaccai*, זכי, 'pure', 'righteous'. First Esdras reads Χορβε, Chorbe, which cannot reflect Zaccai. Zaccai may be a variant of the common Zakā', זכא. An inscription 'belonging to Kisla' ben-Zaka'' was found impressed on a jar handle in the excavations at Bet-Shemesh, and dated to the end of the eighth century BCE (Avigad and Sass 1997: #674). Another inscription, 'belonging to Zakā' ben-Milkom or Milk'az', was found on an Aramaic seal impression dated to the sixth century BCE (Avigad and Sass 1997: #792).

760. Nehemiah agrees with this number, but 1 Esdras reads 705.

2.10 *Bani.* The name is spelled Binnui in Nehemiah. The name in 1 Esdras agrees with Ezra, while the Greek of Ezra and of Nehemiah have Βανουι, Banui, a third form. These are all likely hypocoristics of Benayahu ('Yhwh has built up'). Ostracon 39 at Arad, dated to the seventh century BCE, contains a list of names, one being Ya'azanyahu son of Benayahu (יאזניהו בן בניהו; Aharoni 1981: 68). The similar name Benayah, בניה, with the same meaning, is attested among the Judeans at Elephantine. There is a Benayah father of Hošayah (*TAD* C 3.3:13, sixth century BCE), and a Benayah son of Gaddul (*TAD* D 3.17:4, middle of fifth century BCE). The list in Nehemiah 10 includes both a Bani and a Bunni.

642. Both Nehemiah and 1 Esdras read 648.

2.11 *Bebai.* The name Bībī appears in a witness list on a contract for a loan from Assur dated to the middle of the seventh century BCE (Lipiński 1975: 83, 111). An ostracon from the Wadi Hammamat in Egypt, dated to the eighteenth year of Darius I (503 BCE), reads, 'Blessed be Bebai by (the god) Min', ברך בבי למן (Bongrani Fanfoni and Israel 1994, #2.3). Kornfeld (1978: 35, 119) considers Bebai to be a *Lallname*, that is, a 'mumble-name', a type of nickname that can be found in any language. The names Bebai and Azgad are reversed in the list of Nehemiah 10.

623. Nehemiah reads 628, but 1 Esdras agrees with Ezra.

2.12 *'Azgad.* The descendants of 'Azgad ('Gad is strong', Zadok 1988: 52) are listed among those who returned with Ezra (8.12), and one named 'Azgad is included among the leaders of the people who signed the Amanah (Neh. 10.15). Gad is the god of luck and good fortune, and is mentioned along with the god Meni in Isa. 65.11. 'Azgad is recorded as having an orchard measuring 16 *seah* on a fourth-century ostracon from Idumea (#188, Eph'al and Naveh 1996: 84). The name 'Azgad occurs on a Phoenician tomb inscription from Cyprus dated to the fourth century BCE (Zadok 1988: 278, #72120: 3), at Edfu (Kornfeld 1978: 66), and at Elephantine (*TAD* D 7.57: 5). The latter is on an ostracon dated to the late-third century BCE and refers to one Malkiyah son of 'Azgad.

1,222. Nehemiah reads 2,322, whereas 1 Esdras reads 1,322.

2.13 *'Adoniqam.* 'Adoniqam may mean 'my lord raises up', or 'my lord stands', or 'exists' (Porten, personal communication). The element *qam* may be a theophoric, however, so that the name may mean 'Qam is my lord' (Zadok 1988: 54). Lipiński (2000: 602) suggests that Qam refers to the standing stones, or Beth-els, that represent Aramean and Amorite gods. The element occurs also in 'Azriqam (Neh. 11.15), 'Qam is my help' (Lipiński 2000: 602), which Porten would translate as 'my help exists'. Similarly, Zadok translates Qemuel (Gen. 22.21), as 'Qam is god (El)', rather than 'god exists'. Descendants of 'Adoniqam also returned with Ezra (8.13). The list in Nehemiah 10 reads 'Adonijah ('Yhwh is my lord) in this position rather than 'Adoniqam, perhaps substituting one theophoric for another.

666. This is 667 in both Nehemiah and 1 Esdras.

2.14 *Bagavahya.* Bagavahya is likely the correct pronunciation of this Persian name. (See at v. 2 above.) This would be a different Bagavahya from the one listed there. A Bagavahya is also listed as a signer of the Amanah in Nehemiah 10, and members of this family are listed as returning with Ezra (8.14).

2,056. This reads 2,026 in Nehemiah and 2066 in 1 Esdras.

2.15 *'Adin.* 'Adin is Eden, as in the Garden of Eden. The word means 'delight', 'pleasure'. The name 'Adnah is known at Kuntillet 'Ajrud, an eighth-century BCE oasis and rest site for caravans in the Sinai desert. An ostracon was found there inscribed ''Abdyw (Obadiah = servant of Yhwh) son of 'Adnah' (Zadok 1988: 279). The name is not known at Elephantine. An 'Adin is listed as signing the Amanah (Neh. 10.17).

454. This reads 655 in Nehemiah, but 454 in 1 Esdras as here in Ezra.

2.16 ***'Aṭer of Hezekiah.*** 'Aṭer of Hezekiah, that is, the 'Aṭer who belongs to Hezekiah. One named 'Aṭer is also known among the gatekeepers (Ezra 2.46 = Neh. 7.45). Both 'Aṭer and Hezekiah are listed among the signers of the Amanah (Neh. 10.18). The name apparently means 'left-handed' (Judg. 3.15; 20.16), but as such it must be a nickname, as no one would name a newborn baby 'Lefty'. A contract found at Elephantine (*TAD* B 2.7: 3), dated to November 17, 446 BCE, refers to a Meshullam son of Zaccur son of 'Aṭer.

Hezekiah. Hezekiah, pronounced Yeḥizqîyāh ('Yhwh will strengthen'), is the same name as that of the pre-exilic Judean king, but with the spelling common in 2 Chronicles (28.32; 32.23, 27) rather than that in 2 Kings. It is also the spelling used in the introduction to the books of Hosea (1.1) and Micah (1.1), suggesting that these book titles were added in the postexilic period. The author of 2 Kings refers to that king as Ḥizqiyah, 'Yhwh is my strength'. A coin, dated to c. 370 (Fried 2003a), is engraved '*Yḥzqyw hpḥh'*, Yeḥizqiyahu the governor', using the spelling given here. A seal formerly in the Altman collection, but whose present location is not known, is inscribed לחזק, 'to Ḥazaq', 'strengthened' or 'strong'; that is, a hypocoristic of the above (Avigad and Sass 1997: 97, #153).

98. This reads the same in Nehemiah, but 1 Esdras reads 92.

Kilan, Azetas, Azzur, Hodiah. These four names are missing from both Ezra 2 and Nehemiah 7, and are restored with their numbers from 1 Esdras. The last two names are also included among the signatories of the Amanah in Nehemiah 10 and are in this same location in that list. The first two are the Greek renderings of Semitic names, but it is not clear what the original versions would have been.

'Azzur. The order in Neh. 10.18, 19 [ET 17, 18] is slightly different; it reads ''Azzur, Hodiah, Hashum, and Bezai'. 'Azzur, עַזּוּר, is 'he has been helped'. It may also be a shortened form of עֲזַרְיָהוּ, Azariah, 'Yhwh helped' (Zadok 1988: 114). Jeremiah had an argument with the prophet Hananiah son of 'Azzur (Jer. 28.1), and Ezekiel reports that he saw a Jaazaniah son of 'Azzur in a vision at the east gate of the temple (Ezek. 11.1). A list of names discovered at Elephantine (*TAD* C 4.6: 8), dated to c. 400 BCE, contains the name Kushi son of 'Azzur (כשי בר עזור).

Hodiah. The name Hodiah, הוֹדִיָּה, 'Yhwh is splendor', is missing from Ezra and Nehemiah, but is supplied from the parallel position in Neh. 10.19 [ET 10.18]. In this position, 1 Esdras reads Annias, Αννιας. Talshir (2001: 263, citing Bewer 1922) suggests that Αννιας is a mistake for Audias, Αυδιας, הודיה, Hodiah, which should be in all the lists. A similar name is prominent at Elephantine: הודויה, see below at 2.40. The number 101 is supplied from 1 Esdras.

2.17 ***Beṣai,*** **בצי.** Both Nehemiah 7 and 10 precede the name Beṣai with that of Ḥashum, חָשֻׁם. First Esdras inserts the name Arom, which may be a misreading of Ḥashum, and reads 'the sons of Arom sons of Bezai'. The order in Nehemiah 7 is Ḥashum, Beṣai, and Ḥariph. Ḥashum appears below at 2.19, but a different number of family members is attached. Zadok (1988: 174) states that it is a LB Aramaic name.

323. Nehemiah reads 324, whereas 1 Esdras agrees with Ezra.

2.18 ***Jorah, or Yoreh.*** *Jorah, or Yoreh*, יורה, refers to the blessings of the early rains (Deut. 11.14). A Yorai is listed among the sons of Gad in 1 Chron. 5.13. The name does not occur elsewhere to my knowledge.

Both Nehemiah 7 and 10 as well as 1 Esdras have Hariph/Ariphos instead of Yoreh in this position, with the same number of family members, 112. 1 Esdras thus reflects Nehemiah, rather than Ezra. The name Ḥariph means 'reproach' (e.g. 2 Sam. 21.21) and may be a hypocoristic for 'DN removes my reproach [by providing a son]'. Alternatively, it may be the adjective 'sharp' and be a hypocoristic 'DN is sharp (?)'. Porten (personal communication) finds an interesting connection between Yoreh ('the early rains') and Ḥoref ('winter').

2.19 ***Ḥašum,*** **חָשֻׁם.** *Ḥašum*, חָשֻׁם, is listed as an ancestor of those who divorced their foreign wives in Ezra 10.33, as one of the men who stood next to Ezra when he read the law (Neh. 8.4), and as one of the signers of the Amanah (Neh. 10.19). The name appears earlier in the lists in Nehemiah 7 and 10 and does not appear in 1 Esdras. Talshir (2001: 263) suggests that in copying the names from the list in Nehemiah 7, the author of 1 Esdras must have transposed the names (although she suggests that Arom may be an error for Asom, which is what the Greek of Ḥašum would have been). The name Ḥašum also appears in Genesis as a Temanite who ruled over Edom (Gen. 36.34).

223. Nehemiah 7 reads 328.

2.20 ***Gibbar***. Nehemiah 7.21 reads *Gibeon*, and the text here in Ezra should probably be corrected. If so, then the list of men by town, rather than by family, begins here. Gibeon is identified with Tel el-Jib, 8 km. NW of Jerusalem in the tribal area of Benjamin, on the basis of jar handles found there inscribed *gb'n*. Men from Gibeon are listed among the wall builders in Neh. 3.7 but are not included either among the returnees in 1 Esdras or among the signers of the Amanah in Nehemiah 10. In Neh. 3.7 they are listed under the jurisdiction of the governor of the province Beyond-the-River. See the discussion of Gibeon in the Introduction to Ezra 1–6. Gibeon was inhabited during the Persian period.

Beitar. First Esdras inserts Beitar before Bethlehem, a town that lies 5 km. W of Bethlehem. Although the town name Beitar does not appear in the Hebrew Bible, it appears in the Alexandrine tradition of the LXX in a list of settlements of Judah (Josh 15.59a), alongside Tekoa, תקוע, and אפרתה, Ephrata, that is, Bethlehem (Talshir 2001: 264). It was a site of a stronghold destroyed by the Romans during the Bar Kokhba revolt. The number of family members given for it in 1 Esdras (3,005) is too high and must be an error, as the numbers in the rest of this section are far lower (Talshir 2001: 264). The town lies under the present-day West Bank village of Battir and has not been excavated.

2.21 ***Bethlehem.*** Ezra reads 'sons of Bethlehem', implying that Bethlehem is a personal name, but Nehemiah reads 'men of', implying a town. First Esdras compromises with 'sons from Bethlehem', υἱοὶ ἐκ βαιθλωμην. Lying 5 km. S of Jerusalem, Bethlehem is known traditionally as the site where Rachel died giving birth to Benjamin, and where David and Jesus were born. Because the modern town is located on top of the ancient one, few excavations have been conducted except for the area around the Church of the Nativity. Excavations in the caves beneath the church reveal an Iron Age town dating to the tenth–eighth centuries BCE. Two jar rims from the Persian period and two from the Hellenistic period have also been found, suggesting that there may have been occupation there then (Finkelstein 2008b: 10). The town is not mentioned in Ezra–Nehemiah beyond the lists in Ezra 2 and Nehemiah 7. Bethlehem is well within any map of Persian-period Yehud, but whether it was inhabited then is not likely.

2.22 ***Netophah.*** Netophah is usually identified with Khirbet Badd Faluḥ, near the spring 'Ain en-Natuf, which has preserved the name (Blenkinsopp 1988). It is a well-attested Judean town, on a ridge about 5.5 km. SE of Bethlehem. Two of David's thirty mighty men came from there (2 Sam. 23.28, 29; 1 Chron. 11.30) as did one of the supporters of Ishmael the son of Netaniah (2 Kgs 25.23). It is listed as a levitical city (1 Chron. 9.16) and as a city of temple singers (Neh. 12.28). First Esdras has Νετεβας, reflecting a *b/p* interchange. The town has not been excavated to my knowledge.

56. Nehemiah groups the men from Bethlehem and Netophah together totaling to 188. First Esdras agrees with Ezra, reading 123 for Bethlehem. That would leave 65 for Netophah, but Ezra and 1 Esdras read 56 and 55 respectively.

2.23 ***'Anathoth.*** 'Anathoth, the birthplace of Jeremiah (Jer. 1.1), is a levitical city designated from the tribe of Benjamin for the descendants of Aaron (Josh. 21.18). Abiathar, the last high priest of Eli's family, was expelled to 'Anathoth when he supported Adonijah, Solomon's rival for the throne (1 Kgs 2.26). Jeremiah purchased the field of his cousin Hanamel in Anathoth to demonstrate his faith that the people would return to Judah and Benjamin after the Babylonian Exile (Jeremiah 32). The Arab village 'Anata is 4 km. NE of Jerusalem. A survey reveals extensive Iron II deposits, and some Hellenistic material, but nothing from the Persian period. Some identify the city therefore with Tell Ḥarrube (Ras el-Ḥarrubeh/Kharrubeh) 800 m SSW of present-day 'Anata (Blenkinsopp 1988: 86; Carter 1999: 163). Architectural remains of both the Persian and Hellenistic periods exist in Tell Ḥarrube, but there are few from Iron II, making the association with

Jeremiah's hometown problematic (Carter 1999: 164). On the other hand, a survey found Iron II and Hellenistic shards, but no Persian-period remains (Finkelstein 2008b: 11). Khirbet Deir es-Sidd, 1,400 m E of present-day 'Anata has also been suggested (Nadelman 1994; Finkelstein and Magen 1993: 360), but again there are Iron II deposits but nothing from the Persian period. It is possible that Persian 'Anathoth was not built exactly on the same site as the pre-exilic city, but rather on present-day Tell Ḥarrube (Peterson 1992: 228). Finkelstein suggests that 'Anathoth is under the modern city of 'Anata, and that it simply was not occupied in the Persian period.

All three sites are in the area assigned to Benjamin and would have been within Persian-period Yehud. Both Ezra and Nehemiah read 'the men of 'Anathoth', recognizing the name as a place; 1 Esdras reads 'the ones *from* 'Anathoth', also seeing a place name here. An 'Anathoth is listed as an individual signatory of the Amanah in Neh. 10.19, however.

128. Nehemiah agrees with Ezra here, but 1 Esdras reads 158.

2.24 *'Azmavet.* Although Ezra reads 'the sons of', it is a place name. This site is identified as modern Ḥizmeh, about 8 km. NNE of Jerusalem in the hill country of Judah (Albright 1924). It was inhabited in Iron II, Persian and Hellenistic periods (Finkelstein 2008b: 11). First Esdras has Βαιτασμων, reflecting Nehemiah's Beit-Azmaveth.

2.25 *Kiriath 'Arim.* Although Ezra reads Kiriath 'Arim, קרית ערים, Neh. 7.29 as well as the LXX of both Ezra and Nehemiah have the traditional rendition of Kiriath-Jearim, קרית יערים, as do 1 Esdras and the Peshitta. The MT of Ezra should be emended with the versions and with Nehemiah. Kiriath-Jearim is identified with modern Kiriath-Jearim located 14.5 km. W of Jerusalem in the central hill country near the site of Abū Ghosh on the border between Judah and Benjamin (Finkelstein 2008b: 11). Kiriath-Jearim was strongly inhabited during the Iron II and Hellenistic periods. It was very sparsely inhabited in the Persian period, if at all.

In both Ezra and Nehemiah the towns Kiriath-Jearim, Chephirah and Beeroth are grouped together with 743, indicating the number of returnees from all three towns. In 1 Esdras, Kiriath-Jearim is provided with its own number of returnees—25. The number 743 is then assigned to returnees from the two remaining towns. Joshua 9.17 lists the three towns together with Gibeon as Gibeon, Chephirah, Beeroth and Kiriath-Jearim, and they may have belonged to a Gibeonite–Hivvite enclave NW of Jerusalem (Josh 9.3-7; Blenkinsopp 1988: 87). According to Josh. 18.25-28, all these towns belong to Benjamin, but according to 1 Chron. 13.6, Kiriath-Jearim belongs to Judah. It was on the border between Benjamin and Judah.

Chephira. *Chephira*, כְּפִירָה, has been identified with Khirbat el Kefireh, a 2 hectare tell about 1.6 km. N of Kiriath-Jearim and about 8 km. WSW of Gibeon (Tell el-Jib). The site is located on a steep high spur and is bounded on the north and south by two wadis that join west of the tell to form Wadi

Qotneh, which descends into the Aijalon Valley. It guarded the mid-point of a road that connected Gibeon and Aijalon (Dorsey 1992). Isolated Persian-period potsherds on a surface survey of the site reveal slight Persian-period habitation (Finkelstein and Magen 1993: 209-10, #263). The main period of occupation was the Iron Age; activity at the site in the Persian period was 'weak', but intensified in the Hellenistic period (Finkelstein 2008b: 11).

Be'eroth. The location of Be'eroth, בְּאֵרוֹת, has been disputed, but may be Khirbet el-Burj, near the modern Jerusalem neighborhood of Ramot (Yeivin 1971). Excavations revealed that occupation was strong in the Iron Age but weak during the Persian and Hellenistic periods.

1 Esdras inserts the towns Chadias and Ammid after Be'eroth. The origin of these names is obscure; there is no parallel. Talshir (2001: 266) suggests a possible connection to Ḥadid in Ezra 2.33, for which there is no parallel in 1 Esdras.

2.26 *Ha-Ramah.* Ha-Ramah, הָרָמָה, means 'the height', and was a common name for towns situated on a hill. This town in Benjamin (Josh. 18.25) is usually identified with modern er-Ram, 7 km. N of Jerusalem. Scant Persian-period remains indicate some Persian-period habitation. It was strongly occupied in the Iron Age, weakly occupied in the Persian period, and began to recover in the Hellenistic period (Finkelstein 2008b: 12).

This town in the region of Benjamin may have been where Samuel lived and worked (1 Sam. 7.17). The stories associate him with the nearby towns of Bethel, Gilgal and Mizpah, all in Benjamin. Er-Ram is on the border of the tribal area of Ephraim, and Ramah may be a short form of Ramathaim-Zophim, the Ephraimite town where Samuel's father, Elkanah, was born (1 Sam. 1.1). According to Judg. 4.5, Deborah dwelt between Bethel and Ramah in the hill country of Ephraim, so that Ramah would have been close to the border between Ephraim and Benjamin (Arnold 1992). At the division of the kingdom after Solomon's death, Ramah was a contested border city between Judah and Israel (1 Kgs 15.17-22). The town seems to have served as a staging area for groups of Judeans being deported to Babylon from Judah. The Babylonian captain, Nebuzaradan, had taken Jeremiah to Ramah in chains after the conquest of Jerusalem (Jer. 40.1). It may have been the sight of all the deportees that prompted Jeremiah's lament:

> Thus says Yhwh: A voice is heard in Ramah, lamentation and bitter weeping. Rachel is weeping for her children; she refuses to be comforted for her children, because they are no more (Jer. 31.15).

1 Esdras reads Κιραμας, Kirama, for Ha-Ramah. Talshir (2001: 266) suggests the initial *k* may have evolved through dittography from the final *k* of the preceding εκ, 'from'.

Geba'. Geba' is identified with modern Jiba' or Jaba', 10 km. N of Jerusalem. It was near the northern border of Benjamin (Josh. 18.24-5) and gave rise to the expression 'from Geba' to Beer-Sheba' (2 Kgs 28.3) as indicating the greatest extent of monarchic Judah. A thorough archaeological survey of the site revealed Iron Age and Hellenistic habitation, but no Persian-period material. It was likely not inhabited then.

2.27 *Michmas.* It is spelled here with a samekh, ס; elsewhere in the MT it is spelled with a final sin, שׂ, *s*. It is the town, near Geba', where the Philistines mustered against Saul (1 Sam. 13.11). It is associated with Benjamin in Neh. 11.31.

It is identified with Mukhmâs, 11 km. N of Jerusalem, and with the ancient village of Khirbet el-Hara el-Fawqa, one and one-half km. N of Mukhmâs. That site guards a pass across a deep canyon that runs south to Geba' (Jaba') on the other side. This may be the pass mentioned in 1 Sam. 13.23. Both sites have extensive Persian-period remains.

1 Esdras reads 'Makalon', Μακαλων, which reflects only the first two consonants of the form in the MT but the number of returnees is the same.

2.28 *Bethel and Ai.* Bethel is identified with the modern town of Beitin, about 19 1/2 km. N of Jerusalem, and this identification seems secure (Dever 1992; Koenen 2003: 3-12). Ai is et-Tell ('the ruin'), 3 km. ESE of Beitin. These towns were originally assigned to Ephraim but are listed as Benjaminite in Josh. 18.13, 21 (Koenen 2003: 12-14). Persian-period material is thus far not visible at Bethel, but the ancient town is under the modern one of Beitin, and not all of it can be excavated. Ai was not settled after Iron I (Calloway 1992).

223. Nehemiah reads 123, and 1 Esdras reads 52 for Bethel alone, with no mention of Ai, but see following note.

2.29 *Nebo.* Nebo is called 'the other Nebo' in Neh. 7.33, most likely to differentiate it from the better known Mt Nebo of Moab/Jordan. The name is treated as a place in Nehemiah, but as a person in Ezra (i.e. Ezra reads 'the sons of Nebo', whereas Nehemiah reads 'the men of the other Nebo'). In Ezra 10.43, Nebo's descendants are listed among those who divorced their foreign wives. If a place, it may refer to Nob, the residence of the Elide priesthood after the destruction of Shiloh (1 Sam. 22.11). If so, it would be near Anathoth and would belong to the area of Benjamin. Most scholars identify it with modern Nûba, however, a town in the region of Judah, approximately 5 km. NW of Beth Zur and 3 km. E of Khiret Qeila (Keilah). Beth Zur is identified with Khirbet eṭ-Ṭubeiqah, a fortress city about 32 km. S of Jerusalem, between Jerusalem and Hebron.

1 Esdras reads Βαιτολιω, Baitolio, here. This likely reflects Bethel, but the number of returnees is the number for Nebo. Since neither Ai nor Nebo is represented in 1 Esdras, it appears that part of the text has dropped out (Talshir 2001: 266).

2.30 *Magbish.* The name is missing from Nehemiah 7. The site has not been identified with certainty. It is usually considered to be Khirbet el-Makhiyeh, a rocky hill overlooking the Beth-Shean–Jericho–Shechem–Adam crossroads and the Jordan, Qore and Succoth valleys. Others prefer a slightly more southerly site and identify it with Khirbet Qanan Mugheimis, 2 km. W of Beit 'Alam. First Esdras has Νιφις, Niphis, for Magbish. Only the ending reflects the original, and perhaps a *b*/*p* interchange. The number of returnees given in 1 Esdras is the same as here in Ezra for Magbish, 156.

2.31 ***'Elam.*** This is called 'the other 'Elam', yet the numbers are the same as above (2.7). There is most likely an error somewhere. It has been identified with Khirbet Beit 'Alam, about 10 km. WSW of Beit-Zur in the area of Judah. It has also been identified with Khirbet 'Almit, about 2 km. NE of Anathoth ('Anata). First Esdras gives the name as 'the other Kalamo', Καλαμω ἄλλου, with no number of returnees provided.

2.32 ***Ḥarim.*** *Ḥarim* is listed as the ancestral name of a priestly family in 2.39, but here it is listed among the towns. It has been identified with Khirbet Ḥoron, about 5 km. WNW of Beit 'Alam. Ḥarim, Lod and Ḥadid are missing from 1 Esdras, and Ono is provided there with the number 725, the total amount for Lod, Ḥadid and Ono in Ezra. Part of the text has evidently dropped out from 1 Esdras.

2.33 ***Lod, Ḥadid and 'Ono.*** Lod, Ḥadid and 'Ono. The names in this position in Nehemiah 7 are Jericho, Lod and Sena'ah. Lod (also known as Lydda), in the plain of Sharon, is listed together with Ono as belonging to Benjamin (1 Chron 8.12). Lod is a modern city 18 km. SE of Joffa on the Ayalon Valley (Wadi el-Kabir), near the intersection of the main E–W road from Jerusalem to Jaffa and on the main N–S road from Damascus to Egypt. It is 15 km. SE of Tel Aviv. The presence of the modern town has limited excavations there. Only Early Bronze I material has been found thus far. Lod was likely not located in Persian-period Yehud (see the Introduction). A nearby settlement, Neve Yarak, was occupied in the Iron II, as well as in the Persian and Hellenistic periods, implying the same for Lod (Finkelstein 2008b: 10).

Ḥadid is safely identified with el-Haditheh, 4 miles NE of Lod, known as Adida in the Greco-Roman period (1 Macc. 12.38; 13.13; Jos. *Ant.* 13.203, 392; Blenkinsopp 1988: 87; Finkelstein 2008b: 9). The site was occupied in both the seventh century and in the Persian and Hellenistic periods.

'Ono is a city in the Shephelah, probably to be identified with Kafr Juna, located 1 km. NE of Kafr 'Ana. There was strong habitation in the Persian period at Kafr Juna, but not at Kafr 'Ana (Finkelstein 2008b: 13). As discussed in the Introduction, none of these cities belonged to Persian-period Yehud. First Esdras includes only 'the Other Kalamos' (Elam?) and 'Ono, but the number of returnees is the same. Nehemiah reads 721 instead of 725.

2.34 ***Jericho.*** Jericho, assigned to Benjamin (Josh. 18.21), marks the farthest point E of the area of Persian Yehud. Identified as Tell es-Sulṭân, it is about 16 km. N of the Dead Sea. At a depth of 250 m below sea level, it is the lowest town on the surface of the earth. The site was destroyed in the sixth century BCE by the Babylonians and only lightly resettled in the Persian period. A few seal impressions with the name *yhd, yhwd,* as well as *'wryw/yhwd* (Uriah / Yehud) and *lyhw'zer* (belonging to Yeho'ezer) were discovered there in Persian-period strata. The small settlement there probably formed the northeast border of the province. (See the discussion of Jericho in the Introduction.)

2.35 ***Sena'ah.*** The large number of returnees (3,630) seems suspicious, but all the versions have such high numbers (3,930 in Nehemiah and 3,330 in 1 Esdras). The name may be a corruption of Hassenuah, listed in 1 Chron. 9.7 as the first among the Benjaminites to return to Judah and Jerusalem after the exile. A son of Hassenuah is listed among the wall builders in Neh. 3.3, and a Judah son of Hassenuah, a Benjaminite, was second in command of Jerusalem at the time of Nehemiah (Neh. 11.9). Avi-Yonah (2002: 16) identifies the site with the Migdalsenna of Eusebius, now Khirbet el Beiyudât, and this seems to lie behind its placement on all the atlases. About 12 km. N of Jericho, the site has not revealed any Iron Age remains, however, and is now considered to be the Roman village of Archaelais, the town built by Herod's son (Hizmi 1993). On the ridge just two km. S of Khirbet el Beiyudât lie the ruins of Khirbet el-Auja el-Fauqa, which may be the town of Sena'ah (Murphy-O'Connor 1992: 300-301).

2.36 ***Priests.*** Like every other temple in the ancient Near East, the temple of Yhwh in Jerusalem contained a full hierarchy of temple personnel, from the temple priests *(kōhanîm),* who directly approached the altar and manipulated the sacrificial blood, to menial temple servants (*n*ᵉ*tînîm*), who drew the water and chopped wood for the temple (Leithart 1999). The only ones properly called 'priests', however, were those who participated in the cult per se, that is, who approached the altar and handled the blood. This is consistent with priesthoods everywhere in the ancient Near East, except that elsewhere these priests would also have been the ones who washed, dressed and fed the cult statues (Fried 2004). Excavations at Ugarit, an ancient kingdom on the Mediterranean coast of Syria, uncovered a literature (dating from the fourteenth to the twelfth century BCE) that describes a cultic life very similar to that revealed in the Bible. There, too, the priests (also called *khnm, kōhanîm*) were the primary cultic officials (Urie 1948, 1949). As in Judah, the priests at Ugarit were divided into priestly families; twelve are known from state ration lists (Gray 1965: 211). At Ugarit, the highest ranking priestly family was that of the king. We are told that in Jerusalem, too, at the time of the founding of the state, David's sons were priests (2 Sam. 8.18). The twelve priestly families at Ugarit may have rotated in and out of service month by month, but this is not currently known. (The rotation of priestly families in Jerusalem is discussed below.)

The duties of Yhwh's priests, that is, of the *kōhanîm,* are outlined in Leviticus 1–17, in Numbers 3 and 8 (where they are called the sons of Aaron), and in Ezekiel 40–48 (where they are called the sons of Zadok). Their tasks included collecting the blood, cutting up the slaughtered animal, arranging the pieces of meat on the altar, and sprinkling the blood on it; in short, everything having to do with the altar. Since priestly families were permitted to partake of Yhwh's offerings and to share in the sacrificial meal, priests brought their share of the offering home in reimbursement for officiating. It is interesting to note that there is no attempt here in Ezra 2 (or Nehemiah 7) to bring out the relationship of these priestly houses to either Aaron or Zadok, which we see later in the genealogy supplied for Ezra (7.1-5), for example, and which was so important to Ezekiel (cf. Ezekiel 44; Rudolph 1949: 22; Hunt 2006: 90-98).

2.36 *Jedaiah.* The name Jedaiah, יְדַעְיָה, Yeda'yah or 'Yhwh knew', is common. It is included among the names listed on two ostraca from Arad (Aharoni 1981: #31, #39) dated to the seventh century BCE; on bullae from Tell Beit Mirsim (Avigad 1986: #68, #69) from the same period; and on a bulla from the City of David (Shiloh 1986: #12) dated to the beginning of the sixth century BCE.

Both Ezra and Nehemiah read, 'The priests: the descendants of Jedaiah of the house of Jeshua'. The Chronicler (1 Chron. 9.10-11) provides a list of priestly names beginning with Jedaiah: 'Jedaiah, Jehoiarib, Jakin, and 'Azariah son of Ḥilqiah son of . . .' Commentators interpret the entire sequence as a genealogy even though the words 'son of' are missing for the first four names (e.g. see Knoppers 2004: 495-96). Nehemiah 11 has a similar list. Nehemiah (11.10-11) reads, 'Of the priests: Jedaiah son of Joiarib, Jachin, Seriah son of Ḥiliqiah . . .' (The list of names after Ḥilqiah is the same in both lists.) Jachin (יכין) may be a corruption of *ben* ('son of', בן), since the words look similar (Japhet 1993: 211; Rudolph 1949: 84; *pace* Porten, personal communication [September 3, 2014]). Thus, we could read Jedaiah son of Jehoiarib son of Azariah son of Ḥilqiah. Or better, Seraiah instead of ʿAzariah. The names ʿAzariah and Seraiah, which distinguish the two lists, look identical when the first two letters of 'Azariah are elided. Another priestly genealogy for the pre-exilic period is given in 1 Chron. 5.39-40 (ET 1 Chron. 6.13-14): 'Ḥilqiah fathered 'Azariah who fathered Seraiah who fathered Jehozadaq and Jehozadaq went into exile'. Combining the genealogies suggests that the Jedaiah in our verse (Ezra 2.36) is of the house of Jeshua, the high priest of the restoration period, and that he is the son of Jehoiarib, the second son of Seraiah, and that Jeshua son of Jehozadaq is grandson of that same Seraiah and Jedaiah's cousin.

Jeshua. This is the Jeshua who was the high priest in the time of Darius I and Zerubbabel (*pace* Myers 1965: 169). See note on 2.2. Four of his descendants had taken foreign wives (Ezra 10.18).

973. The reading in Nehemiah agrees with this number; 1 Esdras reads 972.

2.37 *'Immer.* The name *'Immer* is a hypocoristic for 'Amaryahu, 'Yhwh said [a son is born!]'. A Zadok, son of 'Immer, was a priest listed among the men working on the city wall (Neh. 3.28). Two of 'Immer's descendants, Ḥanani and Zebadaiah, were among the priests who divorced their foreign wives (Ezra 10.20). 'Immer, אִמֵּר is listed as 'Amariah in Nehemiah 10. The name 'Immer does not appear in extrabiblical texts, but the name 'Amariah is common. The name 'Amariah / 'Amariahu was found on an inscribed jar handle from early-sixth century Gibeon (Ahituv 2008: 216), and a seal inscribed 'belonging to Yesha'yahu (son of) 'Amariyahu' was found on the surface at Kiriath-Jearim near Jerusalem (Avigad and Sass 1997: #212) and so is undated. Another seal (Avigad and Sass 1997, #449), now in the Israel Museum, bears the legend 'belonging to 'Amaryahu son of Yeho'ab'.

2.38 *Pašḥur.* A Pashḥur, פַּשְׁחוּר, son of 'Immer was active in the time of Jeremiah during the reign of Zedekiah (Jer. 20.1-6). The name is Egyptian (meaning 'son of Horus'). It was also the name of Zedekiah's grandson (Jer. 38.1, 6). The name was common. Gedalyahu ben Pashḥur served as minister to King Zedekiah (597–586 BCE; Jer. 38.1), and a seal impression with his complete name was found intact in recent excavations at the City of David, just meters away from where the seal impression of his colleague, Yehukal ben Shelemyahu (Jer. 37.3), was unearthed three years before (Lefkovits 2008). Another seal found near Jerusalem and dated to the early Persian period reads 'belonging to Pashḥur son of 'Adayahu' (Sukenik 1945: #2). One found in the destruction of Jerusalem reads 'belonging to Pashḥur son of 'Aḥ'amah' (Avigad 1986: #151), and another from Tell Beit Mirsim from the same period reads 'belonging to Pashḥur son of Menaḥem' (Avigad 1986: #152). In the list of priestly names in Nehemiah 10, Pashḥur is preceded by Seraiah, 'Azariah and Jeremiah.

2.39 *Ḥarim.* Ḥarim, 'dedicated', is included here and in Neh. 7.42 as a personal name, but in v. 32 above and in Josh. 19.38 it is listed as a town. It is also cited as a place name on one of the Persepolis Fortification Tablets (Hallock 1969: 692). The name is included among the ancestors of both priests and laymen who had taken foreign wives in Ezra 10.21 and 31, and among the priestly signers of the Amanah in Neh. 10.6. A Malchiah son of Ḥarim is listed among the wall builders in Nehemiah 3. Ḥarim appears as a name only in the book Ezra–Nehemiah and does not appear as a personal name elsewhere to my knowledge.

1,017. The total number of the members of the priestly families, not counting those who could not prove their genealogy (Ezra 2.60-61), is 4,289. It is interesting to note that in contrast to other groups, the numbers of family members for the priests and Levites is identical in Ezra, Nehemiah and 1 Esdras, whereas there are many discrepancies for the other groups.

Jedaiah, ’Immer, Pashḥur, and Ḥarim represent a total of four priestly houses. Nehemiah 12.12-21 lists twenty-one priestly courses or shifts (father’s houses), however, not four; and by the time of the Chronicler (1 Chron. 24.7-12) and of the Qumran community at the Dead Sea (4Q*Mishmarot*) there are twenty-four in all. These courses or shifts (*mishmarot*) rotated in and out of the temple service at fixed periods. According to the calendar at Qumran, each house served a week before rotating out again. The list of only four priestly houses in Ezra 2 may represent an earlier period when there were only four priestly divisions, perhaps each serving a month before rotating out, and rotating in three times a year. The division of the Levites into only three houses (Gershon, Kohath and Merari), for example in Numbers 3, may go back to a period even earlier than the list in Ezra 2.

The use of priestly *phyles* or ‘courses’ that rotate in and out of temple service is known in Egypt from the time of the Old Kingdom (see, e.g., Fried 2004: 58). Other temple personnel also rotated in and out of service. Second Kings 11.9 states that one-third of the temple guards went off duty on the Sabbath and another third came on again, implying a rotation of one-third of the temple personnel each Sabbath. The temple personnel must have included the Levites, since they had their own fields to tend (Neh. 13.10). Except for Pashḥur, the names in Ezra 2.36-39 are included in the complete roster of twenty-four courses in 1 Chron. 24.7-19 and at Qumran (Jedaiah is second, Ḥarim is third, and ’Immer is sixteenth). Pashḥur is missing and may have been absorbed into the house of ’Immer (1 Chron. 9.12). The twenty-one priestly names in Nehemiah 10 include Pashḥur (fourth), ’Immer (’Amariah, fifth), and Ḥarim (tenth). Both Jeshua and Jedaiah are absent from that list. The name of this house may have dropped out inadvertently. Its inclusion in Nehemiah would make twenty-two names there.

2.40 ***The Levites.*** The *Levites* include all noncultic temple personnel. Their duties are spelled out in Ezek. 44.11 as well as in Numbers 3; 4; 8; and 1 Chronicles 9. Although the Levites do not approach the altar, they administered the business that was the temple, managing all of its financial and organizational needs. A partial understanding of the role of the Levites can be gleaned by examining Exodus 36–40. Moses, the Levite, provides the specifications for the altar and all its furnishings. He commissions the artisans and supervises construction, ensuring that everything is built according to specifications (Exod. 39.32-43). He sets up the tabernacle and the altar with all its furnishings, including the garments of Aaron, the high priest (Exod. 40.1-26). He does not manipulate the blood. His are the tasks of the Levites.

A class of cultic personnel at Ugarit, the *qdšm* (literally, the sanctified ones), seem to play a role similar to that of the Levites in Jerusalem (Levine 1963; Clemens 2001: 306-11). Like the Levites, the *qdšm* include all the nonpriestly temple personnel at Ugarit (von Soden 1970: 329). They formed the support staff of the temple at Ugarit, serving and assisting the priests (Clemens 2001: 308). Like the Levites, the *qdšm* also rotated in and out of service. There is a record of a *qdš* becoming a *maryanu*, a chariot warrior, suggesting that temple personnel engaged in other occupations in their time off. Members of priestly families also engaged in other professions at Ugarit (Tarragon 1980: 137), and as this was also the case in Egypt (Fried 2004: 59; 2007b), it was likely true in Jerusalem as well.

Jeshua. This Jeshua (son of 'Azanaiah, Neh. 10.9) is a Levite. The name, meaning 'Yhwh is salvation/deliverance', is common.

Kadmi'el. The name קַדְמִיאֵל means 'El is my ancient one'. It is not known outside of the book of Ezra–Nehemiah to my knowledge.

Of the family of. Literally, 'Of the sons of', *bᵉnê*, בני. First Esdras reads, 'The Levites: the descendants of Jeshua and Kadmiel and Bani and Hodaviah, seventy-four', reading the name 'Bani' rather than *bᵉnê*, בני, 'sons of'. Nehemiah 7.43 reads *bᵉnê*, בני, 'sons of', but with the following name preceded by a lamedh (something impossible in Hebrew if *benai* actually means 'sons of'), suggesting that it should indeed be vocalized there not as *bᵉnê,* but Bani, a personal name (Talshir 2001: 269). Bani is a recognized name in the biblical corpus—Bani the Gadite is listed among David's thirty warriors (2 Sam 23.36); another Bani is included in Ethan's levitical genealogy (1 Chron. 6.31, ET 6.46), and a third is included in the genealogy of a returning Judahite (1 Chron. 9.4, 5). A fourth Bani is listed as an ancestor of several Israelites who divorced their foreign wives (Ezra 10.29, 34). A Reḥum son of Bani is included among the Levites who worked on Nehemiah's wall (Neh. 3.17), and a Bani is included among the Levites who helped the people understand the law (Neh. 8.7) and who signed the Amanah (10.13). Two more were included along with a Bunni as participants in Nehemiah's covenant renewal ceremony (Neh. 9.4). Another Israelite Bani, a leader of the people, is also listed as a signer of the Amanah (Neh. 10.14). The full name, Benaiah, is also known (2 Sam. 23.20, 30).

The name Bani is not observed outside of the Bible to my knowledge, but it may be a hypocoristic. The full name Beniah or rather Beniyahu, 'son of Yhwh', is well attested. A list of names found at Arad dated to the seventh century BCE contains the name 'Ya'azanyahu son of Beniyahu' (Aharoni 1981: 68, #39). A seal found on Cyprus (date unknown) is inscribed 'to Beniyahu son of Ḥor' (Lindberg 1828: 62). Another seal from Tell Beit Mirsim and dated to just before the destruction of Jerusalem (early-sixth century BCE) is inscribed 'belonging to Beniyahu [son of] 'Alyahu' (Avigad 1986: 46, #36). Finally, a seal discovered in the City of David, also dated to just before its destruction, is inscribed 'belonging to Benyahu son of Hoshiyahu' (Shiloh 1986: 28, #31). In addition, a Banuka is attested on a

Persian Persepolis Fortification Tablet (PF 674.18), '*ka*' being a determinative indicating a personal name.

Hodaviah. Hodaviah, הוֹדַוְיָה, probably should be vocalized as Hoduyahu, 'let us praise Yhwh', although Porten and Lund (2002: 340) also vocalize it as Hodavyah. Nehemiah 7.43 reads 'Hodvah' or probably 'Hodu[y]a' in this position, but it is the same name. Although a Levite here, a Hodaviah is listed as a descendant of Benjamin in 1 Chron. 9.7. Another Hodaviah is included among the Levites who helped the people to understand the Law (Neh. 8.7) and one participates in the covenant renewal ceremony (Neh. 9.5). Two men by that name are listed among the Levites who signed the Amanah (Neh. 10.11, 14), and another by that name is listed among the laity there (Neh. 10.19). The name is well attested outside of the Bible. A Hodaviah son of 'Aḥio is referred to in a letter found at Lachish dated to 586 BCE, right before its destruction (Ahituv 2008: 63, Lachish letter 3.17). A bulla inscribed 'to Ḥagab son of Hodayahu' has been found at Tell Beit Mirsim, and is dated to the late-seventh–early-sixth century BCE, right before the destruction of Judah (Avigad 1986: 54, #55). The name is very common at Elephantine. There is a Hodaviah son of Zechariah (*TAD* D 7.20) named in a letter dated to the first quarter of the fifth century BCE; a Hodaviah son of Gedaliah served as a witness to a contract on a loan guarantee, dated December 13, 456 BCE (*TAD* B 3.1); and a Hodaviah son of Zaccur son of Oshaiah witnessed a deposition in a suit dated September 420 BCE (*TAD* B 2.9).

The Levites named in this verse are shown supervising the work of the temple in Ezra 3.9. Again Bani, rather than 'sons of', may be more correct.

74. Whereas the families of the priests and laypeople are each recorded with the number of their family members, the number of the Levites is recorded as a group, not by family. Why so few Levites (74) compared to the large number of priests (4,289)? Even including the singers and the gatekeepers, the total comes to only 341 (or 361 if the totals in Nehemiah 7 are used). The answer may lie in the fact that of the thirteen cities allotted to the priests, that is, to the sons of Aaron, nine are in Judah and four are in Benjamin (Josh. 21.9-12), with no Aaronide cities outside of this area. In contrast, the cities granted to the Levites are all in the north (Josh. 21; Haran 1985: 84-85). The line dividing the Aaronides from the rest of the tribe of Levi is the line dividing north and south. The Levites may have served as priests of northern cultic sites until the fall of the north to the Assyrians in 722 BCE. Most would have been deported into Assyria with the rest of the population—or killed. Some few would have managed to flee south to Judah. The small number of Levites who returned may testify to the small number who had survived the destructions first of Israel in 722 and then of Judah in 586.

2.41 ***The singers.*** Music was a vital part of cultic life throughout the ancient Near East. The Ugaritic cult also employed temple singers, *šrm*. The question is whether musicians were a part of the pre-exilic temple cult. While songs and singing are frequently cited (e.g. Exodus 15, the Song of the Sea), there is no mention of singing or musicians in the descriptions of the cultic services in the books of Exodus, Leviticus, or Numbers. The only descriptions we have in the Bible of the singers' role in the cult are in Chronicles (2 Chron. 5.13), customarily dated to the late-fourth century BCE (Japhet 1993), certifying that music was at least part of the cult of the second temple. Ezekiel (40.44) refers to a special chamber for the singers, but it is not known whether this verse was written by the prophet or was added by a later editor. If written by the prophet, then it likely describes activity of the pre-exilic Jerusalem temple, and we can assume a role for singers there. If not, then it may only describe the postexilic period. It does not bother the Chronicler that there is no mention of singers in the torah literature, since according to him they were only instituted by David for service in the temple (1 Chron. 6.16). There were no singers in the wilderness period. Amos's condemnations of the temple at Bethel suggest, however, that song and music were an integral part of pre-exilic temple service there. Amos (5.21-24) quotes Yhwh as saying:

> I hate, I despise your festivals, and I take no delight in your solemn assemblies. Even though you offer me your burnt offerings and grain offerings, I will not accept them; and the offerings of well-being of your fatted animals I will not look upon. Take away from me the noise of your songs; I will not listen to the melody of your harps. But let justice roll down like waters, and righteousness like an ever-flowing stream.

Amos (8.3) also asserts that on the day of Yhwh, 'the songs of the temple [at Bethel] shall become wailings'. Song was thus part of the pre-exilic temple cult there, and, if so, very likely part of the temple cult in Jerusalem as well, even if not described in the torah literature.

The word of the Chronicler can be accepted for the postexilic period, however. According to the Chronicler, the singers lived in the temple and were on duty day and night (1 Chron. 9.33). This probably means that they rotated in and out of service, since they had their own fields to attend to (Neh. 13.10). The term is more accurately translated 'musicians' rather than 'singers', however, for the Chronicler reports (1 Chron. 15.16) that they 'play on musical instruments, on harps and lyres and cymbals, to raise loud sounds of joy'. At Ugarit, the singers may have been involved in service at both temple and palace (Clemens 2001: 313), and that seems to have been the case in Judah as well. The temple was next to the palace and at the disposal of the king. According to Sennacherib's records, in addition to gold, silver and other costly items, Hezekiah sent to Nineveh 'his own daughters, (his) concubines, and (his) male and female musicians' (Taylor Prism III.48-49, *ANET* 288). Since Hezekiah had the temple's gold and silver at his disposal (2 Kgs 18.15), he may have had the temple's musicians available to him as well, so musicians may have participated in the temple service.

It is interesting to note the different translations for 'singers' used by the authors of Greek Ezra (οἱ ᾄδοντες, *adontes*) and 1 Esdras (ἱεροψάλται, *hieropsaltai*). While the former means 'singers', the latter refers specifically to temple musicians who accompany themselves on a harp or lute (L&S, *ad loc*.). This would be more consistent with the posited temple conditions. The Hebrew word הַמְשֹׁרְרִים *hamšōrr*[e]*rîm* is a polel participle, a form of the word that appears only in Chronicles and Ezra–Nehemiah. There does not appear to be a difference in connotation between this and the usual word for singers (שָׁרִים, *šārîm*; e.g. 2 Sam. 19.36), unless the late form is reserved for temple musicians only.

A question that has puzzled commentators is whether the text in Ezra implies that singers (and other temple personnel) formed a subdivision of the Levites, or if they are to be distinguished from the levitical class. The Hebrew syntax of the list permits either interpretation. It is clear that by the time of the Chronicler, however, the singers and gatekeepers were part of the Levites:

> The Levites, thirty years old and upward, were counted, and the total was thirty-eight thousand. 'Twenty-four thousand of these', David said, 'shall have charge of the work in the house of Yhwh, six thousand shall be officers and judges, four thousand gatekeepers, and four thousand shall offer praises to Yhwh with the instruments that I have made for praise' (1 Chron. 23.3-5).

The Chronicler lists the singers and gatekeepers separately even though he considers both to be Levites. Although some commentators regard this passage as secondary to the work of the Chronicler, Japhet (1993: *ad loc*.) has argued convincingly against this proposition. It is also clear that by the time of at least the final compilation and redaction of Ezra–Nehemiah, the singers were part of the Levites. For example, the singers the sons of Asaph are included among the Levites in Neh. 11.22:

> The overseer of the Levites in Jerusalem was Uzzi son of Bani son of Hashabiah son of Mattaniah son of Mica, of the descendants of Asaph, the singers, in charge of the work of the house of God (Neh. 11.22).

If this note is historical, then at the time of the redaction of Nehemiah, the overseer of the Levites was of the family of Asaph, a temple singer. It is not likely that a member of a lower ranking group in the temple hierarchy would be placed in charge of a higher ranking group. Another verse also shows that at least by the time of the redaction of Ezra–Nehemiah the singers were included among the Levites, as this verse shows:

> Now at the dedication of the wall of Jerusalem they sought out the Levites in all their places, to bring them to Jerusalem to celebrate the dedication with rejoicing, with thanksgivings and with singing, with cymbals, harps, and lyres (Neh. 12.27).

The levitical role in singing and instrumentation is clear here. Moreover, if Neh. 13.5 is from Nehemiah's Memoir, which many accept, then the singers and gatekeepers were owed the same tithes of grain, wine and oil as the rest of the Levites and so, although listed separately, were included in the levitical class at least for the purposes of remuneration:

> The priest Eliashib, who was appointed over the chambers of the house of our god, and who was related to Tobiah, prepared for Tobiah a large room where they had previously put the grain offering, the frankincense, the vessels, and the tithes of grain, wine, and oil, which were given by commandment to the Levites, singers, and gatekeepers, and the contributions for the priests (Neh. 13.5).

The fact that the singers and gatekeepers are listed separately in Nehemiah's memoir indicates that they can be listed separately even though they are all Levites. Whatever the date of the list in Ezra 2 (= Nehemiah 7), we cannot learn of their status from the fact that they are counted separately in it. In addition to the singers who returned under Zerubbabel and Jeshua, additional singers are said to have returned with Ezra (7.7). In order for them to have returned *as singers*, however, they must have been descended from pre-exilic temple musicians. Most people in antiquity took on the profession of their fathers.

Asaph. Only the descendants of Asaph are mentioned among the singers here; it is also the only family of singers cited as present during the temple foundation ceremonies (Ezra 3.10-11). This contrasts with Chronicles, in which three families of singers are listed (1 Chron. 6): Asaph, a descendant of Gershom, son of Levi; Heman, a descendant of Kohath, son of Levi; and Ethan/Jeduthan, a descendant of Merari, son of Levi. Thus, the singers at this point were Levites. It is not clear why only the family of Asaph is included among the original returnees in this list, while the family of Jeduthan is also included in Neh. 11.17. The family of Heman does not appear in Ezra–Nehemiah at all. Psalms 50, and 73–83, credited to Asaph, may indeed be the work of this family of temple singers (Buss 1963).

The name Asaph אָסָף means 'he added', as in '[God] has added (a son)'. It can also mean 'remove', 'take away', as in אָסַף חֶרְפָּתֵנוּ, 'he has removed our reproach' (Isa. 4.1). Thus, God has 'removed our disgrace [by adding a son]' (Avigad and Sass 1997: 485). A Joah son of Asaph was the recorder in the days of Hezekiah (2 Kgs 18.18). A seal found at Megiddo and dated originally to the second half of the eighth century BCE reads 'belonging to Asaph' (Guthe 1906). This seal is lapis lazuli, scaraboid, and unperforated.

Above the name is a winged and kilted griffin wearing the double crown of Egypt facing an ankh (the Egyptian symbol of life) on a pedestal and enclosed in a cartouche. Ussishkin dates it to the tenth century BCE because of the Egyptian epigraphy and iconography (Ussishkin 1994). The name does not otherwise occur outside of the biblical text to my knowledge.

128. First Esdras agrees with Ezra against Nehemiah in the number of returnees here. Myers concludes that the list in Ezra provided the *Vorlage* to the author of 1 Esdras. Hanhart (1974: 75) argues that Nehemiah has the original version. Perhaps the author of 1 Esdras had both Ezra and Nehemiah before him when he composed his text, or the complete Ezra–Nehemiah. (See the articles in Fried 2011.)

2.42 ***Families.*** Literally, 'sons of'. The word 'sons of', בְּנֵי, is absent from Neh. 7.45 and from 1 Esdras.

Gatekeepers. Temple gatekeepers, *tǵrm*, are also known at Ugarit, and may have had the same role (Clemens 2001; Tarragon 1980; Urie 1948). Gatekeepers are also known from the Idumean ostraca, and seven of them conclude with the phrase 'for the gatekeepers', לתרען (Porten and Yardeni 2006: 480). The gatekeepers were some of the most important men in the Jerusalem temple. They were the accountants, in charge of the storerooms, the treasuries, everything that went in or out of the temple, that is, everything that concerned the business of the temple's daily operation:

> They would spend the night near the house of God; for on them lay the duty of watching, and they had charge of opening it every morning. Some of them had charge of the utensils of service, for they were required to count them when they were brought in and taken out. Others of them were appointed over the furniture, and over all the holy utensils, also over the choice flour, the wine, the oil, the incense, and the spices (1 Chron. 9.26-32).

In the pre-exilic period, these tasks were the domain of the priests who guarded the threshold (הַכֹּהֲנִים שֹׁמְרֵי הַסַּף, 2 Kgs 12.9). In the days of Jehoash, for example, they collected the funds that had been donated to the temple, recorded it, and paid it out again in wages for the workers who repaired the building (2 Kings 12). The story of King Josiah's temple repair (2 Kgs 22.4) shows that these gatekeepers, or guardians of the threshold, were in charge of temple funds, as well as of the temple's vessels and its furnishings (2 Kgs 23.4). The official over them had his own chamber in the temple (Jer. 35.4). In the postexilic period the 'guardians of the threshold' were called 'gatekeepers', but they served the same role. Rudolph (1949: 23) disagrees, considering that this was too important a task to leave to members of such a subordinate rank. Nevertheless, the Chronicler portrays the gatekeepers of the return as having inherited the role that their fathers performed as guardian of the thresholds:

> The gatekeepers were: Shallum, Akkub, Talmon, Ahiman; and their kindred. Shallum was the chief, stationed previously in the king's gate on the east side. These were the gatekeepers of the camp of the Levites. Shallum son of Kore, son of Ebiasaph, son of Korah, and his kindred of his ancestral house, the Korahites, were in charge of the work of the service, guardians of the thresholds of the tent, שֹׁמְרֵי הַסִּפִּים as their ancestors had been in charge of the camp of Yhwh, guardians of the entrance (1 Chron. 9.17-19).

The tent mentioned here is not the tent of the wilderness tradition, since the Chronicler viewed these positions as having been established by David and Samuel the Seer (1 Chron. 9.22). It refers rather to the tent that housed the Ark. At the time of the Chronicler (2 Chron. 34.9), these were Levites. A further note in Chronicles clarifies the role of the gatekeepers at the time of the Chronicler in the second temple period:

> The four chief gatekeepers, who were Levites, were in charge of the chambers and the treasuries of the house of God (1 Chron. 9.26).

For 'gatekeepers', 1 Esdras translates οἱ θυρωροί, 'doorkeepers', 'porters', 'the ones who control who may enter a place', whereas Greek Ezra reads τῶν πυλωρῶν, 'gatekeepers'. The first indicates a door of a house or a room, and the second, a city gate, often with military connotations. The Hebrew הַשֹּׁעֲרִים, *haššō'ªrîm*, implies the guardian of a gate of a city or compound, not the doorway of a house. The city gate served as a place of public assembly and debate, and as an administrative center as well. A corpus of letters and administrative lists were found among shards of a broken pottery jar in the remains of a gate tower at Lachish (e.g. Tur-Sinai 1987; Ahituv 2008: 58-91; Ussishkin 2004). The fact that these letters were found at the city gate suggests that city gatekeepers served administrative and archival roles, and not only a military one.

Shallum. The first family of gatekeepers listed here is Shallum. Probably a hypocoristic for Shelemyahu, 'Yhwh has paid, or repaid [for the loss of a child]'. The name is common—both in the Hebrew Bible and at Elephantine. According to a list found at Elephantine, a Shallum son of Menaḥem and a Shallum son of Zechariah each contributed two shekels for Yhw the god on June 1, 400 BCE (*TAD* C 3.15). A Shallum is recorded as delivering barley to Qauskahel on a fourth-century ostracon from Idumea (#139, Eph'al and Naveh 1996: 68).

In pre-exilic Judah, a Maaseiah son of Shallum was the chief keeper of the threshold (chief gatekeeper) in the time of King Jehoiakim. He was important enough to have had a chamber in the temple (Jer. 35.4). His father may have been Shallum son of Tikvah son of Ḥarḥas, the husband of Huldah the prophetess (2 Kgs 22.14), and the keeper of the wardrobe, and thus likely one of the levitical gatekeepers (Yeivin 1941). The title 'keeper of the wardrobe', *ša ina muḫḫi ṣubāti*, is known from Mesopotamian texts (*CAD*

Ṣ 225b), and also from a temple for Baal in Samaria (2 Kgs 10.22). Mesopotamian texts distinguished among those who manufactured, mended and washed clothes for the gods and those who manufactured and cared for human clothing (for a discussion, see Fried 2004: 41). The former were prebendary positions, that is, the holder owned a share in the temple's income. The latter received fixed rations only. This distinction could not have obtained in the temple of Yhwh in Jerusalem, since there was no statue to be dressed. The high priest's wardrobe may have taken on the same status that the wardrobe of the gods did elsewhere, however (Fletcher-Louis 1997). If so, the keeper of the priests' wardrobe would have had a share in the temple income, and would have been eligible to partake of the tithe (e.g. Neh. 13.5); that is, he would have had levitical status, as appears here.

'Aṭer. As levitical gatekeepers, the sons of 'Aṭer are not known outside of this list of returnees in Ezra 2, Nehemiah 7, and 1 Esdras 5. (For a discussion of the name, see above on 2.16.)

The family of Ṭalmon. Ṭalmon (perhaps not 'morning dew', טל) and *'Aqqub* (see below) are gatekeepers listed among the first to return to live in their towns (c. 520 BCE; 1 Chron. 9.17; Neh. 12.25), and also as living in Jerusalem seventy-five years later in the time of Nehemiah (c. 445 BCE; Neh. 11.19). The list in 1 Chronicles 9 may be based on the list at Nehemiah 11, which seems to be the more complete version while the one in Chronicles seems to be an abridgment (Japhet 1993: 203), although usually in text-critical studies, the shorter text is to be preferred. The version at Greek Nehemiah 11 is shorter still, and may be the original one (Knoppers 2003a: 510-11). (One cannot conclude from this that Ezra–Nehemiah was written prior to Chronicles, as the list in Nehemiah 11 could have existed prior to its inclusion in the book. The relationship among all these texts is complex and will be discussed further at Nehemiah 11.) The name Ṭalmon is not known outside of the biblical text to my knowledge.

'Aqqub. 'Aqqub, עַקּוּב, is included along with Ṭalmon among the gatekeepers who returned with Zerubbabel and Joshua according to Neh. 12.25 and who were among those living in Jerusalem in the time of Nehemiah (11.19). The name 'Aqqub also appears among the temple servants, and an 'Aqqub is listed in Neh. 8.7 among the Levites who helped the people to understand the law during Ezra's reading of the law. The name 'Aqqub bar Peṭi was found inscribed on the outside of a jar shard at Elephantine (*TAD* D 11.2). The son's name is Aramaic/Hebrew, while the father's is Egyptian. 'Aqqub is a form of Jacob, יעקב, Ya'aqob. They are hypocoristics of 'Aqqabiah, or Yaqqubiah, 'Yhwh follows after', that is, 'watches over', 'protects'.

Ḥaṭiṭa'. The name Ḥaṭiṭa', חֲטִיטָא, appears in the Bible only here and in the parallel passages at Neh. 7.45 and 1 Esd. 5.28. The name may be Aramaic; it does not occur elsewhere to my knowledge. It may refer to 'grains of wheat', חטה.

Shobai. *Shobai,* שֹׁבָי, is common and may be a hypocoristic for Shobayahu ('Return, O Yhwh'), or Shoba'el ('Return, O God'; Ahituv 2008: 487). The name Hošiyahu ben-Šobai appears on a letter from Meṣad Ḥashavyahu dated to the late-seventh century BCE (Naveh 1960, 1964; Lemaire 1971). An undated seal found in Israel bears the inscription 'belonging to Šobai ben- 'Elzakar' (Schröder 1914). A Shobai ben-Bukhi appears on a distribution list of silver from Edfu, Egypt, of the Ptolemaic period (*TAD* D 8.12). (The son's name is Aramaic, but the father's name is Egyptian.) Recent excavations in Ammon uncovered a seal inscribed *šb' 'mn*, Shobai/'Ammon, possibly indicating that Shobai was the governor of Ammon (Herr 1993; 1999). It is dated to the end of the sixth and the beginning of the fifth centuries BCE, the beginning of the Persian period.

139. Nehemiah records 138 gatekeepers, whereas 1 Esdras reads 139, as here in Ezra.

2.43 *Temple servants.* *Temple servants,* נתינים, *n^etînîm.* The word occurs in the Hebrew Bible only in Ezra–Nehemiah, and 1 Chron. 9.2. It is transliterated οἱ ναθιναῖοι in Greek Ezra and as οἱ ναθινιμ in Greek Nehemiah. The Targum also transliterates the term in 1 Chron. 9.2 rather than translating it (there is no Targum for Ezra–Nehemiah). First Esdras, however, has οἱ ἱερόδουλοι, *hierodouloi,* 'temple servants', 'sacred servants', or 'temple slaves', which is likely the origin of the modern understanding of the term. The Vulgate of 1 Esdras has *sacerdotes servientes,* and the Vulgate of Nehemiah (but not of Ezra) has *ianitores*. Literally, the term *n^etînîm* means donated or dedicated, from the Hebrew verb *ntn,* 'to give'. Rashi, the rabbis, and some modern biblical commentators suggest these include the Gibeonites, who were given *(ntn)* as 'wood-cutters and water-drawers' by Josh. (9.27; e.g. Blenkinsopp 1988: 90):

> So on that day Joshua gave them, וַיִּתְּנֵם, as wood-cutters and as water-drawers for the congregation and for the altar of Yhwh, to continue to this day, in the place that he should choose.

In spite of the creative etiology, this temple role is also known at Ugarit where fifty families and six other individuals are known as *ytnm*. Ugaritic scholars translate the term there as 'temple servitors' based on the translation of the term in the Hebrew Bible (Gordon 1965: 204, Text 301; Gray 1965; Levine 1963). The difficulty with this translation of the Ugaritic is that the Ugaritic text from which this term is taken (UT 301) is just a list of personal and family names headed by the title *ytnm*. The meaning of the role at Ugarit is thus derived solely from the biblical occurrences and offers no independent confirmation. The Ugaritic context demonstrates, however, that it is a profession or class of people, perhaps associated with the temple.

According to the author of Ezra 8, *n*^{e}*tînîm* were lower-level temple personnel whom David (not Joshua) set aside to attend the Levites (Ezra 8.20). In the Persian period, they lived in a house on the Ophel in Jerusalem (Neh. 3.30-31), with the word 'house' curiously in the singular, suggesting a dormitory. Levine (1963) makes much of the fact that the *n*^{e}*tînîm* signed the Amanah (Neh. 10.28), concluding that in spite of their foreign, non-Yawistic names, they were citizens of the Jerusalem temple community. That verse (Neh. 10.28) may have been added to a genuine list of signatories by the redactor, however, and ought not be used to infer historical information (Fried 2005). Levine points out that the names of the *n*^{e}*tînîm* are foreign. I would state that although some are foreign, others are nicknames (like 'Lefty' or 'Freckles'), not the sort of name a parent could give a child at birth. Rather, they suggest names that a master might throw upon a slave on the basis of his looks or some other superficial characteristic, without bothering to inquire what his given name might have been.

Ṣîḥā'. *Ṣîḥā'*, צִיחָא, is spelled plene here in Ezra, but defectively in Neh. 7.46, as צִחָא, *ṣḥ'*, suggesting that the list in Nehemiah is the earlier. First Esdras reads Ησαυ, Esau, the common Greek spelling of Jacob's twin brother. It is also the Aramaic rendering of the common Egyptian name Djeḥo, which appears numerous times in the Aramaic documents from Elephantine with this spelling (Porten and Lund 2002: 406). This Ṣîḥā' may have been the one who was over the *n*^{e}*tînîm* who lived on the Ophel (Neh. 11.21). The name Ṣîḥa' is transliterated as Σουια in Greek Ezra and as Σηα in the Greek of Nehemiah.

Ḥaśûpha. *Ḥaśûpha*, חֲשׂוּפָא, is spelled plene again in Ezra but defectively, Ḥaśūpha, חֲשֻׂפָא, in Nehemiah. The name comes from *ḥśp*, חשף, and means 'the barren one', 'the exposed, or naked one' (e.g. Isa. 52.10). This might express the state the individual was in when he arrived as a slave at the temple. Zadok (1980: 110) suggests that the name refers not to his clothes that were stripped off, but to his skin, that is, that his skin was flaking off, patchy, or rough. The name is not known elsewhere to my knowledge. One named Gišpa', גִּשְׁפָּא, was also over the *n*^{e}*tînîm* (Neh. 11.21), but no one by that name is included among the returnees either here or in Nehemiah 7.

Ṭabba'ot. The name *Ṭabbā'ôt*, טַבָּעוֹת, means 'rings', with *ṭabā'at* being the singular. Slaves are often marked by such rings. A Hebrew slave who opts to remain with his master when his time of release arrives has a hole bored through his ear (Exod. 21.6; Deut. 15.17). The hole was retained by an earring. The name is not known elsewhere to my knowledge.

2.44 *Qeros.* The word *qeros*, קֵרֹס, denotes a clasp or hook used, for example, to connect the curtains of the tabernacle to each other (e.g. Exod. 36.13). This may imply a hook in the slave's nose. As a verb, the root also means 'to stoop' (Isa. 46.1; כָּרַע בֵּל קֹרֵס נְבוֹ, 'Bēl bowed down, Nebo stoops'), and may connote submission. This name appears on an ostracon from pre-exilic Arad that connects the bearer either to the temple there or to the one in Jerusalem. Levine concludes the pre-exilic origin of the *n*[e]*tînîm* from this ostracon (Levine 1969). According to Aharoni, the ostracon in question (Aharoni 1981, #18) reads:

> To my lord Eliashib: May Yhwh seek your welfare. And now, give to Shemaryahu xxx, and to the Qerosi לקרוסי give xxx, and to the matter about which you commanded me, it is completed in the temple of Yhwh.

Aharoni (1981: 36; repeated in Ahituv 2008: 121) considers 'Qerosi' to be a plural gentilic based on the present passage in Ezra (and Nehemiah), that is, that it is a family name of *Nêtinîm*, and not a personal name. Accordingly, Aharoni states:

> The gentilic form *haqqerosi* הקרוסי and the fact of his [the Qerosi] being on a mission at Arad where there was a pre-exilic temple support the hypothesis that at the time of the monarchy, the Nethinim were no longer Temple slaves of inferior degree, but held a position as professionals connected with religious functions.

The difficulty with this hypothesis is that there is no article *ha,* 'the', on the ostracon. The shard reads לקרוסי, which can be pronounced *l*[e]*qerôsî*, meaning 'to Qerosi', or it can be read *lāqqerôsî*, meaning to *the* Qerosi. There is no way to know, so that Qerosi may very well be a personal name, and a common name of a slave.

Si'aha' סִיעֲהָא. The name is Si'aha', סִיעֲהָא, in Ezra, but Si'a', סִיעָא, in Nehemiah. The latter may be a defective spelling, again suggesting that that is the earlier rendition of the list. It reads Σουα, Sua, in 1 Esdras. Zadok (1980: 111) suggests the name may be related to Aramaic *ṣi'ah* 'traveling company, escort', or to the Mandaic plural *ṣi'ata,* 'troops, bands, companies, hordes', and may allude to the nomadic origin of this clan. Or, it could have a Persian origin. *Šiyatiš* is Persian for 'happiness' (Hallock 1969: 758).

Padon. This name is likely from the root פדה, 'to redeem' or 'to ransom'. This temple slave may have been the 'ransomed one'. The name Pedayahu, 'Yhwh redeemed', of which this may be a hypocoristic, is common. Sons of Padayahu are named on a seventh-century BCE inscription from Arad (Aharoni 1981: #49). An undated seal found in excavations at Jerusalem reads *yšm' pdyhw,* Ishma' [son of] Pedayahu (Bliss 1897: 180). An ostracon found at Ḥazor and dated to the eighth century BCE reads, 'belonging to Pady(ahu)' (Yadin 1957/58, Pl. 357 #12). A seal published by Avigad (1992: 27*-31*) of 'unknown provenance' reads לפדיהו בן המלך, 'belonging to Pedayahu, the king's son'. Avigad connects this Pedayahu with the son of Jeconiah and the father of Zerubbabel (1 Chron. 3.18, 19).

2.45 *Lebanah.* Lebanah, לְבָנָה with different vocalizations, means variously 'brick', 'white', 'the moon', or the 'moon god'. Laban is the well-known name of Rebekah's brother and Jacob's father-in-law. Libnah is also the name of a town in Judah. The name may mean 'white', suggesting that the bearer is an albino. It is not attested as a name outside the biblical corpus.

Ḥagabah. The name Ḥagabah, חֲגָבָה, is from *ḥāgāb*, חגב, 'locust', or 'grasshopper' (Lev. 11.22). Surprisingly, the name is known. A *ḥgb bn y'znyhw,* appears in a list of names found at Lachish, dated just before the fall of Jerusalem (G.I. Davies 1991: 346; Lachish letter 1.3). An undated ostracon found at Ḥorvat 'Uza is inscribed *bn ḥgb . . . yhwmlk*. A *bn ḥgby* family of four is listed among the *ytnm* at Ugarit. A seal with the name Ḥagab was recently found in excavations at the northwestern part of the Western Wall plaza in Jerusalem. It was found in a building currently dated to the seventh century BCE. The seal is made of black stone, elliptical in shape, and 1.2 x 1.4 cm. It is adorned with an engraved image of an archer facing right, shooting a bow and arrow. The name of the archer is engraved in the lower right, and reads LḤGB, 'belonging to Ḥagab' (*Bulletin Israel Antiquities Authority,* November 13, 2008).

'Aqqub. The name 'Aqqub is missing in the list of the *n^etînîm* in Nehemiah 7. It is present in 1 Esdras but as Ακουδ, Akkud. Talshir suggests a *beth*/*daleth* confusion (2001: 271). Someone of the same name is included among the gatekeepers. See note on v. 42 above.

2.46 *Ḥagab.* *Ḥagab*. See note on Ḥagabah in the previous verse. First Esdras includes two additional names here, Ουτα and Κηταβ, Outa and Ketab before Ḥagab (where it reads Ḥagaba as above). The names could easily have been omitted from Ezra through homoioteleuton when the scribe's eye skipped to the similar name Ḥagab from Ḥagaba (Talshir 2001: 271). This also seems to have been the case with Neh. 7.47-48, which skips from the first Ḥagaba to the sons of Shalmai, omitting both 'Akkub and the second Ḥagab.

Shalmai. Reading with the *qere* (the *kethib* is Shamlai, as is the corresponding name in Greek Ezra, Σαμαλαι), the *l* and the *m* being switched through metathesis. Nehemiah 7 has Shalmai as does Greek Nehemiah. 1 Esdras reads Subai, Συβαϊ, which may reflect Shobai, Σωβαι (Ezra 2.42; 1 Esd. 5.28). The name *šlmy*, probably Shalmi, appears stamped on a jar (provenance unknown), dated to the second half of the fifth century (Cross 1969). Zadok (1988: 453) suggests the name on the jar is actually *šlmyh*, Shelemyahu, 'Yhwh restores', or some such, since the *h* appears on the next line of the inscription. If so, both Shalmai and Shalmi would be hypocoristics.

Ḥanan. This name appears in all the versions. It is the only name among all the *n^etînîm* to appear in the list of Gibeonites (1 Chron. 8.38; 9.44) belying the assertion that the *n^etînîm* were descendants of the Gibeonites (*pace* Blenkinsopp 1972). If they were, one would expect to see some repetition of the names. The name is common and is a hypocoristic for 'Yhwh is gracious'. There are at least four men of this name at Elephantine alone.

2.47 ***Giddel.*** First Esdras inserts the sons of Cathua, Καθουα, for which no known parallel exists. The name Giddel recurs among the 'sons of Solomon's servants' (Ezra 2.56). First Esdras reads 'the sons of Geddour', Γεδδουρ, in this position and may be a conflation of Giddel and Gaḥar, which follows in both Ezra and Nehemiah but is absent in 1 Esdras (Talshir 2001: 272). Giddel, גִּדֵּל, meaning 'he makes great', is a hypocoristic probably for Gedalyahu, 'Yhwh made great'. Gedalyahu is common both in the Bible and at Elephantine, and elsewhere. The name *gdl* also occurs at Elephantine without the theophoric element (*TAD* D 7.21:2).

Gaḥar. While listed in both Ezra and Nehemiah, Gaḥar is not in 1 Esdras, and occurs nowhere else except in these two lists. Zadok (1980: 112) suggests it means 'red-spotted' and may refer to freckles. Again, 'Freckles' is not a name one would give to a baby.

Re'aiah. *Re'aiah*, רְאָיָה, 'Yhwh has seen', is one of the few Yahwistic names in the list of *n*ᵉ*tînîm*. The name is included in Chronicles as the name of one of the sons of Judah (1 Chron. 4.2) and of a son of Reuben (1 Chron. 5.5). First Esdras has Yairus, Ιαϊρου, the Greek rendition of the very common modern Hebrew name Ya'ir, יאיר (cf. Num. 32.41; Talshir 2001: 272). The name appears on a bulla, published by Avigad, that was offered on the antiquities market (Avigad 1986: 100, #157).

2.48 ***Reṣin.*** *Reṣin*, רצין, is also spelled Rezin in English. This Aramaic name was the name of the King of Aram during the reign of Ahaz of Judah (2 Kgs 16.5-9). First Esdras reads Δαισαν, Daison. This is likely Rezin with a *d/r* confusion, the Hebrew *d*, ד, and *r*, ר, are almost indistinguishable by the time of the Elephantine period (Porten, personal communication [September 10, 2014]).

Neqoda'. Besides being listed here, the sons of Neqoda', נקודא, are included below (v. 59) among those who did not know whether or not they were of the people Israel. First Esdras reads Νοεβα, Noeba. This reflects a *d*/*b* interchange, similar to that in Akoub/Akoud above (Talshir 2001: 272). The root *nqd*, נקד, also means speckled or freckled and may describe the slave in question or his forebears (Zadok 1980: 112). The name is not attested extrabiblically. On the other hand, it could be Persian. A Nakkunda is mentioned in the Fortification Tablets (PF 172.4; 743.4). First Esdras has an additional name, Χασεβα, Ḥaśeba/Ḥašeba.

Gazzam. The sons of Gazzam are mentioned only here and in Nehemiah 7. The root *gzz*, גזז, means to 'shear sheep', so that *gōz*ᵉ*zîm*, גוזזים, would mean 'sheep shearers', perhaps the occupation of this family. Zadok suggests, alternatively, that *gzm* means 'cut off' and refers not to the wool of sheep but to the act of cutting wood, and that these are wood-cutters (1980: 112). This root has also given rise to *gzm*, גזם, 'the cutting, devouring locust' (Joel 1.4; Amos 4.9). First Esdras reads Γαζηρα, Gazera, and the Hebrew root *gzr* also means 'to cut', 'divide', 'to cut off'. The Vulgate of 1 Esdras has *Gaze*. Perhaps this reflects confusion regarding the last letter. The word is not attested elsewhere as a personal name to my knowledge.

2.49 *'Uzza.* 'Uzza, עזא, was the name of the servant of David who was killed when he touched the ark while bringing it up from Kiriath-Jearim to Jerusalem (2 Sam. 6.6). The root עז, *'uz*, means 'he is strong'. With the theophoric Yhwh added as a suffix, it is Uzziah, one of the kings of Judah (2 Chron. 26.3; Isa, 6.1), and added as a prefix it is Yeho'az (Jehoahaz), one of the kings of Israel (2 Kgs 13.1). Gan-'Uzza was the burial place of the Judean kings Manasseh and Amon. The same root (spelled Gaza in English) refers to the coastal area of the Philistines. The name appears on an ostracon found on the slope of a hill above the eastern wall of Arad. It is dated by the orthography to the ninth century BCE (Aharoni 1981: 96, #72). The name also appears on an eighth-century BCE ostracon from Samaria (G.I. Davies 1991: 39, #3.001.5).

Paseaḥ. *Paseaḥ,* 'limping' or 'lame', is also the name (or nickname) of the father of one of the builders of Nehemiah's wall (Neh. 3.6). The Greek of both Ezra and Nehemiah as well as the Vulgate retain the initial *f* sound rather than the hard *p*. First Esdras reads Φινοε, Phinoe, which must reflect Paseaḥ in some way, even though it has a medial *n* instead of *s*. The name is not attested elsewhere. First Esdras inserts Ασαρα, Asara, after the sons of Phinoe, absent in both Ezra and Nehemiah.

Besai. Blenkinsopp (1988: 90) suggests that Besai בסי is Babylonian, as Bi-i-sa-a is attested as a Babylonian woman's name (Tallqvist 1914: 64). It may also come from the Hebrew root בוס, 'to trample'. First Esdras reads Βασθαι, Basthai. The name בסי is attested on a Judean seal obtained on the antiquities market and published by Avigad (G.I. Davies 1991: 152, #100. 247).

2.50 *'Asnah.* The name אַסְנָה, 'Asnah, is missing in Nehemiah, but present in 1 Esdras as Ασανα, Asana. The additional name in 1 Esdras, Asara, may be a repetition of this name (Talshir 2001: 272). The name may be Egyptian; with a feminine ending it is אסנת, 'Osnath, 'belonging to Neith' (the Egyptian goddess; Myers 1965: 14), the name of Joseph's wife (Gen. 41.45). As Aššanka, it appears as a personal name on the Persepolis Fortification Tablets (PF 619.5), the final 'ka' being the determinative for a personal name.

Me'ûnîm. Reading מעונים, the Me'unites, with the *qere* and with Nehemiah 7, rather than Me'înîm with the *kethib*. The name is a gentilic and may refer to a member of a nomadic Arabian people living in the area south of what is present-day Israel, in the northeast of Sinai (Knoppers 2004: 369; Zadok 1980: 113). First Esdras has Μαανι, Maani.

Nephisîm. Reading with the *kethib* (the *qere* reads Nephusîm). The reverse is true of Neh. 7.52. There, Nephushesim is the *kethib*, and Nephishesim is the *qere*. The difference is the *u* or *i* letter, which in this period are nearly impossible to distinguish orthographically in Hebrew. The text in Nehemiah also adds a shin, '*š*', in the penultimate syllable just before the *s*, samekh. According to the genealogies provided in the biblical text, the Nephisîm are related to the Ishmaelites and so are an Arabian group (Gen. 25.15; 1 Chron. 1.31; 5.19). First Esdras has Ναφισι, Naphisi, reflecting the text in Ezra.

2.51 ***Baqbuq.*** A *baqbuq*, בַּקְבּוּק, is a flask or bottle (1 Kgs 14.3; Jer. 19.1, 10). Maybe the bearer of the name was flask-shaped (Blenkinsopp 1988: 91), or perhaps he was a potter who made this type of earthenware vessel. The name is missing from 1 Esdras. Included among the liturgical singers (Neh. 11.17; 12.9, 25) is one named Bakbukiah, 'flask of Yhwh'? The name is not attested extrabiblically, although a Bakapukša is attested on the Persepolis Fortification Tablets (PF 981.3) and a Bagabukša is referred to on the Behistun inscription (DB 4.85).

Ḥaqufa'. Ḥaqufa', חקופא, may be derived from the Arabic *ḥaqafa*, meaning 'bent', 'crooked', 'twisted' (Zadok 1980: 113). First Esdras has two names reflecting this one—Ακουφ and Αχιβα, Akouph and Achiba. The name is not attested extrabiblically to my knowledge.

Ḥarḥur. The sons of Ḥarḥur are listed as the sons of Ασουρ, Asour, in 1 Esdras. The name is Egyptian; the element *Ḥor* refers to the Egyptian god Horus. An Espemet son of Haḥor אספמת בר חחר is listed as a witness for a receipt of silver at Elephantine (*TAD* C 3.4:7).

2.52 ***Baṣlut.*** *Baṣlut*, בצלות, is the name in Ezra, but it is Baṣlit, בצלית, in Nehemiah, suggesting a *waw/yod* (*u* / *i*) confusion. First Esdras reads Βασαλωθ, Basaloth, reading *o* or *u*, in agreement with Ezra. First Esdras inserts Φαρακιμ, Pharachim, a name not included in either of the canonical sources. The word Beṣel, בצל, means 'in the shadow of' or 'in the protection of'. It occurs with the theophoric 'el', אל, in the name Bezalel, the artisan in charge of building the tabernacle (Exod. 31.2). The phrase 'sons of Beṣel', בני בצל, along with the number 3, ///, was found inscribed on the base of a bowl at Arad. The bowl was inscribed all over the base and sides with names and numbers. According to the excavator, it was found in the building next to the entrance of the sanctuary in Stratum VIII and is dated to the end of the eighth century or the beginning of the seventh century BCE (Aharoni 1981: 81, #49).

Meḥida'. The name *Meḥida'*, מחידא, is reflected in all the versions except the Syriac, which has Meḥira, מחירא; even so, emendation may be warranted. The letters *d* and *r* are practically indistinguishable in Hebrew and Aramaic epigraphy at this period. The name Maḥida' is not attested elsewhere; whereas Maḥir is. The word *maḥir* means 'price', 'value' and is a common personal name (1 Chron. 4.11), and a common theophoric component of Babylonian names, for example, ᵈMa-ḫir-aḫ-iddin = 'Maḫir has provided a brother' (Tallqvist 1914: 123). With the meaning 'value', it is attested in the Babylonian name Ma-ḫur-illi, 'valued by the gods' (Tallqvist 1914: 123). Retaining Maḥida, it could be based on the Arabic *ḥada,* 'decline', 'turn aside', 'avoid' (Zadok 1980: 114). It could also be Persian; the name Mahitika (Mahiti + ka, the personal name determinative) is attested among the Persepolis Fortification Tablets (PF 1777.5).

Ḥarsha'. Ḥarsha', חרשא, could be from Ugaritic meaning 'craftsman' (Zadok 1988: 76) or it could be from Aramaic meaning 'deaf' (Zadok 1980: 114). It is not attested beyond Ezra–Nehemiah, nor is it present in 1 Esdras, which reads instead Κουθα and Χαρεα, Cuth and Charea. Neither seems to be a substitution for Ḥarša' (Talshir 2001: 273). Haruš is attested as a personal name on Persepolis Fortification Tablet PF 786.3. A town named Tel-Ḥarsha is listed as a place from where some of the returnees came (Ezra 2.59).

2.53 *Barqos.* *Barqos*, or Barqaws, בַּרְקוֹס, is an Edomite name, meaning 'son of the god Qos/Qaws' the primary god of the Edomites. An ostracon from Arad bears the name [. . .]*qws*, indicating a name whose final component is the theophoric Qws (Aharoni 1981: 52, #26). The ostracon was found in Stratum VI, the last Judahite stratum before the Babylonian conquest (beginning of the sixth century BCE).

Sisera'. Sisera', סיסרא, is the same name as that of the Canaanite general who led the forces against Deborah and Jael (Judges 4 and 5). The name is not attested elsewhere. It is neither Hebrew nor Canaanite. Boling (1975: 94) suggests it is Indo-European, and the bearer may have arrived in Canaan with the Sea Peoples. Freedman suggests it is Indo-Iranian (personal communication). First Esdras reads Σεραρ, Serar. This form of the name may be the original one with the name in Ezra–Nehemiah being influenced by that in Judges (Talshir 2001: 273). Serar is not attested elsewhere either, however. The name *ssr'l, Siser'el*, appears on a seventh-century BCE Aramaic seal (Reifenberg 1950: 44).

Tamaḥ. Tamaḥ, תמח, 'she/you/it will be blotted out'? (Ps. 109.14; Neh. 13.14). The name is not attested elsewhere.

2.54 *Netsiaḥ.* Netsiaḥ or Neṣiaḥ, נציח, means 'eternal (e.g. 1 Sam. 15.29). It may derive from the Aramaic 'shine, be illustrious, be pre-eminent, victorious', or from the Syriac *naṣīḥā*, 'splendid' (Zadok 1980: 114). To my knowledge, it is not attested as a personal name except here and in the parallel passages in Nehemiah 7 and 1 Esdras 5. Našaya is attested as a Persian personal name at PF 335.15, however.

Ḥaṭifa'. *Ḥaṭifa'*, חטיפא, means 'caught', 'seized' (Judg. 21.21; Ps. 10.9; Zadok 1980: 114). The individual may have been kidnapped. The name is not attested elsewhere.

2.55 ***The family of Solomon's servants.*** The last group in the list is of the sons of Solomon's slaves. According to the Deuteronomic historian (1 Kgs 9.20-22):

> All the people who were left of the Amorites, the Hittites, the Perizzites, the Hivites, and the Jebusites, who were not of the people of Israel—their descendants who were still left in the land, whom the Israelites were unable to destroy completely—these Solomon conscripted for slave labor, and so they are to this day. But of the Israelites, Solomon made no slaves; they were the soldiers, they were his officials, his commanders, his captains, and the commanders of his chariotry and cavalry.

The Deuteronomistic writer assumed that there was a group of people who were descendants of a mixed group of Canaanites whom Solomon had enslaved. By the time of the list in Ezra 2=Nehemiah 7, this group was clearly cultic; they are included in the count of N^etînîm, presumably involved in the care and service of the temple and its personnel (see note on v. 43). A primary source of temple slaves in antiquity was warfare. Victorious kings would donate prisoners of war to the temple in gratitude to the god who brought them their victory (Dandamayev 1984a; Haran 1961). The sons of Solomon's servants overwhelmingly bear non-Yhwhistic names (Zadok 1980). This group may have been descendants of such donated temple slaves, not necessarily from those donated by Solomon, but by any Judean king. As Dandamayev points out, the children of slaves were slaves.

Their categorization as a separate group seems to have ended during the Persian period when they became part of the *n^{e}tînîm*. They are cited separately in the list of returnees in Ezra 2, Nehemiah 7 and 11 but not in Ezra 7 or 8, where the *n^{e}tînîm* are listed, nor are they included with the *n^{e}tînîm* as participants in the wall-building effort in Nehemiah 3. Thus, by the time of Nehemiah they were no longer considered a separate group.

Soṭai. *Soṭai*, סטי, may be related to the root *śṭh*, שטה, 'to go astray' (Num. 5.12). It is not attested elsewhere and is missing from 1 Esdras.

Hassopheret. 'The scribe', but it is feminine, and a female scribe seems unlikely. The feminine form of professional titles of males is common, however.

Peruda'. *Peruda'*, פרודא. Nehemiah 7 reads 'Perida', as does 1 Esdras, which may mean 'the mulish one'. The root *prd* also means 'to separate, divide', suggesting 'unique, 'set apart' (Zadok 1980: 115; Noth 1928: 224 n. 3). On the other hand, it may be Persian. Pirrada is attested as a personal name in the Behistun inscription (3.12).

2.56 ***Ya'lah.*** *Ya'lāh*, יַעְלָה, is Arabic meaning 'mountain goat' (Zadok 1980: 115; 1988: 100). An Arabic ostracon in Aramaic script was found in excavations from fourth century BCE Arad inscribed with the similar name Wa'alu ועלו (Aharoni 1981: 167, #40). Zadok (1988: 100) suggests it is an

Arabicized Edomite name. First Esdras reads Ιεηλι, Yeli, suggesting a yod/waw (י/ו), confusion.

Darqon. *Darqon*, דַּרְקוֹן, may stem from Arabic *darūn,* 'hard', or from Arabic *daraqa,* 'walk rapidly, hasten'; or more likely it may be a metathesis of Daqron (from *dqr*, 'to bore, pierce'), a common root in Northwest Semitic personal names (Zadok 1980: 115). First Esdras reads Λοζων, Lozon, suggesting a confusion between Greek L (Λ) and D (Δ). Beyond this, and the ending, the names have really nothing in common.

Giddel. *Giddel* is discussed above (see the note on v. 47). First Esdras reads Ισδαηλ, Isdael, here.

2.57 ***Shephaṭiah.*** *Shephaṭiah*, שְׁפַטְיָה, 'Yhwh has judged', is a common Israelite name (see note on v. 4 above).

Ḥaṭṭil. *Ḥaṭṭil*, חַטִּיל, does not appear as a name elsewhere in the onomastica to my knowledge. It may be a form of the Arabic *ḫaṭala*, 'be loose, base' (Zadok 1980: 115).

Pokeret haṣṣebāyîm. *Pokeret haṣṣ^e^bāyîm.* פֹּכֶרֶת הַצְּבָיִים suggests a title rather than a personal name. *Ṣ^e^bāyîm,* צביים, are gazelles, while פכרת may be from Syriac *pkr* 'to tie up'. The form is a feminine participle, and as such, it may denote the title of the holder of an official position; cf. קהלת, Qoheleth, a feminine form but means 'the preacher', a title of a male. If a title, it could be 'gazelle catcher' or 'the one responsible for the gazelles', a professional title which then became a personal name (*HALOT*, *ad loc.*).

'Ami. 'Amî, אָמִי, is 'Amôn, אָמוֹן, in Nehemiah. The latter is a common Israelite name, meaning 'confirm, trust, support'. As a name it is likely a hypocoristic, 'DN is [my] support'. It is the name of the Judean king, the son of Manasseh (2 Kgs 21.18), and of a mayor of Jerusalem (1 Kgs 22.26). It also refers to the 'master workman' in Prov. 8.30. A letter (*TAD* A 2.7) from an Ami to his mother/sister Atardimri was found at Hermopolis and dated to the late-sixth or early-fifth century BCE. A letter from Arsames to his minister Artahant (*TAD* A 6.7:3) refers to a Cilician person, a slave in Egypt, named Amon, אמון, although Porten and Yardeni vocalize it as the Cilician name, Ammuwana.

There are eight more names belonging to the 'sons of Solomon's servants' in 1 Esdras than are in Ezra and Nehemiah, all occurring at the end of the list in 1 Esdras. The end of the list may have become damaged in transmission and the names lost to the current version of Ezra–Nehemiah (Talshir 2001: 273). The Hebrew/Aramaic form of the names cannot be recovered from the Greek however.

2.58 ***392.*** The numbers of *n^e^tinîm* and of the descendants of Solomon's servants have been combined into one group. Ezra and Nehemiah agree on 392, whereas 1 Esdras has 372.

2.59 ***Tel Melach, Tel Ḥarsha', Cherub, 'Addan, 'Immer.*** I have not been able to locate these places. According to 1 Esdras, however, the last three are not place names, but personal names.

Those who did not know if they were from Israel. This verse proves that it was not necessary to know one's genealogy or to demonstrate membership in the people Israel to join them on the trip to Zion and to be counted among the community of returnees (see note on v. 64 below). This is reminiscent of the 'mixed multitude', עֵרֶב רַב, that went up with the Hebrews from Egypt (Exod. 12.38).

2.60 ***Delaiah.*** Delaiah, דְּלָיָה. This verse is very curious since it puts the names of Delaiah and Ṭobiah, טוֹבִיָּה, together, both provincial governors of provinces of Beyond-the-River in the second half of the fifth century. It is also interesting to find them listed among those who could not prove their ancestry. A Delaiah was the son of Sanballat, governor of Samaria in 445 BCE, the time of Nehemiah. In 407, he was governor himself, and as such, he responded to the plea for help from the Judeans of Elephantine when their temple there had been destroyed (*TAD* A 4.7-9). Ṭobiah was the governor of Ammon when Sanballat and Nehemiah were governors of Samaria and Judah respectively (Mazar 1957). He may have still been governor of Ammon when Delaiah inherited his father's position. If the names indeed refer to these individuals then this part of the verse must have been added by the final redactor, perhaps when the heading was added to the list. The editor may be telling us that he does not know whether Tobiah and Delaiah were part of the people Israel, even though they had Yhwhistic names and even though both their families had married into the family of the high priests of Judah (Fried 2002c).

The occurrence of these two names together may be a coincidence, however. The name Delaiah is not unusual. A Delaiah was an important Judean royal official at the time of Jeremiah and King Zedekiah (Jer. 36.25). An ostracon with this name was found at Lachish, dated to the late-seventh or early-sixth centuries BCE (Aharoni 1968: 168, Pl. 12). The name was also found on a bulla from the City of David, also dated to the late-seventh or early-sixth centuries BCE (Shiloh 1986: 28, #1). The name may mean 'Yhwh has lifted up' (as out of a pit). Greek Ezra inserts the name Boua, Βουα, between Delaiah and Tobiah'.

Ṭobiah. Ṭobiah, 'Yhwh is good', was a very common Judean name. A letter found at Lachish (letter 3.15) dated to 586 BCE, the year of its destruction by the Babylonians, refers to Tobiah, the servant of the king (*ṭbyhw 'bd hmlk*), a title similar to that of the Tobiah in the book of Nehemiah (*ṭbyhw h'bd*, Neh. 2.10; Tur-Sinai 1938: 51; Tufnell 1953: 332; Mazar 1957). The same person may also be referred to in a second letter discovered at Lachish (letter 5.7-8).

Neqoda'. See note at v. 48 above.

2.61 *Ḥavaiah.* Ḥavaiah, חֲבַיָּה, 'Hidden by Yhwh' (Zadok 1988: 30), perhaps in the sense of being kept safe, protected (Job 5.21). Or, it may be 'beloved by Yhwh' like Ḥobab, 'beloved', the name of Moses' father-in-law (Num. 10.29).

Haqqoṣ. *Haqqoṣ*, הקוץ, 'the thorn'? Perhaps it is an error for הקיץ, 'the summer fruit' (*pace* Porten, personal communication). If this Haqqoṣ is the grandfather of Meremoth son of Uriah son of Haqqoṣ who worked on Nehemiah's wall in 445 (Neh. 3.4, 21), and if the Meremoth son of Uriah, the priest, to whom Ezra counted out the temple vessels when he arrived in Jerusalem in 398 (Ezra 8.33) is this same Meremoth son of Uriah who worked on the wall in 445, then the priestly status of the family had been regained. The Meremoth who worked on the walls is not called a priest (although he works among a contingent of priests), so if it is the same man, then the priestly status of his family must have been confirmed between the time of the wall building (445 BCE) and the time of Ezra's arrival in the seventh year of Artaxerxes II (398 BCE), forty-seven years later. This implies that during this forty-seven-year period (445–398) a priest arrived with *urim* and *thummim* (see note on v. 63 below), or more precisely, a high priest appeared in this period with the authority to rule on priestly status. Indeed, by the time of the Chronicler, Haqqoṣ's family line was given charge of the seventh priestly course (1 Chron. 24.10).

If a priest arrived with *urim* and *thummim*, who would it have been? It may have been Yoḥanan, high priest from 410 to 370 BCE, the grandson of Eliashib (Fried 2003a, 2007c; VanderKam 2004). This priest was the only priest in Persian-period Yehud with the authority to mint coins with his name and title on them. If any priest had the power to determine priestly status, it would have been he.

One of the daughters. First Esdras supplies 'the descendants of Jaddus who had married Agia one of the daughters of Barzillai and was called by his name. (1 Esdras actually reads Φαρζελλαιου, Pharzellai, however, instead of Barzillai.) It's impossible to know if the addition is an embellishment by the author of 1 Esdras, or if it had dropped out of the Ezra–Nehemiah text that we have.

Called by his name. It was common for the father of brotherless women to adopt the husband of one of his daughters.

Barzilai the Gileadite. The story of Barzilai the Gileadite is told in 1 Samuel 19, and reiterated in David's last words to Solomon (1 Kgs 2.7). Gilead refers to the territory between the Arnon and the Jabbok rivers, east of the Jordan, which belonged to the tribal area of Manasseh. The phrase 'the Gileadite' is absent from 1 Esdras. The gentilic may not have been in 1 Esdras's *Vorlage* but added to Ezra because of the identical name to connect the bearer to David's benefactor (Talshir 2001: 277).

2.62 ***Unfit for the priesthood.*** Everywhere throughout the ancient Near East, those priests who approached the god had to be members of specific priestly families. Priests who approached the gods in the Babylonian temples of Uruk and Sippar, for example, were selected from only a small number of such families. Temple officials with administrative, but never cultic, functions could be brought in from outside the temple community by the ruling authorities to manage the temple on behalf of the king. These outsiders would then be loyal to the authorities who appointed them, and not to the temple community (Kümmel 1979; Bongenaar 1997; Fried 2004). Priests who approached the god, however, could not be brought in from outside, as their lineage had to be the proper one for the temple. Besides Babylon and Judah, this was also true in Egypt. The Peteesi Petition makes clear that only men whose father served as priest in a particular temple could be appointed to the priesthood of that temple (Fried 2004).

In fact, men of all professions were usually considered fit for an occupation only if their fathers were already in it. Weisberg (1967) discusses a craftsmen's charter from Uruk, Babylon, dated to the reign of Cyrus the Great. The five carpenters (two a father–son pair) were from three agnatic extended families; the thirteen metal engravers (including two brothers) were from four agnatic families; the nine goldsmiths (including a father–son pair) were from four agnatic families. There was no overlap among the families. If a family produced metal engravers, it did not also produce goldsmiths. Family membership was a strong determining factor of one's profession.

2.63 ***Tirshata'.*** The tirshata' (*tiršātā'*), הַתִּרְשָׁתָא, is customarily translated 'the governor' because Nehemiah is given this title in Neh. 8.9 and 10.2, and because he describes himself as the פחה, 'governor', in 5.14. The term *tiršātā'* may come from the Old Persian root, *tarsa*, 'to fear' or 'revere' (Kent 1953: 186), so he is 'the revered one'. First Esdras reads, 'and Nehemiah and Attharias said to them . . .', taking *hattiršātā'* (*ha*, 'the', Tiršata') to be a proper name. The inclusion of Nehemiah with the tirshata' in 1 Esdras demonstrates that the latter's author had the book of Nehemiah in front of him. It is only in the book of Nehemiah (8.9; 10.2) that Nehemiah is called 'the tirshata' '. This passage could not have been derived from Ezra alone, where Nehemiah never appears.

The evidence from Nehemiah indicates that the term refers to the title of the Persian governor of Yehud, suggesting that this Persian appointee had the power to control priestly appointments (this is confirmed in Josephus, *Ant.* 11.298; Grabbe 1992). He apparently controlled even the minutiae of priestly dietary fare. This is consistent with what is known about the relationship between the Persian governors and local priests elsewhere in the Persian Empire (Fried 2004). Persian authorities were deeply involved in the details of everyday life in the areas they ruled. Egyptian documents reveal that Persian officials had to approve the appointment of those nominated for the priesthood, and the applicant often had to pay a fee to the Persian gubernatorial coffers for the privilege (Fried 2004: 80-86). Perhaps Haqqoṣ was unwilling or unable to pay.

The most sanctified food. There were two types of food offered to Yhwh, the 'holy' and the 'most holy' (Lev. 21.22). Numbers 18 elaborates on the difference between them. The 'most holy' offerings were the offerings to Yhwh by fire, whether grain or animal. The leftovers were restricted to the sons of Aaron, the priests (Num. 18.9-10). Other offerings were holy but not 'most holy'. These were the first-fruits of the wine and the grain and the oil, the choice produce of the field and the first-fruits of the land and of the livestock. They could be eaten by anyone in the priest's household who was ritually clean, whether male or female (Num. 18.11-14, 19). These were also made available to those priests whose ancestry was in doubt. In contrast, nonpriests may not eat of the sacred food, even the 'holy' food (Lev. 22.10). By specifying 'most holy' food, the author indicates that those who claimed to be priests but who could not prove their ancestry were to be treated like a member of the priests' household; they may eat the 'holy' food but may not serve at the altar and may not partake of the 'most holy' offerings from it.

Urim and thummim. These are items on the breastplate of the high priest by which he gives judgment (Lev. 8.8; Van Dam 1997; Fried 2007c). It seems that when the verse in Ezra 2 / Nehemiah 7 was written, the high priest did not possess the *urim* and *thummim*. The Talmud (*Yoma* 21b) lists them among the objects present in the first temple that were absent in the second. Maimonides (*Klei Hammikdash* 10.10) argues, however, that the high priest must have had *urim* and *thummim* since these were required apparel. Had they been lacking, the high priest could not have carried out his office. Maimonides suggests that they must have made a breastplate for him with *urim* and *thummim* on them, but that he was not allowed to inquire of them. In any case, if the high priest had no authority to certify the fitness of other priests to serve, then indeed he lacked the basic authority of his office. This verse implies that the Persian governor alone determined who could assume the priesthood. It seems likely that when a priest arose, like Yoḥanan, who was able to seize secular authority for a time, as indicated by his minting a coin, that he was also able to certify priestly appointments. (See the comment above on Haqqoṣ in v. 61.)

2.64 ***The whole community (qāhāl) together.*** Literally, 'as one'. The word *qāhāl* simply means the total gathered, as in Ezra 10.1. There the term includes men, women, and children, everyone who happened to be with Ezra at the time. Some have adduced a second official meaning implied in Ezra 10.7-8, which is discussed there.

42,360. This total is almost twice as large as the sum of the individual groups (26,423, even including the additional totals from 1 Esdras). This number may include women and children whereas the numbers above may include only adult males, or other groups could have dropped out of the text during transmission. First Esdras adds that the total includes only those twelve and over, perhaps in an attempt to clarify the discrepancy. The smaller number may be the actual sum, however, and have been the true population of Judah at the end of the sixth century. Archaeologists have concluded that the population did not reach 40,000 until the end of the Persian period, toward the end of the fourth century BCE (Faust 2007, 2012a). Archaeology also suggests that there was not a single return but a gradual influx of returnees over the two centuries of Persian hegemony and a gradual recovery from the near total devastation by the Babylonians.

2.65 ***Singers.*** Singers always accompanied themselves on instruments. Although the same word is used as in v. 41 above, this group probably consists of noncultic musicians. Music was a vital part of everyday life in antiquity. It was an integral part of wedding festivities (Jer. 33.11), harvest celebrations (Judg. 21.20-21; Isa. 16.10-11), victory dances (Exod. 15.20-21), and at other joyous occasions (Judg. 11.34). These singers were likely to have been family slaves, or they would have been included in the total above.

200. Nehemiah reads 245 singers, as does 1 Esdras. Further, 1 Esdras reads 'harpists and singers'. Pakkala (2004: 137) suggests that this number was taken from the number of mules in Ezra 2.66. The scribe's eye fell to the number of mules and skipped the intervening verse.

2.66 ***Horses and donkeys.*** This verse is missing from Nehemiah 7. It is more likely that it was inadvertently omitted by a late copyist there than that it would be added *de novo* here. (See previous note.)

2.67 ***6,720.*** First Esdras reads 5,520 donkeys. This is the last verse in the list of returnees. No sheep or cattle are included in the total of animals brought to Judah from Babylon, only riding and pack animals.

2.68 ***Patriarchal families.*** Literally, 'heads of fathers' [houses]'. This refers to the extended patriarchal household, the basic unit of civilization in the ancient Near East (Schloen 2001).

To the temple of Yhwh which is in Jerusalem. This clause is not included in the parallel passage in Nehemiah 7. The Nehemiah passage (7.69-72 [ET 70-73]) includes the statement that the *tirshata'* gave to the treasury one thousand drachmas of gold, fifty basins, and five hundred thirty priestly robes', which has no parallel in Ezra. The author may have supposed that the tirshata' referred to in Neh. 7.71 was Sheshbazzar, and his donations to the temple are already listed in chap. 1 (Galling 1964: 104-105). Nehemiah 7 also refers to donations from 'the rest of the people' (Neh. 7.71 [ET 7.72]), a statement not made in Ezra.

The passage in Ezra reads,

> As soon as they came to the temple of Yhwh in Jerusalem, some of the heads of ancestral houses made free-will offerings for the house of God, to erect it on its site. According to their resources they gave to the maintenance fund sixty-one thousand drachmas of gold, five thousand minas of silver, and one hundred priestly robes (Ezra 2.68-69).

Whereas the passage in Nehemiah reads:

> Now some of the heads of ancestral houses contributed to the work. The governor (*hattirshātā'*) gave to the treasury one thousand drachmas of gold, fifty basins, and five hundred thirty priestly robes. And some of the heads of ancestral houses gave into the maintenance fund twenty thousand drachmas of gold and two thousand two hundred minas of silver. And what the rest of the people gave was twenty thousand drachmas of gold, two thousand minas of silver, and sixty-seven priestly robes (Neh. 7.71-72).

Other than the discrepancies regarding the temple (Ezra 2) and the governor (Nehemiah 7), the verses differ only slightly in wording, primarily in the amounts of the donations. If the shorter text is to be preferred as the original one (a common dictum of textual criticism), then the preference would be for the verse in Ezra without the reference to the temple. It is easy to understand that the editor of the Nehemiah material would want to add a reference to the *tirshata'* since he would have regarded Nehemiah as that person (Neh. 8.9; 10.2; cf. Neh. 7.5-7). On the other hand, the author of the list in Ezra might have removed the reference to the governor if he thought it contradicted Ezra 1.11, and added the reference to the temple, so that the verse in Nehemiah could be the original one. More importantly, the narrative context of Nehemiah 7 is of a list of returnees that Nehemiah had found. Nehemiah states (Neh. 7.5), 'I found the book of the genealogy of those who were the first to come back, and I found the following written in it'. Then he quotes the list cited in Ezra 2. Since this is framed as a list of the first returnees, it would not have been a problem, had it been in his *Vorlage,* for the redactor of the Nehemiah memoir to include a verse to the effect that the returnees built the temple on its site. It must have been added by the redactor of Ezra 2, and the verse in Nehemiah is the original one.

On its site. That is, on the location where it had been before. This entire verse (2.68) is not in Nehemiah and was likely added by the author of Ezra 1–6. As stated above, the author of Nehemiah 7 would have retained it, had it been in his *Vorlage*. The verse cannot be used to date the list.

2.69 *Maintenance fund.* Literally, 'the treasury of the work' or 'the treasury of the service'. Although usually translated 'building fund', it does not necessarily imply that it was to contribute to the cost of building the temple. It can equally well refer to the cost of maintaining the daily temple service (cf. Exod. 35.21; Galling 1951: 151).

Gold drachmas **דַּרְכְּמוֹנִים.** The question here is whether these are weights or coins. If the term is Greek, they could be either. The same pair (drachma and mina) is found in a Greek inscription from Xanthus in Lycia. Dated to 338 BCE (Fried 2004: 144-45), the people of Xanthus promise to pay the priest of a new temple 3 half-minas a year (line 17). Further, all those who would become free could pay the god two drachmas and receive their freedom (line 20; Fried 2004: 143).

The following equivalences existed in Greece in the fifth and fourth centuries BCE (L&S 1138; Head 1963: xxxv):

60 minas	1 talent
100 drachmas	1 mina
60 shekels	1 mina
six obols	1 drachma

If in coins, these were all silver. Although the word is 'drachma', commentators routinely interpret it as 'darics' (e.g. the NRSV), because the Persian daric was of gold and the drachma only of silver. Yet, if coins were implied, the type of metal would not have needed to be specified; it would be assumed, so it is more likely that weights are meant. Metals continued to be weighed out as payment throughout the Persian period, even after coins began to be used.

Persia took over Babylon's system of weights and measures. At the time of Nebuchadnezzar the mina weighed between 982.35 and 1,000.9 grams, based on inscribed weights now in the British Museum (Head 1963: xxxvi). When silver and gold were weighed out, the weights were changed, so that only 50 shekels equaled a mina. (This is Ezekiel's complaint when he demands that 60 shekels shall make up your mina [45.12].) That two drachmas equaled a shekel explains the popularity of the didrachma. This two-drachma coin or weight was the basic unit of Aegina and then Athens (Schaps 2004: 105). Although the Greeks began using coins in the sixth and fifth centuries, and even though these coins spread east into Egypt, Phoenicia and the Levant, evidence from hoards suggests that these coins were regarded simply as pieces of silver to be weighed out and cut up if necessary, even up to the fourth century when the Levant began to mint its own coins (Schaps 2004: 106; Fried 2003a).

Slotsky (1997: 133) has recorded what one shekel (approx. 20 grams) of silver could buy at various times throughout the Persian and Greek periods. The earliest time for which she provides a complete record is the end of the first month of Darius II's fifth year, 418 BCE. At that time one shekel of silver (20 grams) could purchase 23 *qû* (1 *qû* = approx. 1 quart) of barley, 16.5 *qû* of dates, and 1 mina of wool (about 2 lbs.). Commodity prices fell sharply during the Achaemenid period, however, since the great kings hoarded silver and gold. Conversely, silver and gold became dearer to the public as time progressed, but all the more available to the king (Slotsky 1997). Even if silver and gold were cheaper at the beginning of the Achaemenid Empire than at the end, at these equivalences the returning exiles contributed about 120 pounds of gold and almost 10,000 pounds of silver to the temple's maintenance fund!

2.70 ***The priests, the Levites, . . . in their [own] towns.*** The translation of this verse is taken from 1 Esdras, as the Hebrew and Greek of both Ezra and Nehemiah are unintelligible as they stand. This verse does not mention the sons of Solomon's servants, suggesting that it was written later, presumably after the sons of Solomon's servants had been incorporated into the *n^{e}tînîm*.

Comments: Ezra 2—The List of Returnees

A. The Literary Purpose of the List

As discussed in the Introduction, the list was likely copied from Nehemiah 7. Why then is the list here? What is its literary function at this point in the narrative? Is it historical, that is, did it exist outside its literary context in Nehemiah, and if so, what would have been its original purpose?

I have discussed in the Introduction to Ezra 1–6, my understanding of these chapters as based on a typical ancient Near Eastern temple-building story, stories that are structured around a fixed template. In the Persian period, a fixed component was a statement regarding the large number of people and the large amount of material that flowed voluntarily in from all over the world to contribute to and to celebrate the god whose temple it was. The temple vessels comprise part of that wealth, and Ezra 1 ends with the statement regarding the large number of vessels brought up from Babylon into the temple. Ezra 2 continues the theme both with a statement that peoples of every status (from priest to laity) stream into Jerusalem to help build the temple and with its statement of the large amounts of gold and silver that the returnees brought to endow the temple's maintenance fund. Such statements are a fixed part of temple building stories of the Persian period (Root 1979; Hurowitz 1985; 1992: 207-10; Boda and Novotny 2010).

Not part of the ancient Near Eastern temple-building story, however, is the inclusion of lists, but the list was a fixed part of Greco-Roman history writing, the probable time of the final redaction of the book. As noted in the Introduction to Ezra 1–6, the list was a popular tool of the Hellenistic historian; and spurious lists were used when actual ones were unavailable (Lateiner 1989: 9; Honigman 2003: 73). Lists were purposely added to the narrative to increase readers' confidence in the historical reliability of the text and in the author's ability to access privileged sources. Indeed the list, whether genuine or fictive, was a favorite device used by Greek historians to bolster the credibility of their history.

The inclusion of the list of returnees at this point in the narrative satisfies two literary purposes therefore. First, it glorifies the temple by describing the immense number of people who streamed in to Jerusalem to participate in building it. Second, the specificity in the names, numbers, family backgrounds, and towns of origin is intended to increase the reader's confidence in the author, in his access to sources, and in the veracity of his report. A third purpose is to illustrate continuity with pre-exilic Judah (Clauss 2011: 111). Each of the families named is presented as descended from those who had been driven out from pre-exilic Judah by Babylon. This is accentuated by the report in v. 59 ('The following are those who came up from Tel-Melach, Tel Ḥarsha', Cherub, 'Addan, 'Immer and could not name the house of their fathers or their genealogy or whether they were from Israel'). Stating that the following could not prove whether they were from Israel stresses that all the rest of those listed were able to prove it.

B. The Historical Purpose of the List

But is the list genuine? Did it exist outside of its literary context, and if so, what was its original purpose? The superscription of twelve names (v. 2) is not part of the original list, and may more likely be simply the names of twelve Judean leaders from the entire Persian period who were known to our author, with the number twelve signifying completeness, as in the twelve tribes of Israel, the twelve apostles, etc. (Mowinckel 1965: 65). They were added to convey the impression that all these great leaders returned with Cyrus at the earliest opportunity. (See below, Comment D. The Chronology Assumed by the Author of Ezra–Nehemiah.)

What about the rest of the list? Torrey regards the entire list as wholly a composition of the Chronicler and not to be taken seriously (Torrey 1970 [1910]: 250). Galling (1951) suggests that the list is historically valid and was compiled to answer Tattenai's request for a list of names of those building the temple (Ezra 5.3, 4, 10). However, it cannot be that Tattenai asked for a list of every family in the community along with the number of members in each. He simply asked for a list of those responsible for building the temple, that is, 'the ones at their head' (Ezra 5.10). Galling (1951: 153) assumes that Tattenai was coming from Samaria and was reacting to the 'great controversy' between Samaria and Jerusalem that is portrayed in Ezra 4.1-4. As will be discussed below *ad loc.*, that dispute is a creation of our author and has no historical value. According to what is most likely a historical letter (see Comment to Ezra 5), Tattenai simply asks for the names of provincial leaders, and we do not have that list.

If not a response to Tattenai's request, what then was the list's original purpose? Ignoring the heading, the list is reminiscent of a list of *ḫadru*s revealed in the Murašû archive, an archive of a banking firm in Nippur, Babylon, whose extant records range from the tenth year of Artaxerxes I (454 BCE) to the first year of Artaxerxes II (404 BCE; Stolper 1985: 23). The Murašû archive reveals that vacant land around Nippur was organized into a system of estates called *ḫadru*s, each held by a group of agnatic relatives. The *ḫadru*s were divided into fiefs, with each fief responsible for contributions of military service to the king's army, the *īlku* or *halak* in Aramaic, and for payment of an annual tax. Whole or fractional fiefs within the *ḫadru*s could be leased or pledged but not alienated. Whoever rented the fief was then responsible for its share of the tax and for furnishing its share of the obligatory soldiers for the army. This was the case everywhere in the empire, and was also the situation in Judah (see more at Nehemiah 5 and Fried 2015c). The list of *ḫadru*s associated with the Murašû firm is revealing: Stolper lists sixty-seven separate *ḫadru*s in Nippur (1985: 72-79). These agnatic holdings were labeled sometimes by ethnic group, sometimes by town of origin, sometimes by profession, but all the labels were prefixed by either 'men of' or 'sons of', exactly as in Ezra 2. One *ḫadru* was simply labeled 'men who were refugees', perhaps men whose origin, profession, or ethnic affiliation were unknown. This seems similar to the case described in Ezra 2.59, 'These are the ones who . . . could not name the house of their fathers or their genealogy or whether they were from Israel'. The list in Ezra 2 may well be organized by *ḫadru*.

The list also suggests a Babylonian context for the term *bêt 'ābôt* ('father's house'). Indeed, we find that in sixth-century Uruk, for example, men were identified by three names, PN_1 son of PN_2 son of PN_3 (Kümmel 1979: 15). The third name was not actually that of the grandfather, but rather went back to either the name of a distant ancestor or to his profession. Those names operated in that society as our family names do today—the name 'Smith' not describing the bearer but the profession of an ancestor. The use of these family names existed throughout Babylonian urban populations beginning in the mid- to late-second millennium and continued into the first century BCE (van de Mieroop 1997: 107). The situation in Babylon may have existed in Judah as well, with *bêt 'āb* referring to a nuclear or three-generational extended family, and *bêt 'ābôt* referring to all those with a common 'family name'. Like people named 'Smith' today, it is not likely that all those people with the same family name were actually blood relatives. Kümmel lists only seventy-seven family names in sixth-century Uruk, which is small for a city estimated at 12,500 inhabitants (Kümmel 1979; van de Mieroop 1997: 108). Moreover, some of these family names were also in use in other cities, such as Babylon. Van de Mieroop therefore considers these to be fictive kinship groups.

In actuality, the main organization of urban society was not the extended family, but the nuclear family (Faust 1999; 2012b). Analysis of texts found in neighboring homes in Babylonian cities reveals that contrary to expectation next-door neighbors were not related by blood. Moreover, people acted as individuals in legal documents, and not as members of larger kinship or professional groups. Nehemiah 5 reveals, for example, that there was no one between the nuclear family and the Persian governor; there was no extended kinship group to intercede between the governor and the individual (Williamson 2000).

If the families here are labeled as the *ḫadru*s were in Nippur, then the towns mentioned in the list would not be places to which the families came when entering Judah but rather their towns of origin, the places from which they had been deported. We do not know the towns to which they came. That they are the places from which they originated, rather than to which they came, is all the more likely since all these towns were inhabited in the Iron Age but not all during the Persian period.

Although the list of names in Ezra 2 may be a list of *ḫadru*s, the list also has a distant parallel to lists among the papyri at Elephantine. All told, nine lists of names have been found on the island (*TAD* C 4.1-9), dating from the middle of the fifth to the beginning of the fourth century BCE. Some lists contain only Egyptian names; one is a list of fourteen Persian names; most contain a mixture of Egyptian, Aramean and Judean names. The purpose of all these lists is unclear; there is no context for them. A long collection account was also found at Elephantine (*TAD* C 3.15), however, that has many similarities to the list in Ezra 2. Dated to June 1, 400 BCE, it has 138 lines of text in Aramaic plus 12 lines of unerased (and apparently unrelated) Demotic. The first two lines read:

> On the 3rd of Phamenoth, year 5: This is (= These are) the names of the [members of the] Judean garrison who gave silver to Yhw the god, each person silver, [2] sh(ekels).

The structure of this list of 128 names is reminiscent of the structure of the list in Ezra 2, except that each name on the Elephantine document is accompanied by the amount donated to the temple (2 shekels), whereas in Ezra, each name is accompanied by the number of family members. In both lists, however, the names are divided into unequal groupings, with some groups receiving an internal subtotal, as in Ezra 2, and some not. Both lists end with a total from all the groups (the one a total number of returnees, the other the total amount donated). As in Ezra 2, different parts of the list at Elephantine are organized differently. Part of the list is organized by family, and part by the divisions of the garrison (called centuries) to which the donor belongs; other groups have no apparent organizing principle:

Group 1. Three names representing three generations of one family.
Group 2. Thirteen names, all belonging to the century of Sin-iddin.
Group 3. Eleven names, all from the century of Nabû-akab.
Group 4. Ninety-one names (no unifying characteristic).

A subtotal of the first four groups is then computed as follows:

> The silver which stood that day in the hand of Jedaniah son of Gemariah in the month of Phamenoth:
> Silver—31 karsh, 8 shekels.
> Herein for Yhw 12 k, 6 sh.
> For Eshembethel, 7 karsh
> For Anathbethel, silver 12 karsh.

That is, the total collected was 318 shekels (10 shekels = 1 karsh), which was then distributed to the three sanctuaries—that of Yhw, Eshembethel, and Anathbethel.

Then two more groups are added:

Group 5. Seven names (no apparent organizing principle).
Group 6. Three names (two Persian), written on the verso.

Not counting the ten names listed after the subtotal, there are 118 names. If each contributed 2 shekels, that equals 236 shekels (= 23.6 karsh). Yet, the subtotal stated is 318 shekels. This is close to, but does not equal, the number of shekels distributed among the three sanctuaries (316). If the additional ten contributors are included, then only 20 more shekels are added, bringing the sum to 256. This is still a long way from 318.

The different procedures for grouping the contributors, the unequal sizes of the groups, the presence of subtotals for some of the groups, and the confusing discrepancy between the stated total and the number achieved by tallying the entries are all traits present in the list in Ezra 2. This does not solve the problems of the two lists, but it does rule out some proposed solutions. It can no longer be assumed that the different mechanism for sorting the entries (by family or by place of origin) implies that Ezra 2 is a composite of several lists. Nor can it be assumed that the discrepancy between the stated total and the amount achieved by tallying the entries implies that errors of transmission have crept in.

It is entirely possible that the similarities between Ezra 2 and *TAD* C 3.15 are more than coincidental. Ezra 2 may also have been a list of contributors to the temple of Yhwh in Jerusalem, reframed by the historian as a list of returnees. The end of Ezra 2 corroborates this impression by providing the total contributed to the temple of Yhwh according to household:

> At the time of their coming to Yhwh's house which is in Jerusalem, some from among the heads of the patriarchal families donated to the house of the god to erect it on its site. They gave to the treasury for the work according to their ability:

Gold: 61,000 drachmas.
Silver: 5,000 minas.
Priestly robes: 100 (Ezra 2:68-69).

An important difference between the list at Elephantine and that in Ezra 2, however, is that the list in Ezra is not a list of personal names but apparently of *ḫadru*s, each giving according to its ability (2.69). This is in contrast to the list at Elephantine, according to which each person gave two shekels. That list has the characteristic of a tax roll, but the list in Ezra may have been a tax roll as well. It may also have been a census. If a census list organized by *ḫadru*s, it becomes clear why only pack and riding animals were enumerated and not cattle and sheep. Each *ḫadru* may have provided riding and pack animals for the army. Cattle and sheep were irrelevant.

It seems then that Ezra 2 may not have been a list of returnees but rather a tax or census list of *ḫadru*s reframed to correspond to the ideology of the biblical historian. The degree to which the list is an ideological reframing is discussed below in Comment E.

In contrast to the collection list at Elephantine, it is not stated here who received the funds. If we knew who received the funds, we could date the list. It may be that in contrast to the situation at Elephantine, the tirshata', the Persian governor, rather than a priest, received the funds and supervised the collection in Judah (v. 63). This is all the more likely if it is a tax or census list. No recipient is named; it may have been Zerubbabel; it may have been Nehemiah, the tirshata', but this cannot be known.

C. The Date of the List

Since we do not know which governor collected the funds, we cannot date the list. It could be from any period. If the information deduced above about Haqqoṣ (discussed at v. 61 above) is correct, however, then the list likely dates from around 500 BCE, in the reign of Darius I, consistent with the heading (they came with Zerubbabel and Jeshua). Zerubbabel would then have been the governor who collected the funds. The amounts listed at the end of the list were donations for the maintenance of the temple, for the temple would have already been built by the time of this census. Because of the remark about Haqqoṣ's lineage, Batten (1913: 73) dates the list to the time of Ezra (398 BCE, in his view). Batten states that 'there is no indication of a concern about the purity of the priesthood before Ezra's time'. However, this denies the resemblance of the priesthood of Yhwh to the priesthoods of every other temple throughout the ancient Near East and Egypt. Every temple was concerned about the genetic purity of the priests who approached the god. Temple officials who participated in the temple administration and management needed no special lineage, but those who approached the god had to be of the appropriate priestly families (see Fried 2004). This concern for priestly lineage was not unique to Judah or to the time of Ezra and does not prevent assigning the list to the period of Darius and Zerubbabel.

If Meremoth, Haqqoṣ's grandson, was as young as fifteen when he worked on Nehemiah's wall in 445, then he would have been sixty-two in 398 when Ezra came to Jerusalem and handed him the vessels. (For the date of Ezra, see the discussion at Ezra 7.1.) If Haqqoṣ was at least sixty years older than his grandson, then in 445 he would have been at least seventy-five. This means he would have been at least twenty in 500, and this may have been the date of the list.

D. The Chronology Assumed by the Author of Ezra–Nehemiah as Compared to the Conventional Chronology

The chronology that forms the background of the book Ezra–Nehemiah, and which is readily apparent in Ezra 2.2, is not the conventional chronology. According to the conventional chronology, the list of the Achaemenid kings from Cyrus to Darius III (called Darius the Persian in Neh. 12.22) spans over two hundred years (from 550 to 333 BCE) and includes ten kings. (The list of Persian kings with their dates is in the Appendix.) The conventional chronology is based on the writings of the Greek historians (Herodotus, Xenophon, etc.), on dated administrative texts from Babylon and Egypt, as well as on the inscriptions of the Persian kings themselves. The conventional chronology is also matched to eclipses of the sun and moon and is correct (Parker and Dubberstein 1956).

The chronology that forms the backbone of the book of Ezra–Nehemiah differs from the conventional one, however. The chronology assumed in Ezra–Nehemiah is revealed in the book of Daniel (11.1-2), dated to the mid-second century BCE. According to the book of Daniel, there were three kings of Persia who succeeded Darius the Mede. The last one (the fourth in the series) was the one who fought Alexander the Great.

> As for me, in the first year of Darius the Mede, I stood up to support and strengthen him [i. e. Darius]. 'Now I will announce the truth to you. Three more kings shall arise in Persia. The fourth shall be far richer than all of them, and when he has become strong through his riches, he shall stir up all against the kingdom of Greece (Dan. 11.1-2).

This is a prediction after the fact (*vaticinium ex eventu*), that is, the writer is writing from the vantage point of the days of Antiochus IV, almost two hundred years after the fall of Persia to Alexander. If, as is likely, his primary information about the chronology of the Persian period came from Ezra–Nehemiah, then we can use these verses in Daniel to understand how the chronology of the Persian period was conceived. Since Darius the Mede does not appear, the three kings mentioned in Daniel must be the three kings named in Ezra–Nehemiah. If the first mention of each king reveals their order, the order of the Persian kings in this reckoning is as follows:

Cyrus (Ezra 1.1), Xerxes (= Ahasuerus; Ezra 4.6), Artaxerxes (Ezra 4.7); and Darius (Ezra 4.24). There is another Artaxerxes whose seventh year is mentioned in Ezra 7.1 and another whose twentieth year is mentioned in Neh. 2.1. Since at most three kings are assumed to cover the entire Persian period after Darius the Mede (per Daniel), it was concluded in late aniquity that Artaxerxes must have been the throne name of every Persian king (cf., the Talmud, *Roš Haš.* 3b; Rashi *ad loc.*). It applied equally to Xerxes and to Darius. The seventh year of Artaxerxes, when Ezra is reported to have come to Jerusalem, is in this view the seventh year of Darius. The temple is consecrated in the twelfth month of Darius's sixth year (Ezra 6.15), and Ezra starts out on his journey a few days later on the first day of the first month of Darius-Artaxerxes' seventh year (Ezra 7.7). That is, the Artaxerxes who is king in Ezra 7–Nehemiah 13 is in fact (according to this way of thinking) Darius the Persian, the same Darius in whose reign the temple was dedicated. This is indicated by the (spurious) genealogy provided for Ezra in 7.1-5, in which it is stated that Ezra is the son of Seraiah, the last high priest of monarchic Judah, and therefore the uncle of Jeshua, the high priest of the restoration. This is why the medieval rabbinic commentator Rashi translates Ezra 6.14 as 'Darius who was called Artaxerxes'. (See further discussion at 6.14 below.)

This yields three Persian kings after Darius the Mede—Cyrus, Ahashuerus (Xerxes) and Darius the Persian. The Persian period is compressed in this way into a very short period. According to this view, Cyrus reigned three years (Dan. 10.1), Ahashuerus-Artaxerxes (Xerxes) reigned twelve years (Est. 3.7), and then Darius-Artaxerxes, at least thirty-two years (Neh. 13.6), for a total of forty-seven years. Nehemiah reports, moreover, that in the 32nd year of (Darius-) Artaxerxes he was recalled to Persia, and after some time he returned to Judah and finished his term, presumably under that same king. This likely was seen as rounding out the Persian period to a nice fifty years. This seems to have been the chronology in the mind of the historian who edited Ezra–Nehemiah, and it explains the order of the kings in Ezra as well as all the names in the heading of the list. With a Persian period of only fifty years from the first return to the advent of Alexander the Great, all the preeminent men of the period could have been contemporaries. Naturally, they all would have returned at the first moment possible under Cyrus. Some—such as Ezra ('Azariah), Nehemiah, and Mordechai—must have returned to Susa at some point since they are reported active there under the Persian kings. Nevertheless, there was no doubt in the narrator's mind at least that if they were alive they would have gone up to Israel immediately under Cyrus even if they went back to Babylon later.[1] (See further at 6.14, below.)

1. The reconstruction proposed here differs slightly from that proposed by the author of *Seder olam*, the rabbinic commentary on the chronology of the world. That chro-

E. The Ideological Purpose of the List

Although the list in Ezra 2 may have been based originally on a tax list of *ḫadru*s, or agnatic households, in Judah, and although it may have stemmed originally from around 500, it has been recast to fulfill an ideological agenda.[2] The people listed in Ezra 2 and Nehemiah 7 as well as in Nehemiah 11–12 are intended to portray the legitimate population of Judah. According to the lists, the people who returned were:

1. the men of the people Israel;
2. the priests;
3. the Levites;
4. the singers,
5. the gatekeepers,
6. the *n^{e}tînîm*, and
7. the sons of Solomon's servants.

This list of population categories is repeated in Ezra 7.7, 24 and Neh. 10.28. Laypeople are grouped together as one. They are the people Israel. The writer provides the names of their ancestors and the names of their places of origin, but other aspects, such as their professions, do not interest him. Nevertheless their professions are real and serve to label some 'father's houses' just as they labeled the *ḫadru*s of Nippur. This can be seen in the list of wall builders in Nehemiah 3. That list has no hierarchical order and includes agnatic households of smiths, perfumers (Neh. 3.8) and merchants (Neh. 3.31), labels that are ignored by the writer of Ezra 2. The list in Ezra 2 does not portray the population as it conceived of itself. That self-perception is revealed in Nehemiah 3. Rather, the list is organized ideologically to express the composition of the 'true Israel'.

The Legitimate Population of a Restored Jerusalem

The authors of Haggai and Zechariah attempted to show that Ezekiel's programmatic ideals were implemented by the restoration community of Judah at the time of Darius (Hanson 1979). The restoration community portrayed in Ezra–Nehemiah also reflects Ezekiel's program for the future (Fried 2008). This can be seen in the population categories that are included and excluded from the population lists. The people listed in Ezra 2 (= Nehe-

nology constricts the Persian period even further—to thirty-four years in total. This is because it assumes that the prophecy in Dan. 11.24-27 refers to the destruction of Jerusalem and the temple under Rome (rather than under Antiochus IV). Since Daniel's 490 years are interpreted to refer to the 656 years between 586 BCE and 70 CE, the Persian period is compressed from two hundred to thirty-four years to make up the shortfall. This was not the concern of the editor of Ezra–Nehemiah, however, or of Daniel. For an interesting discussion of the issues, see First 1997.

2. The following is taken from Fried 2008.

miah 7) as well as in Nehemiah 11–12 comprise the legitimate population of Judah. It can be shown that the population categories used in Ezra and Nehemiah illustrate Ezekiel's notion of the ideal community.[3] According to Ezekiel, the people who return from Babylonian captivity will be first of all the united people Israel (Zimmerli 1979: 563-68). They will not be plagued by tribal divisions:

> Then say to them, Thus says Lord Yhwh: I will take the people of Israel from the nations among which they have gone, and will gather them from every quarter, and bring them to their own land. I will make them one nation in the land, on the mountains of Israel; and there will be one king for all of them. Never again shall they be two nations, and never again shall they be divided into two kingdoms (Ezek. 37.21-22).

Ezekiel's assertion that the dispersed brought back to its own land will be one people, namely Israel, has been reified in all the lists in Ezra–Nehemiah. It is the people Israel who has returned and who participates in the covenant renewal ceremony (Nehemiah 8–10). According to the population lists of Ezra 2 and Nehemiah 7 as well as in Nehemiah 11, the people settled in their towns are not Judeans and Benjaminites but 'the people Israel' (Ezra 2.2 = Neh. 7.7), the sons of Israel (Ezra 2; Neh. 7.72), or simply Israel (Neh. 11.3, 20). This is so, even though outside of these lists the people can be called the people of Judah (e.g. Ezra 4.4; Neh. 11.4) or even 'Judeans' (Ezra 4.23). Moreover, the list in Neh. 7.7 (= Ezra 2.1) begins with twelve names.[4] The number twelve cannot be accidental and likely indicates the writer's attempt to show that all twelve tribes of Israel are represented in the return (Ackroyd 1973: 218; Blenkinsopp 1988: 84).

The rest of the people registered in the lists of Ezra–Nehemiah all belong to the cultic community. As is well known, Ezekiel 1–39 strongly condemns every leadership group in pre-exilic Judah but the priesthood (Duguid 1994: 64). Priests are mentioned only twice in chaps. 1–39 of Ezekiel. In one case (7.26), Ezekiel does not accuse them of anything at all; instruction is said to perish from the priest as a result of the general destruction but not through any fault of his own (Duguid 1994: 65). In the other (22.26), Ezekiel remarks only that the priests failed to make a distinction between the holy and the profane, and that they ignored the Sabbaths, a passage likely dependent on Zeph. 3.4 (Duguid 1994: 72-75). While this is a serious offense (see Lev. 10.10), Ezekiel does not accuse them of the fall of Jerusalem nor blame them for the abominations in the temple. Indeed, he mentions no priest at all when he condemns these abominations (Ezekiel

3. I assume a coherent intention behind Ezekiel 1–39 and 40–48 (for a discussion see Levinson 1976; Niditch 1996; Tuell 1992; Duguid 1994, and the various commentaries).

4. There are only eleven in Ezra 2.2, but most likely one has dropped out through scribal error. There are twelve names in 1 Esdras.

8; Duguid 1994: 68-72). In fact, it is because the priests kept the charge of Yhwh's sanctuary that they will be the head of the community in Ezekiel's restored Jerusalem (44.15); that is, they will judge the people, a role previously reserved for the king and his appointees (44.24). The right to judge and thereby to determine legal precedence gives the priesthood the primary legislative and judicial roles in the restored community. This is evidently the mechanism by which Ezekiel intended the priesthood to wield secular power (Duguid 1994: 80). Correspondingly, in the population lists of Ezra and Nehemiah, priests are preeminent and participate in secular leadership roles. Jeshua son of Jozadak, the high priest, and his fellow priests, along with Zerubbabel, the Davidic heir and Persian governor, are shown building the altar to the god of Israel in the seventh month of the first year of their arrival in Jerusalem (Ezra 3.1-3). He with Zerubbabel and with the rest of the priests and Levites organizes the work on temple construction (Ezra 3.8-9), and he along with Zerubbabel rejects the offer of their enemies to participate in the building process (Ezra 4.1-3). Again, it is Jeshua, the high priest, who along with Zerubbabel the Persian governor, continues work on the temple in spite of efforts to stop it (Ezra 5.1-2). The high priest participates as a leader in every decision of the fledging community. This continues into Ezra 7–10, where Ezra himself is presented as a priest of high priestly lineage (Ezra 7.1-6) and in Nehemiah, where Eliashib, the chief priest, is presented as the indigenous head of the community, in contrast to Nehemiah the (foreign) Persian governor.

The Levites appear second in the population lists, and neither are they condemned in Ezekiel 1–39, the chapters in which the fall of Judah and Jerusalem are described. Ezekiel mentions the Levites for the first time only in chap. 44, in the group of chapters (40–48) in which his program for the ideal restoration community is described. Even though Ezekiel says there that the Levites are responsible for Israel's going astray and tells them that they must bear their guilt for it, he does not deprive them of any of their cultic privileges, and their role is not degraded.[5] They will continue to slaughter the burnt offerings and the sacrifices of the people; they will still be in charge of the sanctuary (44.14) and its gates (44.11):

> They shall be ministers in my sanctuary, having oversight over the gates of the temple, and serving in the temple; they shall slaughter the burnt offering and the sacrifice for the people, and they shall attend on them and serve them (Ezek. 44.11).

5. The role described for them in Ezekiel is that described in Numbers 3, 4, and 18, and I assume that this had been their role from the time of the fall of the northern kingdom (Duke 1988). See Duguid (1994: 83-90) and Min (2004: 55-56), who also recognize that the Levites held this role in the pre-exilic temple. Min states (p. 56) that Ezekiel promises the Levites that they will 'resume their duties as gatekeepers'. See discussion above at v. 40 for the origin of the Levites.

Ezekiel's command is implemented in Ezra–Nehemiah. According to Ezra 6.19, the Levites slaughtered the pascal sacrifice for the people after the dedication of the finished temple:

> For both the priests and the Levites had purified themselves together; all of them were clean. So they slaughtered the Passover lamb for all the returned exiles, for their fellow priests, and for themselves (Ezra 6.20).

The 'they' who do the slaughtering are the Levites. They slaughter it for the people Israel (the returned exiles), for the priests, and for themselves. This is as required by Ezekiel.[6]

Ezekiel also assigns the Levites the critical role of gatekeepers in the restored community (44.11). As gatekeepers, they are to manage the income and outgo of the temple's storerooms and treasuries, and serve as the temple's business managers and accountants (see 1 Chron. 9.26). These are the tasks of those secondary priests whom the Deuteronomic historian refers to as 'the guardians of the threshold' (1 Kgs 12.9; 2 Kgs 22.4; 23.4; 25.18; cf. 2 Chron. 34.9). This is consistent with Ezekiel's relegation to the Levites of the daily management and upkeep of the temple:

> They shall be ministers in my sanctuary, having oversight at the gates of the temple. I will appoint them to keep charge of the duties of the temple, to do all its work, all that is to be done in it (Ezek. 44.11a, 14).

As demanded by Ezekiel, in the restoration community portrayed by Ezra–Nehemiah, Levites are described as having oversight of the daily care of the temple. Everything that is not directly related to the altar is in their

6. *Pace* Min (2004: 75, *inter alia*). There is no attempt in Ezra–Nehemiah to show the Levites as equal to the priests. The priests are always listed separately and before the Levites. As support for his view that the text of Ezra–Nehemiah is biased toward the Levites, Min discusses Ezra 6.20 and proposes that the phrase הכהנים ו, 'the priests and', is not original, but added by a redactor who wanted to keep harmony among the clerical groups. Min (p. 77) argues that the reference to the Levites in this verse proves that this text was originally prolevitical and was later altered to be less so by adding 'the priests'. There is no evidence for such alteration of the text.

The levitical role in slaughtering the pascal sacrifice is spelled out in 2 Chron. 35.10, 11. The Levites slaughter the animal, the priests dash the blood upon the altar, the Levites skin it. This does not show a parity of Levites with priests. As dictated by Ezekiel (and probably also by ancient practice) the priests are the only ones who may approach the altar and handle the blood.

Min (pp. 81-84) also argues for levitical authorship of Ezra–Nehemiah on the basis of the reference to Jeremiah in Ezra 1.1. Jeremiah is a priest, however, not a Levite (Jer. 1.1); Anathoth was one of the cities ceded to the descendants of Aaron, not to the Levites (Josh. 21.13-18). This is affirmed in 1 Chron. 6.42-45 (ET 57-60). The non-Aaronide levitical cities were in the north (Joshua 21); when the north fell, the Levites fled south and joined the temple personnel as second order priests. Anathoth was in Benjamin and in the south when the north fell.

hands. As gatekeepers (Ezek. 44.11a), they guard the gates (Neh. 13.22), and stand with the priests to accept temple donations (Ezra 8.29, 30, 33; Neh. 10.33; 13.13). Moreover, as Ezekiel requires (44.14), the Levites have oversight of the work of the temple:

> They appointed the Levites, from twenty years old and upward, to have the oversight of the work on the house of Yhwh. And Jeshua with his sons and his kin, and Kadmiel and his sons, Binnui and Hodaviah along with the sons of Henadad, the Levites, their sons and kin, together took charge of the workers in the house of God (Ezra 3.8b, 9)—

both outside . . .

> Shabbethai and Jozabad, of the leaders of the Levites, were the ones over the outside work of the house of God (Neh. 11.16)

. . . and inside—

> The overseer of the Levites in Jerusalem was Uzzi son of Bani son of Hashabiah son of Mattaniah son of Mica, of the descendants of Asaph, the singers. He was in charge of the business of the house of God (Neh. 11.22).

Thus, as Ezekiel requires, Ezra–Nehemiah portrays the Levites as engaged in all those temple activities that do not directly relate to the manipulation of the blood upon the altar, a task reserved for the priests.

The population lists in Ezra–Nehemiah place the levitical singers after the gatekeepers. Ezekiel imagined a role for the singers in the temple service, and gave them two chambers inside the rebuilt temple:

> At the inner gate there were chambers for the singers in the inner court, one at the side of the north gate facing south, the other at the side of the south gate facing north (Ezek. 40.44).[7]

Temple singers play a correspondingly strong role in Ezra–Nehemiah. Levitical singers, the sons of Asaph, sing and play music during at the ceremony for laying the temple's foundations (Ezra 3.10, 11):

> When the builders laid the foundation of the temple of Yhwh, the priests with their equipment were stationed to praise Yhwh with trumpets, and the Levites, the sons of Asaph, with cymbals, according to the directions of King David of Israel; and they sang responsively, praising and giving thanks to Yhwh, 'For he is good, for his steadfast love endures forever toward Israel'.

The levitical singers also participate in regular temple services and in other cultic celebrations (Ezra 6.18; Neh. 12.8, 24, 27):

7. *Pace* Zimmerli (1983: 364), who considers 'singers', שרים, to be a misreading for שתים, 'two', and that the word 'singers' is not present in the text.

> As for the Levites, Jeshua, Binnui, Kadmiel, Sherebiah, Judah, and Mattaniah; he and his associates were in charge of the songs of thanksgiving (Neh. 12.8).[8]

> And the leaders of the Levites: Hashabiah, Sherebiah, and Jeshua son of Kadmiel, with their associates over against them, to praise and to give thanks, according to the commandment of David the man of God, section opposite to section (Neh. 12.24).

The singers are given an especially important role at Nehemiah's wall ceremony:

> Now at the dedication of the wall of Jerusalem they sought out the Levites in all their places, to bring them to Jerusalem to celebrate the dedication with rejoicing, with thanksgivings and with singing, with cymbals, harps, and lyres (Neh. 12.27).

In accordance with Ezekiel's prescriptions, the Levites in Ezra–Nehemiah are second-order priests. They are gatekeepers and singers. They never approach the altar; they never manipulate the blood, but as gatekeepers they manage the business of the temple, its income and its outgo.

Still lower in the hierarchy of temple personnel are the *n*^{e}*tînîm* and the descendants of Solomon's servants. Neither group is mentioned in Ezekiel, and it is likely that Ezekiel did not know about them. They are listed only in postexilic sources and may not have been a pre-exilic institution (*pace* Levine 1963: 207-12. See discussion at 2.43-44). Outside of Ezra–Nehemiah, they are mentioned only in 1 Chron. 9.2. The phrase 'descendants of Solomon's servants' may have been an editorial gloss to explain the unfamiliar term *n*^{e}*tînîm.* The numbers of these two groups are totaled together in the population lists (Ezra 2.58 = Neh. 7.60), suggesting they were one group; and the phrase is omitted entirely from other lists of cultic officials (e.g. Ezra 7.24 and 8.24). Although the *n*^{e}*tînîm* are viewed by the author of Ezra 7–10 as having been appointed by David (Ezra 8.20), they are cultic officials of the postexilic period, and so we may add them to Ezekiel's categories of the legitimate population of Judah.

The Personae Non Gratae

The groups omitted from the population lists in Ezra–Nehemiah also reflect Ezekiel's idea of the legitimate people of Israel. Those omitted are the very ones whom Ezekiel considers unwelcome, his *personae non gratae.* Most notably, no secular leader with his title is included in these lists. Zerubbabel is listed (Ezra 2.2); he is even listed first, but no title is ever given him in

8. It is not clear who the 'he' is. As the Masoretes understood the text, it is not Mattaniah since they placed an *atnach* after his name. I suspect that at least they understood the text to refer to Jeshua and his associates.

Ezra (Japhet 1982: 68-71). We see him take a leadership role (Ezra 3.2, 8; 4.3; 5.2), but we only learn he is governor of Judah under Darius I from Haggai (1.1; 2.3). As the son of Shealtiel (Ezra 3.2), he is the Davidic heir, a direct descendant of Jehoiachin, king of Judah, but we only learn this from Chronicles (1 Chron. 3.17-24). Even Sheshbazzar, who is called *nāśî'* in Ezra 1, is excluded from the lists of returnees (Ezra 2.2 = Neh. 7.7). This is because Ezekiel condemns the secular rulers, those whom he refers to variously as king, as *nāśî',* or as shepherd:

> See the rulers (*nāśî'îm*) of Israel! Every one used his power there for the sake of shedding blood (Ezek. 22.6). A conspiracy of the rulers (*nāśî'îm*)[9] [of Jerusalem] is like a roaring lion tearing the prey; they have devoured human lives; they have taken treasure and precious things; they have made many widows within it (Ezek. 22.25).

Ezekiel, referring to the kings as 'shepherds', blames them for the exile:

> You [shepherds of the sheep of Judah] have not strengthened the weak, you have not healed the sick, you have not bound up the injured, you have not brought back the strayed, you have not sought the lost, but with force and harshness you have treaded on them. So they were scattered, because there was no shepherd; and scattered, they became food for all the wild animals (Ezek. 34.4, 5).

Therefore, Ezekiel states that God is against the shepherds (34.10); God himself will be their shepherd (34.11-16). Yhwh alone shall be their king and their shepherd in a restored Judah (20.33; 34.11, 15, 20). In practical terms, this implies a theocracy. Nevertheless, there will also be a role for the Davidic heir:

> I will raise over them one shepherd, my servant David, and he shall feed them: he shall feed them and be their shepherd. And I, Yhwh, will be their god, and my servant David shall be *nāśî'* among them; I, Yhwh, have spoken (Ezek. 34.23-24).

Ezekiel's conception of the restoration of Judah is spelled out in chaps. 40–48, and there the role of the Davidic heir as *nāśî',* shepherd, and as provider for his people is delineated. What does it mean to feed the people, and what does it mean to be a *nāśî'* among them? Whatever it means, it is certain that things will not be as they once were; the king will not have the powers he once did:

> As for you, vile, wicked *nāśî'* of Israel, you whose day has come, the time of final reckoning. Thus says Lord Yhwh: Remove the turban, take off the crown; things shall not remain as they are. Exalt that which is low, abase that which is high. A ruin, a ruin, a ruin I will make it—as has never

9. The Hebrew reads 'her prophets' נְבִיאֶיהָ, an error for 'her princes', נשיאיה.

occurred—until he comes whose right it is; to him I will give it (Ezek. 21.30-32).

The Davidic king who ruled in the monarchic period will be abased in restoration Judah, but he will have a role. He will provide for the flock (34.23, 24), but he shall not rule. Ezekiel states explicitly how the Davidic heir shall provide for the sheep:

> And this shall be the obligation of the *nāśî'* regarding the burnt offerings, grain offerings, and drink offerings, at the festivals, the new moons, and the sabbaths, all the appointed festivals of the house of Israel: he shall provide the sin offerings, grain offerings, the burnt offerings, and the offerings of well-being, to make atonement for the house of Israel (Ezek. 45.17).

The obligations of the Davidic prince continue unabated. In addition to the above, on the first day of the first month he shall also provide a young bull (45.21); on *each* of the seven days of the Passover holiday he shall provide seven bulls and seven rams, plus a male goat (45.23). In addition, he must provide an *ephah* of flour for each bull and for each ram that he offers, plus a *hin* of oil for each (45.24). He must provide this same ration for each of the seven days of the Sukkot holiday as well (45.25). This is what Ezekiel has in mind when he says that the Davidic *nāśî'* will feed the flock. Although the Davidic heir will feed the flock, none but the priests will govern it: 'In a controversy they (the priests) shall act as judges, and they shall decide it according to my laws and my regulations' (Ezek. 44.24a). In any litigation, the priests shall judge, according to their understanding of God's laws and rules. In Ezekiel's plan the priests will thereby obtain secular as well as sacral authority.[10] The *nāśî'* (i.e. the Davidic king), who had ruled in the pre-exilic period, is now abased. He does not judge but merely provides for the cult. Someone else will bear both secular authority (symbolized by the crown) and sacral authority (symbolized by the turban; 21.31, 32).[11] In Ezekiel's program, he who had been abased (or whom Ezekiel saw as having been abased), that someone will now be exalted, wearing both turban and crown. That someone is the high priest.[12] Zerubbabel appears to build the

10. *Pace* Duguid (1994: 54), who argues on the basis of 45.9, that the Davidic heir is still responsible for the judicial system. The command there 'to do what is just and right' does not provide authority to administrate the courts, however. It is no more than a command that would be given to anyone who had oppressed others in the past. Boda maintains (2003: 286-87) that in Ezekiel's plan, the Davidic heir will be a shepherd in restored Judah, but he does not state what powers, if any, this shepherd will have.

11. That the turban indicated here, the מצנפת, is the symbol of the high priest is indicated by Exod. 28.4, 37, 39; 29.6; 39.28, 31; Lev. 8.9; 16.4.

12. Rooke (2000: 19) asks why this double authority should be in the hands of the high priest rather than the king. The statement that what was high will be low and what was low will be high (21.30-32) implies that he who had held supreme authority in the past (i.e. the king) will not hold it in the future; he who had not held it (the high priest),

altar (Ezra 3.2) and the temple (Ezra 3.8; 5.2), but that is all. The Chronicler reports (1 Chron. 3.19) that he had sons (Meshullam and Hananiah), but they are not recorded as playing a role in the restoration community.

The 'people of the land' is another group that is condemned by Ezekiel and that does not appear in the population lists of Ezra–Nehemiah. They are the aristocratic (nonroyal) lay leadership. According to Ezekiel, the 'people of the land' had wronged the poor and the needy—and stand condemned:

> The 'people of the land' (*'am hā'āreṣ*) have practiced fraud and committed robbery; they have wronged the poor and needy, have defrauded the stranger without redress. . . . Therefore I have poured out my indignation upon them; I will finish them off with the fire of my fury. I will repay them for their conduct—declares Lord Yhwh (Ezek. 22.29, 31).

The 'people of the land', like the *nāśî'*, are obviously present in the community of Ezra and Nehemiah (Ezra 4.4; see discussion *ad loc.*), but they are not included in the population lists. They are not part of the legitimate population of restored Israel.

The elders of the house of Israel are also missing from the population registry of Ezra–Nehemiah. Ezekiel holds them, and not the priests, responsible for all the abominations in the temple (Ezek. 8.11, 12; and especially 9.6). He provides them no role in restored Israel (Ezekiel 40–48). They are correspondingly absent from the population lists, although they are certainly present as leaders in the restoration community (Ezra 6.7; 10.8).

Also missing from the list of returnees is the guild of prophets, the *b^{e}nê n^{e}bî'îm*. Of all the groups that Ezekiel condemns, he assigns the prophets the primary responsibility for the fall of Jerusalem:

> My hand is against the prophets, who prophesy falsehood and utter lying divination. They shall not remain in the assembly of my people, they shall not be inscribed in the register of the House of Israel, and they shall not return to the land of Israel. Thus shall you know that I am Lord Yhwh (Ezek. 13.9).

Ezekiel asserts that God is against the prophets. They will not be registered in the list of the population of Israel, and they will not return to the land. This too is borne out in the population lists of Ezra–Nehemiah. No prophets are included in the population roll, even though there certainly were prophets in Persian Yehud. In addition to Haggai and Zechariah, who are explicitly mentioned (Ezra 5.1; 6.14), there were also Malachi and perhaps Joel.

will hold it now. Rooke agrees that in pre-exilic Judah the priest was the servant of the king. The opposite is therefore predicted for restored Jerusalem. Nor does Konkel (2001: 272-79) see a special role for the *nāśî'* other than his responsibility for providing the expenses for the cult and for ensuring fair weights and measures.

Nehemiah also refers to the 'prophetess No'adiah and the rest of the prophets in Judah who wanted to make him afraid (6.7, 14). Ezra 1.1 refers to 'the mouth of Jeremiah', revealing dependence on a source, perhaps 2 Chron. 36.22. As discussed in the Introduction, Chronicles' dependence on the prophetic voice is a major difference between it and Ezra–Nehemiah; four references to Jeremiah appear in the last twenty-five verses of Chronicles alone (Redditt 2008: 230). Nevertheless, the prophets are not listed among the categories of the restored population of Israel. In fulfillment of Ezekiel's word, they are not counted in the register of the returnees.

Ezekiel's mistrust of all secular leadership is felt throughout the book Ezra–Nehemiah. According to the outlook presented in these chapters, Cyrus is trusted but only because he is a puppet whose strings are pulled by God himself (Ezra 1.1, 2). In spite of Cyrus's beneficence, the new arrivals do not depend on earthly leadership. Instead, they immediately build an altar to the god of Israel, offering burnt offerings on it day and night because of the dread upon them of the 'peoples of the lands' (Ezra 3.3). They build the altar and manage to start work on the foundations of the temple (Ezra 3.10, 11), when they are suddenly confronted by enemies, oppressors, that is, the 'people of the land' (Ezra 4.1, 4, 5). These enemies persuade the Persian king Artaxerxes to put a stop to all work on the temple-building project (Ezra 4.21). At Artaxerxes' command, Persian officials arrive with armed force and stop the work (Ezra 4.24). It is only by the decree of the god of Israel that the Persian kings again permit the temple to be completed (Ezra 6.14).

Japhet (1982: 75-76) characterizes the worldview of Ezra 1–6 as, on the one hand, 'one in which kings of Persia determine even the smallest details of the destiny of those peoples under their rule, making the lives of these people dependent on the good will and favor of the Persian kings'. On the other, she argues that Ezra–Nehemiah exhibit 'full acceptance of this situation, and the understanding of it not only as an expression of God's will and his sovereign guidance of the world, but as a divine grace and as God's way of redeeming his people'. Although I agree that this is certainly a realistic picture of life in the Persian Empire (Fried 2004), the writers of Ezra–Nehemiah are preaching a different image. By portraying the restored community as fulfilling the predictions of Ezekiel, they present a world in which it is not the Persian kings who determine the destiny of the Jewish people, and it is not the favor and good will of the Persian kings upon which they must depend, but one in which God is the only king, the true power. God alone pulls the strings of his royal puppets, and it is only his favor and good will that are necessary.

Ezra 3.1-6a

The Prologue (Continued): The Protagonists Are Introduced, the Altar Is Built, Sukkot Is Celebrated

According to Aristotelian rules of rhetoric, the goal of any text is to persuade the reader (*Rhetoric* 1356a1).[1] One way to persuade the reader and to increase his confidence in the reliability of the text was by demonstrating the author's access to relevant sources. This was the purpose of the lists of temple vessels, of returnees, and of donations to the temple. Besides the lists, narrative provides the author with two other modes of persuasion (*Rhetoric* 1356a1-5): first, by leading the reader to identify with the protagonists (*ethos*); and second, by arousing cathartic emotions in him (*pathos*). The prologue therefore introduces the protagonists and attempts to create in the reader a favorable attitude toward them, an attitude that fosters identification (*ethos*). The initial positive attitude should be strengthened by describing the good fortune that the protagonists enjoy, proving they are favored by the gods.

In continuing the prologue begun in chaps. 1 and 2, chap. 3 seeks to focus on individual protagonists—Zerubbabel and Jeshua—and to arouse in the reader a favorable attitude toward them. We read that as soon as the returnees were settled in their towns, they gathered as one man in Jerusalem to build an altar to the god of Israel and to offer burnt offerings upon it according to the law of Moses (Ezra 3.1-6a). Not only do they follow the law of Moses, but they obey the edict of Cyrus too by paying the carpenters and masons their correct fees and by bringing cedar trees from Lebanon by sea to Jaffa as Cyrus had authorized (3.6b, 7). The enthusiasm and concern shown by Zerubbabel, Jeshua and the rest of the returnees for the laws of both God and king are intended to testify to their high moral character.

By starting the story of his major protagonists with the altar-building scene, however, the author has distorted the underlying Mesopotamian temple-building template. He has moved the altar-building scene from its

1. This section is based on Fried 2012a.

usual place at the end of the typical Mesopotamian temple-building story to the prologue of his narrative (see Introduction to Ezra 1–6 for the structure of typical Mesopotamian temple-building stories). In the process, he has transformed the story from a Mesopotamian temple-building account to a Greek one. Building an altar and sacrificing on it before a temple is built is anomalous in the ancient Near East (Hurowitz 1992; Boda and Novotny 2010). Sacrificing on an isolated altar with no temple present at all, however, is typical of Hellenistic and Greek ritual practices. Indeed the sacrificial altar is the only necessary ingredient when establishing a Greek cult site; a temple did not need to be built at all (Burford 1969; Burkert 1985: 55-59; Fried 2013b: 283-300; 2014: 154-61). Moving the altar-building component to the beginning of his story demonstrates a Hellenistic date for its composition. It also allows the protagonists, Zerubbabel and Joshua, to be introduced immediately.

Translation

1. *When the seventh month arrived,*[a] *and the Israelites*[b] *were in their cities,*[c] *the people*[d] *gathered as one man to Jerusalem.*[e] 2. *Then Jeshua son of Jozadak, and his kinsmen the priests, and Zerubbabel son of Shealtiel, and his kin, rose and built*[f] *the altar of the god of Israel, in order to offer upon it whole burnt offerings as is written in the torah*[g] *of Moses, the man of God.*[h] 3. *They founded the altar on its foundations*[i] *because of the terror upon them*[j] *from the peoples of the lands. They sacrificed upon it whole burnt offerings to Yhwh, the burnt offerings of the morning and evening.* 4. *And they observed the festival of Booths, as it is written,*[k] *that is, the sacrifice of the day in* [*its*] *day in* [*its*] *number according to the law of the matter of the day on its day.* 5. *And after that* [*they sacrificed*][l] *the perpetual daily offerings,*[m] *the offerings for the new moons and for all of the* [*other*] *consecrated times of Yhwh,*[n] *and every free-will offering freely offered to Yhwh.* 6. *From the first day of the seventh month*[o] *they began to offer sacrifices to Yhwh.*

Textual Notes

a. **3.1** *When the seventh month arrived.* The verb here is נגע, *nāga'*, which usually means 'to touch', in the usual sense (e.g. Gen. 3.3; 20.6), or 'to strike', as with the plagues (Gen. 12.17). It is used to refer to the arrival of time only here, in other late texts (Ezek. 7.12; Est. 2.12; 9.1), and in the corresponding verse in Nehemiah (Neh. 7.72 [7.73]).

b. *The Israelites.* Literally, 'sons of Israel'.

c. *In their cities.* Ezra actually reads 'in the cities'. The versions (Greek Ezra, Neh. 7.72, Syriac, Vulgate) read 'in their cities', which is likely correct, the letter ה having dropped out, reading בעריהם instead of בערים. First Esdras reads 'each in their own [. . .]'.

The noun is missing, but the use of *idiois* suggests a possessive pronoun in the *Vorlage*, supporting Nehemiah (Talshir 2001: 292).

d. *The people.* Nehemiah 8.1 reads 'all the people'. This phrase is missing in 1 Esdras, reading simply 'they gathered'.

e. *To Jerusalem.* Instead of 'to Jerusalem', 1 Esd. 5.46 reads, 'in the square before the first gate toward the east'. Nehemiah reads, 'to the square which is before the Water Gate'. The Water Gate was evidently the first gate toward the east in front of the temple (Neh. 3.26; 12.37; Eshel 2001: 104). The verse in 1 Esdras was likely copied originally from Neh. 8.1, or from something like it, and refers to Ezra's reading the law. The reference to gates was dropped to fit the narrative of Ezra 1–6, since the gates have not yet been built. See further the discussions at Ezra 7.7 and Neh. 8.1.

f. **3.2** *Rose and built the altar.* First Esdras reads 'prepared the altar'. This may show the influence of וַיָּכִינוּ at the beginning of the next verse, which means 'prepare, get ready' as well as 'set up'. It is easy to mistake יבנו, 'they built', for יכינו, 'they prepared', in an unvocalized text. The verb 'rose' is in the singular, even though it has a plural subject. This is not uncommon, but one could suppose that only Jeshua the high priest is referred to. The verb 'built' is plural, however.

g. *Torah of Moses.* First Esdras reads 'book of Moses'.

h. *Man of God.* The Syriac reads 'the prophet of God' rather than 'man of God'.

i. **3.3** *They founded the altar on its foundations.* Literally, 'They set up the altar in its spot', but the same Hebrew root is used for both the verb and the noun. The word 'original' is not in the text but is implied by the use of the pronoun 'its'. Ezra has a plural for the noun, 'on its foundations', but with a singular sense as in Greek Ezra, 1 Esdras, and the Peshitta.

j. *Of the terror.* The Hebrew reads, literally, 'because in terror upon them'. The Syriac reads 'great fear'. See note on this below.

k. **3.4** *As it is written.* First Esdras reads, 'as commanded in the law'.

l. **3.5** [*They sacrificed*]. This is inserted to make sense of the passage.

m. *Perpetual daily offerings.* Reading the plural with 1 Esdras, Greek Esdras, and the Syriac. The Hebrew is vocalized as a feminine singular construct, interpreting the *tamid* as a noun (the *tamid,* or regular, offering), rather than as an adverb, 'perpetual'. 1 Esdras inserts a reference to the Sabbatical offerings.

n. *Consecrated times of Yhwh.* First Esdras finishes the verse here and connects the rest of the verse to the following.

o. **3.6** *From the first day of the seventh month.* First Esdras reads, 'And all who had made any vow to God began to offer sacrifices to God, from the new moon of the seventh month'. First Esdras customarily interprets a free-will offering as a vow. See note on 1.4.

Notes

3.1 ***When the seventh month arrived.*** No year is specified. Mention of the seventh month is consistent with ancient Near Eastern temple-building stories, which customarily begin 'in a propitious month on a favorable day' (Hurowitz 1992: 225). In Israelite tradition, there is no more propitious month than the seventh, and no more propitious day than the first.

This chapter can be read in two ways. The first is to read it according to the intent of the Hellenistic author, so that we are introduced to the major characters as they set up the altar in the seventh month of the first year of Cyrus. A second way is to try to understand the historical reality that underpins the report. Historically speaking, the following verses, which name Jeshua and Zerubbabel, suggest that the altar was not set up in the time of Cyrus at all but in the time of Darius. The prophets Haggai and Zechariah place Jeshua and Zerubbabel firmly to the time of Darius I (as does 1 Esdras). Historically speaking, Zerubbabel was governor of Judah under Darius; Sheshbazzar, under Cyrus.

According to what is known from ancient Mesopotamian temple-building inscriptions, altars are erected toward the end of the building process, not at the beginning (see Introduction). If the account in Ezra 1–6 is based on the second-temple's actual building inscription, as I have proposed, and if it conformed originally to the typical ancient Near Eastern temple-building account, as I assume, then the account of setting up the altar (Ezra 3.1-6) was moved from near the end of the original building story to here at the beginning. This was done both to conform to the Hellenistic practice in the creation of cult sites and to introduce the protagonists at the beginning of the narrative.

Were gathered. They gathered spontaneously, without anyone assembling them, as one man to Jerusalem as soon as the holy seventh month approached (Gunneweg 1985: 70). This shows God's spirit working within them. As discussed in the Introduction, this verse was taken from Neh. 7.73 and 8.1 when the list itself was copied. It assumes that the people had been living in their towns for a while at least.

3.2 ***Jeshua son of Jozadak.*** See note on Ezra 2.2.

Kinsmen, the priests. As is customary in the ancient Near East and Egypt, members of the priestly caste are all of a single or of very few lineages (see Fried 2004).

Zerubbabel son of Shealtiel. See note at Ezra 2.2. The order of the names of the two men is reversed from the order given in Ezra 2.2, no doubt because the high priest should take control of building the altar to ensure it is done according to specifications.

And his kin. This verse introduces the major characters in the drama. Since Zerubbabel is a descendant of King David (1 Chron. 3.17-19), his kin includes members of the royal family. Neither Jeshua nor Zerubbabel receive a title in Ezra, however, whereas in Haggai, Jeshua is referred to as the high priest and Zerubbabel as the governor of Judah. Gunneweg suggests that this does not imply lack of respect for these offices but that the only authority in these chapters is the torah of Moses, the man of God (Gunneweg 1985: 72). It may be that neither Zerubbabel's title and lineage nor the title and lineage of Jeshua, grandson of the last high priest (1 Chron.

6.14-15), are given in Ezra to show an acceptance of the political situation, that the writer had no aspirations for an independent state, and that the divine will was now actualized through the Persian kings (Japhet 1982: 73).

Alternatively, it may be that the author was keen to follow Aristotle's rules of rhetoric and poetry. In order to create catharsis, the reader must be able to identify with the protagonists. That means they should be ordinary people, neither virtuous nor wicked, but ones who fall between these two extremes (*Poetry* 38.53a1-13). For the author, this demand may rule out the Davidic heir and the high priest. The author seeks to tell the story in a way that enables ordinary people to identify with them. (More on this in the note on Ezra 4.3.)

Whole burnt offerings. This altar is then the large sacrificial altar that stood outside the temple, in contrast to the smaller incense altar that stood inside. The narrator does not mention that a previous altar stood there that had to be demolished, so the original altar had likely been destroyed by the Babylonians. The three biblical laws for constructing the altar may be compared (Heger 1999: 18). They differ both in the material prescribed and in the verb used ('make' or 'build'). They are usually assigned to three different authors:

> If you make for me an altar of *stone*, do not *build* it of hewn stones; for if you use a chisel upon it you profane it (Exod. 20.25) (usually assigned to the E writer, emphasis added).
>
> You shall *make* the altar of acacia *wood*, five cubits long and five cubits wide; the altar shall be square, and it shall be three cubits high. You shall make horns for it on its four corners; its horns shall be of one piece with it, and you shall overlay it with bronze (Exod. 27.1-2) (usually assigned to P, emphasis added).
>
> And you shall *build* an altar there to Yhwh your god, an altar of *stones* on which you have not used an iron tool (Deut. 27.5) (usually assigned to D, emphasis added).

Since the operative word in Ezra 3.2 is 'build' not 'make', the altar referred to here was made of stone, as commanded in Exodus 20 and Deuteronomy 27 (Heger 1999: 18). For altars of wood and bronze (Exod. 27.1-2) or bronze alone (2 Chron. 4.1), the word used is 'make' not 'build'. The Chronicler describes Solomon's altar as made not built, and composed of bronze, following the pattern laid down by P. That the author of Ezra follows a different law, and uses a different verb from that used by the Chronicler, is another indication of two separate authors for Chronicles and Ezra (Heger 1999: 18). It does seem that the author here has the law in Deuteronomy in mind, not the law in Exodus 20, however. According to the Deuteronomist, Moses, the 'man of God' (Deut. 33.1), requires the people to build an altar as soon as they cross over the Jordan (27.4, 5). It may be this command that the author quotes. Building an altar without a temple suggests a late redaction of this Deuteronomic passage and incidentally of all the other passages in Genesis and in Samuel where isolated altars are built (Fried 2013b; 2014: 154-61).

Torah of Moses. The word 'torah' occurs 223 times in various forms in the Hebrew Bible, but most of these do not refer to a written document. Genesis 26.5, for example, quotes God as saying that 'Abraham obeyed my voice and kept my charge, my commandments, my precepts, and my torahs'. Here 'torahs' is plural and cannot refer to a specific written document. In Leviticus it often simply means 'procedure', as in Lev. 6.9, 'this is the torah for the burnt offering', that is, 'this is how to perform the burnt offering'. In these cases, it should probably be translated 'procedure', 'norm', 'right action', 'custom', rather than 'law' in the modern sense of legislated legal requirements. In the passage here in Ezra 3.2, however, the reference is to the 'torah of Moses', and moreover to what was *written* in the 'torah of Moses'. The complete phrase 'torah of Moses' occurs only fourteen times in the Bible, and in ten of these the referent is to a written document. In Nehemiah 8 we have Ezra reading from the 'torah of Moses', so that at some point in the history of Israel the concept of 'torah' changed from meaning 'custom' or 'procedure' to referring to a written law book authored by Moses. Exactly when that change took place is beyond the scope of this commentary, but perhaps it should be assigned to the Hellenistic period when Nehemiah 8 was composed (Fried 2013b: 283-300).

There is a literary contradiction in the mention of the torah of Moses in this passage, however. The implication of Nehemiah 8 is that the people did not know the law of Moses until Ezra read it to them during the time of Nehemiah, that they had never heard of the festival of Sukkoth before, and certainly that they had not previously observed it (Neh. 8.14-18). According to Ezra 3.4, however, they celebrated the festival of Sukkoth as soon as they arrived, sacrificing the correct number of sacrifices on each day of the holiday, as was written in this torah of Moses that they did not yet know and that Ezra had not yet brought!

Man of God. The Hebrew Bible uses this phrase sixty-four times to refer to Moses, David, Samuel, Elijah, Elisha, and several other little-known or unnamed prophets. The epithet is also used of a supernatural angel, a non-human messenger of God, who informed an Israelite woman that she would have a son (i.e. Samson, Judg. 13.6). The unifying characteristic of all these may be their ability to act as God's messenger on earth. The Chronicler calls David a 'man of God' (2 Chron. 8.14), as does the author of Ezra–Nehemiah (Neh. 12.24, 36), portraying him as a prophet, privy to the divine word (Newsome 1975). Outside of the present verse, the Hebrew Bible refers to Moses as a man of God only twice (Deut. 33.1 and Josh. 14.6).

3.3 ***On its foundations.*** That is, its original foundations, the place where it had been during the first temple period. This is crucial in temple building in the ancient Near East. When the temple of Yhw on the Nile island of Elephantine was destroyed in 410, the Judeans requested permission to 'rebuild it on its site as it was formerly' (*TAD* A 4.9:8). See Galling (1961: 70) for the numerous examples from ancient Near Eastern building inscriptions that testify to the importance of erecting temples and altars on the precise spot where they had been before.

Because of the terror upon them. In the clause as it stands, 'terror' is the object of the preposition 'in'. Literally it reads: כי בְּאֵימָה עֲלֵיהֶם מֵעַמֵּי הָאֲרָצוֹת, 'Because in terror upon them from the peoples of the lands'.

1 Esdras has quite a different reading for the verse:

> And some joined them from the other peoples of the land. And they erected the altar in its place, for all the peoples of the land were in enmity against them and were stronger than they; and they offered sacrifices at the proper times and burnt offerings to the Lord morning and evening.

This would imply that even though all of these other peoples were hostile, some of them joined with the Judeans to help set them up the altar, an unlikely scenario. The *Vorlage* to 1 Esdras may have read באים, 'they are coming', instead of באימה, 'in dread' (Talshir 2001: 296). Williamson (1985: 41) proposes an original בא אימה עליהם, 'a dread came upon them', in which the aleph at the end of בא ('it came') and the aleph at the beginning of אימה ('terror') elided through haplography. However the word for 'terror', אימה, is feminine, so instead of בא you would need באה, and it is hard to explain away the absence of the final ה.

From the peoples of the lands. The 'peoples of the lands' are the neighboring peoples round about. (For a discussion of this term, see Comment B below.) The writer adds this verse to provide a rationale for building the altar right away, quite outside of the customary order of temple building (see Introduction to Ezra 1–6, and Comment B below).

The morning and evening sacrifices. The evening sacrifices were carried out in the late afternoon, the morning one, mid-morning. These were the two regular daily sacrifices (Num. 28.4) and were intended to provide the god with the two meals a day that were customary in antiquity (although a light snack was carried along and eaten at mid-day; King and Stager 2001: 67).

3.4 ***According to the law of the matter of the day on its day.*** The laws of the sacrifices for the eight days of Sukkoth (the holiday of 'Booths', or 'Tabernacles') are specified in Num. 29.12-38. They are also referred to in Lev. 23.34-36. (See Comment C below on the holiday of Sukkoth.) Although there is no mention in Ezra that they lived in booths, the holiday is called 'Booths'. (See Comment D below on the purposes of sacrifice in antiquity.)

3.5 *The perpetual daily offerings.* These are the regular daily morning and evening sacrifices.

3.6 *From the first day.* According to the medieval commentator Rabbi David ben Zimra (1462–1572), on the first day of the seventh month a sporadic beginning was made. After the festival of Sukkoth, the full schedule of the sacrifices began in earnest.

Seventh month. We are not told which year. The author wants us to think this all happened right away, in the seventh month in the first year of Cyrus. The seventh month is in the fall, usually around September. The first month is in the spring, usually in April.

Comments

A. The Altar-Building Episode: Ezra 3.1-6

The author of Ezra 1–6 intends to suggest by his arrangement of these chapters that the altar was set up in the seventh month after the arrival of the returnees under Cyrus. Ezra 1 states that the return began in the first year of Cyrus the Great (538 BCE), and the position of chap. 2 implies that the men listed there all returned that same year at their first opportunity. This is so, in spite of the fact that Sheshbazzar is not included in the list of returnees. According to the author, then, they built the sacrificial altar that same year, before even the foundations of the temple were laid (3.6). Thus, from the seventh month of the very first year of their arrival, the first year of Cyrus, they kept the holidays as well as the daily morning and evening offerings, etc., all according to the regulations of the torah of Moses.

There are difficulties in accepting this timetable, however. Ezra 3.1-6a concerns Zerubbabel, the governor of Judah, and Jeshua, the high priest. According to the books of Haggai and Zechariah, these two men were active in the reign of Darius I, not Cyrus, so that this passage regarding the altar must be dated later, to the time of Darius, not Cyrus. Tattenai's letter (Ezra 5) confirms, moreover, that the temple's foundations were laid not by Zerubbabel in the time of Darius but rather by Sheshbazzar in the time of Cyrus, many years before (Ezra 5.16). (For the dates of the Persian kings, see Appendix. For a discussion of the authenticity of Tattenai's letter, see Comment A to Ezra 5.) Tattenai's letter (Ezra 5.2) refers to the time when Zerubbabel and Jeshua *began* to work on the temple, and that was not until temple building had progressed far past the foundations. Indeed, the walls were already high enough for Tattenai to describe their mode of construction (see discussion at 5.8). Thus, we may regard Ezra 3.1-6 as having been inserted secondarily into its present position. This insertion required the addition of the resumptive clause (Ezra 3.6b). Historically speaking, the altar was not built until the reign of Darius.

The nucleus of 3.1-6a was likely moved to its present location from its original position toward the end of the second temple's building inscription. This nucleus consists of Ezra 3.2, 3a. Verse 1 was included when the list of returnees of chap. 2 was copied from Nehemiah 7. Ezra 3.3b was needed to explain why they would set up the altar even before the temple was built. Verses 4-6a were created to show the reader how zealous for the law the protagonists were and to exemplify their good will and dedication, as was required by Aristotelian rules of rhetoric.

Hellenistic rules of rhetoric demand that a writer create a prologue in which he sets the scene and introduces his characters (Wisse 1989: 13).[2] The author should use the prologue to convince his readers of his characters' high moral character and of their good will (Aristotle, *Rhetoric* 1356a1). Ezra 1.1-8 sets the stage, indicating time and place, and detailing the background of the story. Chapter 3 continues the prologue by introducing the characters and detailing their high moral character.

Although building an altar and sacrificing on it before the temple is built is anomalous according to ancient Near Eastern theological understandings, setting up a sacrificial altar is the necessary first step in establishing a cult site in Greece (Burford 1969: 47). Indeed, sacrificing on an isolated altar with no temple present at all is typical of Greek ritual practices. As is clear from any of the Homeric myths, and in contrast to the Mesopotamian gods, Greek gods did not dwell in temples, but lived on Mt Olympus, in the sky, or in Hades. Sacrifices to the gods could be conducted anywhere; the god came to the cult site, participated in the sacrificial meal, and left again (Burkert 1985: 55-59).

By assuming the altar was actually built not in the first year of Cyrus but much later during the time of Darius, it may be possible to discern exactly when it was really set up. Haggai notes, and the priests agree, that when people come into contact with a corpse, their hands become unclean, and, moreover, whatever their hands touched became unclean (Hag. 2.13-14). Haggai states that so it is with this people (i.e. the people working on the temple). This means that their hands and the works of their hands have become unclean apparently from either touching corpses or by touching objects impure from corpse contamination. Haggai states, however, that from this moment on (i.e. from the 24th day of the ninth month of the second year of Darius), Yhwh will bless this people (Hag. 2.18-19). What might have happened on that day? It can only be that somehow impurity from corpse contamination was no longer a problem, that the antidote had become available. To purify oneself of corpse contamination, however, one needs to bring an offering to a priest who slaughters it and sprinkles its

2. Although originally intended for the orator, with the progress of writing, the rules of rhetoric were quickly applied to written texts (Morgan 1998: 190-226).

blood upon the altar (Leviticus 5; Milgrom 1991: 292-307, esp. 299). Since there is no expiation without the altar, it seems likely that on the 24th day of the ninth month of Darius's second year the altar was dedicated.

Haggai 2.18 also seems to imply that the 24th day of the ninth month was the day that the foundations of the temple were laid. If it is maintained that the physical foundations were actually laid under Cyrus and Sheshbazzar, then the 24th day of the ninth month of Darius's second year cannot have been the date of the actual foundation ceremony. However, it may have been the date when a ceremonial second foundation ceremony took place under Zerubbabel. This possibility is suggested by Zech. 4.9, where it states that 'the hands of Zerubbabel have laid the foundation of this house; his hands shall also complete it'. (See comment at 3.12 and note at 5.1.)

As I have suggested in the Introduction, the entire verse Ezra 3.1, which sets the date of the altar building, was copied from Neh. 7.73b, where it introduces Nehemiah 8 and Ezra's reading of the law. The verse is out of place here. Further, Ezra 3.1-6 digresses from the main narrative (Kratz 2005: 59; Pakkala 2004: 140). There is a strong and direct connection between Ezra 1.8 and Ezra 3.7, however, which the lists and the altar building disrupt. A major theme of Ezra 1 is the return to build the temple under King Cyrus, and now in Ezra 3.7 we read of the preparation and procurement of temple building materials according to a grant from that same king. This is the usual order in ancient Near Eastern building inscriptions. Moreover, the biblical writer does not mention any sacrifices at the ceremony when the temple's foundations were laid (Ezra 3.10-13). Sacrifices would certainly have been included in large numbers if the altar had actually been built by then.

B: Because of the Dread of the Peoples' of the Lands

Who did the author mean by 'the peoples of the lands' and why does he say that the Judeans were in terror of them (Ezra 3.3)?[3] The phrase 'the peoples of the lands' appears eighty-one times in the Hebrew Bible in various configurations, single and plural. Ezra 3.3 has it in the plural, but the plural occurs in only twenty-four of these appearances. (See comment at 4.4 for a discussion of the referent for the same term in the singular.) The plural term occurs in two forms: 'the peoples of the land' and 'the peoples of the lands'. Ezra 3.3 has the latter. These plural forms appear only in exilic or postexilic texts, with sixteen of the twenty-four occurrences being in Ezra–Nehemiah and Chronicles (1 Chron. 5.25; 2 Chron. 6.33; 13.9; 32.13, 19; Ezra 3.3; 9.1, 2, 11; 10.2, 11; Neh. 9.24, 30; 10.28, 30, 31). Another five are in postexilic additions to Deuteronomy (e.g. Deut. 28.10) and the Deuteronomic history (e.g. Josh. 4.24; 1 Kgs 8.43, 53, 63). All of these refer to other nations of the

3. The following section is based on Fried 2010b.

world, and they are all neutral or even positive. A typical example is 1 Kgs 8.53, 'For you have separated them [i.e. your people Israel] from among all the peoples of the earth (lit., 'land'), to be your heritage, just as you promised through Moses, your servant, when you brought our ancestors out of Egypt, O Lord God'. The remaining three texts include Est. 8.17:

> In every province and in every city, wherever the king's command and his edict came, there was gladness and joy among the Judeans, a festival and a holiday. Furthermore, many of the peoples of the land (here, Persia) professed to be Judeans, because the fear of the Judeans had fallen upon them.

Ezekiel (31.12), a lament over Assyria:

> Foreigners from the most terrible of the nations have cut it [i.e. Assyria] down and left it. On the mountains and in all the valleys its branches have fallen, and its boughs lie broken in all the watercourses of the land; and all the peoples of the earth [lit., 'land'] went away from its shade and left it.

and a late expansion to Zephaniah (3.20):

> At that time I will bring you home, at the time when I gather you; for I will make you renowned and praised among all the peoples of the earth [lit., 'land'], when I restore your fortunes before your eyes, says Yhwh.

In these texts, the reference is always to non-Judeans/non-Israelites. This is also true of its use in Chronicles. The speech put in the mouth of the Rab Shekah by the Chronicler is typical.

> Do you not know what I and my ancestors have done to all the peoples of the lands? Were the gods of the nations of those lands at all able to save their lands out of my hand? (2 Chron. 32.13).

Here, as elsewhere in Chronicles, the referent is always to non-Judeans/non-Israelites.

The plural form occurs eleven times in Ezra–Nehemiah (Ezra 3.3; 9.1, 2, 11; 10.2, 11; Neh. 9.24, 30; 10.28, 30, 31). In none of these texts is the reader told to whom the term refers except that 'their abominations are like those of the Canaanites, the Hittites, the Perizzites, the Jebusites, the Ammonites, the Moabites, the Egyptians, and the Amorites' (Ezra 9.1), that is, like the abominations of the ancient enemies of Judah and Israel, the peoples with whom the Hebrews shared the land of Canaan in the settlement period. They are from areas that later became the Persian satrapies of Egypt, Cilicia, and Beyond-the-River. Of the texts in Ezra–Nehemiah, the referent is clearest in Neh. 9.30:

> Many years you were patient with them, and warned them by your spirit through your prophets; yet they would not listen. Therefore you handed them over to the peoples of the lands.

The referent here is to the non-Israelite/non-Judean peoples who dominated Israel from the time of her settlement in Canaan. Indeed, this is the referent in the Deuteronomic history, in Chronicles, in Ezra–Nehemiah, and elsewhere. The referent is always to foreign peoples. The authors of Ezra–Nehemiah use the plural forms of the term in the same way that all the biblical authors have used them. There is no indication anywhere that they employ a meaning different from other biblical writers. Grabbe (1998: 138) agrees that the biblical author considers the 'peoples of the land/s' to be foreigners, non-Judeans. Nevertheless, he argues that they were not 'really' foreigners but descendants of Judeans who were never deported. This is an odd statement from one who denies that the section is at all historical (Grabbe 1998: 133). (For a discussion of this claim, see Introduction to Ezra 1–6 on Exile and Return.) If the section is not historical, the referent can only be to what the author intends it to be; there is no external reality, only the text.

To evaluate the historicity of the verse, one must consider first if there were non-Judeans in the vicinity of Persian-period Judah or even within it, and second, if it would have made sense historically for the Judeans to have been afraid of them. If the answer to both questions is yes, then there is no need to posit, as Grabbe does, that the 'real' referent of the term is to the descendants of Judeans who had not been deported. (See the Introduction to Ezra 1–6 for a discussion of the effect of the Babylonian destruction and the population of Judah and Jerusalem after the destruction and at the time of the return.) As discussed in the General Introduction, the Persian province of Yehud was very small and surrounded on all sides by foreign peoples—Edomites, Ammonites, Arabs, Phoenicians. It must be concluded from that discussion that there were indeed non-Judeans and non-Israelites in the near vicinity of Judah. To the foreign peoples listed there, we must add the numerous Persian officials and their families who resided in the provincial capital cities, including Jerusalem, as well as the many foreign soldiers with their families who were billeted throughout the countryside, including the countryside of Yehud (see Briant 2002; and Fried 2004 for discussions of Persian imperial administrative practices). Since the term 'peoples of the land/s' in the biblical corpus always refers to non-Judeans or non-Israelites, and since it is clear that there were non-Judeans and non-Israelites in the areas traditionally considered the land of Judah, it is reasonable to conclude that these foreign peoples were the referent for the term 'the peoples of the lands'. Whether there were or were not descendants of Judeans who had not been deported living within the province of Yehud, there is no reason and no basis for assuming that these were the ones who are referred to. To do so is to impose upon the text something that is not there; it is eisegesis, not exegesis.

The question remains, then, whether it would have been reasonable to be in dread of all the foreigners present in Yehud. Was the Persian Empire safe? The Greek writers emphasize the safety of the provinces, stressing that Persian garrisons were established in every large city and dispersed as well in strategic locations throughout the countryside. They point out, moreover, that the empire was crisscrossed by a network of roads that were all well guarded (Briant 2002: 357-87). Herodotus gives numerous anecdotes to illustrate how scrupulously the roads were monitored, and he is our basic source for our knowledge about the common occurrence of travelers and of the safety of the roads. To quote Herodotus, 'For this, indeed, is what the road is like. All along it are Royal Stages and excellent places to put up; and, as it is all through inhabited country, the whole road is safe' (*Histories* 5.52). Xenophon corroborates this (*Anabasis* 1.9.11-12):

> In Cyrus's province it became possible for either Greek or barbarian, provided he were guilty of no wrongdoing, to travel fearlessly wherever he wished, carrying with him whatever it was to his interest to have.

If each bend in the road were as scrupulously guarded as the Greek writers imply, how realistic would it have been for the returnees to have been in dread of their neighbors, the 'peoples of the lands'? Does the safety of the roads imply safety in the empire generally? No. To answer this question, it is possible to look at areas in the empire where conflict occurred and to determine the causes of the conflict and the nature of the Persian response to it. One area of persistent conflict was Anatolia, an area divided into numerous satrapies and provinces whose borders fluctuated. The Greek histories are replete with examples of the rivalry and competition among the neighboring satraps that this fluctuation elicited. For example, Mitrobates, ruler (αρχον) of Dascylium, taunted Oroetes, viceroy (ὕπαρχος, *hyparch*) of Sardis, for not conquering the island of Samos, just outside his doorstep. In reply, Oroetes killed both the taunter, Mitrobates and his son, as well as Polycrates, ruler of Samos. He thus brought Samos as well as Dascylium under his control (Herodotus, *Histories* 3.127). Immediately Maeandrius, vice-regent of Samos under Polycrates, rebelled against the Persians, who retaliated by killing everyone on the island and turning it uninhabited over to Syloson, Polycrates' nephew (3.145-49). Whether or not the Samosans had welcomed the revolt, they were all killed.

Rivalry, jealousy and brinkmanship among satraps was a major cause of the Ionian revolt too, which lasted over seven years. The people of Miletus may not have favored the revolt, but its men were killed anyway; its women and children were sent to Susa as slaves, and its temples plundered and burnt (Herodotus, *Histories* 6.19-20). The Ionians were not the only deportees in the Persian Empire. Herodotus mentions the Eretrians, who were deported to a village outside of Susa (6.120); and Diodorus writes of

Boeotian and Carian deportees living in villages near the Persian capital (Diodorus 17.110.4-5). The Great Satrap's Revolt also reveals the effect of the persistent rivalry and competition among the satraps. In 367 BCE, the king declared Ariobarzanes, the satrap of Dascylium, a rebel, and ordered Autophradates, satrap of Sardis, by land and Mausolus, satrap of Caria, by sea to attack him (Weiskopf 1989: 40-43). The result was war, deaths and deportations.

In contrast to Asia Minor with its constant fear of wars and revolts, Egypt was fairly stable. Nevertheless, archives from the Nile island of Elephantine reveal that in spite of the ubiquitous presence of Persian garrisons, brigandage was a constant threat. A Demotic letter (*EPE* C4) dated to the 36th year of Darius I (October 5, 486 BCE, month of Payni, day 17) warns the addressee not to leave a shipment of grain unguarded for a moment on the wharf for fear of bandits but to bring it immediately to the storage facility in the house of Osirouer.

Most important to the well-being of any community is the assurance of just courts of law. Greek writers portray the exemplary conduct of the Persian judges. According to Herodotus, Cambyses cut the throat of one royal judge and flayed off all his skin because he had been bribed to give an unjust decision (Herodotus, *Histories* 5.25; 7.194), and Darius crucified another judge for the same offence (7.194). The letters from Elephantine present the opposite picture, however. Bribes were the rule, and judgments were held to be in favor of those making the largest offering (see *TAD* 6.10). An example of the effect of bribes on interethnic relations in the Persian Empire is revealed in a letter from the archive of the Judean garrison at Elephantine (*TAD* A 4.5). According to the letter, dated to 410 (the fourteenth year of Darius II), the priests of Khnum had given the Persian governor, Vidranga, money and valuables, in exchange for which he permitted the Khnum priests to build a covered walkway to their temple, to tear down part of the royal storehouse that was blocking the walkway, to cover over the garrison's well (also on that walkway), and while they were at it, to vandalize the neighboring temple of Yhw. The temple became unfit for use, and the Judeans were unable to bring offerings to their god. In the opinion of the Judean letter-writer, the governor permitted this destruction only because of the gifts of silver and other goods that the priests of Khnum had brought him. Whether or not the perception was accurate, that was the perception. The conflict between the priests of Khnum and those of Yhw points to the role of the Persian administration in adjudicating between rival ethnic groups. Parties resolved conflicts with gifts and bribes to whomever they thought had the power to influence decisions. That the Judeans offered their own gifts to Arsames, the satrap, is seen in another letter (*TAD* A 4.10).

> Your servants—all told 5 persons, men of Syene, who are in Elephantine the citadel—thus say: 'If . . . our temple, the one of Yhw the god, be rebuilt

> in Elephantine the citadel as formerly it was built—we shall give to the house of our lord [i.e. to Arsames] si[lver . . . and] barley, a thousa[nd] *ardabs*' (*TAD* A 4.10).

The rivalry and competition among the satraps of Asia Minor and between the different ethnic groups on the Nile island of Elephantine is also visible among the governors of the provinces of Beyond-the-River. According to the funerary inscription of Eshmun'azor, king of Sidon in the last years of Darius I, land in Beyond-the-River was added to the borders of Sidon in return for favors done the Great King.

> The Lord of Kings [i.e. the Achaemenid ruler] gave to me [i.e. to Sidon] Dor and Jaffa, the mighty lands of Dagon, which are in the Plain of Sharon, in accordance with the important deeds that I did. We added them to the borders of the country so that they would belong to Sidon forever (from the funerary inscription of Eshmun'azor, king of Sidon [early-fifth century; ll. 19-20, *ANET* 662]).

The lands that the Persian king had given to Sidon must have been taken from someone else. The king's transfer of land from one provincial governor to another—as from one satrap to another—could only result in competition and rivalry among them.

The rivalry among the satraps discussed in the Greek writings, the interethnic hostilities revealed in the Elephantine letters, the suspicions with which the governors of Beyond-the-River greeted Nehemiah (see comment at Nehemiah 2), and the competition hinted at in the funerary inscription from Sidon may all have been experienced by the Judean returnees from Babylon. We may well conclude that the threat from the neighboring peoples, the so-called 'peoples of the lands', was real, that the dread of them appropriate.

This does not render the episode of the altar building historic. As discussed in the note to 3.3 and in Comment A above, the section on building the altar was likely moved from its original location toward the end of the building inscription to a point before the foundations were even built. To explain the odd location, the author added the phrase that it was built because of their dread of the peoples of the lands. Although a historical event cannot be claimed, the comment does describe a reality with which the author was familiar and with which he could presume his audience would also be familiar—hostile neighbors and the overwhelming presence of a capricious occupying army.

C. The Holiday of Booths (Sukkoth)

The prescriptions for the holiday of Sukkoth are given in Exod. 23.14-17 (JE); Num. 29.12-38 (P); Lev. 23.34-36, 39-43 (H); and Deut. 16.13-16, 31.9 (D). In Exodus it is not called 'Booths' but the 'holiday of Ingathering', held at the close of the year. The text in Numbers prescribes the sacrifices for each day but does not mention the command to live in booths, nor does the word 'booths' appear in that passage. This may be the text referred to in Ezra 3.4. Although the name of the holiday, 'Booths', is given in Ezra, the command to live in them is not stated; only the sacrifices are mentioned. The holiday of Sukkoth is referred to in 1 Kings 8 without title, simply being called 'the festival of the seventh month'. There is no allusion there either to the practice of living in booths but only to the numerous sacrifices required for the holiday. Neither does Ezekiel's description of the holiday (45.25) include the command to live in booths. He specifies only that the *nāsî'* shall provide for the daily offerings of the festival. Neither does Zechariah (14.16-18) mention living in booths, but only that the winter rains will not come to those who do not observe the holiday.

Both H and D require living in booths, however, and these may be the laws that influenced the author of Nehemiah 8. In that passage, Ezra reads the law to the assembled populace—a reference perhaps to Deut. 31.9 where it is prescribed that the law be read every seven years at the festival of Booths. If Nehemiah 8 is based on the traditions of Deuteronomy, and the one in Ezra 3 on the traditions expressed in Numbers, then the different authors had different holiday traditions, and the traditions had not yet been combined. (See further comment on Sukkot at Nehemiah 8 and the Introduction for a discussion of who wrote Ezra–Nehemiah.)

D. Why Sacrifices and Why Now?

Scholars of comparative religion have identified four possible reasons for sacrifices (Milgrom 1991: 440): (1) to provide food for the god; (2) to assimilate into the celebrant the life force of the victim; (3) to effect union with the deity through the shared meal; and (4) to induce the aid of the deity through the gift. All these reasons are found in the Bible except the second. The biblical text describes the daily, Sabbath, and festival offerings as 'my food, . . . my pleasant aroma' (Num. 28.2), and the aim of the sacred furniture in the tabernacle/temple (i.e. the table for the bread of the presence, the candelabrum, and the incense altar), was to provide food, light, and a sweet aroma for the divine resident (Milgrom 1991: 440). As for the shared meal, that is made explicit in Exod. 24.9-11, in which the elders of Israel share a meal with the deity on top of the mountain in celebration of the consummated covenant. The special offerings, the free-will, and thank offerings exemplify the fourth purpose; they thank God for what he has done in the past and hope that he will continue to provide for the offerer in the future. The primary purpose alluded to in this chapter is to gain the favor of the deity against the presumed power of the neighboring peoples round about, the 'peoples of the lands'. If the sacrificial altar was actually set up just prior to the temple's dedication, as was customary in the ancient Near East, then the altar would have been ready to provide food for Yhwh as soon as the temple was dedicated and he took up residence in his temple again.

Ezra 3.6b-7

The Prologue (Continued): Building Materials Are Obtained and the Positive Attitude toward the Protagonists Is Increased

The Hellenistic Prologue continues as does the ancient Near Eastern temple-building story. Temple building begins. The protagonists follow Cyrus's mandate and pay the workers appropriately, increasing the good will of the reader toward them. Here the text follows the template of Mesopotamian temple-building inscriptions, which always include details of the procurement of building materials especially the wood from Lebanon, which is floated down toward the temple construction area. This is Component C of ancient Near Eastern temple-building inscriptions, and it was included here by the Hellenistic author to increase a positive attitude toward the protagonists, Zerubbabel and Jeshua.

Translation

6b. *But*[a] *the foundations of the temple of Yhwh were not*[b] *laid.* 7. *So they gave silver*[c] *to the quarrymen and to the stone cutters*[d] *and food and drink and oil*[e] *to the Sidonians and the Tyrians to bring cedar wood from the Lebanon to Jaffa by sea, according to the authorization of Cyrus king of Persia to them.*

Textual Notes

a. **3.6b** *But.* This word is usually translated 'and', but can also be translated 'even though' or 'but' depending on the context. I translate it 'but' to convey the idea that it was unusual to have sacrifices before the temple is built.

b. *Not.* First Esdras reads 'not yet', which is the real meaning.

c. **3.7** *Silver.* It is probably anachronistic to translate this 'money' if we are still in the reign of Cyrus. See notes to Ezra 2.69.

d. *Stonecutters* חָרָשִׁים. *ḥārāšîm*. This is usually translated 'carpenters', but as Williamson notes (1985: 42 *ad loc.*) it can have a variety of meanings. Exodus 28.11 suggests a person who works with stone. 2 Chronicles 34.11 states, 'They gave [silver] to the חָרָשִׁים and builders to buy quarried stone and timber'. If there is parallel organization to the verse, then the חָרָשִׁים buy the quarried stone and the builders buy the timber.

e. *Oil.* First Esdras reads χαρρα, *charra,* 'carts', but one MS of 1 Esdras (the B-text) reads, χαρα, *chara*, 'joy'. The translation 'joy' is reflected in the Vulgate, *cum gaudio*, 'with joy'. Rudolph (1949) suggests that *chara* is a misreading of χριμα, 'oil', 'unguent'. Oil is one of the fixed products used for rations at Persepolis, and must be retained.

Notes

3.6b *Foundations of the temple were not yet laid.* The rabbis were concerned that offering sacrifices on the altar prior to building the second temple violated the commandment in Lev. 17.3, 4, which states that whoever sacrifices an animal and does not bring it to the door of the temple (tent of meeting or the tabernacle) is guilty of shedding blood. Sacrificing on an altar without a temple was such an anomalous occurrence in the ancient Near East that it warranted considerable discussion in rabbinic literature (Rabinowitz 1984: 104). See Comment A above on building the altar.

1 Esdras reads 'the temple has not yet been built' rather than 'the foundations were not yet laid'. This is because 1 Esdras incorporates its version of the letter to Artaxerxes in its chap. 2, right after the description of the return under Cyrus and before any mention of Zerubbabel or Jeshua is made. (In the MT, the letter to Artaxerxes occurs in Ezra 4.) According to 1 Esdras, that letter states, 'Let it now be known to our lord the king that the Judeans who came up from you to us have gone to Jerusalem and are building that rebellious and wicked city, repairing its marketplaces and walls and laying the foundations for a temple' (1 Esd. 2.17). According to 1 Esdras, Artaxerxes succeeded Cyrus immediately, and under Artaxerxes the Judeans were building both the city walls and its marketplaces, as well as laying the foundations of the temple. Artaxerxes stops the temple building (but lets the city walls be built), and temple building is not resumed until the second year of Darius (1 Esd. 2.30). Therefore, since the temple's foundations were already laid under Artaxerxes, 1 Esdras now simply says that the temple is not yet finished. (See Appendix for the correct order of the Persian kings and Comment D of Ezra 2 for a discussion of the chronology assumed by the author of Ezra.)

3.7 *So.* This sentence likely continued originally directly from Ezra 1.8 (so also Kratz 2005: 64-65). The list at the end of chap. 1, all of chap. 2, and the first six verses of Ezra 3 are likely an intrusion into an original temple-building story. (See comment below.) In the original story one would have simply translated this word as 'and'. These words are represented identically in Hebrew by a simple prefixed waw, ו.

Kratz's hypothesized original version thus conforms to the building inscription that I assume underlies Ezra 1–6. According to this assumption, the building inscription includes Ezra 1.1-8, omits the list of temple vessels (9-11a), and continues with this verse, Ezra 3.7, to describe the temple-building process that was begun under Cyrus. Ezra 3.1-6 refer to events in the reign of Darius under Zerubbabel and Jeshua, whereas here with Ezra 3.7 we are back in the reign of Cyrus and Sheshbazzar (Ezra 5.16). See discussion in Comment A above.

Quarrymen and the stone cutters. The stones were for the temple's foundations and later for the temple's walls. The walls were to be made of three courses of hewn stone and one course of timber (Ezra 6.4). Cedar beams were to be used in the construction of the walls, the ceilings, and the roof. Other wood was used for paneling the walls. Building foundations were always of stone.

Silver . . . food and drink and oil. These items paid to the Sidonians and Tyrians are typical of allocations to workers reported in the Persepolis tablets (Hallock 1969).

The Sidonians and the Tyrians. The population of Judah and Jerusalem at the time was too small for Judeans to build the temple by themselves. The men who brought the wood would have been paid to participate in the building process. Burford's work on temple building at Epidaurus reveals the importance of foreign workers in temple building (Burford 1969). No city would have had citizens of sufficient competence to conduct all aspects of a temple's construction.

Cedar wood from the Lebanon to Jaffa by sea. These cedar beams were crucial for the construction of a roof of any expanse at all. Thus, a statement of this sort is common to that component of temple-building inscriptions, which describes the acquisition and preparation of building materials, even to sending wood from Lebanon by sea (usually by the Euphrates river) to its destination (see Introduction). The roof of the temple of Yhw in Elephantine, for example, was also composed of cedar beams (*TAD* A 4.7); they too must have been shipped from Lebanon by sea in the manner described here as they did not grow outside of Lebanon.

Authorization of Cyrus. First Esdras reads, 'According to the decree that they had in writing from King Cyrus of the Persians'. This authorization included a grant of money (Ezra 6.4). The authorization mandated, rather than simply permitted, the rebuilding of the temple (Blenkinsopp 1988: 102). As was done everywhere in the Persian Empire, the famous cedar forests of Lebanon had been appropriated by the Persian king and used to supply his building projects (Neh. 2.8; Fried 2004). (See Introduction: Would the Persians Have Ordered the Temple in Jerusalem to be Rebuilt?)

So they gave silver to them. We are not told who the 'they' are. I presume Sheshbazzar and his colleagues supervised the building process acting under Cyrus's orders and with the funds that Cyrus had made available to them.

Ezra 3.8-9

The Prologue (Continued): The Protagonists Take Charge

The Hellenistic Prologue continues here with the author's efforts to increase the positive attitude of the reader toward his two protagonists, Zerubbabel and Jeshua, by revealing the great good fortune that God (or the gods) has bestowed on them. Here he shows them taking charge of the community and of the temple-building process by appointing Levites to their roles in the temple's internal organization (see 1 Chron. 9.24-32). Although it has been moved to the Prologue by our Hellenistic writer, the appointment of temple personnel is actually one of the last details included in a typical ancient Near Eastern temple-building inscription (see Introduction to Ezra 1–6). It is repeated again in its proper place in Ezra 6.18. Jeshua and perhaps also Zerubbabel most likely did appoint temple personnel, but they would have done it when the temple was finished and dedicated in the sixth year of Darius. The work that the temple personnel were to have oversight of was not the construction of the temple or laying its foundations but rather its daily operation. Zerubbabel and Jeshua arrived in Judah only in the second year of Darius I (Haggai and Zechariah 1–6), and were not in Jerusalem during the reign of Cyrus when the temple's foundations were laid.

Translation

8. *Then in the second year of their coming to the house of God, to Jerusalem, in the second month*[a], *Zerubbabel ben-Shealtiel and Jeshua ben-Jozadak and the rest*[b] *of their kin (namely the priests and the Levites and all who came from among the captivity of Jerusalem) began by appointing*[c] *the Levites of twenty years old and above to have charge over*[d] *the work of the house*[e] *of Yhwh.* 9. *Then Jeshua, his sons and his kin, Kadmiel and his sons, the sons of Judah,*[f] *stood as one*[g] *to supervise*[h] *the ones doing the work on the house of God* [*along with*][i] *the sons of Henadad, their sons and their kin, the Levites.*

Textual Notes

a. **3.8** *In the second month.* First Esdras reads, 'the new moon of the second month'.

b. *The rest.* This word is missing from 1 Esdras.

c. *Began by appointing.* All the versions have the verb in the plural except 1 Esdras. Literally, it reads, 'they began and they appointed', where we would expect 'they began to appoint', but the present construction is common in the Hebrew Bible. It is often translated 'they made a beginning and they appointed'.

d. *To have charge over.* This term לנצח has several meanings. It is used in the Psalms and elsewhere to refer to the activity of the leader of a group of musicians or singers. Vocalized differently, it means 'forever' (e.g. Isa. 13.20). The use here to designate a leadership role appears in late texts only, for example, here in Ezra 3.8, 9, and 1 Chron. 23.4. Rashi assumes that the Levites were stationed around the temple building site to sing while the work was going on.

e. *The work of the house of Yhwh.* First Esdras reads simply, 'the work of the Lord'.

f. **3.9** *Jeshua, his sons and his kin, Kadmiel and his sons, the sons of Judah.* Nehemiah 7.43 reads, 'the sons of Jeshua, of Kadmiel, of Bani, and of Hodaviah'. (See the notes on Ezra 2.40.) Nehemiah 10.9, 10 lists among the Levites who signed the Amanah 'Jeshua son of Azaniah, Binnui of the sons of Henadad, Kadmiel, and their associates, Shebaniah, Hodiah . . .' 1 Esdras reads, 'And Jeshua arose, and his sons and kindred and his brother Kadmiel and the sons of Jeshua, Emadabun (Henadad?), and the sons of Joda (Yehudah?) son of Iliadun (?), with their sons and kindred, all the Levites'.

g. *As one.* Greek Ezra omits this phrase.

h. *To supervise.* Rashi translates this as 'to sing', as in the previous verse. The word is missing from 1 Esdras, so that all the named Levites with their sons and kin press forward as one man, that is, equally, to build the temple. To 1 Esdras there are no supervisors and no underlings.

i. [*Along with*]. This phrase is missing, but something like it must belong here to attach the following list of participants to the rest of the verse. The following names are preceded in the manuscripts with a ס, however, indicating that according to the Masoretes, the following begins a new paragraph and should not be connected to the preceding.

Notes

3.8 ***In the second year of their coming to the house of God.*** Or, in the second year *after* their coming. As indicated in the books of Haggai and Zechariah, reference to Zerubbabel and Jeshua brings us to the time of Darius, specifically his second year. Indeed, the reference to the second year here is probably taken from those books. According to the literary context, we are still in the reign of Cyrus, however, and nothing of the temple has yet been built. References to Zerubbabel and Jeshua have been moved to the beginning of the building story to introduce these protagonists and to provide them with the initial great good fortune required by Hellenistic rules of rhetoric. According to Aristotle, the protagonists must experience good fortune, which is then reversed. Indeed, Jeshua and Zerubbabel and all the returnees have the tremendous good fortune to have returned to Judah and have lived to see the day when the foundations of the second temple were laid and the temple built.

Second month. The year is likely counted from Nisan (April), but see the discussion at Ezra 6.15. If beginning in the spring, then the second month would be after the winter rains have passed and the ground dried (Rudolph 1949: 31). Reference to the auspicious second month was likely included to indicate a replication of Solomon's building activities. Solomon also began to build his temple in the second month (1 Kgs 6.1; 2 Chron. 3.2).

Appointing . . . Levites. These two verses are odd here. Temple personnel are not usually appointed until after the temple is constructed (Hurowitz 1992: 56). The description of the foundation ceremony is patterned in part after the Chronicler's description of the dedication of the temple (2 Chron. 5.11-13). Indeed, these two verses (3.8, 9) likely originated in the description of the second temple's dedication on its building inscription but were moved here from their location there to provide a connection to vv. 10-13, the description of the ceremony for the dedication of the foundations (Ezra 3.10-13; see note *ad loc.* below). Since that description mentions levitical singers and musicians, the author thought it necessary to bring up the verse in which Levites are assigned their tasks to a point prior to the description of the foundation-laying ceremony. A second verse was included to show that the Levites were indeed fulfilling the task to which they were assigned. In reality, priests and Levites would have participated as priests and Levites in the foundation-laying ceremony without being appointed to any particular task. Being a priest or a Levite is not something one is appointed to, it is an inherited status. They would need to be appointed to whatever specific task they were to be charged with, of course, but that would only occur after the temple was completed and dedicated.

There is no mention, moreover, of either Zerubbabel or Jeshua at the dedication of the temple (Ezra 6.13-22), which is very strange. Moving these two verses back to the end of chap. 6, their original location, would fix two problems—their anomalous presence here and their anomalous absence there. The verses were moved for the purpose of the plot. According to Hellenistic rules of rhetoric, the protagonists must experience good fortune and joy before their fortunes can be reversed. This is accomplished by allowing them to participate in the ceremony for laying the temple's foundations.

The Levites of twenty years old and above. Twenty is the age of adulthood, when males are able to go to war (Num. 1.3) and pay their taxes (Exod. 30.14). According to Num. 4.43, the Levites begin duty in the sanctuary at age thirty, but according to Num. 8.24, it is at age twenty-five. Rashi harmonizes the texts by suggesting that they began training at twenty-five, but entered actual service at thirty. In 1 Chron. 23.2 the age of obligation is thirty, and in 2 Chron. 31.17, the age appears to be twenty. (For further discussion, see Fleishman 1992.)

3.9 *House of Yhwh.* First Esdras inserts an additional verse at this point: 'And they laid the foundation of the temple of God on the new moon of the second month in the second year after they (Zerubbabel, Jeshua, etc.) came to Judea and Jerusalem'. Apparently this is to clarify that at this point, in the second year of Darius, the foundations were laid. The attempt to lay the temple's foundations earlier had been stopped under Artaxerxes (1 Esd. 2.18) and not continued until the second year of Darius (1 Esd. 2.30). Now, in 1 Esdras, it is the second year (of Darius, apparently), and they can finish laying the foundations. In Ezra, we are still nominally in the reign of Cyrus.

Jeshua, his sons and his kin; Kadmiel and his sons, the sons of Judah. These are the names of the Levites who were appointed over the work of the temple. (Jeshua is both the name of the high priest and of a leading Levite.) The sons of Jeshua (the Levite) and Kadmiel, and the sons of Hodaviah are listed in Ezra 2.40 as the (nonsinging) Levites who returned with Zerubbabel and Jeshua the high priest. Indeed, in almost every list of the Levites in Ezra–Nehemiah (Ezra 2.40; Neh. 7.43; 9.4, 5; 10.10, 11; 12.8; cf. Neh. 3.17, 18) these same few men are listed. It appears to be a stereotypical list of levitical names, and one wonders why there is only this one short list, and where it originated. It may have derived from the list of signers to the Amanah (Nehemiah 10), since that is the only place where Jeshua is given a patronym. If that is the origin of the list of levitical names, then the list does not belong here, and probably does not belong anywhere except in Nehemiah 10. Indeed, if the list of levitical names does not belong here, as seems likely, then it corroborates the suggestion that these verses were written solely to introduce the foundation-laying ceremony.

(Along with) the sons of Henadad, their sons and their kin, the Levites. This entire phrase appears after a mark, ס, indicating the end of a paragraph. The phrase should probably be excised.

Ezra 3.10-11

The Prologue (Continued): The Foundations of the Temple Are Laid and the Good Fortune of the Protagonists Increases

The Aristotelian Prologue and the ancient Near Eastern temple-building inscription both continue apace. Aristotle stresses that an artistically made plot must involve a change, not from bad fortune to good but the other way around, from good fortune to bad (*Poetics* 3853a1.12-15). A change from bad fortune to good 'has none of the qualities that one wants [in a narrative]; it is productive neither of ordinary sympathy nor of pity nor of fear' (*Poetics* 3853a1.1). In the Prologue the author must create protagonists who are neither very bad nor very good, but rather in the middle of these two extremes, people with whom the reader can identify. Then he must show the great good fortune that the gods (or God) have showered on them.

The basis of our story, however, is the ancient Near Eastern temple-building inscription, and the next component is D: the ruler participates in the rites for laying the foundation of the temple. These rites are usually performed according to the prescription of a diviner or prophet.

Translation

10. *So the builders laid the foundations*[a] *of the temple of Yhwh, the priests stood equipped*[b] *with bugles, and the Levites, the descendants of Asaf, with cymbals, stood*[c] *to praise Yhwh according to the directions of David king of Israel.* 11. *They sang responsively*[d] *in praise and in thanksgiving*[e] *to Yhwh because he is good and because his faithfulness on behalf of Israel*[f] *is eternal,*[g] *and all the people shouted a great shout*[h] *in praise to Yhwh because the foundations*[i] *of the house of Yhwh were laid.*

Textual Notes

a. **3.10** *So the builders laid the foundations.* First Esdras reads, 'So the builders built the temple of the Lord'. According to the previous verse of 1 Esdras (v. 57), the foundations were laid on the new moon of the second month of the second year. Now, the temple has been built, and the priests and Levites with their musical instruments are there to dedicate the temple itself, not simply to celebrate laying the foundations.

b. *Equipped.* Literally, 'dressed in their bugles'; see note.

c. *Stood.* Reading the intransitive with the versions. The MT has the transitive form, 'they stationed', יעמידו for יעמדו, 'they stood'. The problem with the transitive form is that there is no object.

d. **3.11** *Sang responsively.* The word ענה in the qal stem as here most often simply means 'answered', but in situations where musical instruments are involved the best interpretation is that they sang or played their instruments responsively. The Greek reads literally, 'they answered each other', whereas 1 Esdras reads simply, 'they lifted their voices'.

e. *In praise and in thanksgiving.* First Esdras renders this 'in hymns of praising'. The word for 'praising', ὁμολογοῦντες, also carries the connotation of 'to acknowledge', which can also be implied in the Hebrew word for 'thanksgiving', הוֹדת.

f. *Israel.* First Esdras reads 'all Israel'.

g. *Because he is good and because his faithfulness . . . is eternal.* This is a stock phrase, occurring nine times in the late texts in the biblical corpus (e.g. 1 Chron. 16.34; 2 Chron. 5.13; 7.3; Pss. 106.1; 107.1; 118.1, 29; 136.1). Further, the phrase 'because his faithfulness . . . is eternal' is even more commonplace, occurring forty times, again always in late texts (Chronicles, Ezra, and late Psalms, but also in Jer. 33.11). The Greek of this common phrase is uniformly rendered ὅτι ἀγαθόν ὅτι εἰς τὸν αἰῶνα τὸ ἔλεος αὐτοῦ, 'because he is good and because his mercy is eternal', but 1 Esdras breaks with the pattern and renders 'good' by χρηστότης, 'uprightness', and 'loyalty', חסד, by δόξα, 'glory', as it does in 1.31 (= 2 Chron. 35.26).

h. *Shouted a great shout.* Actually, made a great noise. First Esdras inserts the phase 'sounded trumpets', since this phrase in the biblical text is usually used with bugle or horn blasts (e.g. Num. 10.1-6). Most probably, the people are shouting and only the priests have the bugles (Num. 10.8).

i. *Foundation.* First Esdras reads 'the temple', not the temple foundations. (See note to 3.10 above.)

Notes

3.10 ***So the builders laid the foundations.*** The text continues in the time of Cyrus. This statement is a common component of Mesopotamian building stories, yet it is odd that only anonymous 'builders' are mentioned here. According to the typical building inscription, the ruler would have led the ritual for laying the temple's foundation, and it would have been carried out according to the prescription of a prophet or diviner. None of these is mentioned. Sheshbazzar is not referred to either. Because of this, Williamson (1985: 79) states categorically that Sheshbazzar did not lay the foundations and that the work did not go on continuously from the reign of Cyrus until the first year of Darius as reported in Tattenai's letter to Darius (Ezra 5.16). Yet, these assertions regarding Sheshbazzar are corroborated by Tattenai's own assessment of the situation (Ezra 5.8), a letter that Williamson accepts as authentic. Blenkinsopp (1988: 122-23) also contends that Sheshbazzar did not participate in temple building. According to him, the statement in Tattenai's letter to Darius regarding Sheshbazzar was fabricated by the Judean community in Jerusalem to gain prestige for the temple. It is likely that Sheshbazzar was indeed in charge when the temple foundations were laid, however, and that he led the foundation ceremony as stated in 5.16. The author deleted the reference to Sheshbazzar when he moved Zerubbabel and Jeshua up from their original position at the temple's dedication in the sixth year of Darius to the present location.

The priests equipped. The Hebrew of this verse has usually been viewed as corrupt since it reads literally 'they were dressed in their bugles'. The NRSV translates 'priests *in their vestments* were stationed to praise the Lord with trumpets'. Rashi translates by 'the priests, elegantly attired, with their bugles'. Maimonides asserts that they were arrayed in their priestly vestments, even though traditionally they were prohibited from wearing them except during the sacrifices (*Klei Hammikdash* 8.12). The Greek versions enable us to understand the text, however. They read ἐστολισμένοι, which carries the meaning 'equipped' as well as 'dressed', so we may simply translate, 'the priests stood equipped with their bugles'. It may be that מלובש, 'dressed', also carried the meaning 'equipped' in the second temple period and that nothing has dropped out of the text. Thus there is no need to supply 'their vestments' with the NRSV or to concern ourselves with what these priests were wearing.

Unaware of this, the rabbis debate whether it was permissible for priests to wear their priestly vestments while outside the temple and when they were not conducting sacrifices. According to Ezek. 42.14, it is forbidden, so the rabbis suggest translating the phrase by 'formally attired'.

Priests are listed here rather than prophets or diviners as would be expected in a typical ancient Near Eastern temple-building inscription. Indeed, the rabbis are troubled by the absence of prophets. Thus, they add them.

> Rabbah b. Hanah said in R. Johanan's name: Three prophets went up with them (the returnees) from the Exile: one testified to them about [the dimensions of] the altar; another testified to them about the site of the altar; and the third testified to them that they could sacrifice even though there was no Temple because the site was holy for all time (*Zebaḥim* 62a).

The absence of prophets here may have something to do with Ezekiel's condemnation of them and his promise that they will not return to Israel (see Comment E to Ezra 2 above).

Bugles. King and Stager (2001: 294) suggest that this is a long straight wind instrument, made of beaten silver or bronze, with a limited range of notes. Rather than translating it as 'trumpet', as is usual, King and Stager suggest that the term ‘bugle’ is more appropriate since in biblical texts this instrument is used more for signaling than for music. Numbers 10.2 describes God’s command to Moses thus: ‘Make two silver bugles; you shall make them of hammered work; and you shall use them for summoning the congregation, and for breaking camp’. Numbers 10.8 designates the bugles for the priests, and it is they, and not the Levites, who play them on religious or semi-religious occasions (although the *‘am hā’āreṣ*, the landed aristocracy, blew them at the dethronement of Athaliah; 2 Kgs 11.14). The best description of the use of the bugle comes from Sir. 50.14-16:

> Finishing the service at the altars, and arranging the offering to the Most High, the Almighty, [the high priest] held out his hand for the cup and poured a drink offering of the blood of the grape; he poured it out at the foot of the altar, a pleasing odor to the Most High, the king of all. Then the sons of Aaron shouted; they blew their bugles of hammered metal; they sounded a mighty fanfare as a reminder before the Most High.

Josephus describes the instrument thus (*Ant.* 3.291):

> Moreover, Moses was the inventor of the form of their horn, which was made of silver. Its description is this: — In length it was little less than a cubit. It was composed of a narrow tube, somewhat thicker than a flute, but with so much breadth as was sufficient for admission of the breath of a man’s mouth: it ended in the form of a bell, like common trumpets. Its sound was called in the Hebrew tongue *Asosra.*

Both Hos. 5.8 and Ps. 98.6 seem to imply that the bugle, *h*^{a}*ṣṣōṣ*^{e}*râ*, is a synonym for the Shophar, yet the latter is typically a ram’s horn, while the former is of hammered silver. The bugle appears only infrequently among the pre-exilic lists of musical instruments and is more common in second temple texts. The instruments listed in 2 Samuel 6, for example, are ‘lyres, harps, tambourines, rattles, and cymbals’. The Chronicler has substituted ‘castanets’ for ‘rattles’ from his *Vorlage* in Samuel and added ‘bugles’.

Asaf. For a discussion of Asaf and the role of the temple singers and musicians in the second temple see the comments on 2.41 above.

Cymbals. The word translated ‘cymbals’, מְצִלְתַּיִם *m*^{e}*ṣiltayim* appears only in Ezra, Nehemiah, and Chronicles, but is synonymous, according to King and Stager (2001: 297), with the *ṣelṣelîm*, צֶלְצְלִים, of 2 Sam. 6.5. They are copper or bronze percussion instruments found in Egypt, the Levant, and Assyria, and representations of them date as early as the third millennium BCE. They have been found in the vicinity of the *Migdal* temple at Megiddo, and a pair measuring 10 cm. in diameter was found in a Canaanite shrine in Hazor. A tiny wire affixed to the center of the cymbal went over the musician’s finger (King and Stager 2001: 297). Jones (1992: 935) describes them as ‘saucerlike plates with pierced centers for wire finger-holds and reflexed rims. They were capable of producing a high-pitched tinkling when struck together.'

According to the directions of David king of Israel. This refers to the tradition described in 1 Chron. 6.16-17 [ET 6.31]. The service described there is a service in a temporary temple provided for the Ark until its permanent habitation, Solomon's temple, could be built for it (Hurowitz 1993). The celebration described here in Ezra, which takes place at the dedication of the temple's foundations, reflects the Chronicler's description of the dedication of Solomon's temple, that is, the finished building, not its foundations:

> Now when the priests came out of the holy place (for all the priests who were present had sanctified themselves, without regard to their divisions), all the levitical singers, Asaph, Heman, and Jeduthun, their sons and kindred, arrayed in fine linen, with cymbals, harps, and lyres, stood east of the altar with one hundred twenty priests who were trumpeters. It was the duty of the trumpeters and singers to make themselves heard in unison in praise and thanksgiving to Yhwh, and when the song was raised, with trumpets and cymbals and other musical instruments, in praise to Yhwh, 'For he is good, for his steadfast love endures forever', the temple, the temple of Yhwh, was filled with a cloud (2 Chron. 5.11-13).

The passage in Ezra (3.10-11), now in the context of the ceremonies held when the foundations were laid, is so similar to the Chronicler's description of the dedication of the temple that it seems likely that this was originally a description of the second temple's dedication and not the ceremony for laying the foundations. The author of Ezra moved it to this spot to embellish the description of the ceremony for laying the foundations and to emphasize the great good fortune of the protagonists. Since that description involved the use of Levites and priests, the verses in which they were appointed (now 3.8, 9) was moved as well.

3.11 ***Faithfulness on behalf of Israel is eternal.*** Laying the foundations of the second temple is proof that God's loyalty to Israel is eternal. The experience of the exile was only an apparent rupture; God's loyalty to Israel is everlasting. This is the ultimate proof of God's good fortune shining upon our protagonists, Zerubbabel, Jeshua, and all the returnees. They have lived to return to the land of Israel; they have lived to see the rebuilding of Yhwh's temple.

Ezra 3.12-13

The Prologue (Continued): Celebration!

The Hellenistic Prologue continues with the description of the great good fortune of the protagonists, giving proof of their favor in the eyes of God. The ancient Near Eastern temple-building inscription also continues.

Here we read the next traditional component of temple building: If a new temple is built near the site of an old one, lamentations are sung by lamentation priests to placate the gods and bridge the gap between the old temple and the new. A stone taken from the old temple is placed in the new one during construction. Lamentations are made for the old temple until the new one is completed. There is no mention of Lamentation priests here in Ezra, but we do read of lamentations.

Translation

12. *And many of the old priests, the Levites, the heads of patriarchal families*[a] *[and] the elders,*[b] *who saw the first temple on its foundations*[c] *(this was the temple in their eyes) continued weeping*[d] *out loud but many [began]*[e] *to raise their voice in a shout*[f] *of joy.* 13. *And none of the people could distinguish the sound of the shout of joy from the sound of the people's weeping; because the people were shouting so loudly, the sound was heard from afar.*

Textual Notes

a. **3.12** *Patriarchal families.* Literally, *father's* [*houses*]. See note on Ezra 2.68. 1 Esdras reads, 'and the leaders, according to their ancestral clans', which is the plain meaning of the Hebrew text.

b. *Elders.* This could also be taken as an adjective and translated 'the older priests, Levites, etc'.

c. *On its foundations.* Revocalizing from 'in its being founded', with the versions.

d. *Continued weeping.* Literally, 'are weeping'. The verb is in the present tense, indicating constant weeping (Rashi).

e. [*Began*]. A finite verb is lacking.

f. *Shout.* First Esdras and the Peshitta interpret this ambiguous word to refer to the blast of musical instruments rather than the shouts of the people.

Notes

3.12 ***Who saw the first temple on its foundations.*** This has been variously interpreted to mean either 'who had seen and remembered the first temple' or 'who saw the ruins of the first temple' right there in front of them. The latter seems more likely to cause the weeping.

This is the temple in their eyes. That is, the former temple was the 'real' temple in their eyes, not the new temple being built. Commentators (e.g. Williamson 1985: 47) often interpret this verse in the light of Hag. 2.3 and vice versa. Haggai 2.3 reads: 'Who is left among you that saw this house in its former glory? How does it look to you now? Is it not in your sight as nothing?'

These commentators assume that Haggai is looking at the temple's foundations rather than at the nearly completed structure. This may not be correct. The scene in Ezra 3 concerns the ceremony for laying the temple's foundations—at the beginning of the temple building project probably in the first or second year of Cyrus. Haggai, prophesying in the second year of Darius, does not talk about laying the temple's foundations. Haggai exhorts the people to 'go up to the hills and bring wood' (1.8). To lay a building's foundations does not require wood, but trenches dug for the foundation stones, and the foundation stones themselves gathered or quarried. It is true that structures at Tel Rehov contained wood in the foundation beams, but this was a lone exception:

> A common feature of these rooms [at Tel Rehov] is the use of wooden logs or beams as a foundation for the walls and floors. The wood was sometimes found to have been laid in several superimposed and interspersed layers. . . . All the beams were carbonized, and in the southern part of the area they were found tilted at a sharp angle down to the east . . . several species . . . elm, olive, acacia, Judas tree, Syrian ash and mulberry. This type of wooden construction serving as a foundation for both mud brick walls and clay and plaster floors is unusual, and unparalleled elsewhere in the Levant. It may have been intended to protect the building against earthquakes, which present a hazard in the Jordan Valley, or it could be the roof of a basement, still unexcavated (Mazar 1999: 21-22).

Haggai did not want wood for building either the temple's foundations or its walls, but rather he wanted it for paneling the inside walls of the nearly finished temple. Haggai commands:

> Is it a time for you yourselves to live in your paneled houses, while this house is a ruin? (חָרֵב). . . . Go up to the mountain and bring wood and build the house, so that I may take pleasure in it and be glorified (אֶכָּבְדָה), says Yhwh (Hag. 1.4, 8).

In other words, you live in paneled houses, but this house still lies unpaneled, unfinished, and consequently uninhabitable. Go to the hills and get wood for the paneling, and finish the house. Haggai puns on the word חרב, translated here as 'ruins', which also means 'drought'. God's house is a ruin, so God calls for a ruin on the land:

> And I have called for a ruin (חרב, dryness, drought) on the land and the hills, on the grain, the new wine, the oil, on what the soil produces, on human beings and animals, and on all their labors (Hag. 1.11).

Yhwh wants wood to glorify the temple, so that he may be glorified in it. The idea that the wood for the beautification of the temple brings glory (כבד) is also seen in Isa. 60.13:

> The glory of Lebanon shall come to you, the cypress, the plane, and the pine, to beautify the place of my sanctuary; and I will glorify where my feet rest.

The glory of the temple is the presence of Yhwh himself. His presence—not its foundation stones—is bound up with the temple's beautification. There is no need to assume that the temple-building project was not yet begun in Haggai's time. According to Tattenai's letter to Darius (Ezra 5), the second temple's foundations were laid by Sheshbazzar in the time of Cyrus. There is no reason to doubt this. Haggai considered the temple to be a ruin because it was still not inhabitable by the second year of Darius.

Continued weeping. The weeping may not have been a spontaneous outburst because of the inadequacy of the new temple. The weeping may have been part of prescribed lamentation rites traditionally conducted for a former temple while a new temple is being built. (For discussion of these lamentation rites, see comment below.) This chapter thus ends with a glorious ceremony when the foundations of the second temple are laid, giving proof of the great good fortune of the returnees, Zerubbabel and Jeshua in particular. They have lived to see it, and they have helped bring it about.

Comment: The Ceremony for Laying the Temple's Foundations

Ezra 3.10-13 narrates the ceremony to celebrate the dedication of the second temple's foundations and may belong to the second temple's original building story. This celebration forms the climax of the chapter and ends the Prologue. As discussed in the Introduction, and in notes at 3.8 and 3.12 above, Ezra 3 as it now stands is intended to describe the good fortunes of the protagonists, Zerubbabel and Jeshua. Ezra 1.1–3.7 introduces them and sets the scene. Ezra 3.8-13 presents them experiencing the high point of their lives: they lead the ceremonies in which the foundations of the second temple are laid. They have lived to witness God's eternal loyalty to the people Israel. Although Levites are described as appointed to their tasks (Ezra 3.8, 9), the actual description of the foundation ceremony (3.11b-13) would not have included the programmed participation of temple personnel. The participants are 'all the people', which of course includes the priests, Levites, elders and lay people.

The scene portrayed here is typical of other ancient Near East foundation ceremonies (Ellis 1968: 32-33), except that there is no mention of prophet or diviner. If the foundations were really laid during the time of Jeshua and Zerubbabel, we surely would read here of the prophesying of Haggai and Zechariah, as we do in Ezra 6.14, the description of the temple's dedication. Jeshua and Zerubbabel had not yet arrived when the foundation stones were laid in the second year of Cyrus. Nor is there mention of sacrifices, which surely would have been included had the altar been erected then. Ezra 3.12, which must be retained as original, notes that the foundation ceremony was accompanied by weeping. This weeping is typical of foundation ceremonies for rebuilding a destroyed temple. When a ruined temple is rebuilt on its former site, lamentations for the old temple are traditionally sung—often led by special lamentation priests—to placate the god whose temple it is and to bridge the gap between the old temple and the new. Thureau-Dangin (1921: 35-59) has published the Mesopotamian *kalû* ritual, the ritual prescribed for rebuilding a temple while the old one lies in ruins. The following are the instructions for the *kalû*, or lamentation priest:

> When the wall of a temple falls into ruin, in order to demolish and then rebuild[1] that temple, . . . the builder of that temple shall put on clean clothes and put a tin bracelet on his arm; he shall take an ax of lead, remove the *maḫritu* brick, and shall put it in a restricted place. You set up an offering table in front of the brick for the god of foundations, and you offer sacrifices; you shall sprinkle every type of (aromatic?) grain; you will pour beer, wine, and milk (over the brick?); you will prostrate yourself (before the brick?). As long as you [they?] demolish and (re)build [the temple] you will offer water (on the brick?). Then the *kalû* priest will make a libation of honey, cream, milk, beer, wine, and [good] oil (over the brick?). The *kalû*-priest [shall recite] the (composition called) '*Enūma Anu ibnū šamē*'. ['When Anu built the heavens . . .'] . . . as long as the demolishing and rebuilding (are going on), offerings and lamentations shall be made and the *kalū*-priest shall not cease strewing (aromatic?) flour and making libations and recitations (Thureau-Dangin 1921: 40-43).

1. Thureau-Dangin (1921, followed by *ANET* 339-42 and Ellis 1968: 184) translates the verb as 'to lay the foundations', interpreting *uš-šu-ši* from *uššu*, 'foundation'. Van Soden suggests rather that the verb is the D stem of *edēšu*, 'to renew' (*AHw*, uššušu(m) III, 1442). It is clear from the final section of the ritual, quoted here, that the rites continue during the entire construction of the building, not only when the foundations of the new temple are laid. The different translations unfortunately give different impressions of the ritual, whether it continued throughout 'demolishing and rebuilding', or only while the foundations were laid. For a different interpretation, see Boda 2006.

The enigmatic term *maḫritu,* 'brick', does not mean 'first brick', as it is often translated, but a previous brick, any previous brick from the former temple (Ellis 1968: 26-29). It cannot be the first brick that was laid when the original temple was built. Bricks cannot be recognized by their inscriptions, as they are usually laid face down. In the *kalû* ritual, the one designated as the builder removes a brick or stone from the old temple and sets it aside. A *kalû* priest makes offerings and sings lamentations over it as long as the old temple is being demolished and the new temple is being constructed. He continues to sing lamentations until the new temple is dedicated. Indeed, the city lament, or *balag*, was composed just for the *kalû* ritual (Jacobsen 1940: 219-24). Its recitation by *kalû* priests was an indispensable part of the ritual accompanying the restoration of a destroyed city's temples. The *balag*-lament includes a vivid description of the city lying desolate and of the 'storm', that is, the attack, that devastated it. The temple is lamented as in ruins and empty until the new temple is finished and dedicated.

Although no specific *kalû* priest is mentioned, the weeping described in Ezra 3.12 may be part of such a lamentation rite, perhaps over a building stone that had been set aside from the ruins of the first temple. Indeed, the *'eben hāri'šâ,* אבן הראשה, that Zerubbabel brings out (Zech. 4.7) may be such a stone from the former temple that had been set aside by the 'builder' during the foundation ceremony (Ezra 3.10a). The phrase אבן הראשה has been translated 'head stone', 'premiere stone', 'first stone', 'top stone'.[2] Yet, there is reason to think it ought to be translated 'former-years' stone', as is also appropriate for the *maḫritu* brick. The dictionaries define ראשה, vocalized *ri'šâ*, the singular of *ri'šôt*, as 'beginning time, early time'. I might suggest also 'former time'. This translation is based on Ezek. 36.11

> I will increase upon you man and beast, they will greatly multiply, and I will cause you to dwell as in your early times (כקדמותיכם), and I will cause more good than your former times (מראשותיכם), and you will know that I am Yhwh.

At some point, when demolishing and rebuilding are finished, the *maḫritu* brick is incorporated into the new building. That act ends the *kalû* ritual. This is necessarily before the walls are paneled. It may be only then that the new temple becomes the temple in actuality; the act of inserting the brick may be what makes the transference complete. Ezra 3.12 suggests that the old temple in ruins was still the 'real' temple in the eyes of the people. Prior to the transfer of the 'former-times' stone, the real temple is the old one, still in ruins. The one who places the *maḫritu* brick into the new building is termed the builder, and according to Zechariah 4, that honor fell

2. 'Top stone', NRSV; 'Premiere stone' (Meyers and Meyers 1987: 228, 248, who consider it to be a stone from the first temple), as does Petersen (1984: 237-42) who refers to it as 'the former stone'.

to Zerubbabel. Zerubbabel's incorporating the 'former-times' stone' into the walls of the new temple can be described as founding (יסד) the temple (Zech. 4.9; Hag. 2.18). Thus, it is most likely that the foundations were laid under Cyrus and Sheshbazzar, but that a refoundation ceremony was held in Darius's second year when Zerubbabel inserted the *maḫritu* brick into the walls of the new temple. Only then would the time have been right for paneling the building, after the *maḫritu* brick was installed.

The *kalû* ritual prescribes that laments be sung for the old temple as long as rebuilding continues, presumably until the new temple is dedicated, even after the *libbitu maḫritu* is placed in the temple walls. Laments for the temple in Jerusalem evidently continued at least into the fourth year of Darius, even after Zerubbabel laid the *'eben ri'šâ* in Darius's second year (Zech. 7.1-3). In the light of the *balag* and the *kalû* ritual, Haggai's and Zechariah's references to the temple still in ruins and to the city still devastated does not indicate that temple building had not been in progress since the return under Sheshbazzar. Ritual laments are prescribed throughout the building process until the new temple is dedicated. Laments and fasting would have continued until the end of Darius's sixth year (Zech. 7.1-3).

Reflections

The greatest good that the Hellenistic author can imagine is that the temple is rebuilt. This was also the feeling of the author of this passage (Jer. 33.10-11):

> This place of which you say, 'It is a waste without human beings or animals', in the towns of Judah and the streets of Jerusalem that are desolate, without inhabitants, human or animal, there shall once more be heard the voice of mirth and the voice of gladness, the voice of the bridegroom and the voice of the bride, the voices of those who sing, as they bring thank offerings to Yhwh's Temple:
>
> 'Give thanks to Yhwh of hosts, for Yhwh is good, for his steadfast love endures forever!'
>
> I will restore the fortunes of the land as at first, says Yhwh.

Ezra 4.1-5

The Plot Begins: Judah's Leaders Make a Terrible Mistake and Temple Building Is Stopped

To Aristotle, the most important aspect of a narrative is the series of events, that is, the plot (*Poetics* 3850a15), and particularly a plot in which the protagonist suffers an unexpected reversal in fortune. This reversal must be from good fortune to bad, for it is only such reversals that arouse pity and fear in the reader. Moreover, the reversal must occur not from the protagonist's wickedness (for then it would not evoke audience identification with him), it must result from his own decision, but a decision that any ordinary person would make, and one that makes him the creator of his own undoing. It must be a decision that has great and negative consequences, a decision that results in a dramatic and negative reversal of fortune. In addition, this reversal must be 'contrary to the reader's expectations', but a logical and necessary consequence of the decision nevertheless (*Poetics* 38.52a4).

The incident told here in vv. 1-5 relates the reversal of fortune that every good (Hellenistic) plot must have. The great good fortune of the protagonists (Zerubbabel, the Persian governor, and Jeshua, the high priest) was in seeing the second temple begun and its foundations laid. Now, through a simple error in judgment, a mistake that anyone could have made, work on the temple is stopped (4.4-5; 4.24). As becomes clear in Ezra 5, this event and the stoppage of work on the temple that results from it are dramatic fictions, designed by the Hellenistic writer to create fear and pity in the reader.

Translation

1. *Enemies*[a] *of Judah and Benjamin*[b] *heard*[c] *that the exiles were building a temple to Yhwh*[d] *the god of Israel.* 2. *They approached Zerubbabel*[e] *and the heads of the fathers' [houses] and said to them, 'Let us build*[f] *with you,*[g] *for like you we have been inquiring of*[h] *your god, and we have been sacrificing to him*[i] *from the days of Esarhaddon,*[j] *king of Assyria, who brought us up here.* 3. *But Zerubbabel, Jeshua, and the rest*[k] *of the heads of the fathers' [houses] of Israel said to them, 'It is not yours, but ours to build*[l] *a temple*

for our god, so we alone[m] *will build*[n] *for Yhwh the god*[o] *of Israel just as King*[p] *Cyrus, king of Persia, had commanded us'.* 4. *So the 'people of the land'*[q] *discouraged*[r] *the people of Judah and made them afraid*[s] *to build,* 5. *bribing officials*[t] *against them to frustrate their plans,*[u] *all the days of Cyrus king of Persia until the reign of Darius king of Persia.*[v]

Textual Notes

a. **4.1** *Enemies*. Perhaps, literally, 'oppressors'. See note below. Most translations read 'when the enemies', but this is not correct according to the grammar, nor is it the interpretation of the Masoretes, who have placed a *sof pasuq* at the end of the verse. Verses 1 and 2 are two separate sentences; the first verse is not a subordinate clause of the second.

b. *Judah and Benjamin.* First Esdras inserts the words 'the tribes', and so reads 'the tribes of Judah and Benjamin'.

c. *Heard.* First Esdras, in contrast to the Hebrew and Greek Ezra, translates by the participle, 'hearing', thus it reads 'upon hearing'. It then introduces a long explanatory clause: 'they came to find out what the sound of the trumpets meant', referring to the trumpets in the previous verse. First Esdras thus supplies a reason for the arrival of the enemies at the building site, not present in the Hebrew.

d. *Yhwh.* Both the Syriac and the Greek texts have 'the Lord, god of Israel', as is usual in these versions.

e. **4.2** *Zerubbabel.* First Esdras adds 'and Jeshua', in view of his presence in v. 3. So do many modern commentators. The name Jeshua is not included in the other versions, however.

f. *Let us build.* Or, 'we will build'. Hebrew has no special hortative form.

g. *With you.* First Esdras ends the verse here and then starts a new one.

h. *Inquiring of.* Consulting, as an oracle. First Esdras has 'we have been heeding', evidently the translator's best guess as to what this word נדרוש might mean (so Talshir 2001: 317). The Syriac has 'we will build', which Hawley (1922) suggests is a copyist's error, writing נבנא for נדרוש.

i. *To him.* The MT has 'and not', לא, but read 'to him', לו, with the *qere* and the versions.

j. *Esarhaddon.* First Esdras reads Ασβασαρεθ, Asbasareth, whereas the Greek Ezra and the Greek of 2 Kgs 19.37 and of Isa. 37.38 have the correct name.

k. **4.3** *The rest.* This word is missing from 1 Esdras.

l. *It is not yours, but ours to build.* Greek Ezra reads, 'It is not for us and for you to build the temple of our god, but we alone will build it'. This is a reasonable translation, since the word in the Hebrew translated here as 'but' also means 'and'.

m. *We alone.* Literally, 'We together'.

n. *Will build.* The Syriac inserts 'a temple'.

o. *The god.* This word is absent from 1 Esdras, resulting in 'we will build for the Lord of Israel'.

p. **4.4** *King.* This first word, 'king', is omitted in the versions.

q. *People of the land.* First Esdras reads 'peoples', in the plural, perhaps connecting this group to those mentioned in 3.3 and elsewhere in Ezra–Nehemiah. Josephus (*Ant.* 11.19) follows 1 Esdras (his source) and interprets these as 'the surrounding nations', but 'primarily the Cuthians', μάλιστα τὸ Χουθαίων', that is, the Samaritans. (See discussion in Ginsberg 1982: 13.)

r. *Discouraged.* Literally, 'weakened the hands'. First Esdras reads ἐπικείμενα, 'pressed hard upon', 'acted against someone urgently'. The primary meaning of this Greek term is 'to be closed (off)', and I suspect it is a rendering of Hebrew סכר, which appears in the next verse. Besides meaning 'bribe', 'pay off', סכר also means 'to stop up', 'dam up', 'close off' (Gen. 8.2; Ps. 63.12).

s. *Made them afraid.* The written Hebrew (the *qethib*) reads, מְבַלַּהִים, 'used up, worn out, exhausted'; the reader is instructed to read the *qere*, מְבַהֲלִים, 'be terrified'. This is missing from 1 Esdras. That text reads simply 'stopped the building'.

t. **4.5** *Officials.* Literally, 'counsellors', 'advisors', but these are counselors or advisors to the king, acting in their official capacity, and so the translation is 'officials'. Josephus interprets correctly as 'the satraps and those in charge' who were corrupted by the bribes.

u. *To frustrate their plans.* First Esdras reads, 'by plots and demagoguery and uprisings they prevented the completion of the building'. This has little relation to the text in Ezra. It may have been supplied by the translator to explain how the Judeans' plans to build were frustrated. The Hebrew Ezra includes the letter to Artaxerxes at this point as an explanation of how the building project was stopped. Since this letter was already included in chap. 2 of 1 Esdras (and we are now in chap. 5 of 1 Esdras), it cannot be used as the explanation here.

v. *Until the reign of Darius king of Persia.* First Esdras reads, 'They prevented them from building for two years, until the reign of Darius'. The second year of Darius I is intended.

Notes

4.1 ***Enemies.*** צרי. Who are these enemies? As discussed in the Introduction, this commentary assumes that Ezra 1–6 was the last section to be added to Ezra–Nehemiah, so that the final author had the text of Ezra 7–Nehemiah 13 before him, including Nehemiah's memoir. In that memoir, the enemies of Judah and Benjamin are stated explicitly. They are the ones labelled 'enemies' by Nehemiah (4.5 [ET 4.11]), that is, the ones who tried to prevent Nehemiah from building Jerusalem's city wall: Sanballat, governor of Samaria; Tobiah, governor of Ammon; and Geshem the Arab, king of the Arab kingdom of Qedar (Neh. 4.1-4 [ET 4.7-11]). These were all Persian satrapal officials, Persian governors of the three provinces surrounding Judah on the north, west and south. They alone would have had the ability to bribe officials to stop progress on the temple as well as on the city wall. They are the ones this author had in mind.

The exiles. That is the community that had returned from exile in Babylon. The exiles who had been deported to Babylon and have now returned are credited with rebuilding the temple because they were the ones who brought with them the temple vessels, the vessels that Nebuchadnezzar had taken from the first temple and deposited in the temple of Marduk. The second temple could not have been built without this tangible evidence of Yhwh's return to Zion. (See the Introduction to Ezra 1–6, the section on the role of the temple vessels.)

Building a temple. First Esdras connects this verse to the one immediately before in which the enemies of the Judeans hear the music of the celebration and come to see what the commotion is about. This may be the implication here as well. In 1 Esdras, however, the ceremony celebrates the temple's completion, whereas in the Hebrew version the preceding verse (3.13) describes the ceremony that celebrates laying the temple's foundations.

Yhwh god of Israel. See comment on Ezra 1.3.

4.2 ***Like you . . . we.*** By the use of explicit pronouns (not grammatically necessary in Hebrew) the author marks a strong separation between the parties (Talshir 2001: 317).

Inquiring of. Literally, 'seeking an oracle from' (Gen. 25.22; Deut. 18.11). The expression 'inquire of Yhwh' or 'inquire of God' usually refers to inquiry through a seer, prophet or medium (e.g. 1 Kgs 22.8; 1 Sam. 28.7). For example, in 1 Sam. 9.9 we read:

> Formerly in Israel, someone who went to inquire (לִדְרוֹשׁ) of God would say, 'Come let us go to the seer', for what we call a prophet today formerly would be called a seer'.

The implication is that Yhwh was the god who could be trusted to provide an accurate oracle.

Your god. 'Your god' and not 'our god', and not even 'Yhwh'. By having the 'enemies' put it this way, the biblical author makes a separation between the two communities of worshipers—the Judeans and their 'enemies'.

We have been sacrificing. To sacrifice an animal to a god required an altar and, in the ancient Near East at least, a temple and its priesthood as well. These would have left physical remains in the ground, but no such remains have been found in the archaeology of either Judah or Samaria that can be dated to any time between the Assyrian conquest and the Persian period (Fried 2002a; Faust 2010). This statement may have been derived from the tradition of 2 Kgs 17.32, but it is not supported archaeologically.

Esarhaddon . . . brought us up here. Esarhaddon, the son of the Assyrian king Sennacherib, ruled Assyria from his father's death in 681 until his own in 669 BCE. He extended Assyria's reach into Egypt; and Manasseh, the son of Hezekiah, and king of Judah from 686 to 642, contributed a contingent to Esarhaddon's building projects (*ARAB* II, p. 265). Esarhaddon's inscriptions indicate that he followed the policy of the Assyrian kings before him. After he conquered Sidon and Tyre, for example, he deported their inhabitants, and brought in other peoples who were from the 'mountain regions and the seashore of the East' (Prism A, *ARAB* II, p. 211). Altogether, twelve separate deportations are credited to him (Oded 1979: 20), so that while we have no explicit information about it, it is possible that he also moved people into areas formerly belonging to the northern kingdom.

By this verse, the biblical writer states that the ones he is calling 'the enemies' of Judah and Benjamin are the Samaritans. According to Judean tradition (2 Kings 17), but not Samaritan tradition, the Samaritans are not part of the people Israel but had been brought into the area by various Assyrian kings. Because the ones who wrote an accusing letter to Artaxerxes against the Judeans are known to have lived in the capital city of Samaria (Ezra 4.17), the biblical author assumes that they must have been descended from those brought into the cities of Samaria from all parts of the Assyrian Empire, and has them make this statement. In fact, this statement is the proof that we do not have an actual quotation here since Samaritans would never have described themselves this way. According to the Samaritans' own tradition they are the original inhabitants of the land of Israel; they had never been deported and had never received foreigners coming into Israel (Anderson and Giles 2005; Hjelm 2000; Knoppers 2013). Moreover, they have been worshiping Yhwh since time immemorial, not simply since the days of Esarhaddon.

4.3 ***Not for you but for us to build.*** This rejection of the offer sets off the events that are described in the rest of the chapter. Those spurned bribe satrapal officials to write accusing letters to the kings of Persia, which result in work on the temple being stopped (4.24). This is the reversal in the good fortune of Zerubbabel and of the rest of the returnees that is demanded by Aristotelian rules of poetry. It results from their own decisions, from their cavalier attitude toward those who simply ask to help with the temple-building process. Those spurned react in anger, becoming enemies.

Although the story was created for a literary goal, it may reflect a strong desire for independence and autonomy from satrapal officials in the author's day under the Ptolemies (Gunneweg 1985: 85).

As Cyrus, king of Persia, commanded us. The reference is to Cyrus's authorization to build the temple (1.3; 3.7; 6.3). This is simply an excuse for the rejection. Since no one else is mentioned in Cyrus's authorization, no one else need participate, but neither is anyone excluded from participating. In fact, it has already been reported that Tyrians and Sidonians participated in bringing material for the temple's foundations (3.7). The purpose here may have been to demonstrate that the temple was pure and that the Samaritans had no role in it (Torrey 1970 [1910]: 235-36; Rudolph 1949: 33).

4.4 ***People of the land.*** These are not the 'peoples of the lands' mentioned in 3.3, where the phrase is in the plural and refers to the neighbouring peoples round about (*pace inter alia* Blenkinsopp 1988: 108; Williamson 1985: 50; Gunneweg 1985: 80). Here it is in the singular and refers to Persian-appointed provincial governors and other satrapal officials. Those are the 'enemies'; they are the ones who wrote the letters to King Artaxerxes and who controlled life in the satrapy. They formed the land-owning aristocracy who had oversight of the land of Beyond-the-River (Rudolph 1949: 33-34). (See Comment C below.)

4.5 *They.* That is, the 'people of the land', the 'oppressors' or 'enemies' of the Judeans.

Officials. Literally, 'advisors'. These are the official advisors to the king or to his satrapal or provincial governors (Ezra 7.28; 8.25), that is, those who had the standing to petition the king directly to stop the work. In the Achaemenid Empire, only the king had the power to permit the work on the temple or to stop it.

Darius king of Persia. There were three kings named Darius in the Persian Empire, so the question of which king is meant has plagued investigators—Darius I (522–486), Darius II (424–405) or Darius III (336–331). Darius I is the only real possibility, however. (See Comment E below as well as Comment D to Ezra 2.) The name is Darayavahuš in Persian, meaning 'He who holds firm the good' (Kent 1953: 180).

All the days of Cyrus king of Persia until the reign of Darius king of Persia. It is hard to know how to understand this phrase. What does the biblical writer know about the reigns of the Persian kings? Historically speaking, Cyrus reigned from 559 to 530, Cambyses, his son, from 530 to 522, Darius I, from 522 to 486 (see the Appendix). The biblical writer does not mention Cambyses, and may not know about him. The author then refers to letters to Xerxes (486–465 BCE) and to Artaxerxes (465–424 BCE), and then he mentions the second year of a king Darius, so might he refer here to Darius II (424–405 BCE). If Darius II were meant, then the order of the kings would be correct, but then we would have Zerubbabel and Jeshua active from the time of Cyrus (530 BCE at the latest) to the time of Darius II, over one hundred years. If Darius I is meant, then the inclusion of these letters to Xerxes and Artaxerxes must be explained. Comment A following the correspondence explains the intrusion of these letters, while Comment E directly below and the note on 4.24 below explains that the Darius here is Darius I.

Comments: Judah's Enemies Stop Temple Construction

A. The Rhetorical Role of the Dispute

As discussed in Comment A to Chapter 3, the first three chapters of Ezra provide the rhetorical prologue to Ezra 1-6. They set the scene and introduce the characters. The reader is supposed to be convinced by now of the author's knowledge of his subject and of his access to archival documents (displayed in Ezra 1-2). He should also be persuaded of the high moral quality, and good will of both the author and of those he portrays – Zerubbabel, Jeshua, and the returnees in general (described in Ezra 3). Also according to Hellenistic rules of rhetoric, the actors are portrayed enjoying unusually good fortune. They have lived to see their return to Judah and the foundations of the second temple being laid (Ezra 3.10-13).

According to Aristotelian rules of rhetoric, this great good fortune must be followed by a reversal from good fortune to bad, and if good fortune is symbolized by the second temple being built, then the reversal of fortune is the stoppage of the building project. Thus, we must have a story now about a stoppage in work on the second temple. Further, again according to Aristotelian rules of rhetoric, this stoppage must come about as a result of an ordinary decision made by the protagonists, a decision that has serious implications for the characters, but a decision that anyone could make. This normal and natural decision must bring about a reversal, moreover, that excites the audience to pity and fear (*Poetics* 3849b25). Accordingly, we read now of the natural, but very ill-advised, decision of Zerubbabel and the community leaders to reject the participation of non-Judeans in the temple-building project (Ezra 4.1-3). This is their unfortunate decision. Those rejected react angrily and respond by 'bribing officials to frustrate [the Judeans'] plan throughout the reign of King Cyrus of Persia and until the reign of King Darius of Persia' (Ezra 4.5). As a result, the building process is summarily stopped until the second year of Darius, arousing pity in the reader. The involvement of the Persian king in the stoppage arouses fear as well.

B. Is the Incident Narrated in Ezra 4.1-5 Historical?

No. The incident was created for a rhetorical effect. In fact, Tattenai's letter to Darius (Ezra 5.8) confirms that there never was an interruption in the temple-building project. According to Tattenai, viceroy at the time of Darius and in charge of the entire half-satrapy of Beyond-the-River (see note at 5.6), '[The temple] is being built of dressed stones with timber laid in the walls. That work is being done quickly and prospers in their hands.' Thus, by the time of Tattenai's writing, most likely in the second year of Darius, there had been no stoppage in the work on the temple, and it was progressing nicely (see discussion at Ezra 5; Gunneweg 1982; 1985: 105). Neither do the writings of Haggai and Zechariah, dated to the beginning years of Darius I, know of any stoppage by Persian authorities or of any dispute with them. Haggai blames the people themselves for their slowness in finishing the temple (Hag. 1.4). (See comment on Ezra 3.12 above.) Nor do these prophets know of any problems with Samaritans nor of any divisions between the returnees and any other group of residents.

The author of Ezra 1–6 created the incident because, writing in the Hellenistic period, he was following Hellenistic rhetorical rules of historiography. He needed a reversal in the great good fortune of the protagonists, and such a reversal could only be a stoppage in the temple-building process. Moreover, the reversal had to result from a normal natural decision of the protagonists, a decision that anyone could make. He created this by having the protagonists reject the *'am ha'areṣ*'s offer of help, resulting in their anger.

C. The 'Am Hā'āreṣ, the 'People of the Land'

Who are these 'people of the land', that is, the *'am hā'āreṣ,* whom the author sees as 'enemies' of the Judeans (4.4)?[1] They offer to help with the labor and presumably with the expenses of building the temple because, they say, they had been worshiping Yhwh since the Assyrian king brought them up here (4.2). After being spurned, they bribe government officials to frustrate the building plans (4.5); they write a letter to Xerxes (4.6), and they join other government officials to write to Artaxerxes (4.9, 10). The redactor glosses the list of the government officials who write the letter (4.9) with the explanation that they were descendants of those who were brought into the area by Assyrian kings (4.10). This gloss makes clear that to the biblical author the letter writers are Samaritans, and they are the 'enemies of the Judeans' (4.1), the *'am hā'āreṣ,* the 'people of the land' (4.4).

Thus, according to the biblical writer, these 'enemies' are the Samaritans and were descended from those who were brought into the area by Assyrian kings (4.2, 10). Many scholars, critical in their evaluation of other portions of the Bible, have accepted the biblical writer's viewpoint here with no discussion (e.g. Gunneweg 1983, 1985; Williamson 1985: 49; Blenkinsopp 1988; Schaper 2000; Barstad 1996, 2003). Williamson states that 'we have no reason to doubt their self-description'.

The book of Ezra uses the term *'am hā'āreṣ* in both its plural and singular forms. (See Comment C to Ezra 3 for a discussion of the meaning of the term in the plural.) Ezra 4.4 is its only instance of the term in the singular, however. According to the biblical corpus, in the pre-exilic period the *'am hā'āreṣ* are found participating in the revolt against Athalia (2 Kings 11); and they intervene after the assassinations of Amon (21.23-24) and Josiah (23.30) to elevate the next king to the throne. They thus comprised the landed aristocracy, the nonpriestly class of free landowning citizens of Judah who participated in the reins of government. They often owned slaves. According to Jeremiah, the king made a covenant with the officials of Judah, the officials of Jerusalem, the eunuchs, the priests and the *'am hā'āreṣ,* who all promised to release their Hebrew male and female slaves (Jer. 34.19).

Gunneweg (1983) argues that the term changed its meaning in the post-exilic period, however. Rather than the powerful aristocracy, they are now the poor—the descendants of those who never left, newly disenfranchised

1. This comment is based on Fried 2006. Please see that article for a full discussion of every occurrence of the term in the biblical corpus.

by the returnees. This claim has been disproven by the archaeology (see Introduction to Ezra 1–6, Exile and Return.), but it is also possible to test it via the biblical text itself. The Priestly writers are usually dated to the post-exilic period, and they include several instances of the term in their writings (Gen. 23.7, 12, 13; Lev. 4.27; 20.2, 4; Num. 14.9).[2] The question is then whether the *'am hā'āreṣ* in the Priestly writings are wealthy landowners or poor and disenfranchised. In Genesis 23, the *'am hā'āreṣ* in Canaan are the Hittites who own land in Canaan. They are the men from whom Abraham buys a section of a field in which to bury his wife. These Hittite *'am hā'āreṣ* sitting at the gate of the city evoke the image of the elders deliberating at the gate in the book of Ruth. As elders, they owned land and participated in the administration of government; yet, they are foreign. They are Hittite, not Israelite; nevertheless, the meaning of the term is the same. They are the landed aristocracy of the area, part of the oligarchy, and Abraham bows to them: וַיָּקָם אַבְרָהָם וַיִּשְׁתַּחוּ לְעַם־הָאָרֶץ לִבְנֵי־חֵת׃, 'And Abraham rose and bowed to the *'am hā'āreṣ*, the Hittites' (Gen. 23.7). In the P version of the story of the spies (Numbers 14) the *'am hā'āreṣ* are those who are dwelling in Canaan, and they are also foreign, non Judean, yet they are people feared, not the lowly disenfranchised: אַךְ בַּיהוָה אַל־תִּמְרֹדוּ וְאַתֶּם אַל־תִּירְאוּ אֶת־עַם הָאָרֶץ כִּי לַחְמֵנוּ הֵם סָר צִלָּם מֵעֲלֵיהֶם וַיהוָה אִתָּנוּ אַל־תִּירָאֻם׃, 'Only, do not rebel against Yhwh; and do not fear the *'am hā'āreṣ*, for they are no more than bread for us; their protection is removed from them, and Yhwh is with us; do not fear them' (Num. 14.9).

In fact, the term refers here to the same people as in Gen. 23.7. They are the non-Israelite landowning aristocracy of Canaan (Levine 1993: 363-64). Joshua and Caleb admonish their people not to fear them as they are 'bread' for the Israelites. The people feared would not be the poor, the disenfranchised slaves, tenant farmers, women, or children. The ones feared would be those wielding power, that is, the landed aristocracy. P recognizes that while some may dread these foreign rulers who presently control the land, he is optimistic, for their protection has turned from them. Yhwh is with the Israelites so long as they do not rebel against him (Num. 14.9). For P, therefore, writing in the Persian period, the identity of the *'am hā'āreṣ* is clear, they are the landed aristocracy, those who control the strings of government, and they are foreign.

This is the meaning of the term in Ezra 4.4; the meaning of the term has not changed. The *'am hā'āreṣ* in the postexilic period are not the poor and disenfranchised but the powerful landed aristocracy. According to Ezra 4, these *'am hā'āreṣ* were the enemies, oppressors (*ṣārê*), of the people of Judah and Benjamin, and they were foreign. They bribed senior government

2. For a discussion of the date of P, see Milgrom 1991; Levine 1993, and references cited there.

officials (Ezra 4.5) to prevent the Judeans from building their temple. They were thus in a position to pay satrapal officials well enough to cause them to frustrate even the plans of Zerubbabel (the Persian appointed governor of Judah) and Jeshua (the high priest). They were not poor rural peasants. They were powerful, well connected, and wealthy. Not only are they described as bribing government officials to frustrate the Judeans' plans throughout the reign of Cyrus until the reign of King Darius of Persia (4.5), but they themselves joined these officials to write accusations against them to the Persian kings (4.6-10).

The biblical writer has the *'am hā'āreṣ* state that they are descendants of those brought into the area by Assyrian kings (4.2). He repeats this again in the letter to Artaxerxes (4.10). This is not likely. The signatories of this authentic correspondence with the Persian kings (see comment on Ezra 4.11-23) were in fact among the highest officials in the satrapal government of Beyond-the-River 'eating the salt of the palace' (Ezra 4.9). As such they would have been appointed by the king from his inner circle in Persia or Babylon, and assigned to the satrapy by the king or his agent (Fried 2004). They would not have been the descendants of those deported into the area by the Assyrians. They would not even have been local. Few local dynasts participated in satrapal government. The Hecotomnids of Caria may be the lone exception to the general rule (Hornblower 1982; Ruzicka, 1992).

Why then did the biblical author have them say that they were descendants of those deported to the area by the Assyrian kings? The answer is simple. The viceroy Reḥum, second in command of the satrapy Beyond-the-River, most likely a Babylonian, was the primary letter writer to Artaxerxes (4.8), and he had his seat of office in the city of Samaria (4.17). The redactor, writing in the Hellenistic period and having his own problems with the Samaritans, assumed that the letter writers were Samaritan, and so concluded based on the traditions of 2 Kings 17 that they had been brought into the area by Assyrian kings. It is not historical.

D. The Enemies of the Returning Judeans

If the *'am hā'āreṣ* were the landed aristocracy of Beyond-the-River, why did the biblical author call them the 'enemies', or the 'oppressors' of the Judeans? Nehemiah's memoir (set in the time of Artaxerxes I) provided the biblical writer with the historical context for the label. According to Nehemiah's memoir, 'enemies' (*ṣārîm*) of the Judeans attempted to prevent Nehemiah from building a city wall around Jerusalem (Neh. 4.1-7). According to the memoir, Sanballat (the governor of Samaria) backed up by his militia, Tobiah (the governor of Ammon), and Geshem or Gašmu, king of the Arab kingdom of Qedar, were the enemies (*ṣārîm*) of Nehemiah and of the Judeans (Neh. 3.33-34 [ET 4.1-2]; Fried 2002c). As royally appointed governors and rulers in their respective provinces, these three men were part of the Persian administrative apparatus in the southern provinces of the satrapy Beyond-the-River. They were thus among the *'am hā'āreṣ* of the area (see Comment C, above), constituting the satrapal administration. According to Nehemiah, they were enemies of Judah, even willing to kill to prevent a wall being built around Jerusalem (Neh. 4.5). Nehemiah's labeling them as 'enemies' (*ṣārîm*) led the author of Ezra 1–6 to label these satrapal officials, these *'am hā'āreṣ*, as enemies as well. Achaemenid provincial governors, such as Sanballat, Tobiah, and Gašmu, had the connections, the power, and the resources required to bribe higher-ranking satrapal officials to frustrate the work on the wall. Indeed, they may have done exactly that. The letter to Artaxerxes included in this chapter more properly belongs to the book of Nehemiah than the book of Ezra since it concerns Nehemiah's wall-building efforts, not the temple (Fried 2012b).

E. Darius King of Persia

Which of three kings named Darius is meant in Ezra 4.5, 24, and chaps. 5 and 6? That is, under which king—Darius I (522–486 BCE), Darius II (424–405 BCE) or Darius III (336–331 BCE)—was the temple completed? We know that Nehemiah was sent to Jerusalem by an Artaxerxes in that king's twentieth year (Neh. 2.1). Artaxerxes grants him timber to build the wall around Jerusalem and to build a house for himself (Neh. 2.8). He is not granted timber to build a temple, however, and in fact it is apparent from Neh. 6.10-11 that there was already a functioning temple in Jerusalem during Nehemiah's tenure. The temple must have been built prior to his arrival. Therefore, it would have been built during the reign of a King Darius who ruled before a King Artaxerxes. Darius I ruled before Artaxerxes I (465–424) and Darius I and Darius II both ruled before Artaxerxes II (405–359). If Nehemiah was governor during the reign of Artaxerxes I, then the Darius would be Darius I; if he was governor during the reign of Artaxerxes II, then it could be either Darius I or II. Nehemiah states that while he was governor of Judah, he left Judah and went to the king in the king's 32nd year. Unfortunately, both kings Artaxerxes I and II ruled for over forty years, so this fact doesn't help to narrow down the choice.

An Aramaic letter dated to the seventeenth year of a King Darius (*TAD* 4.7-9) was found in an archive on the Nile island of Elephantine. It is a copy of a letter sent to Bagavahya, the then Persian governor of Yehud. The letter states that the writers had sent a similar letter three years before to Yoḥanan the high priest in Judah and to Delaiah and Shelemiah, sons of Sanballat, who was governor of Samaria. An answer was received from Bagavahya and from Delaiah. This Sanballat is very likely the one referred to in Nehemiah's memoir. It seems that at the time of this letter, he was elderly and his son was acting on his behalf. Since Sanballat was governor during the reign of an Artaxerxes, the Darius who was king at the time of the Elephantine letter must be a king who ruled after an Artaxerxes—thus, Darius II or III. Since Darius III did not rule seventeen years, this letter must have been written in the seventeenth year of Darius II (407 BCE), and Nehemiah—like Sanballat—must have been governor during the reign of Artaxerxes I, the only Artaxerxes who ruled before Darius II. If Nehemiah was governor under Artaxerxes I, and since at that time the temple was already built (Neh. 6.10-11), the temple must have been built during the reign of Darius I, the only King Darius who preceded Artaxerxes I.

Edelman (2005: 13-25) attempts to make Nehemiah, Joshua and Zerubbabel contemporaries and to argue that the temple was built in the reign of Artaxerxes I, in the time of Nehemiah. According to the biblical text, Jeshua, the first high priest of the return was the grandson of Seraiah, the high priest killed by Nebuchadnezzar. Edelman says that he was really the great-grandson, arbitrarily adding a generation. She also adds generations to the ancestry of Zerubbabel, making him a contemporary of Nehemiah and thereby changing the date of the temple's construction. She seeks to move the date of temple construction to the time of Nehemiah because it does not seem logical to her that a temple would be built in a city without walls and without a population. She states (p. 8), 'It would seem much more logical for the temple to have been re-established at the same time that Jerusalem was rebuilt as a *birah*. It would have been part of the larger building project that established a temple to Yhwh, the local god, for the newly resettled population and local conscripts posted to the garrison to use to honor him.'

The problem with logic is that life doesn't always follow it. According to the archaeological excavations, the temple of Yhwh on Mt Gerizim, for example, was erected by the Samaritans under the Persians, in the mid-fifth century, and was the first structure to be built on the mountain (Magen 2000: 97). Only in the Hellenistic period was a walled city built around it with fortresses and public buildings (Stern and Magen 2000; Magen 2007: 158). Thus, temples can precede cities and city walls, and there is no reason to doubt that the temple was built and dedicated in the reign of Darius I.

Reflections

Our author's idea of the highest good, the positive proof of Yhwh's favor, is the rebuilding of his temple in Jerusalem. Conversely, the worst disaster imaginable is a stoppage of temple construction.

> Happy are those whom you choose and bring near to live in your courts.
> We shall be satisfied with the goodness of your house, your holy temple
> (Ps. 65: 4).

Ezra 4.6-11a

The Plot Thickens: The Enemies of Judah Write Slanderous Letters to the Persian Kings

In this section we are told that the Judeans' enemies write slanderous letters to the king to stop the work on the temple until the second year of Darius (in 520 BCE), but the king they write to is not Cyrus (538–530 BCE), as expected, nor even Darius himself (522–486 BCE), but Xerxes (486–465 BCE) and Artaxerxes (465–424 BCE). This section and the following, which includes the correspondence between Artaxerxes and satrapal officials, is an intrusion. It has nothing to do with the temple but has only to do with building Jerusalem's city wall in the time of Nehemiah! The hostility toward the Judeans seen in the letter is a reaction of satrapal governors and officials to the wall, not to the temple. The Hellenistic writer uses the correspondence with Artaxerxes to create drama in his story. Although a letter to Xerxes and an earlier letter to Artaxerxes are mentioned, they are not supplied, nor are they referred to in 1 Esdras. They may not have existed, and the references to them may simply be a late embellishment to convey the notion that the objection to Judeans restoring their city continued for a long time, over the reigns of many kings (Fulton and Knoppers 2011).

Translation

6. *In the reign of Xerxes,*[a] *at the beginning of his reign, they wrote an accusation against the residents of Judah and Jerusalem.* 7. *And in the days of Artaxerxes,*[b] *Mithradates, Tabe'el, and the rest of his colleagues*[c] *wrote in peace*[d] *to*[e] *Artaxerxes king of Persia.*[f] *The text*[g] *of the request*[h] *is written in Aramaic and translated [into Persian?*[i]*].*

[The following is in[j]*] Aramaic:* 8. *Reḥum the viceroy*[k] *and Shimshai*[l] *the secretary*[m] *wrote a letter regarding*[n] *Jerusalem to Artaxerxes the king, as follows:* 9. *Now*[o] *[say] Reḥum the viceroy, Shimshai the secretary, and the rest of their colleagues*[p]*—the judges,*[q] *the investigators, the Persian officials(?),*[r] *the people of Erech, [that is,] the Babylonians, and the people of Susa, that is,*[s] *the Elamites*[t] 10. *And the rest of the peoples whom the great*

and famous Osnappar settled here in the city of Samaria and in the rest of Beyond-the-River,[u] *and now* 11a. *this is a copy of the letter that they sent to him:*[v]

Textual Notes

a. **4.6** *Xerxes.* Literally, Aḥašwerosh. This verse (Ezra 4.6) has no parallel in 1 Esdras or in Josephus.

b. **4.7** *Artaxerxes.* Vocalized here as Artakhshasta, but elsewhere always as Artakhshast. The *s* is spelled with a sin here but with a samekh in Ezra 7 and in Nehemiah. Grätz (2006) finds evidence in this for two separate authors. First Esdras inserts 'king of the Persians', moving the phrase up from its position in Ezra.

c. *His colleagues.* The written text (the *kethib*) has 'his colleague', but read the plural with the *qere*. First Esdras adds the phrase 'living in Samaria and other places', which clarifies the situation.

d. *In peace.* This is Aramaic. First Esdras interprets it as a personal name, Βεσλεμος, Beslemos, whereas Greek Ezra reads ἐν εἰρήνῃ, 'in peace'. If the word is not interpreted as Aramaic but as Hebrew, then it may be a transliteration of a Babylonian personal name, Bēl-šalmu (Steiner 2007). See note below.

e. *To.* *'al,* עַל. This word is Aramaic.

f. *To Artaxerxes king of Persia.* First Esdras inserts the phrase 'against those who were living in Judea and Jerusalem'.

g. *Text. Ketab.* This word used as a noun (instead of as a verb, 'he wrote') appears only in postexilic texts, primarily in Esther but also three times in Chronicles and once among the Aramaic texts from Elephantine (*TAD* D 23.1). It is Aramaic.

h. *Request.* נִשְׁתְּוָנָא. *ništᵉwānāʿ.* This Persian word appears at Elephantine (*TAD* A 6.1: 3) referring probably to an official request. The word itself does not necessarily connote something written.

i. *Into Persian*? Something must have dropped out here for the verse to make sense. It is possible that the letter was written in Aramaic and translated into Persian for the king. See v. 18.

j. [*The following is in*]. This phrase is missing but is intended, as we have a switch here from Hebrew to Aramaic.

k. **4.8** *Viceroy.* Literally, *bᵉ'ēl ṭᵉ'ēm,* 'hyparch', 'vice-satrap'. Both 1 Esdras and Greek Ezra misinterpret this as a personal name and transliterate rather than translate—Βεσλεμος in 1 Esdras and βααλταμ in Greek Ezra.

l. *Shimshai* The name could mean 'belonging to Shamash, the sun god'; it is similar to the Hebrew name for Samson, 'Shimshon'. Shamash was a very popular Mesopotamian god, but the town of Bet-Shemesh (Temple of the Sun-god) suggests that he had his adherents in Judah as well.

m. *Shimshai the secretary.* First Esdras inserts 'and the rest of their associates, living in Samaria and other places'. This is a summary of vv. 9 and 10, which are omitted from 1 Esdras.

n. *Regarding.* *'al,* עַל. Or maybe it is 'against' Jerusalem.

o. **4.9** *Now.* Literally, 'then', אדין. Probably because a verb is expected here, Greek Ezra interprets the Aramaic *'ādaîn* as the verb 'to judge' from the root 'to judge', *dyn,* דין. Greek Ezra begins τάδε ἔκρινεν, 'thus judged [Reḥum]', translating the word as the verb 'judge' and bringing in the 'thus', τάδε, from the end of the previous verse. Greek and Aramaic letters of the period typically begin ‘thus says’, which is the basis of the Greek translation, and my own. Verses 9 and 10 are not included in 1 Esdras.

p. *Colleagues.* First Esdras reads ‘and the rest of their council (βουλῆς) and judges (κριταί)’. This is all that remains in 1 Esdras of the long list of titles and supposed ethnicities in vv. 9 and 10. This version may be original, except for the notion of a council, but see the following textual note. First Esdras may be interpreting the city of Samaria as a Greek polis, with a self-governing city council. This was not the case anywhere in the Persian Empire, however. (See Fried 2004: 188-93.)

q. *Judges.* Emending *dînāyê* to *dayānayā'*, ‘judges’. Because of v. 10, the Masoretes vocalized this and all the following official titles as ethnicities. Except for mention of the judges, and except to say that the letter was written by people living in Samaria, the entire list of titles and ethnicities included here and in v. 10 is omitted from 1 Esdras. Nor is there any mention there that those now living in Samaria are descendants of those brought up by Assyrian kings. Instead, 1 Esdras simply repeats Ezra 4.17.

Parts of vv. 4.9-11 comprise Fragment 2 of 4Q117 (4QEzra). (See Comment D on p. 229 for my translation of 4QEzra.)

r. *Persian officials.* The word translated here as ‘officials’ is not known from elsewhere and is a guess. Zadok (2007) suggests that these are Lycians, but this does not fit the context, and the linguistic changes required seem tenuous at best.

s. *That is.* Reading די הוא for דהו. דהוא, meaning ‘that is’, appears in an Aramaic graffito from Egypt (from Wadi Hammāmāt; see Dupont-Sommer 1947–48: 105ff.). This is customarily, but incorrectly, read as an ethnicity, Dehavites (Rosenthal 1995: 25, #35).

t. *Judges . . . Elamites.* Greek Ezra transliterates rather than translates these terms, thus interpreting them as peoples. So does Josephus (*Ant.* 11.21), but he changes them into peoples that he knows (peoples of Syria, Phoenicia, Amman, Moab and Samaria).

u. **4.10** *Beyond-the-River.* This is missing from 1 Esdras, which just reads ‘Samaria and other places’.

v. **4.11a** *That they sent to him.* Omitted in 1 Esdras. It is redundant anyway.

Notes

4.6 ***Xerxes.*** Literally, Aḥašweroš, the king in the Esther story. The name is Khshayarsha in Persian, probably meaning ‘hero among kings’ (Kent 1953: 182). He was the son of Darius I, not the father as is erroneously reported in Dan. 9.1. His mother was Queen Atossa, the daughter of Cyrus the Great. Xerxes reigned from 486 to 465 BCE. Although his eldest son was also named Darius, that son never became king. According to Diodorus Siculus (11.69), one named Artabanus assassinated Xerxes and told Artaxerxes, Xerxes’ second son, that his brother Darius had done it. Artaxerxes and Artabanus then killed Darius in revenge. With the oldest son, Darius, out of the way, Artabanus then attempted to kill Artaxerxes, but Artaxerxes got the upper hand and killed him instead, and thus became king. So the story in Diodorus. Neither 1 Esdras nor Josephus includes the notice of a letter to Xerxes.

Beginning of his reign. Parker and Dubberstein (1956: 16-17) report that Darius died in November of 486. Xerxes would have come to the throne in

December or late November of that year, at the earliest. A document from Borsippa in Babylon (*VAS* V 117) is dated to the 22nd day of the eighth month of Xerxes' accession year, that is December 1, 486. In Babylon, regnal years were counted from the first of Nisan, the first month of the Babylonian calendar. Months prior to that belong to the king's accession year. In Persia, however, regnal years are counted from the time the king ascends the throne. There is no accession year (Depuydt 1995). (For a discussion of why letters to Xerxes and Artaxerxes are inserted at this point, see Comment A at the end of the chapter.)

They wrote an accusation. We are not told what is in the letter, or who exactly wrote it. Nor can we know if such a letter actually existed. Unfortunately we know nothing about life in Judah during the reign of Xerxes as our only sources for Judah in the Persian period, Ezra and Nehemiah, do not cover it. Josephus dates the events of Ezra 7–10 and of Nehemiah to Xerxes and not Artaxerxes, but he has no reason for doing so other than to try to straighten out the bewildering chronology. He has no information for this period other than the biblical text.

Against the residents of Judah and Jerusalem. This phraseology indicates an external point of view. The accusations were not written against 'us' but against 'them', against those people who live in Judah and Jerusalem. This external point of view will become progressively accentuated as the text moves into Aramaic (Arnold 1996).

4.7 ***Artaxerxes.*** Artaḥshasta in the Hebrew, Artakhshatha in Persian. 'Arta' means 'law, justice', and refers to the archangel attending the god Ahuramazda. The suffix 'khshatha' means 'kingdom', or 'power', so the name might be 'having a kingdom of justice' (Kent 1953: 171). Artaxerxes I, Xerxes' second son, ruled from 465 to 423. Josephus omits the correspondence from Xerxes, and changes Artaxerxes' name to Cambyses in order to obtain the correct chronological order of the Persian kings—Cyrus, Cambyses, Darius. (See Appendix for the dates of the Persian kings.)

Mithradates. Not the same man who was Cyrus's treasurer, but see the note on 1.8 for the derivation of this common Persian name.

Ṭabe'el. The god or God (El) is good. This common Babylonian name is *Ṭa-a-bu-il* or *Ṭa-a-bu-ilī*, 'The god or the gods is/are good' (*CAD* Ṭ, 34).

His colleagues. This Aramaic word appears only here in the Hebrew Bible, but it is common in the Aramaic letters of Elephantine. One letter (*TAD* A 4.7: 1) reads, 'to our lord Bagavahya, governor of Yehud, [from] your servants Yedaniah and his colleagues (כנותה)'. Here in Ezra the Aramaic word has a Hebrew personal pronoun suffix rather than an Aramaic one. The word entered Aramaic from the Akkadian *kinattu,* 'a person of equal status as you', that is, a colleague (Rosenthal 1995: 62).

In peace. Since antiquity, exegetes have asked whether this is the personal name Beshlam or the phrase 'in peace'. The word *beshlam*, meaning ‘in peace’, occurs frequently throughout the late-sixth- or early-fifth-century Aramaic letters from Hermopolis as part of the phrase ‘let me/us see your face in peace’. It was recently argued, however, that here it refers to the Babylonian name Bēl-šalāmu, meaning ‘the god, Bēl, has reconciled (himself to us)’ (Steiner 2007). Although Babylonians served in very high positions throughout the Persian Empire, it is difficult to see a Babylonian supervising a Persian, as would be implied by listing the Babylonian Bēl-šalāmu before the Persian Mithradates. It may be more plausible that this word is Aramaic, like the rest of the letter, and means something like ‘in fellowship’, or perhaps it is a shortened form of the full expression, ‘let us see your face in peace’. Either of these would fit the context. Josephus omits all the letter writers except for Rathymos (Reḥum) and Semelios (Shimshai).

Order. The word here is the Persian *nishtevan,* and is usually translated ‘letter’. In the Hebrew Bible it occurs only here and in Ezra 7.11, to refer to the instructions from Artaxerxes to Ezra. Extrabiblically, it occurs in a similar context in a letter (*TAD* A 6.1:3) from Arsames, the Persian satrap of Egypt, to one of his officials. Schwiderski (2000: 346) declares that the word ‘written’ that appears here after the word ‘order’ is redundant. The word *nishtevan* does not imply a written document, however, but may just mean ‘order’, ‘instruction’ (Williamson 1985: 54). When it is written that fact is made explicit as here and as in the Elephantine letter where we read נשתונא כתיב, which Porten translates as ‘a rescript was written’. In Ezra 7.11, we read פַּרְשֶׁגֶן הַנִּשְׁתְּוָן, ‘a copy of the order’, implying a written copy of an oral order.

And translated. Like the previous one to Xerxes, this letter is not included, unless (as suggested by Steiner 2006) all the following is the letter that they sent. It was presumably written in Aramaic, as are most of the extant chancellery letters from the Persian period (whether from Egypt or from Bactria). Perhaps it was translated into Persian for the king’s benefit.

The following is in Aramaic. This passage may refer to the following letter, or it may refer to the fact that the rest of chap. 4, all of chap. 5, and chap. 6 up through v. 18 are in Aramaic. Hebrew begins again in 6.19. (See Note on 4.24 below and Comment A to Ezra 5.1-2 for a discussion of the use of Aramaic in the narrative that frames the letter.)

4.8 ***Reḥum.*** A Babylonian Judean name (Zadok 1979: 48). As his title implies, he was the second highest official in the satrapy Beyond-the-River, second only to the satrap. Babylonians of Judean descent, like other Babylonians, were active in the highest levels of government in the Persian empire (Stolper 1984).

Viceroy (bᵉʿēl ṭᵉʿēm). (Greek *hyparch.*) See Introduction for a discussion of this title. That these viceroys, or hyparchs, had soldiers under them is confirmed by Herodotus (*Histories* 7.26), for when he states that Xerxes orders all the army to come to him in Sardis from Cappadocia, he adds,

'Now which of the *hyparchs* brought the most splendidly appointed army to win the rewards of the king, I cannot say'.

Secretary. Literally, 'scribe'. Signing after the viceroy was the chancellery secretary, Shimshai. As in Egypt (*TAD* A 6.1), he would have been a native, since unlike other satrapal officials, the secretary was often required to interact with the local population (Fried 2004: 86-87). Each of the satrapal viceroys had such a secretary by necessity (Herodotus, *Histories* 3.128).

Reḥum . . . and Shimshai . . . wrote a letter. How many letters were written? There was one to Xerxes (4.6); there was one to Artaxerxes written by Mithredates, Tabe'el, and their colleagues (4.7); and a third, also to Artaxerxes, written by Reḥum and Shimshai and their colleagues (4.8). This last is the only one whose text is included. First Esdras omits the letter to Xerxes, and combines the names of the letter writers in 4.7 and 8, so that it mentions only one letter, the one included in the biblical text. The response from Artaxerxes in 1 Esdras is to Reḥum and Shimshai, and so it is only to the third letter. The author of 1 Esdras telescoped the various introductions in Ezra into one.

Steiner (2006) maintains that the core of Ezra 4–6 is one long archival document, with the letters to and from Darius (Ezra 5.6–6.12) incorporated as an appendix at the end of the letters to and from Artaxerxes. This would explain the reverse chronological order of the letters, that is, why the letters to and from Darius I come after the letters to and from Artaxerxes. According to Steiner (2006: 674), the biblical author stuck this one long archival document into his text in its entirety. The letters do not form one long archival document, however, as there is narrative separating them (Ezra 4.24–5.5).

4.9 ***Judges.*** Writing after the satrapal secretary were the judges. As is evident from the Babylonian and Egyptian evidence, satrapal judges were appointed by the king or his agent and were called royal judges, or judges of the king (*TAD* B5.1: 3). The so-called provincial judges, in contrast, were appointed by the satrap (*TAD* A5.2; Porten 1996: 136 n. 19). According to Herodotus (3.31), the royal or satrapal judges were 'a body of Persian men picked [by the king] who held office till death or till some injustice is detected in them'. The judges who wrote the letter with Reḥum, the viceroy, thus functioned at the satrapal level, and so were Persian (or Babylonian) men appointed by the king himself or by his imperial agent. After the Achaemenid occupation of Babylon, for example, all local judges were replaced by Persians (Dandamayev and Lukonin 1989: 122-23). The 'judge of the [Babylonian] canal of Sîn', for example, was the Persian Ishtabuzanu; later his son, Humardātu, took over the post. A document on the receipt of a loan of 45 *mina* of silver by Marduk-naṣir-apli of the Babylonian House of Egibi was registered in the presence of the Iranian judge Ammadātu. This was also true in Egypt. In both the Elephantine archives and the Arsames letters, every named judge was either Iranian or (rarely) Babylonian. There were no Egyptian judges for the Egyptians, nor were there Judean judges for the Judeans. This was also the situation in Beyond-the-River. The judges listed here, like the rest of the satrapal officials, were not local but were from Susa and Uruk, central locations of power in the Achaemenid Empire.

Investigators. The fourth title in the list of writers, listed after the viceroy, the scribe, and the judges, is that of the *aparsatkāya*, 'investigators'. The title is likely from the Old Persian root **u*- 'well' and **frasta* 'questioned', 'investigated', plus the Aramaic suffix *kāya* (Kent 1953: 176). The use of Persian titles demonstrates the complete Persian nature of the administrative and judicial systems, a fact that held true for every satrapy of the Achaemenid Empire.

4.10. ***And the rest of the peoples whom . . . the great and famous Osnappar settled here. . . .*** Osnappar may have been great and famous at one time, but now no one knows who he is! Guesses abound. The most popular is Assurbanipal, king of Assyria, 669–630 BCE. According to Millard (1976: 11),

> Identification with Ashurbanipal can hardly be doubted, even if the process of change cannot be traced fully at present. Shift of final *l* to *r* may be a sign of Persian influence, as in Old Persian *Babiruš* for Babylon, or it may be a Semitic shift. The loss of medial *rb* could be attributed to scribal or oral ellipsis in the absence of any more definite proposal. Despite these changes, the Assyrian sibilant remains in initial Ashur [i.e. Os], as in Esarhaddon (Ezra 4.2).

This verse, 4.10, is a gloss, that is, an explanatory note added by the biblical author. It is not part of the original letter that begins in v. 11 (Williamson 2008). This verse and the one before it were inserted secondarily into the letter since they interrupt the natural flow of the text. The text should go directly from v. 8 to v. 11b, that is, from 'as follows' (v. 8) to 'to King Artaxerxes' (v. 11b). It is possible that v. 9 was written on the outside of the letter as the address, and that when the biblical writer inserted v. 9 into his text he added v. 10 by way of explanation. Verse 10 is a gloss by which the biblical author attempts to make clear that the letter writers are the same group of people whom he has previously labelled both as 'enemies of the Judeans (4.1) and as the 'people of the land', the *'am hā'āreṣ*, the 'landed aristocracy', that is, as the Samaritans (4.4). Nevertheless, the letter writers who are listed in v. 9 were satrapal officials. Primary among them was the *bᵉ'ēl ṭᵉ'ēm*, the highest official of the satrapy next to the satrap himself (Briant 2002; Fried 2004). They were not Samaritans.

Much of our information on satrapal officials in the Persian Empire comes from Egypt (Fried 2004). Except for the Egyptian scribes and accountants who interacted with the local population, all the officials in the Egyptian satrapy were from Iran or occasionally Babylon. Pherendates, the satrap of Egypt under Darius I, Achaemenes, Egypt's satrap under Xerxes and Artaxerxes, and Arsames, under Artaxerxes and Darius II, were all Persian. Their chief assistants were either Persian or Babylonian, as were the judges, heralds, provincial governors, garrison commanders, and the commanders of the separate military detachments. In fact, every official, every judge, of Achaemenid Egypt whose name we know was either a Persian, a Babylonian, or a Judean from Babylon or Persia (*TAD*; Briant 2002; Fried 2004; 2006: 132 n. 12; 2013c). For example, after the Persian conquest of Egypt, the Egyptian Khnemibre, chief of public works of Upper and Lower Egypt under the pharaohs, was demoted. Under the Persians he reported to the Iranian Atiyvaya, *śariś* of Persia (Posener 1936: 117-30; Bongrani Fanfoni and Israel 1994). This was true in every case that we know of except the scribal class. An early letter to Arsames (*TAD* A 6.1) provides the titles of some officials in the satrapal hierarchy. The verso reads,

> [To] our lord Arsames [w]ho is in Egypt, [from] your servants Achaemenes and his colleagues the heralds; Ba[gadana and his colleagues] the judges; Peteisi and his colleagues the scribes of the province of Pamunpara/Nasunpara, Harudj and his colleagues the scribes of the province of...

The herald, Achaemenes, and the judge, Bagadana, in the Egyptian satrapal court were both Iranian, as were their colleagues, the rest of the heralds and judges. Only the provincial scribes, Peteisi and Harudj, were Egyptian. Except for the scribes and the chief accountant, there were no Egyptians evident among the officials in the satrapal court in Egypt. The ones who held power in Achaemenid Egypt were ethnic Iranians and some Babylonians, including the occasional Babylonian Judean. They were not Egyptian. This was the pattern throughout the empire. As elsewhere, the satrapal officials of Beyond-the-River, the ones who wrote accusing letters to the king, were Persians and Babylonians. Appointed by the king or his agent, they were sent to the satrapy Beyond-the-River to administer it.

To the list of satrapal officials, the redactor has glossed 'and the rest of the people whom the great and famous Osnappar deported and settled in the cities of Samaria and the rest of Beyond-the-River' (4.10). The biblical author assumed that these satrapal officials were descendants of those brought into the area by Assyrian kings because Reḥum, the primary letter writer, had his seat of office in Samaria, the capital city of the province of that name (4.17). The author, writing in the Hellenistic period, assumed that since the letter writers were located in Samaria, they must have been Samaritan and therefore (based on the tradition of 2 Kings 17) they had been brought into the area by Assyrian kings. This is not likely. The men listed as signatories were among the highest officials in the satrapal government of Beyond-the-River 'eating the salt of the palace' (Ezra 4.9). As such they would have been appointed by the king from his inner circle in Persia and

Babylon and sent to the satrapy by the king himself (Fried 2013c). They would not have been the descendants of those deported into the area by the Assyrians. Few local dynasts participated in the government of satrapies. The Hecotomnids of Caria may be the lone exception to the general rule (Hornblower 1982; Ruzicka 1992). (See Comments B and C below, as well as Fried 2006; 2013c).

4.11a ***A copy of the letter that they sent to him.*** The date of this letter to King Artaxerxes is not known, but the relationship between it and Nehemiah's effort to build Jerusalem's city wall is near certain and will be discussed further at Nehemiah 2. Nehemiah addresses this king in the twentieth year of his reign, 445 BCE (Neh. 2.1). The letter included here in Ezra 4 is apparently a reaction to Nehemiah's arrival and his wall-building efforts, and so can be dated to that same year (445 BCE; Fried 2012b). We can assume that it was Sanballat, Tobiah, and Gashmu who bribed Reḥum to petition the king.

Rudolph (1949: 45) asks why these satrapal officials wrote directly to the king, bypassing the satrap of Beyond-the-River. He suggests that this was because the satrap, Megabyzus, had rebelled against King Artaxerxes I and that the officials were concerned that the Judeans were involved in that revolt and that was why they were building the wall (so also Blenkinsopp 1988: 114; Clines 1984: 77; Olmstead 1948: 313; Williamson 1985: 62). The story of Megabyzus's rebellion is told only in the work of Ctesias, however, and is considered 'untrustworthy' (Hoglund 1992: 162-64), and 'fictionalized' and 'unbelievable' (Briant 2002: 320, 578). According to Ctesias, Megabyzus participated with Achaemenes, satrap of Egypt, to put down an Egyptian revolt. The revolt was successfully repressed, but during it Achaemenes, Xerxes' son, was killed. After the revolt, Megabyzus returned to Damascus where he had his office as satrap of Beyond-the-River, and from where, according to Ctesias, he seceded from the empire. Again according to Ctesias, King Artaxerxes sent several armies against him, but after Megabyzus defeated them all, the king eventually pardoned him. No other Greek writer refers to this revolt, and certainly they would have done so since he was said to have used Greek mercenaries in his rebellion. Moreover, it is extremely unlikely that Artaxerxes would have pardoned anyone, particularly a satrap, if he had rebelled against him in this manner, even if he was married to Artaxerxes' sister.

There is no need to posit a reason for not writing to the satrap. Reḥum, the second in command of the satrapy, would have been able to contact the king directly without having to go through his satrap first. This is especially true if the satrap had been called back to Susa at the time, leaving Reḥum in charge.

Comments

A. The Use of Aramaic in the Framing Narrative (4.8-11, 24)

It is understandable that the included correspondences with the Persian kings Artaxerxes and Darius would be in Aramaic as it was the official language of the Persian Empire. Letters between Persian satraps and their officials in satrapies as far apart as Egypt and Bactria testify to the ubiquity and the importance of Aramaic as the official international language. Thus, the correspondence, whether genuine or fictional, would have been put into Aramaic just to convey authenticity. What puzzles is the language of the framing narrative. The letter itself does not begin until v. 11b, yet vv. 8-11a, not part of the letter, are also in Aramaic.

The narrative that frames the correspondence in Ezra 4 includes v. 24 as well, and it too is in Aramaic. This verse has been called a resumptive repetition, that is, it repeats v. 4 of this chapter and resumes the narrative, bringing it back to the events of vv. 1-5 and the reign of Darius. Nevertheless, while it repeats the sense of v. 4, v. 4 is in Hebrew, whereas v. 24 is in Aramaic. (This is discussed extensively in the note to v. 24 below, and in Comment A to Ezra 5.)

B. Who Was Artaxerxes?

The letter that follows is an objection to building the city wall around Jerusalem (4.12), and so was written in the time of Nehemiah, and the king in question is Artaxerxes I (465–425 BCE), the son of Xerxes and the grandson of Darius I. (See Comment E directly above on Darius and the Appendix for the dates of the Persian kings.) The beginning of his reign was marked by revolts. The first, put down in short order, was by a brother who was satrap of Bactria. The second, in Egypt, was in response to the news that Xerxes had been assassinated (Diodorus 11.71.3-6; see note on Sheshbazzar at Ezra 1).

Artaxerxes died in 425, having sired only one legitimate son, Xerxes II. He had several sons by concubines, however, and one such, Sogdianus, assassinated his half-brother and named himself king. Another half-brother, Ochus, had received the Bactrian satrapy and married a half-sister, daughter of a third concubine. Ochus managed to win over the support of the head of Sogdianus's cavalry, and when Ochus declared himself king with the throne name Darius II, Sogdianus gave himself up and was executed. The execution of other brothers and a cousin followed.

Ezra 4.11b-24

The Proof: The Letter to King Artaxerxes and the Horrible Result

Now begins the correspondence between satrapal officials of Beyond-the-River and King Artaxerxes I. Even though Ezra Chapters 1-6 are about the construction of the second temple in Jerusalem culminating in the temple's dedication in the sixth year of Darius I (515 BCE; see Comment E below),[1] correspondence with Kings Xerxes (4.6; Darius's son) and Artaxerxes I (4.7; Darius' grandson) are included here –correspondences which concern the city wall (4.12) and have nothing to do with the temple. Interpreting Ezra 1-6 according to Hellenistic rules of rhetoric, however, explains why the letters about the city wall were included in this temple building story. (See Comment A below.)

Translation

11b. *To Artaxerxes the king, (from) your servants the men of Beyond-the-River:*[a]

12. *Let it be known to the king*[b] *that the Judeans who came up from you*[c] *to us have come to Jerusalem. They are rebuilding that rebellious and evil city—they have ordered the walls*[d] *to be completed*[e] *and are searching out*[f] *its foundations.*[g] 13. *Now, let it be known to the king*[h] *that if this city will be built and her walls completed, neither rent, tribute, nor corvée*[i] *will be paid, and the wealth*[j] *of my king*[k] *is being harmed.*[l] 14. *Now, inasmuch as we have partaken of the salt of the palace*[m] *it is not proper for us to witness the humiliation*[n] *of the king, therefore we send and inform the king*[o] 15. *that*[p] *one should search in the book of memoranda*[q] *of your fathers. You will find in the book of memoranda*[r] *and then you will know that this city is a rebellious city, harming kings and states, insurrection*[s] *being made in it from long ago. On account of this, this city was destroyed.* 16. *We are letting the king know that if this city is built and her walls completed, then you will not have a share in Beyond-the-River.*[t]

1. This section is based on Fried 2012a; Fried 2013a.

17. *The king sent a response*[u] *to Reḥum the viceroy*[v] *and Shimshai the secretary and the rest of their colleagues who dwell in Samaria and the rest of Beyond-the-River:*

Greetings![w] *And now:* 18. *The letter*[x] *that you sent to us*[y] *was translated*[z] *and read before me.*[aa] 19. *An order was issued by me and they searched and found that from long ago this city has been rising up against kings and rebellion and insurrections*[bb] *have been made in it.* 20. *Mighty*[cc] *kings were over Jerusalem and governed all of Beyond-the-River,*[dd] *and rent, tribute, and corvée were given to them.* 21. *Now, issue an order*[ee] *to stop these men. This city shall not be built until an order will be issued by me.*[ff] 22. *Be warned against acting negligently about this,*[gg] *lest harm grow to the injury of kings.*

23. *As soon as a copy of the letter of Artaxerxes the king was read before Reḥum*[hh] *and Shimshai the secretary and their colleagues, they rushed to Jerusalem, to the Judeans, and stopped them with force of arms.*[ii]

24. *Then the work on the temple of the god which is in Jerusalem was stopped, and remained stopped until the second year of Darius king of Persia.*

Textual Notes

a. **4.11b** *Beyond-the-River.* Beyond-the-River is the name of the satrapy after Babylon was made a separate province under Xerxes. First Esdras reads Coelesyria and Phoenicia, Κοίλῃ Συρίᾳ καὶ Φοινίκῃ (1 Esd. 2.13), which reflects the name of the province in Hellenistic times. (See Introduction for a discussion of satrapal borders.)

b. **4.12** *To the king.* First Esdras reads 'to our lord the king', which is customary in the Aramaic letters that we have from Elephantine.

c. *From you.* This is in the singular. First Esdras reads the plural, perhaps the royal plural.

d. *The walls.* First Esdras inserts 'its agoras', that is, 'its marketplaces', perhaps through dittography seeing שוק, 'marketplace', for שור, 'wall'.

e. *Ordered the walls to be completed.* The *kethib* is אשכללו, the *qere* is שכלילו. If we were to read the *qere* as a loan word from the Akkadian š*uklulu*, 'to complete', 'to perfect', it would have to be translated as 'they completed the walls'. This cannot be correct, since according to 4.13 and 16, the walls were not yet completed. It is possible to read the *qere* as the causative shaphel of *kll*, 'to complete', yielding 'they caused the walls to be completed', which still implies completed walls. On the other hand, one may read the *kethib* and not the *qere*. In this case, you have an aphel of √*škll*, which would also imply the causative of 'to complete' in the past. In either case, we have the past tense of the causative form of a verb that means 'to complete', when the sense ought to be that the walls have not yet been completed. Hence, my translation. The Syriac reads simply *škllw*, שכללו, 'they completed'.

f. *Searching out.* יַחִיטוּ, *yaḥîṭû.* This is a loan word from the Akkadian *ḫâṭu*, 'to explore', 'to survey', 'examine', 'search' (*pace* Rosenthal 1995: #178). It is often used in Akkadian building inscriptions to indicate the search for the old foundations in order to build the new edifice upon them. Esarhaddon says *temenšu labīri aḫiṭ abrēma,* 'I carefully searched out its old foundations' (*CAD* Ḫ. 161). The Greek texts have 'laying' and 'lifting up' the foundations, illustrating that the Greek translators did not understand the word. The Syriac has *šrrw*, 'they made firm', 'established'.

g. *Foundations*. For this translation, see Edelman (2005: 156-59 *apud* Sidney Smith 1945).

h. **4.13** *Now let it be known to the king.* This redundant phrase is missing from 1 Esdras.

i. *Rent, tribute, and corvée.* Greek Ezra and 1 Esdras translate all three terms with the one word φόροι, 'tribute'. They seem to have been unable to distinguish them.

j. *Wealth.* אַפְּתֹם, *'aptōm.* From Old Persian *apputammu* (Zadok 2007).

k. *My king.* Literally, 'kings', with a Hebrew plural ending, which cannot be right in an Aramaic text. Moving the final mem to the next word results in 'my king', with the next word becoming a participle.

l. *Is being harmed.* Literally, 'will cause harm', in the third person feminine singular, implying that the subject must be the (rebuilt) city. There is no object, however. Moving the mem from 'kings' to the following verb creates the present passive participle מתהנזק. This would be a present passive participle of the haphel, which is not otherwise attested in biblical Aramaic (Rosenthal 1995: 46). Greek Ezra reads 'this injures kings'; 1 Esdras reads 'and they will even oppose kings'. The Syriac translates the Hebrew literally.

m. **4.14** *Inasmuch as we have partaken of the salt of the palace.* Literally, 'We have been salted with the salt of the palace'. This phrase is omitted from all the Greek versions, probably as incomprehensible. First Esdras inserts 'inasmuch as the building of the temple is now going on', interpreting היכל as referring to the temple rather than the palace, but it is clear that the phrase either was not understood or not there.

n. *Humiliation.* Literally, 'the nakedness'. Greek Ezra reads 'the indecent act'. This phrase is missing in 1 Esdras. The Syriac has צערא, 'pain', 'suffering'.

o. **4.15** *The king.* First Esdras has, as before, 'our lord, the king', as is usual in letters to superiors.

p. *That.* First Esdras inserts 'if it seems good to you', which is appropriate.

q. *Book of memoranda.* First Esdras reads 'books', plural, and omits 'memoranda'.

r. *Book of memoranda.* This second appearance of this phrase is not in the versions.

s. *Insurrection.* וְאֶשְׁתַּדּוּר, *eshtadur.* This word is unknown; the translation is based on 4.19, where it appears in parallel with מרד, 'rebellion'. Rosenthal (1995: 63) proposes it is from a hypothetical Persian **ā(x)šti-drauga,* 'breach of the peace'. Greek Ezra inserts, 'there were in the midst of it from very old time refuges for *runaway* slaves'.

t. **4.16** *You will not have a share in Beyond-the-River.* Greek Ezra reads, 'you will have no peace', omitting 'Beyond-the-River'. First Esdras reads, 'you will no longer have access to Coelesyria and Phoenicia'.

u. **4.17** *Response. Pitgam.* פתגם. Probably of Persian origin. Rosenthal (1995: 63) suggests it is from **pati-gāma*, 'message', 'word'. The versions translate simply with a verb, 'the king responded'.

v. *The viceroy, hyparch,* בעל טעם, *b^{e}'ēl ṭ^{e}'ēm.* Greek Ezra transliterates this as if it were Reḥum's last name. First Esdras also assumes it is a name, but of a third person. It also inserts an explanation of Reḥum's status here as 'the one in charge of reporting on matters'.

w. *Greetings.* This word is omitted from 1 Esdras.

x. **4.18** *Letter.* See textual note at 4.7. For some reason Greek Ezra translates here and elsewhere as ὁ φορολόγος, 'tribute carrier (?)'. The Vulgate has *accusationem,* a literal interpretation of what was sent.

y. *To us.* The royal 'us'. First Esdras reads 'that you sent to me'.

z. *Translated.* This is a guess. The word *meparaš* means 'explained', 'interpreted', 'taken apart'. This word is missing in the versions.

aa. *Read before me.* First Esdras reads, 'I have read the letter that you sent me'.

bb. **4.19** *Insurrections.* This is the same word that appears in 4.15. Greek Ezra translates the word both here and in 4.15 as a place of refuge. It reads, 'desertions take place within [the city]'.

cc. **4.20** *Mighty.* First Esdras inserts 'and harsh'.

dd. *Beyond-the-River.* Again, 1 Esdras explains the term by translating it as 'Coelesyria and Phoenicia'.

ee. **4.21** *Issue an order.* That is, I command you, Reḥum and Shimshai, to issue an order. First Esdras reads, 'I issue an order'.

ff. *Until an order will be issued by me.* This phrase is absent in 1 Esdras, so no possibility of a change in the future is implied there.

gg. *Be warned against acting negligently about this.* First Esdras reads, 'To take care that nothing more be done about this'. It seems that the translator did not understand the Aramaic *shalu,* שלו, *negligence,* interpreting it as the relative pronoun, shin, ש, plus the negative.

hh. **4.23** *Before Reḥum.* Syriac inserts his title following the name.

ii. *Force of arms.* Both Greek Ezra and 1 Esdras add 'with cavalry', which may be original.

Notes

4.11b *The men of Beyond-the-River.* The names of the senders have already been stated in vv. 9 and 10, but would have been included here in the original letter. The original salutation was probably as in 1 Esdras and as in Ezra 4.17, something like, 'From your servants, Reḥum the viceroy, Shimshai the secretary, the judges, and their associates who live in Samaria and in the rest of the province Beyond-the-River'. If this was based on an archival copy of the letter that was sent, then the salutation may have been abbreviated.

The Vulgate inserts *salutem dicunt,* 'greet you saying'. The fact that such a greeting formula is missing here is odd. If based on an archival copy of a letter that was sent to the king, however, then the greeting, like the names of the senders, could also have been omitted (Steiner 2006: 680). In Jedaniah's archive, found in Elephantine, there was an archival copy of a letter sent from Jedaniah in which the name of the addressee and the salutation is missing (*TAD* A 4.10). Steiner adduces other parallels from archives in Ugarit.

4.12 *The Judeans who came from you to us.* There may have been an influx of Judeans from Babylon or Susa to Judah during the reign of Artaxerxes I that is unknown to us. More likely it refers to Nehemiah and the Judeans and others who may have accompanied him. Although the archaeology of Judah indicates that Judeans were coming to their homeland all throughout the Persian period, it seems that only during the reign of Artaxerxes did the population of Judah become such that it became desirable to build a city wall around its capital city. Only the larger cities had walls; the smaller ones did not (Stern 1982). (See comment at Nehemiah 3.) Some have argued that the reference to 'the Judeans who came from you' is a reference to the mission of Ezra, who came up from Babylon in the seventh year of a king Artaxerxes (e.g. Williamson 1985: 63). This is not likely, however, since Ezra comes to a city whose walls and gates were already built (see comment at Ezra 7.1 and at Neh. 8.1).

4.13 ***Rent, tribute, and corvée (mindâ, b^e^lô, and h^a^lāk).*** These terms are Akkadian but continued to be used in the Persian tax system and beyond, except for *b^e^lô,* which is not attested in post-Achaemenid texts (Grabbe 2006). Indeed the use of the term *b^e^lô* confirms that the letter was written originally in the Achaemenid period.

Rent (mindâ). The first word in the series is *mindâ,* from the Akkadian *mandattu.* Examination of the occurrence of the word in extrabiblical Achaemenid era literature sheds light on its meaning. The word occurs several times in the Elephantine papyri, most often in the customs account (*TAD* C3.7) to indicate payment for use of the Nile river paid in silver or in kind by ships passing through it, payment that is always transferred to the royal storehouse. Texts from the Murašu archive also indicate the numerous canals and reservoirs in the area of Nippur that the king controlled and leased out and on which the *mandattu* was paid. The same seems to have been true of the Nile river in Egypt. No ship passed through it without paying the *mindâ* rent to the Achaemenid king. The Great King controlled the waterways.

The word also occurs in the Arsames archive. According to one text, Arsames had assigned land in Egypt to another member of the Achaemenid royal family, Varuvahya. Varuvahya writes, probably from Susa, to complain that he has not been receiving the *mandattu* that are due on his domains.

It also occurs in a letter from fourth-century Bactria. Although the letter is fragmentary, we are able to read the phrase *mindat hammelek* (Naveh and Shaked 2012: *ADAB* A8). The letter seems to be from the satrap of Bactria, Akhvamazda, to Bagavant, one of his provincial governors. In the letter Akhvamazda complains that he has not received the *minda* due on the royal property, just as Varuvahya complains that he has not received the *minda* due on his. The *minda* is rent, in this case on property in Bactria owned by the Achaemenid king. The satrap seems to have been responsible for collecting the rents on royal property and forwarding it to the king. Thus we see the *minda,* or *mandattu,* owed on land belonging to the royal family in both Egypt and Bactria. The passage in Neh. 5.4, where the same phrase is used, indicates that the king also owned land in Judah and had rented it out to the Judeans (see discussion there, forthcoming; and Fried 2015c).

Tribute (b^e^lô). The second word is *b^e^lô*, and comes from the Akkadian *biltu*. It does not appear in any Aramaic extrabiblical texts to my knowledge, but in Akkadian inscriptions it is most often used to indicate tribute paid by foreign subjects to a conquering king.

Corvée labor (h^a^lāk). The last of these three words is *h^a^lāk*. We know very well what this is. This term is derived from the Akkadian *ilku* (Hoftijzer and Jongeling 1995: 283; Rosenthal 1995, #188; van Driel 2002: 254; Lemaire 2007: 63; Naveh and Shaked 2012: 30; Fried 2015c). The *ilku* is corvée service, military or otherwise, that is owed to a king or governor as part of rent on land that has been encumbered in this way (van Driel 2002: 254-59; *CAD* I-J: 73). Often the *ilku* is remunerated in kind or in silver, so that someone else can be paid to perform the *ilku* service instead of the renter. A good example of *ilku* service is known from the Murašu archive (fifth century BCE, Nippur, Babylon). One text concerns an agreement in which a certain Gedaliah promises to fulfill the *ilku* service on cavalry land (*bît sîsî*) belonging to his father, and Rîmût-Ninurta son of Murašu agrees to provide all the equipment necessary including a horse (Cardasçia 1951: 179-82). It is clear that the *ilku* service there is military.

Another example occurs in a letter drawn from the Arsames archive, in fifth-century Egypt (*TAD* A 6.11). The satrap, Arsames, a member of the Persian royal family, had estates that he controlled and parceled out in Egypt (in addition to the ones he had in Babylon, as the Murašu documents reveal). The letter shows that Arsames could assign these estates to whomever he pleased or he could keep them for himself. The holding that he had assigned to Peṭosiri and then gave over to Peṭosiri's son Pamun was a fief on which the *ilku* service was owed.

The *ilku* is also referred to in a letter from Akhvamazda, the satrap of Bactria, to one of his governors, Bagavant, in the sixth year of Artaxerxes III (352 BCE; Naveh and Shaked 2012: *ADAB* A1). According to that letter, Bagavant, the Persian governor of a province in northern Bactria, had detained a group of camel drivers (line 3) in order to make them pay the *ilku*. The master of the camel drivers complained to Akhvamazda, the satrap, that the camel drivers were his servants, his apprentices, that they were guarding the camels of the king and that they were not obligated for the *ilku* tax. Although we are not told in the letter just why they were not obligated nor why the governor thought that they should have been obligated, we may suppose that the act of guarding the king's camels fulfilled their *ilku* service (Shaul Shaked, personal communication [July 12, 2013]). These letters confirm that throughout the empire, land was held by the king or members of his royal family and allotted to ordinary people in return for service, military or otherwise, or for a fee in exchange for service. We may conclude that the reference to the *ilku* (*h^a^lāk*) in Ezra shows that the same process existed in Judah in the Achaemenid period.

Will not be paid. According to the response of the Judeans to Tattenai (Ezra 6.4), Cyrus agreed to let the costs of the temple be paid for out of the royal treasury. This did not free them from other obligations, however. Cultic officials were released from these obligations upon Ezra's arrival (Ezra 7.24), but this would have been after the city wall was built and after these letters here in Ezra 4 had been written. (See comment to Ezra 7 on the date of Ezra's arrival.)

4.14 ***Inasmuch as the salt of the palace is our salt.*** That is, inasmuch as we are on the king's payroll. Persepolis Fortification Tablets (Hallock 1969) reveal that salt was a common component of ration lists. Salaries (which incidentally derives from the word 'salt') were most often paid in kind, that is, as rations, although silver could also be used. The implication may mean, therefore, that since the writers receive rations from the king, that is, since they were on his payroll, they only had his best interest at heart. Because salt was universally used as a preservative, biblical references to a 'covenant of salt' (Lev. 2.13; Num. 18.19; 2 Chron. 13.5) imply a permanent relationship. Eating the 'salt of the palace' thus implies a permanent bond of fealty.

4.15 ***Book of memoranda of your fathers.*** This reference to a memorandum that refers to a rebellion of Jerusalem may be to the Chronicles of the Babylonian kings since there were no other Judean rebellions except the ones against Babylon. We read in these chronicles, for example, a year-by-year account of the activities of King Nebuchadnezzar of Babylon from his accession year in 607 BCE to Kislev (December) of his eleventh year in 594 when the tablet breaks off. If we could have read it until the end, however, we would have read of the Judean revolt against Babylon and Nebuchadnezzar's conquest of Judah in 588–586 BCE. For Nebuchadnezzar's seventh year we read, for example,

> The seventh year: In the month of Kislev (December 598 BCE) the king of Akkad mustered his army and marched to Hattu (i.e. to the west). He encamped against the city of Judah (*āl ia-a-ḫu-du*) and on the second day of the month of Adar (March, the twelfth month of the year) he captured the city and seized its king. A king of his own choice he appointed in the city and taking the vast tribute he brought it to Babylon (*ABC* 5.11-13; Grayson 2000: 102).

This account refers to events in 597 BCE. Compare the biblical text:

> Jehoiachin was eighteen years old when he began to reign; he reigned three months in Jerusalem. His mother's name was Nehushta daughter of Elnathan of Jerusalem. He did what was evil in the sight of Yhwh, just as his father had done. At that time the servants of King Nebuchadnezzar of Babylon came up to Jerusalem, and the city was besieged. King Nebuchadnezzar of Babylon came to the city, while his servants were besieging it. King Jehoiachin of Judah gave himself up to the king of Babylon,

> himself, his mother, his servants, his officers, and his palace officials. The king of Babylon took him prisoner in the eighth year of his reign (i.e. Nisan, April, the first month of Nebuchadnezzar's eighth year). The king of Babylon made Mattaniah, Jehoiachin's uncle, king in his place, and changed his name to Zedekiah (2 Kgs 24.8-17).

Because the tablet of the Chronicles of the Babylonian kings breaks off, we do not have Babylonian records of the revolt against Babylon or of the final destruction of Judah in 586.

On account of this, this city was destroyed. The reference is clearly to the revolt against Nebuchadnezzar in 586 BCE. A record would have been available to Artaxerxes, although it is now lost to us. This type of accusation sent to the king was part and parcel of life in the Achaemenid Empire. Each official tries to prove his own loyalty by condemning the other. (See Comment B to Ezra 3.1-6a.)

4.16 ***You will not have a share in Beyond-the-River.*** That is, if the Judeans build a wall around Jerusalem, they will rebel, and you will lose the city and the province. The threat was expanded hyperbolically to imply that not only would the king lose the minor province of Judah but that he would lose all of Beyond-the-River as well.

The letter was written in response to an attempt in the time of Nehemiah to build a wall around Jerusalem; but why? Why did a city wall arouse such anxiety on the part of satrapal officials? In fact, any change in the status quo was met with distrust and suspicion among the various satraps and vice-satraps of the Persian Empire, and routinely responded to by sending accusations of rebellion and sedition to the king. The response of the king was always the same—to believe the accusations. (See Comment B to chap. 3 above.) We read of a similar event and a similar response that occurred much later in the Roman period during the reign of Claudius (41–54 CE):

> Agrippa fortified the walls of Jerusalem on the side of the New City at the public expense, increasing both their breadth and height, and he would have made them too strong for any human force had not Marsus, the governor of Syria, reported by letter to Claudius Caesar what was being done. Claudius, suspecting that a revolution was on foot, earnestly charged Agrippa in a letter to desist from building the walls; and Agrippa thought it best not to disobey (Josephus, *Ant.* 19.326-27).

The Syrian legate Marsus, whose authority included the province of Judah, wrote to the emperor to protest the fact that the Judean governor, King Agrippa, was rebuilding and refortifying the walls around Jerusalem. The emperor ordered the building process to be stopped. In this case the apprehension is understandable. At the time various eastern provinces of the Roman Empire (including Parthia and Armenia) were planning to rebel against Rome. Josephus explains Agrippa's rebuilt fortifications as due to the latter's concern that Judah would become Rome's major defensive line when those neighboring provinces started to rebel. Even so, it was natural for the legate and the emperor to assume instead that Agrippa’s fortifying the wall indicated that Judah was preparing to join the rebels. This was the case being made here against the Judeans by Reḥum, *b*^{e}*‘ēl ṭ*^{e}*’ēm* of Beyond-the-River.

4.17 ***The king sent a response to Reḥum the viceroy and Shimshai the secretary.*** The king’s response is only to the letter from Reḥum and Shimshai. Neither of the other letters mentioned in this chapter is included in the response.

Samaria. The fact that Reḥum, the satrapal viceroy, and Shimshai, his secretary, wrote from the town of Samaria indicates that the seat of power second only to that of the satrap was located in that city. This has led some scholars (e.g. Alt 1953; Würthwein 1936) to assume that the Persian province of Yehud was under the control of Samaria until the time of Nehemiah. Rather, the entire satrapy of Beyond-the-River was under the control of the satrap, who had his office in Damascus, and then under the viceroys, one of whom had his office in Samaria. (See comment on Ezra 5.3 and the Introduction.)

4.18 ***Translated and read before me.*** The implication is not necessarily that Artaxerxes could not read. Rather, this phrase was often used in letters to imply that the writer was of such exalted status that he would not have to read it himself (Wente 1995).

4.19 ***Has been rising up.*** A present participle is used, indicating ongoing or repeated action in the past. Most likely the events referred to are the two rebellions against the Babylonians, in 597 and 586 BCE.

4.20 ***Mighty kings.*** The mighty kings who ruled Jerusalem and collected rent, tribute, and corvée labor from them evidently did so while the city was not walled, that is, after the Babylonian conquest. These would have included all the Persian kings who preceded Artaxerxes on the throne. Yet, this is not how Persian kings spoke of their ancestors. We have two inscriptions of Artaxerxes. One begins:

> I am Artaxerxes, . . . son of Xerxes the King, grandson of Darius, an Achaemenian (*$A^{1}Pa$;* Kent 1953: 153).

Another reads:

> I am Artaxerxes the Great King, King of Kings, King of Countries, son of Xerxes the King, of Xerxes [who was] son of Darius the King (*$A^{1}I$*; Kent 1953: 153).

Artaxerxes would not have simply mentioned previous ‘mighty kings’, but would have referred to Xerxes, his father, and Darius, his grandfather, by name (Hoglund 1992: 58-59).

This verse seems to imply that these mighty kings ruled all of Beyond-the-River from Jerusalem and is thus a reference to David and Solomon. The verse was supplied by the biblical writer and is not part of an authentic letter from Artaxerxes. (See comment below on the authenticity of the letter.)

Rent, tribute, and corvée labor were given to them. The response from the king repeats the letter that was sent to him, which is typical of correspondence from this period.

4.21 ***Issue an order.*** That is, I command you to issue an order to the troops that you have garrisoned within your provinces.

To stop these men. To go out and physically stop them.

This city shall not be built. The command from the king is to stop the Judeans from building their city wall. It has nothing to do with the temple.

Until an order will be issued by me. This allows the king time to examine the situation more thoroughly if he has a mind to.

4.22 ***Lest harm come to the injury of kings.*** This is the end of the king's letter. The goal of the letter writers met with success.

4.23 ***Read before Reḥum and Shimshai the secretary and their colleagues.*** It was read out loud so that the whole group could hear it at once.

This verse and the one following are not part of the correspondence with Artaxerxes but were written by the biblical writer to tie the letters into the story being told, the story of how the perfidious Samaritans stopped the *temple* from being built. That story is not historical; there was no halt to the temple's construction, as can be seen from Tattenai's letter (Ezra 5.8). The biblical author created the story of a stoppage to the temple's construction to add drama to the text and used this letter about work on the city wall being stopped as proof that satrapal officials would do such things.

Rushed to Jerusalem. Reḥum and Shimshai would not have personally rushed to Jerusalem, but with all haste they would have sent messengers to the governors of the neighboring provinces ordering them to lead the soldiers garrisoned in their provinces to Jerusalem and to stop the city wall from being built. The provincial governors so ordered would have included Sanballat, governor of Samaria, Tobiah, governor of Ammon, and Geshem, king of the Kedarite Arab kingdom (Neh. 2.19; 4.1-2 [ET 4.7-8]; cf. 3.34 [ET 4.2]), the same ones who instigated Reḥum's letter to the king in the first place. As seen from the Bactrian correspondence, these governors would each have led their troops personally. Every provincial governor had soldiers garrisoned in his province who were subject to his command (Fried 2002c, 2004, 2013c, in press a; Naveh and Shaked 2012; see Comment C below.)

Stopped them. That is, they stopped them from building the wall in the reign of Artaxerxes I, not from building the temple in the reign of Darius. If this letter is a reaction to Nehemiah's efforts to build Jerusalem's city wall, the stoppage was only temporary. According to the book of Nehemiah, the wall was completed and dedicated (Neh. 12.27-43). This is confirmed by Jesus Ben Sira, writing around 200 BCE: 'The memory of Nehemiah also is lasting; he raised our fallen walls, and set up gates and bars, and rebuilt our ruined houses' (Sir. 49.13). The archaeology is disputed, however (Finkelstein 2008a, 2009; Fried 2012b).

Force of arms. Nehemiah's view of the situation is told in Nehemiah 4 [ET 4.7-23]. (See Comment C below.) The lack of a city wall would have kept most people from living in the city and thus would have prevented its growth and development. Indeed, prior to Nehemiah the city was desolate (Neh. 7.4).

4.24 ***Then the work on the house of the god which is in Jerusalem was stopped,... until the second year of Darius.*** In closing chap. 4, the biblical writer repeats the final clause of Ezra 4.5-6 in 4.24. He repeats it in Aramaic, however, not in Hebrew, the language of those verses. (See Comment A above and Comment A to Ezra 5 for a discussion of the use of Aramaic in the narrative framing the Aramaic letters in Ezra.) In spite of the fact that the intervening correspondence is with King Artaxerxes and concerns the city wall in the time of Nehemiah, the three framing verses (4.5, 6, 24) refer to King Darius of Persia (Artaxerxes' grandfather) and the time of Zerubbabel in the second year of Darius's reign.

Ezra 4.4-5 states,

> So the 'people of the land' (the *'am hā'āreṣ*) would discourage the people of Judah and make them afraid to build, bribing officials against them to frustrate their plans all the days of Cyrus king of Persia until the reign of Darius king of Persia.

Ezra 4.24 concludes the first phase of the narrative:

> Then the work on the temple of the god which was in Jerusalem was stopped, and remained stopped until the second year of Darius king of Persia.

Commentators point out that the repetition of the final phrase of 4.5 in 4.24 is a resumptive clause that signals that the intervening material is an insertion (e.g. Clines 1984: 82; Blenkinsopp 1988: 115; Williamson 1983; 1985: 57). A resumptive clause occurs when an author inserts material into a text and repeats the sentence on either side of the inserted material to indicate the insertion. The resumption allows the reader to pick up the narrative where it had left off. The intervening material is regarded as parenthetical and the repeated verses as a set of parentheses. Although Ezra 4.24 does not repeat 4.5 exactly, it still serves as a *Wiederaufnahmen*, a resumptive clause (Clines 1984: 82; Williamson 1985: 57; Blenkinsopp 1988: 115). Ezra 4.4-5 states that the *'am hā'āreṣ* bribed officials and so frustrated the plans of the Judeans from the time of Cyrus up until the reign of Darius. Ezra 4.24 states that building remained stopped until the second year of that same Darius. The intervening verses, vv. 6-23, while parenthetical, are not irrelevant. They are meant to demonstrate exactly how the *'am hā'āreṣ* would have frustrated the plans of the Judeans during all these years. They were the type of people not only to bribe officials but also to write accusing letters to the kings. They were the type to stop temple construction in the reign of Darius since they stopped the wall building in the reign of Artaxerxes. The resumptive clause, Ezra 4.24, brings the narrative back to the literary present, back to the second year of Darius I when the second phase of the narrative begins.

Historically speaking, work on the temple was never stopped. Ezra 5.8 records in Tattenai's letter to Darius I, written probably in that king's second year, that 'the house of the great god is being built of hewn stone, and timber is laid in the walls; the work is being done diligently and prospers in their hands'. Thus, work had been progressing slowly but steadily since the foundations were laid eighteen years before. (The reliability of Tattenai's letter is discussed in the context of chaps. 5 and 6.)

Although v. 24 is a resumptive repetition that picks up the narrative where it left off in vv. 4 and 5, and although it is provided by the biblical writer, there is a major difference between it and vv. 1- 5 that is seldom brought out (but see Arnold 1996; Berman 2006, 2007). Verses 1-5 above are in Hebrew and speak of building the temple of 'our god' (4.3), and of 'Yhwh, the god of Israel' (4.1, 3); v. 24, in contrast, is in Aramaic and refers to 'the house of the god which is in Jerusalem'. These are the words of the Cyrus edict, of a non-Judean, an outsider. In fact, as is discussed in the context of the Cyrus edict (Ezra 1.4), it is not clear whether to translate this as 'the house of the god *which* is in Jerusalem' or 'the house of the god *who* is in Jerusalem'. In either case, it is not the temple of 'Yhwh, the god of Israel' or even the temple of 'our god' that is referred to. The Aramaic language, the language of Persian officials, rather than the native Hebrew, as well as the words used, are intended by the biblical writer to provide a feeling of an external official voice and to increase the sense of helplessness in the reader. The stoppage was brought about by factors outside of the control of either the protagonists or the Judean community.

The narrative as well as the proof of the veracity of the narrative are concluded. The reader is meant now to be in a state of pity for the protagonists and in a state of fear and apprehension for their safety in the face of the attack by the soldiers of the neighboring provincial governors.

Comments

A. Why were Letters of Complaint about the City Wall Included Here in a Temple Building Story?

The biblical author has accused unnamed 'enemies', the *'am hā'āreṣ*, of bribing officials to stop the Judeans from working on the temple of YHWH until the second year of the reign of Darius. According to Aristatelian laws of rhetoric, the accusation narrated in 4.1-5 should now be followed by proofs, and it is. The author cites a letter that enemies of the Judeans sent to King Xerxes (4.6), a second letter that another group of enemies sent to King Artaxerxes (4.8), and a third letter (4.11b-16) that a third group sent to that king along with his response to it (4.17b-22). The latter correspondence is provided in full. These letters were included because, in contrast to poetry, in Hellenistic historiography rules of forensics also apply. Historical narrative is essentially a legal accusation, and it must be followed by a proof of the accusation's veracity. Aristotle describes two types of proofs: internal and external. The internal proof is the argument, and may either be deductive (by syllogisms) or inductive (by examples). In lieu of any internal proof, the author may take refuge in external proofs. External proofs are provided by witnesses, documents, written contracts, letters, etc. The letters in Ezra 4 constitute an external proof.

The authenticity of the letter is discussed below. The question at issue here is how the *'am hā'āreṣ*'s correspondences with Xerxes and Artaxerxes (son and grandson of Darius) support the truth of the author's claim that these enemies of the Judeans prevented them from building their temple in the time of Cyrus up to the second year of that same Darius, many years before? The answer is they do not, nor can they. The letter to Artaxerxes, quoted in full, was written to complain about the city wall being built, not about the temple (4.12). The biblical author evidently did not have direct evidence available to him regarding the stoppage of work on the temple. Had he had such direct proof, he would have provided it. Indeed, as commentators have long known, this is the best indication of the letter's authenticity. If the biblical author had forged the letter, he would have placed it in the time of Darius and it would have referred to the temple, not the wall (*pace* Gunneweg 1985:85). What the cited letters were intended to do is to demonstrate not that these men in particular, but that the *'am hā'āreṣ* in general were the sort of people to write slanderous letters to prevent the temple from being built. The proof offered here is that they wrote such slanderous letters in the time of Artaxerxes to prevent Jerusalem's city wall from being built. That shows that they were the type who would make this sort of attack. According to Aristotle, when praising or accusing a man in a judicial proceeding, it is necessary to show that his acts are intentional, and this is all the easier if it can be shown that he is in the habit of doing such things (*Rhetoric* 1367b20). Aristotle advises that, 'even if a man has not actually done a given good [or bad] thing, we may bestow praise [or blame] on him, if we are sure that he is the sort of person who *would* do it' (*Rhetoric* 1367b33). By showing just what the *'am hā'āreṣ* had done in the time of Artaxerxes, the letters demonstrate the character of the *'am hā'āreṣ* in general, and show just what they are in the habit of doing. Once the devious character of this sort of person has been demonstrated, he can be blamed for other similar actions for which no actual external proofs are available.

B. Is the Correspondence with Artaxerxes Genuine?

Is the correspondence being offered as proof of the perfidy of the *'am hā'āreṣ* genuine?[2] Private letters between individuals have been part and parcel of Greek history-writing since Herodotus (van den Hout 1949: 25-28). Van den Hout examines nine letters which Herodotus quotes, but concludes that 'no one will doubt that Herodotus never saw the letters of which he presents the direct text' (van den Hout 1949: 28; West 1985). Van den Hout argues that Herodotus includes the letters not because the subjects of his history wrote them and he happens to have them, but to enliven the story. This could certainly be the case here. Rosenmeyer (2001: 46) suggests however that letters in historical works play the same role as do reported speeches. Letters were a device that allowed speeches to take place between people who were far apart. As Thucydides makes clear moreover, the historian is obligated to make the speeches and letters that he employs reflect the gist of what was actually said or written (I.22). Letters should not be the creation of the historian *ex nihilo*, rather they should ideally express the thoughts of the writers, even if they are necessarily in the words of the historian (Fornara 1983: 142-45).

The major argument for its authenticity is that it does not fit the narrative (Grabbe 2006: 544-46; Williamson 2008; Gunneweg 1985: 86). If it were a forgery created by the biblical writer, then it would have been addressed to Darius, not to Xerxes or Artaxerxes, and it would have dealt with the construction of the temple, not the city wall.

Gunneweg (1985: 86) points out in addition that none of the literary characteristics of the biblical author are present in the correspondence. There is no reference to priests or Levites, or to the heads of fathers' houses. This suggests that the letters were not created by the biblical writer but simply used by him to make his point that Persian satrapal officials were the enemies of Judah and Benjamin. Comment B to Ezra 3 above describes just how common accusations from various satrapal officials to the king were. No one was safe. The letters in Ezra 4 need to be seen in this context.

2. This section is based in part on Fried 2012b.

Even Torrey (1970 [1910]), who believes that the Aramaic documents are forgeries, agrees that they were not written by the Chronicler (whom he considers to have written Chronicles and Ezra 1–6). He argues that the transition between 4.7 and 4.8 is so awkward that it betrays the hand of a different writer. 'The Chronicler, composing freely, could not possibly have proceeded in this way' (1970 [1910]: 159). Torrey notes, further, that the Chronicler could not have concealed his own writing style and personality throughout the long section of Ezra 4.8–6.14. To Torrey, the whole of this section was composed as a novella by someone writing at the time of the Chronicler (mid-third century in his view) and incorporated by the Chronicler into his narrative.

Torrey includes 4.24 as part of the original novella, which he assumes pre-existed the book of Ezra. He is able to do this because he assumes that the Darius under whom the temple was dedicated was Darius II. The language in 4.24 repeats the language in 4.5, however, which Torrey sees as betraying the hand of the Chronicler. If so, 4.24 was also written by the biblical author who added it when he incorporated the letters. Ezra 4.8–6.14 cannot have been composed originally as one long novella.

Orthography of the correspondence. To argue that the Artaxerxes correspondence is a Hellenistic forgery, Torrey points to a number of discrepancies between the orthography of the late-fifth-century Aramaic documents from Elephantine and that of the letters in Ezra that purport to be from the same period (Torrey 1970 [1910]: 161-66; so also Schwiderski 2000; Grabbe 2006).[3] One example is that the fifth-century BCE documents from Elephantine consistently use זי, *zî*, as the relative pronoun, the root of the demonstrative pronoun, and as the sign of the genitive, whereas the letters in Ezra always use the later form, די, *dî*. However, Aramaic witnesses a gradual sound change during the Achaemenid period itself from ז to ד, *z* to *d*, and both *dî* and *zî* can appear in the same letter (e.g. *TAD* A 2.3; Folmer 1995: 49-63; Muraoka and Porten 1998: 2-6). Moreover, as Muraoka and Porten point out (p. 3),

> Most instructive is . . . *TAD* B 3.4, which (incorrectly) has זין וזבב, *zîn vezavov* ([legal] 'suit or process') (line 17) yet reads (correctly) דין ודבב, *dîn vedavov* (in lines 12, 13, and 14). The spelling with *z* is best interpreted as a hypercorrection: On the alert for the common misspelling by ד, *d*, for the correct ז, *z*, the scribe inadvertently writes *zayin* instead of the correct *dalet*. This would indicate that, by 437 BCE when the document was drawn up, the sound in question was considered better represented by ד (*dalet*) than by ז (*zayin*).

Thus, by the fifth century, *z* and *d* seem to represent close to the same sound. Moreover, a recently published ostracon dating probably to the last third of the fourth century BCE is entitled *ledikrôn*, לדכרון, 'memorandum', with a *d* instead of a *z* (Lemaire 2006: 420-23). Gropp (1990: 169-87) also notes דנה

3. This section is based on Fried 2012b.

d^e^*nâ* alongside זנה *z*^e^*nâ* in the fourth-century BCE Samarian papyri. The use of the daleth instead of the zayin in the letter to Artaxerxes therefore is not conclusive.

Grabbe (2006) argues that the letters are likely Hellenistic forgeries because of the presence of Hellenistic second- and third-person *plene* plural pronominal suffixes in the Aramaic letters in Ezra instead of the Achaemenid-period defective forms. We also see an unexpected final nun. That is, we see כון *kôn* and כום, *kôm,* instead of the expected כם *km*; and הון *hôn* and הום *hôm*, instead of the expected הם *hm*. Muraoka and Porten (1998: 53-54) show, however, that these plural morphemes occur with both final nun and mem in the Egyptian papyri. Most of the examples of final nun are from the Hermopolis papyri, which are late-sixth or early-fifth century, but Muraoka and Porten interpret them as precursors of the corresponding forms that appear in later Aramaic dialects. There is moreover פרסכן ('your salary'—defectively written but with final nun, and addressed to a single man!) in a letter dated to the second quarter of the fifth century, as well as להן ('to them', masculine) and ביניהן ('between them', masculine), defectively written but with final nun. These both appear in letters from the Judean garrison at Elephantine (last half of the fifth century). Regarding a final *m* or *n,* therefore, no consistency should be expected. As for *plene* or defective spelling, Muraoka and Porten note frequent use of the *plene* spelling of the morpheme הום, *hôm,* in the letter from the Judean garrison to the governor of Judah (עליהום, זניהום, לנפשהום; all in *TAD* A 4.7 and 8). The only morphemes that are not attested in the Egyptian papyri until the third century are הון and כון, *plene* spelling with a nun suffix.

How does the Artaxerxes correspondence stand up to these criticisms? A major difficulty in understanding the letter to Artaxerxes is the garbled beginning. The actual letter does not start until 4.11b. There we have:

> עַל־אַרְתַּחְשַׁשְׂתְּא מַלְכָּא עַבְדָיִךְ אֱנָשׁ עֲבַר־נַהֲרָה וּכְעֶנֶת . . .
>
> To King Artaxerxes: Your servants, the people of the Province Beyond-the-River. And now . . .

The response to it begins in 4.17:

> פִּתְגָמָא שְׁלַח מַלְכָּא עַל־רְחוּם בְּעֵל־טְעֵם וְשִׁמְשַׁי סָפְרָא וּשְׁאָר כְּנָוָתְהוֹן דִּי יָתְבִין בְּשָׁמְרָיִן
> וּשְׁאָר עֲבַר־נַהֲרָה שְׁלָם וּכְעֶת . . .
>
> The king sent word to Reḥum the viceroy and Shimshai the secretary and the rest of their colleagues who dwell in Samaria and the rest of Beyond-the-River—Greetings! And now…

The word for 'to' in both the original letter and the response is עַל, typical of official Achaemenid period letters, a form replaced by ל- in the Hellenistic period (Folmer 1995: 621-29). Schwiderski (2000: 355) agrees that the typology of the address formula in both this letter and in the response to it

(4.17) gives no opportunity to doubt their authenticity. The marker כְּעֶנֶת, 'and now', which appears here (4.11b) and in the response (4.17), is also typical of Achaemenid-period correspondence, disappearing in the Hellenistic period when it is replaced by ש in Hebrew and די in Aramaic. This lends additional credence to the genuineness of the letters (Williamson 2008; cf. Schwiderski 2000: 155-64, 250-52). Moreover, the term בלו, which appears in the first letter (4.13), stems from the Akkadian *bilṭu* and is not attested in later Aramaic, another indication that the letter was written originally in the Achaemenid period (Grabbe 2006: 558). Also important for evaluating the letter is the lack of greeting in 4.11b. This is typical of Achaemenid-period correspondence (*inter alia*, *TAD* A 6.2; *TAD* A 6.14; Shaked 2003: 28). A letter reported by Shaked, for example, from the satrap of Bactria to the local governor is dated to the reign of Artaxerxes III. It reads simply, 'From Akhvamazda to Bagavant. And now'.

The letter to Artaxerxes ends in 4.16. There are no plural second- or third-person plural pronominal suffixes in it to speak against its authenticity.

As Schwiderski (2000: 376) points out, however, both the names of the senders and the salutation are missing from v. 11, so this cannot be the original beginning of the letter. This lack is common in archival copies of letters that had been sent out. Since the response in 4.17 is directed to Reḥum and to Shimshai, these names must have been part of the prescript of the original letter. Therefore, if we include these names from v. 8 and add the customary salutation from the Elephantine letters (e.g. *TAD* A 6.1) we may read:

*על מראן אַרְתַּחְשַׁשְׂתְּא מַלְכָּא עַבְדָיִךְ רְחוּם בְּעֵל־טְעֵם וְשִׁמְשַׁי סָפְרָא וֶאֱנָשׁ עֲבַר־נַהֲרָה
שלם מראן אלה שמיא שגיא ישאלו בכל עדן וּכְעֶנֶת . . .

*To our lord Artaxerxes the king, your servants Reḥum the Viceroy, Shimshai the Secretary, and the men of Beyond-the-River, may the god of heaven seek after the welfare of our lord abundantly at all times, and now . . .

The verse introducing Artaxerxes' response (4.17), on the other hand, was likely added by the biblical author or expanded by him. It contains the late Hellenistic morpheme הון (כנותהון). Although it is 'unthinkable' that the name of the king as sender would be omitted, it is possible that the biblical writer displaced it to incorporate the letter into its narrative context (Schwiderski 2000: 357). More crucial for rejecting the authenticity of the verse, however, is the late plural morpheme 'their colleagues'.

Nevertheless, since the prescript contains the genuine Achaemenid-period morphemes -על, 'to', and וּכְעֶת, 'and now', which disappear later, I suggest that the verse has simply been expanded by the biblical writer and should simply read: '[Artaxerxes the king] to Reḥum the viceroy and Shimshai the secretary, and now . . .'. By removing the intervening phrase with the Hellenistic greeting שְׁלָם, '*šᵉlām*', and the late plural suffix הוֹן in 'their colleagues', כְּנָוָתְהוֹן, the prescript is rendered into official Achaemenid-period chancellery style.

Artaxerxes' response properly begins only in 4.18, however, but the response also contains the Hellenistic morpheme הון, *hôn* in v. 20. This verse, which seems problematic anyway (see note *ad loc.*), is likely an addition. Except for 4.17 and 20, therefore, there are no suspicious morphemes in the text of the two letters. The response is admittedly more doubtful than the letter to the king, but there are no orthographic or stylistic reasons to remove any other verses from it or to reject the letter as a whole. Schwiderski (2000: 375) argues in contrast that the echoes of older forms (על, 'to', and וּכְעֶת, 'and now') were included only to lend an appearance of originality and that all that is relevant for dating is the most recent form. Admittedly the response from Artaxerxes has been updated in the Hellenistic period. These are not sufficient grounds for rejecting the entire letter as fiction, however, since the offending verse and half-verse can so easily be removed.

The tenor of the letter. Besides the orthography, Grabbe (2006: 545) finds the letter to Artaxerxes 'rude', 'not what one would expect from loyal subjects to the emperor'. However, we may compare this letter to one that Harpagus sent to Cyrus, quoted in full by Herodotus (1.123).

> Son of Cambyses, may the gods watch over you. Else you never had such luck. Now take vengeance on Astyages, who is your murderer. For in his intention toward you, you are dead, and it is only thanks to the gods and to me that you are alive. . . . If you will now listen to me, you will be king of all the land that now Astyages rules. Persuade the Persians to revolt, and do you lead their army against the Medes. If I am appointed by Astyages as his general against you, everything will go your way; if some other of the Median noblemen, still it will be the same. For these noblemen will desert him and join you and try to depose him. Know, then, that this is all ready here; do as I tell you, and do it quickly!

It is true that Cyrus was not yet emperor, and only likely to become so. Still, it is not at all polite or deferential. The letter from Pausanias to Xerxes, quoted in full by Thucydides (1.128.7), is similar.

> Pausanias, the Spartan commander, wishing to do you a favor, sends you back these men whom he captured with the spear. And I make the proposal, if it seems good to you also, to marry your daughter and to make Sparta and the rest of Hellas subject to you. And I am able, I think, to accomplish these things with the help of your counsel. If any of these things pleases you, send a trusty man to the sea and through him we shall in future confer.

The letters quoted by Herodotus or Thucydides differ in form or style from the letters quoted in Ezra. Indeed, in the letter from Pausanias to Xerxes the addressee is not named, and there is no greeting formula. (Notice also the switch between third and first person in referring to himself.) In the letter quoted by Herodotus, the name of the sender is not mentioned. It should be pointed out that although Persia was famous for its mail service, most letters were not sent by it. Letters were sent by couriers, trusted agents, who would have been able to relate who had sent the letter and who was to receive it.

The title b^{e}ʿēl ṭ^{e}ʿēm. Grabbe (2006: 545-46; following Schwiderski 2000: 190-93) argues that the biblical writer does not realize that the term *b^{e}ʾēl ṭ^{e}ʾēm*, which I have translated variously as 'viceroy', or 'hyparch', in Artaxerxes' response, is not a title at all but simply designates the one responsible for the letter. (It literally means 'owner of the decree'.) In an Aramaic letter from Elephantine, an ʿAnani is said to be *b^{e}ʾēl ṭ^{e}ʾēm* (*TAD* A 6.2: 23), but Schwiderski (2000: 190) argues that Anani's official title was 'scribe', or 'secretary', since he is denoted '*the* scribe', ספרא, with the definite article. Because he is not denoted *the b^{e}ʾēl ṭ^{e}ʾēm* (with the definite article), the statement that he was *b^{e}ʾēl ṭ^{e}ʾēm* (*TAD* A 6.2: 23) only means that he was responsible for that letter. It is not a title. Schwiderski bases his opinion on other letters from Elephantine that say that PN knows this order, PN ידע טעמא (e.g. *TAD* A 6.10: 10).

In fact, the title *bēl ṭè-e-mu* appears on a Babylonian tablet (BM 74554) dated to the 24th day of the sixth month, of the 36th year of Darius I, that is, October 4, 486 BCE (Stolper 1989a; Heltzer 1992). On the tablet, which is a record of a transfer of barley, two men are each given both the titles 'scribe' and *bēl ṭè-e-mu*, and it appears that they both served directly under the satrap of Babylon and Beyond-the-River, one served as viceroy in charge of Babylon and one as viceroy in charge of Beyond-the-River. (See note at 4.8, above, and Introduction.)

The role of the correspondence. Finally, J.L. Wright (2004: 35-43) objects that the correspondence with Artaxerxes was created *de novo* simply to propel the narrative. The Artaxerxes of Nehemiah's authentic memoir, as portrayed in Nehemiah 2, knows nothing of any previous edict to stop the wall-building efforts and knows nothing of Jerusalem being a rebellious and seditious city, harmful to kings. Further, in Nehemiah, the king sends letters to governors of Beyond-the-River (Neh. 2.7, 8), but there is no letter to Reḥum and Shimshai indicating that his previous order has been rescinded and that Nehemiah now has permission to build the city walls. The problem of the date of the letter in relation to Nehemiah's governorship will be discussed at Nehemiah 2. For now, we may suppose that the correspondence between satrapal officials and King Artaxerxes regarding Jerusalem's city wall occurred when Nehemiah began to build Jerusalem's city wall and was written during Nehemiah's governorship (Fried 2012b). In sum, there is no reason to reject the authenticity of these two letters, omitting 4.20 and emending 4.17.

C. Did Satrapal Officials Stop Work on Jerusalem's City Wall?

The entire correspondence between satrapal officials and the king is typical of affairs in the Achaemenid Empire. Rivalry, jealousy and brinkmanship among satraps and governors and the willingness of the kings to accept any accusation as truthful were well known. (See Comment B to Chapter 3.1-6a above, and Fried 2010b).

Therefore it would have been completely expected for Artaxerxes to have ordered a stop to the wall-building efforts upon accusations of sedition. It is also likely that this would have been carried out by means of soldiers garrisoned in the provinces (again see Comment C to Chapter 3 above and Fried 2012b). In fact, we have in Nehemiah 4 Nehemiah's response to the threat of an attack on him by these provincial troops:

> But when Sanballat and Tobiah and the Arabs and the Ammonites and the Ashdodites heard that the repair of Jerusalem's walls was going forward and the gaps were beginning to be closed, they were very angry, and all plotted together to come and wage war against Jerusalem and to cause chaos in it (Neh. 4.1-2 [4.7-8]).
>
> And our enemies, צָרֵינוּ, said, 'They will not know or see anything before we come upon them and kill them and stop the work' (Neh. 4.11).

Nehemiah does not want to blame Artaxerxes for this attack, but he does recognize that his enemies are the provincial governors Sanballat, Tobiah, and Geshem (who were evidently the ones who bribed the satrapal officials Reḥum and Shimshai to write to the king). Provincial governors could not broach an attack on another Persian governor without the express authority of the king. In spite of the fact that the king himself would have ordered the attack, it was customary in these situations for the accused party to defend himself. This was the case with Ariobarzanes (see again Comment B to Chapter 3 and Fried 2010b). Accordingly, Nehemiah also prepared to defend himself as described in Nehemiah 4. 'So we prayed to our god, and set a guard as a protection against them day and night' (Neh. 4.3 [ET 4.9]).

Some scholars consider it unlikely that provinces in the Achaemenid Empire would have the temerity to attack one another. Mowinckel suggests that an internal mutiny against Nehemiah (4.4) was expanded by later writers into an external threat (Mowinckel 1964b: 24). Kellermann sees in this entire chapter the imprint of a Deuteronomistic 'holy war', although he considers it genuine anyway (Kellermann 1967: 18). Gunneweg thinks that a simple exaggeration on Nehemiah's part turned an actual though minor skirmish into a war (Gunneweg 1987: 81). Seeing these events against the backdrop of events in the Achaemenid Empire, however, warrants an acceptance of their historicity.

D. The Translation of 4QEzra (4Q117)

By way of an appendix to this chapter, I report two fragments of Ezra 4 and one of Ezra 5–6 that were found among the Dead Sea Scrolls at Qumran (Ulrich 1992; the translation is my own). First Esdras has not been found at Qumran.

Fragment 1. Ezra 4.2-6 (1 Esdras 5.66-70)

1. [Like you, we seek your] go[d and to him we have been sacrificing since the days of Esarhaddon, king of Assyria, who brought us up]

2. [here. And] Z[rubbabel and Joshua and the rest of the heads of the patriarchal clans of Israel said] to them ['It is not for you, but for us, to build]

3. [a house for our god.] For w[e alone will build to Yhwh the god of Israel just as King Cyrus the king of Persia commanded us.]

4. [But the *'am*] *hā'āreṣ* dis[couraged the people of Judah making them afraid to build. So they bribed]

5. [officials against them] to frustrate their plans [all the days of Cyrus king of Persia until the reign of Darius king of Persia.]

6. [And during the reign of Xerxes, at the begin]ing of his reig[n]

Fragment 2. Ezra 4.9-11 (No 1 Esdras parallel)

1. [the scribe and the rest of the]ir [collea]gues—the ju]ges [. . . . .]

2. [and the people of Susa, that is, the E]lamites and the rest of the natio[ns . . . .]

3. [. . . . .] and the rest of Beyond-the-River. And now [this is a copy of the letter that they sent to him:]

4. [To Artaxerxes the K]i[ng] Your Servants, men of Beyond-[the-River, and now . . . . .]

Fragment 3. Ezra 5.17–6.5 (1 Esdras 6.20-25)

1. . . .

2. [Cyrus the king issued a decree to build] this [h]ouse of God in Jeru[salem. Now let the king send us his pleasure in the matter.]

3. [Then, Darius the king issued a de]cree, and he searched in the arc[hives in Babylon where the records were deposited but] a document [was found]

4. [in Ecbatana, the capital of Media] the province and thus was writ[ten within it a memorandum: In the first year of Cyrus]

5. [the king, King Cyrus decr]eed: (Concerning) the house of the god in Jerusalem, let [the] house [be built, a site where sacrifices may be sacrificed]

6. [and its foundations laid. Its heigh]t, sixty cub[i]ts, its width, sixty cubits, [three] layers of [rolled stone]

7. [and one layer of wood. Expense]s will be paid from the royal palace. And moreover,] gold [and silver] vessels of the hou[se of the god]

8. [which Nebuchadnezzar brought out] from the temple which is in Jerusalem and which were carried to Baby[lon, they shall be restored and brought]

9. [to the temple which is in Jerusalem to its place], and you shall deposit (them) in the house of the god. (*vacat*). And now [. . .

Ezra 5.1-2

Deus ex Machina: Haggai and Zechariah Encourage the Builders

Zerubbabel and Jeshua had made the ill-advised decision to reject the offer of the 'people of the land' to help with the temple-building project (Ezra 4.1-4). Thus spurned, these *'am hā'āreṣ* reacted in anger and—according to the plot of our story—connived to bribe satrapal officials to write to the king and to stop the building project. We read that the building activity was stopped until the second year of Darius (4.24). This dramatic reversal in fortune resulted only from the very natural but terrible decision of Zerubbabel, the primary protagonist, and therefore conforms to Aristotelian rules of tragedy. If we were telling only a tragedy, our story would stop here, but we know that the temple was in fact rebuilt and indeed stood strong even while this story was being written and read. (The book of Ezra was found at Qumran, and so was written and copied in the days of the second temple before its destruction by the Romans.) In stories where the true (but nontragic) ending is known to the audience, Greek writers sometimes found it necessary for a god to appear (lowered down on a crane) to untangle the tragic plot and bring the matter to its rightful and god-desired conclusion. The god from the crane, *deus ex machina,* is supplied here by the prophesies of Haggai and Zecharia to bring the story to its appropriate conclusion.

The following verses, and indeed the rest of this chapter as well as the first part of chap. 6, take place in the second year of Darius. These two chapters through v. 18 of Ezra 6 are in Aramaic. (See Comment A below for discussion.)

Translation

1. *Then*[a] *the prophets Haggai the prophet*[b] *and Zechariah son of Iddo prophesied*[c] *to the Judeans who were in Yehud and in Jerusalem in the name of the god of Israel*[d] *[who was] over them*[e]. 2. *Then Zerubbabel son of Shealtiel and Jeshua son of Yozadak rose*[f] *and began to build the temple of God*[g] *which*[h] *is in Jerusalem and with them were the prophets of God*[i] *supporting them.*

Textual Notes

a. **5.1** *Then.* Literally, simply 'and'. First Esdras inserts the phrase 'In the second year of the reign of Darius'. This is not necessary in the Hebrew, because the time is stated in the preceding verse.

b. *Haggai the prophet.* It is not clear why this redundant title is added after Haggai and not after Zechariah. It may be in place of the missing patronymic (Rudolph 1949: 46). It is missing in 1 Esdras.

c. *And the prophet Haggai . . . prophesied.* A singular verb is used here with a plural subject as is often the case in Hebrew and Aramaic. The Vulgate reads the verb in the plural.

d. *God of Israel.* First Esdras reads κυρίου θεοῦ Ισραηλ, 'the Lord, god of Israel'.

e. [*Who was*] *over them.* That is, over the prophets. Or, the phrase could mean 'about them', referring to the prophetic words about the Judeans. The preposition *'al* is ambiguous.

f. **5.2** *Rose.* First Esdras reads a singular verb here.

g. *God.* First Esdras inserts 'the Lord God'.

h. *The temple of the god which.* Or, 'the temple of the god who'. The relative pronoun is the same in Hebrew and Aramaic whether it refers to the temple or the god. See discussion at 1.3.

i. *God.* First Esdras reads 'the Lord' instead of 'God'.

Notes

5.1 ***Then.*** The verb-first construction, which we have in this verse, is intended to convey a continuation of the narrative from the previous verse. To the biblical author, there is no break in the action. He intends the prophesying to be understood as a direct response to the royal command in the previous chapter (4.21) to stop work on the temple. Historically speaking, there was no such command. Haggai and Zechariah report no command to stop work on the temple in their own prophetic books. In fact, the letter to Artaxerxes reported in Ezra 4 does not deal with the temple at all but with the city wall. It was work on the wall that was ordered stopped, not work on the temple (Fried 2012b).

Prophesying in the name of the god implies communication from the deity who is to take up residence in the temple. This is a vital component of every temple-building project, but usually it appears as part of the initial decision to build, not at this late stage in the building process. (See note at Ezra 1.1 and Comment B below on the rhetorical role of the prophets in Ezra.)

The prophet Haggai. Some of Haggai's words are collected in the book bearing his name. They are dated to the second year of Darius I and include exhortations to complete the temple of Yhwh in Jerusalem. Except for that book, the name Haggai appears in the biblical corpus only this once, although a Haggi is listed among the children of Gad (Gen. 46.16 and Num. 26.15), and a Haggit was a wife of King David and mother of Adonijah. The name comes from the root *ḥag* (like the Arabic *haj*), meaning 'pilgrimage festival', as in a pilgrimage to a holy site.

And the prophet Zechariah son of Iddo. Some of Zechariah's words are collected in chaps. 1–8 of the book bearing his name. They are dated to the second and fourth year of Darius I and concern the dedication of the temple and the installation of Jeshua the high priest (see Comment A of Chapter 3). Zechariah, whose name means 'Yhwh remembered', is identified as the son of Iddo here in Ezra, but in Zech. 1.1 he is the son of Berechiah son of Iddo. The phrase 'son of Iddo' in Ezra may simply be intended to identify the family, as it appears to have been a well-known priestly one (cf. Neh. 12.4, 16). Mention of Haggai's and Zechariah's prophesying places the events in the second year of Darius when all of Haggai's and most of Zechariah's prophesying occur. The author of Ezra 1–6 may have had access to the prophetic books of Haggai and Zechariah (Williamson 1985: 75).

Haggai's and Zechariah's prophesying was most likely occasioned by the arrival in Jerusalem of Zerubbabel, the grandson of the last king of Judah, and by Jeshua, the grandson of the last high priest. It may have been their presence that convinced Haggai and Zechariah that it was now the right time to complete the temple (Bedford 2001). It is impossible to understand the burst of prophetic activity on the part of Haggai and Zechariah in the second year of Darius if Zerubbabel, heir to the Davidic throne, had been in Jerusalem during all the previous eighteen years (Japhet 2006: 207). It can only have been their arrival that aroused such prophetic fervor and messianic hopes (see Hag. 2.23). The list of names in Ezra 2.2, which includes Zerubbabel, does not stem from the time of Cyrus but from the time of Darius I (see note and comments to Ezra 2 above).

In the name of the god of Israel. To speak in the name of someone is to speak the words that that person tells you to say. Deuteronomy 18.18-22 makes clear exactly what it means to speak in the name of Yhwh:

> 'I will raise up for them a prophet like you [i.e. like Moses] from among their own people; I will put my words in the mouth of the prophet, who shall speak to them everything that I command. Anyone who does not heed the words that the prophet shall speak in my name, I myself will hold accountable. But any prophet who speaks in the name of other gods, or who presumes to speak in my name a word that I have not commanded the prophet to speak—that prophet shall die.' You may say to yourself, 'How can we recognize a word that Yhwh has not spoken?' If a prophet speaks in the name of Yhwh but the thing does not take place or prove true, it is a word that Yhwh has not spoken. The prophet has spoken it presumptuously; do not be frightened by it.

The name of the god, Yhwh, does not appear in the entire Aramaic correspondence (Ezra 4.8–6.18). The Elephantine documents suggest that this was typical of conversation with non-Judeans, which the use of the Aramaic language attempts to mimic. (See Comment A below on the use of Aramaic in the narrative sections of Ezra 5.)

Over them. The word 'them' could refer to the Judeans or to the prophets.

5.2 ***Zerubbabel son of Shealtiel and Jeshua son of Yozadak . . . began to build.*** (For these men, see notes at 2.1 and 3.8, and Comment A of Chapter 3 on the altar building.) According to Tattenai's letter (Ezra 5.8), construction on the temple has been on-going continuously since the time of Cyrus, but only now in the second year of Darius I do Zerubbabel and Jeshua appear to take charge of the building process. This verse does not know about Jeshua's and Zerubbabel's previous involvement in laying the temple's foundations (Ezra 3.8). If this verse is original to the second temple's building inscription, as is likely, then Jeshua and Zerubbabel did not participate in laying the foundations; they began to participate only at this point, in the second year of Darius, when the walls were already high enough for Tattenai to report their construction (see note at 5.17 below). The foundations were laid by Sheshbazzar in the time of Cyrus (Ezra 5.16).

This is the last mention of Zerubbabel in the book of Ezra, and there is a great deal of (idle) speculation surrounding his apparent disappearance. See Comment C below.

Prophets of God supporting them. The prophets strengthened the builders with moral support and encouragement. The biblical writer does not name the prophets here, but we can assume that Haggai and Zechariah are meant (see 6.14), unless the writer wants the reader to assume that large numbers of prophets were inspiring the workers. Their words are not quoted; perhaps the implied reader has access to their books. Lack of the prophetic words is a strong indication that these chapters were not composed by the Chronicler, who surely would have taken this opportunity to compose a prophetic speech (See the Introduction on the author of Ezra 1–6 and on the relationship of Ezra–Nehemiah to Chronicles.)

In contrast to Haggai and Zechariah, the writer of Ezra does not see in either the temple's rebuilding or in the presence of Zerubbabel or Jeshua a promise of a messianic age (see Hag. 2.20-23; Zech. 6.12, 13). God is at work, surely (Ezra 1.1), in bringing about the rebuilding and in the return of the people, and we are to praise his steadfast loyalty (3.11); but that is all.

Comments

A. Why Are These Verses and the Entire Narrative That Frames the Royal Correspondence in Aramaic?

The letter from Tattenai to Darius which follows is naturally in Aramaic, the official language of the Persian Empire, but this would not require the surrounding narrative to be in Aramaic as well. Various theories have been proposed to explain the Aramaic of the surrounding narrative. Kratz (2005: 52-54) suggests that the story told in Ezra 5.1–6.15 is a complete, well-rounded narrative, written in Aramaic and that this narrative was the basis on which Ezra 1–4 rests. Zerubbabel and Jeshua are introduced in 5.2 as if they were unknown to the reader, although we have already encountered them in Ezra 3. This can only mean, writes Kratz, that chap. 5 was written first. Others have also argued that the biblical writer used an Aramaic source comprising chaps. 4–6, and either copied it exactly, so Torrey (1970 [1910]: 157-61), or rearranged the chapters from their original chronological order to create a more positive ending (so Porten 1978-79; Rudolph 1949: 47; Gunneweg 1982; Williamson 1985: xxiii; Blenkinsopp 1988: 116).

Most convincing to commentators is the non-Judean character of the Aramaic, the so-called 'external' voice of the author (Arnold 1996; Berman 2006, 2007). Rather than Haggai and Zechariah prophesying 'to us', they prophesy 'to the Judeans who were in Judah and in Jerusalem' (5.1). Rather than speaking of 'the house of Yhwh', it is 'the house of the god which [or who?] is in Jerusalem' (5.2). Rather than Tattenai and his associates coming 'to us' and speaking 'to us', they come 'to them', and speak 'to them' (5.3). Finally we read, 'so then *we* asked them, 'what are the names of the men who are building this building?' (5.4). Nearly every commentator emends this to 'then *they* asked them', but it actually reads, 'we asked them' (Berman 2006). All throughout, the voice is that of non-Judeans, and, particularly, it is the voice of the Persian officials who came with Tattenai to inquire about the building process.

The distance created by this type of phrasing is enhanced even more by the use of the Aramaic language, the official language of the Achaemenid Empire. The phrasing and the language are rhetorical devices used by the biblical author himself writing in the Hellenistic period to increase fear and apprehension in the reader. The reader should feel not only that he is reading an official report, but that he, like the Judeans in the story, are subject to the capricious whims of the Achaemenid kings. Only God stands between him and them.

B. The Rhetorical Role of the Prophets

According to the biblical writer, it was only the prophetic voice, speaking in the name of God, that changed the course of events and enabled the temple to be completed in spite of the royal command (5.1, 2, 5). Their prophesying ensured that the eye of 'their god' would be upon the elders of the Judeans (5.5). I have suggested above in the Introduction and the Excursus following Ezra 2 that the writer of Ezra–Nehemiah was a follower of Ezekiel and that the population groups included in the list of returnees in Ezra 2 were only those sanctioned by Ezekiel. The prophets had encouraged rebellion against Babylon during the reigns of the last kings of Judah and did not foresee that they would be destroyed as a result. Ezekiel (writing after the fall) condemns them:[1]

> My hand will be against the prophets who see false visions and utter lying divinations; they shall not be in the council of my people, nor be enrolled in the register of the house of Israel, *nor shall they enter the land of Israel*; and you shall know that I am the Lord Yhwh. Because, in truth, because they have misled my people, saying, 'Peace', when there is no peace; and because, when the people build a wall, these prophets smear whitewash on it (Ezek. 13.9-10).

Ezekiel blames the prophets for the fall of Judah and predicts that they would not return to Judah. Accordingly they are missing from the list of returnees (Ezra 2; Nehemiah 7). Nevertheless, in spite of this, here we have in Ezra 5.1 a reference to the very prophets whom Ezekiel condemns, and moreover the writer implies that work on the temple commenced only because of their prophesying. How can the writer be a follower of Ezekiel and still make use of the prophetic voice in this way?

This commentary has suggested that the underlying scaffolding of Ezra 1–6 is the ancient Near East building inscription. On top of the original building inscription that the author had at his disposal, he superimposed a Greek tragedy, a tragedy whose primary purpose was to incite pity and fear in the audience. Pity and fear were to be created by a twist of the plot line so that the initial good fortune of the protagonists is reversed purely as a result of their own unwise decisions. The scene in which Zerubbabel rejects the offer of the *'am hā'āreṣ* to aid in building the temple relates just such a calamitous decision and results in the requisite dramatic downturn of their fortunes and an apparent halt to the temple-building project. That scene (4.24) in which the temple building project is halted is intended to arouse pity and fear in the reader.

Like many Greek plays that are dramatic retellings of known events, however, our story's positive ending is already known to the reader. The intended reader already knows that the temple stands, and therefore was built. The problem for the author then was how to get from the low point of the drama, the downward turn of Zerubbabel's fortune, to the known outcome of the rebuilt temple. To Aristotle, the better plays end unhappily; there should be no reversal from bad to good fortune again. Had our story ended there with the stoppage of the temple, and the temple remaining forever in ruins, it would have been the perfect tragic ending that Aristotle favors. There is a problem in retelling familiar stories, however, when the true positive ending is already known to the audience. Indeed, in Greek tragedies, the god was sometimes necessary just to let the audience know

1. This section is based on Fried 2013a.

what that rightful conclusion was supposed to be. In Sophocles' *Philoctetes*, for example, Heracles appears to tell both the protagonists and the audience what it is that the gods desire, namely, that Philoctetes would go with Odysseus to conquer Troy. In Euripides' *Electra,* the play describes the creation of a putatively new cult for the Furies, who had miraculously just appeared, but it was a cult nevertheless whose rites were already well known to the audience. This was a common way to bring the past action of the play into the audience's present (Rehm 1992: 70-71). Although the appearance of the god (lowered by means of a crane onto the stage), known in Latin as the *deus ex machina,* 'the god out from the machine', became a standard device in Greek tragedy to straighten out a snarled plot, Aristotle (*Poetics* 1454a33–1454b9) objected to the device:

> In character portrayal also, as in plot construction, one should always strive for either the necessary or the probable, so that it is either necessary or probable for that kind of person to do or say that kind of thing, just as it is for one event to follow the other. It is evident, then, that the dénouements of plots also should come out of the character itself, and not from the 'machine' as in the Medea or with the sailing of the fleet in the Aulis. . . . let there be no illogicality in the web of events.

The 'god from the machine' was, by definition, an event that did not come out of the character of the *dramatis personae*, nor was it ever an event that followed necessarily and logically from preceding events. It was always extraneous to both character and plot. Aristotle thought that tragedies should end unhappily, and the only purpose of the god's appearance was to avoid the natural unhappy ending.

When the story's happy ending was already well known, the presence of a sort of *deus ex machina* could not always be avoided. Indeed, the technique is not unknown in biblical literature. The dramatic rescue of Isaac from Abraham when an angel (or God himself) stays Abraham's hand is one such example of the magical and unexpected appearance of a god. Indeed, if the story were acted, the angel would have to have been lowered down by a crane (Genesis 22). Because the audience knows that Isaac survived to sire children, the author cannot have him sacrificed. The only way out of the dilemma, apparently, was to have a god appear, save Isaac, and grant Abraham numerous blessings to boot.

Similarly, a very nonflamboyant type of *deus ex machina* is depicted here in Ezra 5. The audience (or reader in this case) knows that the temple was eventually built, and so in spite of the fact that temple construction had apparently been stopped by order of the king himself, the author must somehow get over to the period of the temple's completion and dedication. According to Judean theology, however, the aniconic god cannot appear on a rooftop, lowered down by a crane. Instead, the author unexpectedly brings in the prophets Haggai and Zechariah to prophesy. The text relates that as soon as they prophesied (5.1), Zerubbabel and Jeshua rose and proceeded to build the temple (5.2). This is a type of *deus ex machina*; there is nothing in any of the previous events or in the cast of characters included thus far (in which the prophets are noticeably absent) that would make this event a logical and necessary outcome. Their appearance is totally unexpected, and, in Aristotle's terms, illogical. Tattenai enters immediately at that crucial moment to investigate (5.3) and reports back to Darius that the temple is progressing 'quickly' and that the work 'prospers in their hands' (5.8). There is no evidence in Tattenai's letter that the work had been stopped, nor could there be, since his letter was written in the reign of Darius I, and the putative stoppage occurred in the reign of Darius's grandson, Artaxerxes I. Saying that, however, denies the role of the *deus ex machina,* denies the magical effect of the prophets, and denies the intention of the writer. By having the prophets prophesy, the writer creates a type of *deus ex machina.* The prophesying brings God in to lead the action to its God-desired ending—the completion and dedication of his temple. Moreover, like the role of the *deus* in Greek tragedy, the role of the prophets here, and Zerubbabel and Jeshua's immediate involvement in temple construction afterwards, informs the reader what God's true desire is—that his temple be completed.

C. The Putative Disappearance of Zerubbabel

This is the last appearance of Zerubbabel in the text. He is noticeably missing from the temple's dedication ceremony in the sixth year of Darius (Ezra 6.16-17). This has spawned a great deal of speculation. Albertz (1994: 445) writes the following:

> The building of the temple, which began in difficult conditions, at the same time manifested the instability of the compromise made with the Persians. It sparked off the glowing expectations of a revolution in world history and a national restoration which attached themselves to Zerubbabel of the house of David. The situation seemed so dangerous to the Persians that the satrap Tattenai paid a personal visit to Jerusalem to sort things out (Ezra 5.3-17). While he allowed the rebuilding after consultations with the court (6.1-15), this was probably only on condition that Zerubbabel be withdrawn and that the dangerous prophetic movements be stopped or effectively controlled.

Although Albertz does not cite him, this theory of Zerubbabel's disappearance because of messianic pretensions goes back to a 1954 article by Waterman, 'The Camouflaged Purge of Three Messianic Conspirators'. Waterman bases his argument on a text from the book of Zechariah (Zech. 6.9-14):

> The word of Yhwh came to me:
>
> Collect silver and gold from the exiles—from Heldai, Tobijah, and Jedaiah—who have arrived from Babylon; and go the same day to the house of Josiah son of Zephaniah.

> Take the silver and gold and make crowns, and set [one] on the head of the high priest Joshua son of Jehozadak; say to him (i.e. to Joshua): 'Thus says Yhwh of hosts: Behold the man whose name is Branch: for he shall branch out in his place, and he shall build the temple of Yhwh.
>
> 'It is he who shall build the temple of Yhwh; he shall bear royal honor, and shall sit upon his throne and rule. There shall be a priest on his own throne, and a council of peace shall exist between the two of them.
>
> And the [other] crown shall be the temple of Yhwh as a reminder for Heldai, Tobiah, Jedaiah, and Josiah son of Zephaniah.'[2]

Two crowns are made, and one is to be placed on the head of Joshua the high priest. Thus, the high priest receives the symbol of supreme secular authority, and it is removed from Zerubbabel, the Davidic heir. This is the reversal predicted by Ezekiel (21.29-32). What happens to the other crown? It is put in the temple as a reminder that the true king is Yhwh. It seemed obvious to many, however (e.g. to Waterman and Albertz), that the second crown was for Zerubbabel but that his name had been purged because of fears of a revolution against Persian rule. To Albertz it was this that sparked Tattenai's visit to Jerusalem, and it was not simply part of a routine inspection of the satrapy at the start of Tattenai's appointment in the beginning of Darius's reign.

In point of fact, however, Zerubbabel does not disappear from our text nor does he disappear from Judah in the second year of Darius. We read the following in Ezra 3.1-6a:

> When the seventh month came, and the Israelites were in the towns, the people gathered together in Jerusalem. Then Jeshua son of Jozadak, with his fellow priests, and Zerubbabel son of Shealtiel with his kin set out to build the altar of the god of Israel, to offer burnt offerings on it, as prescribed in the law of Moses the man of God. They set up the altar on its foundation, because they were in dread of the neighboring peoples, and they offered burnt offerings upon it to Yhwh, morning and evening. And they kept the festival of Booths, as prescribed, and offered the daily burnt offerings by number according to the ordinance, as required for each day, and after that the regular burnt offerings, the offerings at the new moon and at all of Yhwh's sacred festivals, and the offerings of everyone who made a free-will offering to Yhwh. From the first day of the seventh month they began to offer burnt offerings to Yhwh.

The text does not state what year this is, only that it is the seventh month. According to the chronology of the book of Ezra, it refers to the seventh month of the first year of their return to the land, that is, in 538 BCE, the first year of Cyrus as king of Babylon. Since the text continues by saying that the foundations of the temple were not yet laid (Ezra 3.6b), this seems a natural interpretation. We learn from Tattenai's letter, however, that the foundations

2. Translation suggested by Meyers and Meyers 1987.

were laid by Sheshbazzar, not Zerubbabel, and that Zerubbabel and Jeshua do not arrive in Jerusalem until the second year of Darius. It could only have been the excitement of the arrival of Zerubbabel, the Davidic heir, and Jeshua the grandson of the last high priest of Judah, that stimulated the prophecies of Haggai and Zechariah (Bedford 2001). According to Ezra 5.2, Zerubbabel and Jeshua began to participate in the temple-building process only then, in the second year of Darius, and this would have been the time of their arrival in Jerusalem. Since the sacrificial altar is actually one of the final stages of the temple-building process in the ancient Near East (see Introduction to Ezra 1–6), we may date Ezra 3.1-6a to Darius's second year not to Cyrus's (see Comment A to Ezra 3.1-6a). Moreover, Darius's order to Tattenai that 'the governor of the Judeans and the elders of the Judeans shall have a free hand to rebuild this house of God on its site' (Ezra 6.7) implies that Darius did not perceive the governor to be a threat and he may be forgiven for forgetting his name (Williamson 1985: 76). There was no purge; Zerubbabel does not disappear. There was only a bit of text moved from its original position near the end of the temple-building story to its beginning.

Ezra 5.3-5

Tattenai, the Viceroy of Beyond-the-River, Investigates Jerusalem

In terms of the story, the order had been given to stop work, and work on the temple had stopped until now in the second year of Darius (4.24). At this point the prophets begin to prophesy, and the work begins to go forward again in spite of the royal order. Now, in the midst of all this illegal activity, Tattenai, governor in charge of the entire half-satrapy of Beyond-the-River, shows up to investigate Judah and Jerusalem.

This event is intended to create fear and pity in the mind of the reader, and we as readers should let ourselves feel that fear and that pity. At the same time we know intellectually that no stoppage on the temple was ever ordered and that the building activities were not actually illegal. It was only the work on the city wall that was stopped. That stoppage we will not hear about until the book of Nehemiah.

Translation

3. *At that time Tattenai,*[a] *governor*[b] *of Beyond-the-River,*[c] *Shethar-Boznai,*[d] *and their colleagues came to them saying thus to them: 'Who gave you an order to build this house and to complete this paneling?'*[e] 4. *Then thus we said to them:*[f] *'What are the names*[g] *of the men who are building this building?'* 5. *But the eye of their god was on the elders of the Judeans,*[h] *and they did not stop*[i] *[them] until a report would go to Darius*[j] *and they would have an order*[k] *returned about this.*

Textual Notes

a. **5.3** *Tattenai.* First Esdras reads 'Sisinnes'.

b. *Governor.* פחה, *peḥâ.* First Esdras reads *eparch,* ἔπαρχος. The titles *hyparch* and *eparch,* common in the Greek writings, indicate someone in charge of an area of any size who reports to someone else, be it to another hyparch or to the Great King. See note.

c. *Beyond-the-River.* First Esdras reads 'Syria and Phoenicia'.

d. *Shethar-Boznai.* This may be a corruption of the common Persian name Shatibarzana, 'desiring joy' (Rosenthal 1995: 103). Both a Shatibarzana and a Shatibara (bearing joy) appear in the Elephantine papyri.

e. *This paneling.* The Aramaic or, more likely, the Persian word ארשנא, *'uršana*, appears several times among the Aramaic papyri from Elephantine but is still not fully understood. From the papyri it appears that it refers to something that is made of wood and can burn up, that can be taken, and that can be used in conjunction with a boat, a house, or a temple. First Esdras translates the term as 'roof', but that would not fit the Elephantine texts. Greek Ezra reads 'wealth', but this would not fit the Elephantine texts either. Both the Vulgate and the Syriac translate it as 'walls', which is not something that can be taken but which is close to the term 'paneling' for the walls, which is proposed here. 'Paneling' would fit all the contexts (Mowinckel 1964a).

f. **5.4** *Then thus we said to them.* This phrase is missing in 1 Esdras.

g. *What are the names?* 1 Esdras reads, 'Who are the builders who are finishing these things?', omitting the word 'names'. Greek Ezra retains 'What are the names' but instead of 'who are building this building' reads 'who are building this city'.

h. **5.5** *But the eye of their god was on the elders of the Judeans.* First Esdras reads, 'The elders of the Judeans had favor, the captives being under the supervision of the Lord'. Greek Ezra reads, 'But the eyes of God were upon the captivity of Judah'. The Aramaic for 'elders', *śby,* שבי, is orthographically identical to the Hebrew word for 'captives', *šby,* שבי. The translator of 1 Esdras attempts to get both meanings into the verse. Greek Ezra refers to the 'eyes' of God, in the plural. Perhaps it intends God's two eyes or perhaps the author has seven eyes in mind (see Zech. 4.10).

i. *They did not stop* [*them*]. There is no object for this transitive verb. First Esdras puts this in the passive: 'They were not prevented from building . . .'

j. *A report went to Darius.* Literally, 'until a decision went to Darius'. First Esdras reads, 'until a report was sent to Darius to inform [him] about them', that is, about the Judeans.

k. *Order.* See note at 4.7. The word itself does not necessarily imply something written. Greek Ezra reads 'tribute gatherer' for this Aramaic/Persian word, as it does in 4.18 and 4.23.

Notes

5.3 ***At that time.*** The biblical author intends for the reader to assume that Tattenai's investigation resulted from the fact that building was continuing, even though it had been expressly forbidden by the king (4.21-24).

Tattenai. A cuneiform tablet found in Babylon and dated to 502 BCE refers to the servant of 'Ta-at-tan-nu, governor (*piḫatu*) of Ebir-nari', that is, to 'Tattenai governor of Beyond-the-River' (Ungnad 1941). Tattenai is stated on this tablet to be in charge of the half-satrapy of Beyond-the-River in the twentieth year of Darius. According to the tablet, moreover, he has the same official title that he bears in the book of Ezra. If in the twentieth year, so he was apparently also in this role eighteen years earlier in 520, in the second year of Darius, when he is said to have investigated Jerusalem. Ungnad sees in the reference to Tattenai here proof that the information in the book of Ezra should not be 'shoved aside' as unreliable (Ungnad 1941: 243). Tattenai was evidently the *hyparch* of the sub-satrapy Beyond-the-River under Uštanu, who was satrap of the combined province Babylon and Beyond-the-River from March 521 to June/July 516 BCE, if not later as well (Stolper 1989a: 290). Uštanu's seat of office would have been the city of Babylon; Tattenai's would most likely have been Damascus. Babylon and Beyond-the-River are last attested as a single satrapy in October of 486 BCE, two months before the death of Darius I (Briant 2002: 544). Xerxes very likely divided them into the two separate satrapies of Beyond-the-River and Babylon when Babylon revolted in 479 BCE.

Their colleagues. These are high officials in Tattenai's office; their specific title is given in v. 6 below. Fleishman (1995: 83) suggests that these may be governors of other provinces in Beyond-the-River, but there is no evidence for this. Satrapal and sub-satrapal courts would have had their full complement of officials. Nehemiah (5.17) claims to have had 150 people at his provincial court, that is, who ate at his table.

Came to them. According to the letter, Tattenai spoke to anonymous 'elders of the Judeans'. The implication of the introduction to the letter, supplied by the biblical writer, is that Tattenai came to interrogate Zerubbabel, Jeshua, and the prophets of God.

Complete this paneling. That this is the correct translation of this Persian term and that the temple was already at the point of paneling the inside temple walls by 520 BCE are clear from Haggai's demand that the people go to the hills and get wood to beautify the temple building (Hag. 1.8). See discussion at 3.12 above.

5.4 ***We said to them.*** That 'we' is written here rather than the 'they' to which it is usually emended is a purposeful attempt by the biblical writer to create distance between the Persian officials who came to Jerusalem and the implied reader who identifies with the Judeans in Jerusalem. The greater the distance the writer can create between these officials and the reader, the greater the threat that the reader will perceive, and the greater the catharsis when the temple is finally dedicated.

5.5 ***Elders of the Judeans.*** This foreign-sounding phrase also creates distance between the point of view of the narrator and that of the implied reader and adds to the experience of threat. If he were writing from the Judean point of view, we would have written 'the heads of [fathers'] houses' as he does elsewhere (1.5, etc.). See note below at 5.9.

The eye of their god. The use of the phrase 'their god' rather than 'our god' is also used purposefully by the biblical writer, again to create distance—and fear—between the narrator and the implied reader. This distance also creates a feeling of objectivity, that the writer is quoting an external source, and that these are not his own words. Thus, even an objective external writer can see that the eye of their god, the Judean god, is watching over the Judeans.

Comment: Why Did Tattenai Inspect the Temple?

If Tattenai's letter is authentic (see below), then Tattenai must have investigated Jerusalem and seen the temple in the process of being built. If the events described in Ezra 4.1-5 are not historical, as argued *ad loc.*, then why would he have needed to investigate Jerusalem at all? The reason, though not mentioned in the text, is clear from general Persian administrative practices. It is incumbent upon every Persian official to know every detail about everything that occurs in his jurisdiction. This is apparent from the Arsames letters dealing with Achaemenid Egypt and from the letters to Bagavant, dealing with Achaemenid Bactria (Blenkinsopp 1988: 120; Fried 2004; Shaked 2004; Naveh and Shaked 2012).

Tattenai's visit occurred during the reign of Darius I, and obviously before his sixth year, when the temple was dedicated. It could not have been before Darius's second year in office. The Behistun inscription describes Darius's tumultuous first year, in which he was continually beset by rebellions. Only in his second year, when the rebellions ended, would Darius have had the time to organize his empire and appoint satraps, hyparchs and governors. After Cyrus's death in battle in 530 BCE, Cambyses his son became king. When Cambyses died suddenly in 522, Darius seized the throne by killing Cyrus's younger son, Smerdis. He spent the first year of his reign putting down one rebellion after another (see the Behistun inscription; Kent 1953). It was only in the second year of his reign that he would have been able to turn his attention to the organization of his empire. During his first year he would have fired (or more probably killed) those officials who had been appointed by Cyrus and Cambyses (and who would have supported Smerdis), and by his second year he seems to have appointed new ones loyal to himself (Briant 2002; Fried 2004). The second year of Darius would then have been Tattenai's first year in office and the first time in which he would have been able to tour the sub-satrapy of Beyond-the-River and to bring himself up to date on the events in his jurisdiction. By informing the king and seeking his approval, Tattenai was simply doing his job. Nothing sinister should be read into the questions; nothing happened anywhere in the Persian Empire without the knowledge and approval of the king. The king's interest in the temple would have been more than cursory, however, since temples in the empire provided a major source of revenue to the king (see Introduction).

Ezra 5.6-17

The Viceroy of Beyond-the-River Reports to the King

Tattenai, the viceroy of the combined satrapy Babylon and Beyond-the-River, in charge of Beyond-the-River, writes his report to King Darius.

Translation

6. *[The following is] a copy*[a] *of the letter that Tattenai, Governor of Beyond-the- River, Shethar-Boznai and their colleagues, the examiners*[b] *of Beyond-the-River, sent to Darius the king:* 7. *They sent a message*[c] *to him, and thus it was written in it:*[d]

To Darius the King: All peace![e]

8. *May it be known*[f] *to the king*[g] *that we went*[h] *to the province of Yehud*[i] *to the house of the great god.*[j] *It is being built of dressed stones*[k] *with timber*[l] *laid in the walls. The work is being done quickly*[m] *and prospers in their hands.*[n] 9. *Then we asked*[o] *those elders: Thus we said to them: 'Who gave you an order to build this house and to complete its paneling'?*[p] 10. *We also asked them their names in order to inform you so that we might write down the names of the men who are at their head.* 11. *Thus they responded*[q] *to us, saying:*

'We are the servants of the god of heaven and earth[r] *and we are rebuilding this house*[s] *that had been built many years ago. A great*[t] *king of Israel had built and perfected it.* 12. *But because our fathers angered*[u] *the god of heaven,*[v] *he gave them into the hand*[w] *of Nebuchadnezzar king of Babylon, the Chaldean,*[x] *who destroyed*[y] *this house and deported the people to Babylon.* 13. *However, in the first year of Cyrus, king of Babylon,*[z] *King Cyrus issued an order*[aa] *to rebuild the house of this god.*[bb] 14. *Furthermore, the vessels*[cc] *of the house of the god*[dd] *which were of gold and silver that Nebuchadnezzar had taken from the temple in Jerusalem and had deposited in the temple of Babylon,*[ee] *King Cyrus took them out from the temple of Babylon and they were delivered to a man named Sheshbazzar*[ff] *whom he had made governor.*[gg] 15. *He said to him, 'Take these vessels,*[hh] *go,*[ii] *deposit them in the temple in Jerusalem, and let the house of the god*[jj] *be built on its site'.* 16. *Then that Sheshbazzar came and laid the foundations of this house*

of the god[kk] *in Jerusalem. From then until now it has been under construction, but it is not yet finished'.*

17. *Now if it pleases the king,*[ll] *let it be investigated in the royal treasury*[mm] *if there is there*[nn] *in Babylon an order of King Cyrus*[oo] *to build the house of the god which is in Jerusalem, and let the king send us his pleasure in the matter.*

Textual Notes

a. **5.6** *Copy*. Greek Ezra reads, 'An explanation of the letter'. The translator misunderstood the Persian *paršegen*. See note at 4.11.

b. *Examiners.* אֲפַרְסְכָיֵא. *Aparskaya.* The title is likely from the Old Persian root **u*- 'well' and **parsa* 'examine', plus the Aramaic suffix *kāya* (Kent 1953: 198). This word is similar to *aprastakāya* in 4.9, above, which we have translated 'investigators', but the Persian roots are slightly different. One is *fraθ,* 'investigate', the other is *parsa,* 'examine' (Kent 1953: 198). It probably does not simply mean 'Persians', אֲפָרְסָיֵא, with the added *ka* meaning 'the ones who', as suggested by (Rosenthal 1995: 189). Greek Ezra interprets the word as an ethnic group, the Apharsachaeans. First Esdras translates as 'appointed officials'.

c. **5.7** *Message.* See note at 4.17 for a discussion of this Persian word.

d. *They sent . . . written in it.* This entire phrase is omitted in 1 Esdras. It is redundant.

e. *All peace*! This is a greeting formula, שלמא כלא. The word 'all', כלא, is an appositive in construct with the preceding noun and appears in this way in Aramaic letters from the fifth century BCE (Fitzmyer 1997: 210-14). The exact phrase שלמא כלא does not occur at Elephantine, however (Schwiderski 2000: 365). First Esdras misinterprets the role of the 'all' and connects it to the following line, so that it reads, 'let all be known to the king'.

f. **5.8** *Let it be known.* First Esdras reads 'let all be known', bringing the 'all' from the line above.

g. *To the king.* First Esdras reads 'to our lord the king', as frequently occurs in official correspondence.

h. *We went.* אֲזַלְנָא ends in the letter aleph, א, used as a vowel. This is a late form and does not appear among the Aramaic documents at Elephantine, suggesting that the spelling has been updated by the copyist in the Hellenistic period.

i. *The province of Yehud.* First Esdras reads 'the area of Judea', without applying a political title to the area. It also inserts the phrase 'and when we entered the area of Judea and the city of Jerusalem we came upon the elders of the captives of the Judeans in the city of Jerusalem'. It is an attempt to fill in a perceived gap. See note. Again we have שבי, interpreted both as 'elders' and 'captives'.

j. *To the house of the great god.* This phrase is not present in 1 Esdras. Rather, 1 Esdras reads, 'we found the elders of the captives building in the city of Jerusalem a great new house of the Lord'. 'Great' modifies 'house' there, not the god as here in Ezra.

k. *Dressed stones.* First Esdras reads 'polished stones'.

l. *Timber.* First Esdras reads 'costly timber'.

m. *Quickly.* The exact meaning of this term is not known; others translate by 'diligently' or 'thoroughly'. The word appears in a document from Elephantine (*TAD* A.6.13:4) in which the satrap Arsames tells his assistant to 'release the rent of the domains of PN *'osparnā'*. Porten and Yardeni translate it 'in full', but that would not fit the context of the letter in Ezra. First Esdras translates it as 'quickly', and Greek Ezra by 'dexterously'. These would fit all the contexts.

n. *Prospers in their hands.* First Esdras adds, 'the work is being completed with splendor and care'.

o. **5.9** *We asked, we said.* These verbs also have an aleph at the end used as a vowel, which indicates a modernizing of the spelling in the Hellenistic period.

p. *Complete its paneling.* First Esdras reads 'strengthen the work'. It does not repeat 5.3 as both Ezra and Greek Ezra do.

q. **5.11** *They responded.* Literally, 'they returned a word'. This circumlocution is common also in Hebrew. The term for 'word' is the Persian *pitgama.*

r. *God of heaven and earth.* First Esdras reads 'the Lord who created Heaven and Earth'.

s. *We are rebuilding this house.* This statement is missing from 1 Esdras, leaving the connection between the present building and the former one only implied, not stated.

t. *Great.* First Esdras inserts 'and mighty'

u. **5.12** *Angered.* First Esdras reads instead 'in rebelling, sinned against'.

v. *The god of heaven.* First Esdras reads 'the Lord of Israel, the one of heaven', or 'the one living in heaven'.

w. *Hand.* Both 1 Esdras and Greek Ezra have 'hands', plural.

x. *The Chaldean.* First Esdras reads 'king of the Chaldeans', based on the *kethib* rather than the *qere.*

y. *Destroyed.* 'Pulled down'. Based on the Greek, κατέλυσεν (Clines 2009: 305; see Prov. 28.28). First Esdras reads καθελόντες ἐνεπύρισαν, 'pulled down and burned'.

z. *In the first year of Cyrus.* First Esdras clarifies with 'in the first year that Cyrus reigned over the country of Babylon'. That is, he had been king of Persia before he added Babylon to his realm.

aa. *Issued an order.* First Esdras simply reads 'wrote' and not even 'wrote an order', which is odd. Perhaps whatever the king writes is an order by definition.

bb. *Of this god.* This phrase is missing in 1 Esdras.

cc. **5.14** *The vessels.* First Esdras reads 'the holy vessels', as in 1.7.

dd. *The house of the god.* This phrase is missing from 1 Esdras but is implied by the adjective 'holy'.

ee. *The temple in Babylon.* First Esdras reads 'his own temple', which is accurate.

ff. *To a man named Sheshbazzar.* First Esdras reads 'to Zerubbabel and Sanabassaros'. Zerubbabel is inserted here because in the Story of the Three Youths (1 Esdras 3–4) Darius gives Zerubbabel the vessels that Cyrus 'vowed' to return to Jerusalem.

gg. *Whom he had made governor.* First Esdras simply says 'Sanabassaros the *hyparch*', omitting 'whom he had made'. Greek Ezra has 'Sasabassar the treasurer who was over the treasury'. In Ezra 1.8, Greek Ezra refers to Sasabassar as *archon* over Judah, and Mithradates as treasurer.

hh. **5.15** *He said to him, 'Take these vessels'.* As is usual, the Hebrew has direct speech and 1 Esdras indirect, reading, 'He commanded him to take these vessels'. There is no need to emend.

ii. *Go.* This is omitted as redundant in 1 Esdras.

jj. *House of the god.* First Esdras has 'this house of the Lord'.

kk. **5.16** *House of the god.* Again 1 Esdras reads 'the house of the Lord'.

ll. **5.17** *If it pleases the king.* First Esdras reads 'If it is judged acceptable, O King'.

mm. *Royal treasury.* First Esdras reads 'the royal library'.

nn. *There.* The word is omitted from 1 Esdras; it is awkward.

oo. *Cyrus.* Some manuscripts of 1 Esdras read 'of the Lord the king', instead of 'of Cyrus the king'. This is simply mistaking *kuriou,* 'Lord', for *kurou*, 'Cyrus'.

Notes

5.6 ***Copy of the letter . . . sent to Darius the king.*** This verse and the next are in Aramaic, as is the letter itself. The use of Persian words for 'copy' and for 'investigators', the list of senders, and the fact that the phrase 'to Darius the king' is written with the preposition *'al* for 'to', which is characteristic only of Persian-period documents, suggest that this verse was taken from the original letter or perhaps from the outside of the rolled-up scroll.

Beyond-the-River. This is the half-satrapy representing half of the former Babylonian Empire, the second half of the combined satrapy of Babylon and Beyond-the-River. This large satrapy was split in two in the reign of Xerxes. The area indicated is west of the river Euphrates.

5.7 ***To Darius the King, 'All peace!'*** The word for 'to' is *l-* rather than the *'al*, or *'el*, used in the previous verse. This usage does not appear until the Hellenistic period (Schwiderski 2000: 360). The phrase 'all peace', *š^elāmā' kollā'*, has no parallel in Achaemenid era letters either, but is very similar to the Hellenistic πολλὰ χαίρειν, 'many greetings!' (Schwiderski 2000: 365-68; Grabbe 2006: 547). This verse was evidently written in the Hellenistic period by the biblical author to introduce the letter.

5.8 ***The great god.*** This phrase appears on two texts from the Persepolis Fortification Tablets (Hallock 1969). These texts from Persepolis, one of the three capitals of the Persian Empire, deal with the administrative transfer of food commodities in the years between 509 and 494, the 13th to the 28th year of Darius I. One text (Number 353) refers to a delivery of two *marriš* of beer for the god Adad and two more for 'the great god', making a total of four. Another (Number 354) refers to a delivery of 3 BAR of grain for the libation of 'the great god'. The great god is not named in these texts, and the phrase seems to be a circumlocution for any unknown god.

Williamson (1985: 68) emends this verse to read, '. . . we went to the province of Judah and found *the elders of the Judeans in the city of Jerusalem* building the house of the great God'. Blenkinsopp (1988: 118) emends the verse to read, 'we went to the house of the great God. We discovered *that it was being rebuilt by the Judean elders in the city of Jerusalem.*' These emendations follow the text of 1 Esdras (see textual note) but are not necessary.

Dressed stones. The Aramaic *gll* is often understood to be from the Hebrew root *gll,* meaning 'rolled', the stones being so big they must be rolled rather than lifted. However, Akkadian and Aramaic texts from Persian Persepolis speak of *aban galalu*, that is, '*galalu*-stones', in contexts that suggest that the stones are smoothed or polished or dressed in some way. The use of an apparently Persian word suggests an Achaemenid date for its writing.

With timber laid in the walls. The type of construction, spelled out in Ezra 6.4 as three courses of dressed stone and a course of wood, was common in the ancient Near East (Thomson 1960). It affords protection against earthquake and provides a degree of elasticity in the case of uneven settling of the stones. Timber was placed in the walls from the middle of the wall upward, since it is primarily the upper reaches of the building that are vulnerable to earthquakes and because wood was too costly to put everywhere (Faust, personal communication [June 14, 2007]). Therefore, for Tattenai to know the manner of construction, the building must have progressed quite far.

Quickly. This Persian word, *'osparnā',* occurs frequently in the correspondence of Arsames, satrap of Egypt during the reign of Darius II. It is not known later, and so testifies to the authenticity of this part of Tattenai's letter.

Prospers in their hands. It is clear from Tattenai's report that the Judeans have progressed a good deal in the building process. Although not completed, the building process has progressed far beyond simply the foundations. The third-person plural suffix of the word 'their hands', בִּידְהֹם, *bydhm*, is spelled defectively, a spelling that went out of style toward the end of the Achaemenid period. This early form provides additional evidence of the authenticity of the letter. Whereas a late copyist may update the spelling to the more 'modern' one, it is not likely that a writer in the Hellenistic period would deliberately use archaic forms.

Most compelling, however, is the fact that this letter knows of no stoppage at any time between the start of the building process in the time of Cyrus and now, in the second year of Darius, eighteen years later. This certainly testifies to the authenticity of the letter, or at least that it was not written for the sake of the story.

5.9 ***We asked those elders.*** What elders? In fact, no elders in particular. The phrase 'the elders' is a circumlocution referring to any free citizen who is perceived to be in charge (Dandamayev 1995: 28-29). Gunneweg (1985: 100) states that without a phrase similar to the one added in 1 Esdras that 'we encountered the elders of the returnees building in the city of Jerusalem' the reference to the 'elders' hangs in the air. It is clear that the author of 1 Esdras thought so, and accordingly added the phrase to fill in the perceived gap.

1 Esdras also adds a reference to the city of Jerusalem, which is missing from our text. Gunneweg suggests this indicates that the letter is not authentic. The biblical writer who wrote it knows, however, that the reader will understand that the temple of the 'great god' is naturally the temple in Jeru-

salem. As discussed in the Introduction to this commentary, the province of Yehud was quite small, and consisted primarily of a city and its environs. Further, without a city wall, not built for another sixty-five years, it is not clear that the Persian officials would have considered the name of the city worth mentioning.

Japhet (2006: 68) asks how likely it would have been for Tattenai, Darius's newly appointed governor of Beyond-the-River, to negotiate directly with the elders of the Judeans. Would he not have turned to his own subordinate Zerubbabel, the governor of Judah? Indeed, it is not likely; however, negotiation is not portrayed here but only an interrogation. Further, if Tattenai was appointed hyparch of Beyond-the-River at the same time that Zerubbabel was appointed governor of Judah, that is, in 520, the second year of Darius I, then Tattenai would not have supposed that Zerubbabel would know the answer to his questions any more than he would. Tattenai would have had to ask those elders of the Judeans who had been there since the time of Cyrus. There is no need to posit a 'democratizing' tendency on the part of the biblical author (*pace* Japhet 2006: 68).

Who gave you an order? They are not being asked to show a written proof. Indeed, the expectation of the authors of the letter is that the written proof, if any, would lie in the royal treasury in Babylon, not with the Judeans in Yehud. (See note on Ezra 1.1.)

Complete its paneling. This verse and the previous one provide the source for the narrative in 5.3-5. (See discussion at 5.3 and at 3.12 above.)

5.10 ***Their names*** **שְׁמָהָתְהֹם.** The third-person plural suffix 'their' is spelled defectively, another indication that the letter was written originally in the Achaemenid period and was a source to the biblical writer.

Write down the names. The list of names is not included in our text. Williamson (1985: 78) speculates that the list forms the basis of the names in Ezra 2.

Their head **בְּרָאשֵׁיהֹם.** The suffix 'their' is spelled defectively here as well, a spelling indicative of the Achaemenid period and pointing to the authenticity of the letter.

5.11 ***God of heaven and earth.*** This exact title appears only here in the Hebrew Bible, but similar titles appear frequently in Persian-period biblical texts (Rofé 1990). (For the title 'god of heaven', see comments to Ezra 1.2.) We read, 'God Most High, owner of heaven and earth' in Gen. 14.19, 22; and 'I swear by Yhwh, god of heaven and god of earth' in Gen. 24.3.

This house had been built many years ago. A great king of Israel had built and perfected it. A similar argument was brought by the Judeans of Elephantine in 407 BCE when they requested permission to rebuild their destroyed temple (*TAD* 4.7 and 8:13-14):

> During the days of the kings of Egypt our fathers had built that temple in Elephantine the fortress and when Cambyses entered Egypt he found that

> temple built. And they overthrew the temples of the gods of Egypt, all (of them), but no one damaged anything in that temple.

The Judeans of Elephantine refer to their temple's implicit authorization by Cambyses, and the Judeans of Jerusalem refer to the explicit authorization by Cyrus (Rothenbusch 2012: 99).

5.12 ***Because our fathers angered the god of heaven.*** This theology was ubiquitous throughout the ancient Near East. If a temple was destroyed it could be only because the god whose temple it was became angry with his worshipers. To believe otherwise was to confront the possibility of a powerless god, something unthinkable. (See Introduction.)

5.14 ***To a man named Sheshbazzar.*** Literally, 'Sheshbazzar, his name'. Blenkinsopp (1988: 122) suggests that this way of referring to Sheshbazzar was rude and indicates that he had already become '*persona non grata* to the Persian authorities'. In fact, this construction is common in Achaemenid-period letters and inscriptions to refer to someone who was not expected to be known to the reader. Darius's Behistun inscription (1.28), for example, states that 'A son of Cyrus, *Cambyses his name*, of our family, was king here'. Among the Aramaic documents from Elephantine, we have the record of an adoption (*TAD* B 3.9:3-5). The document states that '*Jedaniah his name*, son of Taḥwa, . . . shall be my son'. Steiner (2006: 644-45) argues that the construction had a very short life span within Aramaic. The construction is unattested after the Achaemenid period, another indication of the date of the document.

Sheshbazzar whom he had made governor. This is where we learn that Sheshbazzar was the governor of Judah, and that Judah was already a separate province from the first year of Cyrus. (See note on 1.8 above.)

5.15 ***He said to him, 'Take these vessels'.*** For a discussion about whether the temple vessels would have survived and have been in a state capable of being returned, see discussion in the comment to Ezra 1 above. This use of direct speech is common in Achaemenid-era memoranda. A memorandum discovered at Elephantine (*TAD* A 4.9:2) also quotes direct speech in the second-person singular:

> Memorandum of what Bagohi and Delaiah said
> to me, saying: Memorandum: You may say in Egypt . . .

In fact, the use of direct speech is characteristic of an Achaemenid date for the letter. Direct speech gave way to indirect speech only in the Hellenistic period, as can be seen from the translation in 1 Esdras. Rothenbusch (2012: 96) writes that it is 'hardly conceivable' ('Es ist aber kaum vorstellbar') that the elders would know the exact words that Cyrus said to Sheshbazzar and not be able to produce a copy of the decree authorizing the rebuilding. In fact, they may have made themselves such a memorandum, similar to the memorandum that Jedaniah, priest of the temple of Yhw, made for himself, which reflected a conversation authorizing him to plead his case to Arsames. A copy of such a memorandum in the hands of the Judeans would not have convinced Tattenai however. He would have needed more official proof.

He (Cyrus) said to him . . . let the house of the god be built on its site. For a discussion the historicity of Cyrus's concern for a temple in far-off Judah, see comment to Ezra 1.

Sheshbazzar came and laid the foundations. Many scholars (e.g. Williamson 1985; Blenkinsopp 1988) assert that the Judeans were lying here to Tattenai, and that really Zerubbabel had laid the foundations (but see the discussion at Ezra 3 above, as well as Japhet 2006: 183-232). It is not likely that the Judeans would have lied to Tattenai about this. Darius took the throne in a military coup against Cambyses' brother, Smerdis, the second son of Cyrus the Great. His first year was spent in a series of wars against those rebelling against him (see Darius's Behistun inscription; Kent 1953). It was only in the second year of his reign that he was able to turn to administrative affairs and to appoint satraps and under-satraps of the satrapies and governors of the provinces. At that time he appointed officials who would be loyal to himself and not to the family of Cyrus and Cambyses (Fried 2004; Briant 2002). Tattenai and Zerubbabel would have both been appointed in Darius's second year at the earliest. Tattenai would have made a routine tour of inspection at the time of his appointment. Since he describes everyone as working rapidly (5.8), the visit must have occurred after Haggai had chided them for not working hard enough on the temple-building project (Hag. 1.2), that is, it must have been after the sixth or seventh month of Darius's second year, and so after Zerubbabel has already arrived (Hag. 1.1). It is not possible that the Judeans would have claimed that Sheshbazzar had laid the foundations if Zerubbabel had really laid them when Zerubbabel was standing right there!

From then until now it has been under construction, but it is not yet finished. There is no awareness in Tattenai's letter of any of the events described in 4.1-5, nor is there any awareness that the work had been stopped. If the letter is authentic, then neither the stoppage nor the events described in 4.1-5 are historical. Indeed, the fact that the letter contradicts the narrative intent of the author indicates that it is genuine. If it had been created by the biblical writer, he would have written it to conform to his narrative. (See comment on the historicity of Tattenai's letter.) The only work that was ordered stopped was the work on the wall in the time of Nehemiah (Ezra 4.23), not the work on the temple.

The reply of the elders to Tattenai is reminiscent of the letter (*TAD* A 4.7, 8) sent to the governor of Judah from the Judean garrison at Elephantine when their temple of Yhw at Elephantine was destroyed. After recounting the events surrounding the temple's destruction by the Persian governor of the island, Jedaniah, the high priest of the temple, writes that Cambyses had left the temple of Yhw in peace when he conquered Egypt (*TAD* A 4.7:13-14), implying his approval of the building, and that, therefore, the argument goes, no one had the right to tear it down. The reply of the Judeans to Tattenai is similar: it was approved by Cyrus; therefore no one had the right to stop its construction.

Gunneweg (1985: 103) sees two separate independent traditions here that the biblical author skillfully merges: one tradition in which the temple was stopped, and one in which it continued uninterrupted. It is clear from the author's use of the letter regarding the stoppage of work on Jerusalem's city wall in Ezra 4, however, that in fact he had no tradition regarding any stoppage of the temple. He created the story *de novo* to add drama and suspense to his narrative (Fried 2012a).

5.17 ***Treasury.*** First Esdras reads 'library'. Ezra reads בְּבֵית גִּנְזַיָּא, *bêt ginzayyā'*, 'in the house of the treasury', or 'treasury house', from *ganza,* the Persian word for 'treasury'. We know that there was a treasury (*ganza*) house at Persepolis. A hoard of cuneiform tablets found at the site in the early 1930s confirms that a royal treasury existed at Persepolis under the command of the *ganzabara*, the treasurer. It housed both silver and all the archival tablets that tracked the income and disbursements of the silver. The tablets at Persepolis also tracked the income and disbursements of grain, animals, spices, wine and beer, as well as silver, at local treasury houses all across the empire. The Judean garrison at the Nile island of Elephantine received monthly rations paid from the royal treasury at Elephantine, and the customs collected on Nile traffic was among the funds deposited in the treasury.

Since the treasury tablets were intended to record the income and disbursements of royal property, a request to search the records of the royal treasury implies that Tattenai assumed that a permission to build a temple would necessarily have included an authorization of funds.

Babylon. Babylon was the capital of the combined satrapy Babylon and Beyond-the-River, so it was natural to search in Babylon's treasury building first.

Comment: Is Tattenai's Letter to Darius (Ezra 5.7b-17) Authentic?

Most important for the evaluation of the letter is that the information provided in it conflicts with the narrative of Ezra itself (Grabbe 2006: 546). According to the letter, Sheshbazzar laid the temple's foundations, whereas the narrative has Zerubbabel and Jeshua laying them (Ezra 3). Moreover, the letter knows of no disputes with either Samaritans or satrapal officials; it knows of no malicious attempts to stop temple construction, nor does it know of any royal order to stop the building project as is described in Ezra 4. According to Tattenai, by the second year of Darius the work has been progressing nicely and prospers in their hands. He quotes the reply of the Judeans that the temple has been under construction continuously from the time the foundations were laid under Sheshbazzar and Cyrus until the present time, during Tattenai's investigation, most likely in the second year of Darius. These discrepancies provide primary evidence that the biblical writer did not compose the letter. Indeed, scholars agree that this letter is perhaps the oldest and most authentic section in Ezra 1–6, and indeed the oldest section of Ezra–Nehemiah (Pakkala 2004: 3; Kratz 2005: 53-55; Grabbe 2006: 546-48, 563). The correspondence with Darius is independent of the events described in Ezra 4 and not a reaction to it.

Further, the request for Darius's order vis-à-vis the Jerusalem temple is completely in agreement with Achaemenid decision-making practices. Local provincial governors could do nothing without satrapal approval, and the satrap could do little without consulting the king. A letter sent from Akhvamazda, satrap of Bactria, to Bagavant, one of his provincial governors, is dated to 3 Sivan, the eleventh year of Artaxerxes III, or June 21, 348 BCE (*ADAB* A4, Naveh and Shaked 2012: 96-99). In the letter, Akhvamazda responds affirmatively to Bagavant's request to release the troops at his disposal temporarily from building the city wall of the city of Nikhšapaya and to use them instead to gather in the harvest before the locusts consumed it. It is clear from this letter that the Persian governor had no autonomy whatsoever. The governor could not decide by himself to halt the wall-building efforts in order to collect the harvest before the locusts ate it. He had to request permission from his satrap and then await his satrap's response. Lack of local autonomy in the Persian Empire is repeatedly mentioned by the Greek authors as well. Diodorus states, for example (15.41.5), that the Persians took so long in preparing to put down the Egyptian revolt that the Egyptians were ready for them when they came. The long delay in attacking Egypt was due to the fact that the Persian generals had to refer all questions to the king and then await his reply before they could carry out any action. This type of activity is visible here in Tattenai's correspondence with Darius.

The orthography of the letter also points to a Persian-period composition. In his discussion of the authenticity of this letter, Grabbe points out that a major tool of evaluation is the spelling of the second- and third-person pronominal suffixes (Grabbe 2006: 546-48; see comment on the authenticity of the letter to Artaxerxes in Ezra 4 above). These tend to be spelled defectively in Achaemenid-period texts but are spelled fully in Hellenistic documents. All the second- and third-person plural forms in the present letter are spelled defectively, consistent with an original Achaemenid composition. Whereas it would be common for a Hellenistic copyist or for the biblical author himself to update the spelling, it would be very unlikely for someone composing the letter *de novo* in the Hellenistic period to use archaic spelling. These forms provide crucial evidence for the authenticity of the letter. In spite of these indications of an original letter composed in the Achaemenid period, as is described in the notes, the salutation and the spelling of the 'we' form of the verbs have been 'modernized'.

Ezra 6.1-5

Darius Searches the Archives and the Temple Is Rebuilt

According to Tattenai's letter, the temple had been approved originally by Cyrus. Therefore, if the Judeans were telling the truth, there should be some record of it in the archives. Would Cyrus have left such a record? After waiting on pins and needles for Darius's response, it is finally returned.

The framing narrative continues in Aramaic to increase the distance between the narrator and the reader and so prolong the tension.

Translation

1. *Then Darius the king issued an order and they searched in the scroll house where the treasures are deposited in Babylon.* 2. *And in Aḥmeta, in the capital*[a] *of the province of Media, a scroll was found, and thus was written on it:*

Memorandum:[b]

3. *In the first year of King Cyrus, Cyrus the king issued an order:*

'[Regarding] the house of the god[c] *in Jerusalem, let the house be built—a place where they sacrifice sacrifices*[d] *and [where] its fire-offerings*[e] *are brought.*[f] *[Let] its height [be] 60 cubits; its width 60 cubits.* 4. *[Let it be composed of] three courses*[g] *of dressed stone*[h] *for one*[i] *course of wood.*[j] *Let the expenses be paid from the house of the king.*[k] 5. *Moreover, the vessels*[l] *of the temple of the god*[m] *of gold and of silver which Nebuchadnezzar took out from the temple which was in Jerusalem and brought to Babylon, let them go back; let each go to the temple which is in Jerusalem to its own place.*[n] *You shall deposit [them]*[o] *in the temple of the god.*

Textual Notes

a. **6.2** *In the capital.* In the documents at Elephantine, the parallel phrase is written ביב בירתא, 'in Yeb (= Elephantine) the capital', rather than as here, 'in Aḥmeta, in the capital'. Williamson (2004: 216) and Rudolph (1949: 54) suggest therefore that the *b*-

before *bîrtā'*, was added through dittography and should be dropped. It should probably read 'in Aḥmeta the capital' rather than 'in Aḥmeta, in the capital', as it is translated here.

b. *Memorandum.* This is spelled דִּכְרוֹנָה, *dikrônâ,* rather than זכרן *zkrn,* as we find at Elephantine. Not only is the word spelled fully in the biblical text, rather than defectively as at Elephantine, a daleth, ד, is substituted for the zayin, ז. Either the word was added or its spelling updated in the Hellenistic period. It is missing from 1 Esdras.

c. **6.3** *The god.* First Esdras naturally has 'the Lord'.

d. *Sacrifices.* This word is omitted in 1 Esdras. See following note.

e. *Its fire-offerings.* The consonantal text, אשוהי, *'eššôhî,* is most likely 'its fires', masculine plural of אשא, 'fire', with masculine singular suffix 'his'. The difficulty is that the Masoretes have vocalized it as if it were אֻשּׁוֹהִי, *'uššôhî,* 'its foundations'. The ambiguity is resolved by the next word. (See following textual note.) First Esdras reads 'where they sacrifice by means of eternal fire'. Greek Ezra reads, 'Also he set up its foundation, in height sixty cubits; its breadth sixty cubits', misconstruing אשוהי in the same way that the Masoretes did (unless the Masoretes were basing their vocalization on the Greek text).

f. *Are brought.* מְסוֹבְלִין. This word also poses difficulties. It has variously been considered a shaphel passive participle of *ybl,* 'to bring', or a poel passive participle of *sbl,* 'to bear', 'carry', or 'endure', and thus, by extension, 'to maintain', 'sustain'. Clines (1984: 91) and Williamson (1985: 68) translate the phrase as 'its foundations shall be retained', whereas Blenkinsopp (1988: 123) translates it 'where fire-offerings are brought'. Rather than seeing the verb from either the Aramaic *sbl* or *ybl*, as is usual, it should most likely be seen as the Aramaic passive participle of the Akkadian *zubbūlu,* 'to carry'. It should probably be vocalized *mesubblin*, rather than *mesoblin,* as the Masoretes do.

g. **6.4** *Courses.* נִדְבָּךְ, *nidbāk,* is from the Akkadian *nadabāku*, meaning a 'course' or 'layer' of bricks or stones.

h. *Dressed stone.* First Esdras reads 'polished stone', whereas Greek Ezra reads 'three strong courses of stone'. (See textual note at Ezra 5.8 above.)

i. *One course.* Read the Aramaic *ḥad,* 'one', rather than Aramaic *ḥadat,* 'new'. Clines (1984: 92) points out that new or unseasoned wood placed in the walls would be disastrous!

j. *Wood.* First Esdras reads 'new native wood'.

k. *House of the king.* First Esdras reads 'Cyrus the king'.

l. **6.5** *The vessels.* First Esdras reads 'the holy vessels'.

m. *The temple of the god.* First Esdras reads 'the temple of the Lord'.

n. *To its place.* First Esdras reads 'to the place where it had been'.

o. [*Them*]. The object is understood.

Notes

6.1 ***(Then) Darius the king issued an order.*** Although it is commonly thought that this verse and the following were composed by the biblical writer to connect Tattenai's letter to Darius's response (Gunneweg 1985: 105; Blenkinsopp 1988: 127), it is more likely that these verses (except for the word 'then') were part of the original official response and formed the introduction to the quotation of Cyrus's memorandum.

Scroll house where they deposit the treasures. See notes at 5.17 above for a discussion of the role of this type of building.

Babylon. As stated in the note on 5.17 above, these royal treasury houses were placed in every provincial capital throughout the empire. It was natural to assume that if Cyrus gave the order when he first became king of Babylon, then the order would have been stored at the royal treasury there.

6.2 ***In the capital.*** The term is *birtā'* in Aramaic and is well attested in Aramaic inscriptions and texts of the Persian Empire (Lemaire and Lozachmeur 1987, 1995). Although the term is usually translated 'fortress', the cities given this title have more than a simple military function. They also play an important administrative role over a country or province (Lemaire and Lozachmeur 1987, 1995; Briant 1978–79). It is the *birtā'* that houses not only a military garrison but also the hall of archives including surveys and censuses, courtrooms, a treasury building, storage centers for taxes paid in kind, often a mint, the place of residence of the governor or military head, as well as a temple for the local god(s). The *birtā'* was the provincial capital.

Aḥmata, in the capital of the province of Media. Hamadan is the modern name of this Iranian city located in the Zagros mountains between Tehran and Baghdad. Known by the Old Persian name Hagmatana ('gathering place') or by its more familiar Greek name, Ecbatana, it was the capital of the Median Empire until the fall of the Medes to Cyrus (550 BCE). Because of its location at the foot of Mt Orontes, it provided a cool summer retreat for the Persian kings. Xenophon states (*Cyrop.* 8.6.22) that Cyrus spent the winters in Babylon, the springs in Susa, and the summers in Ecbatana (Hamadan). According to Herodotus (1.98), Hamadan was surrounded by seven concentric walls, each one higher than the next. Within the innermost circle stood the royal palace and the treasuries. The location of the memorandum in the treasury house at Hamadan rather than Babylon suggests that Sheshbazzar was commissioned during the summer months of Cyrus's first year. It also suggests that the search was made in the treasury houses of all the cities wherever they thought Cyrus might have placed it. The implication is that they did due diligence in making the search.

In the Gadatas inscription (Fried 2004: 108-19, with references), Darius I reprimands Gadatas, most likely satrap of Lydia, because he was not conforming to the wishes of Darius's 'ancestors' (most likely Cyrus). If the reprimand is authentic, as I think it is, it demonstrates the intention of Darius to discover and to uphold the edicts of his predecessors.

Scroll. Grätz (2006: 412, citing Gunneweg 1985: 107) states that the biblical author makes a factual error ('sachlichen Fehler') when he refers to a scroll. They both claim that the Persians would have used a clay tablet and that referring to a scroll betrays a Hebrew/Aramaic custom rather than a Persian one. Because of the transient nature of both papyrus and leather, it cannot be known whether clay tablets were more prevalent among the Persians or not, and Grätz's and Gunneweg's certainty in this regard is surprising. Briant (2002: 423) laments, in fact, that the archives of clay tablets found at Persepolis yield only a tiny portion of what once must have been stored there. He supposes that a significant portion of the administrative records is missing because it was written on perishable materials. Missing, for example, are all documents recording the reception and disbursement of foodstuffs and clothing, which surely would have been included.

The tablets frequently mention, moreover, scribes writing on parchment and parchment documents. The correspondence between the satrap Pherendates and the priest of the temple of Khnum, for example (which dates to the time of Darius I), is on papyrus, and it is only because of the dry climate of Egypt that it was preserved (see Fried 2004: 80-86). Moreover, that correspondence refers to 'record *books*', that is, 'scrolls', not tablets. The use of the word 'scroll' cannot be assumed to be an 'error', nor to imply a non-Persian usage.

Memorandum. This is most likely to be understood as the official minutes of a meeting between Cyrus and Sheshbazzar, his governor. It is not a memorandum of an 'edict'; there was no edict. It was simply an order given to Sheshbazzar alone to take charge of rebuilding the temple of Yhwh in Jerusalem and to return the temple vessels to it. A similar memorandum of a meeting was found in the archive of Jedaniah, the high priest of the temple of Yhw at Yeb (= Elephantine; *TAD* A 4.9). That memorandum is as follows:

> Memorandum of what Bagavahya and Delaiah said to me [i.e. to Jedaniah]:
> Memorandum:
> You may say in Egypt before Arsames:
> 'Concerning the altar-house of the god of heaven that is in Yeb the capital:
> It was built from long ago, from before Cambyses, which that evil Vidranga tore down in the fourteenth year of Darius the king.
> [This is] in order to rebuild it on its site as it was formerly, so that meal and incense will be offered on that altar just as it was formerly done.'

This memorandum, found in Jedaniah's archive, is dated to some time after 407 BCE, during the reign of Darius II. Bagavahya was then the governor of Yehud, Delaiah the governor of Samaria, and Arsames the satrap of Egypt. There was no other notice in Jedaniah's archive, but since according to the archaeologists the temple was rebuilt in the last decade of Darius II (von Pilgrim 1999), Arsames must have acquiesced to it. His acquiescence would necessarily have been in writing, but it is not extant. All that exists at present is Jedaniah's personal memorandum of what Bagavahya and Delaiah told him to say before Arsames. It is written on papyrus.

6.3 ***Where its fire-offerings are brought.*** The torah speaks often of 'offerings by fire' (e.g. Lev. 2.3, 10; etc.). The torah also knows of an eternal fire on the altar (Lev. 6.6 [ET 6.13]). So the text here in Ezra may refer to those offerings. However, fire-offerings would have particularly resonated with the Persian Zoroastrians, for whom fire was one of the manifestations of the godhead. Even in pre-Zoroastrian times, Iranians would offer the fat of the entrails of the sacrificial animal to the sacred fire, and no animal could be slaughtered without this ritual element (Boyce 1996: 153). If the letter is authentic, then it would be natural for the Persian king to mention in it the offerings to a perpetual fire.

Among the Zoroastrians, the hearth fire was considered worthy of sacrifice and prayer, and it was not allowed to go out until the master of the household himself died (Boyce 1996: 154). When a family moved, the hearth fire was carried in a pot, remaining lit. The necessity that a fire be constant from dwelling to dwelling is also evoked in 2 Macc. 1.19-22 (as pointed out by Talshir 2001: 253 n. 2):

> When our ancestors were being led captive to Persia, the pious priests of that time took some of the fire of the altar and secretly hid it in the hollow of a dry cistern, where they took such precautions that the place was unknown to anyone. But after many years had passed, when it pleased God, Nehemiah, having been commissioned by the king of Persia, sent the descendants of the priests who had hidden the fire to get it. And when they reported to us that they had not found fire but only a thick liquid, he ordered them to dip it out and bring it. When the materials for the sacrifices were presented, Nehemiah ordered the priests to sprinkle the liquid on the wood and on the things laid upon it. When this had been done and some time had passed, and when the sun, which had been clouded over, shone out, a great fire blazed up, so that all marveled.

It is not clear why the reference is to Nehemiah in the 2 Maccabees passage. Goldstein (1983: 173-76) suggests that Zerubbabel had become assimilated to Nehemiah, and that the deeds of Zerubbabel are described. This miracle implies that to the author of 2 Maccabees, Yhwh had indeed entered the second temple.

Its height, 60 cubits; its width 60 cubits. At 18 inches to a cubit, this would be 90 feet high (over seven stories) and 90 feet wide. These measurements are preposterous as they stand; the text must have become garbled in transmission, yet, all the versions repeat this. Further, its length has dropped out. Williamson (1985: 68) emends to 60 cubits long (90 feet), 20 cubits wide (30 feet), and 30 cubits high (45 feet), following 1 Kgs 6.2, the dimensions of Solomon's temple. This is most likely what the text's author had in mind. These also approximate the dimensions of the temple at ʿAin Dara, in northern Syria, the closest parallel to Solomon's temple (Monson 2000: 20). ʿAin Dara's dimensions were 98 feet long and 65 feet wide, but its height cannot be determined from the ruins. These dimensions include storage and other chambers along its two sides and in back.

6.4 ***Three courses of dressed stone for one course of wood.*** According to Tattenai's report, the temple was being built according to Cyrus's specifications. The language in the memorandum is not the same as in Tattenai's letter, however; one is not simply a copy of the other, as they would have been had they both had the same author. They seem to be independent attestations.

It may be hard to imagine that Cyrus would give such explicit instructions for a temple in far-off Judah for a god he did not know (Isa. 45.4). However, such micro-management seems to be characteristic of the Persian Empire. This tendency is exhibited everywhere. Among the documents found in the archive of Arsames, for example, is a letter from the satrap (*TAD* A 6.2) in which he quotes a request from a boat holder for permission to make repairs on the boat. Arsames provides a complete listing of all the materials agreed to for repairing the boat (down to the 150 nails that were each three handbreaths long and the 275 nails that were each ten handbreaths long), and a statement that word shall be sent to the accountants of the treasury (*gnz'*), so that the materials will be given to the chief of the carpenters. The care with which Arsames the Egyptian satrap oversees the repair of a boat is certainly consistent with the care with which Cyrus oversees the repair of a Judean temple.

Let expenses be paid from the house of the king. For a discussion of the likelihood that the Persian king would pay for the temple, see the Introduction. Diodorus Siculus states (16.40.2) that the city of Thebes, in Greece, finding itself impoverished, 'Artaxerxes III, readily acceding to the request (of Thebes), made a gift to (that city) of 300 talents of silver'. One way to calculate the modern equivalent to a talent is by military pay. During the Peloponnesian war, a talent was the amount of silver needed to pay the crew of a trireme for one month. Hellenistic mercenaries were commonly paid one drachma for every day of service. A drachma was half a shekel. At 6,000 drachmas to a talent, and assuming a crew of roughly 200 rowers paid at the basic pay rate of a junior enlisted member of the U.S. armed forces (E-2), a talent would be worth nearly $300,000 in today's prices.

Moreover, the Persian kings were not the only kings to fund the Jerusalem temple. Josephus reports (*Ant.* 12.137-41) that King Antiochus III guaranteed 'an allowance of sacrificial animals, wine, oil, and frankincense to the value of twenty-thousand pieces [i.e. drachmas] of silver'. Josephus quotes Antiochus further that 'it is my will . . . that the work on the temple be completed, including the porticoes and any other part that it may be necessary to build. The timber, moreover, shall be brought . . . from Lebanon with the imposition of a toll-charge'. According to 2 Maccabees, Seleucus IV followed his father's custom, and King Seleucus of Asia defrayed from his own revenues all the expenses connected with the service of the sacrifices (2 Macc. 3.3).

Rather than finding proof of the custom of royal support for local temples in view of these gifts cited by Hellenistic authors, Grätz (2006: 410-12) finds in the reference proof of the nonauthenticity of Cyrus's memorandum and proof of its origin in the Hellenistic period. He assumes that the Hellenistic kings were the first kings to rule through gifts and not through harshness. In fact, however, gifts were a major mechanism by which the Persians ruled their realm (Briant 2002: 302-23; Kuhrt 2007: 633-63). (See the Introduction to Ezra 1–6 for Persian support of local temples.)

6.5 ***Let them go back.*** (For a discussion of the return of temple vessels see Introduction.) The return of the gods of conquered temples is routine when a new king wants to ingratiate himself with his new subjects. When the Ptolemies inherited Egypt from Alexander, who had conquered the Persians, they stressed in a series of edicts that the cult statues that Cambyses had removed would be returned. Devauchelle (1995) cites four inscriptions from the period of the Ptolemies that describe the return of cult statues from Syria back to Egypt. The earliest example is Ptolemy I's so-called 'Stele of the Satrap', dated to the seventh year of the reign of the minor, Alexander IV, son of Alexander the Great, that is, 312 BCE. Lines 3-4 state: 'He has brought back the statues of the gods found in Syria, as well as all the objects, all the works of the temples of Upper and Lower Egypt, and he has returned them to their place'.

The second example is the Stele of Pithom, which dates to the sixth year of the reign of Ptolemy II (279 BCE). Lines 10-11 state:

> The king went in the country of Syria. After he had reached Palestine, he found there the gods of Egypt in great number. He carried them back to Egypt. They went with the king of Upper and Lower Egypt, Master [of the Two Lands], Ptolemy, to *Khemty*. His Majesty sent them to Egypt. They were received by the guardians of Egypt in joy according to the order of these gods. . . . They came there to the place of His Majesty, before these gods. They found that it was the statue of the Nome of Harpon of the west. They passed there ten days with His Majesty. The gods of Egypt went to Egypt; the gods of Pithom-Tcheku remained there; it is their place for eternity.

A third, the Canopus Decree, is in both hieroglyphics and demotic. It is dated to the ninth year of Ptolemy III (238 BCE). Line 6 says: 'The divine images that the vile Persians had carried out of Egypt, after His Majesty had marched against the Asiatic countries, he saved them, he brought them to Egypt and put them in their place in the temples where they had been placed before'. Finally, the Decree of Raphia, in demotic, dated to the sixth year of Ptolemy IV (217 BCE), says, in lines 21-23:

> He gave every care to the images carried out of Egypt toward the lands of Syria and Phoenicia at the time when the Persians were damaging the temples of Egypt. He ordered them to be searched for with care. Those which were found were more than those which his father had [already] carried back to Egypt, he had them carried back to Egypt, celebrating the feast, offering sacrifices before them. He had them conducted to the temple from which they had been carried before.

It is clear that this theme had become a literary topos among the Ptolemies. Even so, it is certainly possible that Cambyses had confiscated cult images when he destroyed the Egyptian temples and taken them with him from Egypt. The capture of foreign gods typically accompanied conquest. In order to ingratiate themselves with their new subjects, the Ptolemies made a show of returning them. This pattern can also be seen in the Cyrus Cylinder. It too stresses Cyrus's return of the Babylonian gods to their rightful places. The fact that the second temple in Jerusalem was actually rebuilt suggests that Cyrus did return its cult vessels. (See Introduction.)

You shall deposit [them]. The switch to second-person singular suggests that the archival record is a copy of a personal note to Sheshbazzar. If the original building permit had been given to Sheshbazzar it would explain why the Judeans did not have their own copy of it. Although not explicitly stated, Sheshbazzar would not have traveled the distance from Ecbatana to Jerusalem by himself, but would have been accompanied by Judeans and their families, especially priestly families to care for the vessels and to supervise the temple-building project.

Comment: Is Cyrus's Memorandum (Ezra 6.2-5) Authentic?

This memorandum is the basis on which the biblical writer wrote the description of the return under Sheshbazzar in Ezra 1. What we have here is not an empire-wide decree, but an order from Cyrus, no doubt to Sheshbazzar, to rebuild the temple of the god in Jerusalem and to take the temple vessels back and deposit them in that temple.

Grabbe (2006) has examined the Aramaic letters in Ezra most thoroughly and most recently, so it is worthwhile to continue in dialogue with him on the authenticity of these letters. Unfortunately, there are no plural suffixes in Cyrus's memorandum by which to date the composition, nor is there an address to compare against known address formulae. The text moves directly to the memorandum, and so must be evaluated by its contents, not its style. In agreement with Grabbe, it seems unlikely (if not impossible) for the temple to be built without a Persian official giving his permission, so some such statement along the lines of what we have is necessary. Grabbe argues further, however, that orders for rebuilding 'would have come from the local governor or perhaps the satrap, but would hardly be a matter with which the Persian king would concern himself'. This statement underestimates the degree to which the Persian Empire was micromanaged by those at the top. (See Fried 2004, and note at 6.4 above.) There is no evidence of autonomy by any Persian official anywhere in the Persian Empire; each deferred to those above him. The Egyptian satrap Pherendates, for example, who served under Darius I, is recorded as supervising the choice of the high priest of the temple of Khnum in Elephantine, a temple far from the seats of power in Egypt. Not only were the priests of Khnum prevented from appointing whomever they wished as high priest, but Pherendates states that his choice of high priest is 'in accordance with that which Darius [I] has ordered' (see Fried 2004: 83). The Persian Empire is best understood as a huge bureaucracy, with no local autonomy anywhere. Thus, it is not surprising at all that the king would have to approve the rebuilding of a temple in Judah.

Grabbe also argues that even if the king approved it, the probability is small that the Persian government would pay for the building. Yet, we know that Persian kings did pay occasionally to support local temples. (See Introduction.) Moreover, the Persepolis tablets record the delivery of various goods for use in the service of a number of gods, including Babylonian, Elamite, and Persian gods, all supported equally from the imperial treasuries (Hallock 1969; Williamson 2004: 221; Koch 1988).

Grabbe also finds it impossible that the temple vessels would still be preserved a century and a half after they were looted, but they certainly would have been preserved if they had been kept as a trophy in the Esagila, the temple of Marduk in Babylon (see Introduction).

Tellingly, the language of Cyrus's memorandum that is quoted in Darius's letter is not the same as the language used in Tattenai's letter to Darius. One is not simply a copy of the other as would have been the case if they had the same author. They seem to be independent attestations, and thus suggestive of the authenticity of each. In view of all this, and in view of the fact that we have seen the memorandum genre at Elephantine, it seems plausible that a genuine memorandum by Cyrus is being quoted here, albeit with problems in transmission regarding the dimensions of the temple.

Ezra 6.6-12

Darius Confirms Cyrus's Memorandum and Orders Work on the House of the God in Jerusalem to Continue

With great relief we now read Darius's positive response to the request to rebuild the temple in Jerusalem.

Translation

6. *Now [say to] Tattenai, governor of Beyond-the-River, Shethar-Boznai, and their*[a] *colleagues, the investigators,*[b] *who are in Beyond-the-River: Be satisfied.*[c] 7. *Leave the work on this house of god alone. Let the governor of the Judeans*[d] *and the elders of the Judeans build this house of god*[e] *on its site.*

8. *Now from me an order is issued*[f] *concerning what you will do together with*[g] *these elders*[h] *of the Judeans in order to build this temple for the god.*[i] *From the royal accounts*[j] *of the tribute*[k] *of Beyond-the-River*[l] *let the expenses*[m] *be paid quickly*[n] *to these men*[o] *in order not to stop [the work].*[p] 9. *And whatever is needed—young bulls, rams, lambs—for burnt offerings for the god of heaven,*[q] *and wheat, salt, wine, or oil,*[r] *as the priests who are in Jerusalem say,*[s] *let it be given to them day by day,*[t] *without fail,*[u] 10. *so that sweet-smelling sacrifices*[v] *may be offered to the god of heaven*[w] *and so that they may pray for the king and his children.*[x] 11. *I am issuing an order*[y] *that any person who alters this decree*[z] *let a beam be pulled out of his house*[aa] *and let him be affixed and beaten*[bb] *upon it and his house made a heap of ruins.*[cc] *on account of this.* 12. *May the god*[dd] *who causes his name to dwell there*[ee] *overthrow any king or people who dares*[ff] *to cause a change*[gg] *to harm this temple of the god*[hh] *which is in Jerusalem. I, Darius, have issued a decree. Let it be carried out quickly.*[ii]

Textual Notes

a. **6.6** *Their,* not 'your'. This is spelled *plene*, that is, הום-, a spelling characteristic of the Hellenistic period, indicating editing in the Hellenistic period. The use of 'their' rather than 'your' has confused commentators, but see Note. First Esdras reads the whole in the third person, 'So Darius commanded Sisinnes . . . and Sathrabuzanes . . . and *their* associates . . .'. Greek Ezra reads 'you', plural.

b. *Investigators.* See textual note at 5.6.

c. *Be satisfied.* Literally, 'You keep far from there'. It is an Aramaic idiom common in the Elephantine papyri, meaning 'Be satisfied with the outcome [of a court decision]', 'have no complaints against' someone. It is not to be taken literally, but it is clear that the versions did not understand the idiom and translated it literally as 'be far from there'. First Esdras reads third person here, 'So he commanded Sisinnes'; it also adds Zerubbabel's name to make Zerubbabel present.

d. **6.7** *Governor of the Judeans.* First Esdras adds 'Zerubbabel, the servant of the Lord'. Greek Ezra reads the 'leaders' of the Judeans.

e. *Temple of the god.* First Esdras reads 'temple of the Lord' as is typical of it.

f. **6.8** *From me an order is issued.* This is normal Aramaic. First Esdras reads 'I command' and inserts the phrase 'that building be done completely'.

g. *Together with.* Literally, 'with'. This is expressed in all the versions, rather than 'for', as in most English translations. First Esdras inserts ἀτενίσαι, literally, 'look intently', which probably means 'take care', that is, 'take care to help build the temple of the god' (Talshir 2001: 260).

h. *These elders.* As is usual, 1 Esdras reads 'those who returned from captivity'. (See note at 5.5.)

i. *To build a temple for this god.* First Esdras reads instead 'until the temple of the Lord is finished'. As Talshir (2001: 360) points out, the translator is intent that the work be pursued until the end.

j. *Accounts.* נִכְסַי, *niksê,* from the Akkadian *nikkasu,* 'accounts', 'account record' (*CAD* N II.224). First Esdras reads 'strict accounting', but the Greek term also carries the meaning of the 'assessed sum', that is, the result of the accounting (L&S). The Greek term is used this way also in 2 Macc. 9.16. Greek Ezra reads 'property'.

k. *Tribute.* See note at 4.13 above.

l. *Beyond-the-River.* First Esdras reads 'Greater Syria and Phoenicia', as is usual in this translation.

m. *Expenses.* נִפְקְתָא. *Nipk*ᵉ*tā'.* In the biblical text, this word appears only here and in 6.4, above, but it appears often at Elephantine. It is not expressed in 1 Esdras. The implication of 1 Esdras is that not all the expenses will be paid, but a fixed assessed sum is to be transferred from the tribute of Greater Syria and Phoenicia.

n. *Quickly.* אספרנא. *'osparnā'.* See textual note at 5.8. First Esdras translates it here as 'careful', modifying 'accounting'. Greek Ezra translates it similarly, but there it modifies 'given', that is, 'carefully given to those men'.

o. *To these men.* First Esdras adds 'that is, to Zerubbabel the governor'.

p. *In order not to stop* [*the work*]. The object is understood. First Esdras does not translate this phrase but inserts at the beginning of the verse 'until the work on the temple of the Lord is finished'.

q. **6.9** *God of heaven.* First Esdras reads 'for the Lord'.

r. *Wheat, salt, wine, or oil.* First Esdras inserts 'regularly every year'.

s. *Say.* First Esdras reads 'dictate', which may be too strong for the meaning.

t. *Given to them day by day.* First Esdras reads 'to consume every day'.

u. *Without fail.* First Esdras reads 'without dispute', 'without quibbling'.

v. **6.10** *Sweet-smelling sacrifices.* First Esdras reads 'libations', that is, 'drink offerings'.

w. *To the god of heaven.* First Esdras reads 'to the most high god', that is, to El Elyon, and adds 'for the sake of the king and his children', so that both the sacrifices and the prayers are for the sake of the king and his children.

x. *Children.* Or perhaps just 'sons'. Aramaic, like Hebrew, does not distinguish between these. First Esdras reads 'that they may pray for their lives'.

y. **6.11** *I am issuing an order.* Literally, 'From me is issued an order'. First Esdras reads simply 'I ordered', although some manuscripts have 'he ordered', in the third person.

z. *Alters this decree.* First Esdras reads 'transgresses what was said above and also written so that it becomes null'. This clarifies the meaning of the Aramaic. Behind the translation stands the assumption that the actual order is what is stated verbally. The written document is simply proof of what was stated.

aa. *His house.* First Esdras clarifies with 'his own house'.

bb. *Affixed and beaten.* The actual phrase is 'impaled and beaten', which does not make sense since there is no point in beating someone already impaled. It may refer to crucifixion. The word 'beaten' is missing from the versions, so perhaps it ought not influence the translation. Greek Ezra reads, 'He shall be lifted up and set up on it', which implies 'impaled'. First Esdras has 'hung' on it, implying crucifixion.

cc. *Heap of ruins.* The exact meaning of this word נְוָלוּ, n^{e}*wālû*, is not known. Some translate 'dunghill'. It may be related to the Akkadian *nâlu,* 'to lay flat', as in 'he laid the army of GN flat like a reed' (*CAD* N 1. 205). See also, Dan. 2.5; 3.29. Both 1 Esdras and Greek Ezra translate instead 'his property to become the king's'.

dd. **6.12** *May the god.* First Esdras reads 'May the Lord'.

ee. *Who causes his name to dwell there.* First Esdras reads 'whose name is called there'. Greek Ezra reads, 'May the god whose name dwells there'.

ff. *Dares.* Literally, 'sends forth his hand' (translation suggested by Jerusalmi 1982: 35).

gg. *To cause a change.* Probably with the connotation 'to violate an order'. See Dan. 6.9, 12; 7.25.

hh. *Overthrow* (ימגר) . . . *to harm* (לחבלה) *the temple of this god.* First Esdras reads 'destroy' for 'overthrow'.

ii. *Quickly. 'osparnā'.* See textual note at 5.8.

Notes

6.6 ***Now.*** This transition is specific to Achaemenid epistolary style and appears nowhere in Hellenistic-era letters, thus supporting the authenticity of the letter. This is common in the letters from the Bactrian satrap Akhvamazda to his governor Bagavant. They all begin, 'From Akhvamazda to Bagavant, and now . . .'. There is no salutation, no greeting formula. Lack of salutation and a note beginning with 'now, do this!' also appear in private letters, especially informal ones written on ostraca (Schwiderski 2000: 361). We read, for example (*TAD* D 7.9), 'Now, regarding the gift that Uriah gave me for the libation, give it to Gemariah son of Ahio . . .'.

Now (say to) Tattenai. Darius is dictating his response to the scribe, but also to the messenger who will carry the message to Tattenai in Jerusalem.

The written text is most often simply a mnemonic to help the messenger remember the text. The messenger then read the text to the recipient.

Be satisfied. Literally, 'you keep far from there'. This common expression is prevalent among the Aramaic documents at Elephantine (e.g. *TAD* B 2.9). It is used to indicate that someone is satisfied with the outcome of a suit or other dispute and withdraws from all further claims. For example:

> . . . our hearts are satisfied herein from this d[a]y forever. I, Menahem and Ananiah, we are far from you from this day forever. We shall not be able—we or our sons or our daughters or our brothers or a person who is near us or a member of our town—they shall not be able to bring suit or process against you (*TAD* B 2.9:9-11).

This passage defines what it means to be far from someone in Aramaic legal texts; it does not literally mean to keep physically distant from someone. Darius is simply telling Tattenai and his colleagues to refrain from instituting a suit against them (Botta 2009: 96-136).

6.7 *Governor of the Judeans.* Darius does not name him. He may not have remembered his name since it is not reported in Tattenai's letter. Commentators (Clines 1984: 93; Blenkinsopp 1988: 127) suggest that the phrase is a gloss since it is not well integrated into the sentence, and vv. 8 and 14 below refer only to the elders. If Darius did not remember whom he appointed governor in the obscure province at the edge of the empire he would not have remembered that he was a Judean, and could not suppose that he would be allowed to participate in building a temple to the Judean god.

Elders. This is not the term of our author, who prefers 'heads of fathers' [houses]'. The word occurs in Ezra–Nehemiah only in the Aramaic documents and in Ezra 10.8, 14. In the latter passage the elders are seen acting in conjunction with officials and magistrates, Persian appointees. They were from the heads of prominent families and would have had influence over the Judeans (Dandamayev 1995: 28-29). They were now being commissioned to take charge, along with the Persian governor, of the work on the temple.

6.8 *From me an order is issued.* The speaker is Darius.

Let the expenses be paid from the royal accounts. These are the expenses for constructing the temple. Darius here validates and confirms Cyrus's command (6.4). There is external evidence to the effect that Darius honored the decrees of his predecessor. The Gadatas inscription records Darius's letter to Gadatas, probably a keeper of royal gardens in Lydia (I have argued for the authenticity of the inscription at some length in Fried 2004: 108-19).

In the letter (ll. 19-29) Darius chastises Gadatas for not honoring previous agreements:

> I will give to you, if you do not change,
> proof of my offended anger.
> Indeed, you have exacted tribute from

> the gardener-priests of Apollo,
> and you even assigned [them] profane land to dig,
> not recognizing my
> ancestors' purpose on behalf of the god
> who spoke to the Persians
> only truth. . . .

According to this inscription, Darius was angry at Gadatas for forcing the priests of Apollo to pay tribute and to engage in corvée labor (i.e. to work on profane land, land not dedicated to the god Apollo) evidently in violation of an agreement between the Apollo priests and Darius's ancestor. Who is Darius's ancestor? Neither Darius's Behistun inscription nor the writings of the Greek historians record a relationship between the Apollo priests in Lydia and any of Darius's ancestors. Herodotus (1.46-55) discusses Cyrus's dealings with the Apollo priests of Lydia, however, so that the ancestor that Darius speaks of must have been Cyrus, who preceded him as king of the Persian Empire. Cyrus must have made an agreement with the priests of Apollo that neither tribute nor corvée labor would be exacted from them, and Gadatas had evidently violated it, to Darius's embarrassment.

The letter from Darius quoted in the Gadatas inscription reveals that Darius honored an agreement between Cyrus and the priests of Apollo, a foreign god. Similarly, the letter from Darius quoted in Ezra shows Darius honoring an agreement between Cyrus and the priests of Yhwh to the effect that expenses for building the temple be paid from royal revenues. Darius limits his losses by requiring that expenses be paid out of the income to the satrap of Beyond-the-River, that is, the income of Tattenai himself.

The restoration of sanctuaries that one's predecessor destroyed is an important commitment of the usurper to show he is accepted by the gods (see Introduction, and Fried 2002b). The gods' subsequent return to their sanctuaries is interpreted as revealing their satisfaction with the new ruler. Darius's Behistun inscription reads, for example:

> Thus says Darius the King: . . . I made the sanctuaries which Gaumata the Magian destroyed as before. . . . I brought back what had been taken away (DB 1.62-70).

Darius emphasizes here that he restored the temples that Gaumata had destroyed when he rebelled against Darius.

The Egyptian priest Udjaḫorresnet also reports that both Cambyses and Darius funded the restoration of the temple of Neith in Sais, Egypt, 'as it was before'. About Cambyses, Udjaḫorresnet states:

> I made a petition to the majesty of the King of Upper and Lower Egypt, Cambyses, about all the foreigners who were occupying the temple of Neith, in order to have them expelled from it, so as to let the temple of Neith be in all its splendor as it had been before. His majesty commanded

> to expel all the foreigners who occupied the temple of Neith to demolish all their houses and all their unclean things that were in this temple [compound].
>
> When they had carried [all their] personal [belongings] outside the wall of the temple [compound], his majesty commanded to cleanse the temple of Neith and to return all its personnel to it, the - - - and the hour-priests of the temple. His majesty commanded to give divine offerings to Neith-the-Great, the mother of god, and to the great gods of Sais, as it had been before.
>
> . . .
>
> [His majesty] established the presentation of libations to the Lord of Eternity in the temple of Neith as every pharaoh had done before (ll. 18-22, 28, Lichtheim 1980: 38-39).

According to Udjaḫorresnet, Cambyses (who had defiled the temple when his soldiers occupied it) ordered the soldiers out and paid for its cleansing and for the restoration of the sacrifices. (Also see Introduction for additional evidence of Persian support for local temples.) There is no need to doubt that Achaemenid rulers sometimes rebuilt destroyed temples, and that this would have included the temple to Yhwh in Jerusalem.

In order not to stop [the work?]. It may have been this phrase in Darius's letter that led the biblical author to assume that Darius was reacting to a threat that work on the temple was to be stopped. This may have led him to create the incident in Ezra 4.1-5 and to use the letter to Artaxerxes as proof of the malevolent intensions of the 'enemies' of the Judeans.

6.9 ***Whatever is needed.*** This bit of exaggeration may have been added by the biblical writer, writing in the Hellenistic period, to argue before the Ptolemaic or Seleucid king that ample support for the temples had precedence among the Persians.

God of heaven. For this title, see the note at Ezra 1.2.

As the priests who are in Jerusalem say. The use of the Hebrew word *kōhēn* for priests כָּהֲנַיָּא (though Aramaicized) betrays the biblical writer. The normal Aramaic word for priest is *kamrā'*, a term appearing throughout the Aramaic documents from Elephantine. This whole verse was updated by the biblical writer in the Hellenistic period.

Let it be given to them. The fact that the word for 'to them', לְהֹם, is spelled defectively suggests that a basis for this verse is original to the letter but has been expanded upon.

6.10. ***Sweet-smelling sacrifices*** **(*nyḥwḥyn*).** Blenkinsopp (1988: 127) suggests this phrase is 'of Judean origin' since a Persian would not know it. Yet Persian kings were intimately involved in the affairs of the various peoples of their empire. This is particularly revealed in the so-called Passover letter (*TAD* 4.1) found in the archive of Jedaniah, high priest of the temple of Yhw at Elephantine: The letter reads:

[To my brothers Je]daniah and his colleagues the Judean ga[rrison,] (from) your brother Ḥanan[i]ah.

May God/the gods [seek after] the welfare of my brothers [at all times.]

And now, this year, year 5 of King Darius (II), it has been sent from the king to Arsa[mes . . .]:

. . . Now, you thus count four[teen days in Nisan and on the 14th at twilight ob]serve [the Passover] and from the 15th day until the 21st day of [Nisan observe the Festival of Unleavened Bread. Seven days eat unleavened bread.

Now,] be pure and take heed. [Do] n[ot do] work [on the 15th day and on the 21st day of Nisan.] Do not drink [any fermented drink. And do] not [eat] anything of leaven [nor let it be seen in your houses from the 14th day of Nisan at] sunset until the 21st day of Nisa[n at sunset. And b]ring into your chambers [any leaven which you have in your houses] and seal (it) up during [these] days. [. . .]

[To] my brothers Jedaniah and his colleagues the Judean garrison, your brother Ḥananiah s[on of PN].

The letter is quite fragmentary; the left half of the scroll is missing. It seems clear though that a letter has been sent from Darius II to Arsames, his satrap in Egypt, to permit, nay command, the Judeans in Elephantine to obey the Passover traditions and to abstain from work on the first and seventh day of the holiday.

One of the Persepolis Fortification Tablets (PF 348), moreover, records a donation of 3 *marriš* of wine for the divine *tamšiyam* ceremony of the Elamite earth god, Khumban. The meaning of *tamšiyam* is not clear, but it is considered analogous to *nyḥwḥyn*, with both meaning 'providing pleasure', that is, 'a satisfaction offering' (Williamson 2004: 223). All these texts show royal involvement in the minutia of the empire.

God of heaven. See note at 1.2.

The king and his children. According to this passage, Darius guarantees sums for a daily offering (out of the revenues of the half-satrapy Beyond-the-River) so that prayers may be said daily on behalf of himself and his family. This is not to be construed as funding the twice daily regular offering or the special Sabbath or holiday offerings. Rather, this is to fund an additional daily offering, whatever the priests direct, that prayers may be said on behalf of the king and his family. Indeed, prayers on his behalf and paid for by him were not unique to Darius. We read that the first Judean war against Rome began when Eleazar, son of Ananias the high priest and captain of the temple in Jerusalem, persuaded those priests who officiated in the temple services to accept no gift or sacrifice paid for by a foreigner. Josephus reports (*War* 2.409): 'This action laid the foundation of the war with the Romans; for the sacrifices offered on behalf of that nation [i.e. Rome] and the emperor were in consequence rejected'. Those sacrifices, offered twice daily and paid for by the emperor, were in addition to the regular sacrifices.

Grätz (2006: 410-11) argues, however, that it was only in the Hellenistic period that the king gave gifts to the temple in response to prayers said on their behalf. It was only then that the kings attempted to rule through gifts rather than through harsh measures. It is true that, for the most part, the funds that the indigenous kings had donated to their local temples now, under the Persians, went the other way, that is, from the temples to the Persian kings (Fried 2004). Still, prayers would be offered on behalf of the king or officials in response for favors. The Judeans of Elephantine sent a letter to Bagavahya requesting that he send a letter to Arsames, the Persian satrap of Egypt, requesting both permission and funds to rebuild their temple after it had been destroyed (*TAD* A 4.9); in return, the Judeans promised to offer prayers on his behalf:

> We shall offer the meal-offering, the incense and the holocaust on the altar of Yhw the god in your name and we shall pray for you at all times—we and our wives and our children and the Judeans, all of them who are here.

The temple in Jerusalem was not the only one that Darius supported with gifts and funds. The inscription of Udjaḫorresnet (Lichtheim 1980: 37; lines 1-2) indicates that Darius also contributed to the temple of Osiris in Sais:

> An offering that the King (Darius) gives to Osiris who presides over the Sanctuary: A thousand of bread, beer, oxen and fowl, clothing, myrrh, and unguent, and every good thing, for the *ka* of the one honored by all the gods, the chief physician, Udjaḫorresnet.

It can be assumed that the priests of the temple of Osiris in Sais offered in exchange prayers for Darius's continued good health.

We read moreover in the Cyrus Cylinder: 'May all the gods whom I have resettled in their sacred cities daily ask Bel and Nebo for a long life for me'.

6.11 ***Any person who alters this decree.*** Darius ends his letter to Tattenai with a curse upon anyone who alters the decree or who sends his hand against the 'house of this god'. Grabbe (2006: 549) objects that it is not likely that the Persian king would imagine that anyone would disobey his order and that he would not be so solicitous of the Judeans to set such a fierce threat to possible opposition. To Grabbe, this passage simply records what the Judeans would have wanted the king to say. In fact, such curses are a common component of ancient Near Eastern temple-building inscriptions (see Introduction; Ellis 1968; Hurowitz 1992).We read, for example, on the inscription of Yahdun-Lim, king of Mari (1810–1793 BCE), at the site of his new temple to Shamash:

> As for the one who destroys this temple . . . may the god Enlil . . . make his kingship smaller than that of any king. May the god Sin . . . inflict on

> him a great curse. May the god Nergal . . . smash his weapon. . . . May the god Ea . . . assign him an evil destiny, and may the goddess bride Aia . . . put in a bad word about him before Shamash forever. May the god Bunene . . . cut his throat, may he take away his progeny and may his offspring and descendants not walk before the god Shamash.

Let him be affixed and beaten upon it. To attack a temple set up by Cyrus and Darius (or really any temple in the Persian Empire) would be an act of rebellion against the king. What Darius is guaranteeing to do to one who destroys this temple is only what he did to every rebel, as spelled out in the Behistun inscription:

> Says Darius the King: Thereafter this Phraortes with a few horsemen fled. . . . I sent an army in pursuit; Phraortes, seized, was led to me. I cut off his nose and ears and tongue and put out one eye; he was kept bound at my palace entrance, all the people saw him. Afterward I impaled him at Ecbatana; the men who were his foremost followers, those at Ecbatana I flayed and hung out their hides stuffed with straw (DB II.70-8).

His house made a heap of ruins. The Hittites appears to have had a similar law (HL #173a).

> If anyone rejects a judgment of the king, his house will become a heap of ruins.
>
> If anyone rejects the judgment of the king's representative, his head will be cut off.

Since a king has higher authority than any of his representatives, perhaps 'house' here should be interpreted as 'household', and that a punishment may be in view like that dealt out to Achan in Josh. 7.16-20 in which all the members of the family were killed and their houses torn down (Gurney 1990: 76). Alternatively, it may be that the two statements are really one, that the king and his representative stand for one person, and that he who rejects the judgment of either has both his house (not household) reduced to ruins and his head cut off. This would mimic exactly what Darius threatens, both death to the individual (not his family) and the destruction of his house.

6.12 ***May the god who causes his name to dwell there.*** Darius's letter seems to have been emended a bit to conform to Deuteronomic theology. Presumably Darius simply said, 'May the god who dwells there'. It is expected that the god who lives there will defend his house from kings or people who attack it, and such imprecations were commonly invoked whenever temples were built. One such curse is found at the end of a trilingual stele found at Xanthus, Lycia (dated 340/339 BCE). It commemorates the dedication of a temple to the Carian god Kandawats built on the grounds of a temple dedicated to the Lycian twins Apollo and Artemis, and to their mother Leto.

> If a man ever removes [anything from the property of] Kandawats, the god, or from his priest, then let him be removed from Kandawats, the god, and from his companion, and from the gods Leto, Artemis, Hšatrapati (= Apollo), and the others. [Regarding] anyone who removes [anything], these gods will requite it from him (ll. 20-27, Aramaic version).
>
> If anyone alters [anything], he will have sinned against Leto and against her kinsmen and against the Nymphs.
> Pixadarus shall be in charge (ll. 30-35, Greek version).

Here again, the gods are expected to defend any temple built on their property, even a foreign one. Pixadarus, the Persian satrap of Caria, who set up a temple to the Carian god Kandawats on the land of a Lycian temple to Leto, did not hesitate to ask the Lycian gods to protect even this temple of an interloper. (For a discussion of the Xanthus inscription, see Fried 2004: 140-54, and references cited there.) This is normal language for temple building inscriptions.

Richter (2002) has recently suggested that the Deuteronomic formula, usually translated 'to cause his name to dwell there', is really a mistranslation of a common Mesopotamian saying 'to place, or inscribe, his name there'. The god is simply 'taking ownership' of the property and writing his name on it; it has nothing to do with the metaphorical 'indwelling' of the name. The difficulty with applying the Mesopotamian understanding of the phrase to this letter is that the Mesopotamian parallels she adduces are all on memorial steles, votive offerings, etc. They are not on temples. Richter counters that the temple itself is the memorial for Yhwh's name, arguing that the Deuteronomic expression 'to build a house for Yhwh's name' (1 Kgs 5.17, 19; 8.17-20, 44, 48) does not mean a place for the name to dwell but a place that will enhance the god's reputation. Van Seters (2003) agrees that we should take seriously the Mesopotamian meaning of the phrase 'to place one's name there' and assume it means the place where the god has caused his name to be written. That place, to Van Seters, is the torah, and the temple is then the house of the torah, the document on which Yhwh's name is written. This is an interesting idea, but, in any case, the phrase cannot be authentic to Darius. It is more likely that the letter was simply emended.

Overthrow* (ימגר)*... to harm* (לחבלה) *the temple of this god. These same two Aramaic words are used in reference to the temple at Elephantine (*TAD* A 4.7:13-14), increasing the likelihood of the letter's authenticity.

> When Cambyses [came] to Egypt, he found this temple [of Yhw at Elephantine] built, and the temples of the gods of Egypt—all—they overthrew (מגרו), but nothing in this temple was harmed (חבל).

Let it be carried out quickly. This Persian word, *'usfarna,* occurs frequently in the correspondence of Arsames, satrap of Egypt during the reign of Darius II. It is not known later, and so is consistent with the authenticity of Darius's response.

With this phrase, the letter from Darius ends.

Comment: Is Darius's Reply to Tattenai (Ezra 6.6-12) Authentic?

Schwiderski (2000: 361) concludes that the authenticity of the opening (6.6) of Darius's response to Tattenai is 'certainly not in question', although it mimics direct speech rather than a formal letter. In his thorough discussion of the Aramaic letters in Ezra, however, Grabbe finds a number of points in Darius's response to Tattenai that 'arouse suspicion' (Grabbe 2006). As pointed out in the note to 6.6, the letter begins with the marker 'now', but without an address. Such a form occurs in ostraca, not in official letters. It seems likely that the address or prescript had been included in the beginning of the letter, prior to the quotation of the Cyrus memorandum, but that it was omitted by the biblical writer when he inserted the letter into his narrative. There is no greeting, but letters from Akhvamazda, satrap of Bactria, to Bagavant, his governor (*ADAB* A1-6) all begin, 'From Akhvamazda to Bagawant: And now', with no greeting or salutation.

Regarding formal characteristics, Grabbe notes that the word in the first verse of Darius's response, 'their colleagues', וכנותהון, is spelled *plene*, indicating that this part of the letter at least was touched-up in the Hellenistic period. Grabbe also points out that the early form is attested in 6.9, להם, which supports the authenticity of that portion of the letter.

Grabbe objects to the order to Tattenai to 'keep away from' the Judeans and Jerusalem. He considers it too harsh (so also Blenkinsopp 1988: 127). In fact, this is a standard expression in the Aramaic legal contracts from Elephantine (e.g. *TAD* B 5.2:8; 2.10:4). It simply means that the individual shall be satisfied with the outcome of the decision and will not sue or get an injunction against the other. Its use is consistent with an authentic letter of Darius (see note at 6.6).

Grabbe also sees a problem in the term 'elders' in 6.7-8. He quotes Japhet (1982, 1983) who argues that the author of Ezra–Nehemiah is 'democratic' and therefore would not mention a governor, but would only mention 'elders'. He concludes therefore that the reference to 'governor' in 6.7 argues for the authenticity of the letter, but that the reference to 'elders' in 6.7 and 8 argues against it. In fact, the term 'elders' is not the language of the biblical writer, who routinely uses the phrase 'heads of fathers' [houses]' to indicate the leaders of Judah (e.g. 1.5; 2.68; 3.12; 4.2). The term 'elders' appears originally in Tattenai's letter to Darius (5.9). Darius then uses the term in his response (see note above at 6.6) but adds the phrase 'the governor of the Judeans'. In any case, since the use of the term 'elders' is not typical of the biblical writer, it speaks in favor of the authenticity of the letter, not against it.

Grabbe takes further issue with the fact that the letter seems to suggest that Darius is willing not only to pay for building the temple (6.8) but that he also seems to be giving open-ended permission for temple personnel to receive from him whatever they want, just by asking (6.9). This verse has clearly been embellished by the biblical writer. The original letter most likely limited the expenditures and restricted them to funds that will come out of Tattenai's receipts (6.8). It is Tattenai's income that is reduced, not that of the king. As for the daily sacrifice on behalf of the king (6.9), it may not originally have implied additional animals, but rather simply that prayers should be said on behalf of the king and his family during the regular sacrifice.

Grabbe does not accept, moreover, the authenticity of Darius's curse at the end of his letter. In fact, such a curse for the protection of a temple is part of the genre by which temple-building stories are understood (see the Introduction as well as the note above at 6.12). The curse applies not only to kings living at the time of Darius but to all future kings, and was a necessary component of temple-building inscriptions.

One may conclude, therefore, that the letter from Darius is at base genuine, but v. 9 especially has been thoroughly embellished by the biblical writer in the Hellenistic period.

Ezra 6.13-22

The Temple Is Completed and Dedicated with Joy; Passover Is Celebrated at the New Temple

We come now to the final stages of the second temple's building story, we ought to read now the last five components of the typical ancient Near East building inscription. These should include (1) a description of the completed temple and its furnishings; (2) a statement that the king has built the temple as the god commanded; (3) a description of the ceremony dedicating the finished building; (4) a statement that the god has been installed in his temple and has taken up residence in it; and (5) the appointment of temple personnel. We find all these components here except for two. Surprisingly, we have no description of the completed temple or its furnishings and no statement that the god has entered his temple and taken up residence.

Translation

13. *Then Tattenai,*[a] *governor*[b] *of Beyond-the-River,*[c] *Shethar-Bozenai, and their colleagues*[d] *according to that which Darius the king sent, thus they quickly did.*[e] 14. *The elders of the Judeans*[f] *built and prospered by the prophesying of Haggai the prophet and Zechariah son of Iddo.*[g]

They completed[h] *building it by the decree of the god of Israel*[i] *and by the decree*[j] *of Cyrus, Darius, and Artaxerxes king*[k] *of Persia.* 15. *This temple*[l] *was completed on the [twenty]-third day of the month of Adar which was in the sixth year of the reign of Darius the king.*

16. *Then the people of Israel—the priests, the Levites, and the rest of the people of the exile*[m]*—celebrated the dedication of this*[n] *temple of God with joy.*[o] 17. *At the dedication of this*[p] *temple of God, they sacrificed 100 bulls, 200 rams, 400 lambs, and as a purification-offering*[q] *for all Israel, 12 male goats according to the number of the tribes*[r] *of Israel.* 18. *They established*[s] *the priests in their divisions and the Levites in their courses*[t] *for the service of the god who is in Jerusalem*[u] *as is written in the book of Moses.*[v]

19. *Then the returnees*[w] *celebrated the Passover on the fourteenth of the first month.* 20. *Because the priests and the Levites had purified them-*

selves together,[x] *all of them were pure,*[y] *so they slaughtered the Pesach sacrifice for all the returnees, for their brothers the priests, and for themselves.* 21. *The people Israel ate*[z]*—the ones having returned from exile and anyone who would separate himself*[aa] *from the impurities of the nations of the land [to join himself]*[bb] *to them in order to inquire of Yhwh, the god of Israel.*[cc] 22. *They celebrated the holiday of Matzoth seven days with joy*[dd] *because Yhwh had made them joyous*[ee] *and had turned the heart of the king of Assyria*[ff] *to them in order to encourage them in the work of the temple*[gg] *of God, the god of Israel.*

Textual Notes

a. **6.13** *Tattenai.* As before, 1 Esdras interprets this name as Sisinnes; Greek Ezra reads Thanthana.

b. *Governor.* Both Greek Ezra and 1 Esdras translate this as *eparch,* ἔπαρχος (Ezra 6.13).

c. *Beyond-the-River.* Again 1 Esdras reads 'Greater Syria and Phoenicia'.

d. *Colleagues.* Greek Ezra reads 'fellow servants'.

e. *Quickly. 'osparnā'.* See note at 5.8. The versions translate it as 'carefully'. First Esdras adds, 'they (Tattenai *et al.*) supervised the holy work with very great care'.

f. **6.14** *The elders of the Judeans.* First Esdras inserts 'together with', that is, Tattenai supervised the work together with the elders of the Judeans, etc. Greek Ezra adds 'and the Levites', and 1 Esdras adds 'The chief officers of the temple', both absent in Ezra.

g. *And Zechariah son of Iddo.* He is not referred to here as a prophet, but it is understood.

h. *Completed.* See note on 4.13.

i. *The god of Israel.* First Esdras reads 'the Lord, god of Israel'.

j. *Decree.* This is in the singular in the Hebrew and in the versions. First Esdras reads 'by the decree of the Lord, god of Israel, and the consent of the kings', differentiating the roles of the kings and God. Greek Ezra reads 'consent' for both.

k. *King.* The Hebrew reads 'king' in the singular, but perhaps we should read 'kings' with the versions.

l. **6.15** *This temple.* Many manuscripts of 1 Esdras have 'this holy temple'.

m. **6.16** *The rest of the people of the exile.* First Esdras reads 'And the rest of those joining the people of the exile'. It may be based on 6.21.

n. *This.* This demonstrative is missing from the versions.

o. *Celebrated the dedication of this temple of god with joy.* First Esdras has instead 'according to what was in the law of Moses'. The dedication of the temple is not mentioned in 1 Esdras until the following verse.

p. **6.17** *This.* This demonstrative is missing from all the versions.

q. *Purification offering.* Incorrectly translated as 'sin-offering' in all the versions, it is used to purify the altar prior to the dedication ceremony.

r. *Tribes of Israel.* First Esdras reads 'leaders of the tribes of Israel'.

s. **6.18** *Established.* First Esdras reads 'The priests and Levites stood', making them the subjects of the verb.

t. *Divisions . . . courses.* First Esdras reads 'the priests and the Levites in the *phyles*', 'tribes', not making a distinction between 'divisions' and 'courses'. First Esdras also inserts 'arrayed in their vestments'.

u. *The god who is in Jerusalem.* First Esdras reads 'for the Lord God of Israel'.

v. *Book of Moses.* First Esdras adds 'and the gatekeepers at each gate'. This is the last verse of the Aramaic section.

w. **6.19** *Returnees.* Literally, 'sons of the exile'. First Esdras reads 'sons of Israel, the ones out of captivity'. This verse is in Hebrew, and the rest of the chapter continues in Hebrew.

x. **6.20** *Because the priests and the Levites purified themselves together.* In 1 Esdras this is part of the preceding verse.

y. *All of them were pure.* First Esdras reads, 'Not all of the returned captives were purified, but the Levites were all purified together'.

z. **6.21** *The people Israel ate.* Greek Ezra supplies το πασχα, 'the Passover'.

aa. *And any who separated himself.* First Esdras deletes the initial 'and', implying only one group of people, not two, as in Ezra.

bb. [*Joined*]. This word is missing in Ezra, but since the following phrase, 'to them', is present, something like this is implied.

cc. *To inquire of Yhwh, the god of Israel.* First Esdras reads simply 'to inquire of the Lord'.

dd. **6.22** *With joy.* First Esdras reads 'rejoicing before the Lord'.

ee. *Yhwh had made them joyous.* This phrase is missing in 1 Esdras, perhaps it is redundant.

ff. *King of Assyria.* First Esdras reads 'king of the Assyrians', which makes better sense.

gg. *Temple.* This word is missing in 1 Esdras, so that 1 Esdras reads 'for the work of the Lord, god of Israel.

Notes

6.13 ***They did quickly.*** The biblical author repeats the words of the letter to show that there was full compliance with Darius's instructions. He continues in Aramaic using as his sources probably the second temple's bilingual building inscription as well as the correspondence between Tattenai and Darius.

6.14 ***Elders of the Judeans.*** This phrase is taken from Darius's letter; it is not the language of the biblical writer who would have written 'heads of fathers' [houses]'. Noticeably missing is a reference to Zerubbabel the governor and Jeshua the high priest, but see Comment A below. The biblical author mentions them in his preface to Tattenai's letter, but they are missing here in his description of the reaction to Darius's response. A reference to the governor therefore was likely missing from Darius's letter as well. It is hard to attribute this omission to a 'democratizing' tendency on the part of the biblical author, however (*pace* Japhet 1982, 1983), since he mentions them both earlier. (See Comment A below on the absence of Zerubbabel and Jeshua from 6.13-22.)

Built and prospered. This again repeats and summarizes Tattenai's letter to Darius.

Haggai the prophet and Zechariah son of Iddo. This refers back to 5.1.

By the decree of the god of Israel and by the decree of Cyrus, Darius, and Artaxerxes. This statement conforms to Component F of typical temple-building inscriptions. It is stated that the temple has been built by the decree first of the god whose temple it is and then of the reigning monarch in whose reign the temple was built. It is odd, therefore, that the name of the god is missing, that he is only 'the god of Israel', without a name. It may be that this section quotes from the Aramaic section of the temple's bilingual building inscription and that the reference in it is to 'the god of Israel', rather than using his name.

Consistent with ancient Near Eastern temple-building inscriptions, the reigning monarchs under whose reign the temple was completed are mentioned, not the governor, even though he is Zerubbabel, the Davidic heir. Zerubbabel could not order the temple completed; as governor of Judah, he could only act under the orders of Tattenai and Darius.

A crux is the inclusion of Artaxerxes among the kings who 'decreed' that the temple be finished when the temple had already been completed and dedicated in the reign of his grandfather, Darius I. Some have argued that his inclusion demonstrates that the temple was really built in the time of Darius II, Artaxerxes' son (e.g. Becking 1998; Edelman 2005), but this is not possible (see comment at 4.5, above). Others have argued that the biblical author did not know the true order of the Persian kings, or thought that there was only one Darius, namely Darius II, the one who came after Artaxerxes, or even Darius III (e.g. Meyer 1965 [1896]: 14). It is more likely, however, as many commentators have noted (Williamson 1985: 83-84; Blenkinsopp 1988: 129; Eskenazi 1988: 41), that this verse constitutes a grateful recognition that Artaxerxes did finally give approval for the completion of the city wall (Neh. 2.9) and an acknowledgement that in the process of building and dedicating the wall, the temple was dedicated anew (Neh. 12.27-47). Moreover, according to the text as we have it, Artaxerxes had stopped not only the completion of the wall but the temple as well (5.23, 24), so that the biblical writer must have reasoned that the king must have relented and given permission for its completion, since it was in fact completed. His name would not have been part of the original building inscription, however, but could have been added to it when Artaxerxes became king. It could also have been added by the biblical author when he inserted the correspondence between that king and the satrapal officials. As Eskenazi notes, the verse serves as 'a retrospective and proleptic summary' of all of Ezra–Nehemiah.

King of Persia. The Hebrew has 'decree' and 'king' in the singular. Eskenazi suggests that the intent of the singular verbs is to stress that there was only one decree, God's, and that the kings of Persia act as one in consort with it.

6.15 ***[Twenty-]third day of the month of Adar.*** First Esdras reads 'the 23rd day of the month of Adar', whereas Ezra refers to the third day. Both the dedication of the altar (Ezra 3.4) and the dedication of the first temple (1 Kgs 8.64-66) are closely connected with the festival of Sukkot, whereas if the second temple's dedication had been on the third of Adar (the twelfth month), it would have been only loosely connected with the coming Passover holiday in the middle of the first month, the fourteenth of Nisan (Talshir 2001: 375). If the dedication had been on the 23rd of Adar, as in 1 Esdras, however, the celebration for the temple's dedication would have extended into the Passover holiday. According to the Babylonian Talmud (*Šab.* 87b), when the desert tabernacle was dedicated, the eight-day priestly ordination ceremony (Lev. 9) was followed by a twelve-day ceremony to dedicate the altar, which was in turn followed by the celebration of the Passover on the fourteenth of Nisan (Hurowitz 2006). According to this reasoning, the tabernacle was dedicated on the 23rd of Adar. This was likely the situation at the dedication of the second temple as well, so that it too would have been dedicated on the 23rd of Adar, as is stated in 1 Esdras, followed by an eight-day ordination of the priesthood, a twelve-day ceremony to dedicate the altar, and then the preparation for Passover. This conflicts with the order of events currently in the biblical text, however, in which the altar was dedicated prior to even laying the temple's foundations. It is argued above (Ezra 3), though, that building and dedicating the altar so early cannot be historical.

A choice of the third or the 23rd of Adar also depends on which year it was. Adar of Darius I's sixth year was in March of either 516 or 515 BCE (for the problem of the year, see following Note). If 515 BCE, the third of Adar fell on a Saturday (Shabbat), and the 23rd fell on a Friday (the day of preparation for Shabbat), neither of which are very likely. The year 516 BCE was a leap year, and there was a second Adar. In 516 BCE, the third of Adar I was a Sunday and the 23rd a Monday; the third of Adar II was a Monday and the 23rd a Sunday. Any of these four days is possible. It seems most likely, however, given the close connection with the Passover in the following verses, that the dedication was held on the 23rd of Adar II in 516 BCE. This was a Sunday, April 11. The following verses seem to imply that the twelve-day dedication of the altar preceded the ordination of the priesthood.

It should be noted that contrary to the normal usage of the biblical author, the Babylonian month name, Adar, is used here, rather than giving the month as a number, that is, 'the twelfth month', as he does elsewhere (3.1, 6, 8). This suggests a different author. The month name Adar may have been taken from the original building inscription, while the passages that state the month as a number were written by the biblical writer.

Sixth year of the reign of Darius the king. When was this year? There are several ways of counting regnal years (Depuydt 1995: 193). The Babylonians counted the first year of a king's reign from the first of Nisan, the first New Year's Day of his reign, to the last day of that year at the end of Adar. The period from the time he ascends the throne to that first New Year's Day is counted as his accession year. A second method of computing regnal years was used in Egypt—namely, the method of antedating, or predating. In this method, the period between the time when the new king ascends the throne until the first New Year's Day is counted as year one. Year two begins on New Year's Day. A third method is apparently the one used by the Persians (Bickerman 1980: 90; Depuydt 1995). This counts the first year from the time the new king ascends the throne until the anniversary of that date in the following year. There is no accession year. Thus, as Bickerman points out, the regnal years for the Persian kings were counted from the spring New Year in Babylon, from the fall New Year in Egypt, and from the date of accession at the Persian court. It is usually assumed that the Persian province of Judah followed the Babylonian counting system, so that regnal years began in the spring. If so, Adar of Darius's sixth year would have fallen in March of 515 BCE. Judah evidently counted Persian regnal years as they did at the Persian court, however. This is why Kislev (the ninth Babylonian month) of Artaxerxes' twentieth year falls before Nisan (the first Babylonian month) of that same twentieth year (Neh. 1.1; 2.1); Artaxerxes' regnal years were counted from the date of his accession to the throne, which occurred in Kislev (mid-winter).

Thus, to know the year in which the Adar of Darius's sixth year occurred according to the Persian system of counting, we need to know the date of his accession. According to the Behistun inscription, he slew the pretender Gaumata (i.e. Smerdis, Cambyses' brother) and declared himself king on the tenth day of the seventh month of 522 BCE (September 29 on the Gregorian calendar). The sixth year of his reign would then be from the seventh month of 517 to the seventh month of 516 BCE. Adar of that sixth year would fall in 516, an entire year before Adar of Darius's sixth year according to the Babylonian calendar. For the reasons cited in the previous note, it is more likely that the temple was dedicated on 23rd of Adar II, 516. This corroborates the assumption that during the period of Persian domination, the system of accounting regnal years in Judah was that of the Persian court.

The temple was thus 'under the scaffolding' from 538 to 516, twenty-two years, due to the extreme poverty of the community in spite of the assurances of both Cyrus and Darius. This long duration in building the temple, from the first year of Cyrus king of Babylon to the sixth year of Darius, may have caused the biblical writer to seek an explanation and to imagine a bitter struggle with the Samaritans.

This temple stood until the year 70 CE, 586 years, when it was destroyed by Rome.

6.16 ***Then the people of Israel . . . celebrated the dedication of this house of god with joy.*** This statement is Component G of typical temple-building inscriptions. The author may be quoting from the Aramaic section of the temple's bilingual inscription. The different inscriptions of multilingual building inscriptions represent independent texts; they are not translations of one another. The trilingual inscription for the temple at Xanthus in Lycia, for example, includes inscriptions in Greek, Aramaic and Lycian. While the Lycian and the Greek may be translations of each other, the Aramaic differs completely.[1]

The people of Israel—the priests, the Levites, and the rest of the people. This is the traditional division of the people Israel also described in Ezra 2: priests, Levites, and the lay tribes of Judah and Benjamin. Priests and Levites are from the tribe of Levi; and to the writer, these three tribes together comprised all that remained in the land of Israel of the people Israel. The biblical author did not consider the Samaritans part of the people Israel, but descended from those brought into the region from abroad by Assyrian kings (Ezra 4.2). This phrase is likely an addition by the biblical writer and was not in the building inscription. The elders are not mentioned again in this section of Ezra.

6.17 ***100 bulls, 200 rams, 400 lambs.*** This type of statement describing the dedication celebration is very typical of ancient Near Eastern temple-building inscriptions. The dedication of Solomon's temple, as described in both Kings and Chronicles, includes a large number of offerings called offerings of well-being (*šᵉlāmîm*; 1 Kgs 8.63). Although it is not stated, it may be assumed that the 100 bulls, the 200 rams, and the 400 lambs are also offerings of well-being. The numbers offered are in inverse relationship to the value of the animal. Only males are offered, of course, since the females were too valuable.

Twelve male goats according to the number of the tribes of Israel. This takes account of the ten tribes of Israel still in exile. The temple belongs to them as well, though they were not there to participate in its dedication.

As a purification-offering for all Israel. The dedication of Solomon's temple, as described in both Kings and Chronicles, makes no mention of a sin or purification offering. However, a goat as a purgation-offering is brought by the leader of each of the twelve tribes at the time of the dedication of the wilderness tabernacle (Num. 7.87). Rainey (1970; also Levine 1993: 263-64) explains that the administrative order of donations and disbursements (as set forth here and in Numbers 7) may not have corresponded to the actual order of the sacrifice. Rather, in the inauguration of the cult, the *ḥaṭṭā't,* the

1. The Greek was used to decode the Lycian, which is imperfectly known.

purification or purgation offering, preceded the other sacrifices. It was a preparatory cleansing ritual to assure that the sanctuary was fit for sacrificial activity. (To call it a 'sin-offering' is a mistranslation and misunderstanding. See Milgrom 1991: 253-92.) Thus according to the priestly writer of Numbers, a purification-offering must be included; whereas according to the Deuteronomist, one needs only offer the sacrifices of well-being (*šᵉlāmîm*). It appears that at least by the time of writing Ezra 6, the book of Moses (see next verse), which prescribes rules for dedicating the temple, included traditions from both the Priestly and the Deuteronomic schools.

At this point the god is supposed to be ushered into his new home to take up residence, but there is no mention of it. In the second temple period, with the ark of Yhwh absent, the temple vessels may have substituted as the proof of Yhwh's presence (see Introduction and Fried 2003b; 2004: 158-77). Cyrus apparently ordered Sheshbazzar to take Yhwh's vessels from the temple of Marduk, to bring them to Jerusalem, and to install them in their rightful place in the temple of Yhwh there (1.8; 5.15). Surprisingly, we are not told that he did so. Tattenai's letter reports that Sheshbazzar brought them to Judah, but of course there was no temple then, no installed priesthood, nowhere to put them when he arrived. According to Mesopotamian tradition, however, they should have been housed in a temporary temple until the permanent one was dedicated, at which point the vessels should have been brought out of their temporary housing and restored to their permanent abode (Hurowitz 1993). If this occurred, their installation would have been part of the second temple's building inscription, but the author of Ezra does not report it.

Hurowitz (2006) suggests that the biblical writer refrained from reporting the installation of the temple vessels or of any other icon of the god because he was among those who believed that the second temple was devoid of an immanent divine presence (*b. Yoma* 21b). It is difficult to imagine that an author would write at least six chapters to describe the building and dedication of a temple built for a god who would not deign to inhabit it. Hurowitz may be partly right in that this author may not have believed that the temple vessels represented the god, and therefore did not report their installation.

Immediately after the dedication and the celebration of the Passover, we have the story of Ezra's arrival, however (Ezra 7 and 8). Although Ezra brought some vessels with him, and although he deposited them in the temple (8.33), we are not told that these were from the original temple in Jerusalem, and, moreover, this was not the purpose of his visit. According to the biblical writer, he came to bring the torah (7.10). In fact, the climax of the book of Ezra–Nehemiah is the story of Ezra reading the law to the populace, as described in Nehemiah 8. That story is surrounded in the book of Nehemiah with the larger story first of building and dedicating the city wall and then of rededicating the temple (Nehemiah 6–12). It is that larger story that describes the ceremony in which the god is finally brought into his temple and takes up residence in it. The icon of the god evolved from the ark in monarchic times, to the temple vessels at the time of the return (Isa. 52.7-12), to the book or torah of Moses at the time of writing Ezra–Nehemiah (van der Toorn 1997; Fried 2008, 2013b; Tigay 2013). See further at Nehemiah 12.

6.18 ***They set up the priests in their divisions and the Levites in their courses.*** This statement is among the last components of typical ancient Near Eastern temple-building inscriptions. Temple dedications are normally followed by the installation of the temple's personnel, so that now, after the dedication, is the appropriate time to appoint the priesthood and set them up in their divisions. It is only when the temple is dedicated that the rotation of temple personnel is established. In the original building inscription this verse was likely preceded by the two verses that are now in Ezra 3.8b, 9:

> Then Zerubbabel ben-Shealtiel and Jeshua ben-Jozadak and the rest of their kin (namely the priests and the Levites and all who came from among the captivity of Jerusalem) began by appointing the Levites of twenty years old and above to have charge over the work of the house of Yhwh. And Jeshua, his sons and his kin, Kadmiel and his sons, the sons of Judah, stood as one to supervise doing the care of the house of God (along with) the sons of Henadad, their sons and their kin, the Levites.
>
> They established the priests in their divisions and the Levites in their courses for the service of the god who is in Jerusalem as is written in the book of Moses.

Thus, according to the proposed reconstruction of the second temple's original building inscription, Jeshua and Zerubbabel were present at the temple's dedication. (See Comment A below.)

The book of Moses. This phrase concludes the Aramaic portion of Ezra 1–6 and concludes as well the story of the building and the dedication of the second temple. This would have ended the second temple's actual building inscription, which may also have been written in Aramaic or have been bilingual, Aramaic and Hebrew. The foundations have been laid (3.10), the altar set up on its original site (3.3), the Persian kings who supported the temple building project are thanked (6.14), the temple is dedicated with pomp and circumstance (6.16-17), and temple personnel are appointed (3.8b, 9; 6.18). (See comments below for the inclusion here of 3.8b and 9).

6.19 ***Then the returnees celebrated the Passover on the fourteenth of the first month.*** With this verse, the text returns to Hebrew and continues in Hebrew through to the end of the chapter. The story of building and dedicating the temple is over. We must wait for the remaining chapters of Ezra–Nehemiah to read the story of the installation into it of the torah of Moses, Yhwh's icon. The building inscription would have ended with the previous verse, and so the author reverts to Hebrew. It may be only coincidence that the temple's dedication occurred in Adar, enabling the dedication ceremony to continue into the celebration of the Passover. With the Passover celebration, the temple cult is inaugurated once more in Israel. The description of the Passover celebration would have been familiar to the reader and would have brought the story up to his own time. (See Comment B below on the inauguration of the cult.)

6.20 ***They slaughtered the Pesach sacrifice.*** The 'they' refers to the Levites. Because the priests and Levites were all recently purified, they could celebrate the Passover on the fourteenth day of the first month, as was usual. The emphasis on purity in connection with their celebrating the Passover at its proper time has to do with the law in Num. 9.9-11:

> Yhwh spoke to Moses, saying: 'Speak to the Israelites, saying: Anyone of you or your descendants who is unclean through touching a corpse, or is away on a journey, shall still keep the Passover to Yhwh. In the second month on the fourteenth day, at twilight, they shall keep it; they shall eat it with unleavened bread and bitter herbs.'

The Chronicler reports, moreover, that after the fall of the northern kingdom, Hezekiah was forced to celebrate the Passover in the second month because not enough of the Levites had sanctified themselves to perform the sacrifice (2 Chronicles 30).

6.21 ***All who would keep himself separate from the cultic impurities of the nations of the area.*** Thus, not only the returnees, but anyone else who was willing to separate himself from the customs of the nations round about and to join the Judeans was also permitted to eat the Passover sacrifice and to participate in the inauguration of the cult. Who were these others? It must be kept in mind that the Persian Empire had foreign soldiers and Persian officers garrisoned everywhere throughout the empire, including Judah and Jerusalem (Tuplin 1987b; Briant 2002; Fried 2004, 2006, 2010b). Some of these may have joined themselves to the Jerusalem cult.

6.22 ***The festival of Matzoth.*** It appears that during the Persian period at least (if not earlier, and if not originally) the Passover holiday and the festival of Matzoth were two separate holidays. In Lev. 23.4-6 we read:

> These are Yhwh's appointed festivals, the holy convocations, which you shall celebrate at the time appointed for them. In the first month, on the fourteenth day of the month, at twilight, there shall be a Passover offering to Yhwh, and on the fifteenth day of the same month is the festival of unleavened bread [festival of Matzoth] to Yhwh; seven days you shall eat unleavened bread.

The existence of two separate holidays is confirmed by the so-called Passover letter (*TAD* 4.1), quoted above (at 6.10). Days begin at sunset. According to that letter, from sunset on the fourteenth to sunset on the fifteenth is the holiday of Passover, or maybe the holiday of the Paschal sacrifice. The festival of Unleavened Bread, חג המצות, follows immediately at sunset on the fifteenth and lasts until sunset on the twenty-first, but for all seven days, the Judeans both in Judah and at Elephantine abstained from leavening in both their bread and their drink.

Assyria. Why is the king of Assyria mentioned rather than the king of Persia? The king of Assyria stands for the source of all the Judeans' difficulties 'until today' (Neh. 9.32), but now it appears that for the moment at least, the heart of a foreign king has been turned toward the Judeans.

Comments

A. What Happened to Zerubbabel and Jeshua?

Many commentators have suspected a purge, but it is unlikely. Had the Persians suspected rebellious activity, they would have destroyed the temple itself, the seat of the apparent fomentation. They would not have allowed its completion. It is more likely that Zerubbabel and Jeshua did not disappear, that they were present at the dedication, but that they simply disappeared from the text. It is noted above in the discussion of Ezra 3 that the verses there were out of order in comparison with typical ancient Near Eastern building inscriptions. In typical inscriptions, the altar is set up only toward the end of the building process. Priests and temple personnel, moreover, are appointed only after the temple is completed and dedicated. It is suggested there that the altar was dedicated not in the first year of Cyrus but in the second year of Darius, as would be more usual, and that temple personnel were appointed only in Darius's sixth year, after the temple's dedication, as would be appropriate—not when the foundations were being laid. If so, if that was their original position in the second temple's actual building inscription, the inscription that very likely underlies these chapters, then we may move Ezra 3.8b-9 (the appointment of temple personnel) to what was likely its original place in the inscription. If we move those verses to their appropriate spot according to the ancient Near Eastern temple-rebuilding template, then we will have moved them to between 6.17 and 6.18. The description of the dedication would then read as follows:

> 6.16 Then the people of Israel—the priests, the Levites, and the rest of the people of the exile celebrated the dedication of this temple of God with joy. 6.17. At the dedication of this temple of God, they sacrificed 100 bulls, 200 rams, 400 lambs, and as a purification-offering for all Israel, 12 male goats according to the number of the tribes of Israel.
>
> 3.8b Then Zerubbabel ben-Shealtiel and Jeshua ben-Jozadak and the rest of their kin (namely the priests and the Levites and all who came from among the captivity of Jerusalem) began by appointing the Levites of

> twenty years old and above to have charge over the work of the house of Yhwh.
>
> 6.18 They set up the priests in their divisions and the Levites in their courses for the service of the god who is in Jerusalem as is written in the book of Moses.
>
> 3.9 Then Jeshua, his sons and his kin, Kadmiel and his sons, the sons of Judah, stood as one to supervise the maintenance of the house of God (along with) the sons of Henadad, their sons and their kin, the Levites.

When we put the verses back to what was likely their original position in the second temple's actual building inscription, we find that Zerubbabel and Jeshua have not disappeared at all. They are there, appointing cultic personnel and placing them in their divisions for the care of the newly dedicated temple.

B. The Inauguration of the Cult

The description of the Passover holiday that follows brings the story into the audience's own time. We are told that the Levites killed the Passover sacrifice for themselves, for the priests, and for all Israel, and with joy they celebrated the holiday for seven days. This was the usual way of celebrating the Passover holiday in the second temple period. The throngs arriving yearly for the holiday in second temple times is alluded to both in the New Testament and in Josephus (e.g. *Ant.* 3.249).

The story of the inauguration of the cult and the celebration of the Passover is marked with joy. This section forms the epilogue of the Hellenistic narrative that overlays the ancient Near Eastern building inscription. Besides bringing the account into the audience's own time, the epilogue is designed to put the reader in a positive frame of mind. This it certainly does.

Reflection

What Yhwh started when he 'stirred up' the spirit of Cyrus is now completed twenty-two years later. What Yhwh wants, he brings to completion, but not without the help of human hands. The biblical author is quite cognizant that without people willing to leave the safety of Babylon for a strange new land, without their willingness to invest in the future, nothing would have happened. Change comes only for those who are willing to step out of their comfort zone and take a chance on God.

Ezra 7–10

Introduction to Part II: The Story of Ezra's Arrival in Jerusalem and the Mass Divorce

Immediately after the temple's dedication, we read of Ezra's arrival in Jerusalem. He is presented to the reader of chap. 7 as both a scribe and a priest. According to the biblical text, he arrives in Judah and Jerusalem with the thought only to teach torah (the laws of Moses). Apparently he comes with a mandate from King Artaxerxes to do so, as well as a command from him to inspect Jerusalem according to the law of God which he has in his hand and to appoint judges and magistrates to enforce these laws. This relationship with the torah is Ezra's most important and most enduring characteristic, and the reason why Ezra appears in postbiblical Jewish, Christian, Samaritan and Islamic texts (Fried 2014: 28-147). It also is the reason why biblical scholars have attributed to Ezra the origin of Judaism (Fried 2014: 148-70; 2015b).

Soon after Ezra's arrival, officials approach him, complaining about the treachery of the people Israel in their many intermarriages with the 'peoples of the lands' (Ezra 9.1-2). Ezra reacts to the news with shock: he tears his hair and beard, rends his clothes, and fasts until evening. He is afraid to pray to God, stating that he is too ashamed and embarrassed to lift his face to him. 'Our iniquities have risen higher than our head', he says. Ezra argues that we had been driven off our land because of our sins, and have only now returned, and we are again provoking God with this treachery. After warning the people that these intermarriages might cause them to be driven off their land again, the people agree to a mass divorce. This story is told in Ezra 9–10.

According to the book of Ezra, Ezra arrives in Judah in the seventh year of a King Artaxerxes but scholars are divided over which Persian King Artaxerxes is meant of the four who bore that name (again, see the Appendix). The debate is primarily between Artaxerxes I (465–424 BCE) and Artaxerxes II (405–359 BCE). If the historical Ezra arrived in the seventh year of Artaxerxes I, then he preceded Nehemiah (who arrived in 445 BCE, the twentieth year of that king). If he arrived in the seventh year of Artaxerxes II, then he followed him. The date of Ezra's arrival is explored in the discussion on Ezra 7, but it is concluded there that the reign of Artaxerxes II is most plausible. This means that contrary to the order of their presentation in the biblical texts, and contrary to the intent of the biblical writer, the historical Ezra followed Nehemiah by almost half a century!

The Arrangement of Events in Ezra–Nehemiah

The highlight of Ezra–Nehemiah does not occur until Nehemiah 8 when Ezra reads to the assembled populace the torah of Moses that he brought with him from Babylon. The reading is followed by a long confessional prayer (Nehemiah 9) and a so-called covenant renewal ceremony in which the representatives of the assembled populace sign an Amanah, an agreement, primarily to care for the temple of Yhwh, but also to keep the Sabbath and to prevent their children from marrying with foreigners (Fried 2005). The intent of the editor who wrote the story of the reading of the law is revealed in his arrangement of the events.[1] He has sandwiched the reading of the law and his whole covenant renewal ceremony (Nehemiah 8–10) between two lists of the male population of Judah and Jerusalem (Nehemiah 7 and Nehemiah 11–12). Next he prefaces his first population list (Nehemiah 7) with Nehemiah's account of his trip to Judah to rebuild the city wall, an account of the wall building itself and the portion of Nehemiah's memoir that ends with the comment that the wall is completed and the doors hung (Neh. 7.5). He follows the second population list in Nehemiah 11 and 12 with a description of the wall's dedication, the ascent onto the wall, and the ceremonial celebration, the temple sacrifices, and the installation of temple personnel (Neh. 12.27-47). This author has thus surrounded his covenant renewal ceremony first, and most nearly, with a list of the population of Judah, and, second and outermost, with the creation, completion and dedication of the city wall. The wall has become a fence, not only around the people but around the temple and within the temple, the torah. Inside the dedicated wall is the rightful population of Judah, and in the center of that population is the torah, the icon of Yhwh himself. All of this is prefaced first by an account of building, dedicating and refurbishing the temple (Ezra 1–8), and then with the account of purifying and legitimating the population (Ezra 9–10). Ezra's reading of the law described in Nehemiah 8 is a consequence of the rebuilt temple (Ezra 1–6) and of the newly purified population of Judah (Ezra 7–10).

As discussed in the Introduction, the author of Ezra 7–10 is likely the author of Ezra 7–Nehemiah 13. His sources included a copy of Artaxerxes' original letter commissioning Ezra, an Ezra story (perhaps written by Ezra himself or a subordinate as a report to the king), and Nehemiah's memoir (again, perhaps written by Nehemiah himself).

1. This section is derived from Fried 2008.

Ezra 7.1-10

Ezra: Priest, Scribe, and King's 'Ear'

The first ten verses of Ezra 7 function as an introduction to the person of Ezra and foreshadow the story to be told in Ezra 7–10 and Nehemiah 8. Ezra is identified as a member of the high-priestly family and as a scribe skilled in the law of Moses. These first ten verses provide his genealogy (vv. 1-5), his profession (v. 6), his origin (v. 6), the date of his departure from Babylon and arrival in Jerusalem (vv. 8-9), as well as the purpose of the journey (v. 10) (Mowinckel 1965: 18).

The issues surrounding this passage are numerous and include its literary unity, its authorship, its relationship to the rest of the story of Ezra, and its relationship to the preceding six chapters. Williamson (1983, 1985) has suggested that Ezra 1–6 was added secondarily to a text that already included Ezra 7–Nehemiah 13 in pretty much the form that we have, and that is basically the approach followed here. The author of Ezra 7.1-10 is assumed here to be the one who created Ezra 7–Nehemiah 13. He combined the Nehemiah memoir with a previously existing Ezra story, added the various lists, and created a continuous narrative from Ezra 7.1 to Nehemiah 13 as we have it. In the process he wrote Nehemiah 8–10, the so-called covenant renewal ceremony, which includes Ezra reading the torah of Moses to the assembled crowd (Nehemiah 8).

Nevertheless, there are intrusions into these introductory verses (7.1-10), perhaps from the author who appended Ezra 1–6 to it. This later writer would have been the one to preface Ezra's introduction with the phrase 'after these things' in 7.1. There are other interpolations as well that may also reflect his handiwork. He may have been the one to add Ezra's genealogy, which is intrusive, as well as v. 7, which also stands out from its context and reflects his interest in the cultic orders (as he is also assumed to have copied the list of returnees from Nehemiah 7 into Ezra 2).

Williamson (1985) explains these intrusions in the introduction not as stemming from the editor who appended Ezra 1–6, but from the author of Ezra 7–Nehemiah 13 himself. He suggests that this author had before him Ezra's authentic memoir, a first-person account, which he edited, changing parts of it to third person. Whether there was an original first-person account, a so-called Ezra memoir, has been a topic of discussion at least since Torrey's (1896) article on the historical value of Ezra–Nehemiah. The issue will be discussed throughout the rest of the commentary, but even if so, it is difficult to see a reworked Ezra memoir underlying this passage in Ezra 7.1-10. It is more likely that the author of Ezra 7–Nehemiah 13 created this passage purely on the basis of the Artaxerxes letter and that the intrusions were added by a later author. (See Comment B below.)

Translation

1. *After these things, in the reign of Artaxerxes*[a] *king of Persia, Ezra*[b] *son of Seraiah, son of Azariah, son of Hilkiah,* 2. *son of Shallum, son of Zadok, son of Ahitub,* 3. *son of Amariah, son of Azariah, son of Meraioth,* 4. *son of Zerahiah,*[c] *son of Uzzi, son of Bukki,* 5. *son of Abishua, son of Phinehas, son of Eleazar, son of Aaron the high priest—* 6. *this Ezra went up from Babylon.*

He was a scribe[d] *skilled*[e] *in the torah of Moses which Yhwh, god of Israel, had given; and the king gave him everything he requested*[f]*, as the hand of Yhwh his god was upon him.*[g] (7. *Some from among the people Israel, and from among the priests, the Levites, the singers, the gatekeepers, and the temple servants went up*[h] *[with him] to Jerusalem in the seventh year of Artaxerxes the king.*) 8. *And he entered*[i] *Jerusalem in the fifth month. It was the seventh year of the king.* 9. *For on the first of the first month he ordered*[j] *the ascent from Babylon, and on the first of the fifth month he entered*[k] *Jerusalem because the good hand of his god was upon him.*[l] 10. *For Ezra had set his heart*[m] *to inquire of the torah of Yhwh*[n] *to do [it],*[o] *and to teach in Israel*[p] *statutes and ordinances.*

Textual Notes

a. **1.** *Artaxerxes.* The text reads אַרְתַּחְשַׁסְתָּא throughout Ezra 7 and Nehemiah, as compared to אַרְתַּחְשַׁשְׂתָּא in Ezra 4 and 6.14. The word is pronounced the same, Artachshasta; in both cases, only the spelling is slightly different, the second שׂ (*ś*, sin) is replaced by a ס (samekh). At Elephantine the spelling is different still, ארתחשסש, Artachshasash.

b. *Ezra.* Both Hebrew and Greek grammar require a verb here. Both Greek Ezra and 1 Esdras supply one, but it is absent in the Hebrew.

c. **7.4** *Azariah, Meraioth, Zerahiah.* These names are missing from 1 Esdras.

d. **7.6** *Scribe.* Greek Ezra and 1 Ezra both use the word γραμματεύς, which is used for 'scribe' throughout the New Testament.

e. *Skilled.* First Esdras reads εὐφυής, 'naturally suited'.

f. *The king gave him . . . everything he requested.* First Esdras reads, 'and the king showed him honor, for he found favor before the king in all his requests' (1 Esdras 8.4). See note.

g. *The hand of his god was upon him.* This phrase is absent in 1 Esdras.

h. **7.7** *(They) went up.* First Esdras reads συνανέβησαν (1 Esd. 8.5), 'they accompanied, went up with [him]', which is implied, but not present in the Hebrew or Greek Ezra. The Vulgate of 1 Esdras reads *ascenderunt simul cum ipso*, 'they went up together with him', but the Latin of Ezra is just *ascenderunt*, 'they went up'.

i. **7.8** *He entered Jerusalem.* All the versions read 'they entered' to harmonize with the previous verse. Rudolph (1949: 67) proposes that it was originally ויעל, 'he brought up', referring to Ezra, and not ויעלו, 'they went up', but there is no textual support for this. This phrase is absent in 1 Esdras.

j. **7.9** *Ordered.* יְסֻד. This verb meaning 'to found' (e.g. Ezra 3.10, 11) should be emended to יִסַּד, 'to order', 'command', as in Est. 1.8 and in 1 Chron. 9.22. This verb is translated in Greek Ezra as ἐθεμελίωσεν, 'he established'. First Esdras simply reads 'they went out', ἐξελθόντε.

k. *He entered.* First Esdras maintains the plural and reads 'they arrived'.

l. *Because the good hand of his god was upon him.* First Esdras retains the reference to the entire group of returnees and reads 'according to the successful journey that the Lord had given them'.

m. 7.**10** *Set his heart.* First Esdras reads, 'for Ezra possessed great knowledge'.

n. *To inquire of the torah of Yhwh.* First Esdras reads, 'so that he omitted nothing from the law of the Lord'. Did the translator have a different text, or is he paraphrasing?

o. *To do it.* This phrase is also omitted from 1 Esdras. Either the translator thought it was superfluous, or he had a different text.

p. *In Israel.* First Esdras reads 'taught all Israel'; Israel is the recipient of the teaching, not the place.

Notes

7.1 ***After these things.*** This phrase would have been added by the author who wrote and appended Ezra 1–6 to the beginning of the story of Ezra–Nehemiah. A form of this phrase occurs twelve times in the Hebrew Bible. Whenever it occurs, its use suggests that the exact chronological relationship between the events was not clear to the writer. In every case, however, the second, subsequent event occurs within the lifetime of the protagonist of the first event. (See, for example, Gen. 15.1; 22.1, 20; 39.7; 40.1; 48.1.) It is instructive to consider 1 Kgs 21.1 and the corresponding version in the LXX 20.1. The phrase 'after these things' is present in the Hebrew 21.1 but absent in the LXX. This is because 1 Kings 21 in the Hebrew relates an event in the life of Ahab, the protagonist of the previous chapter. Indeed, the purpose of the phrase is to tell you so. The protagonist of 1 Kings 19 is Elijah, however. Not being about the same protagonist, the phrase is omitted in the Greek.

This implies that the events of Ezra 7–Nehemiah 13 were construed by the author of this phrase as occurring within the lifetime of Darius, the main protagonist of Ezra 6. Indeed, the Talmud (*Roš Haš.* 3b) understands the name, Artaxerxes, the name of the king at the time of both Ezra and Nehemiah, to be the throne name of every Persian king, and so also the throne name of Darius. This seems to have been the view of the biblical writer as well. Thus, the events of this chapter, which occur in the first month of the seventh year of Artaxerxes, were intended by this phrase to be read as following immediately upon the events of Adar, the twelfth month of Darius's sixth year. The phrase 'after this' should be read as 'shortly after this' from the point of view of the literary construction of the story. In the mind of its author, no chronological separation existed between the temple's rebuilding and dedication and Ezra's intention to bring the law to Jerusalem (Gunneweg 1985: 121).

In the reign of Artaxerxes. This was likely the original beginning of the Ezra story before it was combined with chaps. 1–6 of Ezra (Kapelrud 1944: 8; Mowinckel 1965: 18). Which of the four kings of Persia who took this throne name is intended—Artaxerxes I (465–424 BCE), Artaxerxes II (405–359 BCE), Artaxerxes III (358–338 BCE), or Artaxerxes IV (338–336 BCE)? A crux of Ezra studies has been the identity of the king under whom the historical Ezra served. The reader must keep two separate issues in mind simultaneously, however—the identity of the historical Artaxerxes under whom Ezra and Nehemiah each served and that of the Artaxerxes in the mind of the biblical writer. The Artaxerxes that the biblical writer has in mind is likely Darius I. (See further at Comment D at Ezra 2). For the historical Artaxerxes, see Comment B below. Nevertheless, to whichever of the four historical Artaxerxes we assign the activity of Ezra, there will be a large gap in time from the dedication of the temple in 516 to the seventh year of any of them, a gap of which the biblical author was unaware. In fact, the phrase 'after these things' contradicts the phrase 'in the reign of Artaxerxes'.

The spelling of the king's name differs slightly from that used in Ezra 4 and 6.14 above. There it is ארתחששתא, whereas here, throughout Ezra 7, and in Nehemiah it is spelled ארתחשסתא. This is a minor orthographic, stylistic difference, since both spellings yield the same pronunciation. The difference can be attributed to different authors, one who wrote Ezra 1–6, and another who wrote Ezra 7–Nehemiah 13.

Ezra. The name Ezra is probably a shortened form of 'Azariyahu, 'Yhwh is my helper', a very common name. Normal Hebrew syntax requires a verb at this point in the verse, however, but it is missing, displaced to v. 6. This suggests that the long genealogy that intervenes between the initial adverbial phrase and the verb was added secondarily. See following note.

Son of Seriah . . . son of Aaron. Ezra's genealogy is nearly identical to the high-priestly genealogy in 1 Chron. 5.29ff. [ET 6.3ff.], except that six names are omitted from the center of this list (Amariah—Johanan):

1 Chronicles 5.29-41 [ET 6.3-15]	**Ezra 7.1-5**
Aaron	Aaron
Eleazar	Eleazar
Phinehas	Phinehas
Abishua	Abishua
Bukki	Bukki
Uzzi	Uzzi
Zerahiah	Zerahiah
Meraioth	Meraioth
Amariah	
Ahitub	
Zadok	
Ahimaaz	
Azariah	
Johanan	
Azariah	Azariah
Amariah	Amariah
Ahitub	Ahitub
Zadok	Zadok
Shallum	Shallum
Hilkiah	Hilkiah
Azariah	Azariah
Seraiah	Seraiah
Jehozadak	Ezra

The Chronicler states that the Jehozadak who ends the list in Chronicles is the very same one who was exiled (1 Chron. 5.49 [ET 6.15]). Seraiah, his father, would therefore have been the one who was killed by the hand of the Babylonian king at Riblah (2 Kgs 25.18-21), although the Chronicler does not mention this.

By providing this genealogy its author declares that this Ezra was the son of the last high priest of Judah, brother of the Jehozadak who was exiled, and uncle of the Jeshua son of Jehozadak, the high priest of the restoration period under Darius. The concern to put Ezra in the period of the restoration and to connect him to Jeshua the high priest betrays the author of Ezra 1–6. The absence of the six names in the middle of Ezra's genealogy cannot imply that Ezra is closer by six generations to Aaron, Moses' brother, than Jehozadak was. Since the Zadok who was omitted, along with his father

Ahitub and his son Ahimaaz, are the three priests whom we know about through the stories of David and Solomon (see 2 Sam. 8.17; 15.2), it is possible that the Chronicler added these famous names to the shorter list that appears in Ezra (so Japhet 1993: 151). It is also possible that these three names were omitted from the list in Ezra due to haplography, that is, the scribe's eye jumped to the exact set of three names (Amariah, Ahitub, Zadok) which are repeated further down on the list. Since middle names on a list are more likely to be lost when repeating a list than the names at either the beginning or the end, it is more likely that the longer list in Chronicles is the original one, and that the author of our passage used the genealogy in Chronicles to give Ezra a high-priestly pedigree.

Aside from the missing six names, the genealogy is the same as the one in Chronicles, so whoever supplied the genealogy apparently assumed that Ezra was the son of that Seraiah who was high priest at the time of the destruction of the first temple by Nebuchadnezzar. The genealogy is intended to demonstrate that Ezra is a legitimate descendant of Aaron, a member of the high-priestly family, son of the last high priest, brother of Jehozadak, and uncle of Jeshua ben Jehozadak, the high priest of the restoration period.

If Ezra did in fact arrive in Judah during the reign of any king Artaxerxes, however, then historically speaking, it is impossible for him to be the uncle of Jeshua son of Jehozadak. It may be that Ezra's father was actually named Seraiah, and the biblical writer assumed him to be the Seraiah who was the last high priest under the Judean monarchy, and so supplied the appropriate genealogy. If so, then Ezra's true genealogy was not known to the author, and he may not have been of the high priestly line or even a priest at all (*pace* Rudolph 1949: 71). The genealogy provides no information about any ancestors who may have resided in Babylon with him (Knoppers 2009). Only first temple ancestors are listed, suggesting his true genealogy was not known. Moreover, even if Ezra arrived in 458, in the seventh year of Artaxerxes I, he could not have been the son of someone who lived in 586, 125 years before. This genealogy is reasonable only if the biblical author assumes that Artaxerxes was the throne name of Darius. According to this understanding, since the second temple was dedicated nearly seventy years after the destruction of the first one, Ezra could have been about seventy-one when he led a group back to Judah (see Comment D at Chapter 2 above).

It is less likely that this genealogy was taken from Ezra's actual memoir and that several generations fell out when the scribe's eye skipped from the Seraiah, the last high priest, to the Seraiah who was Ezra's father (*pace* Rudolph 1949: 66; and in der Smitten 1973: 8). It is more likely that since genealogies have specific purposes, a genealogy going back to Aaron, the first high priest, was supplied for a reason that has nothing to do with the historical Ezra (so also Kapelrud 1944: 20). The historical Ezra may not even have been a priest. The phrase 'the priest' is added after Ezra's name in Ezra 10.10, but is not present in the corresponding text in 1 Esd. 9.7, even though 1 Esdras expands Ezra's priestly role everywhere, even making him a high priest, ὁ ἀρχιερεύς (1 Esd. 9.39, 40), when he is never called this in the Hebrew (Pakkala 2004: 42-43). It seems likely therefore that had the phrase 'the priest' been present in 1 Esdras's source at Ezra 10.10, 1 Esdras would have included it, suggesting that his genealogy and references to him as a priest were added late in the transmission process and that originally he was known simply as scribe.

7.6 ***This Ezra went up.*** We finally get to the verb. This is very awkward in Hebrew. Normal Hebrew syntax requires the verb to be either at the beginning of the sentence or in second position, after an adverbial phrase. The long genealogy pushes the verb uncharacteristically to the end of the sentence and forces a repetition of the subject with 'this Ezra'. The awkward syntax demonstrates the secondary nature of the insertion of the genealogy into the narrative (Noth 1987: 63).

***Skilled scribe* סופר מהיר.** This phrase appears in Ps. 45.2 [ET 45.1], and a similar usage of the adjective 'skilled' occurs in Prov. 22.29. Most notably, the complete phrase occurs as a description of the sage Aḥiqar in the so-called *Parables of Aḥiqar*. That text, of Mesopotamian origin, was found in a fragmentary copy in Aramaic on the Nile island of Elephantine dating to the late-fifth century BCE (*TAD* C 1.1). Although the narrative mentions the Mesopotamian god Shamash and the Syrian god El, the document circulated in the Judean community at Elephantine. The text consists of a narrative followed by a set of parables or proverbs—that is, the words of Aḥiqar. Aḥiqar is also referred to in the book of Tobit (1.21, 22; 2.10; 11.18; 14.10), not only in the Greek apocrypha but also in the Aramaic version found at Qumran (4QTob^{aram}). According to the *Parables*, Aḥiqar was, like Ezra, a 'skilled scribe', סופר מהיר, but also advisor to Sennacherib (705–681 BCE), the king of all Assyria and bearer of his royal seal (*TAD* C 1.1:1-3). According to the book of Tobit, Sennacherib's son Esarhaddon (681–669 BCE) had placed Aḥiqar over all the accounts of his kingdom and had given him authority over his entire administration (Tob. 1.21). The language of the parables indicates they were composed around 700 BCE, before the time of Sennacherib, but the language of the narrative that frames the parables are much later, from the sixth century BCE (Kottsieper 2008: 120). The story of Aḥiqar was likely well known to the author of Ezra and to his readers, and the description 'skilled scribe' may have been intended to convey to readers a similarity between the two men and suggest that Ezra's relationship to Artaxerxes was the same as Aḥiqar's to Sennacherib and Esarhaddon, and that Ezra, like Aḥiqar, was also the bearer of traditional wisdom.

The office of scribe was crucial to the functioning of bureaucratic empires such as the Assyrian and the Persian. Scribes fulfilled many functions, from writing letters and contracts for the illiterate majority of the population (as is witnessed by Jer. 36.32 and the Aramaic papyri from Elephantine [*TAD* B; Botta 2009]) to serving in high administrative positions in provincial, satrapal, and royal administrations (see the note to Ezra 4.9 above and the articles in Gammie and Perdue 1990; Perdue 2008). Nehemiah appointed Zadok, the scribe, as one of the treasurers over the temple storehouse to serve under Shelemiah, the priest, probably as chief accountant and record keeper of the temple funds (Neh. 13.13). Beyond their bureaucratic and administrative functions, scribes were considered to be steeped in the wisdom traditions and the scholarly training of their cultures. Ben Sira (38.24–39.11) describes the role of the scribe, as well as his status in society. He uses the term γραμματεύς, the same title that Ezra receives in Greek Ezra. These two images of the scribe, the court official and the wisdom scholar, play out in the biblical traditions of Ezra: the first in the letter from Artaxerxes (see below at v.14), and the second in the descriptions of the biblical author (see below at v. 10 and Nehemiah 8, as well as Comment C).

Torah of Moses. What does it mean to be a scribe skilled in the torah of Moses? Or rather, what did it mean to the biblical writer? Did it mean someone who knew the general wisdom traditions believed to have been handed down since Moses, in the same way that Aḥiqar knew the wisdom traditions of his culture? Or, did it mean someone who could copy and read the same scroll that is read in Jewish synagogues today? The identity of this torah of Moses that Ezra reads to the populace in Nehemiah 8 has been an issue in biblical scholarship since the days of Wellhausen. (See comment at Nehemiah 8).

Hand of Yhwh his god was upon him. This phrase 'the hand of Yhwh', or 'the hand of God' or some form of it, occurs frequently in Ezra–Nehemiah (Ezra 7.6, 9, 28; 8.18, 22, 31; Neh. 2.8, 18). It may have been drawn originally from the Nehemiah memoir (Neh. 2.8, 18), which the biblical author certainly had at his disposal (Kapelrud 1944: 23; Kellermann 1967: 58; Williamson 1985: 92). Both texts (Ezra and Nehemiah) might be based on Ezekiel, however (Ezek. 1.3; 3.22; 37.1; 40.1; Fishbane 1990: 441) since Ezra–Nehemiah reflects a strong dependence on Ezekiel (Fried 2008). The phrase is not in 1 Esdras, suggesting this is a late insertion into the Ezra story.

Everything he requested. This phrase is often viewed as an attempt to outdo the Nehemiah passage (Neh. 2.7-8; e.g. Rudolph 1949: 72; Kellermann 1967: 58; Williamson 1985: 92). Since we have no record of Ezra having requested anything from the king, the biblical writer may have taken this phrase from the Nehemiah memoir. Nehemiah requests that the king provide letters of safe passage to the governors of Beyond-the-River, as well as a letter to Asaph, the keeper of the king's forest, for timber for his own house and for the city wall (Neh. 2.8). The king agrees to supply these letters, an act that Nehemiah attributes to the 'gracious hand of my god upon me' (Neh.

2.8). J.L. Wright (2004: 340) sees all of Neh. 2.8 as added very late to Nehemiah's memoir since it interrupts the flow of the text, but the Persepolis tablets (Cameron 1948; Hallock 1969) as well as the Arsames documents (*TAD* A 6.9) show that both Ezra and Nehemiah would have needed such letters of safe passage from the king to the governors in the satrapy Beyond-the-River in order for them to travel safely through those provinces. The letters would also have guaranteed supplies for everyone in the party at each of the rest stops along the way. These rest stops were part of the imperial road system and guaranteed by the governor of each jurisdiction.

7.7 ***Some . . . went up.*** Here we have an abrupt change in the subject of the verb from the singular, referring only to Ezra and used everywhere else in these introductory verses (1-10), to the plural, so it should be understood as a parenthetic expression. For a discussion of the cultic terms, see notes at Ezra 2. This verse was inserted by a later author.

Singers and gatekeepers. Singers and gatekeepers are not mentioned in Ezra 8, suggesting that this verse is derived from the list of personnel in Nehemiah 7 (= Ezra 2), and is not original to the Ezra story.

Seventh year. It is not entirely clear where the narrator gets this number from in the current Ezra story that we have (Ezra 7.27–10.44). The year may have been in Ezra's memoir (if such existed) but left out when it was incorporated into Ezra–Nehemiah (Rudolph 1949: 73; Schneider 1959: 131). More likely it was supplied by the author who appended Ezra 1–6 and who wanted to portray Ezra as arriving in Jerusalem immediately after the dedication of the temple in Darius's sixth year. In other words, this date is not reliable, but we use it anyway for lack of any other.

7.8 ***Fifth month.*** Assuming he took the northern route and did not go across the desert, the trip would have been about 1,750 kilometers. Taking four months at least to do this trip implies he walked and averaged about 18 kilometers a day, or 11 miles, which is certainly doable. Leaving in the first month, March/April, means he started after the rainy season and would have arrived before it became unbearably hot. (See further at Ezra 8.)

Seventh year. The repetition of the phrase 'seventh year' plus the change in the subject from singular to plural in v. 7 and now here in v. 8 back to singular again suggests that v. 7 is an interpolation, interpolated by someone interested in the temple personnel.

7.9 ***First of the first month.*** This day is presumed to be the day Ezra determined to go to Jerusalem, not the day that he actually left (see textual note above). That day was the twelfth of the first month (Ezra 8.31), the month of Nisan (April 16, 398 BCE; Parker and Dubberstein 1956: 34). (See comment C below and note at 8.31.)

Ascent. The author uses an expression that has otherwise been used to indicate Yhwh's bringing the people up out of Egypt (e.g. Lev. 11.45; Josh. 24.17; Jer. 2.6; Mowinckel 1965: 20).

The good hand of his god was upon him. See above at v. 6.

7.10. ***Inquire of the torah of Yhwh.*** The expression 'inquire of Yhwh', or 'inquire of God', usually refers to inquiry through a seer, prophet or medium (e.g. 1 Sam. 9.9; 1 Kgs 22.8; 1 Sam. 28.7). Here it is inquiry of the torah of Yhwh. Because later we read (Neh. 8.1) that 'they told Ezra the scribe to bring the book of the torah of Moses which Yhwh commanded Israel (וַיֹּאמְרוּ לְעֶזְרָא הַסֹּפֵר לְהָבִיא אֶת־סֵפֶר תּוֹרַת מֹשֶׁה אֲשֶׁר־צִוָּה יְהוָה אֶת־יִשְׂרָאֵל), we should probably assume that a book is meant here in Ezra 7.10 as well. If so, then the book of the law had become an oracular device by which to inquire of Yhwh (Fishbane 1985: 245). A precise description of this activity is found in 1 Macc. 3.48:

> καὶ ἐξεπέτασαν τὸ βιβλίον τοῦ νόμου περὶ ὧν ἐξηρεύνων τὰ ἔθνη τὰ ὁμοιώματα τῶν εἰδώλων αὐτῶν.
>
> And they opened the book of the law (torah) to inquire into those matters about which the nations consulted the images of their gods.

If this analysis is correct, by the time this passage in Ezra was written the book of the law of Yhwh had taken on a hypostatic character (in der Smitten 1973: 10) and had become the icon of the god Yhwh from which one can obtain oracles (van der Toorn 1997; Tigay 2013: esp. p. 331). A major question is when this would have been, but it cannot be answered at the present state of our knowledge. (See Comment A below.)

To teach in Israel statutes and ordinances. According to the biblical writer, presumably the author of Ezra 7–Nehemiah 13, this is the purpose of Ezra's trip; and according to the writer, like Nehemiah's trip, it is self-initiated, not imposed from above (Gunneweg 1985: 127). That is, it was not Artaxerxes' idea to send him, but as with Nehemiah, it was Ezra's own. Ezra is described here not as wanting to teach Yhwh's laws *to* Israel, but *in* Israel. If it were *to* Israel, he could have remained in Babylon and taught the commandments to the Judeans who remained there. It seems that to the author, the holiness of the land demanded a greater adherence to the torah than was required in Babylon.

Comments

A. Why the High Priestly Genealogy?

It is clear from the syntax that Ezra's genealogy going back to Aaron, the first high priest, is a late insertion into the text, so the question is why was it added.[1] Ezra is never shown in a priestly role throughout the books Ezra and Nehemiah. He is not shown performing sacrifices, slaughtering animals,

1. This section is based on Fried 2013b.

nor is he even shown inside the temple except to spend a fretful night in the chambers of Yoḥanan, the actual high priest in the time of Ezra (Ezra 10.6; Fried 2003a). Why then add the high priestly genealogy if not to show him in the role of a priest?

According to the biblical writer, the purpose of Ezra's trip to Judah was to teach law and ordinance in Israel (Ezra 7.10). In this view, Ezra came to Jerusalem for the express purpose of studying and teaching torah, the Mosaic law code, in Israel. He came, moreover, not just to teach it but 'to inquire, לדרוש (*lidᵉrôš*), of the torah of Yhwh' (Ezra 7.10). This choice of word suggests, as noted above, that the scroll itself had become an oracular device (Fishbane 1985: 245; Tigay 2013; Fried 2013b), a medium through which God may be accessed, an icon of the god Yhwh.

This explains the necessity of the high-priestly genealogy. As an icon of Yhwh, only priests, indeed perhaps only the high priest, could touch the torah to avoid the sacred contagion that surrounded it. We see this concept of sacred contagion, for example, in the story describing the ark's being brought up to Jerusalem (2 Sam. 6.2-7), for the ark too was a medium by which Yhwh could be accessed:

> David and all the people with him set out and went from Baale-Judah, to bring up from there the ark of God, which is called by the name: 'Yhwh of Hosts Who Is Enthroned on the Cherubim'. They carried the ark of God on a new cart, and brought it out of the house of Abinadab, which was on the hill. Uzzah and Ahio, the sons of Abinadab, were driving the new cart with the ark of God; and Ahio went in front of the ark. . . .
>
> When they came to the threshing floor of Nacon, Uzzah reached out his hand to the ark of God and grasped it, for the oxen shook it. Yhwh's anger was kindled against Uzzah; and God struck him there because he reached out his hand and touched the ark; and he died there beside the ark of God.

Uzzah died because he touched the ark without being of the priestly caste. The same contagion is seen in the attitude toward the torah scroll (Lim 2010: 501-15). The rabbis knew that Ezra's torah would defile the hands if taken out of the temple. According to the Tosefta (*Kelim* BM 5.8; *apud* Goodman 1990: 102),

> Ezra's book [i.e. the torah scroll that he brought to Jerusalem] when taken out (of the temple) defiles the hands, and not only Ezra's book, but also the Prophets and the Five Books (of the Writings?).

This notion of 'defiling the hands' implies a tradition of a sacred contagion inherent in the torah scroll. This contagion is conveyed not by the meaning of the laws and commandments written on the scroll, but it is a contagion inherent in the scroll itself, a physical contagion dangerous to all but the high priests to whom, according to Josephus, Ezra's torah was entrusted (*Contra Apion* 1.29; Barton 1997: 108-21; Goodman 1990: 99-107; Lim 2010).

The torah scroll as the icon of the god is revealed again in the description of the torah reading in Nehemiah (Neh. 8.5-6):

> And Ezra opened the book in the sight of all the people, for he was standing above all the people; and when he opened it, all the people stood up. Then Ezra blessed Yhwh, the great god, and all the people answered, 'Amen, Amen', lifting up their hands. Then they bowed their heads and bowed down (יִשְׁתַּחֲוּוּ) to Yhwh with their noses to the ground.

The verb יִשְׁתַּחֲוּוּ, *yištaḥ*^{a}*wū*, to bow down, is used numerous times in the Hebrew Bible, often to denote respect; David, for example, bows down before King Saul (1 Sam. 24.9). However, it is also the very action that Moses takes when Yhwh stands before him on Mt Sinai (Exod. 34.8) and that Bilam makes before the angel of Yhwh (Num. 22.31). It is thus a reaction to the presence of the divine. This is the only time in the Hebrew Bible that people are shown bowing down before a text, however, and it conveys more than simple respect. The ceremony described in Nehemiah 8, in which the people bow down before the torah scroll when Ezra lifts it up, suggests that at the time of writing this passage the torah scroll had become more than a simple piece of text, more than simple wisdom literature. It had been exalted into the physical manifestation of Yhwh's presence, his location on earth (Niditch 1996: 106). Here too in Ezra 7.10 as in Neh. 8.1-6 the torah scroll is seen as an epiphany of the god Yhwh and a medium through which he may be accessed. It is because Ezra holds, touches and reads from the torah scroll (Nehemiah 8) that he must be given a high-priestly genealogy.

B. Ezra as Teacher of Torah

Ezra set his task not only to inquire of the torah of Yhwh but 'in order to do and to teach in Israel statute and ordinance' (Ezra 7.10). Since Nehemiah 8 is the only passage that actually shows Ezra teaching statutes and ordinances in Israel, this verse in Ezra 7 is intended to foreshadow the story of Ezra's reading the law told in Nehemiah. The author of this verse then was the one who wrote the story of the law reading and indeed the entire covenant renewal ceremony (Neh. 8–10) and inserted it into the middle of Nehemiah's memoir. This verse (7.10) is echoed by Neh. 8.1, in which Ezra is told to bring the torah scroll. In Neh. 8.1, Ezra the *sofer* (scribe) is told to bring the *sefer* (the book of the torah of Moses) and to read it to the people assembled before him in Jerusalem.

The similarity between the two verses is striking:

Ezra 7.6	*Nehemiah 8.1*
This Ezra went up from Babylon	They told
He was a ready scribe	*Ezra the scribe* to bring the book
of the torah of Moses	*of the torah of Moses*
which Yhwh god of Israel gave	*which Yhwh commanded Israel*

The biblical writer, who introduces Ezra in Ezra 7.1-10 and arranged all of Ezra 7–Nehemiah 13, wrote in the Hellenistic period (see Introduction). He assumed that Ezra had brought a copy of the original Mosaic torah with him to Jerusalem. He apparently based this assumption on the Persian word *dātā'*, which appears several times in Artaxerxes' letter (7.12, 14, 21, 25, 26; discussed below). At the time of his writing in the Hellenistic period, this word had been incorporated into the Hebrew and Aramaic languages with a completely different meaning than it had originally meant under the Persians. Instead of the term referring to *ad hoc* royal decrees that had only temporary validity and restricted applicability as it did under the Achaemenids, a permanent written law code was now in mind. The change in meaning is visible in the Aramaic portions of Daniel, likely written over the course of the third century BCE. The original Persian understanding of the term is employed in Dan. 2.9, for example, where it refers to a decree of the king applicable only once and only to Daniel (Hartman and Di Lella 1978: 13). The later Hellenistic meaning is employed in Daniel 6, however. There, the several references to the *dātā'* of the Persians and the Medes suggest a permanent collection of codified laws. This is not historical since no such law code ever existed anywhere in the Persian Empire (Dandamayev and Lukonin 1989: 116-17). It represents a completely Hellenized understanding of law. Nevertheless, the appearance of the word in Artaxerxes' letter to Ezra confirmed to the biblical author that Ezra brought the torah of Moses to Judah. That phrase 'the torah of Moses' never appears in Artaxerxes' letter, however. (See the next section below on Artaxerxes' letter.)

C. Which Artaxerxes?

The historical order of Ezra and Nehemiah has been a vexing problem since 1890 when Hoonacker first raised the issue (Hoonacker 1890: 151-84, 317-51, 389-400; Rowley 1963: 211-45; Lebram 1987). Comment D of Ezra 4 explains that the Artaxerxes who reigned during the governorship of Nehemiah when Jerusalem's city wall was being built was Artaxerxes I. Therefore the difficulty has been in determining whether the historical Ezra preceded or followed Nehemiah, that is, did he arrive in the seventh year of Artaxerxes I, II, or III, 458 BCE, 398 BCE, or 351 BCE?

According to the biblical text, Ezra enters Jerusalem in the seventh year of a king Artaxerxes. The events told in the book of Ezra last one year, the first day of the first month (Ezra 7.7) until the first day of the first month of the following year (Ezra 10.17). Apparently after a twelve-year pause, about which nothing is said, Nehemiah arrives to build a city wall around Jerusalem (Neh. 2.1). Ezra is not mentioned in the first seven chapters of Nehemiah but appears suddenly in Nehemiah 8 to read the law that he had brought twelve years earlier. Nehemiah, on the other hand, is not mentioned at all in Nehemiah 8, except 8.9, where it is briefly stated that Nehemiah is the governor (lit., tirshata'). Ezra does not appear again until Nehemiah 12, where, in addition to the inclusion of his name among the list of returnees, he is briefly mentioned among those celebrating the wall's dedication (Neh. 12.36b). Outside of these few instances, Ezra and Nehemiah never interact, suggesting that they were not actually contemporaries at all but only placed together by the biblical writer (*pace* Demsky 1994).

Ezra is said to have brought with him exemptions from taxes and corvée labor for the cultic personnel of the temple of Yhwh in Jerusalem (Ezra 7.24). Indeed, temple priests were such a common source of corvée labor that the Persians would build their fabulous gardens, *paradēsū*, near temples just to have a handy source of labor nearby (Dandamayev 1984). If the passage in Ezra 7.24 is historical, then these exemptions would also have included release from corvée labor, a type of release fairly common in the Persian Empire. Cyrus remitted taxes and corvée labor for Babylon when the city opened its gates to him (Cyrus Cylinder, lines 25-26). Gadatas, the governor of Lydia, had exacted tribute and corvée labor from the priests of Apollo, contrary to Darius's wishes (Gadatas letter, lines 19-29; see Fried 2004: 110-16). Evidently Cyrus had promised them exemption from both, and Darius intended for the promise to be kept. Furthermore, the priest of the Carian god, King, at Xanthus in Lycia was granted exemption from public burdens, that is, taxes and corvée labor, by Pixadarus, the last Persian satrap of Caria and Lycia (Xanthus stele, line 11, Greek text; see Fried 2004: 142-43).

Such is the case here as well. If this verse is historic, then these exemptions released the cultic personnel from both taxes and corvée labor (see discussion at Ezra 7.34 and Fried 2015c). Work on city walls is always corvée labor; in fact, Neh. 4.4 refers to the failure of the strength of the *śabbāl,* סַבָּל, a 'gang of workmen at forced, that is, corvée, labor' (*HALOT* I, p. 741). The same term at 1 Kgs 5.29 (ET 5.15) also refers to corvée labor (Cogan 2001: 230). The term is from the Akkadian *sablu,* 'corvée party' (*CAD* S. 4). It is not likely that temple priests would have participated in building the city wall if they had been granted an exemption from such duties only thirteen years before. If Ezra 7.24 is historical, then Ezra must have followed Nehemiah and granted cultic personnel release from such duties only in 398 BCE, the seventh year of Artaxerxes II, or 351 BCE, the seventh year of Artaxerxes III. He could not have arrived before him. Some have objected (namely, D. Fleming and H.G.M.Williamson, personal communications) that Nehemiah states that he secured the willing cooperation of the people and that the wall building was therefore not corvée labor. This is admittedly how Nehemiah portrays the situation, but the reader is not obligated to trust Nehemiah's version as an unbiased portrayal of reality (Clines 1990: 124-64). The reference to the temple chambers of Jehoḥanan grandson of Eliashib (Ezra 10.6) confirms a date in the time of Artaxerxes II, however (Fried 2003a). See note *ad loc.*

Ezra 7.11

The Hebrew Introduction to Artaxerxes' Letter to Ezra

Ezra 7.11 introduces Artaxerxes' letter. Written by the biblical author, the introduction is in Hebrew, whereas the letter itself is in Aramaic. According to the letter's introduction, we have before us a copy of an order that the king gave to Ezra, appointing him to his position in Judah (v. 14). The letter would also have acted as a letter of introduction to the governors of the various provinces through which he traveled as he journeyed from Babylon to Judah. Nehemiah (2.7) requested such a letter in order to guarantee himself safe passage as he traveled from Susa to Jerusalem. Such a letter (*TAD* A 6.9), dated to the end of the fifth century BCE, was found in Egypt. It is a letter from Arsames, the satrap of Egypt, guaranteeing one of his officials safe passage and provisions from the governors of the various provinces that he would traverse in his journey from Susa back to Egypt. The letter authorizes the various governors to dispense rations for him and his companions as well as fodder for the horses at each stop on the way. Without such a letter, travel was impossible.

Admittedly, Artaxerxes' letter as presented here does not do that. It does not state that the various governors should provide rations at each of the rest stops encountered on the way. It does state that the travelers have the permission of the king to travel to Judah from Babylon (v. 13), that the silver and gold and the vessels that they are carrying are sent from the king and his counselors (vv. 15-20), implying that they are not to be confiscated. These statements should guarantee safe passage through the territories. Still, it is not the sort of letter one would expect, and so scholars have debated its authenticity since the time of Wellhausen (1957 [1878]) at least. This is discussed in Comment A below. The letter serves primarily as a letter of introduction to the officials in Beyond-the-River, introducing Ezra to the treasurers in the satrapy (7.21), and to the governors of the various provinces in it (8.36).

Translation

11. *This is a copy of the order[a] that the king Artaxerxes gave to Ezra[b] the priest–scribe,[c] scribe of the words of the commands of Yhwh and his laws concerning Israel:*

Textual Notes

a. **7.11** *Copy of the order.* See textual note at 4.7 above. The words for 'copy' and 'order' are Persian.

b. *That the king Artaxerxes gave to Ezra.* First Esdras 8.8 reads, 'the edict of Artaxerxes, the king, reached Ezra'. The participle used, προσπεσόντος, occurs in official documents to mean 'to reach someone, to fall into someone's hands'. This is not a direct translation but does not imply a different text (Z. Talshir 1999: 256-57). Batten (1913) construes this to mean that the letter was delivered to Ezra, perhaps while he was at the river Ahava (Ezra 8.15).

c. *The priest–scribe, scribe. . . .* First Esdras reads 'the priest and the official reader', ἀναγνώστην, not 'scribe'. Other versions include the word for 'scribe' only once. Greek Ezra reads 'the scribe of the book'.

Notes

7.11 ***Copy of the order.*** That is, the author implies that the following letter was originally a written copy of an oral order. See note on 4.7 above. This verse is written in Hebrew by the biblical writer to introduce Artaxerxes' letter, written in Aramaic.

Ezra the priest–scribe, scribe of. . . Commentators have been perplexed at the repetition of the word 'scribe' here (the repeated word is omitted in all the versions) and have offered numerous paraphrases. Blenkinsopp (1988) translates it as 'Ezra the priest, the scribe, *versed* in matters concerning the commandments. . .'. Williamson (1985) translates, 'Ezra, the priest, the scribe, one *learned in* . . .'. Rudolph (1949) repeats the word but translates the phrase as 'to the priest, the scholar ('Gelehrte'), scholar ('Gelehrte') in the words . . .'. Schwiderski (2000: 353) translates it 'the scribe, the scholar' ('den Schreiber, den Gelehrten'). Pakkala (2004: 32) suggests that the whole second half of this verse (beginning with the repeated 'scribe') is a secondary addition to the original to provide Ezra an additional honor lacking in the first half of the verse. This is not necessary; the insertion of a comma renders the entire sentence, with repeated word, sensible.

Scribe of the words of the commands of Yhwh and his laws concerning Israel. This refers to the torah of Moses (cf. v. 6 above). The biblical author has a written text in mind (Pakkala 2004: 33). By 'scribe' here we mean 'copyist', not 'author' or 'composer'. Wellhausen (1957 [1878]: 407-

10) and Meyer (1965 [1896]: 60-61) argue that Ezra was the author of the Priestly portions of the Pentateuch and the one who compiled the original documents into a single Hexateuch (Genesis to Joshua). This is not what the biblical writer who assigns it all to Moses has in mind (7.6; cf. 3.2; 6.18; Rudolph 1949: 68); so by 'scribe' we should think here of scholar and teacher, as well as copyist. The biblical writer's conception of Ezra's involvement with the text is as described in 7.10, that is, his goal was to inquire of it. The word used for 'to inquire of' in that passage conveys the magical supernatural power of the text. (See above at 7.10, below at 7.12, 14, and at Comment D.)

Gave to Ezra. The king gave this letter to Ezra to carry with him as a letter of introduction to the people he would meet on the way and to the officials in Judah when he arrives to take up his duties.

Ezra 7.12

Salutation

This begins the letter proper and is in Aramaic.

Translation

12. *Artaxerxes, King of Kings, to Ezra, priest, scribe*[a] *of the word*[b] *of the god of heaven. (May it be fulfilled!).*[c] *And now . . . ,*[d]

Textual Notes

a. **7.12** *Scribe.* First Esdras translates as 'reader', as above, so 'reader of the law', not 'writer of the law'.

b. *Word.* This Persian term *dātā'* is translated as νόμος, *nomos,* in Greek Ezra and 1 Esdras, and by the word 'law' in English translations. See note.

c. *May it be fulfilled!* גְּמִיר. Except for Greek Ezra, the versions read some form of שלם, 'greetings!', most likely in an attempt to smooth over a difficult term. (So also Schwiderski 2000: 370). Greek Ezra reads, 'May the word be completed and its answer'.

d. *And now.* First Esdras 8.10 omits this phrase, inserting instead the phrase 'and with benevolence I am deciding'. The Syriac also omits the phrase.

Notes

7.12 ***Artaxerxes.*** For the identity of this king, see Comment B above. The scholarly dispute is between Artaxerxes I and II. This commentary favors the second king of that name who reigned between 405 and 359 BCE. That is, if the letter is genuine, Ezra arrived in Jerusalem after Nehemiah.

King of Kings. This phrase is common to the inscriptions of all the Persian kings, including those of Artaxerxes I and II (Kent 1953).

To Ezra. The form for the word 'to' is -לְ, *l,* a form characteristic of addressees in letters of the Hellenistic and Roman periods, not the Achaemenid (Schwiderski 2000: 362). Thus the letter has at least been updated in the Hellenistic period. This is also seen in the remainder of the verse. (See following note.)

Priest. The word כָּהֲנָא used here is the normal Hebrew word for 'priest', *kōhēn*, with an Aramaic determinative. It is not the Aramaic word for priest, *kūmrā',* כמרא (Hoftijzer and Jongeling 1995; *TAD* D 18.1; 18.2). Rather than indicating that the Hebrew word had become a recognized official title in the Achaemenid chancellery (so Rudolph 1949: 73), the appearance of the Hebrew word suggests instead that this word has been added by the biblical writer and Ezra's identity as priest was not known, or at least not relevant, to the king.

Scribe of the word. The term translated as 'word' here is the Persian term *dātā'*. This Persian word typically was used to refer to the word of the Achaemenid kings and of their god Ahuramazda (Wiesehöfer 2013: 49-50). See Comment B above on Ezra as teacher. The use of the word 'scribe' to imply someone who writes or copies law codes is consistent with the biblical writer's Hellenistic concept of law as a written document, but is not consistent with something that a Persian king would have understood, since there were no written law codes in the Achaemenid Empire. (See Comment B below on the role of law codes.)

Of the god of heaven. The phrase 'god of heaven' was customarily used by Judeans to refer to their god when speaking both among themselves and with non-Judeans. Non-Judeans also used this phrase when referring to Yhwh (see note at Ezra 1.2).

(May it be fulfilled!). Or, Be fulfilled! גְּמִיר The Aramaic word גמיר, from the root גמר, means 'to complete, fulfill'. I suggest that this is an interjection by an early copyist and should not be construed as part of the letter. It is the perfect passive of the pe'il form.

And now. The marker כְּעֶנֶת, 'and now', is typical of Achaemenid period correspondence, disappearing already in the Hellenistic period when it was replaced by ש, *š* in Hebrew, and די, *dy* in Aramaic. This lends credence to the genuineness of at least parts of the letter (Williamson 2008; Schwiderski 2000: 155-64, 250-52). The original form of this first verse, the letter's salutation, was most likely simply 'Artaxerxes, King of Kings, to Ezra the scribe, and now'.

Ezra 7.13-26

The Body of the Letter

Now begins the body of the letter and Artaxerxes' decree. The first part permits any of the people Israel (including the priests and Levites) who wish to travel with Ezra to accompany him to Jerusalem (v. 13). The second part defines Ezra's new role as King's Eye or Ear, the episkopos of Judah and Jerusalem (v. 14). The third section authorizes Ezra and those traveling with him to bring to the temple in Jerusalem the silver and gold that the king has donated to it (vv. 15-20).

Verse 21 begins a second embedded letter. This letter is from King Artaxerxes to all the treasurers in the satrapy Beyond-the-River. It authorizes expenditures from the income of the satrapy to meet Ezra's requests up to a certain amount (vv. 21-23) and releases temple personnel from taxes and corvée labor (v. 24). The final section commands Ezra to appoint judges throughout the satrapy and authorizes punishment of those on whom the judges allocate it (vv. 25-26).

Translation

13. *From me it is decreed*[a] *that any in my kingdom from the people of Israel*[b] *and its priests and Levites who volunteer to go to Jerusalem with you may go.* 14. *Accordingly,*[c] *[you]*[d] *are being sent from before the king and his seven counselors*[e] *to act as the King's Ear*[f] *over Judah and Jerusalem by means of*[g] *the word of your god*[h] *which is in your hand;* 15. *and*[i] *to carry the silver and gold*[j] *that the king and his counselors*[k] *have voluntarily donated*[l] *for the god*[m] *of Israel whose dwelling is in Jerusalem,* 16. *and all the silver and gold that you will find in the whole province of Babylon along with the free-will offerings of the people and the priests, freely offered for the house of their god which is in Jerusalem.*

17. *According to this*[n] *you shall quickly*[o] *acquire with this silver [and gold]*[p] *bulls, rams, and their grain offerings, and their libation offerings*[q] *and you shall offer them on the altar on the house of your god*[r] *which is in Jerusalem.* 18. *Whatever will be good to you and to your colleagues*[s] *to do*

with the rest[t] *of the silver and the gold*[u] *do it*[v] *according to the will of your god.*[w]

19. *The vessels*[x] *that are given to you for the service of the house of your god deliver safely before the god of Jerusalem.*[y] 20. *The rest of the requirements of the house of your god which fall upon you to give,*[z] *give from the treasure house of the king.*

21. *I, Artaxerxes the king, decree to all the treasurers who are in Beyond-the-River*[aa] *that all that Ezra the priest and scribe*[bb] *of the word of the god of heaven*[cc] *will ask of you, you shall quickly do,*[dd] 22. *up to 100 talents of silver, 100 kors of wheat, 100 baths of wine, 100 baths of oil,*[ee] *and salt without counting.*[ff] 23. *All that is commanded by the god of heaven*[gg] *let it be done zealously*[hh] *for the house of the god of heaven*[ii] *lest Wrath come upon the realm of the king and upon his children.*[jj] 24. *We inform all of you that [regarding] all the priests, Levites, singers, gatekeepers, temple servants, and cult officials of this house of God, neither rent, tribute, nor corvée is authorized to impose upon them.*

25. *Now, you, Ezra, according to the wisdom of your god*[kk] *which is in your hand*[ll], *appoint*[mm] *magistrates and judges*[nn] *who may become judges for all the people who are in Beyond-the-River—to all who know the word of your god. Whoever does not know, you [judges and magistrates] will instruct*[oo]. 26. *All who do not obey the word of your god and the word of the king*[pp] *let judgment be quickly executed on him, either for death, or flogging,*[qq] *or fine, or imprisonment.*

Textual Notes

a. **7.13** *From me it is decreed.* The Syriac reads, 'I command and set down the law'.

b. *From the people Israel.* First Esdras reads instead 'from the Judean people', although the translator does not avoid using the term 'Israel' elsewhere (e.g. 8.61 = Ezra 9.1). He also adds 'and others from our kingdom', implying non-Judeans as well.

c. **7.14** *Accordingly.* See note. Greek Ezra and the Syriac omit this phrase. First Esdras inserts an additional phrase: 'as many as consider it, let them go with you'.

d. [*You*]. The expected subject is missing, but the verb, 'being sent', is the masculine singular passive participle, so the 'you' (singular) may be supplied.

e. *Seven counselors.* First Esdras reads 'just as has been decided by me and by the seven friends, counselors'.

f. *To act as King's Ear over.* That is, to act as *m*ᵉ*baqqēr,* inspector, episkopos, over Judah and Jerusalem. See note below. Greek Ezra reads ἐπισκέψασθαι, 'to be the episkopos'. First Esdras also reads ἐπισκέψωνται, 'to act as episkopos', but in the third-person plural, 'that they may act as episkopos', referring strangely to Ezra and everyone who goes with him.

g. *By means of.* The single preposition ב, *b,* while usually translated as 'in', is also used to indicate the dative case, so one may translate with Greek Ezra as 'through', or 'by means of'. First Esdras uses ἀκολούθως, 'in accordance with', 'in conformity with', which is an interpretation.

h. *Word of your god.* This term (*dātā'*) is customarily translated as 'law'. See note below.

i. *And.* Greek Ezra inserts 'and for the house of the Lord'.

j. *Silver and gold.* First Esdras reads 'gifts' here but below reads 'gold and silver'.

k. *King and his counselors.* First Esdras reads 'which I and my friends', indicating a switch to first person.

l. *Voluntarily donated.* First Esdras reads 'volunteered' in the first-person singular.

m. **7.15** *God.* First Esdras reads 'Lord' as usual to refer to Israel's god.

n. **7.17** *According to this.* כָּל־קֳבֵל דְּנָה. See note at 7.14. Greek Ezra reads 'and for everyone who arrives'. Was there a different *Vorlage?* Or was this phrase unfamiliar to the translator? It is missing in the other versions.

o. *Quickly,* אָסְפַּרְנָא, *'osparnā'*. See textual note at 5.8 above. The word is omitted in 1 Esdras.

p. *Acquire with this silver* [*and gold*]. Gold is omitted, perhaps by accident. Greek Ezra reads 'order, according to this letter', with no mention of either silver or gold. First Esdras reads, 'gather together the gold and the silver for bulls, etc.', suggesting that 'gold' was in the *Vorlage.*

q. *Their grain offerings, and their libation offerings.* Instead of this phrase, 1 Esdras reads 'and what goes with them'.

r. *Your god.* First Esdras reads 'their Lord'.

s. **7.18** *Colleagues.* Literally, 'brothers'.

t. *The rest.* This phrase is omitted in 1 Esdras.

u. *Silver and the gold.* This is transposed to 'gold and silver' in 1 Esdras.

v. *Do it.* This imperative is in the plural in the Hebrew and all the versions, but in the singular in 1 Esdras.

w. *Your god.* Again, this is in the plural 'you' in the Hebrew and all the versions except 1 Esdras, where it is in the singular.

x. **7.19** *The vessels.* First Esdras reads 'the holy vessels of the Lord'.

y. *Deliver safely before the god of Jerusalem.* This whole phrase is missing from 1 Esdras; perhaps it has dropped out by accident (Talshir 2001: 404).

z. **7.20** *Which falls upon you to give.* First Esdras reads 'which you consider necessary'.

aa. **7.21** *Beyond-the-River.* First Esdras reads 'Syria and Phoenicia'.

bb. *Scribe.* First Esdras again has 'reader'.

cc. *Words of the god of heaven.* Again, 'words' (*dātā'*) is translated 'law', νόμος, in all the versions. See note on 7.14. First Esdras reads 'God Most High' instead of 'god of heaven'.

dd. *Quickly do.* First Esdras adds 'for him'.

ee. **7.22** *100 baths of oil.* This dropped out of 1 Esdras, no doubt by accident.

ff. *Salt without counting.* First Esdras reads 'salt in abundance'. This is not the meaning of the Aramaic, which simply means 'not recorded, not given a receipt for'.

gg. **7.23** *All that is commanded by the god of heaven.* First Esdras reads, 'All that which is according to the law of God'.

hh. *Zealously.* This is the Persian loan word אַדְרַזְדָּא, *'adrazda',* from Old Persian **drzdra* (= Avestan *zrasda,* Rosenthal 1995: 63). This word does not occur in later Aramaic.

ii. *God of heaven.* First Esdras reads 'God Most High'.

jj. *Lest Wrath come upon the realm of the king and upon his children.* Greek Ezra reads, 'lest any one make an attack on the house of the god of heaven, lest at any time there shall be wrath against the realm of the king and his sons'. This interprets 'wrath' in two different ways—a physical attack, and as an unspecified 'wrath'.

kk. **7.25** *Your god.* None of the versions include the adjective 'your'; all read 'the wisdom of God'. It is even omitted from the NRSV translation. The versions include the possessive adjective 'your' after god in the second part of the verse however.

ll. *Which is in your hand.* This phrase is missing in 1 Esdras, and Z. Talshir (2001: 408) suggests it was not in the translator's *Vorlage.*

mm. *Appoint.* Interestingly, Rashi, the medieval biblical commentator, interprets this word, מַנִּי, *mennî*, as the comparative 'than', *min.* He translates the verse 'according to the wisdom of your God in your hand, which is greater than all the judges and magistrates of Beyond-the-River'.

nn. *Magistrates and judges.* The first word here is the Hebrew word for 'judge', while the second is the Aramaic. They thus refer to the same office. Greek Ezra translates the first word as γραμματεῖς, scribes, also lawyers, experts in the law, that is, the very title this version applies to Ezra. First Esdras translates the first word as 'judges' but the second as 'jurors', those who actually sit in judgment in Athenian court cases.

oo. *You [judges] will instruct.* The Aramaic verb is in the plural here; only 1 Esdras puts it into the singular. I supply 'judges' as the probable subject of the verb. See note.

pp. **7.26** *Word of your god and the word of the king.* The versions translate 'the *nomos* of your god and the *nomos* of the king', which may not mean 'law' but rather 'command', 'order'.

qq. *Flogging.* Greek Esdras reads simply παιδεία, 'instruction', 'training', 'chastisement', and this is likely the basis for Porten's translation of the word in *TAD* A6.3. First Esdras reads τιμωρία, 'vengeance', 'retribution', or 'punishment'.

Notes

7.13 ***From me it is decreed.*** See note to 4.19 above. This phrase is typical of Aramaic letters from a superior to an inferior.

The people of Israel. See note to 1.3. It is not likely that a genuine letter of Artaxerxes would use or know the word 'Israel', since *Yehud* was the name by which the province was known. Moreover, the 'people Israel' as distinguished from the 'priests and Levites' is a concept familiar to the biblical writer (cf. Ezra 2) but not to a king of Persia. The word used for 'people' here is עַמָּה, *'ammâ* [= *āh*], with a he, *h,* at the end. The he is sometimes used instead of the final aleph to indicate the determined state of the noun, that is, to indicate the word 'the'. In Aramaic a final he can also indicate a masculine singular possessive suffix, 'his', however. If the word 'Israel' is removed as an intrusion by the biblical writer, and if we translate it as 'his people', instead of 'the people', then we would have 'all who wish of any of his people may go', which is more likely, but does not fit easily with the 'with you', since one would want in that case 'with him'.

And its priests and the Levites. This phrase is also an expansion inserted by the biblical author. As noted above (v. 12), it is unlikely that the Persian king or his chancellery would use the Hebrew word *kōhānîm* for 'priests', when the normal Aramaic word for 'priest' would do. Nor is it likely that they would know the term 'Levites', peculiar to the Jerusalem cult. The author of this passage has a strong interest in both priests and Levites, and has inserted these terms in the text of Ezra–Nehemiah at every opportunity (Min 2004: 41-47, see esp. tables 2.1 and 2.2).

Who volunteers. This word does not appear in any of the Aramaic documents from Achaemenid Egypt, and is probably not Aramaic but Hebrew with an Aramaic vocalization. It was likely added by the biblical writer.

It appears then that the entire verse is suspect. It may be that the king's intention was for Ezra to travel alone or with only a few servants, as was typical of the 'King's Ears', very likely Ezra's role. (See following note.)

7.14 ***Accordingly,*** **כָּל־קֳבֵל דִּי,** ***kol qᵒbēl dî.*** This precise phrase does not occur in the imperial Aramaic documents that we have, that is, either in the correspondence from Arsames, satrap of Egypt, to his subordinates, or in the letters from Akhvamazda, satrap of Bactria, to his governor (Shaked, personal communication), so the phrase may be foreign to imperial Aramaic (Janzen 2000: 628). It may have been added later to connect this verse to the previous when the previous verse was added. On the other hand the similar phrase, לקבל, *loqᵒbēl,* 'accordingly', or לקבל זנה, *loqᵒbēl zᵉnâ,* 'according to this', is common in Persian period documents. For example, the following phrase is typical (*TAD* A 6.2:22-23):

> Now, Arsames says thus: 'You, do according to that (לקבל זנה) which the accountants say, as order has been issued'.

The phrase כָּל־קֳבֵל דִּי is frequent in the Aramaic passages in Daniel, dated to at least the third century; so rather than a late addition we may have a simple updating of a Persian period original with the addition of the word *kol,* and the substitution of *dî* for *zî*.

From before the king. This phrase מן קדם, 'from before', 'from the presence of', occurs numerous times in Aramaic inscriptions where an authority is always the object of this prepositional phrase (Hoftijzer and Jongeling 1995: 989). It also occurs frequently in the Aramaic portions of Daniel (seven times), with either God or the king as object (Polaski 2004: 658 n. 34).

His seven counselors. This has become a literary topos, a popular ascription to the Persian monarch by non-Persian writers; see Est. 1.14. According to both Herodotus (3.84) and the Behistun inscription (5.68) there were seven men who cooperated with Darius when he slew Gaumata (Smerdis), and Darius commanded whoever may be king after him to protect the families of those men. Nothing else, no special privileges are mentioned in either text. Herodotus (3.83-87) corroborates the inscription with a story about how these seven helped Darius become king, and relates later (3.118) that those seven could enter unannounced into the king's quarters. Yet, he also tells (3.119) the story of Darius ordering the execution of one of these seven with all his family for treachery, without having to obtain permission or consult with the other six. Some commentators (e.g. Williamson 1985: 101; Blenkinsopp 1988: 148; Gunneweg 1988: 131) have seen in these seven a permanent advisory council to the king, and others (e.g. Godley 1982: 41 n. 2, quoting Est. 1.14) have seen in them a standing body of seven royal judges who serve for life. Neither Herodotus nor anyone else describes a limit to the number of royal judges. These same scholars also cite Xenophon (*Anabasis* 1.6.6) to show that Cyrus the Younger brought 'seven of the noblest Persians among his attendants' when an erstwhile supporter was found to be unfaithful. This does not point to a standing body of seven men, or that these seven first supporters of Darius had any permanent status at all. The number seven is a magic number, selected by Greek authors when the number was not known or irrelevant. There is no mention of them in any document attributed to the Persians themselves. The king was sovereign, and did not share power (Briant 2002: 130-37). This reference to the seven advisors was added by the biblical author to lend putative Persian coloring to the missive.

He is being sent. Literally, 'being sent' in the passive participle, masculine singular. The same phrase appears in Dan. 5.24, where the hand that writes 'is being sent' from God himself. The same construction also occurs in the so-called Passover letter at Elephantine (*TAD* A 4.1:2), where word is 'being sent' from Darius the king to Arsames, satrap of Egypt, a word having royal authority. Parallels have been seen between the Aramaic term *shaliach,* 'the one sent', שליח, and the Mishnaic statement that 'the one being sent by a person is like that person' (*m. Ber.* 5.5; cf. John 13.16; Polaski 2004: 659; Agnew 1986: 83). If so, it implies that the one being sent has permission to act in the role of the sender, so that being sent by Artaxerxes would automatically place Ezra in an official, perhaps even a royal, role. Just as the hand in Daniel 5 acts as God's own hand, so Ezra is being described as standing in, as Artaxerxes' agent, for the king himself. Indeed, this is the role of the so-called 'King's Ear'; he is to be received as the king himself.

To act as the 'King's Ear'. The Aramaic infinitive here, לְבַקָּרָא, *l^ebaqqārā'*, means 'to act as a *m^ebaqqēr*', that is, as an inspector (Steiner 2001).[1] Both Greek versions translate with the verb ἐπισκέπτομαι, which according to Liddell and Scott (definition 5) means 'to hold the office of episkopos' (ἐπίσκοπος), one who 'watches over, as overseer, or guardian, specifically, as the King's Eye'. This was a common office throughout the empire; satrapal and provincial governments were under the constant supervision of the 'ears' and 'eyes' of the king (Xenophon, *Cyrop.* 8.2.10-12; Hirsch 1985: 131-34; Dandamayev 1993). These agents were independent of the satraps and other local authorities and reported any seditious speech or act directly to the king. We may assume that the Judeans in Alexandria who translated the text into the Greek understood the Aramaic term and its role since it functioned in the same way

1. The following section is based on Fried 2014: 12-21.

at contemporary Qumran (Gehman 1972; Thiering 1981). The episkopos was common in the Athenian Empire; these officers were sent out by Athens to inspect subject states on an *ad hoc* basis (Liddell and Scott, ἐπίσκοπος; Steiner 2001; see map of Athenian Empire below, p. 370). They toured the conquered territories to ensure that they continued to function in the interests of the empire (Balcer 1977). Episkopoi had no enforcement capabilities, but exercised their influence through persuasion or, if necessary, by means of the local Athenian garrison commanders and their garrisons posted throughout the empire. According to one decree promulgated in Erythrai, 453/452 BCE, the Episkopoi were to oversee (with the assistance of the Athenian garrison posted there) the selection of 120 Erythraian city-council members, and supervise the investigation into their qualifications for the role. According to a further decree, c. 447 BCE, Episkopoi in the allied states throughout the empire were directed to supervise the collection of the annual tribute to Athens.

The Athenian office of episkopos was based on that of the Achaemenid 'King's Eye' or the 'King's Ear' (Balcer 1977: 255-56). These ubiquitous 'King's Ears' are mentioned in a draft petition (*TAD* A 4.5:9-10) from the Judean garrison on the Nile island of Elephantine dated to c. 410 BCE, the reign of Darius II. The beginning of the letter is missing, so it is not known to whom it is addressed. It reads in part as follows:

> If inquiry be made of the judges, police, or the Ears who have been appointed in the province of Tshetres, then it will be known to our lord according to that which we say.

It can be seen from this that the King's Ears were a fixed part of the investigative apparatus of a province. This was what the historical Ezra was appointed to be.

In the Hebrew of the Damascus Document at Qumran, as in the Aramaic of Artaxerxes' letter, the office was known as the *m*ᵉ*baqqēr,* מבקר (CD 9.16-23; 13.7-19; 14.8-12; 1QS 6.12, 20; Thiering 1981). Like the episkopos, the *m*ᵉ*baqqēr* cross-examined prospective members of the Qumran community (1QS 6.10-11), and those who were admitted had to hand over all their property to him (6.20). A text indicating some of the duties of the office (CD-A XIII 15-20; XIV 8-20; Martínez and Tigchelaar 1997: 595) states:

> And no one should make a purchase or sell anything without informing the *m*ᵉ*baqqēr* of the camp; he shall proceed in consultation, lest they err. And likewise with regard to anyone who marries a woman, it should be with consultation [with the *m*ᵉ*baqqēr*]. And likewise he shall pay attention to anyone who divorces . . .
>
> On his [i.e. the *m*ᵉ*baqqēr's*] authority, the members of the assembly shall enter, each one in his turn, and any matter in connection with any dispute or judgment that any man needs to say to the assembly should be told [first] to the *m*ᵉ*baqqēr*.

According to Xenophon (*Cyrop.* 8.6.13-16), the King's Eye

> makes the circuit of the provinces . . . to help any satrap that may need help, to humble any one that may be growing rebellious, and to adjust matters if any one is careless about seeing the taxes paid or protecting the inhabitants, or to see that the land is kept under cultivation . . . and if he cannot set it right, . . . it is his business to report it to the king. . . .

The 'King's Eye' or the 'King's Ear' worked outside the official apparatus of the governmental bureaucracy, reporting directly to the king. He traveled throughout the empire rarely with soldiers or imperial guards (Balcer 1977: 262). Ezra, the *shaliach,* or emissary, of King Artaxerxes, was sent to Judah to *l^{e}baqqēr,* that is, to function as the *m^{e}baqqēr,* that is, as the Eye and Ear of the king in Judah and Jerusalem. His duties would include those enumerated by Xenophon: humbling any who grew rebellious and seeing to it that taxes were paid, that the land was cultivated (and taxes paid on it), that order was maintained and that the people were protected from brigands. His only authority, however, came from the expectation that he would report what he saw to the king.

This commentary proposes that Ezra followed Nehemiah and arrived in the reign of Artaxerxes II (see note on 7.24, and Comment B below). If so, he arrived in 398 BCE, the seventh year of that king; and as I have suggested elsewhere (Fried 2003a), during the high priesthood of Yoḥanan the priest (410–c. 368 BCE). This is the same high priest who killed his brother Yešua in the temple because the then Persian governor, Bagavahya, favored this brother for the priesthood over him (Josephus, *Ant.* 11.297; Fried 2003a). This murder, and the friction between the high priest and the governor, would certainly have been on Ezra's list of items to investigate.

Over Judah and Jerusalem. The phrase 'and Jerusalem' may have been added by the biblical writer (so Blenkinsopp 2009: 154), although Jerusalem as the capital of the province and the seat of the provincial office would have been the town where Ezra would have been stationed.

By means of the word of your god. The Persian word *dātā',* which I translate here as 'word', is translated as 'law' in every other translation of Ezra. This is not the correct translation of this Persian term, however (see textual note at v. 12 above). It is based on the translation νόμος, *nomos*, of the word *dātā'* in the Greek versions, which in turn is typically rendered by 'law' in English. *Nomos* can also be translated as 'custom', 'convention', 'usage', and this is more appropriate in societies without a written legal code such as the Achaemenid Empire.

What then would have been meant by the phrase 'by means of the *dātā'* of your god'? There are two ways to consider this: one according to how the biblical writer would have interpreted it, and another according to how King Artaxerxes might have intended it in an authentic letter. If the entire letter is a fictitious creation of the biblical writer, then the meaning of the phrase is clear. It refers to the written torah of Moses (see comments at vv. 6 and 10 above). In this understanding, the Achaemenid ruler, Artaxerxes, is sending Ezra to Judah and Jerusalem to determine the extent to which the law of Moses is being obeyed. Indeed, this has been the customary interpretation of the verse. The question had been only whether it was a new law that Ezra composed himself or one with which the people of Judah and Jerusalem were already familiar (Rudolph 1949: 74 *inter alia*). The pseudepigraphical *4 Ezra* shows Ezra dictating from angelic revelation the twenty-four books of the Hebrew Bible plus seventy secret texts, all of which had been lost (Fried 2014: 65-88). Thus, by the Roman period Ezra had earned the title of the 'second Moses' in Judean tradition.

However, if the letter is authentic, or even if this verse alone is authentic, then we are asking an entirely different question, since it is not likely that the holder of the office of King's Ear, a recognized position in the Persian administrative apparatus, would have required a knowledge of Judean law—or indeed of any local law—to perform his task. What then would Artaxerxes have meant by the phrase 'by means of the *dātā'* of your god'? The only way to understand the passage is to examine the Old Persian meaning of the term.

Based on the wide variety of Persian period inscriptions and court cases available (Wiesehöfer 2013; Fried 2014: 11-21; in press b), it must be concluded that the *dātā'* of the king refers to the king's orders and decrees, not to a written law code that did not exist in Achaemenid Iran (Dandamaev and Lukonin 1989: 116-17). The *dātā'* of the king refers to his words, his pronouncements, his *ad hoc* royal decrees and edicts; primarily, however, it refers to justice and the general right order and right action that the god establishes on the king's behalf (Wiesehöfer 2013). The *dātā'* of the god is the right order that Ahuramazda has established. Similarly, the *dātā'* established by Ezra's god also can only refer to right order, justice, fairness, with each person in his proper place as described in the Persian inscriptions. This is what the *dātā'* of Ezra's god refers to—right order, justice, fairness, with each person in his proper place. By his god-given knowledge of right order, justice and fairness, Ezra, like all the other Eyes and Ears of the king, will know whether each person in the province is behaving as the king would wish it.

Which is in your hand. Given the preceding discussion, if the letter is authentic, it should not be assumed that that which Ezra holds in his hands is something physical, a written law code, although this is certainly how the biblical writer understood it (see Nehemiah 8). The expression 'in your hand', however, is used commonly throughout the ancient world to convey the notion of being 'under your control'. In Darius's Behistun inscription we read, 'The lie made [these nine kings] rebellious, . . . afterwards

Ahuramazda put them into my hand; as was my desire, so I did unto them' (DB 4.36). More pertinent perhaps is the following Akkadian example:

> dinam ša ina qatikunu ibaššu šuḫiza
>
> try the case according to the judgment that is in your hands (*CAD* Q 189).

A judgment cannot exist literally in the hands of the judges, but does exist in their minds and hearts. This is similar to the command to 'try the case according to your best judgment'. Accordingly we may translate Ezra 7.14 as:

> You are being sent to serve as King's Ear in Judah and Jerusalem by means \of the god-given knowledge of right action that you possess.

This command does not restrict Ezra's activity as episkopos, that is, as the King's Eye. He is not to go about determining if the inhabitants were following Mosaic law, or even if the cult of Yhwh was conducted properly. None of this would have been in the interest of the king. Assuming a historic letter from Artaxerxes, then Ezra was to help any governor in the satrapy Beyond-the-River that needed help, to humble anyone that may be growing rebellious, to adjust matters if anyone in charge was careless about seeing that the taxes were paid or was lax about protecting the inhabitants; then, if he could not set it right, he was to report back to the king. That was the job of the King's Eye or Ear.

It should be pointed out that both those scholars who accept the legitimacy of the letter (e.g. Meyer 1965 [1896]; Rudolph 1949; Myers 1965; Clines 1984; Williamson 1985; Blenkinsopp 1988) and those who do not (Torrey 1970 [1910]: 157, 261; Gunneweg 1985: 129; Lebram 1987; Grabbe 1998: 143-153; Janzen 2000; Becking 2001; Pakkala 2004; Grätz 2009; Blenkinsopp 2009) assume that the letter's purpose was to legitimize and authorize Mosaic law for Judeans in Beyond-the-River, or at least in Judah, and this is certainly how the biblical writer understood it. This commentary considers this to be the case only if the letter is not authentic. If the letter is an authentic letter from the Achaemenid king Artaxerxes, and not the creation of the biblical writer, then the purpose of the letter was to notify the governors and treasurers of Beyond-the-River of Ezra's appointment as episkopos, as the King's Eye or Ear. (See Comment A for a discussion of the authenticity of the letter.)

7.15 ***And to carry the silver and gold that the king and his counselors have voluntarily donated for the god of Israel whose dwelling is in Jerusalem.*** The use of the Hebrew word 'voluntary' rather than the Aramaic equivalent, as well as the phrase 'god of Israel', leads to the suspicion that this verse was added secondarily, likely by the same biblical writer who added v. 13. It is easy to understand that the biblical writer would not have imagined that the king would send Ezra to Judah empty handed, without gifts for the god who lives there.

7.16a. And all the silver and gold that you will find in the whole province of Babylon. This is a bit farfetched to consider as a genuine component of a letter of Artaxerxes; moreover, it breaks the connection between the gifts of the king (v. 15) and the gifts of the people mentioned in the second half of this verse (v. 16b; Pakkala 2004: 34). The half-verse 16a should be viewed as a late addition to the letter, even later than when v. 15 was added. This suggests a text that was updated not just once, but continually, over long periods of time.

Babylon became a separate satrapy during the reign of Xerxes and was then no longer half of the satrapy of Babylon and Beyond-the-River. As a central satrapy, Babylon was very influential in the Persian administration, supplying numerous high officials to the Achaemenid bureaucracy (Stolper 1984). This use of the label 'province' may have been an attempt by the Judean writer to denigrate the ancient enemy of Judah (so Gunneweg 1985: 132). More likely, it simply signifies a political area with no technical meaning.

7.16b. Along with the voluntary offerings of the people and the priests, offered for the house of their god which is in Jerusalem. This second half of the verse continues directly from v. 15, and belongs to an earlier addition to the letter. The morpheme for 'their' in 'their god' is spelled defectively, and belongs to a Persian period orthography that went out of date in the Hellenistic period (Grabbe 2006). Again the Hebrew word for 'priests' is used.

7.17 ***According to this* כָּל־קֳבֵל דְּנָה.** See note for 'accordingly' at 7.14. According to this decree.

Quickly,* אָסְפַּרְנָא, *'osparnā'. See note for this word at Ezra 5.8. This word is not attested in late Aramaic (Grabbe 2006: 558) and so demands a Persian period stratum for this verse, for related verses, and therefore for the letter as a whole.

Acquire with this silver [and gold]. If the word 'gold' has not simply dropped out by accident, then this verse could also be translated 'purchase with this money', for the verb *qny* means both 'acquire' and 'purchase', and the noun *ksp* came to mean both 'money' and 'silver'. Very early on, silver became the medium of exchange against which other prices were measured. Diaries of Babylonian commodity values survive from 567 BCE, the 37th year of Nebuchadnezzar, to 61 BCE, the last surviving example (Slotsky 1997: 1-5). These record on a monthly basis the purchase value of one shekel of silver in terms of barley, dates, mustard, sesame and wool. In view of the presence of both silver and gold in the following verse, it is likely that the omission is not original. This verse expresses the notion that Ezra and his group did not need to bring sacrificial animals with them, but could purchase them when they arrived.

Their grain offerings and their libation offerings. The reference to their grain and their libation offerings is to the grain and libation offerings that accompany the animal sacrifices. This is stated clearly in 1 Esdras, which substitutes the phrase 'and what goes with them' for the phrase 'their grain and libation offerings'. The orthography of the morpheme 'their' was updated in the Hellenistic period, if the whole phrase was not actually added then to make the offerings consistent with current temple practice. It is not likely that the Persian king would know the practice of the grain or drink offerings, whereas animal sacrifices were ubiquitous throughout the ancient Near East.

And you (sg.) shall offer them on the altar of the house of your (pl.) god which is in Jerusalem. The word for 'your god' is plural and written in the older orthography of the Persian period. First Esdras reads 'their god', which would refer to the people in Babylon who had contributed the funds. That may be the original reading, although the plural 'your' may reflect the 'you and your colleagues' of the following verse.

If the sums collected are to be freely offered to the temple (vv. 15 and 16), Pakkala (2004: 34) questions why their use was to be restricted to the sacrifices. It must be recognized that the sacrifices were the most expensive part of the service and that the offerings that the god did not eat, the god's leftovers, went to feed the entire temple staff and their families. This verse must be considered an addition to the basic letter by the biblical writer who added v. 13 however. It may have been among the first additions to the text, added during the Persian period.

7.18 ***To you and to your brothers.*** The reference in this verse to 'silver and gold' connects this verse to vv. 15 and 16b and thus to v. 13. According to this assumed writer, Ezra's brothers could refer to the priests that accompany him on his trip, or it could simply refer to all his compatriots who accompany him.

The rest of the silver and the gold. The notion that there is some silver and gold left after having purchased the sacrificial animals is odd, since there is no end to the number of animals one could buy (Pakkala 2004: 34). The intent of the initial amount may have been for a special ceremony after a safe arrival in Jerusalem (cf. 8.35; so Williamson 1985: 102).

According to the will of your god. The word used here for 'will' is not Aramaic but Hebrew, confirming that this verse has been added by a Judean writer (Janzen 2000; Shaked, personal communication [2011]). The morpheme 'your' in 'your god' is written defectively (i.e. without a vowel letter), indicating that the addition of this verse was made in the Persian period.

7.19 ***The vessels that are given to you for the service of the house of your god.*** There is no intimation here that these were among the vessels taken during the attack on Jerusalem by Nebuchadnezzar; those were returned under Cyrus. (See comment on the temple vessels at Ezra 1.) According to the text of 1 Esdras, however, the vessels taken by Nebuchadnezzar were not returned by Cyrus but merely set aside by him to be returned later. These were then finally returned by Zerubbabel. The 'your' in 'your god' is singular.

Deliver safely before the god of Jerusalem. There is nothing linguistic in this verse to prevent it being seen as original to a letter from Artaxerxes, except that the word for 'that', *dy,* is a Hellenistic spelling of the Persian period *zy.* The word for 'you' is back in the singular again; only Ezra is addressed.

7.20 ***The rest of the requirements of the house of your god which falls upon you to give, give from the treasure house of the king.*** There is nothing linguistic in this verse that prevents it from being seen as part of an original letter from Artaxerxes. The word 'your' is again in the singular and so addresses only Ezra. Ezra is being given permission from the king to withdraw from the royal treasury in Jerusalem whatever is incumbent upon him to give to the temple. That is, Ezra was going to Jerusalem as a royal official, so if his presence there incurred obligations toward the temple, the king was willing to provide it. He does not offer to pay all the expenses of the temple, but only those expenses that fall upon Ezra to pay. This suggests that the king had in mind a rent or a tithe of some sort, for which Ezra would have been obligated when he arrived (Fried 2003c). We read later (10.6) that Ezra spends a night in the rooms of Yoḥanan, [grand]son of that Eliashib who was the high priest under Nehemiah and who was now the high priest himself (see note at Ezra 10.6). The high priest's chambers in the temple were very likely the grandest in all Jerusalem; and if they had been lent to Ezra for the duration of his stay, it might very well fall upon Ezra to return the honor with a commensurate gift.

7.21 ***I, Artaxerxes the king, decree to all the treasurers who are in Beyond-the-River that . . .*** This begins a new letter directed toward all the treasurers of the provinces in the satrapy of Beyond-the-River (see the Introduction for the boundaries of the satrapy and the provinces included in it; see Steiner 2006 for a discussion of embedded letters in antiquity).

Aramaic inscriptions on mortars, pestles and plates found in the treasury at Persepolis name two men who held the title treasurer (*gnzbr*) in succession, each referred to as the treasurer 'who is in the [satrapy] Arachosia' (*hrḥwty*) (modern Afghanistan), and at least seven other men who held the title sub-treasurer (*'pgnzbr*, transcribing Iranian **upaganzabara*) (Stolper 2000). The inscriptions indicate three or more places characterized as the capital city (*byrt'*) of provinces within the satrapy and which housed the treasury buildings of the provinces. The satrapal treasurers were associated with all three capital cities, while the sub-treasurers were associated with one capital each. These texts imply a regional organization in the satrapies, with a central treasurer for each satrapy, and subtreasurers charged with overseeing the treasury of the provincial capitals within the satrapy. The order of Artaxerxes to 'all the treasurers in

Beyond-the-River' is consistent with this image of many regional centers in the satrapy charged both with disbursals of the king's treasure and with levying and collecting tribute.

The letter to Ezra continues in v. 25, after the interpolation. Ezra's task, as stated there, is to appoint judges for the entire satrapy Beyond-the-River. This will be discussed below *ad loc.*, but for now it must be recognized that these judges were paid, and their allowances would have come from the royal treasuries in each of the provinces of the satrapy in which they were to serve.

Janzen (2000: 627) asserts that the particle דִּי, 'that', which introduces the command of Artaxerxes, is never used to introduce speech in any extrabiblical Persian-period official correspondence. He concludes that this passage cannot be authentic. Yet, we see the same construction in *TAD* A 6.13:4-5:

> כעת ארשם כן אמר אנתם הנדרז עבדו לחתובסתי פקיד ורוהי **זי** עד מנדת בגאי זי ורוהי
> אספרן והדאבגו יהנפק
>
> Now Arsames says thus: You, issue instruction to Ḥatubasti, official of Varuvahya, *that* he release the rent of the domains of Varuvahya quickly and the accrued increment.

This construction is identical to that in our verse except that the older *zy* is used, not *dy*. It is rare in Biblical Hebrew, but does occur in some texts (e.g. Est. 3.4; Job 36.24; 37.20; 1 Chron 21.18; contrast 2 Sam. 24.18). More importantly, it occurs in Persian inscriptions. The Persian word *tya*, 'that', regularly introduces direct and indirect speech (DB 1.32, 52; DNa 38f; DNb 8, 10, 19).

All that Ezra the priest. Here again we have the Hebrew word for priest, *kāhᵃnâ,* albeit with Aramaic pronunciation rather than the normal Aramaic word *kūmrā'.* This passage and the rest of the verse are therefore an addition by the biblical writer.

And scribe of the word of the god of heaven. For the phrase 'the god of heaven' see the note at v. 12 above and at 1.2. It appears to be a way of referring to Yhwh between Judeans and non-Judeans.

Will ask of you (plural), you (singular) shall quickly do. The spelling of the morpheme 'you' here in 'ask of you' has at least been updated in the Hellenistic period, if the whole passage was not supplied then by the biblical writer. The difficulty is that the 'you' in 'you shall do' is in the singular. This verse has become corrupt.

7.22 ***Up to 100 talents of silver, 100 kors of wheat, 100 baths of wine, 100 baths of oil, and salt without counting.*** The amount of silver has seemed impossibly large. It has been suggested that 100 talents would weigh more than three tons! Scholars generally suggest an error in transmission (e.g. Blenkinsopp 1988: 151; Grabbe 1998: 138-141; Clines 1984: 104, Williamson 1985: 103). The amount is considered especially high since the tribute of the entire satrapy Beyond-the-River paid to the king's coffers was only 300 talents (Herodotus, *Hist.* 3.91). Yet, Diodorus Siculus states (16.40.2) that 'Artaxerxes III, readily acceding to the request (of the city of Thebes in Greece), made a gift (to Thebes) of 300 talents of silver'. The amount of 100 talents may not be extraordinary considering the great wealth of the kings of Persia. In fact, the Persian kings hoarded silver, so that one shekel of silver could buy on the average nearly 80 liters of barley (Slotsky 1997: 51).

It has been assumed that the 100 kors of wheat were for the temple's cereal offerings; the 100 baths of wine for its drink offerings; the oil and salt to accompany the temple offerings, as well as the oil for the temple lamp (Williamson 1985: 103). The silver would have been to purchase the animal offerings. If so, these amounts would have supplied the temple for about two years.

There is no mention in vv. 21-22, however, that these items were for the temple. This embedded letter is addressed to all the treasurers in all the provinces of the satrapy, and they would not have been enlisted to support the temple in Jerusalem when they had temples in their own provinces to support. These amounts were more likely to have been sums allocated by the provincial treasurers for the judges and magistrates in the provinces whom Ezra was about to appoint. They are exactly the kinds of items that are listed as payments to officials in the Persepolis Fortification and Treasury Tablets (Cameron 1948; Hallock 1969; 1985). Official receipts of the Achaemenid Empire reveal that officials were most often paid in grain and wine, but were beginning to be paid in silver as well. While not numerous, payment of oil as part of the monthly rations to officials is not unknown (Hallock 1969 : 234, PF 795). The word for oil here in the Artaxerxes rescript, מְשַׁח, *m*ᵉ*šaḥ*, has no cultic connotations. It is simply the normal word for 'oil', 'fat', 'goose fat', 'resin', 'pine wood', any cooking oil, or perfumed oil (Hoftijzer and Jongeling 1995: 699; *TAD* A 4.7:20). Grain, drink and oil were also used in Judah to serve as rations to the Sidonians and Tyrians for bringing cedar from Lebanon (Ezra 3.7). The Persepolis Fortification Tablets do not mention salt. Perhaps it was distributed as rations but not counted.

7.23 ***All that is commanded by the god of heaven let it be done zealously for the house of the god of heaven.*** Since there is virtually no limit to the desires of the 'god of heaven' (as interpreted by his priests), this verse is not likely part of an original letter from Artaxerxes. Moreover, it contradicts the concrete limits specified in the previous verse. The previous verse states, moreover, that the treasurers should do all that Ezra asked of them, but now it has been elaborated to include all that the god asks (i.e. all that the priests ask). The word translated here as 'zealously', however, אַדְרַזְדָּא, is from the Old Persian *azrazda*, a word that does not appear in later Aramaic.

The word has the connotation of 'zealous, religiously eager, devoted', and is most often used in references to Ahuramazda (e.g. Yasna 31.1). This suggests that the phrase 'let it be done zealously' is original to the letter.

Lest Wrath come upon the royal kingdom and its sons. The wording here is consistent with Persian thought. Zoroaster did not envision Ahuramazda to be all-powerful. Rather, the god received his power from the devotion and sacrifices of his followers. A Zoroastrian daily prayer can be rendered as follows: 'Arise for me, Lord! By your most holy spirit, O Mazda, take to yourself might through devotion, swiftness through good gift-offerings, potent force through truth, protection through good purpose' (Boyce 1992: 74). Mankind's devotions and offerings help Ahuramazda defeat evil.

Janzen (2000: 629) suggests, however, that the reference to 'wrath' in the passage is unknown in epigraphic Aramaic, but appears frequently in Biblical Hebrew. It is part of Official Aramaic, however, appearing in the story of Ahiqar (*TAD* C 1.1:85) only with the spelling *kṣp,* rather than *qṣp,* as here (Hoftijzer and Jongeling 1995: 532, 1022). The spelling here has been Hebraicized. The hostile 'Wrath' (*Aeshma*), the generic night demon, is central to Zoroastrian thought (Yasna 29.2; 30.6; 48.12; Boyce 1984: 35), as is the verse itself.

The relationship of this passage and of the following verses to 2 Chron. 19.4-11 has been often commented on, for there one reads that Jehoshaphat, king of Judah, appointed judges in all the fortified cities of Judah (2 Chron. 19.5; cf. Ezra 7.25), and that he charges the judges to instruct the people (cf. Ezra 7.25) so that 'wrath' may not come upon them (2 Chron. 19.10; cf. Ezra 7.23). The Chronicler also distinguishes, moreover, between the 'matters of Yhwh' and the 'matters of the king', which many have seen as a parallel to 'the law of your god' and the 'law of the king' in Ezra 7.26. (See more at v. 26 below.) Admittedly, this passage could have been derived from the passage in Chronicles, but it is also possible that the Chronicler used the Artaxerxes letter as a template when he composed his story about Jehoshaphat, a story not in Kings (Frei 1996: 55).

7.24 ***We inform all of you that.*** The 'we' is the royal we, the king. The 'you' is plural and is written in the defective spelling common to the Achaemenid period. It addresses all the royal treasurers of the satrapy Beyond-the-River. We know from the Elephantine papyri (*TAD* A-D) and the Persepolis tablets that each provincial capital had a royal treasury house in which income from taxes was stored (usually in kind, sometimes in silver), and from which monthly rations to provincial employees were paid (Stolper 2000). Scribes attached to the storehouse kept records of receipts and disbursements, and the treasurers at each location levied the taxes and approved the disbursements.

The priests, Levites, singers, gatekeepers, temple servants. The list of these temple personnel would have been added by the biblical writer as a gloss on 'officiants of the house of the god', which follows. The king would not have known these Hebrew titles.

And officiants of the house of the god. This is the normal word in Official Aramaic for one who serves a god. It is applied, for example, to a priest of Osiris on a funeral stele (*TAD* D 20.5).

Neither rent, tribute, nor corvée is authorized to impose upon them. The words used (מִנְדָּה, בְלוֹ, וַהֲלָךְ, *mindâ* or *middâ, b*^{e}*lô,* and *h*^{a}*lāk*) are types of taxes common in the Achaemenid Empire. For a discussion of the terms see note on 4.13 above. The word for 'them' is written in the defective spelling of the Achaemenid period. Once we delete the specific words for the Judean cult officials, there is no linguistic reason for rejecting this verse.

Exemption of temple officials from taxation and tribute was not unusual in the Persian Empire; these were usually given as a *quid pro quo* for services rendered to the Great King. The exemptions to the priests of Apollo in Asia Minor (Fried 2004: 108-19), to the priests of Neith in Egypt (Fried 2004: 63-65), and to the priests of Marduk in Babylon (Fried 2004: 20-24) are other examples. The exemption from the *ilku,* or *h*^{a}*lāk,* tax is an exemption from corvée labor (Lemaire 2007; Fried 2015c). If the letter, or this passage, is historical, then Ezra would necessarily have come to Jerusalem after Nehemiah—in the seventh year of Artaxerxes II (398 BCE). Nehemiah had the priests help build Jerusalem's city wall, thus imposing corvée labor upon them (Neh. 3.1; Heltzer 2008: 78; Lemaire 2007). He could not have done this had Ezra previously given them an exemption.

7.25 ***Now, you, Ezra.*** The name is repeated because of the embedded letter to the treasurers of the provinces of Beyond-the-River that intervened.

According to the wisdom of your god. Much ink has been spilled over this verse. Scholars see it as following upon and expanding v. 14, and assume that the wisdom of Ezra's god refers to the written Mosaic law that Ezra has carried with him from Babylon (e.g. Batten 1913; Rudolph 1949: 74; Kidner 1979: 63; Blenkinsopp 1988: 151). They point to an apparent equating of wisdom with torah in the biblical texts (see Deut. 4.5, 6; Pss. 37.30, 31; 119.98) and assume that that equation is operating here. However, whereas the laws of Yhwh bring wisdom and discernment and provide good instruction, none of these verses implies that torah is wisdom itself (Sanders 2001). The equation of torah with wisdom occurs only in Sir. 24.23, a text from the early-second century BCE, certainly later than when Ezra–Nehemiah was written.

There are again two ways to read this verse. If the letter or even this verse is fictive, composed by the biblical writer, then it would most certainly mean that the Persian Empire has authorized a written torah law in Judah and Jerusalem (Nehemiah 8).

However, if we read the letter as a genuine authorization from the Persian king to Ezra, his new episkopos, then this verse elucidates v. 14, and demonstrates that the wisdom of Ezra's god is indeed the meaning of the 'word' (*dātā'*) of Ezra's god, that they are indeed one and the same. Nevertheless, this does not imply it is embodied in a physical written code. Rather, this intangible wisdom of God is key to achieving right order, justice and fairness, with each person in his proper place (Gunneweg 1985: 137). This is what wisdom and right order are; there is no distinction between them because there was no notion in Persia or anywhere in the ancient Near East of a written law code with prescriptive validity (Dandamayev and Lukonin 1989: 116-17; Wiesehöfer 2013).

Which is in your hand. See the comment at this expression in v. 14 above. The phrase does not refer to a physical object that one holds in one's hand. It simply means 'to possess' the wisdom of God, or divine wisdom.

Appoint magistrates and judges. Literally, judges and judges, the first in the Hebrew and the second in the Aramaic. We should omit the first word as a gloss by the biblical writer.

Who may become judges for all the people who are in Beyond-the-River. This is Ezra's primary task; he was to appoint judges. These are the so-called royal judges (since he was an agent of the king) who were to judge all the people in the satrapy Beyond-the-River, not just Judeans (for the boundaries of the satrapy, see Introduction). These judges would undoubtedly have all been Persian, except perhaps for an occasional Babylonian. Texts from Persian-period Egypt reveal that ethnic Persians took over the judicial systems of all the areas they conquered. Indeed, a passage from a letter from Elephantine cited above reveals how completely Persian the judicial system was in Persian-period Egypt:

> If inquiry be made of the judges, police, and (King's) Ears who are appointed in the province of Tshetres, it would be [known] to our lord in accordance to this which we say (*TAD* A 4.5:9-10).

The word for Ears, literally, 'hearers', is *goškiaya,* from the Old Persian **gaušaka*, and the word for 'police' is *typatya',* from the Old Persian **tipati.* Texts from Elephantine reveal that the judges, police and intelligence officers were all ethnic Persians (plus one Babylonian). (The entire list of Persian official titles including judges and police is listed in Dan. 3.2.) Greek authors report that the Persian kings sent Persians into the conquered countries to serve as judges (Dandamayev and Lukonin 1989: 122). This is confirmed by Babylonian cuneiform tablets, as well as Elamite texts from Persepolis (Dandamayev and Lukonin 1989: 118 n. 12, 122). This was also the situation in Egypt, where every named judge was either Persian or Babylonian. There were no Egyptian judges. Egyptians, Judeans and Arameans in Egypt all appeared before Persian judges. These judges were either royal appointees (judges of the king, *TAD* B 5.1:3) or satrapal appointees (judges of the province, *TAD* A 5.2:4, 7). Indeed, the installation of Persian judges and a Persian court system (in addition to the garrisons of foreign soldiers that enforced the judges' decisions) was the major way in which the king and the satraps enforced their decrees (Fried 2013c; in press a).

It might be claimed that Babylonians and Egyptians gave their children Persian names, and that these were not foreign judges but local, but this was not the case. The Aramaic documents, for example, reveal only two Egyptians who gave their sons Persian names: Bagadāta son of Psamshek (*TAD* B 4.3:24; B 4.4:20) and Bagadāta son of Ḥori (Lozachmeur 1998); one Aramean: Varyzata son of Bethelzabad (*TAD* B 3.9:11); one Babylonian: Bagadata son of Nabukudurri (*TAD* B 2.1:18); and one Judean: Arvaratha son of Yeḥonatan (*TAD* B 4.4:21). Also, if Ostanes is the physical brother of an ʻAnani in Judah (*TAD* A 4.7 and 8:18), then a second Judean had an Iranian name. This is out of tens of thousands of names, strongly implying that those with Persian names were Persian. Moreover, Nabukudurri was a detachment commander at Elephantine, and so may have been Persian himself. It appears that Ezra, as the royal episkopos, was charged by the king with the task of appointing these royal Persian judges for the entire satrapy Beyond-the-River. This is similar to the task of the Athenian episkopos who was sent to Erythrai to 'help' appoint the members of the *boulē,* that city's governing body (Balcer 1977).

Appointing judges throughout the satrapy did not give Ezra 'unlimited power' in the satrapy. He would not have had the power to dismiss them, for example, since once appointed these royal judges served for life unless removed by the king himself.

To all who know the words (dātê) of your god and to all who do not know, you (pl.) will instruct. If we consider the letter fictive, or the verse fictive, then we translate *dātê* as 'laws' and assume that Ezra is to appoint Judean judges who will exact punishment upon those who do not abide by Mosaic law, that is, who eat pork, etc. If so, then the implication is that this was intended to apply only to Judeans. If we consider the letter to be an authentic decree from Artaxerxes, however, then *dātê* needs to be translated as it is translated everywhere throughout the Persian Empire, as 'words', or 'dictates', that is, as *ad hoc* royal decrees with no implication of a written law code and with no cultural or ethnic connotations. There would be no implication in an authentic use of the term that those who know how to behave correctly would only be Judeans who refrain from eating pork. Rather, an authentic usage would refer to all people, Judeans and non-Judeans alike throughout the satrapy, all those who know how to act appropriately in an ordered society.

The subject of the verb switches to the plural here, so it is not Ezra who is addressed or at least not only Ezra. It is most likely the judges whom Ezra will appoint who are meant here. They are to instruct those who have behaved aberrantly, that is, anyone who would appear before them. The 'instruction' would occur by means of the measures listed below. The switch in addressee indicates that this phrase is either secondary or has been disturbed. Moreover, the plural is spelled *plene*, and so has at least been updated in the Hellenistic period. Perhaps there was an original third letter addressed from the king to the judges that Ezra would appoint (as there was a second letter from the king to the satrapal treasurers) that became corrupted when added to the original letter. Or, it could have been a secondary addition by the biblical writer. It coheres very poorly with the rest of the passage.

The thought that the king would allow Ezra to enforce Mosaic law on the whole satrapy of Beyond-the-River has led many scholars to see the letter as a forgery. Batten (1913: 307-308) states, for example:

> It is absolutely out of the question that such enormous powers would be conferred upon a Jewish priest, making him really the supreme authority in the whole Syrian province, with power to impose even the death penalty. . . .
>
> Ezra is here clothed with all of the power of the Persian king in the whole of Syria, yet he was unable to effect a single divorce except by a pathetic appeal to the people.

This common interpretation is incorrect. Ezra himself would not have adjudicated the cases; he had no power himself to impose any penalty whatsoever. These powers were invested only in the Persian judges whom Ezra, as agent of the king, appointed and who served for life. Ezra, as episkopos, acted only as the Eyes or Ears of the king. His power came from his reports to the king.

7.26 ***The word (dātāʾ) of your god and the word (dātāʾ) of the king.*** The pertinent question is how the word (*dātāʾ*) of Ezra's god and the word (*dātāʾ*) of the king were assumed to relate to each other. Were these one and the same? Yes. There can be no doubt but that the Achaemenid kings considered their pronouncements (i.e. the *dātāʾ* of the king) to be guides to 'right actions', and identical with the pronouncements of any god, even a foreign god (Wiesehöfer 2013).

We have the names of royal judges who served in the Achaemenid Empire in both Babylon and Egypt, and they were never native—not in Babylon and not in Egypt (Babylonian judges served in Egypt but not in Babylon). We must assume therefore that the royal judges appointed to serve in Judah would not have been native either, but Persian, or Babylonian. These foreign judges would not have known nor would they have cared to know local laws or customs (even if codified); rather, they judged by their own standards of right and wrong (and, of course, also according to the desires of the one who submitted the largest bribe; see Fried 2001; 2010b).

For death, or flogging, or fine, or imprisonment. The word translated here as 'flogging', שְׁרֹשִׁי, *šᵉrōšî*, has been translated both as 'banishment' and as 'flogging'. If it is assumed to be from the Hebrew root *šrš*, which means 'root', then the word would be translated as 'uprooted', 'banished'. It is more likely from the Avestan word *sraošya*, however, meaning 'strike', or 'beat'. We see it in Aramaic as סרושיתא, *s^erôšîtā'*, in a request from a Persian official in Egypt to Arsames, the satrap of Egypt, that the eight slaves who had run away be flogged. Porten (*TAD* A 6.3:6) translates the word as 'chastise', thus avoiding translating it, but runaway slaves are more likely to be flogged when found than banished or verbally chastised. That Nehemiah in his role as governor of Judah did resort to flogging (Neh. 13.25) lends support to this translation.

All of these are Persian sanctions, indicating again that we are dealing here with a completely Persian judicial system (see Fried 2013c; in press a; in press b).

The letter should end with a statement to the effect that the letter is from Artaxerxes the king to Ezra, with the name of the scribe who wrote the letter and the date. Perhaps the biblical writer omitted it when he incorporated the letter into his narrative.

Comments

A. Is the Letter from Artaxerxes Genuine?

I include here my version of the probable original authentic letter from Artaxerxes. There is nothing in the following verses that prevents them from being viewed as stemming from the Persian king. See further at Comment B below.

Artaxerxes, King of Kings, to Ezra the scribe, now ***14****. [you]are being sent from before the king to act as the King's Ear over Judah by means of the word of your god which is in your hand.* ***19.*** *The vessels that are given to you for the service of the house of your god deliver safely before the god of Jerusalem.* ***20.*** *The rest of the requirements of the house of your god which fall upon you to give, give from the treasure house of the king [which is in Jerusalem].*

21. *I, Artaxerxes the king decree to all the treasurers who are in Beyond-the-River that regarding the cultic officiants of the house of the god [in Jerusalem], neither rent, tribute, nor corvée labor is authorized to impose upon them.*

25. *Now, you, Ezra, according to the wisdom of god which is in your hand, appoint judges who may become judges for all the people who are in Beyond-the-River.* ***26.*** *All who do not obey the words of god and of the king let judgment be quickly executed on him, either for death, or flogging, or fine, or imprisonment.*

[From Artaxerxes, King of Kings, to Ezra the scribe, year seven of the king.]

B. The Role of Law Codes in Antiquity

As discussed above, evidence shows that the Persians installed a completely Persian judicial system throughout all the areas that they conquered, including predominantly ethnic Persian judges, police, and 'Eyes and Ears' of the king (Fried 2001). If so, what laws would these ethnic Persian judges have enforced? The phrase 'the *dātā'* of your god and the *dātā'* of the king' in Artaxerxes' letter (Ezra 7.26) parallels the phrase in the Demotic Chronicle #225: 'the law (*hp*) of Pharaoh and of the temple' (Spiegelberg 1914, col. C, line 11). According to the Demotic Chronicle, Darius ordered the satrap of Egypt to send to him in Susa 'wise individuals from the ranks of warriors, priests, and scribes'. These men were to compile 'the *hp* of Pharaoh, the temples, and the people' applicable in the country at the time of the Persian conquest. While often translated 'law', the basic meaning of the word *hp* is 'customary right', or 'customary observance or act' (Nims 1948: 243-60). Indeed, *hp* most often refers to tradition, right action, the norm (Bontty 1997).

There were, in fact, no written laws in Egypt for Darius to codify. What he likely codified and put into Aramaic was a copy of cadastral land surveys to indicate the borders of the great landed estates of the various institutions for purposes of taxation (Redford 2001: 135-59). Thus, the so-called Demotic Chronicle actually refers to the codification of the procedures, mechanisms and titles of personnel involved in running those Egyptian institutions, such as the temples, that were productive of wealth (Cruz-Uribe 2003: 47-50). These enabled the Persian satrap and the provincial governors to know, for example, who among the temple personnel was responsible for the management of the finances and who would be responsible for each temple's payment of taxes. Achaemenid collection and codification of this type of data are also revealed in the Murašu archives of Babylonia (Kuhrt 1988: 112-38; Kuhrt and Sherwin-White 1987: 69-78; Stolper 1985; Joannès 1990: 173-89).

If there were no written law codes anywhere in the Persian Empire, then how did the judicial system operate? The case of Peteesi in Egypt is typical. His story concerns events from the reign of Psammetichus I through Cambyses, thus under both native Egyptian and Persian judicial systems (Griffith 1909; Vittmann 1994, 1998). Peteesi was a priest at the Temple of Amun at Teuzoi (El-Hîbeh) under Darius I. According to Peteesi's petition, every wrong done his family (and there were many over the years) necessitated a trip down river to plead his case to the district governor. The governor heard both sides and meted out his decision; he never cited a law or referred to any royal pronouncement. The literary *Tale of the Eloquent Peasant* also illustrates the Egyptian judicial system (Shupak 1992: 1-18). A peasant, wronged, took his case to the district head who personally adjudicated it. No law is cited. Nor was there a trained judiciary. The pharaoh or his agents judged or appointed others to do so on an *ad hoc* basis; litigants argued their own cases. These procedures continued under the Persians (Allam 1972: 245-47). As there were no professional judges, there was no professional law school. District officials judged according to their own ideas of fairness and right.

The Egyptian legal system differed little from that of the ancient Near East, even though law collections were common there.[2] These collections proclaimed the rulers' concern 'to make justice prevail in the land, to abolish the wicked and the evil, to prevent the strong from oppressing the weak' (Roth 1997: 13-22, 77). Inscribed on stelae set up in temples or in marketplaces, or buried as foundation deposits in temple walls, these law collections demonstrated the ruler's concern to establish truth and justice in the land. The Code of Hammurabi (c. 1750) is an oft-cited example, but only one of many such lists (Westbrook 1985: 247-64). These collections date as far back as the reign of Ur-Namma (c. 2100 BCE) and continued into the Neo-Babylonian period and later (c. 700 BCE). Even while new collections were promulgated, old ones were copied and studied in the scribal schools as much as a thousand years later. Dozens of copies of some collections are still extant.

The term 'law code' to refer to these collections is a misnomer. The goal of modern law codes is to provide a complete and comprehensive list of all the laws and prescriptions that govern a legal jurisdiction. To this end, they are continually revised and updated. The ancient law collections are not codes. They are notoriously incomplete. Whole areas of law are missing; yet, they are not updated. This is because custom was the actual law that governed. 'The lacunas—considerable—in the legislation prove that the juridical rules, necessary for all societal life, can be found only in custom' (Cardasçia 1990: 62-63). Assyriologists who study these texts have noted this. There are no laws directly dealing with arson, treason, theft of livestock, surety, barter, murder, manumission, or sale. These omissions are even more surprising when placed against the tens of thousands of court cases. Problems and conflicts arise that are never mentioned in the codes. Yet, the codes were not updated to account for them.

More importantly, among the thousands of court cases extant, none refers to any passage from these collections, even when the case concerned a subject the collections covered. Moreover, many cases were resolved entirely differently from that suggested by the collections, as if these collections did not exist. One example is the case of the hungry *nadîtu*. This case is often cited as an example of the king's role in creating law. The text in question is a letter (extant in four copies) sent from the king Samsuiluna (1749–1712 BCE) to the judges of Sippar. (Samsuiluna took office immediately after

2. This section is based on Fried 2001.

Hammurabi's death, and so right after the erection in Babylon of the stele of Hammurabi's Code.) The letter is a response to two problems the judges had put before the king. One problem concerns *nadîtu* women cloistered in the temple of Shamash in Sippar without dowry or support. They were forced to depend on the food supplies of the palace. Samsuiluna ordered that henceforth the cloister of Shamash would not admit women without adequate support: 'If a *nadîtum* of Shamash is not taken care of, I ordered not to let her enter the Cloister' (lines 16, 17). This expressly contradicts #180 of Hammurabi's Code.

Lafont states that this text offers 'exceptional testimony about the method whereby law was created'. Previous documents have shown the king acting as judge, but 'no text has hitherto described the concrete method whereby law was created' (Lafont 1994: 97). According to Lafont, 'the king rescinds the lenient rules of the code. From now on, the support of a cloistered *nadîtum* is an exclusive duty of her family, the state refusing to care for them. Therefore, the rescript changes Hammurapian law'. This is also the view of Janssen, who states that 'the letter bears testimony of the origin of new laws' (Janssen 1991: 11). In fact, the letter is no different with respect to the code from the thousands of court cases referred to above. The letter does not refer to the code, and makes a decision as if the code did not exist. Samsuiluna changed the criterion for admitting women to the cloister. This fact is irrelevant to the Code of Hammurabi. The code itself remained unchanged. It continued to be copied as it was for a thousand more years. This letter shows that the king had the power to change long-standing procedures and customs. It also demonstrates the nonresponsiveness of the law codes. The codes were separate from the life of the people.

Indeed, the notion of a written law as binding on judges was not part of the understanding of either Egypt or the ancient Near East. As is often pointed out, there is no Akkadian word for 'law'; and such expressions as 'to observe the law', 'the validity of the law', or even 'convicted according to law # x' never appear (Landsberger 1939: 219-34). The law collections of the ancient Near East were scribal treatises drawn up and published as instances of justice—justice in the abstract. They were intended to reassure the populace that the king was concerned to install justice in the land. This was the view everywhere in the Achaemenid Empire and in the mind of the king.

C. Did Ezra Create Judaism?

Modern biblical scholars have tended to credit Ezra with the creation of Judaism, and some have even claimed that without Ezra's bringing the torah to Jerusalem, Judaism could not have existed.[3] This line of thought goes

3. This section is based on Fried 2015b.

back to Eduard Meyer (1965 [1896]), a late-nineteenth-century historian, and before that to the seventeenth-century scholars Hobbes (1588–1679 CE) and Spinoza (1632–1677 CE), who asserted that Ezra not only brought the torah to Judah but in fact that he had written it. In his influential *Prolegomena to the History of Israel,* Wellhausen maintains that 'the law first became 'canonical only through the influence of Ezra and Nehemiah' (Wellhausen 1957 [1878]: 2). 'Canonical validity was given to the torah by a single public and formal act [described in Nehemiah 8–10], through which it was introduced as the Magna Carta of the Jewish communion'. Following quickly on Wellhausen's heels was Meyer (1965 [1896]), who argues in *Die Entstehung des Judentums* (*The Origin of Judaism)* that Judaism was a creation of the Persian Empire. Without the Persian Empire and Artaxerxes' mandate of torah law, there would have been no Judaism.

Unfortunately, this view persists in modern scholarship. Blum (1984; 1990: 333-60; 2002: 231-77) proposes that the Pentateuch is a combination of two independent epic works (each composed of smaller units), a priestly (PK or Priestly composition) and a Deuteronomic (DK or Deuteronomic composition). These were combined only under Persian influence because under Ezra and the Persians the Pentateuch became the official law code for Jews, especially those Jews in Judah. This assumption is based on a misreading of the Artaxerxes letter in Ezra 7 in which *dātā'* is interpreted as the torah of Moses. Modern scholars regularly repeat this view even when claiming that the letter itself is fictive (!) (e.g. Albertz 2003: 467; Blenkinsopp 1992: 239-42; 2009; Carr 2007: 39-56; Crüsemann 1996: 336; Frei 1996: 8-131; 2001: 5-40; Hagedorn 2007: 56-76; Schmid 2007a). The origin of Judaism cannot be found in Artaxerxes' letter, nor in the fictional story of Ezra's reading the torah of Moses in Nehemiah 8 (Fried 2014: 8-27, 148-70). Scholars must look elsewhere.

Ezra 7.27-28a

Ezra Reacts to his Appointment

The following verses (Ezra 7.27–9.15) begin a first-person account in Hebrew, and many scholars (e.g. Williamson 1985: xxviii-xxxii; Clines 1984: 6-7, 106-107) have dubbed this section 'The Ezra Memoir'. The question is whether the story of Ezra is based on the historical Ezra's memoir, even if reworked, or if it is entirely a fictive construction of the biblical writer. Writing in 1910, Torrey, gives a resounding 'Fiction!' to this question (Torrey 1970 [1910]: 240). He argues that the whole 'Ezra Memoir', from Ezra 7.27 to 10.44, plus the extended story of Ezra in Nehemiah (Neh. 7.70–10.40), was written by the same biblical writer, the language being the same throughout. That is, he contends that both the sections written in the first person (Ezra 7.27–9.15, customarily attributed to Ezra himself), as well as the sections written in the third person (Ezra 10; Nehemiah 8), were all written by the same person. He concludes that this writer could not have been Ezra, and that there was no real Ezra at all. The biblical writer used the first person solely to imitate the authentic first-person memoir of Nehemiah and to lend authenticity to his report.

In a detailed linguistic study, Kapelrud (1944: 95) too finds no differences between the linguistic features of the first-person and third-person texts, and agrees they were all written by the same person. This was obviously not Ezra since Ezra would not refer to himself in the third person. He too concludes that there was no person Ezra. Mowinckel claims that the use of first person as a literary technique has 'seduced' ['verleitet'] the reader into accepting the first-person narrative as Ezra's authentic memoir (Mowinckel 1965: 11; Noth 1987: 187ff.; for a discussion of the effect of person, see Eskenazi 1988: 129-35). Mowinckel (1965: 13) finds reason to accept an actual Ezra behind the text, however. He does not think that a biblical writer, writing in Jerusalem, would know about a river Ahava (Ezra 8.15), or about a cult place called Casiphia nearby where Levites might be found (Ezra 8.17). Mowinckel sees in the first-person account an underlying text that has been added to by a second biblical writer, and concludes that therefore there must have been an underlying source. He attributes this underlying source to Ezra. Evidence for a basic first-person account that has been added to, however, does not prove that this underlying text was written by the historical Ezra, or even that there was an Ezra.

Dor (2006: 13-98) has recently argued for several authors of Ezra 9 and 10 based on the different use of person and on the different vocabularies in the texts. Yet, even she notes a strong connection in terms of similarity of vocabulary between the introduction to the prayer in Ezra 9 (9.1-5) and parts of Ezra 10, in spite of the difference in person used (first person in Ezra 9, and third in Ezra 10). Between the prayer itself and Ezra 10, she finds only a weak connection.

The alternation between first and third persons in literary texts has been studied recently with respect to the narrative in Acts (Campbell 2010: 385-407). The so-called 'we' passages occur in the last half of the book and alternate there with 'he' passages, that is, with a third-person narrative. The presence of the 'we' passages has indicated to traditional readers an eye-witness account. A survey of ancient literature makes clear, however, that the use of first or third person in antiquity differs from our own. Thucydides, who wrote the *History of the Peloponnesian War* in the mid-fifth century BCE, customarily refers to himself, an actor in the events, in the third person (e.g. *Hist.* 1.1.1; 2.70.4; 5.26.1). The use of third person to describe events in which the author himself takes part was intended to lend an air of detachment and of objectivity to the narrative. Thucydides also uses first person to refer to himself when he claims that he has interrogated his sources carefully, has lived through it all, and understands it all (e.g. 1.1.3; 1.20.1; 1.21.1). Thus, the same author makes use of both first and third person to refer to himself depending on his literary goals. Polybius, writing in the second century BCE on the rise of Rome to power, makes use of both first and third persons in the same way that Thucydides does, referring to himself now in first person singular, now in the third person. He also uses first person plural occasionally, most notably in his prayer to the gods for his safe return from Rome (39.8.3-8). Polybius explains the variety of his choices for grammatical person: —'so that we do not offend by . . . continuously mentioning our name, or that we should fall into a boorish rhetorical style without being aware of it by constantly interjecting "of me" or "on account of me"' (36.12.3). Thus, alternation in person was also used to avoid undue repetition.

Given the fact that most scholars find no real linguistic differences between the 'I' and 'he' passages in the narrative of Ezra 7.27–10.44, we may conclude that the choice of person in Ezra (as well as the choice of vocabulary) has to do only with the rhetorical goals of the writer and cannot help us to determine if there was or was not such a historical person who is being described. Third person was used in contemporary literature to indicate objectivity, while first person was used to indicate personal integrity and trustworthiness. These characteristics are seen in the Ezra narrative. The first-person singular account in 7.27–9.5 indicates not only Ezra's personal integrity, trustworthiness and personal involvement in the affairs he describes, but it also lends historicity and an aura of reliability to the narrative. The author then, like Polybius, switches from first person singular to first person plural in his prayer (Ezra 9.6-15) in order to convey solidarity and identification with his people. The account in Ezra 10 of the mass divorce of mixed marriages is described in the third person, distancing the main character, that is, Ezra, from the events described, while conveying objectivity and detachment. Ezra's detachment is emphasized further in that the impulse for the mass divorce is put in the mouth of Shecaniah ben Jehiel, and not of Ezra himself. The unity of style across the 'I' and 'he' passages makes it possible, therefore, that one person wrote both, referring to Ezra now in first person and now in third. The fact that the 'we' passages in Acts do not cohere with Paul's actual letters reminds us, however, that the use of first person is a rhetorical strategy and does not necessarily indicate the historicity of the protagonist or an authentic memoir. Nor does it indicate the opposite, as Thucydides' histories reveal.

Translation

27. *Blessed*[a] *be Yhwh*[b] *the god of my fathers*[c] *who put something like this in the heart of the king to glorify the house of Yhwh*[d] *which is in Jerusalem* 28a. *and who extended kindness upon me*[e] *before the king*[f] *and his advisors,*[g] *and before all the mighty commanders*[h] *of the king.*

Textual Notes

a. **7.27** *Blessed be Yhwh.* The Vulgate to 1 Esdras introduces the passage with '*et dixit Ezras scriba'*, 'and Ezra the scribe said'.

b. *Yhwh.* First Esdras reads 'the Lord alone'.

c. *The god of my fathers.* First Esdras omits this phrase.

d. *The house of Yhwh.* First Esdras reads simply 'his house'. Since Yhwh is the subject of the verb, the 'his' must refer to Yhwh's own house.

e. *Who extended kindness.* The word for kindness is חסד, *ḥesed*, variously translated as 'steadfast love', 'loyalty', 'covenant loyalty'. First Esdras paraphrases with 'he honored me'.

f. *Before the king.* Greek Ezra reads 'in the eyes of the king', an interpretation.

g. *Advisors.* This word is missing in the Syriac. First Esdras adds 'and all his friends'.

h. *The mighty ministers.* First Esdras reads μεγιστάνων, literally, 'great ones'. This was a common title in Ptolemaic Egypt for friends of the king (Harvey 2011: 181).

Notes

7.27 ***Blessed be Yhwh.*** Ezra thanks Yhwh, not the king. We have moved back into Hebrew after the Aramaic of the letter. The reader is not told who is speaking, or what king is referred to. Neither this verse nor the following can be understood without the preceding letter. Only the Latin Vulgate translation of 1 Esdras perceives a difficulty and prefaces the phrase with 'and Ezra the scribe said'. If there was an original first-person account that the biblical author incorporated into his narrative, it could not have begun this way. These verses were included in the story by the biblical author who inserted Artaxerxes' letter in order to connect the letter to the story of Ezra.

Who put something like this in the heart of the king to glorify the house of Yhwh. Nothing in Artaxerxes' letter indicates a desire to glorify the temple, except the gifts that the king gives for Ezra to take there, so this must be what is referred to. There is no mention of Ezra's being appointed to run a check on the community. This phrase mimics Neh. 2.12 and 7.5.

7.28a ***Before the king and his advisors, and before all the ministers of the king, the warriors.*** The advisors are Artaxerxes' advisors that are mentioned in the letter (vv. 14 and 15). As discussed above (*ad loc.*), reference to the king's advisors is not likely original, suggesting that this verse too was written by the biblical author. The Hebrew *gibbōrîm* for 'warriors' is used to describe David's mighty warriors (e.g. 1 Chron. 11.11).

Ezra 7.28b–8.14

Those Who Went Up with Ezra

This list purports to be a list of those who went up with Ezra, but is basically a repeat of those who went up at the beginning (Ezra 2; Nehemiah 7). It is not a new list. Ezra the episkopos would have gone up to Jerusalem with only a few others to accompany him, as was usual for this office.

Translation

7.28b. *I took courage because the hand of Yhwh my god was upon me and I gathered some among Israel leaders*[a] *to go up with me.* 8.1. *These are the heads of their fathers [houses]*[b] *and the genealogy*[c] *of those going up with me from Babylon*[d] *in the reign of Artaxerxes, the king*[e]*:*

2. *Of the sons of Phinehas—Gershom; of the sons of Itamar—Daniel;*[f] *of the sons of David—Hattush.*

3. *Of the sons of Shecaniah . . .*[g] *of the sons of Parosh*[h]*, Zecharia, with him were registered*[i] *to Zecharia 150.*

4. *Of the sons of Paḥath-Moab*[j] *—Eliehoenai*[k] *son of Zerachiah, and with him 200 men.* 5. *Of the sons [of Zattu]*[l] *Shecaniah*[m] *son of Jahaziel, and with him 300 men.*

6. *Of the sons of Adin,*[n] *Ebed son of Jonathan, and with him fifty men.*[o]

7. *Of the sons of Elam,*[p] *Jeshaiah son of 'Athaliah,*[q] *and with him seventy men.*

8. *Of the sons of Shephatiah,*[r] *Zebadiah*[s] *son of Michael, and with him eighty*[t] *men.*

9. *Of the sons of Joab*[u]*, Obadiah son of Jehiel,*[v] *and with him 218*[w] *men.*

10. *Of the sons of [Bani],*[x] *Shelomith son of Josiphia and with him 160*[y] *men.*

11. *Of the sons of Bebai,*[z] *Zecharia son of Bebai, and with him twenty-eight men.*

12. *Of the sons of Azgad,*[aa] *Johanan son of*[bb] *Hakkatan*[cc] *and with him 110 men.*

13. *And the last of the sons of Adonikam,*[dd] *and these are their names: Eliphelet, Jeiel, and Shemaiah, and with them sixty*[ee] *men.*

14. *And of the sons of Bigvai,*[ff] *Uthai and Zaccur,*[gg] *and with them seventy men.*

Textual Notes

a. **7.28** *Leaders.* Literally, 'heads'.

b. **8.1** *Heads of their fathers'* [*houses*]. See note to 1.5. Greek Ezra adds a second explanatory 'their leaders', which seems to have been in the *Vorlage* to 1 Esdras as well, but which translates it as 'their divisions'. The Syriac reads, 'These are the names of the heads of their fathers'.

c. *The genealogy.* Greek Ezra and 1 Esdras add 'their leaders'.

d. *From Babylon.* This phrase appears confusingly at the end of the verse in the Hebrew, reading 'the king from Babylon'. Greek Ezra and the Vulgate translate it literally. First Esdras changes to the more appropriate word order.

e. *The king.* Greek Ezra reads 'king of kings'.

f. **8.2** *Daniel.* First Esdras reads 'Gamelos', perhaps reflecting Gamliel.

g. **8.3** *The sons of Shecaniah . . .* First Esdras reads 'the son of Shecaniah', in the singular, which may further define Hattush (Talshir 2001: 412). This is probably the correct reading, so that Parosh begins the list of laypeople. Otherwise, the sons of Shecaniah are missing.

h. *Parosh.* Parosh is the first family listed here, and also first in the list in Ezra 2 (Nehemiah 7).

i. *Were registered.* Greek Ezra reads 'and with him a company'. The Vulgate reads 'with him the number of men, 150'.

j. **8.4** *Paḥath Moab.* The Syriac reads 'governor of Moab', which is a literal translation. This family is second in this list but third in the list in Ezra 2 (Nehemiah 7). The family of Araḥ is listed between Shephatiah and Paḥath-Moab in Ezra 2 (Nehemiah 7).

k. *Eliehoenai.* The Syriac splits it into two names.

l. **8.5** Of the sons [of Zattu]. This is present in Greek Ezra and 1 Esdras and should be added here. If so, this family is listed third here, and sixth in Ezra 2 (Nehemiah 7).

m. *Shecaniah.* Syriac reads 'Shecaniah son of Gido son of Jahaziel'.

n. **8.6** *Adin.* The family of Adin is listed fourth here, but in Ezra 2 (Nehemiah 7) it is listed thirteenth.

o. *Fifty men.* First Esdras reads '250 men'.

p. **8.7** Elam. The family of Elam is listed fifth here, and also fifth in Ezra 2 (Nehemiah 7).

q. *Athaliah.* First Esdras reads 'Gotholiou', but likely the ע with which 'Athaliah begins is guttural, and so the G should also be read as a guttural. Syriac reads 'Nataniah'.

r. **8.8** *Shephatiah.* The family of Shephatiah is listed sixth here, but second in Ezra 2 and Nehemiah 7.

s. *Zebadiah.* First Esdras reads 'Zarias'. The Syriac reads 'Zecharia'.

t. *Eighty.* First Esdras reads 'seventy'.

u. **8.9** *Joab.* The family of Joab is listed seventh here, but in Ezra 2 (Nehemiah 7) this family is listed as part of the family of Paḥath-Moab.

v. *Jeḥiel.* First Esdras reads 'Jezelus'.

w. *218.* First Esdras reads '212'.

x. **8.10**. *Of the sons of* [*Bani*]. Both Greek Ezra and 1 Esdras read 'of the sons of Bani, son of Shelomith', and this should be added here as well. If so, the family of Bani is listed eighth here, and eighth in Ezra 2. Nehemiah 7 reads the family of Binnui.

y. *160.* The Syriac reads '260'.

z. **8.11** *Bebai.* The family of Bebai is listed ninth here and in Ezra 2 (Nehemiah 7).

aa. **8.12** *Azgad.* The family of Azgad is listed tenth here and in Ezra 2 (Nehemiah 7).

bb. *Son of.* First Esdras reads Ioanes Akatan, reflecting perhaps 'Johanan the small one'.

cc. *Hakkatan,* or 'the small one'. Syriac reads 'Zechariah'.

dd. **8.13** *Adonikom.* The family of Adonikam is listed eleventh here and in Ezra 2 (Nehemiah 7).

ee. *Sixty.* First Esdras reads 'seventy'.

ff. **8.14** *Bigvai.* The family of Bigvai is listed twelfth here and twelfth in Ezra 2 (Nehemiah 7).

gg. *Zaccur.* This is what is read, the *qere.* Zabud is actually written, the *kethib.* First Esdras reads 'Uthai son of Istalcurus'.

Notes

7.28b *Then I took courage.* Pakkala (2004: 54) proposes this verse as the beginning of the Ezra story, but as he himself points out, since we do not know who is speaking, the verse depends on the verses preceding the letter, that is, Ezra 7.1-10. He draws our attention to the opening verses of the apocryphal book of Tobit:

> This book tells the story of Tobit son of Tobiel son of Hananiel son of Aduel son of Gabael son of Raphael son of Raguel of the descendants of Asiel, of the tribe of Naphtali, [2] who in the days of King Shalmaneser of the Assyrians was taken into captivity from Thisbe, which is to the south of Kedesh Naphtali in Upper Galilee, above Asher toward the west, and north of Phogor.
>
> [3] I, Tobit, walked in the ways of truth and righteousness all the days of my life. I performed many acts of charity for my kindred and my people who had gone with me in exile to Nineveh in the land of the Assyrians (Tob. 1.1-3).

The book begins in the third person by introducing Tobit, the main character. It provides his genealogy, his tribal affiliation, and tells how he came to be in Nineveh. It then continues with Tobit speaking in the first person. This is what we have in Ezra, omitting the letter. An Aramaic version of Tobit was found at Qumran among the Dead Sea Scrolls and is usually dated to between 300 and 170 BCE, the probable time or a little after the time of the composition of Ezra–Nehemiah. In spite of the use of various voices and the mixture of third and first person, scholars have concluded that the entire story of Tobit was written by one author (Moore 1996: 21-2; Fitzmyer 2003: 42-45). The fictional book of Tobit reminds us that a first-person account does not guarantee a historic text. The fact that the Ezra in the Ezra story has little in common with the Ezra of the letter, however, that he is not described as investigating Judah or appointing judges, supports the independent character of both the Ezra story and of the letter, and increases the likelihood that the story pre-existed its incorporation into the biblical narrative.

As the hand of Yhwh my god was upon me. See note at Ezra 7.6 above.

I gathered among Israel. The people Israel living in Babylon. See note at 1.3 above.

Leaders. The word is literally 'heads'. Although the word is not in construct, and although the word 'heads' meaning 'leaders' or 'chiefs' is common throughout the Hebrew Bible (e.g. Exod. 18.25; Deut. 1.15), it is likely that it refers here to the 'heads of fathers' houses' of the following verses. This entire section is based on the list in Ezra 2 (= Nehemiah 7) and is not part of an original Ezra story. The list of names is an expansion of Ezra 7.7, which foreshadows and summarizes it.

8.1 ***Heads of their fathers [houses].*** See comment at 1.5.

And the genealogy. Since no genealogy is actually given, it is probably better to read 'and their companies' with 1 Esdras.

In the reign of Artaxerxes, the king. These words show that this phrase, and perhaps this whole section, was not composed in connection with Ezra 7, or the date would be superfluous. The verse reads literally, 'these are the heads of fathers' [houses] and their genealogy who went up with me in the reign of Artaxerxes the king from Babylon' suggesting that the phrase 'in the reign of Artaxerxes the king' was inserted secondarily and awkwardly since it cannot be that Artaxerxes would be called the 'king from Babylon' (Batten 1913: 318). The thread of the narrative that ends in 7.28a is picked up again with a resumptive repetition only in 8.15. The list of those going up with Ezra and the introduction to it were likely added to the Ezra story by a late author who inserted 7.7 and the story of the search for the Levites (8.15-20).

8.2 ***Of the sons of Phinehas—Gershom; of the sons of Itamar—Daniel.*** Because they are listed before even Hattush, the son of David, it is assumed that the Phinehas mentioned here is descended from the Phinehas who was the son of Eleazar the son of Aaron, and that the Itamar mentioned is descended from Aaron's other son who lived to have children. If so, Phinehas and Itamar represent the priesthood. This is not assumed by the translator of 1 Esdras. (See textual note at 8.15 below.) If these are indeed priests, then in contrast to the list in Ezra 2 (Nehemiah 7) the priests are listed first.

Of the sons of David—Hattush. After the priests comes Hattush of the royal line. This shows the attitude of this author who views the priesthood as more important than the line of David. The recognition that Hattush is of the line of David conflicts noticeably with the reluctance of the author of Ezra 1–6 to state that Zerubbabel was also of the line of David.

3. ***Of the sons of Shecaniah . . . of the sons of Parosh . . . 14. And of the sons of Bigvai, Uthai and Zaccur, and with them seventy men.*** The author of this list is keen to present twelve families of laypeople preceded first by sons of the two high-priestly families, and then by the scion of David. As discussed above and in the textual notes, the list of names of the laity here is nearly identical to that of the list in Ezra 2 (Nehemiah 7). Two family names are missing here that are in that list, Arah and Zaccai. These may have been omitted by accident, or they may have been omitted so that only twelve lay families are included. The absence of Levites, singers, gatekeepers and temple servants must be considered a purposeful omission on the part of the author to enable Ezra to search for them in Casiphia (Ezra 8.17) and so prove how concerned he was for the cult and for the appropriate personnel to carry the vessels to be dedicated to the temple. Indeed, the entire purpose of the list may have been just that—to allow the search for the Levites.

Ezra 8.15-35

Ezra Brings Gifts to Jerusalem and Reports Back to the King

The journey from Babylon to Jerusalem was arduous and long, over 1,000 km. (some estimate 1,400–1,500 km.; e.g., Rudolph 1949: 84), described here as taking four months. Before embarking on the trip, Ezra needs to make sure that there will be Levites accompanying him to transport the vessels that will be dedicated to the temple on their arrival (see comment on the Levites below). Ezra also proclaims a fast to petition the good graces of God for safety on the trip. As Gunneweg remarks (1985: 152), the description of the preparations for the trip takes up more room in the account than any description of the trip itself. In fact, of the trip itself, nothing is said. We are not told how they traveled, whether on foot or by wagons, whether they brought food or intended to obtain it on the way. We are not given their itinerary; we are not told of the adventures they had, the battles they fought (8.31), sights they saw, the people they met, the stories they heard. This part of the journey was not considered relevant. All that was relevant is the fact that the gifts from the king, especially the sacred vessels, were safely delivered to the temple upon their arrival. It seems, therefore, that the chapter is based on Ezra's historical report to the king stating only that he had arrived safely and that the king's gifts for the temple had also arrived safely and were counted out to the appropriate officials in Jerusalem. (See Comment C below.) We may suppose, moreover, that as episkopos he would have traveled with only a few people; they would have ridden on horseback, and the trip would have been much shorter than the four months assumed by the biblical writer (Ezra 7.8).

Translation

15. *I gathered them to the river that runs to Ahava*[a] *and we camped there three days. I noticed the people and the priests, but of the sons of Levi,*[b] *I did not find any there.* 16. *So I sent for Eliezer, Ariel*[c]*, Shemaiah,*[d] *Elnathan, Jarib, Elnathan, Nathan,*[e] *Zechariah, and Meshullam, leaders,*[f] *and for Joiarib and Elnathan,*[g] *who had discernment.* 17. *I ordered*[h] *them to Iddo,*[i] *the*

head at the place Casiphia,[j] *and I put into their mouths words*[k] *to say to Iddo, [to] his brothers*[l] *[and to] the temple servants at the place Casiphia, to bring us ministers*[m] *for the temple of our god.* 18. *And they brought us,*[n] *because the good*[o] *hand of our god was upon us, a man*[p] *of discernment*[q] *of the sons of Mahli son of Levi son of Israel, namely*[r] *Sherebiah*[s] *with his sons and his kin, eighteen.*[t] 19. *And [they brought]*[u] *Hashabiah*[v] *and with him, Isaiah of the sons of Merari,*[w] *his kin and their sons, twenty.* 20. *And of the temple servants whom David and his commanders*[x] *allotted to serve the Levites, the temple servants were 220, all of them designated by name.*[y]

21. *Then I called there a fast by the river Ahava to humble ourselves*[z] *before God*[aa] *in order to seek from him a direct path*[bb] *for ourselves*[cc] *and our little ones and all our possessions.*[dd] 22. *Because I was embarrassed to ask from the king foot-soldiers and cavalry*[ee] *to help us*[ff] *from enemies on the way because we had said to the king, quote: The hand of our god is over all who seek him for good and his power and his anger are against all who forsake him.*[gg] 23. *We fasted and petitioned our god for all this, and he was moved toward us [by our entreaties].*[hh]

24. *Then I set apart twelve*[ii] *of the commanders of the priests, as well as Sherebiah, and Hashabiah,*[jj] *and with them of their kin—ten*[kk]. 25. *I weighed out for them the silver and the gold and the vessels*[ll]*—the contribution*[mm] *for the house of our god that the king, his advisors, his commanders, and all Israel there had raised.* 26. *I weighed out into their hand:*

Silver—650[nn] *talents*

Silver vessels—100, . . .[oo] *talents*

Gold—100 talents.

27. *Gold bowls—twenty—[worth] about 1,000 darics.*[pp]

Two[qq] *finely polished bronze vessels—as precious as gold.*[rr]

28. *And I said to them, 'You are holy to Yhwh*[ss] *and the vessels are holy, and the silver and the gold is donated voluntarily to Yhwh the god of your fathers.* 29. *Watch over them and keep them until you weigh them out before the officers of the priests and the Levites and the officers of the patriarchal families of Israel in Jerusalem, that is, at the storerooms*[tt] *of the house of Yhwh.'*[uu] 30. *So the priests and Levites accepted the responsibility for*[vv] *the silver, the gold, and the vessels*[ww] *to bring [them]to Jerusalem to the house of our god*[xx].

31. *We started out from the river Ahava*[yy] *on the twelfth of the first month to go to Jerusalem, and the hand of our god*[zz] *was upon us, and he rescued us from the enemy hand*[aaa] *and from ambush*[bbb] *along the way.* 32. *We came to Jerusalem and rested there three days.*

33. *On the fourth day,*[ccc] *the silver, and the gold, and the vessels*[ddd] *were measured*[eee] *out at the house of our god into the hand of the priest Meremoth, son of Uriah, and with him Eleazar son of Phinehas, and with them were Yozabad son of Jeshua and Noadiah*[fff] *son of Binnui,*[ggg] *the Levites* 34. *By* *number and by weight of everything, all the weight was recorded.* 35. *At that time*[hhh] *the exiles,*[iii] *the ones who came up from the captivity, offered to the god of Israel*[jjj] *twelve young bulls for all Israel, 96 rams, 77 young rams,*[kkk] *and twelve male goats for a purgation offering.*[lll] *All this was a burnt offering to Yhwh.* 36. *They gave the king's orders to the satraps as well as to the governors of Beyond-the-River who then praised*[mmm] *the people and the house of the god.*

Textual Notes

a. **8.15** *That runs to Ahava.* In 8.21, 31, the river is called Ahava. First Esdras reads 'the river that is called Theras'.

b. *Of the sons of Levi.* First Esdras reads 'among the sons of the priests and of the Levites'. The status of Phinehas and Itamar as priests is not stated in the text, but is assumed.

c. **8.16** *Ariel.* First Esdras reads 'Idouel', confusing r, ר, for d, ד, a common confusion. Syriac reads 'Arani'.

d. *Shemaiah.* First Esdras inserts Maasmas before Shemaiah.

e. *Elnathan, Nathan.* The Vulgate reads 'the elders Elnathan and Nathan'.

f. *Leaders.* Literally, 'heads'. The use of this word is the same as in 7.28. First Esdras adds 'and learned'. Greek Ezra reads simply 'men'. Syriac omits 'leaders' here, but adds at the end, 'these all were leaders'.

g. *Joiarib and Elnathan.* This seems to be a variant of Elnathan and Jarib listed earlier, and may not indicate additional men. Perhaps we should read 'especially Elnathan and Joiarib who had discernment'. First Esdras combines all the men into one group and labels them all as 'leading men of understanding'.

h. **8.17** *I ordered them.* This is what the tradition tells us to read, the so-called *qere*. The *kethib*, what is actually written, is 'I sent them out'. First Esdras reads simply, 'I told them to go'.

i. *To Iddo.* The word for 'to' is Aramaic *'al*, not Hebrew *'el*. The Aramaic word for 'to', *'al*, is actually the Hebrew word for 'on', so Greek Ezra translates it with ἐπὶ, the Greek word for 'on'.

j. *Casiphia.* Greek Ezra reads 'leader in silver', since *kesep* is the normal Hebrew word for silver.

k. *I put into their mouths words.* First Esdras reads simply, 'I commanded them to tell Iddo'.

l. *Iddo* [*to*] *his brothers* [*and to*]*the temple servants.* Greek Ezra omits 'Iddo'. All the versions read 'to their brothers', in the plural. Since Iddo is in charge, he is not likely a temple servant; so the text needs emending.

m. *Ministers.* Greek Ezra reads 'singers'.

n. **8.18** *They brought.* Greek Ezra reads, 'they came'.

o. *Good.* First Esdras reads 'mighty', 'powerful'.

p. *A man.* First Esdras reads 'men'.

q. *Discernment.* Probably moral discernment; see note. Greek Ezra transliterates rather than translates as σαχωλ (*sachōl*).

r. *Namely.* The word 'and' is used here. The direct object marker *'et*, to indicate that this is one whom they brought, is missing.

s. *Sherebiah.* Greek Ezra omits the name, reading 'he came at the beginning'.

t. *Eighteen.* The Syriac reads 'twelve'.

u. **8.19**. *And* [*they brought*]. This phrase 'they brought' is not in the text, but the direct object marker *'et* before the name Hashabiah, וְאֶת־חֲשַׁבְיָה, indicates that Hashabiah is the object of 'they brought' in v. 18. See note.

v. *Hashabiah.* First Esdras reads 'Hashabiah and Annunus and his brother Isaiah'.

w. *Merari.* First Esdras reads 'Hananaiah'.

x. **8.20**. *His commanders.* The Syriac omits this phrase.

y. *All of them designated by name.* First Esdras specifies, 'the list of all their names was reported'.

z. **8.21** *To humble ourselves.* First Esdras reads 'a fast for our youths'.

aa. *Before God.* First Esdras and the Vulgate read 'before our Lord'.

bb. *A direct path.* First Esdras reads 'a successful journey'.

cc. *Ourselves.* First Esdras adds 'and those who were with us'.

dd. *Possessions.* First Esdras reads 'our cattle'.

ee. **8.22** *And cavalry.* First Esdras adds 'and an escort'.

ff. *To help us.* First Esdras explains by saying 'to keep us safe'.

gg. *And his power and his anger are against all who forsake him.* First Esdras omits this phrase.

hh. **8.23** *He was moved toward us.* First Esdras explains, 'And we found him merciful'. The Latin reads, 'and our way prospered'.

ii. **8.24** *Twelve.* First Esdras reads 'twelve men'.

jj. *As well as Sherebiah and Hashabiah.* Reading with 1 Esdras. Hebrew Ezra and all the other versions read 'namely Sherebiah, Hashabiah', but these are explicitly said to be Levites, not priests.

kk. *Ten.* First Esdras reads 'ten men'.

ll. **8.25** *Vessels.* First Esdras reads 'holy vessels'.

mm. *The contribution.* First Esdras omits this word.

nn. **8.26** *Six hundred and fifty.* The Syriac reads '150'.

oo. . . . . The number of talents has dropped out. The versions leave out the word 'talents' and just record 100 silver vessels.

pp. **8.27** *Darics.* If a value, then a daric; if a weight, then a drachma. Greek Ezra reads, 'weighing about 1,000 drachmas'.

qq. *Two.* First Esdras reads 'twelve', which may be correct.

rr. *As precious as gold.* First Esdras reads 'that glittered like gold', which may be original.

ss. *Yhwh.* All the versions read 'to the Lord' at both instances.

tt. **8.29** *Storerooms.* A side room of the temple; see 1 Chron. 9.26; Neh. 13.5. The word here is anomalously preceded by the article, even though it is in the construct.

uu. *Yhwh.* The versions read 'our Lord'.

vv. **8.30** *Accepted the responsibility for.* Literally, 'accepted the weight of'. First Esdras omits the term.

ww. *Vessels.* First Esdras adds 'that had been in Jerusalem', meaning that these were the vessels that Nebuchadnezzar had taken. In that version, Cyrus had put them aside, but had not actually sent them. This compensates for the lack of any reference in Ezra 1 to what happened to the vessels.

xx. *Our god.* First Esdras reads 'the Lord'.

yy. **8.31** *The river Ahava.* First Esdras again reads 'the river Theras'.

zz. *The hand of our god.* First Esdras reads 'the mighty hand of our Lord'.

aaa. *The enemy hand.* First Esdras reads 'from every enemy'.

bbb. *From ambush.* First Esdras omits.

ccc. **8.33** *On the fourth day.* Greek Ezra reads, 'and it came to pass, on the fourth day'.

ddd. *Vessels.* First Esdras omits this word.

eee. *Measured out.* Literally, 'weighed out', but the sentence continues in the next verse reading 'by number and by weight'.

fff. *Noadiah.* First Esdras reads 'Moeth'.

ggg. *Binnui.* First Esdras reads 'Sabannos'.

hhh. **8.35** *At that time.* I moved this phrase from the end of the previous verse to the beginning of this one. See note.

iii. *The exiles.* First Esdras omits this phrase; it is redundant.

jjj. *To the god of Israel.* First Esdras reads 'to the Lord'.

kkk. *77 young rams.* First Esdras reads 72, which might be original, as it is divisible by 12.

lll. *Purgation offering.* First Esdras reads 'thank offering', or 'salvation offering'. The Syriac reads 'an offering for forgiveness of sin'. See note on 6.17.

mmm. **8.36** *Praised.* Literally, 'lifted up', נָשָׂא, '*nāśʼā*', 'to lift up', but with a variety of meanings. Both Greek Ezra and 1 Esdras read ἐδόξασαν 'praised', 'honored', 'glorified'.

Notes

8.15 ***I gathered them.*** Literarily, this verse continues directly from Ezra 7.28b. The 'them' here whom Ezra gathered are the leaders referred to in 7.28. The intervening list of names was supplied by a later author based on Ezra 2 or Nehemiah 7. Historically, this verse begins Ezra's report to the king.

The river Ahava. It is not known where this river is; perhaps it is one of the many irrigation canals that run through Babylon. Rudolph suggests it could not have been too far from the city of Babylon (1949: 81).

But of the sons of Levi, I did not find any there. For the role of the Levites in the temple cult, see discussion at Ezra 2.40 above, and the comment below. This whole section regarding the Levites (8.15b-20) is a late insertion by the biblical writer who has made many such insertions of the Levites into the basic text (Pakkala 2004: 59; Min 2004). According to the story, Ezra is keen to include Levites on his trip, but he makes no use of them (see note on vv. 24-25 below).

8.16 ***Eliezer, Ariel, Shemaiah, Elnathan, Jarib, Elnathan, Nathan, Zechariah, and Meshullam, leaders, and for Joiarib and Elnathan who had discernment.*** There is quite a bit of repetition of the names within this verse; it has become garbled in transmission.

Casiphia. The town of Casiphia has been identified with Tel Kašap, which may refer to the Assyrian town Kassappi (Leuchter 2009; Deller 1990). However, this town is located on the Greater Zab River, two kilometers north of where the river empties into the Tigris. It seems awfully far from Babylon, on the Euphrates, if that is indeed where they started from.

Rudolph (1949: 83) asks what sort of place it was that was known to be a gathering place for Levites, whether it was a type of cult place or a school for Levites. Or was it a full-fledged temple to Yhwh (Joong 1996)?

8.17 ***Ministers.*** This is a general term for all those who served at the temple, not only Levites.

8.18 ***They brought to us, because the good hand of our god was upon us, a man of discernment of the sons of Mahli son of Levi son of Israel, namely Sherebiah with his sons and his kin, eighteen.*** The direct object marker to indicate whom 'they brought to us' does not appear in front of Sherebiah, but only Hashabiah in the next verse. This verse may have been inserted by the levitical author to foreshadow his reference to the Levites in Nehemiah 8. Sherebiah is described here as a man of discernment, *śekel*, and in Nehemiah 8 he is listed among the Levites who put discernment, *śekel,* and understanding in the minds of the listeners. He appears prominently in Nehemiah 9 as well as among those who sign the Amanah in Nehemiah 10, but the name does not appear in any of the lists of Levites in Chronicles, nor among the wall builders in Nehemiah 3, nor among any of the texts that might belong to Nehemiah's authentic memoir.

Because the good hand of our god was upon us. Taken perhaps from the Nehemiah memoir, the phrase expresses the relief that indeed Levites would be accompanying them on the trip. This good fortune is attributed to God alone.

Mahli. Mahli is listed as a son of Merari in Exod. 6.19 and 1 Chron. 6.4 [ET 6.19]. It is not clear why the sons of Mahli are listed separately from the sons of Merari, since the sons of Mahli are sons of Merari.

8.19 ***As well as Hashabiah.*** The name Hashabiah is preceded by the direct object marker and so is the original object of the verb 'they brought to us' in v. 18. The name *Sherebiah* and the entire previous verse were added secondarily.

Merari. Merari is listed as a son of Levi in Exod. 6.16; 1 Chron. 6.1 [ET 6.16]). It is their identification as belonging to the sons of Merari that is relevant for the levitical task of carrying the sacred vessels during travel. See comment below on the Levites.

8.*20* ***Temple servants.*** See note to Ezra 2.43.

All of them designated by name. This is the last verse of the insertion.

8.21 ***I called a fast there at the river Ahava.*** This repeats v. 15, closing the parenthesis that marked the long late insertion regarding the search for the Levites. The word 'there' and 'river Ahava' are redundant (Pakkala 2004: 59). 'River Ahava' was added when the insertion was added to make clear what 'there' refers to.

A fast is called in situations of dire threat and extreme emergency. For example, we read the following in the book of Judges when the Benjaminites killed 18,000 armed Israelite men in battle:

> Benjamin moved out against them from Gibeah the second day, and struck down eighteen thousand of the Israelites, all of them armed men.
>
> Then all the Israelites, the whole army, went back to Bethel and wept, sitting there before Yhwh; they fasted that day until evening. Then they offered burnt offerings and sacrifices of well-being before Yhwh (Judg. 20.25-26).

We also read of David fasting to importune God to save the life of his child:

> Yhwh struck the child that Uriah's wife bore to David, and he became very ill. David therefore pleaded with God for the child; David fasted, and went in and lay all night on the ground. The elders of his house stood beside him, urging him to rise from the ground; but he would not, nor did he eat food with them (2 Sam. 12.15-17).

We can imagine therefore the terror that Ezra was experiencing if he has called a fast. He was forced to put his faith in God because he was too embarrassed to ask for an armed escort.

A direct way. Besides the fear of bandits, there was also the fear of getting lost, of wandering around, of having to travel longer than would have been necessary. A straight or direct path is desired so that Yhwh's trip from Babylon to Jerusalem would be hastened

> A voice cries out: 'Prepare Yhwh's way in the wilderness, make straight in the desert a highway for our god' (Isa. 40.3).

Not only Yhwh's return trip from Babylon to Judah would be hastened, but that of his people as well. Recall Psalm 107 with Clines (1984: 111):

> O give thanks to Yhwh, for he is good; for his steadfast love endures forever.
>
> Let Yhwh's redeemed say so, those he redeemed from trouble and gathered in from the lands, from the east and from the west, from the north and from the south.
>
> Some wandered in desert wastes, finding no way to an inhabited town; hungry and thirsty, their soul fainted within them.
>
> Then they cried out to Yhwh in their trouble, and he delivered them from their distress; he led them by a direct way, until they reached an inhabited town (Ps. 107.1-7).

And our little ones. It is not likely that a Persian episkopos would be traveling with small children as that would certainly have impeded his travel. This phrase was likely added by the biblical writer to imitate the trip to Judah described in Ezra 2.

8.22 ***I was embarrassed to ask from the king foot soldiers and cavalry.*** Ezra eschews the king's protection for God's.

The original reason for being too embarrassed to ask for an armed escort may have been that the king was responsible for ensuring that all the roads were safe. Herodotus (5.35; 7.239) and Xenophon (*Anab.* 1.11.13) extol the safety of the roads, and the Persepolis Fortification Tablets confirm that there were very few large parties on the roads, indicating no necessity for armed guards (Tuplin 1987a: 110ff.). Commentators have generally viewed Ezra's rejection of an armed guard as the biblical writer's attempt to outdo Nehemiah's accompaniment of foot soldiers and cavalry on his trip to Jerusalem (Neh. 2.9), but Nehemiah in his role of governor is bringing this force with him to take over the citadel in Jerusalem, he is not bringing them for his personal protection (Fried 2002a).

8.23 ***He was moved toward us [by our entreaties].*** The positive outcome of the journey implies that God was moved by the prayers and the fasting.

8.24 ***I set apart twelve of the commanders of the priests, [as well as] Sherebiah, and Hashabiah, and with them of their kin—ten.*** The phrase 'as well as' is not here. The text actually says, 'commanders of the priests, *namely* Sherebiah and Hashabiah', indicating that originally Sherebiah and Hashabiah were the chief priests, not Levites. The temple vessels were evidently placed into the hands of the twelve priests, not Levites.

[As well as] Sherebiah and Hashabiah. As a result of the insertion regarding the Levites, we must emend the text to make them Levites. Thus now, there are twenty-four leaders, not twelve. Responsibility for all these valuables was placed in the hands of twelve unnamed priestly officials plus twelve Levites headed by Sherebiah and Hashabiah. Perhaps one should imagine a long train of ox-drawn wagons, with these twenty-four in charge of the wagons bearing gifts. The insertion of these names here would have been by the author who inserted v. 18 above. Gunneweg (1985: 154) suggests that if we have no priests' names, then we should not expect names of Levites either. The entire search for Levites at Casiphia, as well as the addition of these names, was the work of an editor with levitical interests and was not part of an original Ezra story (so also Pakkala 2004: 59-63).

8.25 ***I weighed out for them.*** Weighed out and counted out, so that it would be known upon arrival whether any were missing. They would be weighed and counted again at the temple in Jerusalem.

The silver and the gold and the vessels. These large amounts have probably been embellished during the course of transmission.

There is no mention here of a torah scroll. If Ezra were indeed carrying a torah scroll, that too would have been given all the care that the gold and silver were given. The author of the basic Ezra story knows nothing of a torah scroll and is not the author of Ezra 7.1-10 nor of Nehemiah 8. This suggests an independent Ezra story that preceded its incorporation into the book Ezra–Nehemiah.

The king, his advisors, his commanders, and all Israel there had raised. This inclusion of 'advisors, commanders, and all Israel' is an addition by the biblical writer. The king operated alone.

8.27 ***1,000 darics.*** The daric was of solid gold and weighed about 8.3 g. (Briant 2002: 408-409).

And I said to them, 'You are holy to Yhwh'. Ezra uses the name of the god when reporting his conversation to the priests, but otherwise he refrains and says simply 'our god'.

8.29 ***Commanders of the priests and the Levites and the commanders of the patriarchal families of Israel in Jerusalem, that is, at the storerooms of the house of Yhwh.*** This verse was very likely embellished by the biblical writer. It probably originally referred only to 'commanders at the house of Yhwh'. Again, we have Ezra's use of the god's personal name when reporting his conversation with the priests.

8.30 ***The priests and Levites accepted the responsibility.*** That is, they accepted full responsibility for the full weight (and number) of the donations to the temple.

The phrase 'and Levites' is likely another late addition. Pakkala (2004: 62) suggests that this whole section regarding the consignment of the silver, gold, and holy vessels into the hands of the priests (and Levites) was a later addition by the same author who added the story of the search for the Levites. He points out that it breaks the flow of the narrative. They entreated God for a safe journey in v. 23; and then in v. 31, they leave. The point is a theological one. Ezra rejects an armed guard and entrusts the huge amounts of gold and silver to the priests (and Levites) instead. Nevertheless, the king would have given his emissary gifts for the temple at his destination, and it is reasonable to suppose that these sacred vessels would have been placed under the care of priests at least.

To the house of our god. Normally Ezra does not name the god; it is just 'our god'. Only when he reports his direct speech to the priests does he refer to the god's name. See Comment below.

8.31 ***We started out from the river Ahava on the twelfth of the first month.*** According to Ezra 7.9 they began their journey on the first of the first month, Nisan. They had been camping by the river Ahava for three days when Ezra noticed that there were no Levites (8.15). It must have taken the remaining days to go to Casiphia and persuade Levites to join them (8.16-20), and then to weigh out and to load the vessels and the other goods for the trip (8.24-30).

It is very curious, however, that a group under the leadership of Ezra, a 'scribe skilled in the law of Moses', would begin a four-month-long journey two days before the Passover holiday. It may be that the biblical writer assumed the laws of Deuteronomy to be in force, so that the Passover could only be celebrated in Jerusalem (Deut. 16.5-7); or, if Casiphia were indeed a Yahwistic cult place as has been suggested (Joong 1996), Ezra could have celebrated the Passover there. It is more likely, however, that the author of this passage and indeed of the original portions of the chapter did not know about the holiday of Passover. He would have at least mentioned it if he knew of it. The author may have been Ezra himself, the royal episkopos, an Ezra who knew nothing of either the holiday of Passover, or of a torah scroll; but see comment on the Passover below.

He rescued us from the enemy hand and from ambush. It is very disappointing that the author has not chosen to tell us any of these adventures, but they would not have been relevant in a report to the king.

8.32 ***We came to Jerusalem.*** No drama here, just a simple statement. According to Ezra 7.8, 9 they arrived in the fifth month. That is not stated here. This is much too long for an episkopos on horseback. The choice of the fifth month might be the biblical author's way to indicate a reversal of the fall of the temple in the fifth month (2 Kgs 25.8, 9).

And we rested there three days. This seems to be a literary topos. The phrase 'three days' appears sixty-six times in the Hebrew Bible! They camped at Ahava three days (8.15), and Nehemiah too rests three days after his arrival in Jerusalem (2.11). Still, it is not unreasonable.

8.33 ***The silver, and the gold, and the vessels were measured out.*** Finally we read that the vessels holy to Yhwh (v. 28) are deposited in the temple. This may be the verse that is missing from the temple's dedication. We are never told what happened to the vessels that Sheshbazzar brought up from Babylon. Perhaps the present verse was displaced from the story of the temple's dedication to the story of Ezra.

The verse is in the passive voice and does not say 'we measured out'. The consonantal text of the verb (but not its vocalization) נשקל, *nšql,* can be read either way, as a third-person singular perfect passive voice ('it was measured out'), or as a first-person plural imperfect active voice ('we measured out'). Since there is no normal accusative marker to indicate that the words for 'the silver, and the gold, and the vessels' are in the accusative case, the objects of the verb 'we weighed', we must conclude that they are the subjects of the verb, and we must read 'were weighed' as it is vocalized. The fact that the verb is singular even though the subject is a string of objects is not unusual. The author uses the passive to make plain that it was the priests (and Levites) who were in charge of the items when they were weighed out, not Ezra personally.

There is no mention of a torah scroll among the items deposited in the temple. The author of this passage does not know that Ezra was supposed to be bringing one with him. In fact, there is no mention of such a torah scroll in all of Ezra 8–10; the author of the Ezra story does not know Ezra 7.1-10 or Nehemiah 8. This is *prima facie* evidence of an independent Ezra story.

Meremoth, son of Uriah. See note on Hakkoz at 2.61 above.

Meremoth, son of Uriah, and with him Eleazar son of Phinehas, and with them were Yozabad son of Jeshua and Noadiah son of Binnui, the

Levites. The names of those receiving the items are listed so that these may be later contacted if any items have gone astray.

8.34 ***By number and by weight.*** This continues from the previous verse; the silver, gold, and vessels were measured out by number and by weight into the hands of the priests and Levites there to receive them.

8.35 ***At that time the exiles, the ones who had come up from the captivity.*** I moved the phrase 'at that time' from the end of the previous verse to the beginning of this one because the grammar requires that v. 35 be in the pluperfect. The pluperfect is intended to convey the notion that the sacrifices and the celebration were on the occasion of the items having been deposited in the temple.

The statement of the sacrifices seems to mark the end of a section of text, and those who argue that Nehemiah 8 belongs here suggest that this verse either opened or closed that chapter (e.g. Rudolph 1949: 85; Clines 1984: 115; Williamson 1985: 116; Blenkinsopp 1988: 172). See Comment A to Ezra 9.

Bulls for all Israel, 96 rams, 77 (or 72) young rams. These sacrifices and the celebration are in response to the deposit of the sacred vessels in the temple. They thus serve the same function as did the sacrifices in response to the dedication of the temple in Ezra 6. They signify the joy inherent in the fact that proper worship has been restored to the temple. The joy is from the deposit in the temple of the sacred vessels that were 'holy to Yhwh'.

Rudolph (1949: 85) suggests plausibly that this verse may have been added by the biblical writer to suggest that the command in Artaxerxes' letter (7.17) was carried out immediately upon Ezra's arrival. According to the rabbis (*Ter.* 15b; *Hor.* 6a), however, the offerings brought here do not conform to any torah laws about offerings and would not ordinarily have been performed. They conclude that Ezra, as a prophet, could have issued a temporary ruling and permitted these offerings. This verse is likely an addition by the biblical writer and was not part of Ezra's original report to the king.

8.36 ***They gave.*** Ezra sent messengers to the satrap and to each of the vice-satraps and governors in Beyond-the-River to introduce himself to them and to relay the king's orders in his regard. He also sent messengers to each of the satraps he encountered along the way to convey the king's orders to them as well. See below at 'satraps'. This is the last sentence of Ezra's report to the king.

The king's orders. The word translated as 'orders' here is *dātā'*, the same word used in Ezra 7.14, 21, 25 and 26. It simply means 'orders', literally, the king's 'words', and does not refer to any law code, written or otherwise.

Satraps. The Hebrew word here in the plural. The singular is אֲחַשְׁדַּרְפָּן, *'ᵃḥašdarpān*, from the Persian *χšaθrapavan*. The satrap is the head of the satrapy, and in the satrapy of Beyond-the-River there would have been one only satrap. The fact that this word is in the plural suggests that

Ezra gave the king's orders to each of the satraps whose satrapy he crossed on the way to Beyond-the-River as well as to each of the governors in the satrapy in which he was to do his work, that is, the satrapy of Beyond-the-River.

Who then praised the people and the house of the god. The text is not clear on who praised the people, but it may be supposed that the governors are meant. The usual translation 'supported' implies that the governors of the various provinces actually contributed to the upkeep of the Jerusalem temple, which is not likely. The translation offered here is based on the Greek texts. Again, Ezra does not use the name of the god when reporting to the king as it would not have meant anything to him.

Comments

Comment A. Why Levites?

It is clear what the role of the Levites, in particular the sons of Merari, was and why Ezra needed them so badly. They were to be in charge of bringing to Jerusalem the gold and silver and all the vessels that were being dedicated to the temple of Yhwh. This was the traditional role of the sons of Merari as listed in Num. 3.36-37; 10.17:

> The service assigned to the sons of Merari is the frames of the tabernacle, the bars, the pillars, the bases, and all their accessories—all the service pertaining to these; also the pillars of the court all around, with their bases and pegs and cords.
>
> When the tabernacle was taken down, . . . the sons of Merari, who carried the tabernacle, set out.

Thus, they were responsible for taking the tabernacle apart when it traveled, for carrying and guarding its various components during the travel, and for setting it up again once it rested. The other groups of Levites had responsibility for the vessels in preparation for the service itself, but the sons of Merari were specifically designated in charge of the tabernacle and its components during the travel. The author of this section in Ezra could not imagine bringing holy vessels to the temple in Jerusalem without the sons of Merari to carry and guard them during the journey.

It must be noted that there is no reference to the torah of Moses here, no citation of verses in Numbers regarding the role of the Levites, no indication that the sons of Merari were needed in order to conform to what was written in the torah of Moses. The author of this passage follows the prescriptions not only of Numbers but of Ezekiel. He too saw the Levites as a second-order priestly caste (44.10-11). More importantly, perhaps, is that unlike Ezekiel, this author did not feel their presence required justification, or explanation. It was just the way things were supposed to be and needed to be. A written law code was not necessary.

Comment B. The Non-Passover at the River Ahava

Choi (2010: 60-61) begins his discussion of Passover in second temple texts with 2 Chronicles 30. The Passover celebration there is in the context of Hezekiah's cleansing the temple and renewing the cult. As Choi points out, there is no mention of the Exodus or of the people's liberation from Egypt, rather it is a temple rededication ceremony. The Chronicler records how the people celebrated the festival of Matzoth with so much joy and gladness that they added another seven days onto the seven days they already observed (2 Chron. 30.23). In Chronicles, Passover and the festival of Matzoth symbolize a return to the proper worship of Yhwh, to the right people celebrating it, that is, the entire people Israel from both the north and the south, and to the right place—Jerusalem. Moreover, neither in Josiah's celebration of the Passover in 2 Kings 23 nor in that celebration as described in 2 Chronicles 35 is there a mention of the exodus from Egypt. They are both presented in the context of renewal of temple worship. This is also the context of the Passover celebration in Ezra 6; it too is celebrated as part of the rededication of the temple, with no mention of the exodus or of the liberation from Egypt. It marks the beginning of living correctly on the land, in the same way that the Passover celebrated in Josh. 5.10-12 does. This understanding of the Passover holiday as a holiday to celebrate the renewal of correct worship in the land of Israel leaves no room for Ezra to have celebrated it on the banks of the river Ahava or at Casiphia, cult site or no.

Comment C. A Hypothesized Original Report of Ezra

Evidence suggests that there was an original account that was later added to by the biblical writer, an account that knows nothing of a torah scroll or of the traditional understanding of the holiday of Passover as an exodus from Egypt. The proposed reconstruction suggests that the chapter was originally simply Ezra's report to the king that he arrived safely in Jerusalem, that all the gifts that the king had donated to the temple also arrived safely, that they were counted out to the appropriate cultic officials, and that the king's orders regarding Ezra were handed over to the appropriate officials:

To Artaxerxes the king, from your servant Ezra, the King's Ear, and now: I gathered among Israel leaders to go up with me. I gathered them to the river that runs to Ahava and we camped there three days. I called there a fast by the river Ahava to humble ourselves before God in order to seek from him a direct way for ourselves and all our possessions, because I was embarrassed to ask from you foot soldiers and cavalry to help us from enemies. I set apart twelve of the officials of the priests, and I weighed out for them the silver and the gold and the vessels—the contribution for the house of our god that you had raised. And I said to them, 'Watch over them and keep them until you weigh them out before the commanders of the priests at the house of Yhwh'. So the priests accepted the responsibility for the silver, the gold, and the vessels to bring [them]to Jerusalem to the house of our god.

We started out from the river Ahava on the twelfth of the first month to go to Jerusalem, and the hand of our god was upon us and he rescued us from the enemy hand and from ambush along the way. We came to Jerusalem and rested there three days.

On the fourth day the silver, and the gold, and the vessels were measured out at the house of our god into the hand of the priest Meremoth, son of Uriah, and with him Eleazar son of Phinehas, and with them were Yozabad son of Jeshua and Noadiah son of Binnui, the Levites, by number and by weight, of everything, all the weight was recorded. We also gave your orders to the satraps as well as to the governors of Beyond-the-River who praised the people and the house of the god.

To Artaxerxes the king, from your servant Ezra, year 7 of the king.

Ezra 9.1-2

Ezra Begins his Activities in Beyond-the-River

As in the first section of the book of Ezra (Ezra 1–6), Ezra 7–10 also begins with a trip of exiles—priests, Levites, and laypeople—from Babylon to Jerusalem, laden with gifts and valuable items for the temple. Also, as in the first section, upon arrival, the returnees are informed of unexpected difficulties that threaten to overturn their good fortune. Instead of a threat to the temple-building project, however, since the temple has been completed, this time it is a threat to their very existence on the land—their intermarriages.

Ezra has arrived in Jerusalem, and the returnees have celebrated their safe arrival with a 'burnt offering to Yhwh'. Now Ezra begins his real work, the purpose for which he was sent. According to Artaxerxes' letter, Ezra was sent to act as episkopos and in that role to appoint judges for the satrapy. He is never shown doing so, however. Instead, he is shown concerned only with the intermarriages that have taken place between 'the people Israel' and the 'peoples of the lands'. Is this concern and the forced mass divorce that follows historic? If so, was it demanded by the Achaemenid rulers? Or, was it a result of internal Judean pressures, pressures independent of the Persian government? Or, is the whole event fiction, a creation of the biblical writer? But then, if so, why was it written?

It is customarily argued that Nehemiah 8, the story of Ezra's reading the law to the assembled populace, was originally set between chaps. 8 and 9 of Ezra. In Ezra 9.1-2 officials report to Ezra that the people Israel has not separated itself from the 'peoples of the lands'. Most commentators assume that their motivation could only have come from the story of Ezra's reading the law, the torah, a story that is not told until Nehemiah 8. Indeed Williamson asserts 'that since Torrey's time only the most extremely conservative . . . have rejected the view that Nehemiah 8 . . . originally stood with Ezra 7–10' (1985: xxx). Without the account of the reading of the law, the officers' complaint to Ezra seems unmotivated. Others maintain, however, that the story of the reading of the law in Nehemiah 8 was written for its present location in Nehemiah and never appeared as part of the Ezra story (e.g. VanderKam 1992; Wright 2004: 321-30). (See Comment A below for a discussion of the location of Nehemiah 8.) As discussed above in the Introduction to Ezra 7–10 and further in Comment A below, it is the position of this commentary that the story of Ezra's reading the law was created *de novo* for its present location in Nehemiah and was not part of an original independent Ezra story. (See further at Nehemiah 8 and Fried 2008.)

Translation

9.1 *When these [things] had been done, officers approached me, saying: 'The people Israel, the priests,*[a] *and the Levites have not separated themselves from the peoples of the lands,*[b] *whose abominations are like those of*[c] *the Canaanites, Hittites, Perizzites, Jebusites, Ammonites, Moabites, Egyptians, and Amorites,* 2. *for they have taken some of their daughters as wives for themselves and for their sons, and intermingled the holy seed with the peoples of the lands,*[d] *and the hand of officers and prefects was the first in this faithlessness'.*

Textual Notes

a. **9.1** *The priests.* First Esdras reads 'the leaders and the priests'.

b. *The peoples of the lands.* First Esdras clarifies 'the other peoples of the lands'.

c. *Whose abominations are like those of.* Literally, simply 'like the abominations of'.

d. **9.2** *Peoples of the lands.* As above, 1 Esdras clarifies, 'like the other peoples of the lands'.

Notes

9.1 ***When these [things] had been done.*** This should be read as 'immediately after these [things] had been done'. It is the author's intention that the reader should understand that the officers approached Ezra immediately upon his arrival.

There is no need to posit the interpolation here of Nehemiah 8, even though most commentators argue that without its interpolation this verse appears unmotivated. They do not see a reason why officers would approach Ezra with their complaint about the intermarriages without their first being taught the Mosaic prohibition against it. The difficulty with this supposition is that, as we will see further below, there is no prohibition in the extant torah against intermarriage, no way to learn from it that intermarriage is forbidden. In fact, many biblical heroes did intermarry (e.g. Moses, Joseph), and the prohibition in Deuteronomy 7, which is customarily referred to, is only a prohibition against seven specific peoples, most of whom no longer existed in the time of Ezra; it is not a blanket condemnation of all intermarriage.

The officers (śārîm) approached me. The officers approached Ezra apparently in his role as the Persian episkopos. Who were these officers (*śārîm*)? There are two possibilities. Either they were Persian officials or local Judean leaders. The reader should keep both possibilities in mind: the first, that they were Persian officials, is likely the historically correct interpretation; the second, that they were Judean leaders, is the interpretation of the biblical writer who edited an original independent Ezra story.

The basic meaning of the term *śar* is that of a military officer or commander. Thus, he was a Persian official since the military was an arm of the empire. In Gen. 21.22, 32, for example, the *śar ṣābā'*, שַׂר צָבָא, is the general of the army (Levine 2000: 96). In Exod. 1.11 the שָׂרֵי מִסִּים, *śārê missîm*, the 'officers of a workforce', are so called because of the soldiers with whom they ensure the compliance of the workers. In Exod. 18.21, Jethro tells Moses to appoint commanders שָׂרֵי, *śārê*, of thousands, of hundreds, or fifties, and of tens to judge the people (cf. 2 Chron. 1.2; 8.9, 10). This reflects the organization of the Persian military (Herodotus, *Hist.* 7.81), as is well attested in the records from the Persian garrison at the Nile island of Elephantine (fifth–fourth centuries, BCE). Those who approached Ezra then were military commanders who ruled the province under the Persian governor, and so they were Persian appointees, as was the case throughout the empire. This interpretation is substantiated by Neh. 3.9, which refers to שַׂר חֲצִי פֶּלֶךְ יְרוּשָׁלָםִ, 'the commander of half the workforce of the district of Jerusalem' (Demsky 1983). He too would have been an officer in the Persian military, appointed by Nehemiah, the Persian governor.

Persian military officers approached Ezra on his arrival because of his role as the newly appointed Persian episkopos. They would have done so, however, only if intermarriage had previously been proscribed by the king. They would have wanted to absolve themselves quickly of complicity and point the finger at others, since Ezra would find out about it soon anyway. The issue then would be whether the Great King would have proscribed intermarriage, and if so, what sort and why? This is discussed in Comment B below.

The possibility that they were local Judean leaders who approached Ezra and that their concern was only that Judeans were marrying non-Judeans is the interpretation of the biblical writer. This is also the assumption of nearly every commentator. This view is discussed in Comment A at the end of Ezra 9.

The third possibility—that the incident is not historical—begs the question of why it was written. Was there some event or some circumstance in the Hellenistic period that aroused concern regarding the number of intermarriages, a concern that was then retrojected back into the Persian period? Josephus may provide a key to the answer:

> [Ezra] found a great many of the posterity of Jeshua the high priest, and of the priests and Levites, and Israelites, who had a greater regard to the observation of the law than to their natural affection, immediately cast out their wives, and the children which were born of them; and in order to

> appease God, they offered sacrifices, and slew rams, as oblations to him (*Ant.* 11.152).

If the mass divorce is not historical but had been written much later, during the persecutions of Antiochus IV, for example, it may have been written to provide encouragement to the people to maintain their ancestral traditions in the face of any hardship and to keep away from foreign ways.

The people Israel. See note on Ezra 1.3. The term Israel is not one that Persian military commanders would have known or used. Indeed, except for the first phrase ('the officers approached me') and perhaps the final phrase of 9.2 ('the hand of the officers [*śārîm*] and the prefects [*śᵉgānîm*] was the first in this faithlessness'), the entire chapter is the work of a biblical writer who supplemented Ezra 7–Nehemiah 13 with pious additions. It is not part of the original Ezra story that resumes in 10.2.

The priests. Although included by the biblical writer as part of his normal description of Israel as people, priests, and Levites, the priests, particularly the family of the high priests, are listed among those who married non-Judeans (Ezra 10.18; Neh. 13.28). Moreover, the family of the high priests did not sign the Amanah, the agreement in Nehemiah 10 promising to prevent their sons or daughters from marrying the 'peoples of the lands' (Neh. 10.31 [ET 10.30]; Knoppers 2009). One may see the refusal of that family to cooperate with this imperial demand as a political struggle between local dynasts and Ezra and Nehemiah, the Persian appointees who commanded the intermarriage ban (Fried 2002c).

The Levites. See note on Ezra 7.7. This phrase is also a contribution of the biblical writer. It would not be a statement by Persian officials.

Have not separated themselves. That is, have intermarried with them.

From the peoples of the lands. For the identity of these foreigners see comment on Ezra 3.3. It is odd indeed that in chap. 3 the arrivals are shown afraid of them, and now in the time of Ezra they are portrayed as marrying them! See further discussion at 9.11.

Whose abominations are like those of the Canaanites, etc. The term 'abominations' refers to foreign, non-Yahwistic, religious practices (e.g. Ps. 106.35). Most commentators translate this as 'have not separated themselves from the peoples of the lands with their abominations, from the Canaanites, etc.' (so the NRSV) to imply that all these peoples are still in the land and that it is these people from whom the people Israel has not separated themselves, but this is not correct. Most of the nations listed were no longer extant at the time of Ezra. See note below.

Whose abominations are like those of the Canaanites, Hittites, Perizzites, Jebusites, Ammonites, Moabites, Egyptians and Amorites. This is clearly the writing of the biblical writer and does not belong to an authentic statement that Persian officials would make. It is loosely similar to the passage in Deut. 7.1-6:

> When Yhwh your god brings you into the land that you are about to enter and occupy, and he clears away many nations before you—the Hittites, the Girgashites, the Amorites, the Canaanites, the Perizzites, the Hivites, and the Jebusites, seven nations mightier and more numerous than you—and when Yhwh your god gives them over to you and you defeat them, then you must utterly destroy them. Make no covenant with them and show them no mercy.
>
> Do not intermarry with them, giving your daughters to their sons or taking their daughters for your sons, for that would turn away your children from following me, to serve other gods. Then the anger of Yhwh would be kindled against you, and he would destroy you quickly.
>
> But this is how you must deal with them: break down their altars, smash their pillars, hew down their sacred poles, and burn their idols with fire.
>
> For you are a people holy to Yhwh your god; Yhwh your god has chosen you out of all the peoples on earth to be his people, his treasured possession (Deut. 7.1-6).

Whereas Deuteronomy refers to seven nations: the Hittites, the Girgashites, the Amorites, the Canaanites, the Perizzites, the Hivites and the Jebusites, the book of Ezra refers to the abominations of eight nations: the Canaanites, Hittites, Perizzites, Jebusites, Ammonites, Moabites, Egyptians and Amorites. The first four nations mentioned in Ezra are also mentioned in Deuteronomy 7, but the last four, the Ammonites, Moabites, Egyptians and Amorites are not. Indeed, the first four nations mentioned in Ezra had already disappeared by the Persian period, but the last four presented a constant threat to tiny Yehud. Regarding the last, the name of the Amorites had changed in meaning over the centuries. In the time of the Judean monarchy, the name in Assyrian texts referred to all the western peoples in Syria and the Levant. In Persian period Babylonian texts, however, the term referred to the peoples of North Arabia (Van Seters 1972: 64-81).

Indeed, these last three nations (or four, if we count the Arabs) were not forbidden marriage partners according to the biblical writers. King David descended from a Moabite woman (Ruth 4.10-22). Rehoboam, the first king of Judah after King Solomon, was the son of an Ammonite woman, and this did not affect either his legitimacy or his ability to rule (1 Kgs 14.21). This is in spite of the command in Deut. 23.3:

> No Ammonite or Moabite shall be admitted to Yhwh's assembly. Even to the tenth generation, none of their descendants shall be admitted to Yhwh's assembly.

We also see that Abraham had married an Egyptian (Gen. 21.9-10):

> Sarah saw the son of Hagar the Egyptian, whom she had borne to Abraham, fondling her son Isaac. So she said to Abraham, 'Cast out this slave

> woman with her son; for the son of this slave woman shall not inherit along with my son Isaac'.

Indeed, the command in Deuteronomy cannot be interpreted as a general prohibition against marriage with all non-Israelites, since we see that Moses himself married a Midianite woman (Exod. 2.15-22):

> But Moses fled from Pharaoh. He settled in the land of Midian, and sat down by a well. The priest of Midian had seven daughters. . . . Moses agreed to stay with [him], and he gave Moses his daughter Zippora in marriage. She bore him a son, and he named him Gershom; for he said, 'I have been an alien residing in a foreign land' (Exod. 2.15-22).

And an Ethiopian woman:

> While they were at Hazeroth, Miriam and Aaron spoke against Moses because of the Cushite woman whom he had married—for he had indeed married a Cushite woman (Num. 12.1).

Midianites and Ethiopians (Cushites) were evidently not forbidden since they are not listed among the seven Canaanite nations. Neither were the Egyptians. Joseph marries an Egyptian, and she bears him two sons, Manasseh and Ephraim, the eponymous ancestors of the two main tribes of the northern kingdom (Gen. 41.45, 50-52).

> Pharaoh gave Joseph the name Zaphenath-paneah; and he gave him Asenath daughter of Potiphera, priest of On, as his wife. . . . Joseph had two sons, whom Asenath daughter of Potiphera, priest of On, bore to him. 51 Joseph named the firstborn Manasseh, . . . 52 The second he named Ephraim.

The marriage to the daughter of the high priest of On is given as proof of Joseph's valor and importance, and the biblical writer provides no condemnation of this marriage. Nor is there doubt about the status of the offspring; they are certainly Israelite and Hebrew. Those biblical writers saw nothing wrong with these unions per se. A problem occurs only if the foreign wife turns the heart of the Israelite away from following God (1 Kgs 11.1-3).

> King Solomon loved many foreign women along with the daughter of Pharaoh: Moabite, Ammonite, Edomite, Sidonian, and Hittite women . . . Solomon clung to these in love. Among his wives were seven hundred princesses and three hundred concubines; and his wives turned away his heart.

This fear that foreign wives may turn the hearts of their husbands from Yhwh may be what is behind the concern shown by the biblical writer of Ezra 9.1, but it is not stated explicitly (except in Neh. 13.26).

9.2 ***For they have taken their daughters as wives for themselves and for their sons.*** This is the explanation of what is meant by 'not separating'.

The holy seed. This is another indication of the biblical writer; it is not a statement that Persian officials would have made. It is a reference to Isaiah 6, the only other place where this phrase occurs:

> Then I said, 'How long, my Lord?' And he said: 'Until cities lie waste without inhabitant, and houses without people, and the land is utterly desolate; until Yhwh sends everyone far away, and vast is the emptiness in the midst of the land. Even if a tenth part remain in it, it will be burned again, like the pistachio tree or an oak whose stump remains standing when it is felled. The holy seed is its stump (Isa. 6.11-13).

According to the Isaianic passage, the 'holy seed' refers to the tenth part of the people Israel who remained in the land after Yhwh had sent everyone else away in exile. The word translated 'stump' is *maṣṣebet,* or memorial stone. In other words, by the time of the return from exile the holy seed, the seed of Israel, will only be a memory of what it once was.

Deuteronomy 7.6, quoted above, provides the definition of what it means to be 'holy': 'For you are a people holy to Yhwh your god: Yhwh your god has chosen you out of all the peoples on earth to be his people, his treasured possession'. The Hebrew word *qādoš,* translated as 'holy', actually means 'dedicated', 'set aside'. People are termed holy when they dedicate themselves to Yhwh alone and to his commandments. Holiness is contingent on behavior; it is not intrinsic or genetic. Gentiles are not 'defiled', or 'impure' (Hayes 2002: 20). This is made clear by the ability of Gentiles to bring sacrifices in the same way that an Israelite does:

> An alien who lives with you, or who takes up permanent residence among you, and wishes to offer an offering by fire, a pleasing odor to Yhwh, shall do as you do. As for the community, there shall be for both you and the resident alien a single statute, a perpetual statute throughout your generations; you and the alien shall be alike before Yhwh.
>
> You and the alien who resides with you shall have the same law and the same ordinance.

If non-Judeans were considered intrinsically impure, unholy, defiled, they would not have been allowed to offer sacrifices nor to approach the altar. Nor does Nehemiah see anything wrong with buying grain and other foodstuffs from foreigners:

> If the peoples of the land bring in merchandise or any grain on the sabbath day to sell, we will not buy it from them on the sabbath or on a holy day (Neh. 10.32).

The biblical writer can label the Judeans living on the land after the return from exile as 'holy' because they had been redeemed. Since Yhwh is just and since Yhwh is in charge, bad things only happen to bad people; good things happen only to good people. The people had merited a return to the land and have continued to live on it peacefully. That is the proof that until recently they had been living a life dedicated to Yhwh's ordinances, a holy life.

To continue on the land, however, they must remain so dedicated, but this requires separation from peoples with different gods and different practices and traditions. The land belongs to Yhwh. According to biblical theology, it was the previous peoples' relationship to other gods and their indulging in non-Yahwistic cultic practices that led to their being cast out. This was why the people Israel too were cast out as well (2 Kings 17).

> Do not defile yourselves in any of these ways, for by all these practices the nations I am casting out before you have defiled themselves. Thus the land became defiled; and I punished it for its iniquity, and the land vomited out its inhabitants.
>
> But you shall keep my statutes and my ordinances and commit none of these abominations, either the citizen or the alien who resides among you (for the inhabitants of the land, who were before you, committed all of these abominations, and the land became defiled); otherwise the land will vomit you out for defiling it, as it vomited out the nations that were before you (Lev. 18.24-28).

Living a holy life means separation from non-Yahwistic practices, and this was the requirement for living on the land.

> But I have said to you: You shall inherit their land, and I will give it to you to possess, a land flowing with milk and honey. I am Yhwh your god; I have separated you from the peoples (Lev. 20.24).

It is this fear of being cast out from the land again that likely motivated the biblical writer whenever he lived. This can be seen in the prayer of Ezra that the writer supplied (see below).

The hand of the officers (śārîm) and the prefects (s^{e}gānîm) was the first. This phrase likely stems from the original Ezra story, after the interpolation by the biblical writer. For the identity of the officers, see note at 9.1. The word translated as 'prefect' is Aramaic and occurs numerous times among the Aramaic papyri from Elephantine. It is a general label for Persian satrapal officials who operated on a level at or just above the provincial governors (Lemaire 2007). In Dan. 3.2, 3, etc., for example, they are listed just after the satrap in the imperial hierarchy, and right before the provincial governors. According to the report, the first to intermarry were Persian military and satrapal officials. If historic, the complaint to Ezra would have been part of an official report submitted to him upon his arrival.

Who would these Persian military officers and prefects have been marrying? Apparently they were marrying into the families of local Judeans. If historical, such fraternization would have been against the wishes of the Great King or it would not have been reported to Ezra.

The hand . . . was the first. The use of the singular 'hand' rather than 'hands' is intended to indicate that these officials have been acting in concert.

Faithlessness. See the following section for a discussion of this term.

Comments

Comment A. The Original Location of Nehemiah 8–10

Beginning with Torrey (1970 [1910]: 253-55) scholars have been convinced that Nehemiah 8 should be inserted between Ezra 8 and Ezra 9 (e.g. Rudolph 1949: 143; Clines 1984: 180-81; Williamson 1985: xxx; Blenkinsopp 1988: 44; Pakkala 2004, 2006). Torrey complains that Ezra arrives in the seventh year of Artaxerxes in order to teach and administer the law (Ezra 7.10, 14, 25), but does not do so until thirteen years later, in Artaxerxes' twentieth year (Nehemiah 8). In Ezra 9, officials approach Ezra to inform him that the people have breached the law, implying that it was already known to them, and so Ezra must have taught it. Yet, according to the present narrative, this teaching does not occur for another thirteen years! Torrey recommends inserting Neh. 7.70–8.18 at the end of Ezra 8. With Nehemiah 8 inserted after Ezra 8, Ezra arrives on the first day of the fifth month (Ezra 7.9) and reads the law on the first day of the seventh month (Neh. 8.2), two months later. The mass divorce then begins three months after that, on the first day of the tenth month (Ezra 10.16).

As discussed above, however, there is really nothing in the torah that provides a blanket prohibition of intermarriage, and so the reading of the law cannot motivate the officials' complaint. One could read the entire torah without ever concluding that all foreign marriages were prohibited. More importantly, however, neither the officials who approach Ezra nor Ezra himself in his prayer (see following section) refers to a written (or unwritten) law code. Ezra's prayer to God refers to Judeans' having 'abandoned your (i.e. Yhwh's) commandments that you commanded by the hand of your servants *the prophets'* (Ezra 9.10-11). This is a reference to an oral tradition, not to a written law code, and especially not to a law code that had just been read. In fact, there is no evidence that the author(s) of Ezra 7.27–10.44 knew anything of a written code of law. It is more likely that the author who wrote Ezra 7.1-10 and who incorporated the embellished letter from Artaxerxes into his text arranged the chapters of Ezra 7–Nehemiah 13 as we have it and in doing so wrote *de novo* the covenant renewal scene of Nehemiah 8–10 in which Ezra reads a law scroll to the populace. (The present layout of Ezra 7–Nehemiah 13 is discussed above in the Introduction to Part II, the story of Ezra, and in Fried 2008.)

Besides apparently motivating the officials' complaint, another reason why scholars associate Nehemiah 8 with the Ezra story is the way the dates are cited. The dates are cited in Ezra in the same way that they are cited in Nehemiah 8, but these differ from the way they are cited in the Nehemiah memoir. In Neh. 1.1, 2.1 and 6.15 the months are cited by name (Kislev, Nisan, Elul), but in Nehemiah 8 the month is cited by number—it is the seventh month, as in Ezra (7.8, 9; 8.31; 10.9, 16). All that this proves, however, is that the author of the Nehemiah memoir (= Nehemiah?) is not the author of Nehemiah 8. Nehemiah 8–10 was inserted secondarily into its position to create a covenant renewal ceremony; its author most likely was the author of Ezra 7.1-10.

There is further evidence to indicate that Nehemiah 8 was not written by the authors of the material that we have in Ezra 7.27–10.44. This is shown by the choice of the Hebrew word to express the verb 'to assemble' (J.L. Wright 2004: 327). The word used for 'assembled' in Neh. 8.1 is based on the root *'āsap,* אסף, and it is used twice more in the same pericope (Neh. 8.13; 9.1). It appears only once in all of Ezra 7–10 (Ezra 9.4), and this is in the prayer, a late insertion (see Comment A in the following section). The word used most commonly in Ezra 7–8 and 10 for 'to assemble' is based on the root קבץ, *qbṣ*, and it is used five times (Ezra 7.28; 8.15; 10.1, 7, 9). It is unlikely that the author of the original Ezra story in Ezra 7.28–10.44, who uses קבץ most consistently (twice in Ezra 7–8 and three times in Ezra 10) would now use only אסף in an intervening chapter (the law reading in Neh. 8 and the prayer in Ezra 9). The author of the Ezra story is not the author of Nehemiah 8 (so also Rendtorff 1984, 1999; VanderKam 1992: 55-75). The author of Ezra 7.1-10, who included and embellished Artaxerxes' letter, is very likely the author of Nehemiah 8, however, and most likely the author of the prayer as well. He would have been the one who wove the Ezra and the Nehemiah stories together.

Scholars who require that Ezra cite a law in order to demand a mass divorce are imposing modern notions of law codes on an ancient Near Eastern society. Administrative or legal practices in Near Eastern antiquity were not based on law codes. Indeed, there were no written law codes in the true sense of the term anywhere in the ancient Near East, including in the Persian Empire (Fried 2001; Dandamayev and Lukonin 1989: 116-17). (See discussion at Comment B to Ezra 7.)

Comment B. The Mass Divorce

Why would Persian officials complain to Ezra, the new episkopos, about intermarriages between Persian prefects and military commanders and local Judeans if intermarriage was not a violation of a law code? They would only have done so if a ban on such marriages was ordered by the Great King. Although there is no specific information regarding the Achaemenids, such intermarriage bans were commonly used in antiquity to control subject populations (Fried 2002c). Akbar, one of the descendants of Genghis Khan, established a military occupation in China and forbade intermarriage among the various ethnic groups there (Duverger 1980: 12). Lucius Aemilius Paullus, Roman general in 168 BCE, divided Macedonia into four separate provinces and forbade intermarriage and land ownership across the boundaries (Livy 45.29; Shallit 1975: 41). The deified Augustus established a code of rules for the administration of the Privy Purse (BGU 210, at the Berlin Egyptian Museum), a code maintained for two hundred years. This code consisted of over one hundred laws that greatly restricted interaction among the ethnic groups, including the higher caste Greeks (Lewis 1983: 32-33; Bagnall and Frier 1994: 28-29). The goal was *divide et impera.*

A similar ban on intermarriages was enacted in contemporaneous imperial Athens (Fried 2009; 2015a). In 451–450 BCE, Pericles, a prominent and influential statesman and general in Athens, persuaded the Athenian assembly to pass a law that required that for anyone in the empire to be considered an Athenian citizen he had to have two Athenian parents. According to Plutarch (*Pericles* 37.2), this was a law 'about bastards', not about citizenship per se. Aristotle also reports on the law:

> And in the year of [the archonship of] Antidotus, owing to the large number of the citizens, an enactment was passed on the proposal of Pericles prohibiting a person from having a share in the city who was not born of two citizens (*Ath. pol.* 26.3).

For the first time, Athenian citizens now had to prove descent from an Athenian mother, that is a woman whose father was a citizen. Those unable to prove this were reckoned as bastards. Though not often stated, this law recognized for the first time the status of the Athenian woman, and may have even elevated it (Osborne 1997: 3-33). The decree of 451/450 was followed by a public scrutiny (διαψηφισμός) in 445 BCE, when the Egyptian king sent grain to be distributed to Athenian citizens.

> And so [in 445] when the king of Egypt sent a present to the people [of Athens] of forty thousand measures of grain, and this had to be divided up among the citizens, there was a great crop of prosecutions against citizens of impure birth by the law of Pericles, who had up to that time escaped notice and been overlooked, and many of them also suffered at the hands of informers. As a result, a little less than five thousand were convicted and sold into slavery, and those who retained their citizenship and were adjudged to be Athenians were found, as a result of this selection, to be fourteen thousand and forty in number (Plutarch, *Pericles* 37.3-4).

According to Philochoros, 4,760 Athenians were struck from the citizenship rolls then as being of 'impure origin' (οἱ τῷ γένει μὴ καθαροί) and not

The Athenian Empire at its Greatest Extent, c. 450 BCE. Map courtesy of Karl Longstreth of the University of Michigan Map Library.

entitled to the grain (Jacoby 1923: 119; Davies 1977–78: 105-21). Deprived of their rights as citizens, they had no recourse to the protection of the courts; if murdered, their family had no right of vengeance. Many fled or were exiled. Confiscation of property and often loss of life followed even those allowed to remain in Athens. Those who sued for their citizenship rights and lost their suit were executed. These laws were allowed to lapse during the Peloponnesian wars, but in 403 BCE they were reinforced and strengthened. Another census and mass exile ensued. Manville characterizes these periodic 'scrutinies' as 'reigns of terror' (Manville 1997: 184). Davies notes the constant status anxieties that are reflected in contemporary tragedies.

Laws elaborating on the prohibition of intermarriage between Athenians and foreigners followed upon Pericles' citizenship law. Two laws in particular are noteworthy, both quoted in Demosthenes, *Against Neaira* 59.16, 52.

> If a foreign man lives as husband with an Athenian woman in any way or manner whatsoever, he may be prosecuted before the *thesmothetai* by any Athenian wishing and entitled to do so. If he is found guilty, both he and his property shall be sold and one-third of the money shall be given to the prosecutor. The same rule applies to a foreign woman who lives with

> an Athenian as his wife, and the Athenian convicted of living as husband with a foreign woman shall be fined a thousand drachmas (Demosthenes, *Against Neaira* 59.16).
>
> If any Athenian gives a foreign woman in marriage to an Athenian citizen, as being his relative, he shall lose his civic rights and his property shall be confiscated and one-third shall belong to the successful prosecutor. Those entitled may prosecute before the *thesmothetai,* as in the case of usurpation of citizenship (Demosthenes, *Against Neaira* 59.52).

These laws indicate that a mandatory divorce took place for all marriages between an Athenian and non-Athenian, whether male or female. According to the law, the foreigner living as a spouse with an Athenian would be sold into slavery, and his or her property confiscated (with one-third given to the man who brought the suit). Since women did not give themselves in marriage, anyone giving a foreign woman to an Athenian in marriage was subject to sanctions. This was then the situation in fifth- and fourth-century BCE Athens.

Why was this law enacted in Athens? One problem with foreign marriages was that of inheritance. Sons of foreign women, or rather, grandsons of foreign men, could wind up inheriting land in Athens. Technically speaking, women did not inherit, but wealthy women received a premortem inheritance through their dowries, and these could include lands and estates, as well as sums of money easily turned into land. Women without brothers also received a postmortem inheritance. In this way, a woman served as a conduit, conducting her father's estate to her sons. Sons of brotherless women were often adopted into the household of their maternal grandfather, and if the women were foreign, these non-Athenian grandsons could wind up owning land in Athens and achieving civil power there. Merton sums up the problem with intermarriage succinctly:

> Endogamy is a device which serves to maintain social prerogatives and immunities within a social group. It helps prevent the diffusion of power, authority, and preferred status to persons who are not affiliated with a dominant group. It serves further to accentuate and symbolize the 'reality' of the group by setting it off against other discriminable social units. Endogamy serves as an isolation and exclusion device, with the function of increasing group solidarity and supporting the social structure by helping to fix social distance which obtains between groups (Merton 1941: 362; *apud* Smith-Christopher 1994: 247).

According to this theory, the ban on intermarriage is instituted by the higher-ranking social group in order to maintain its power and authority and to prevent it from diffusing to other groups. This is borne out by modern sociological data (Smith-Christopher 2002). The majority of interracial marriages in twentieth-century America, for example, consisted of professional and educated black men 'marrying up' to nonprofessional women of the white higher-status culture. Studies of intercaste marriages in India also predominantly involved a professional male of a lower caste and a nonprofessional woman of a higher caste. Data also show that Jewish–Gentile intermarriages in Europe between 1876 and 1933 consisted predominantly of Jewish males and Gentile females. Smith-Christopher suggests that the intermarriages in fifth- and fourth-century Judah consisted primarily of lower-caste Judean men 'marrying up' by marrying higher-status non-Judean women. These would have been the daughters of foreign satrapal or military officials stationed in Judah. The higher-status group of satrapal officials and military commanders would have wanted to preserve their power, status and authority and to prevent them from being diffused to the local population. It would have been the reason for Persia to ban daughters of satrapal officials and military commanders from marrying Judeans. Persia would have wanted to prevent its power, status and authority from diffusing to members of the subjected populations.

The law in Athens succeeded in sharply reducing foreign marriages. While common before, they are unknown after Pericles' law of 450 (Osborne 1997: 3-33). Moreover, charges of 'impure birth' and 'treachery' (viewed as the same thing in Athens) were the most common allegations scrawled on potsherds used to ostracize politicians from the city. The main effect of the law, however, was on the large number of men serving in garrisons posted in cities throughout the Athenian Empire. In prohibiting their fraternization with locals, the law prevented families in other locations from accessing property and power in Athens through the marriage of their daughters to Athenians. If Athenian men married abroad, their children could not be Athenians and would not inherit Athenian land. Claims of kinship could never lead non-Athenians to power or influence in Athens.

A second purpose of the ban in Athens may have been to prevent Athenians from forming dynastic alliances with wealthy families from other states—not only those with which Athens had hostilities, such as Sparta, but also with those dependent states paying tribute to the coffers of the Athenian League (Humphreys 1974: 93-94; Samons 2007: 14). Any of these alliances could easily have upset the balance of power. Such alliances would provide a power base outside of Athens, a power base that could threaten Athenian hegemony. It must be remembered that marriage constituted a gift exchange and an alliance between the bridegroom and the bride's father (Brosius 1996: 70; Finley 1955), it was not a random event.

The Persians seemed to have had the same concern about foreign marriages since they were generally avoided under the Achaemenids (Briant 2002: 83, 501). Whereas intermarriages were common between the ruling Mermnad dynasty and the Sardian aristocracy of Asia Minor before the

Persian conquest (680–547 BCE), for example, they are completely absent from the documentation of the Achaemenid period. Cambyses II, Cyrus's son, entered into marriages with the daughters of both Persian nobles and non-Persian royalty (e.g. the daughter of Pharaoh), but he was the last to do so (Brosius 1996: 45-64). Darius I, the usurper, married the wives of his predecessors, Cambyses II and Bardiya (Smerdis), and also their sisters, but only to emphasize his right to the throne. His successors all married within the royal family (half-sisters or close cousins). Other members of the royal household married offspring of Persian satraps and Persian military commanders not only to strengthen the bonds between them and the king (Brosius 1996: 37-39) but also to prevent Persian officials in the satrapies from marrying local women (Balcer 1993: 273-342). There are no instances of dynastic marriages—marriages to bind the Achaemenid royal household with their diplomatic neighbors (Balcer 1993: 281). Marriages between Persian officials and local dynasts were frowned upon, and perhaps banned, since these could create alliances that would exert a centrifugal force away from the central power base in Susa and threaten the status quo.[1] All provincial governors had garrisons and militias at their disposal to control the populace and to collect taxes and tribute from them to send on to Susa. These resources tended to increase the desire of local governors for independence and autonomy (Fried 2002c; Briant 1978–79). Marriages between ruling Persian governors and local dynasts would have pooled these resources and threatened resistance against Persia. Nehemiah, the Persian governor, fulminated against marriage alliances between local Judean dynasts and Persian satrapal officials from Samaria (Neh. 13.23-29). He may have feared a power base and source of wealth independent of himself as emissary of the king (Hoglund 1992: 226-40; Fried 2002c; 2015a; *pace* Eskenazi 2006).

Persian officials would then naturally have approached Ezra, the new episkopos, to complain about the numerous intermarriages that were taking place in Judah, especially since '[Persian] military officers and prefects (הַשָּׂרִים וְהַסְּגָנִים) were the first in this wrong' (Ezra 9.2). The power and authority of high-ranking Persian satrapal and military officials were

1. Balcer (1993: 282-84) knows of two Persian women who married non-Persians. One Darius gave along with a house and estates as a reward to a Greek for his support against the Ionians (Herodotus 6.41). Another reported by Diodorus Siculus (11.44), which Balcer doubts. Another case is one in which King Alexander I of Macedon gives his sister along with a great sum to the Persian Bubares in order to stop a Persian attack (Herodotus, *Histories* 5.21). Two Persian men married non-Persians (Artabanos II and Cyrus the Younger). Both of these men were in revolt against their king (Artaxerxes I and II respectively).

in danger of being diffused to the low-ranking subject population of the Judeans. Members of the priestly family of Eliashib, for example, had intermarried with the family of Sanballat, the Persian governor of Samaria, (Neh. 13.28; Josephus, *Ant.* 11.2), and also with the family of Tobiah, Persian governor of Ammon (Neh. 13.4; *Ant.* 12.4). Other members of the Judean nobility had also married into the Tobiad family (Neh. 6.18). That both the Tobiads and the family of Sanballat were Yahwists made these dynastic liaisons acceptable to the high-priestly family of Eliashib, if not to the Persian administration.

Ezra 9.3-15

Ezra Reacts to the News of the Intermarriages and Prays

Ezra reacts in a stereotyped response of mourning; he tears his clothing and pulls hair from his head and beard. Speaking in the first person plural, he admits his guilt, the guilt of his ancestors, and the continuing guilt of his community. The words he uses are *beged* and *ma'al*, both signifying willful rebelliousness against God, usually translated as treachery or faithlessness. Only willful sins need to be confessed, not ones committed inadvertently (Lev. 5.15), and this was a willful sin, and so the confession (Milgrom 1991: 301-302). Only after confession can the guilt offering, the *'āšām,* be brought (Ezra 10.19). For inadvertent sins, the *'āšām* may be brought without any need for confession. Ezra's confession turns the deliberate sin into an inadvertent one, qualifying it for the *'āšām*. This need for confession before God or human was required for expiation throughout the ancient Near East. Ezra, in his role as priest and leader of the community, was empowered to make confession on its behalf (Lev. 16.21). The community then brought the *'āšām* (Ezra 10.19).

But why is intermarriage viewed as so disastrous? It is never treated so elsewhere in the biblical text. (See note at 9.1 above.) By referring to intermarriage with the foreign peoples living in and around Judah as *beged* and *ma'al,* the author of Ezra likens intermarriage to idolatry, to forsaking Yhwh, and to the supreme act that threatens Israel's continued existence on the land. Intermarriage may not itself be idolatry but was evidently feared as a gateway to it.

The different vocabulary used in Ezra 9 and 10 to express the same ideas will be pointed out in the notes to Ezra 10, *ad loc.,* but they strongly imply that these two chapters were not written by the same author (Dor 2006: 18-20). The prayer in Ezra 9 and the introduction to it were added to an original Ezra story by a second writer as an elaboration of Ezra 10.6:

> Then Ezra got up from before the house of God, and went to the chamber of Jehohanan son of Eliashib. He did not eat bread or drink water, for he was mourning over the faithlessness (*ma'al*) of the exiles (Ezra 10.6).

Although the prayer and its introduction are written in the first person, the vocabulary suggests they were not composed by the same author who compiled Ezra 7–Nehemiah 13. They are not part of the original Ezra story (so also Pakkala 2004). (See Comment A at the end of Chapter 10 for a discussion of the original Ezra story.)

Translation

3. *When I heard this matter I tore my robe*[a] *and my cloak*[b] *and pulled hair from my head and beard and sat desolate.*[c] 4. *Then all who trembled at the words*[d] *of the god of Israel on account of the faithlessness of the returned exiles*[e] *gathered to me while I sat desolate until the evening sacrifice.*

5. *At the evening sacrifice*[f] *I rose from my fasting,*[g] *and with my robe*[h] *and cloak*[i] *torn I got on my knees*[j] *and spread out my hands*[k] *to Yhwh my god.*[l] 6. *Then I said, 'Oh, my god,*[m] *I am embarrassed and ashamed*[n] *to raise, O God, my face to you,*[o] *because our sins have increased to above our heads,*[p] *and our guilt has grown to the skies.* 7. *From the days of our ancestors until this day we have been in great guilt, and because of our sins*[q] *we,*[r] *our kings, our priests,*[s] *have been handed over into the hands of the kings of the lands*[t] *by the sword, by captivity, by plunder, and by visible shame.*[u] 8. *And now, for barely a moment,*[v] *there has been mercy from Yhwh our god who has left us a remnant*[w] *in order to give us a stake*[x] *in the place of his holiness*[y]*and to brighten our eyes, O our god,*[z] *and to rejuvenate us*[aa] *a little in our servitude.*[bb] 9. *For we are slaves,*[cc] *but in our servitude God has not abandoned us and has extended upon us steadfast love before the kings*[dd] *of Persia to rejuvenate us*[ee] *to raise up the house of our god,*[ff] *to repair its ruins,*[gg] *and to give us a protective wall in Judah and in Jerusalem.*

10. *And now,*[hh] *what shall we say, our god, after this,*[ii] *that we have abandoned your commandments* 11. *that you commanded by means of*[jj] *your servants the prophets saying: "The land which you are entering to inherit is a land polluted*[kk] *by the pollutions of the peoples of the lands*[ll]*, by their abominations which fill it from corner to corner*[mm] *with their uncleanness.* 12. *And now, do not give your daughters to their sons, and their daughters do not marry to your sons, and never inquire after their health*[nn] *or welfare*[oo] *so that you may be strong and eat the bounty of the land and leave it for an inheritance for your children*[pp] *forever."* 13. *And after all that has come upon us due to our evil deeds and our great guilt, you have held back, [punishing] us less than our sins*[qq] *and have given us a remnant*[rr] *like this.* 14. *Shall we return*[ss] *to violating your commandments and marry with the peoples of these abominations*[tt]*? Will you not be angry against us until our destruction and there will be no remnant or survivor?*[uu] 15. *Yhwh, god of Israel, you are just because we are left a remnant as on this day. We are here before you in our guilt,*[vv] *although no one can stand before you on account of this.'*

Textual Notes

a. **9.3** *Robe.* It is not known what type of garment this refers to. All the versions read 'clothing', in general and plural rather than trying to translate each separately.

b. *Cloak.* Greek Ezra reads 'and trembled'; 1 Esdras reads 'clothing and holy garment'. First Esdras conceives of Ezra as a high priest and gives him the high priestly garment.

c. *Desolate.* First Esdras reads, 'I sat down in anxiety and grief', which renders explicitly what the Hebrew is trying to describe.

d. **9.4** *Words.* The versions all read 'word'.

e. *The returned exiles.* First Esdras omits this phrase.

f. **9.5** *At the evening sacrifice.* First Esdras omits this. It is redundant.

g. *Fasting.* Greek Ezra translates as 'humiliation', which is another meaning of the Hebrew, but not the one intended.

h. *Robe.* See note at v. 3a.

i. *And cloak.* As in v. 3, Greek Ezra reads 'and trembled', and as in v. 3, 1 Esdras reads 'holy garment'.

j. *Got on my knees.* The Hebrew actually says, 'kneeling on my knees'. First Esdras reads simply 'I kneeled'.

k. *Spread out my hands.* The Syriac adds 'in prayer' after this phrase.

l. *My god.* Greek Ezra and the Syriac read 'the god'. First Esdras omits the word.

m. **9.6** *My god.* The versions all read 'Oh LORD'.

n. *Embarrassed and ashamed.* Syriac simply reads 'ashamed'.

o. *To raise, O God, my face to you.* First Esdras reads 'before your face'.

p. *Heads.* The Hebrew is in the singular, 'head'. The versions all read 'heads', plural.

q. **9.7** *Our sins.* First Esdras reads 'our sins and the sins of our fathers'; the Syriac reads 'because of the increase in our sins'.

r. *We.* First Esdras adds 'we with our kin'.

s. *Our priests.* Greek Ezra reads 'our children', which may be original.

t. *Of the kings of the lands.* The Syriac reads 'into the hand of the enemy'.

u. *And by visible shame.* Literally, 'with shame on my face'. The Syriac omits.

v. **9.8** *For barely a moment.* Greek Ezra omits this phrase. First Esdras reads, 'And now how much has mercy come to us'.

w. *Remnant.* First Esdras reads 'a root'.

x. *Stake.* Literally, tent peg. Greek Ezra reads 'support'. First Esdras reads 'a name'. The Syriac reads 'a place'.

y. *The place of his holiness.* First Esdras reads 'your sanctuary'.

z. *O our god.* Greek Ezra omits. First Esdras reads, 'And to uncover a light for us in the house of the Lord our god'.

aa. *To rejuvenate us.* Greek Ezra reads 'making us alive a little', which is the literal translation. First Esdras reads 'giving us food'.

bb. *In our servitude.* First Esdras reads 'in the time of our servitude'.

cc. **9.9** *For we are slaves.* 1 Esdras omits this phrase.

dd. *Kings.* Some Greek manuscripts plus the Vulgate and the Syriac read 'king'.

ee. *Rejuvenate.* First Esdras reads, 'so that they (i.e. the Persian kings) have given us food'. The Syriac adds 'today'.

ff. *The house of our god.* First Esdras reads 'our sanctuary'.

gg. *To repair its ruins.* First Esdras reads, 'and [they] raised Zion from desolation', referring to the Persian kings.

hh. **9.10**. *And now.* Greek Ezra omits this phrase.

ii. *After this.* First Esdras reads 'having these things'.

jj. **9.11.** *By means of.* Literally, 'by the hand of'.

kk. *Polluted.* Greek Ezra reads, 'a land from which the nations are being removed because of their pollutions'.

ll. *Peoples of the lands.* First Esdras reads 'the other peoples of the land', which is the intention.

mm. *From corner to corner.* First Esdras omits.

nn. **9.12** *Never inquire after their health or welfare.* First Esdras and Greek Ezra read, 'never seek peace with them'. The word *shalom* means both 'health' and 'peace'.

oo. *Welfare.* First Esdras omits this word. Greek Ezra reads, 'never seek their peace or their good'.

pp. *For your children.* The Syriac adds 'to inherit forever'.

qq. **9.13** *Less than our sins.* Greek Ezra and 1 Esdras read, 'you have alleviated our sins', or 'made our sins less onerous'.

rr. *A remnant.* First Esdras reads 'offspring', 'descendants'. Greek Ezra reads 'salvation', which is another meaning of the Hebrew here. The Syriac reads, 'you have counted our sins less than they are'.

ss. **9.14.** *Shall we return?* All the versions read, 'but we turned back'.

tt. *Peoples of these abominations.* Greek Ezra reads simply 'the peoples of the lands'. Maybe that is original. First Esdras reads 'by mixing with the immorality of the peoples of the lands'. The Syriac adds 'and do the deeds that they do', which is certainly the implication of the text.

uu. *Be no remnant or survivor.* First Esdras reads, 'leaving us neither descendants, seed, or name'.

vv. **9.15**. *Here before you in our guilt.* The Syriac reads, 'we stand before you and confess our guilt'.

Notes

9.3 My robe and my cloak. It is not known what types of garments these refer to. It is interesting to note, however, that both these words are homonyms. The word translated 'robe' here is בֶּגֶד, *beged,* the normal word for clothing, but it can also mean 'treachery', 'faithlessness', or 'fraud' (e.g. Isa. 24.16). Similarly with מְעִיל, *m*^{e}*'îl,* 'cloak.' The root מעל, *ma'al,* is used right in the next verse (9.4; cf. 10.2 and 10.12), where it means 'to act unfaithfully'. So we have two puns here to tell the reader exactly what the mourning is all about—the treachery and faithlessness of Israel.

Tore my robe and my cloak and pulled hair from my head and beard. Not only are these stereotypical signs of mourning, but they refer especially to mourning for someone who has died unexpectedly or horribly. We read in Gen. 37.29 that 'when Reuben returned to the pit and saw that Joseph was not in the pit, he tore his clothes'. It is also used after a horrible disaster. This ritualized mourning can also seen in the description of the desolation of Moab after the destruction by the Babylonians.

> For every head is shaved and every beard cut off; on all the hands there are gashes, and on the loins sackcloth. On all the housetops of Moab and in the squares there is nothing but lamentation (Jer. 48.37-38).

It is also a sign of remorse and regret. We read that when King Josiah 'heard the words of the book of the law, he tore his clothes' (2 Kgs 22.11), and God relented of his plan for the king:

> Because your heart was penitent, and you humbled yourself before Yhwh, when you heard how I spoke against this place, . . . and because you have torn your clothes and wept before me, I also have heard you, says Yhwh. Therefore, I will gather you to your ancestors, and you shall be gathered to your grave in peace (2 Kgs 22.19-20).

The goal of the self-immolation is the same—to show repentance and contrition and so to avert the evil decree.

Sat there desolate. Ezekiel uses the same language in Ezek. 3.15 and elsewhere, altogether over twenty times. This supports the suggested affinity of the author of Ezra–Nehemiah with Ezekiel.

9.4 ***All who trembled at the words of the god of Israel.*** The word for 'tremble' here is *ḥārēd,* from which we get the label *Haredim*, the ones who 'tremble' at God's word. See also Isa. 66.5. The trembling connotes great fear. Both these terms are part of the language of Ezekiel:

> I will make many peoples appalled at you [i.e. Pharaoh]; their kings shall shudder because of you. When I brandish my sword before them, they shall tremble every moment for their lives, each one of them, on the day of your downfall (Ezek. 32.10).

The evening sacrifice. There were generally two sacrifices, representing the two regular meals of the god, mid-morning and twilight (see Numbers 28). The word used here is *minḥâ,* which refers specifically to the grain used to accompany the sacrificial meat, but generally connotes the afternoon sacrifice. The occasions of the daily sacrifices were used to indicate the time of day (see 1 Kgs 18.29; Dan. 9.21).

9.5 ***I got on my knees and spread out my hands to Yhwh.*** We see this description of prayer also in 1 Kings:

> Now when Solomon finished offering all this prayer and this plea to Yhwh, he arose from facing the altar of Yhwh, where he had been crouching on his knees with his hands spread out toward heaven (1 Kgs 8.54).

And a similar description of Daniel:

> Daniel . . . continued to go to his house, which had windows in its upper room open toward Jerusalem, and to get down on his knees three times a day to pray to his god and praise him, just as he had done previously (Dan. 6.10).

There is no description here of the position of his hands. At the eighth-century caravanserai at Kuntillet 'Ajrud in the Sinai, a large storage jar was found with a picture incised on it of five standing figures all in a row facing right with their hands raised in what the excavator interprets as a gesture of prayer (Meshel 1979). They are standing, however, not on their knees. The description of Elijah in prayer differs slightly: 'Elijah went up to the top of Carmel; there he bowed himself down upon the earth and put his face between his knees' (1 Kgs 18.42). This image is similar to that of Jehu, king of Israel, bowing down before the king of Assyria on the Black Obelisk, currently in the British Museum. Most instances of prayer in the Hebrew Bible do not record the stance of the one praying.

9.6 ***Our sins . . . our guilt. . . . handed over into the hands of the kings of the lands.*** The proof that 'our ancestors' have sinned and have been guilty of tremendous wrongdoing is that they had been put under the control of the kings of the lands—the northern kingdom to the kings of Assyria and the southern kingdom to the kings of Babylon and all of them now to Persia.

The first act of contrition is admitting the sin. It is an attempt to clear away the past so that the relationship may start anew (Miller 1994: 251).

9.7 ***By the sword, by captivity, by plunder, and by visible shame.*** This is the mechanism by which God (of course) handed the people Israel over to the kings of the lands. A poignant description can be found in the biblical book of Lamentations.

9.8 ***For barely a moment.*** That is, for the few years from the time of the return in 538 BCE until now, a very brief period in the mind of the biblical writer. (See comment at the end of Ezra 2 on the chronology assumed by the biblical writer.)

There has been mercy. God has been merciful and brought the Judeans to their own land.

And has left us a remnant. And has allowed a remnant to remain after all the destruction, and has returned this remnant to their own land.

A stake. Literally, a tent peg. Metaphorically, a secure position, which cannot be pulled down or blown away. The stake is the temple, the place of his holiness. We may compare this to the iron pegs that were placed in the foundations of Babylonian temples to symbolize the secure relationship between the builder (usually the king) and the god (Clines 1984: 123; Ellis 1968: 46-93). However, as Batten notes (1913: 333), the fact that this could all be undone again by the people's sins speaks to the terrifying impermanence of the stake.

In the place of his holiness. This refers to the temple. We read in Psalm 24:

> The earth is Yhwh's and all that is in it, the world, and those who live in it;
> for he has founded it on the seas, and established it on the rivers.
> Who shall ascend Yhwh's hill? And who shall stand in his holy place?

> Those who have clean hands and pure hearts, who do not lift up their souls to what is false, and do not swear deceitfully.
> They will receive blessing from Yhwh, and vindication from the god of their salvation.

Brighten our eyes. This implies rejuvenation and is the visible sign of it. See, for example, the story of Saul and his son Jonathan in 1 Samuel 14:

> Now Saul committed a very rash act on that day. He had laid an oath on the troops, saying, 'Cursed be anyone who eats food before it is evening and I have been avenged on my enemies'. So none of the troops tasted food.
> 25 All the troops came upon a honeycomb; and there was honey on the ground.
> 26 When the troops came upon the honeycomb, the honey was dripping out; but they did not put their hands to their mouths, for they feared the oath.
> 27 But Jonathan had not heard his father charge the troops with the oath; so he extended the staff that was in his hand, and dipped the tip of it in the honeycomb, and put his hand to his mouth; and his eyes brightened.
> 28 Then one of the soldiers said, 'Your father strictly charged the troops with an oath, saying, "Cursed be anyone who eats food this day". And so the troops are faint.'
> 29 Then Jonathan said, 'My father has troubled the land; see how my eyes have brightened because I tasted a little of this honey' (1 Sam. 14.24-29).

To rejuvenate us. Literally, to renew our lives. To give us something to live for. God has been gracious to us. Part of a penitential prayer, which this is, is recognition and thanksgiving for all of God's gracious acts in spite of the fact that the penitent has not deserved it.

9.9 ***For we are slaves.*** Make no mistake about it, the Judeans under foreign rule were slaves, unable to plan their own destiny, and working only for the good of their Persian masters. A friend of mine visiting from Poland when it was still part of the Soviet Empire gave me their description of a Polish cow: 'A Polish cow is so big that it eats grass in Warsaw but gives milk in Moscow'. That is national slavery.

God has not abandoned us and has extended upon us steadfast love. The proof that God has not abandoned us and the proof of his steadfast love are God's return to Zion and his taking up residence once more in the place of his holiness. Recognition of the continuing relationship between God and the Judean people in spite of their sin and the ensuing exile was crucial for the penitential prayer. The exile is punishment for sins committed, but throughout it all, God has not abandoned them even in their exile. They were exiled from the land but not from God.

Before the kings of Persia. In the sight of the kings of Persia.

And to give us a wall in Judah and in Jerusalem. The wall here is not a city wall (which uses a different Hebrew word), but a *gādēr*, a wall that might surround a garden to prevent it from being trampled (Isa. 5.5). It is metaphoric here, and probably stands for truth, or righteous living; compare Ezekiel's condemnation of the prophets for not building a *gādēr* to defend the people:

> Your prophets have been like jackals among ruins, O Israel.
> [They] have not gone up into the breaches, or repaired a wall (*gādēr)* for the house of Israel, so that it might stand in battle on the day of Yhwh (Ezek. 13.4-5).

9.10. ***That we have abandoned your commandments.*** This is the crux of their problem.

9.11 ***That you commanded by means of your servants the prophets.*** In the ancient Near East, prophets were believed to have a direct link to the gods and to be their mouthpieces. Ezra appears to quote Deuteronomy. It can be seen, however, that though the wording is similar, it is not a direct quote. It has been argued recently that Ezra–Nehemiah 'assume a fixed written torah' and a 'fully developed literary torah text, such as Deut. 7.1-6' (Schmid 2007a: 237). As the comparison shows below, this is not the case:

Ezra 9.11-12	Deuteronomy 7.1-4
The land that you are entering to inherit is a land polluted by the pollutions of the peoples of the lands, by their abominations which fill it from corner to corner with their uncleanness. And now, do not give your daughters to their sons, and their daughters do not marry to your sons, and never inquire after their health or welfare so that you may be strong and eat the bounty of the land and leave it for an inheritance for your children forever.	When Yhwh your god brings you into the land that you are about to enter and occupy, and he clears away many nations before you . . . and when Yhwh your god gives them over to you and you defeat them, then you must utterly destroy them. Make no covenant with them and show them no mercy. Do not intermarry with them, giving your daughters to their sons or taking their daughters for your sons, for that would turn away your children from following me, to serve other gods. Then the anger of Yhwh would be kindled against you, and he would destroy you quickly.

The text in Ezra is not a literal quote from a fixed text. The text is evidently not fixed at this point. Moreover, Ezra does not claim to be quoting a text here, only a prophetic tradition. A full discussion of this important issue is deferred to the discussion at Nehemiah 8.

Peoples of the lands. For the identity of these people, see the discussion at 3.3. We must remember that in addition to the foreign peoples at every border of the small province of Yehud, there were foreign soldiers garrisoned right in Jerusalem or near it in Ramat Raḥel. Every major city had Persian garrisons billeted in it, garrisons manned not with local soldiers, but foreign ones (Tuplin 1987b). These foreign garrisons brought with them altars for their own gods. We read, for example, of a temple to Yhw for the Judean soldiers garrisoned in Elephantine, in upper Egypt, a temple to Nabu for the Babylonian soldiers also billeted there, and a temple to the Carian god, King Kaunios, for the Carian garrison stationed in Xanthus, Lycia (Fried 2004). In addition to the foreign soldiers in Jerusalem, there were Persian officials, judges, accountants, etc., who would have lit their fire altars to Ahuramazda. Intermarriage with any of these or their daughters threatened to turn Judeans away from Yhwh. In fact, we have one such case in Elephantine Egypt. There the marriage of a local Egyptian man to the daughter of one of the foreign Judean soldiers stationed there resulted in the Egyptian man changing his name from the Egyptian 'Esḥor' (*TAD* B2.9) to the Hebrew 'Nathan' (*TAD* B2.10), indicating a conversion to worshiping the foreign god of his foreign wife. He evidently left the Egyptian community and joined the community of the foreign garrison. Intermarriage with the forces of the occupying army may not have been frequent. Once a foreign soldier marries into a family of the indigenous population, his loyalties change, and he cannot do his job.

9.12 ***Never inquire after their health or welfare.*** The author thus adds a prohibition against even minimal conversation or social interaction. The words are quoting Deut. 23.7, but there it is directed against only Ammonites and Moabites 'because because they did not meet you with food and water on your journey out of Egypt, and because they hired against you Balaam son of Beor, from Pethor of Mesopotamia, to curse you'. Ezra expands it to include all foreigners (cf. Neh. 13.1-3; Fishbane 1985: 114-29; Olyan 2004). This goes beyond what Nehemiah permitted, since under him Judeans regularly engaged in commerce with others (Neh. 13.16), but it does not match in severity that demanded by Deuteronomy. Ezra does not require that they be 'defeated' or 'destroyed', as that would be impossible.

9.13 ***You have held back, [punishing] us less than our sins and have given us a remnant like this.*** In spite of our sins, you have been gracious and merciful, and have given us a remnant and have restored us to our land and to your sanctuary.

9.14 ***Will you not be angry against us until our destruction and there will be no remnant or survivor?*** Explicit here is the very real fear that violating God's commandments would result in the people's total destruction, leaving them without remnant or survivor. Thus, to this writer, it would not be the failure to remit the required tribute to Persia that could lead to their destruction but their intermarriage with foreigners.

9.15 ***You are just.*** As Miller says (1994: 257), the heart of the confessional prayer is the acknowledgment of God's justice and the rightness of his decrees.

We are here before you in our guilt. We acknowledge that in spite of everything, we have sinned again. That is, we have married foreigners.

Comments

Comment A. The Existential Threat

Williamson (1985: 159) finds the episode of the mass divorce to be one of the 'least attractive' parts of the Hebrew Bible. He and other commentators see ugly racial overtones (e.g. Williamson 1985: 130-32; Blenkinsopp 1988: 176; Mowinckel 1965: 34-35). Mowinckel, for example, likens the attitude to Nazism. Janzen (2002) argues that foreign women were expelled because they were viewed as dangerous to the community, and that what resulted was a 'witch hunt', a purification ritual.

Some commentators rationalize and explain that intermarrying with the 'peoples of the lands' would imply adopting some of their religious practices (e.g. Myers 1965: 77). Since the restored community was to be a religious one, it needed to establish strict criteria for membership in order for the distinctive elements of the Jewish faith to survive (e.g. Ackroyd 1973: 253; Blenkinsopp 1988: 177; Fensham 1982: 125; Williamson 1985: 160). The foreign women are emphasized rather than foreign men because the mother teaches her beliefs to her offspring; those who grow up to follow Jewish practices are more likely to have had Jewish mothers (Holmgren 1987: 73).

A third group of exegetes sees the opprobrium attached to 'mingling the holy seed' as an exegetical elaboration of the older idea of Israel as a 'holy people', an idea frequent in both the Deuteronomic and the Holiness materials (Exod. 19.6; Lev. 20.26; Deut. 14.2; e.g. Fishbane 1985: 114-29; Olyan 2000: 83; 2004; Hayes 2002: 19-59). In Ezra's reference to the seven forbidden Canaanite nations (Ezra 9.1), Fishbane (1985: 115-16) sees a clear allusion to Deut. 7.1-6, where the prohibition against intermarriage is justified 'because you are a holy people' (עַם קָדוֹשׁ). The addition of the Ammonites, Moabites, Egyptians and Amorites is simply the addition of the four peoples prohibited from entering the congregation of Yhwh (Deut. 23.3-8; cf. Neh. 13.1-3). The antidote of divorce expels those who had entered the congregation of Yhwh illegally. Since these peoples were forbidden up to the tenth generation, it follows that their children are forbidden as well. It is the fear of defiling the land and of being expelled from it again, combined with their immersion in a sea of alien peoples, that leads the returnees not only to zealously follow torah law but also to extend it to a new situation through exegesis. In contrast, Klawans (1995; 2000: 43-46) argues that the restoration community believed that the moral practices of the neighboring peoples defile the land and that such defilement would lead to exile. Separating from the peoples of the land is a separation from such defiling practices. However, it cannot be fear of the practices that led to the mass divorce, or there would have been provision for conversion or for other demonstration of relinquishing foreign ways. As both Olyan and Hayes point out, an impermeable boundary is created independent of the behavior of the foreigner.

The biblical writer who wrote this prayer seems to have seen in the Judeans' intermarriages a threat to their very presence on their land. He presents Ezra exhibiting shock and dismay upon hearing the news, and characterizes his response as one of extreme mourning—Ezra fasts, pulls out his hair, and tears his garments (Ezra 9.3, 5). As noted above, this stereotypical mourning rite is also seen in the description of the desolation of Moab after their destruction by the Babylonians. The goal of the self-immolation in all these cases is the same—to show repentance and contrition and so to avert another evil decree.

The temple's destruction and the exile of the people demonstrated God's anger. The Babylonians were an unwitting tool of the god of heaven; like the Assyrians before them, they were the rod of Yhwh's anger (Isa. 10.6). Rather than the exile being caused by repeated rebellions against Babylon and failures to pay the tribute owed her (2 Kgs 24.1, 20), the biblical writers (both of Ezra and of the book of Kings) internalized the guilt and concluded that the people must have sinned against God. To the writer of Kings, the exile was a just punishment, because Zedekiah, the king, 'did what was evil' and 'Jerusalem and Judah so angered Yhwh that he expelled them from his presence' (2 Kgs 24.20). The author of Kings leaves the precise reason for God's anger unspecified; it is some nameless 'evil' of their king that brought about the destruction and the exile. The author of Ezra on the other hand states that the exile was caused by the sins of the whole people, not just their king, and by their failure to keep the commandments (Ezra 9.13, 14).

This is expressed in the Judeans' explanation to Tattenai of how their temple came to be in ruins in what is likely an authentic letter:

> Because our ancestors had angered the god of heaven, he gave them into the hand of King Nebuchadnezzar of Babylon, the Chaldean, who destroyed this house and carried away the people to Babylonia (Ezra 5.12).

God is always in control; whatever may happens, it happens only because God wills it. God is just. Evil is deserved. The only conclusion that can be derived from misfortune, injury, or death is that the victim had sinned (Crenshaw 2005: 117-31). Bad things do not happen to good people (*pace* Kushner 1981); indeed, the fact of the injury or death proves that the person had sinned. If 'bad things' happened to 'good people', then it would mean that either God was not just or that God was not in charge and had no power. Either conclusion was untenable, and for that matter unbiblical. Although the view is questioned in the biblical book of Job, it had a long reign. We see it here in this prayer, most likely written in the Hellenistic period as the latest addition to the text. (See following comment.)

Ezra brings the torah to Judah, but whether or not the people already knew the commandments in it, they were still responsible for them. Ezra states, 'shall we break the commandments again' (9.14)? In other words, it is because we have broken the commandments in the past that we were cast out of the land; shall we risk breaking them again when doing so might cause God to destroy us entirely?

> After all that has come upon us for our evil deeds and for our great guilt, seeing that you, our god, have punished us less than our iniquities deserved and have given us such a remnant as this, shall we break your commandments again and intermarry with the peoples who practice these abominations? Would you not be angry with us until you destroy us without remnant or survivor (Ezra 9.13, 14)?

This fear that foreign wives may turn the hearts of their husbands from Yhwh may be what is behind the concern shown by the biblical writer, but it is never stated explicitly (except in Neh. 13.26). What is explicit, however, is the fear that violating God's commandments would result in the people's total destruction, leaving them without remnant or survivor (Ezra 9.14).

According to the biblical writer, the antidote to sin and to God's expected response to it is obedience to the law. To this end, the people agree to form a new covenant with Yhwh and to put away their foreign wives according to torah (Ezra 10.3). This ability to change one's ways, to repent, to send away the foreign element, and to make a new covenant emphasizes God's patience and compassion as well as man's free will. Indeed, no event or situation in the narrative present is explained in Ezra–Nehemiah as a consequence of the sin of the intermarriages (Japhet 2003: 442). This may be because the mass divorce has averted the awful decree.

Comment B. History and Story

In the absence of recording devices one should not expect stories of the past to be history in the sense that we know it. Thucydides (460–c. 395 BCE) states the problems of creating an accurate recounting of even contemporaneous events (*Hist.* 1.22):

> As to the speeches that were made by different men, either when they were about to begin the war or when they were already engaged therein, it has been difficult to recall with strict accuracy the words actually spoken, both for me as regards that which I myself heard, and for those who from various sources brought me reports. Therefore the speeches are given in

> the language in which, as it seemed to me, the several speakers would express, on the subjects under consideration, the sentiments most befitting the occasion, though at the same time I have adhered as closely as possible to the general sense of what was actually said.

Thucydides admits to putting words into the mouths of his historical characters, words that they might have said, words appropriate for the occasion, but even so words that Thucydides himself had written. This is what we have here. That this was done to biblical stories as well is amply demonstrated in the book of Esther. The Hebrew version of Esther has no prayers, but the translation into Greek has one that the translator put into the mouth of Mordechai and a long one that he put into the mouth of Esther. Comparing the Hebrew and Greek versions of Esther (and Daniel) shows how texts grew and how subsequent authors felt free to add and embellish the stories they received. We read in Ezra 10.6 that Ezra 'rose', so he must have been on his knees, and if on his knees, he must have been praying. It is natural then for the Hellenistic author to insert the words that he 'must have' prayed as another Hellenistic author did with Mordechai and Esther.

Ezra 10.1-17

The Mass Divorce

This episode may be one of the saddest in the Hebrew Bible. The case of Athens, described in a comment to Ezra 9, shows the full force of the edict. As in any divorce (note the case of Tamar, Genesis 38), however, the divorced woman would have gone back to her parents' home and the children born to her would then have been adopted into her father's household (Cohn-Haft 1995: 1). It would not have been as in the case of Hagar and her son Ishmael (Genesis 16, 21), who were simply sent out into the desert to fend for themselves. See comment below. Nor is there any intimation that the divorced wives were sold into slavery, as at Athens.

The narrative picks up in 10.2 directly from Ezra 9.1a, 'after these things'. Everything in between is a late insertion. According to the basic narrative, there is no crowd around Ezra, only the few officials who approach him. (See Comment B at the end of the chapter for a discussion of the original Ezra story.)

Translation

1. *(As Ezra prayed and made his confession weeping and throwing himself down*[a] *before the house of God,*[b] *a very large crowd of men, women, and children from Israel*[c] *were gathered to him. The people too wept in great numbers.)*

2. *Shecaniah son of Jehiel of the Elamites*[d] *addressed Ezra,*[e] *saying:*
'We have acted faithlessly with our god[f] *and have had foreign women*
from the peoples of the land dwell with us. But even now there is hope[g]
for Israel about this. 3. *So now,*[h] *let us make a pact*[i] *with our god*[j] *to*
send out all the women[k] *and the ones born of them according to the*
advice of my lord[l] *and of the ones who tremble*[m] *at the command of*
our god, and let it be done according to the law.[n] 4. *Stand up!,*[o] *for*
this is your responsibility,[p] *but we are with you. Be strong and act!'*

5. *So Ezra*[q] *stood up and had the officers of the priests, of the Levites, and of all Israel swear to act according to this matter, and they swore.*

6. *Then Ezra*[r] *got up from before the house of God*[s] *and went to the temple chamber*[t] *of Yehoḥanan son of Eliashib and spent the night there.*[u] *Bread he did not eat and water he did not drink, for he was in mourning over the faithlessness*[v] *of the exiles.* 7. *So they sent out a herald in Judah*[w] *and Jerusalem to all the exiles that they should gather in Jerusalem:*[x]

8. *'Anyone who does not come in three days*[y] *according to the advice of the officials and the elders*[z] *will have all his (movable) property confiscated and he will be separated from the community of the exiles'.*[aa]

9. *So all the men of Judah and Benjamin*[bb] *were gathered to Jerusalem on the third day. It was the ninth month on the twentieth*[cc] *of the month, and all the people*[dd] *sat*[ee] *in the square of the house of God shivering*[ff] *on account of the matter*[gg] *and from the rains.*[hh]

10. *Then Ezra the priest*[ii] *rose and said to them, 'You have been faithless*[jj] *and have had foreign women dwell with you to increase the guilt of Israel.* 11. *And now confess*[kk] *to Yhwh, god of your fathers,*[ll] *and do his will, and separate yourselves from the peoples of the land and from the foreign women.'* 12. *Then the entire gathering answered and said*[mm] *with a loud voice,*[nn] *'Yes, it is incumbent upon us to do*[oo] *according to your word.*[pp] 13. *But, the people are many, and this is the time of the rains,*[qq] *and we have no strength to remain outside. The work*[rr] *is not for one day, and not for two, since many of us have transgressed in this matter.* 14. *Let our officers over the entire community stay here, and let any who in our cities has taken foreign wives come at the appointed time*[ss] *and with them the elders of each city and its judges until the fierce anger of our god is turned away from us on account of*[tt] *this matter.'*[uu] 15. *Only Jonathan son of Asahel and Jahzeiah son of Tikvah opposed this,*[vv] *and Meshullam and Shabbethai the Levite supported them.*

16. *And so the exiles did. Ezra the priest . . .*[ww] *men, heads of patriarchal families, were separated*[xx] *according to the house of their fathers, and all of them [recorded] by name.*[yy] *They sat down*[zz] *on the first day of the tenth month to investigate*[aaa] *the matter.* 17. *They finished with all the men who had taken foreign wives by the first day of the first month.*

Textual Notes

a. **10.1** *Throwing himself down.* It is a participle, and one wonders how many times he can do it. Greek Ezra repeats 'praying' here. Perhaps 'lying prostrate' is the better translation, with Williamson (1985).

b. *House of God.* First Esdras reads 'sanctuary'.

c. *From Israel.* First Esdras reads 'from Jerusalem', which makes better sense. The Syriac reads, 'the children were weeping'.

d. **10.2** *Of the Elamites.* First Esdras reads 'of the sons of Israel', that is, of the Israelites.

e. *Ezra.* The Syriac reads 'the scribe'.

f. *Our god.* First Esdras reads 'our Lord'. The Syriac reads 'our Lord God'.

g. *Hope.* Greek Ezra reads ὑπομονή, 'steadfastness', 'fortitude'. The Vulgate reads *paenitentia,* 'sorrow', 'repentance', 'guilt'.

h. **10.3** *And now.* First Esdras and the Vulgate omit this phrase.

i. *Let us make a pact.* First Esdras reads, 'Let us make an oath'.

j. *With our god.* First Esdras reads 'to the Lord'.

k. *Women.* First Esdras reads 'foreign women', a qualifier missing in the Hebrew.

l. *According to the advice of my lord.* Greek Ezra reads 'as you would wish'. First Esdras reads 'as seems good to you'. Both texts imply Ezra. The vocalized word actually reads *adonai,* אֲדֹנָי , the way the word Yhwh is vocalized. Nevertheless, Yhwh is always written with the tetragrammaton, יהוה, in the Hebrew Bible. By removing the Masoretes' vocalization we read *adoni,* ' my Lord', with the versions (*pace* Pakkala 2004: 97).

m. *The ones who tremble.* Greek Ezra reads 'rise and terrify them', or, 'rise, and make them tremble!' 1 Esdras reads 'and to all who obey the law of the Lord'.

n. *According to the law.* This phrase is absent in both 1 Esdras and the Syriac, ending with 'let it be done'. It is likely a very late addition.

o. **10.4** *Rise.* First Esdras adds 'take action!' This is likely original. The Syriac is similar, reading 'be firm!'

p. *For this is your responsibility.* The Syriac reads, 'for it is on your account that this matter has been decided', a paraphrase.

q. **10.5** *Ezra.* The Syriac adds 'the scribe'.

r. **10.6** *Ezra.* The Syriac again adds 'the scribe'.

s. *From before the house of God.* First Esdras reads 'from the court of the temple'.

t. *Chamber.* Greek Ezra reads 'treasury'.

u. *And spent the night there.* The Hebrew actually reads, 'and went there', וילך שם, which makes no sense since he has already arrived. We correct with 1 Esdras and the Syriac to the orthographically similar 'and spent the night there', וילן שם.

v. *Faithlessness.* First Esdras reads 'great lawlessness'.

w. **10.7** *In Judah.* First Esdras reads 'in the whole of Judah'.

x. *Jerusalem.* The Syriac adds 'the capital'.

y. **10.8** *In three days.* First Esdras reads 'in two or three days'.

z. *Advice of the officials and the elders.* First Esdras reads 'according to the decree of the ruling elders'.

aa. *Community of the exiles.* The Syriac reads 'from the people Israel', an interpretation.

bb. **10.9.** *Judah and Benjamin.* First Esdras reads 'of the tribe of Judah and Benjamin'.

cc. *Twentieth.* The Syriac reads 'the tenth'. Probably an error.

dd. *People.* The Syriac reads 'all the people of the Lord'.

ee. *Sat.* The Syriac reads 'gathered', which is probably the real meaning.

ff. *Shivering.* Greek Ezra reads, instead, 'with their wailing'. The Syriac reads 'quaking and shivering because of the matter'.

gg. *On account of the matter.* First Esdras omits. The Vulgate reads 'because of their sin', which explains the text.

hh. *And from the rains.* The Syriac omits this.

ii. **10.10** *The priest.* First Esdras omits the title. It is likely not original, but late.

jj. *Faithless.* The Syriac expands saying, 'you have been false with God'.

kk. **10.11** *Confess.* The Hebrew word is a homonym, meaning literally 'give praise', or 'give thanks', but also 'confess'. Greek Ezra and the Syriac translate it as 'give praise'. First Esdras reads 'confess and give praise'.

ll. *Your fathers.* Greek Ezra and 1 Esdras read 'our fathers'.

mm. **10.12** *Said.* The Syriac adds 'to Ezra'.

nn. *With a loud voice.* Greek Ezra omits this.

oo. *Yes, it is incumbent upon us to do.* The Syriac reads, 'Acceptable is everything that you tell us to do in truth'.

pp. *According to your word.* Greek Ezra reads, 'your word is powerful upon us to do', moving the word 'loud', 'great', to modify 'word'. The Syriac reads 'your beautiful word'.

qq. **10.13** *Time of the rains.* First Esdras reads, 'It is the winter season'.

rr. *The work.* First Esdras reads 'our work'.

ss. **10.14** *At the appointed time.* The Syriac reads 'for a moment in prayer'.

tt. *On account of.* The Hebrew reads 'Until this matter', עַד לַדָּבָר הַזֶּה; עַד must be corrected to עַל, 'on account of this matter'.

uu. *This matter.* The Syriac reads 'this oath'.

vv. **10.15** *Opposed this.* Literally, 'stood against this'. Greek Ezra reads 'were with me on this', reading 'with me', עמדי, instead of 'they stood', עָמְדוּ. This might be the original reading however.

ww. **10.16** . . . *men.* The Syriac reads 'ten men'. Something has dropped out here.

xx. *Ezra the priest . . . were separated.* First Esdras and the Syriac read, 'Ezra the priest selected for himself', reading 'separated' in the active voice rather than the passive/reflexive (niphal). This may be correct.

yy. *All of them by name.* The Syriac reads, 'and all of them were called by name', making the text explicit.

zz. *They sat down.* Greek Ezra reads 'they returned', a reading based on a simple switch in the pointing.

aaa. *To investigate.* The text actually reads 'for Darius', *l^eDaryôš,* rather than '*lidrôš*'.

Notes

10.1 ***As Ezra prayed and made his confession.*** The language switches into third person from the first person of the previous two chapters. As described in the Introduction to Ezra 7–10, the third person was used by ancient authors in an attempt to distance the main character, here Ezra, from the events described, and to convey objectivity and detachment (Campbell 2010). This verse is inserted by the author of the prayer to connect the prayer to the rest of the text.

A very large crowd of men, women, and children from Israel were gathered to him. The reader might imagine that Ezra created quite a scene to draw the crowd. This verse refers to the crowd gathered to Ezra in 9.4. That entire episode including the prayer was added late to the Ezra story. This verse, 10.1, was added when the prayer was inserted to connect the prayer to the story. The vocabulary used in Ezra 10 is so different from that used in Ezra 9 that two different authors are implied (Dor 2006).

The word translated 'crowd' is *qāhāl*, קָהָל. There have been attempts to imply that this word has a political meaning, like an official assembly (e.g. Oswald 2012), but since women and children are explicitly mentioned as present, then it is simply a crowd, with no political connotations.

10.2 ***Shecaniah son of Jehiel.*** Although there is a switch from first person to third, this verse is likely part of the original Ezra story, picking up after 9.1a. Shecaniah would thus have been one of the officials who approached Ezra. Though from Elam, and an Elamite, Shecaniah has a Judean name and patronym, suggesting Judean ancestry. By putting the impulse for the mass divorce into the mouth of Shecaniah ben Jehiel and the other officials who approached Ezra when he arrived (9.1), and not in the mouth of Ezra himself, Ezra's detachment and neutrality are emphasized.

Of the Elamites. Elam was a central province of Achaemenid Iran; its capital, Susa, was the primary capital of the Achaemenid Empire. Nehemiah too, though of Judean descent, was also an Elamite, being from Susa. Shecaniah's origin in Elam suggests that, like Nehemiah, either he or his father or both were Persian officials sent to Judah to serve in an official capacity there. It would have been in this capacity that he approached Ezra, the episkopos. (See comment on Ezra 4.9 for officials from Elam.)

We have acted faithlessly with our god. The word *ma'al* is used here, suggesting that this passage was put into the mouth of Shecaniah by the author of the prayer.

Foreign women. This phrase, נָשִׁים נָכְרִיּוֹת, is used seven times in Ezra, but exclusively in Ezra 10 (2, 10, 11, 14, 17, 18, 44). It never appears in Ezra 9, strongly implying two separate authors (Dor 2006: 18). In Ezra 9, the word used to refer to the women whom Judeans were not to marry is always 'daughters of the peoples of the lands' (9.1-2, 11-12).

The peoples of the land. The phrase used, *'ammê hā'āreṣ,* appears in Ezra 10 twice (10.2, 11) but it appears nowhere else in Ezra in this form with the word for 'land' in the singular. In Ezra 9 it is always 'peoples of the lands', with 'lands' in the plural (Ezra 9.1, 2, 11). In turn, that form, with 'lands' plural, does not appear in Ezra 10. Again, this implies two separate authors. The referent would be the same for both these plural forms, however, and is as it is in Ezra 3.3.

We have caused foreign women from the peoples of the land to dwell [with us]. The word translated 'have caused to dwell with us', וַנֹּשֶׁב, from לְהוֹשִׁיב, *lᵉhôšîb*, the verb 'to dwell' in the causative voice (hiphil). It is not the normal word for 'marry'. The use of this term is intended to imply that a legitimate marriage did not take place but that they were only 'living together'. This verb in this sense is unique to Ezra 10 (Dor 2006: 20). It occurs in Ezra 10 five times (2, 10, 14, 17, 18) but never in Ezra 9. In Ezra

9 the verbs used are *nāśā'*, נָשָׂא, the normal word for 'to take a wife' (9.2, 12), and *l^ehithattēn*, לְהִתְחַתֵּן, the normal word for 'to marry' (9.14). The verb *nāśā'* occurs in Ezra 10 only once (10.44) and *l^ehithattēn* does not appear in Ezra 10 at all. The use of a unique vocabulary in Ezra 10 for 'to take a wife' or 'to marry' again indicates two separate authors of Ezra 9 and 10.

Shecaniah's own father, Jehiel, counted himself among those men who had taken foreign wives (10.26). Did Shecaniah instigate this mass divorce to remove his step-mother and the children born to her from their family and from a possible inheritance?

Hope for Israel about this. The use of the word 'Israel' is the language of the biblical writer who wrote Ezra 9, the introduction to Ezra 7, Nehemiah 8, etc., and which he has now put into the mouth of Shecaniah the Elamite.

10.3 ***Let us make a pact with our god.*** That is, 'let us swear', or, 'let us make an oath'. The word used is *b^erît,* usually translated 'covenant'. It is 'loaded' language. It may have been used here by the biblical writer to foreshadow the torah reading in Nehemiah 8, or it may be original to the Ezra story and used here, as is often the case, purely in its secular meaning (e.g. Gen. 1.27, 32; 1 Kgs 15.19; 20.34).

To send out all the women and the ones born of them. There is nothing in the torah that we have that requires this. Either the plan is Shecaniah's (so Batten 1913: 340) or the plan was Persia's, and Shecaniah, a Persian official from Elam, was following orders. This term 'to send out', לְהוֹצִיא, occurs only in Ezra 10.3, 19, and not in Ezra 9.

Why is only a divorce of foreign women spoken of, not foreign men? In patrilocal societies the women live with their husbands, and if their husbands are foreign, they may no longer have been living in the area. If Judean women had married Persian satrapal and gubernatorial officials, as is evident, there may not have been anything that Ezra could do about it except banish them both (see Neh. 13.28). Only in the case of Judean men marrying the daughters of foreign soldiers or officials would the couple have remained in Judah and be subject to Ezra's decrees.

According to the advice of my lord. The phrase 'my lord' here refers to Ezra, not God. Shecaniah refers to Ezra politely as his lord.

Of the ones who tremble at the command of our god. This phrase refers back to 9.4, the author of that verse adding it to the present scene in order to imply that the crowd who gathered in Ezra 9 is still gathered around Ezra here. In the original version of the Ezra story that is proposed in this commentary, Ezra 9 was added later, and so there is no crowd about Ezra, just a few officials, including Shecaniah the Elamite.

Let it be done according to law. The word translated 'law' here is *tôrâ.* It is notable that this is the only occurrence of the word *tôrâ* in the entire Ezra story (Ezra 7.28–10.44), and it occurs in the mouth of Shecaniah, not Ezra. Moreover, the entire phrase is missing from both the passage in 1 Esdras and that in the Syriac, implying that it is a very late addition to the text (Pakkala 2004: 95).

Even if we include the term as part of an original Ezra story, a written law of Moses is not referred to here. Shecaniah's request should more likely be translated, 'let it be done rightly'. The meaning of *tôrâ* would then be as it is in the rest of the biblical canon—that is, as 'teaching', 'instruction', 'right behavior', 'custom', 'tradition' (e.g. Prov. 6.20, 'do not abandon the teaching [*tôrâ*] of your mother' אַל־תִּטֹּשׁ תּוֹרַת אִמֶּךָ). (Indeed the word is translated as 'teaching' here in Ezra by the Jewish Publication Society.) No written set of laws is implied; rather the term would connote time-honored custom in handling cases of divorce. This means providing the women with their *ketubah,* their written marriage contract entitling the women to the return of all the items of their dowry, plus any other items or funds promised them by their husbands that was written in their marriage contract at the time of the betrothal (Lemos 2010). See Comment B below.

10.4 ***Stand up, for this is your responsibility.*** 'Get to work, this is your job'. Shecaniah reminds Ezra that it is up to Ezra to organize this; it is not up to Shecaniah. As episkopos, Ezra would have the task of supervising the edicts of the king and reporting back to him. The threat to report back gave Ezra all the authority he needed. Of course, he also could depend on the satrapal judges he appointed as well as the commanders of the garrisons stationed in the cities.

10.5 ***Ezra . . . had the officers of the priests, of the Levites, and of all Israel swear to act according to this matter, and they swore.*** This is often translated 'had the leading priests, the Levites, and all Israel swear' (e.g. the NRSV; Williamson 1985: 151; Blenkinsopp 1988: 189), implying that the entire people as well as the leading priests swore. The Hebrew actually says that only the officers swore, but they were officers over 'all Israel', inluding over the priests and the Levites (so also Clines 1984: 127). There is no huge assembly here; we have only a few Persian officials who met with Ezra shortly after he arrived. Nevertheless, they would have been the officials in charge of all Yehud (over the priests, Levites and laity). It is these officials who swear.

Ezra does not trust the officials to implement Shecaniah's proposal voluntarily as it will be difficult and complicated, so he makes them swear to implement it. There is no indication here of community agreement, or of a consensus of the community. Community members are not present and do not speak. Shecaniah the Elamite recommends a mass divorce of foreign wives, and Ezra in response has the officers of Yehud swear to act according to this matter, that is, to swear that they will implement this decision to institute a mass divorce, and so they swore. In fact, they had no choice since Ezra was sent to carry out the orders of the king and he had a garrison behind him to enforce his orders.

It is likely that the reference to 'the priests, the Levites, and all Israel' was inserted here by the same person who added the redundant verse Ezra 7.7. In any case, these are officials over the entire community of Yehud, and they would have been Persian appointees.

10.6 ***Then Ezra got up from before the house of God.*** This verse was likely what prompted the bulk of Ezra 9. If Ezra 'got up', then he must have been on his knees, and so must have been praying. In the context of Ezra 10, however, Ezra has simply gotten up and left the group of officials he was meeting with and moved to his room inside the temple.

And went to the temple chamber of Yehoḥanan [grand]son of Eliashib. This verse is one of the reasons for concluding that Ezra came to Jerusalem after Nehemiah in 398 BCE, in the seventh year of Artaxerxes II, and not before him in 458 BCE, in the seventh year of Artaxerxes I, in spite of the order of the books. Eliashib was high priest at the time of Nehemiah (Neh. 3.1), and so his grandson, Yehoḥanan, was high priest at the time of Ezra. The names of the last four priests of Judah prior to Alexander's conquest are given in Neh. 12.22 (Jonathan in Neh. 12.11 is an error for Yehoḥanan; see VanderKam 1991; 2004: 43-111; Fried 2003a). We know of the high priest Yehoḥanan from a coin imprinted with his name and title and from a reference to him in the Aramaic papyri at Elephantine. Although both Eliashib and Yehoḥanan were common names, it is not likely that any but the high priest would have had an apartment in the temple, nor is it likely that Ezra would have been a guest of any other priest (Clines 1984: 127). Other priests served in courses (*mishmarot*) that rotated in and out of the temple service at fixed periods and so were not always present. (See comment at Ezra 2.39.) The high priest remained constant, however, so he would have needed an apartment in the temple in addition to his own house near the temple where his family would have dwelled (Neh. 3.20).

Bread he did not eat and water he did not drink, for he was in mourning over the faithlessness of the exiles. Commentators have wondered why Ezra continued to fast when the 'whole community' just swore to divorce their foreign wives. Blenkinsopp finds this action redundant with the description of the general assembly that met a few days later (Ezra 10.9-12), and attributes the repetition to the Chronicler's combining various sources (Blenkinsopp 1988: 189). Pakkala agrees (2004: 96), arguing that vv. 5 and 6-9 are two separate additions to the basic text since Ezra makes all the people swear in v. 5 and makes them swear again in v. 11. However, if we recognize that only the few officials swore to implement Shecaniah's proposal and that the people as a whole were not involved (and were not there), then there is no contradiction or repetition. Ezra is in mourning and fasting because of the big job ahead of him in convincing the *people* that they were going to have to divorce their wives and expel their own children.

Faithlessness of the exiles. From the point of view of the biblical writer, the exiles had merited the supreme good fortune of living in Judah; they had been redeemed from Babylon. Now they are threatening to spoil it all and to be cast out among the nations again by submitting themselves to foreign influences. From the point of view of Ezra the episkopos, both the Judeans and Persian satrapal officals (who were the first in this faithlessness) had disobeyed a Persian demand not to marry (Fried 2002c; 2015a).

10.7 ***So they sent out a herald in Judah and Jerusalem.*** The 'they' who sent out the herald were the Persian officials, the subject of v. 5, who were now implementing the decision that they had just agreed to. It is often assumed that it was the assembly, the *qāhāl*, who had the power to send out heralds, order attendance, confiscate property, and order divorces (Myers 1965: 132; Blenkinsopp 1988: 175; Oswald 2012). This would give it quite a bit of authority, suggesting a type of self-rule. Yet, it was not the *qāhāl*—consisting as noted above of men, women and children—that had the judicial power to give such orders, but the *śārîm*, the imperially appointed military commanders. Nor was it the elders (*pace* Clines 1984: 128; Williamson 1985: 154). See comment on the elders below at v. 8.

To all the exiles. That is, the entire community of Israel living in Judah and all others who may have joined up with them from among the non-Judeans living there (Ezra 6.21). As discussed in the Introduction, the archaeology of Judah and Benjamin reveals that the number who had remained in the land after the Babylonian conquest and resultant devastation from war, pestilence and famine was negligible. Those who managed to survive the devastation fled. After the recovery under the Persians, Judeans returned not only from Babylon but also from all the places to which they had escaped. The foreigners living in Judah would have been many, however, including, most prominently, members of the foreign garrisons located near every large city, plus all the foreign officials, prefects, judges, military commanders and other dignitaries sent by the king to manage the province. (See Introduction.)

That they should gather in Jerusalem. They need to gather to hear the announcement of the provincial officials. The root for 'gather' is √קבץ, *qbṣ*, which occurs three times in Ezra 10 (1, 7 and 9), but not in Ezra 9. In Ezra 9 the root used for 'gather' is √אסף, *'sp,* again implying different authors.

10.8 ***Anyone who does not come in three days.*** The province was small enough that this would be enough time.

According to the advice of the officers and the elders. The word here is 'advice', 'counsel', not 'order', as it is usually translated. In point of fact, however, the officers could give orders because they had the soldiers of the garrisons to enforce them; elders could only advise. Dandamayev (1982) has studied the *šībū*, the elders, in Neo-Babylonian and Persian period Babylonian texts. A city's elders were those male citizens who owned land within the city's districts. They were entitled to sit as witnesses in the *puḫru*, the city assembly. They did not speak or otherwise participate in the proceedings, however, but served as witnesses only. (See comment below on the role of the assembly.)

The references to the elders here show them in their normal role as witnesses in cases of confiscation of property and divorce proceedings; no other form of participation is implied. Both the instigation for the divorces as well as the sanctions imposed for those failing to comply were by order of the *śārîm*, the military officers, not the elders (9.1; 10.5, 7). Court cases were tried by provincial judges; the elders serve only as witnesses to them (10.14). As in Mesopotamia, decisions are stated as made in the name of the officials and the elders, but the elders did not speak during the proceedings. This role for the elders is exhibited in Ruth 4.1-6. Elders were called to serve as witnesses to transactions, but they did not participate directly in them.

Will have all his (movable) property confiscated. The word for property here, *r*ᵉ*kûš*, רְכוּשׁ, refers to movable property only. The word translated 'confiscated' is *ḥerem*. Traditionally this would mean that items would be handed over to the god (i.e. to the priesthood; Lev. 27.21; Num. 18.14). In a Persian context it is not clear; perhaps the property is handed over to the Persian authorities and sent on to Susa, since this is one of the punishments listed in Ezra 7.26.

Separated from the community of the exiles. This threat of banishment here is one of the reasons sometimes given for the translation of שְׁרֹשִׁי, *š*ᵉ*rōšî*, in Ezra 7.26 as 'banishment' rather than as 'flogging'. It is not likely, however, that Ezra or the Persian officials would feel themselves limited by the punishments listed in Artaxerxes' letter. We see that Nehemiah, in his role as Persian governor of Judah, not only flogged but also plucked out the hair of the head and the beard of those who had married foreign women (Neh. 13.25; Heltzer 1995–96).

What does separation from the community entail? It does not seem to mean outright exile, but rather a loss of citizenship. We have no description of this in Judah, but parallels in the contemporary Greek context are instructive (Blidstein 1974). In Athens, the affected person could not bring a suit in a court of law, and this may be what is meant here. In the Persian Empire, courts were controlled by Persian appointed judges, so they would certainly be able to enforce such a ban if that is what is intended. The affected person would then have had no way to redress his grievances; if someone stole from him, for example, he could not accuse him in a court of law.

10.9 ***So all the men of Judah and Benjamin were gathered to Jerusalem.*** They did not come voluntarily but 'were gathered' (passive voice) by the force of the edict.

It was the ninth month. This is mid-winter, cold and rainy.

While all the people sat in the square of the house of God. Although it says 'all the people', only adult males would have had to come, and only they are referred to as having 'been gathered'. The square would have been the paved courtyard in front of the temple on the temple mount.

Shivering on account of the matter. The word translated 'shivering' here is not the same word as used in 9.4 or 10.3 above. They were shivering from the rain and from the fear of what may be in store for them.

10.10 ***Then Ezra the priest rose and said to them.*** Pakkala (2004: 96) assumes that this verse originally followed immediately after 10.4. Shecaniah asks Ezra to stand (v. 4), and now in v. 10, he stands. Shecaniah asks Ezra to resolve the issue, and he does here in v. 10. In Pakkala's mind (so also Blenkinsopp 1988: 189), the issue is resolved twice, first in v. 5 when everyone agrees to send out their foreign wives, and now again in vv. 10-14. It is more likely that in v. 5, as stated there, only the officials were present, and that only they swore. They swear not to send out their own foreign wives, but rather to enforce a mass divorce on the population, according to Shecaniah's proposal. To that effect, the officials sent out a herald to gather the people in Jerusalem so that the people may hear the decision of the officials. They have now been gathered. Ezra rises and speaks to the entire (male) population for the first time.

'You have been faithless and have had foreign women dwell with you'. Ezra repeats here the words of Shecaniah (10.4). This is one reason for thinking that all the verses between 10.4 and 10.10 were a late insertion. Once we understand though that the entire community in Judah was not present in 10.4, but only Yehud's Persian officials, then we can see the need for the intervening verses.

To increase the guilt of Israel. These are also the words of Shecaniah. The presence of the word 'Israel' indicates the biblical writer. The word is foreign to a Persian context. The biblical writer has reframed a likely Persian edict as a religious issue.

10.11 ***'And now confess to Yhwh, god of your fathers, and do his will, and separate yourselves from the peoples of the land and from the foreign women'.*** See comment at Ezra 9 on the role of confession. For the identity of the 'peoples of the land/s' see the comment on Ezra 3.3.

The issue for the historian is whether in fact there was a mass divorce in Judah, and if so, was it at the instigation of the Persian ruler, as is supposed in this commentary, or was it at the instigation of the Judean religious leadership. By giving Ezra the title of priest, by inserting the prayer, and by framing the divorce as 'doing the will of Yhwh', the biblical writer attempts to present this as an internal Judean matter instituted by the priestly establishment. Historically speaking, however, Ezra and Nehemiah were Persian officials, Persian functionaries, committed to doing the will of Persia and committed to keeping the provinces quiet and to avoid creating unnecessary problems for her. Since Pericles instituted the same exact process of a mass divorce in contemporary Athens, for Athenian imperial purposes, it is reasonable to suppose that Persian officials instituted a mass divorce in Judah for the same imperial purposes. (See comment at the end of Ezra 9 on the mass divorce and Persian concerns.) It would not, therefore, have been Yhwh's will, but Persia's, although the biblical writer may have seen these as the same. Yhwh's will is exerted through those he sets over the Judean people. Merton's (1941) summary of the purposes for enforcing endogamy holds not only for Athens but for Persia as well (see comment at Ezra 9). The social prerogatives and immunities that were intended to be maintained by Persian edicts against intermarriage with the local Judean population were the prerogatives and immunities of the Persian officials, judges, garrison commanders, and even the common Persian soldier doing his military service far away from home in the Persian province of Judah. It was these prerogatives that Persian officials, such as Ezra and Nehemiah, attempted to preserve.

10.12 ***Then the entire community answered and said with a loud voice.*** The word translated here as 'community' is translated in the Greek versions as ἐκκλησία, *ekklēsia*, which in a Greek context indicates an official legislative body. That is not the implication of *qāhāl*, however.

Albertz argues that the popular assembly, the *qāhāl,* was 'summoned now and then when important decisions were due' (1994: 447). He refers to this verse in Ezra and to Neh. 5.7, 13. The image in Nehemiah 5 is the same as in this verse. Commentators suppose that the agreement expressed here in v. 12 was preceded by discussion and a vote, resulting in consensus, but that is not what is being described. In the Persian Empire the assembly was never called to obtain its opinion. Assemblies were called to hear the edicts of the king, satrap, or governor. This is what is shown here and in Nehemiah 5. The people were assembled only to hear Ezra's or Nehemiah's pronouncements. See Comment A below on the role of the assembly and the references cited there.

'Yes, it is incumbent upon us to do according to your word'. This is the response of the assembly, 'yes, we have to do what you say', or literally, 'yes, it is upon us to do what you say'. There is no choice here. The men assembled here were not asked their opinion; they were gathered to hear the orders of the Persian administration under whom they were living.

10.13 ***But.*** But (we do not really want to do this, let's stall . . .').

The people are many, and this is the time of the rains, and we have no strength to remain outside. The work is not for one day, nor for two, since many of us have transgressed in this matter'. In other words, let's postpone all of this as long as we can.

10.14 ***Let our officials over the entire community stay here.*** Literally, 'let our officials who are over the entire community stand'. Rashi translates, 'remain with the congregation', but that would imply their splitting up and traveling to each of the towns where the people lived. The NRSV reads, 'Let our officials represent the whole assembly', but represent them how?

More likely, 'let them stand' means 'let them [the Persian officials] stay here in Jerusalem' while everyone else returns to his own town to decide what to do.

And let any who in our cities has taken foreign wives come at the appointed time. Only those who have taken foreign wives need return to Jerusalem.

And with them the elders of each city and its judges. When they return, let them return with the elders of their own city and their own judges (not Persian appointed ones). Perhaps these will advocate for those accused of marrying foreign women.

Until the fierce anger of our god is turned away from us on account of this matter. Until this matter is solved. This is likely an addition from the author of Ezra 9.

10.15 ***Only Jonathan son of Asahel and Jahzeiah son of Tikvah opposed this.*** The phrase translated here as 'opposed this' is literally 'stood upon this', עָמְדוּ עַל־זֹאת, *'āmᵉdû 'al zō't*, which in modern Hebrew actually means 'insisted on this'. However we must translate it as 'stood up against this', as in 1 Chron. 21.1, וַיַּעֲמֹד שָׂטָן עַל־יִשְׂרָאֵל, 'Satan rose up against Israel', and as in 2Chron. 20.23, וַיַּעַמְדוּ בְּנֵי עַמּוֹן וּמוֹאָב עַל־יֹשְׁבֵי הַר־שֵׂעִיר, 'the Ammonites and Moabites rose up against the inhabitants of Mount Seir'. Although opposition is being expressed, we do not know exactly to what. Are they opposed to the postponement, or are they opposed to the whole process of enforcing the divorce? We do not know who these two men were, but they do not appear among the men cited for having married foreign women (Ezra 10.18-43). Perhaps they had married foreign women and refused to appear before the judges in Jerusalem. Or, perhaps they had not married foreign women at all.

The opposition of these men was not sufficient to affect the outcome, since they had all admitted (v. 12) that they were obligated to do what Ezra had announced to them, that they would have to divorce their foreign wives. This was mere grumbling.

And Meshullam and Shabbethai the Levite supported them. That is, they supported Jonathan son of Asahel and Jahzeiah son of Tikvah in their opposition. Both Meshullam and Shabbethai are common names, and since their patronyms are not given we cannot know who they are exactly. A Meshullam was sent with several other 'leaders' to Iddo at Casiphia to try to encourage some Levites to join Ezra in the trip to Judah (Ezra 8.16). A

Meshullam of the descendants of Bani is listed among those who had married foreign women (10.29). A Meshullam son of Berechiah son of Meshezabel worked on Jerusalem's city wall (Neh. 3.4, 30) as did a Meshullam son of Besodeiah (Neh. 3.6). The daughter of Meshullam son of Berechiah had married a foreigner, the son of Tobiah the Ammonite, the Persian appointed governor of Ammon (Neh. 6.18). A Shabbethai is listed among the Levites as being over the outside work on the temple (Neh. 11.16), and one is listed among the Levites in Nehemiah 8 who helped the people understand the law (Neh. 8.7); it may be the same one, but the name is common.

10.16 ***And so the exiles did.*** Everyone went home to their villages, and those men who had married foreign women returned to Jerusalem at the appointed time with their elders and their judges.

Ezra the priest . . . men, heads of patriarchal families, were separated according to the house of their fathers, and all of them [recorded] by name. The versions tend to put the verb in the active voice with Ezra as the subject. According to the versions, Ezra separated the men who returned to Jerusalem according to their patriarchal families. The verse seems odd, and has likely become corrupted in transition. It may have been inserted to explain why the list that follows records each man according to his 'father's house'.

They sat down on the first day of the tenth month to investigate the matter. The men who admitted to having married non-Judean women returned to Jerusalem about ten days later, on the first day of the tenth month, or December 26 of 398 BCE, according to the Gregorian calendar. Did they return alone, or did they come with their wives and children?

It is not clear who the 'they' are who are said to investigate the matter. If they were the 'heads of fathers' houses', referring to the subject of the previous verse, then it is odd that they needed to return to Jerusalem to do this. Why could they not have done all this in the cities where they lived? In most societies of the ancient Near East, including Persian period Egypt from which most of our records come, judges were not involved in a divorce. Divorces were simply between a man and a woman; they would stand before an assembly and one or the other would say, 'I hate you'. If a woman felt that her marriage contract was not being honored properly, however, then she or rather her father or guardian could bring a suit before a judge. In Persian Egypt, from which we have the most data, all the judges were Persian, so in Judah as well, the suit would have been brought before the judges whom Ezra appointed, not before the 'heads of fathers' houses'.

10.17 ***They finished with all the men who had taken foreign wives by the first day of the first month.*** This is April 23, 397 BCE, four months later. The year 397 BCE was a leap year, and a second month of Addaru was added at the end of the year (March 24–April 22; Parker and Dubberstein 1956: 34).

What would have taken so long? According to the edict, only those men who admitted having married foreign women needed to arrive in Jerusalem (v. 14), so what needed to be adjudicated? If they were only recording the names of the men who appeared, it could not have taken four months (or even three, if no leap year). Did they straggle in over the four months and that is what took so long, or did everyone arrive on the first day of the tenth month, and it was the investigations themselves that took so long? If only those who admitted marrying foreign women appeared in Jerusalem, what was there to investigate? Perhaps this is an allusion to disputes over the *ketubahs,* the marriage contracts that detailed what the wife was to receive in the event of a divorce.

Comments

Comment A. The Role of the Assembly in the Ancient Near East and Persia
Legislation in the ancient Near East and Persia resulted from the king's decree, or from the decrees of his agents, the mayors, provincial governors, and numerous other officials he appointed and who spoke in his name. This was so, even though Mesopotamia had a tradition of local assemblies (*puḫru*). These assemblies did not create law. A search among the Neo-Babylonian and Persian documents for the Akkadian terms *puḫru* (assembly) and *paḫāru* (to assemble) reveals this institution's purpose.[1] A *puḫru* was called for judicial decisions only: a sheep was stolen, or land needed to be reassigned. The parties to the transaction testified before judges who alone pronounced the decision. The scribe drew up the case; the witnesses (*mār banī*) signed the document to certify that the trial had occurred and the decision was rendered as described. The parties called to testify in the case did not sign the document as witnesses to the trial, although the same term was used (*mukinnu*). Members of the assembly (*puḫru)* who signed the tablet never spoke during the proceedings. They simply witnessed the trial and its outcome. There were often between twenty and thirty men signing as witnesses. These men formed the *puḫru,* the assembly. (The only exceptions to this come from literary texts; see van de Mieroop 1997: 118-41; 1999: 139-61; Bloom 1992; Fleming 2004: esp. p. 235.)

That there were no legislative assemblies means there was no occasion when an assembly met to discuss, for example, a new law, a new tax, or a new canal. There is no hint of self-rule in any of these texts. The king or satrap made the decisions regarding these matters. The district leader called an assembly to hear the decision and to rubber stamp its assent, but the

1. I am indebted to Martha Roth, Tim Collins, and Linda McLarnan of the Chicago Oriental Institute for their help in searching their database. This section is based on Fried 2001.

assembly did not contribute to the decision-making process. There is no evidence of local participation in city governance anywhere in Mesopotamia and nowhere in the Achaemenid Empire.

This is illustrated by the Judeans at Elephantine in Achaemenid period Egypt. Tuplin suggests that the Judean community assembly at Elephantine was a judicial body that acted to adjudicate land disputes (Tuplin 1987a: 111). Yet all the land disputes mentioned in the papyri were in fact resolved by judges during judicial proceedings. The cases he cites in reference to local assemblies (*TAD* B 2.6, B 3.3, and B 3.8) are in fact all gatherings to witness marriage and divorce proceedings. A party proclaimed in front of the assembled men that the couple was divorced, or that one party agreed to fulfill an obligation if a divorce did occur. As in Babylon, those assembled at Elephantine served as witnesses only.

Oswald (2012) has recently argued that the evidence from Persian period Mesopotamia or Egypt is not relevant because the image revealed in the Pentateuch and in Ezra–Nehemiah displays the type of assembly that was in force in Greece. In Greece, the men present in the assembly voted, and legislation was actually created. He cites in particular a verse in which, he claims, 'the people pass the resolution to bring into force the so-called Covenant Code' (Oswald 2012: 6). That passage reads as follows:

> Moses came and told the people all of Yhwh's words and all the ordinances; and all the people answered with one voice, and said, 'All the words that Yhwh has spoken we will do' (Exod. 24.3).

This is not the image of a vote taken by citizens after hearing the pros and cons of the matter. This is the image of an official (Moses) informing the people of a king's (i.e. God's) edicts, and their assent. This is not the picture of a democracy. So also in Ezra 10.9. Oswald finds in Ezra 10 the image of an assembly that 'formally appoints a committee to investigate and solve the matter [of the mixed marriages]' (Oswald 2012: 7).

It may be the Greek translation, ἐκκλησία, *ekklēsia*, for 'assembly' (Ezra 10.12) that has given commentators the notion that we have here in Persian period Judah the beginnings of democracy. While admitting that Judah was ruled by a Persian governor who reported to the satrap, and also admitting that under the governor were Persian officials, *śārîm*, who administered each of nine administrative units within the province, Albertz (1994: 446-47) argues for 'Jewish self-government' below this Persian administrative apparatus. He claims that this consisted of 'a council of elders' and a 'priestly college' that advised the governor. He bases his theory on a letter, *TAD* A 4.7, 8, from the Persian garrison on the Nile island of Elephantine to these groups. The letter is dated to 407 BCE and is addressed to the Persian governor of Yehud, Bagavahya. The letter refers to a previous letter sent three years before that was addressed to the same governor and 'to

Yehoḥanan, the high priest, and to his colleagues the priests who are in Jerusalem, and to Ostanes, the brother of Anani, and to the nobles of the Judeans, חרי יהודיא. Albertz concludes from this that these were government officials with real power. This is a lot to conclude from a single letter that only expresses the hope that those appealed to will use whatever personal influence they may have to appeal to the satrap of Egypt, Arsames, to permit the temple at Elephantine to be rebuilt. There is no indication in the letter that those addressed had any actual authority. The only power in the Persian Empire was the king, and the satraps who carried out his bidding. The idea that other powers existed, or that the king shared power, cannot be supported. Governors carried out the orders of the satrap, who carried out the orders of the king, as the Aramaic documents from Bactria and Elephantine make abundantly clear. Provincial governors did not even have the authority to release the soldiers under them from building a city wall so that they could rescue a harvest from the locusts (Naveh and Shaked 2012; Fried 2004; 2013c; in press a). There were no independent institutions in the Achaemenid Empire. Men were assembled to hear decrees and to witness the decisions of imperial officials. That is all.

Comment B. The Mass Divorce

All marriages, even marriages between Judeans and non-Judeans, would have required that in the event of a divorce the woman be given her rights as enumerated in her *ketubah*, her written marriage contract. Several of these documents are visible in the archives from Persian period Elephantine and include intermarriages (*TAD* B 2.5; 2.6; 3.8). One of these (B 2.6) is the marriage contract of the daughter of a member of a foreign garrison who was marrying a local Egyptian man. Their divorce would have involved honoring the contract and the return to the woman's father of the dowry that he had given to her husband upon marriage, all of which is carefully enumerated (Levick 2012: 101). Not to do so risked the anger and possible revenge of the woman's father and brothers; in fact it was fear of this anger that restrained a number of divorces. A case in Athens is relevant. A husband, Phrastor, learned that his wife, Phano, was not an Athenian citizen, and 'threw her out', *ekbalonta* (Cohn-Haft 1995: 4). The woman's father, Stephanos, sued to get her dowry back, and when that failed, he attempted to receive at least the interest on it. Evidently that too failed. The case shows, however, that even marriages that may not have been considered legitimate to begin with did involve a dowry that belonged to the woman's father upon divorce.

Japhet (2007) compares the situation of the women in Ezra to Hagar (Gen. 6.1-16; 21.9-23). As Japhet admits, Hagar was no actual wife but simply his slave. She had no marriage document and no dowry. Thus, it cannot be asserted that the situation of Hagar is analogous. Japhet argues that Shecaniah's term for divorce, that is, 'put out', לְהוֹצִיא (10.3), implies an annulment, 'as if the marriage never took place' (Japhet 2007: 151). Shecaniah's proposal, Japhet suggests, is to turn them all into secondary wives, regardless of their social class, and to put them out—all according to the law—without the hassle of a formal divorce. The concept of annulment may be anachronistic, however; I know of no such cases in antiquity. If there was a marriage, then there is a marriage document, a *ketubah*, and so a divorce settlement. A wife may not be reclassified as a slave in order to void her marriage contract. The comparison with the case of Phrastor and Phano, quoted above, is apt. Phrastor uses the same sort of vocabulary as does Shecaniah—'throw out!' 'Throwing out' is the same as a divorce, however, since in neither society, Athens or Jerusalem, does the husband have to supply a reason for terminating the relationship. In both cases, however, there is the matter of the marriage contract, and the dowry. These documents always provided for the woman in the event of divorce, no matter the reason for it. If the divorce was done according to the law (as Shecaniah requires), then the woman received her dowry, and she returned with her children and her dowry to her father's house, her children adopted into her father's family.

Ezra 10.18-44

The Judean Men Who Married Foreign Women

Of the men who married foreign women, the high priestly family is listed first (10.18), then the rest of the priests (10.19-22), then the Levites (10.23-24), and finally the rest of the people, termed here Israel (10.25-43).

Translation

18. *It was found among the sons*[a] *of the priests*[b] *who had taken foreign*
wives—of the sons of Jeshua son of Jozadak and his kin: Maaseiah, Eliezer,
Jarib,[c] *and Gedaliah.*[d] 19. *They pledged to send away their wives, and their*
guilt offering was a ram[e] *of the flock for their guilt.* 20. *Of the descendants*
of Immer: Hanani and Zebadiah.[f] 21. *Of the sons of Harim: Maaseiah, Eli-*
jah, Shemaiah, Jehiel, and Uzziah.[g] 22. *Of the sons of Pashhur: Elioenai,*
Maaseiah, Ishmael, Nethanel, Jozabad,[h] *and Elasah.*[i]
23. *Of the Levites: Jozabad, Shimei, Kelaiah (that is, Kelita), Pethahiah,*
Judah,[j] *and Eliezer.*[k] 24. *Of the singers: Eliashib.*[l] *Of the gatekeepers: Shal-*
lum, Telem,[m] *and Uri.*[n]
25. *And of Israel: of the sons of Parosh: Ramiah,*[o] *Izziah, Malchijah,*
Mijamin,[p] *Eleazar, Malchijah,*[q] *and Benaiah.* 26. *Of the sons of Elam: Mat-*
taniah, Zechariah, Jehiel,[r] *Abdi, Jeremoth, and Elijah.* 27. *Of the sons of*
Zattu:[s] *Elioenai,*[t] *Eliashib,*[u] *Mattaniah,*[v] *Jeremoth, Zabad,*[w] *and Aziza.*[x]
28. *Of the sons of Bebai: Jehohanan, Hananiah, Zabbai,*[y] *and Athlai.*[z] 29. *Of*
the sons of Bani:[aa] *Meshullam,*[bb] *Malluch, Adaiah, Jashub, Sheal,*[cc] *and*
Jeremoth. 30. *Of the sons of Pahath-Moab*[dd]*: Adna,*[ee] *Chelal,*[ff] *Benaiah,*[gg]
Maaseiah, Mattaniah, Bezalel,[hh] *Binnui,*[ii] *and Manasseh.* 31. *The sons*[jj] *of*
Harim:[kk] *Eliezer,*[ll] *Isshijah, Malchijah, Shemaiah,*[mm] *Shimeon,*[nn] 32. *Benja-*
min, Malluch, [and] Shemariah.[oo] 33. *Of the sons of Hashum: Mattenai,*[pp]
Mattattah, Zabad,[qq] *Eliphelet, Jeremai,*[rr] *Manasseh, and Shimei.* 34. *Of the*
sons of Bani:[ss] *Maadai,*[tt] *Amram,*[uu] *and 'Uel,*[vv] 35. *Benaiah,*[ww] *Bedeiah,*[xx]
Cheluhi,[yy] 36. *Vaniah,*[zz] *Meremoth,*[aaa] *Eliashib,* 37. *Mattaniah, Mattenai,*[bbb]
and Jaasu.[ccc] 38. *Of the sons of Binnui:*[ddd] *Shimei,*[eee] 39. *Shelemiah, Nathan,*
Adaiah,[fff] 40. *Machnadebai,*[ggg] *Shashai, Sharai,*[hhh] 41. *Azarel,*[iii] *Shelemiah,*[jjj]
Shemariah,[kkk] 42. *Shallum,*[lll] *Amariah,*[mmm] *and Joseph.* 43. *Of the sons of*

Nebo:[nnn] *Jeiel,*[ooo] *Mattithiah,*[ppp] *Zabad,*[qqq] *Zebina,*[rrr] *Jaddai,*[sss] *Joel, and Benaiah.*

44. *All these had married foreign women, and there were among them women who had provided*[ttt] *children.*

Textual Notes

a. **10.18** *Among the sons.* First Esdras omits 'the sons'.

b. *Of the priests.* First Esdras adds 'who had gathered', implying that the ones who did not gather could not be investigated.

c. *Jarib.* The Syriac reads 'Yonadab'.

d. *Gedaliah.* First Esdras reads Ιωδανος, Jodanos, which seems similar to the Syriac rendition of Jarib, with a *d*/*n* reversal.

e. **10.19** *Ram.* First Esdras reads this in the plural, which would make more sense.

f. **10.20** *And Zebadiah.* First Esdras adds 'Maneis, Shemaiah, Jeriel, and Azariah'. It is supposed that Maneis is a misunderstanding of *mibnei,* מבני, 'of the sons of', and Jeriel may represent Jehiel (Talshir 2001: 472).

g. **10.21** *Of the sons of Harim.* This verse is omitted from 1 Esdras and is assimilated to the preceding, probably through scribal error (Talshir 2001: 472).

h. **10.22** *Jozabad.* First Esdras reads Ωκιδηλος, Okidelos.

i. *Elasah.* First Esdras reads Σαλθας, Salthas.

j. **10.23** *Judah.* First Esdras reads Ωουδας, which suggests Huda, הודה, a common name (Talshir 2001: 473).

k. *Eliezer.* First Esdras reads Ιωανας, Joḥanan, suggesting that this was in 1 Esdras's *Vorlage.*

l. **10.24** *Eliashib.* First Esdras inserts Βακχουρος, Bakouros, after Eliashib. It may reflect Zacur.

m. *Telem.* First Esdras reads Τολβανης, Tolbanes, which suggests Talmon, rather than Telem (Talshir 2001: 474).

n. *Uri.* Greek Ezra reads 'Odoué'. First Esdras omits this name.

o. **10.25** *Ramiah.* First Esdras reads Ιερμας, Jermas.

p. *Mijamin.* The Syriac reads Binjamin.

q. *Malchijah.* This second citing of Malchijah is kept in the Vulgate and the Syriac, but is substituted by Ασαβια, *Hashabiah,* in both Greek Ezra and 1 Esdras.

r. **10.26** *Jehiel.* First Esdras reads here Ιεζριηλος, Jezrielos.

s. **10.27** *Zattu.* First Esdras reads Ζαμοθ, Zamoth.

t. *Elioenai.* First Esdras reads Ελιαδας, Eliadas.

u. *Eliashib.* First Esdras reads Ελιασιμος, Eliasimos.

v. *Mattaniah.* First Esdras reads Οθονιας, Othoniah. The initial M is missing here.

w. *Zabad.* First Esdras and the Vulgate read Σαβαθος, Zabeth.

x. *Aziza.* First Esdras reads Ζερδαιας, Zerdaias. The Syriac reads Uzi.

y. **10.28** *Zabbai.* First Esdras reads Ζαβδος, Zabdos.

z. *Athlai.* First Esdras reads Εμαθις, Emathis.

aa. **10.29** *Bani.* First Esdras reads Μανι, Mani. The Syriac inserts 'Baki'.

bb. *Meshullam.* First Esdras inserts Ωλαμος, Olamus; perhaps the beginning of the name is missing. The Syriac reads 'from Shulom', interpreting the initial *m* as the particle מ, *m*, 'from'.

cc. *Sheal.* First Esdras reads Ασαηλος, Asaeilos.

dd. **10.30** *Pahath-Moab.* The Syriac reads שלטן מואב 'Saltan Moab', 'the ruler of Moab', translating 'Pahath', 'governor', literally. This name, or tribal group, is missing from 1 Esdras.

ee. *Adna.* First Esdras reads 'Addi'. Since 'Pahath-Moab' is missing from 1 Esdras, 'Adna', or 'Addi', becomes the name of the tribal group (Talshir 2001: 477). First Esdras inserts Νααθος, 'Naathos', perhaps from the *na* at the end of 'Adna' (Talshir 2001: 477). The Syriac reads 'Zadlia''.

ff. *Chelal.* First Esdras reads Λακκουνος, 'Lakkounos', an *L* and *K* interchange?

gg. *Benaiah.* First Esdras reads Ναΐδος, 'Naidos'.

hh. *Bezalel.* This name is missing in the Syriac. First Esdras reads Σεσθηλ, 'Sesthel'.

ii. *Binnui.* First Esdras reads Βαλνουος. The Syriac reads *benai*, 'sons of'.

jj. **10.31** *The sons of.* It should read 'Of the sons of' with all the versions.

kk. *Harim.* First Esdras reads Αννᾳν, 'Annan'.

ll. *Eliezer.* First Esdras reads Ελιωνας, 'Elionas'. In 10.27 above, 1 Esdras interpreted the name 'Elioenai' as 'Eliadas'.

mm. *Shemaiah.* First Esdras reads Σαββαιας, 'Sabbaias', suggesting an *m*/*b* interchange (Talshir 2001: 478).

nn. *Shimeon.* First Esdras adds Χοσαμαιος, 'Kosamaios', after 'Shimeon', or 'Simon', actually in Greek.

oo. **10.32** *Shemariah.* This verse is missing from 1 Esdras. The Syriac reads 'Shemaiah'.

pp. **10.33** *Mattenai.* First Esdras reads Μαλταννᾳιος, 'Maltannaios', substituting an *l* to avoid a double *tt* (Talshir 2001: 478).

qq. *Zabad.* The Syriac reads 'Zakur'. The *k* and *b* are nearly identical in the Syriac, as are the *r* and *d*, and of course only the consonantal text is represented.

rr. *Jeremai.* This name is missing from 1 Esdras.

ss. **10.34** *Bani.* 1 Esdras inserts Ιερεμιας, 'Jeremai', which was missing from the previous verse. The Syriac reads 'Baki'. Since the clan 'Bani' is listed already in 10.29, Hawley (1922: 68) suggests that the MT should be emended here to 'Baki' with the Syriac, but perhaps it should be emended to Bagavahya (Bigvai); see note.

tt. *Maadai.* The Syriac reads מדראי, 'Madara'i', probably due to a *r*/*d* confusion.

uu. *Amram.* First Esdras reads Μαηρος, 'Maeiros'.

vv. *'Uel.* The versions all read 'Yoel' (i.e. 'Joel'); so perhaps the MT should be corrected.

ww. **10.35** *Benaiah.* First Esdras reads Μαμδαι, 'Mamdai'.

xx. *Bedeiah.* The Syriac reads simply 'Badi'. First Esdras reads Πεδιας, 'Pediah', revealing a *p*/*b* interchange.

yy. *Cheluhi.* This name is omitted in 1 Esdras.

zz. **10.36** *Vaniah.* Greek Ezra reads Ουιεχωα, Ouiechoa, replacing the internal *n* with the Greek χ, 'chi'. First Esdras reads Ανως, 'Anos', mistaking the initial waw for the Hebrew word 'and', which is simply the letter waw. The Syriac reads ונהעיל, 'Vanah'il'.

aaa. *Meremoth.* Greek Ezra reads Ιεραμωθ, 'Ieremoth', or 'Jeremoth', missing the initial *m*. First Esdras reads Καραβασιων, 'Karabasion'. Interpreting the initial 'Ka' as from Greek *kai,* 'and', and assuming a *b*/*m* interchange may help explain the name.

bbb. **10.37** *Mattaniah, Mattenai.* These two names seem to be combined in 1 Esdras in Μαμνιταναιμος, 'Mamnitanaimos'.

ccc. *Jaasu.* This is the same as the Hebrew word *ya'su*, 'they made', which is translated in Greek Ezra not as a name but as the Greek equivalent ἐποίησαν, '*epoiēsan*', 'they made'. First Esdras reads Ελιασις, 'Eliasis', which may be the full theophoric of the name 'God made' rather than 'they made' (Talshir 2001: 480).

ddd. **10.38** *The sons of Binnui.* First Esdras adds another name, Ελιαλις, 'Elialis', missing in Ezra.

eee. *Shimei.* Greek Ezra reads 'and the sons of Shimei'.

fff. **10.39** *Adaiah.* The Syriac reads 'Azariah'. The name is missing from 1 Esdras.

ggg. **10.40** *Machnadebai.* This name is missing in 1 Esdras, reading instead, 'And the sons of Εζωρα', 'Ezora'. The Syriac reads מכיזב, 'Machizab',

hhh. *Sharai.* This name is omitted from 1 Esdras.

iii. **10.41** *Azarel.* First Esdras reads Εζριλ, 'Ezril', and inserts Αζαηλος, 'Azaeilos', not present in the other versions.

jjj. *Shelemiah.* The name is missing in both 1 Esdras and the Syriac.

kkk. *Shemariah.* First Esdras reads instead Σαματος, 'Samatos'.

lll. **10.42** *Shallum.* 'Shallum' is missing from 1 Esdras.

mmm. *Amariah.* First Esdras reads Ζαμβρις, 'Zambris'.

nnn. **10.43** *Nebo.* First Esdras reads Νοομα, 'Nooma'.

ooo. *Jeiel.* The name is missing from 1 Esdras. The Syriac reads נבעיל, 'Nab'il'.

ppp. *Mattithiah.* First Esdras reads Μαζιτιας, 'Mazitias'.

qqq. *Zabad.* Greek Ezra reads 'Zedem'. The Syriac reads 'Zakur'. See note at 10.27.

rrr. *Zebina.* The name is missing from 1 Esdras.

sss. *Jaddai.* The name is missing in the Syriac.

ttt. **10.44** *Who had provided children.* Read with Greek Ezra and the Syriac. The MT reads literally, 'who had put children', which makes no sense. First Esdras reads, 'All these had married foreign women, and they sent them away with their children'.

Notes

10.18 ***Among the priests who had taken foreign wives—of the sons of Jeshua son of Jozadak and his kin: Maaseiah, Eliezer, Jarib, and Gedaliah.*** These are the family of the high priest himself. But we should not be surprised, since we already know of such intermarriages from the reports of Nehemiah and Josephus.

The priests are named first in this list, in contrast to the list in Ezra 2 (Nehemiah 7), where they are listed after the people of Israel.

10.19 ***They pledged to send away their wives.*** The phrase translated 'pledged' is literally 'they gave their hand'. We are not told if they actually did send them away however.

Their guilt offering was a ram of the flock. This is the *'āšām* offering (see the Introduction to Ezra's prayer, above). The fact that the guilt offering is a ram may allude to the fact that the guilt was incurred unknowingly, that is, that the people had not known that there was a ban on intermarriage. The law of the ram for the guilt offering is explained in Lev. 5.17-19:

> If any of you sin without knowing it, doing any of the things that by Yhwh's commandments ought not to be done, you have incurred guilt, and are subject to punishment. You shall bring to the priest a ram without blemish from the flock, or the equivalent, as a guilt offering; and the priest

> shall make atonement on your behalf for the error that you committed unintentionally, and you shall be forgiven.
> It is a guilt offering; you have incurred guilt before Yhwh.

A guilt offering is also to be brought in cases where the sinner sinned knowingly but feels guilty (Lev. 5.21-26 [ET 6.1-6]):

> Yhwh spoke to Moses, saying:
> When any of you sin and commit a trespass against Yhwh by deceiving a neighbor in a matter of a deposit or a pledge, or by robbery, or if you have defrauded a neighbor, or have found something lost and lied about it—if you swear falsely regarding any of the various things that one may do and sin thereby—when you have sinned and realize your guilt, and would restore what you took by robbery or by fraud or the deposit that was committed to you, or the lost thing that you found, or anything else about which you have sworn falsely, you shall repay the principal amount and shall add one-fifth to it. You shall pay it to its owner when you realize your guilt. And you shall bring to the priest, as your guilt offering to Yhwh, a ram without blemish from the flock, or its equivalent, for a guilt offering.

The presentation of a ram to the priest as a guilt offering implies an admission of guilt. If the transgression is against another human being, the code demands full restitution to the offended party plus one-fifth added to it. If a divorce ensues, the offended party is naturally the woman's father or her brother, if no father is living. If the divorce was according to traditional custom, then the husband would have had to repay his wife's father not only the full amount of the *ketubah*, her marriage contract, but perhaps also add one-fifth to it. One wonders how willing the husband would be to implement this, but the non-Judean fathers might have been more willing to receive their daughters back with one-fifth added to the *ketubah*.

10.20 ***Of the descendants of Immer: Hanani and Zebadiah.*** Now begins the list of members of priestly families not of the family of the high priest. The family of Immer is also listed first in the list of returnees (2.37) among the priestly families not of the high priest.

10.21-22 ***Of the sons of Harim: . . . 22. Of the sons of Pashhur.*** These two priestly families are reversed in the list in Ezra 2.

10.23 ***Of the Levites: Jozabad.*** When Ezra arrived in Jerusalem he weighed out the gifts for the temple into the hand, among others, of Jozabad son of Jeshua, the Levite. The name is common, however, meaning 'gift of Yhwh', and we do not have the patronym here.

Kelaiah (that is, Kelita). The name Kelaiah is unknown elsewhere, but a Levite Kelita helped explain the torah to the assembly during the reading of the law (Neh. 8.7) and also signed the Amanah (Neh. 10.11). If it is the same one, then he signed the Amanah after having divorced his wife.

10.24 ***Of the singers: Eliashib.*** This verse refers to Eliashib, a levitical singer. The name is common, giving force to the contention of some that when Ezra went to the temple chamber of Jehohanan son of Eliashib (Ezra 10.6) that it was not the Eliashib who had been high priest during the time of Nehemiah. (See discussion *ad loc.)*

Of the gatekeepers: Shallum, Telem, and Uri. Shallum and Talmon are listed as gatekeepers in the list of returnees (Ezra 2.42). Telem is a short form of Talmon.

10.25 ***And of Israel:*** These men, having confessed to marrying foreign women, are still part of the people Israel, the people whom the god Yhwh addresses. (See note on Ezra 1.3.)

The names of the laity are divided according to the names of the families that were construed as making up the people Israel.

Sons of Parosh. The sons of Parosh are listed first among the laity in Ezra 2 and 8 as well (Ezra 2.3; 8.3), and a Parosh is listed first among the signers of the Amanah in Nehemiah 10 (Neh. 10.14). Indeed, the family of Parosh is listed first in every list of laity. A Pedaiah son of Parosh is listed among the wall builders in Nehemiah 3 (3.25).

10.26 ***Of the sons of Elam: Mattaniah, Zechariah, Jehiel.*** Elam is listed fifth in Ezra 2 and 8, but second here and third in Nehemiah 10. It is hard to know if this means anything. One is tempted to assume that the Elamites increased in status as a result of the status of Shecaniah son of Jehiel of the Elamites (10.2). Jehiel here is likely Shecaniah's father, and this assumption that Shecaniah's own father had married a foreign woman gives rise to plenty of conjecture about the reasons that Shecaniah encouraged this mass divorce. (See comment on 10.3-5).

10.27 ***Of the sons of Zattu.*** Zattu is listed third both here and in Ezra 8, but sixth in Ezra 2. He is listed fourth in Nehemiah 10.

10.28 ***Of the sons of Bebai.*** Bebai is listed fourth here, but ninth in every other list.

10.29 ***Of the sons of Bani.*** Bani is listed fifth here, but eighth everywhere else.

10.30 ***The sons of Pahath-Moab.*** Pahath-Moab is listed sixth here, but third in Ezra 2 and second in Ezra 8 and Nehemiah 10. A Hasshub son of Pahath-Moab repaired a section of Jerusalem's city wall and the Tower of the Ovens (Neh. 3.11).

10.31-32 ***The sons of Harim: . . . , Malchijah, . . .*** Harim is listed seventh here among the families of Israel, but is listed among the cities in Ezra 2.32 and not among the families of laity. Harim is also the name of a priestly family (Ezra 2.39; 10.21). A Malchijah son of Harim is included among the laity who helped repair Jerusalem's city wall in the time of Nehemiah (Neh. 3.11). He may be the same one who is listed here forty-seven years later as having a foreign wife.

10.33 ***Of the sons of Hashum.*** Hashum is listed eighth here, but seventeenth in Ezra 2 and sixteenth in Nehemiah 10.

10.34 ***The sons of Bani.*** Bani is listed twice, and perhaps the second listing should be emended to Bagavahya, which is present in all the other lists but missing from this one. In both Ezra 2 and 8, the name is listed twelfth (2.14; 8.14), and in Nehemiah 10, it is listed tenth. Here it is the ninth family name in the list.

10.38 ***Of the sons of Binnui.*** Binnui is listed tenth here, but is not listed in the other lists as a family name except in Nehemiah 7 as an alteration of Bani. There it is listed eighth.

10.43 ***Of the sons of Nebo.*** Nebo is listed eleventh here in the list of family names, but in Ezra 2 he is listed last after the list of cities. He is not named in any of the other lists in Ezra or Nehemiah except, of course, in Nehemiah 7 (v. 33) where he is listed as a place ('the men of the other Nebo').

10.44 ***All these had married foreign women, and there were among them women who had provided children.*** Unlike the wording in 1 Esdras (see textual note), this passage does not state that these men had actually divorced their foreign wives.

Comments

A. The Original Ezra Story

There were at least two authors of Ezra 7–Nehemiah 13. The first one used an authentic letter from Artaxerxes II to create Ezra 7 and an authentic report from Ezra the episkopos to that king to create parts of Ezra 8.15-36. I have appended those hypothesized letters at the end of Chapters 7 and 8 respectively. Very likely that author also wrote the story of the divorce in Ezra 10. By removing the pious intrusions by the author of the prayer of Ezra 9, we have what may have been the original story of the divorce:

> Then military officers approached Ezra, saying, '. . . have taken some of their daughters as wives for themselves and for their sons and the hand of the officers and prefects was the first in this . . .' (Ezra 9.1-2).
>
> Then Shecaniah son of Jehiel, of Elam, addressed Ezra, saying:
> 'We have had foreign women from the peoples of the land dwell with us, but even now there is hope . . . in spite of this. So now, let us make a pact . . . to send out all the women and the ones born of them, according to the advice of my lord . . . ; and let it be done according to the law.
> Stand up! This is your responsibility, but we are with you. Be strong and act!' (Ezra 10.2-4).
>
> So Ezra stood up and had the officers . . . swear to act according to this matter and they swore.
> Then Ezra got up from before the house of god, and went to the temple-chamber of Yehoḥanan son of Eliashib, and spent the night there. . . .

> Then they sent out a herald in Judah and Jerusalem . . . that [the men of Judah and Benjamin] should gather in Jerusalem:
>
> 'Anyone who does not come in three days, according to the advice of the officials and the elders, will have all his (movable) property confiscated, and he will be separated from the community . . .'
>
> All the men of Judah and Benjamin were gathered to Jerusalem on the third day. It was the ninth month, on the twentieth of the month and all the people sat in the square of the house of God shivering on account of the matter and from the rains.
>
> Then Ezra . . . rose and said to them, 'You have trespassed and married foreign women. . . . Now . . . separate yourselves from the peoples of the land and from the foreign women.'
>
> Then the entire gathering answered and said with a loud voice, 'Yes, it is incumbent upon us to do according to your word. But the people are many, and this is the time of the rains, and we have no strength to remain outside. The work is not for one day and not for two, since many of us have transgressed in this matter.
>
> Let our officers over the entire community stay [here]; and let any who in our cities has taken foreign women come at the appointed time, and with them the elders of every city and its judges. . . .'
>
> Only Jonathan son of Asahel and Jahzeiah son of Tikvah opposed this, and Meshullam and Shabbethai the Levites supported them.
>
> And so [they] did. Ezra . . . men. . . . They sat down on the first day of the tenth month to investigate the matter.
>
> They finished with all the men who had taken foreign wives by the first day of the first month (Ezra 10.5-17).

In removing the prayer and other pious intrusions by that second biblical author, all internal Judean motivation is also removed. The original demand for the divorce comes from Persian military officers and prefects, including Shecaniah ben Jehiel, an Elamite, who perhaps was, like Nehemiah, from Susa. It was enforced by Ezra, the Persian episkopos.

B. The Mass Divorce—Fact or Fiction?

There are no extrabiblical data either to confirm or to deny the story in Ezra. It seems reasonable to conclude, however, that since the Athenian Empire desired to impose and did impose a ban on intermarriage on the people of contemporary Athens, then the Persians would have had the same desires for the same reasons and have had the same powers to impose a similar ban on Persians posted throughout their empire. Whether they actually did or not, we do not yet know. It is likely, however, since marriages between Persian officials and members of the local populations seem to have been frowned upon. There is no known case of a marriage between Persians and Greeks in Asia Minor, for example, even though Persians were densely populated in the area (Briant 2002: 501). It must be emphasized that marriages were not random events, but alliances between families. All marriages were arranged.

It is equally possible, of course, for the entire story to be a fabrication of a Hellenistic writer. He would have written it in order to encourage his fellow Judeans to stay away from foreigners with their Hellenizing influences. There are hints in the story of opposition to the decree. The men who assembled in Jerusalem agreed that they had to do as Ezra commanded them and divorce their foreign wives (10.12), but they put up various objections—it was too cold and rainy; it would take too long, etc. (10.13). They proposed that everyone should return to his own town, but that the Persian officers must remain in Jerusalem (10.14a). All those who had taken foreign wives would then return at the appointed time with their (own) elders and judges (10.14b). Sketched out this way, it may be that Ezra 10 is hiding a story of resistance to foreign rule and its arbitrary foreign demands. In the context of the prayer in Ezra 9 the story is completely different. That story is not one of resistance. Ezra is not presented as the Persian episkopos, but as a Judean trying to bring the people back to Yhwh, the god whom they had deserted by their intermarriages. Ezra is shown bringing the law to Jerusalem (Ezra 7), convincing the people that they had sinned (Ezra 9) and demanding that they right the wrong done Yhwh and divorce their foreign wives, which they do (Ezra 9–10). The people have righted the wrong; their relationship with Yhwh has been corrected through the *'āšām* offering, and all is right with the world.

Appendix: The Achaemenid Rulers

1.	Cyrus II (the Great)	559–530
2.	Cambyses II	529–522
3.	Bardija	522 (6 months)
4.	Nebuchadnezzar III	522 (2 months)
5.	Nebuchadnezzar IV	521 (3 months)
6.	Darius I (the Great)	522–486
7.	Xerxes I	486–465
8.	Artaxerxes I	465–424
9.	Darius II	424–405
10.	Artaxerxes II	405–359
11.	Artaxerxes III	358–338
12.	Artaxerxes IV	338–336
13.	Darius III	336–331

Alexander III (the Great) 330–323

Bibliography

Abu Assaf, A.

1993 'Der Tempel von 'Ain Dara in Nordsyrien', *Antike Welt* 24: 155-71.

Ackroyd, Peter R.

1973 *I and II Chronicles, Ezra, Nehemiah* (Torch Bible commentaries; London: SCM).

1987 'The Temple Vessels: A Continuity Theme', in *Studies in the Religious Tradition of the Old Testament* (ed. Peter R. Ackroyd; London: SCM Press): 45-60.

Agnew, Francis H.

1986 'The Origin of the NT Apostle-Concept: A Review of Research', *JBL* 105: 75-96.

Aharoni, Yohanan

1968 'Trial Excavation in the "Solar Shrine" at Lachish: Preliminary Report', *IEJ* 18: 157-69.

1981 *Arad Inscriptions* (Jerusalem: Israel Exploration Society).

Ahituv, Shmuel

2008 *Echoes from the Past: Hebrew and Cognate Inscriptions from the Biblical Period* (Jerusalem: Carta Jerusalem).

Albertz, Rainer

1994 *A History of Israelite Religion in the Old Testament Period.* II. *From the Exile to the Maccabees* (trans. John Bowden; Louisville, KY: Westminster John Knox).

2003 *Israel in Exile: The History and Literature of the Sixth Century B.C.E.* (trans. D. Green; Studies in Biblical Literature, 3; Atlanta, GA: Society of Biblical Literature).

Albrektson, Bertil

1967 *History and the Gods: An Essay on the Idea of Historical Events as Divine Manifestations in the Ancient Near East and in Israel* (Lund: C.W.K. Gleerup).

Albright, William F.

1924 'Alemeth and Azmaveth', *AASOR* 4: 156-57.

Allam, Schafik

1972 'Richter', in *Lexikon der Aegyptologie* 5 (Wiesbaden: Harrassowitz Verlag): 245-47.

Alt, Albrecht

1953 'Die Rolle Samarias bei der Entstehung des Judentums', in *Kleine Schriften zur Geschichte des Volkes Israel* 2 (ed. Albrecht Alt; Munich: Beck): 316-37.

Amiran, Ruth, and Zev Herzog

1997 *Arad* (Tel Aviv: Tel Aviv University).

Anderson, Gary A.
1987 *Sacrifices and Offerings in Ancient Israel: Studies in their Social and Political Importance* (Harvard Semitic Museum Monographs, 41; Atlanta, GA: Scholars Press).
Anderson, Robert T., and Terry Giles
2005 *Tradition Kept: The Literature of the Samaritans* (Peabody, MA: Hendrickson).
Andrews, D.K.
1964 'Yahweh the God of the Heavens', in *The Seed of Wisdom: Essays in Honour of Th. J. Meek* (ed. William Stewart McCullough; Toronto: University of Toronto Press): 45-57.
Aristotle
2005 *Poetics and Rhetoric* (trans. W. Rhys Roberts; New York: Barnes & Noble Classics).
Arnold, B.
1992 'Ramah', *ABD* 5: 614.
1996 'The Use of Aramaic in the Hebrew Bible: Another Look at the Bilingualism in Ezra and Daniel', *JNSL* 22: 1-16.
Avigad, Nahman
1958 'New Light on the MṢH Seal Impressions', *IEJ* 8: 113-19.
1959 'Some Notes on the Hebrew Inscriptions from Gibeon (review article)', *IEJ* 9: 130-33.
1986 *Hebrew Bullae from the Time of Jeremiah: Remnants of a Burnt Archive* (Jerusalem: Israel Exploration Society).
1992 'A New Seal of a "Son of the King"', *Michmanim* 6: 27*-31*.
Avigad, Nahman, and Benjamin Sass
1997 *Corpus of West Semitic Stamp Seals* (Jerusalem: Israel Exploration Society).
Avi-Yonah, Michael
1961 *Oriental Art in Roman Palestine* (Rome: Centro di studi semitici, Istituto di studi del vicino Oriente, Università de Roma).
2002 (1966) *The Holy Land: A Historical Geography from the Persian to the Arab Conquest (536 B.C.–A.D. 640)* (Jerusalem: Carta).
Bagnall, Roger S., and Bruce W. Frier
1994 *The Demography of Roman Egypt* (Cambridge: Cambridge University Press).
Balcer, Jack Martin
1977 'The Athenian Episkopos and the Achaemenid "King's Eye"', *The American Journal of Philology* 98: 252-63.
1993 *A Prosopographical Study of the Ancient Persians Royal and Noble C. 550–450 B.C.* (Lewiston, NY: Edwin Mellen Press).
Barkay, Gabriel
1985 'Excavations at Ketef Ḥinom in Jerusalem (Hebrew)', *Qadmoniot* 17: 94-107.
Barstad, Hans
1996 *The Myth of the Empty Land: A Study in the History and Archaeology of Judah during the "Exilic" Period* (Oslo: Scandinavian University Press).
2003 'After the "Myth of the Empty Land": Major Challenges in the Study of Neo-Babylonian Judah', in *Judah and the Judeans in the Neo-Babylonian Period* (ed. Oded Lipschits and Joseph Blenkinsopp; Winona Lake, IN: Eisenbrauns): 3-20.
Barton, John
1997 *The Spirit and the Letter: Studies in the Biblical Canon* (London: Society for Promoting Christian Knowledge).

Batten, Loring W.

1913 *The Books of Ezra and Nehemiah: A Critical and Exegetical Commentary* (ICC; Edinburgh: T. & T. Clark).

Beaulieu, Paul-Alain

1993 'An Episode in the Fall of Babylon to the Persians', *JNES* 52: 241-61.

Becking, Bob

1998 'Ezra's Re-enactment of the Exile', in *Leading Captivity Captive: "The Exile" as History and Ideology* (ed. Lester L. Grabbe; JSOTSup., 278; Sheffield: Sheffield Academic Press): 40-61.

2001 'The Idea of Thorah in Ezra 7–10: A Functional Analysis', *ZABR* 7: 273-86.

Bedford, Peter Ross

2001 *Temple Restoration in Early Achaemenid Judah* (Supplements to the Journal for the Study of Judaism; Leiden: Brill).

Berger, P.R.

1971 'Zu den Namen *ššbṣr* und *šnṣr*', *ZAW* 83: 98-100.

Berman, Joshua

2006 'The Narratorial Voice of the Scribes of Samaria: Ezra IV 8–VI 18 Reconsidered', *VT* 56: 313-26.

2007 'The Narratological Purpose of Aramaic Prose in Ezra 4.8–6.18', *Aramaic Studies* 5: 165-91.

Bewer, Julius A.

1922 *The Literature of the Old Testament in its Historical Development* (New York: Columbia University Press).

Bickerman, E.J.

1946 'The Edict of Cyrus in Ezra 1', *JBL* 65: 249-75.

1980 *Chronology of the Ancient World* (London: Thames and Hudson, rev. edn).

Blenkinsopp, Joseph

1972 *Gibeon and Israel: The Role of Gibeon and the Gibeonites in the Political and Religious History of Early Israel* (Cambridge: Cambridge University Press).

1988 *Ezra–Nehemiah: A Commentary* (Old Testament Library; Philadelphia, PA: Westminster Press).

1992 *The Pentateuch: An Introduction to the First Five Books of the Bible* (Anchor Bible Reference Library; New York: Doubleday).

2000 *Isaiah 1–39* (Anchor Bible, 19; New York: Doubleday).

2009 *Judaism: The First Phase. The Place of Ezra and Nehemiah in the Origins of Judaism* (Grand Rapids, MI: Eerdmans).

Blidstein, Gerald J.

1974 ''Atimia: A Greek Parallel to Ezra X 8 and to Post-Biblical Exclusion from the Community', *VT* 24: 357-60.

Bliss, F.J.

1897 'Thirteenth Report on the Excavations at Jerusalem', *PEFQS* 29: 180.

Bloom, J.A.

1992 *Ancient Near Eastern Temple Assemblies* (dissertation, Annenberg Research Institute, University of Pennsylvania, Philadelphia, PA).

Blum, Erhard

1984 *Die Komposition der Vätergeschichte* (Wissenschaftliche Monographien zum Alten und Neuen Testament, 57; Düsseldorf: Neukirchener Verlag).

1990 'Die Komposition der jüdischen Tora und die persische Politik', in *Studien zur Komposition des Pentateuch* (ed. Erhard Blum; BZAW, 189; Berlin: de Gruyter): 333-60.

2002 'Esra, die Mosetora und die persische Politik', in *Religion und Religionskontakte im Zeitalter der Achämeniden* (ed. Reinhard G. Kratz; Gütersloh: Gütersloher Verlagshaus): 231-77.

Boda, Mark J.

2003 'Reading between the Lines: Zechariah 11:4-16 in its Literary Contexts', in *Bringing Out the Treasure: Inner Biblical Allusion in Zechariah 9–14* (ed. Mark J. Boda and Michael H. Floyd; JSOTSup, 370; Sheffield: Sheffield Academic Press): 277-91.

2006 'From Dystopia to Myopia: Utopian (Re)Visions in Haggai and Zechariah 1–8', in *Utopia and Dystopia in Prophetic Literature* (ed. Ehud Ben Zvi; Helsinki: Finish Exegetical Society): 210-48.

Boda, Mark J., and Jamie R. Novotny

2010 *From the Foundations to the Crenellations: Essays on Temple Building in the Ancient Near East and Hebrew Bible* (AOAT, 366; Münster: Ugarit-Verlag).

Bolin, Thomas M.

1995 'The Temple of יהו at Elephantine and Persian Religious Policy', in *The Triumph of Elohim: From Yahwisms to Judaisms* (ed. Diana Vikander Edelman; Grand Rapids, MI: Eerdmans): 127-42.

Boling, Robert G.

1975 *Judges* (AB, 6A; Garden City, NY: Doubleday).

Bongenaar, A.C.V.M.

1997 *The Neo-Babylonian Ebabbar Temple at Sippar: Its Administration and its Prosopography* (PIHANS, 80; Leiden: Nederlands Historisch-Archaeologisch Instituut te Istanbul).

Bongrani Fanfoni, L., and F. Israel

1994 'Documenti achemenidi nel deserto orientale egiziano (Gebel Abu Queh—Wadi Hammamat)', *Transeuphratène* 8: 75-93.

Bontty, Monica M.

1997 *Conflict Management in Ancient Egypt: Law as a Social Phenomenon* (PhD diss., University of California at Los Angeles).

Borger, R.

1959 'An Additional Remark on P.R. Ackroyd, JNES XVII, 23-27', *JNES* 18: 74.

1996 *Beiträge zum Inschriftenwerk Ashurbanipals* (Wiesbaden: Harrassowitz Verlag).

Botta, Alejandro F.

2009 *The Aramaic and Egyptian Legal Traditions at Elephantine: An Egyptological Approach* (Library of Second Temple Studies, 64; London: T. & T. Clark).

Boyce, Mary

1982 *A History of Zoroastrianism*. II (Leiden: Brill).

1984 *Textual Sources for the Study of Zoroastrianism* (Chicago: University of Chicago Press).

1992 *Zoroastrianism: Its Antiquity and Constant Vigour* (New York: Mazda & Bibliotheca Persica).

1996 *A History of Zoroastrianism*. I. *The Early Period* (HdO, 8; Leiden: Brill).

Briant, Pierre

1978–79 'Contrainte militaire, dépendance rurale et exploitation des territoires en Asie achéménide', *Index* 8: 48-98.

2002 *From Cyrus to Alexander: A History of the Persian Empire* (trans. Peter T. Daniels; Winona Lake, IN: Eisenbrauns).

Briend, J.
1996 'L'édit de Cyrus et sa valeur historique', *Transeuphratène* 11: 33-44.
Brosius, Maria
1996 *Women in Ancient Persia (559–331 BC)* (Oxford Classical Monographs; Oxford: Clarendon Press).
Bunimovitz, S., and Z. Lederman
2003 'The Final Destruction of Beth Shemesh and the *Pax assyriaca* in the Judahite Shephelah', *Tel Aviv* 30: 3-26.
Burford, Alison
1969 *The Greek Temple Builders at Epidauros: A Social and Economic Study of Building in the Asklepian Sanctuary during the Fourth and Early Third Centuries B.C.* (Liverpool Monographs in Archaeology and Oriental Studies; Liverpool: Liverpool University Press).
Burkert, Walter
1985 *Greek Religion* (trans. John Raffan; Cambridge, MA: Harvard University Press).
Buss, M.J.
1963 'The Psalms of Asaph and Korah', *JBL* 82: 382-91.
Calloway, Joseph A.
1992 'Ai', in *ABD* 1: 125-30.
Cameron, George G.
1948 *The Persepolis Treasury Tablets* (Chicago: University of Chicago Press).
Campbell, William Sanger
2010 'The Narrator as "He," "Me," and "We": Grammatical Person in Ancient Histories and in the Acts of the Apostles', *JBL* 129: 385-407.
Cardasçia, Guillaume
1951 *Les archives des Murašû, une famille d'hommes d'affaires à l'époque perse (455–503 av. J.-C.)* (Paris: Imprimerie nationale).
1958 'Le statut de l'étranger dans la mesopotamie ancienne', *Recueils de la société Jean Bodin: L'étranger* 9: 105-17.
1990 'La coutume dans les droits cunéiformes', *Recueils de la societé Jean Bodin* 51: 61-69.
Carr, David M.
2007 'The Rise of Torah', in *The Pentateuch as Torah: New Models for Understanding its Promulgation and Acceptance* (ed. Gary N. Knoppers and Bernard M. Levinson; Winona Lake, IN: Eisenbrauns): 39-56.
Carter, C.E.
1999 *The Emergence of Yehud in the Persian Period: A Social and Demographic Study* (Sheffield: Sheffield Academic Press).
Cazelles, Henri
1983 '587 ou 586?', in *The Word of the Lord Shall Go Forth* (ed. C.L. Meyers and M. O'Connor; Winona Lake, IN: Eisenbrauns): 427-31.
Chadwick, Jeffrey R.
2005 'Discovering Hebron: The City of the Patriarchs Slowly Yields its Secrets', *BAR* 31.5: 24-33, 70.
Charlesworth, James
in press 'Announcing a Dead Sea Scrolls Fragment of Nehemiah', *Maarav*.
Choi, John H.
2010 *Traditions at Odds: The Reception of the Pentateuch in Biblical and Second Temple Period Literature* (Library of Hebrew Bible/Old Testament Studies, 518; New York: T. & T. Clark).

Clauss, Jan
2011 'Understanding the Mixed Marriages of Ezra–Nehemiah in the Light of Temple-Building and the Book's Concept of Jerusalem', in *Mixed Marriages: Intermarriage and Group Identity in the Second Temple Period* (ed. Christian Frevel, Christian; London: T. & T. Clark): 109-31.
Clemens, David M.
2001 *Sources for Ugaritic Ritual and Sacrifice.* I. *Ugaritic and Ugarit Akkadian Texts* (Münster: Ugarit-Verlag).
Clines, David J.A.
1984 *Ezra, Nehemiah, Esther* (The New Century Bible Commentary; Grand Rapids, MI: Eerdmans).
1990a *What Does Eve Do to Help?: And Other Readerly Questions to the Old Testament* (Sheffield: JSOT Press).
1990b 'The Nehemiah Memoir: The Perils of Autobiography', in *What Does Eve Do to Help?: And Other Readerly Questions to the Old Testament* (ed. David J.A. Clines; Sheffield: Journal for the Study of the Old Testament Press): 124-64.
1994 'Haggai's Temple, Constructed, Deconstructed and Reconstructed', in *Second Temple Studies.* 2. *Temple and Community in the Persian Period* (ed. Tamara C. Eskenazi and Kent H. Richards; JSOTSup., 175; Sheffield: Sheffield Academic Press): 60-87.
2009 *The Concise Dictionary of Classical Hebrew* (Sheffield: Sheffield Phoenix Press).
Cogan, Mordechai
1974 *Imperialism and Religion: Assyria, Judah and Israel in the Eighth and Seventh Centuries B.C.* (Missoula, MT: Scholars Press).
2001 *I Kings* (Anchor Bible, 10; New York: Doubleday).
Cogan, Mordechai, and Hayim Tadmor
1988 *II Kings* (Anchor Bible, 11; New York: Doubleday).
Cohn-Haft, Louis
1995 'Divorce in Classical Athens', *The Journal of Hellenic Studies* 115: 1-14.
Crenshaw, James L.
2005 *Defending God: Biblical Responses to the Problem of Evil* (Oxford: Oxford University Press).
Cross, Frank M., Jr
1963 'The Discovery of the Samaria Papyri', *Biblical Archaeologist* 26.4: 110-21.
1969 'Judaean Stamps', *EI* 9: 26f., pl. V: 3, 4.
1998 'A Reconstruction of the Judean Restoration', in *From Epic to Canon: History and Literature in Ancient Israel* (ed. Frank M. Cross, Jr; Baltimore, MD: Johns Hopkins University Press): 151-72.
Crüsemann, Frank
1996 'Human Solidarity and Ethnic Identity: Israel's Self-Definition in the Genealogical System of Genesis', in *Ethnicity and the Bible* (ed. Mark G. Brett; Leiden: Brill Academic Publishers): 57-76.
Cruz-Uribe, Eugene
2003 'The Invasion of Egypt by Cambyses', *Transeuphratène* 25: 9-60.
Curtis, E.L., and A.A. Madsen
1910 *A Critical and Exegetical Commentary on the Books of Chronicles* (ICC; Edinburgh: T. & T. Clark).

Dandamayev, Muhammad A.

1982 'The Neo-Babylonian Elders', in *Societies and Languages of the Ancient Near East: Festschrift in Honor of I.M. Diakonoff* (ed. Muhammad A. Dandamayev; Warminister: Aris & Phillips): 38-41.

1984 'Royal Paradeisoi in Babylonia', *Orientalia—J. Duchesne-Guillemin emerito oblata: Hommages et opera minora* 9: 113-17.

1984 *Slavery in Babylonia, 626–331* (trans. V. Powell; DeKalb, IL: Northern Illinois University Press).

1993 'Courts and Courtiers: In the Median and Achaemenid Periods', in *Encyclopaedia Iranica* 6: 356-59.

1995 'Babylonian Popular Assemblies in the First Millennium B.C.', *Bulletin of the Canadian Society for Mesopotamian Studies* 30: 23-29.

Dandamayev, Muhammad A., and Vladimir G. Lukonin

1989 *The Culture and Social Institutions of Ancient Iran* (Cambridge: Cambridge University Press).

Davies, G.I.

1991 *Ancient Hebrew Inscriptions: Corpus and Concordance.* I (Cambridge: Cambridge University Press).

Davies, John K.

1977-78 'Athenian Citizenship: The Descent Group and the Alternatives', *Classical Journal* 73: 105-21.

Deller, Karlheinz

1990 'aB Kaštappum, mA Kaltappu, nA Kassappa/i', *NABU* 3: 61-62.

Demsky, Aaron

1983 '"Pelekh" in Nehemiah 3', *IEJ* 33: 242-44.

1994 'Who Came First, Ezra or Nehemiah?', *HUCA* 65: 1-19.

Depuydt, Leo

1995 'Evidence for Accession Dating under the Achaemenids', *JAOS* 115: 193-204.

Deutsch, Robert, and André Lemaire

2000 *Biblical Period Personal Seals in the Shlomo Moussaieff Collection* (Tel Aviv: Archaeological Center Publications).

Devauchelle, Didier

1995 'Le sentiment anti-perse chez les anciens Égyptíens', *Transeuphratène* 9: 67-80.

Dever, William G.

1971 'Archaeological Methods and Results: A Review of Two Recent Publications', *Or* 40: 459-71.

1992 'Tell Beitin', in *ABD* 1: 651-52.

Dion, Paul E.

1983 'Šašbassar and Sas-nûrî', *ZAW* 95: 111-12.

Dor, Yonina

2006 *Did They Really Divorce the Foreign Wives?: The Question of the Separation in the Days of the Second Temple* (Hebrew) (Jerusalem: Magnes Press).

Dorsey, David

1992 'Chephirah', *ABD* 1: 898.

Driel, G. van

2002 *Elusive Silver: In Search for a Market in an Agrarian Environment; Aspects of Mesopotamia's Society* (Nederlands Instituut voor het Nabije Oosten te Leiden, 95; Leiden: Nederlands Instituut voor het Nabije Oosten).

Driver, Samuel R.
1913 *An Introduction to the Literature of the Old Testament* (Edinburgh: T. & T. Clark).
Duguid, Iain M.
1994 *Ezekiel and the Leaders of Israel* (Leiden: Brill).
Duke, R. K.
1988 'Punishment or Restoration? Another Look at the Levites of Ezekiel 44:6-16', *JSOT* 40: 61-81.
Dupont-Sommer, André
1947-48 'Une inscription inédite de l'Ouâdi Hammâmât', *RA* 41: 105.
Duverger, Maurice
1980 'Le concept d'empire', in Maurice Duverger, *Le concept d'empire* (Paris: Presses universitaires de France).
Edelman, Diana
2005 *The Origins of the "Second" Temple: Persian Imperial Policy and the Rebuilding of Jerusalem* (London: Equinox).
Ellis, R.S.
1968 *Foundation Deposits* (New Haven, CT: Yale University Press).
Else, Gerald F.
1967 'Introduction to Aristotle's *Poetics*', in *Aristotle's Poetics* (Ann Arbor, MI: University of Michigan Press): 1-14.
Eph'al, Israel
1978 'The Western Minorities in Babylonia in the 6th–5th Centuries B.C.: Maintenance and Cohesion', *Orientalia* 47: 74-90.
Eph'al, Israel, and Joseph Naveh
1996 *Aramaic Ostraca of the Fourth Century BC from Idumaea* (Israel Exploration Society; Jerusalem: The Hebrew University/Magnes Press).
Eshel, Hanan
1987 'The Late Iron Age Cemetery of Gibeon', *IEJ* 37: 1-17.
2001 'Jerusalem in the Days of Nehemiah—A Proposal for a New Reconstruction (Hebrew)', in *New Studies on Jerusalem: Proceedings of the Seventh Conference, December 6th 2001* (ed. Avraham Faust and Eyal Baruch; Ramat Gan: Ingeborg Rennert Center for Jerusalem Studies): 97-110.
Eskenazi, Tamara Cohn
1988 *In an Age of Prose: A Literary Approach to Ezra–Nehemiah* (Atlanta, GA: Scholars Press).
2006 'The Missions of Ezra and Nehemiah', in *Judah and the Judeans in the Persian Period* (ed. Oded Lipschits and Manfred Oeming; Winona Lake, IN: Eisenbrauns): 509-29.
Fantalkin, Alexander
2004 'The Final Destruction of Beth Shemesh and the *Pax assyriaca* in the Judahite Shephelah: An Alternative View', *Tel Aviv* 31: 245-61.
Fantalkin, Alexander, and Oren Tal
2006 'Redating Lachish Level I: Identifying Achaemenid Imperial Policy at the Southern Frontier of the Fifth Satrapy', in *Judah and the Judeans in the Persian Period* (ed. Oded Lipschits and Manfred Oeming; Winona Lake, IN: Eisenbrauns): 167-97.
Faust, Avraham
1999 'Differences in Family Structures between Cities and Villages in Iron Age II.', *Tel Aviv* 26: 233-52.

2003 'Judah in the Sixth Century B.C.E.: A Rural Perspective', *PEQ* 135: 37-53.
2004 'Social and Cultural Changes in Judah during the 6th Century BCE and their Implications for our Understanding of the Nature of the Neo-Babylonian Period', *Ugarit Forschungen* 36: 157-76.
2006 *Israel's Ethnogenesis: Settlement, Interaction, Expansion, and Resistance* (London: Equinox).
2007 'Settlement Dynamics and Demographic Fluctuations in Judah from the Late Iron Age to the Hellenistic Period and the Archaeology of Persian-Period Yehud', in *A Time of Change: Judah and its Neighbours in the Persian and Early Hellenistic Periods* (ed. Yigal Levin; London: T. & T. Clark): 23-63.
2010 'The Archaeology of the Israelite Cult: Questioning the Consensus', *BASOR* 360: 23-35.
2011 'Deportation and Demography in Sixth Century B.C.E. Judah', in *Interpreting Exile: Interdisciplinary Studies of Displacement and Deportation in Biblical and Modern Contexts* (ed. B.E. Kelle, F. Ritchel Ames, and J.L. Wright; Atlanta, GA: Society of Biblical Literature): 91-103.
2012a *Judah in the Neo-Babylonian Period: The Archaeology of Desolation* (Society of Biblical Literature: Archaeology and Biblical Studies, 18; Atlanta, GA: Society of Biblical Literature).
2012b *The Archaeology of Israelite Society in Iron Age II* (Winona Lake, IN: Eisenbrauns).

Fensham, F. Charles
1982 *The Books of Ezra and Nehemiah* (NICOT; Grand Rapids, MI: Eerdmans).

Finkelstein, Israel
2008a 'Jerusalem in the Persian (and Early Hellenistic) Period and the Wall of Nehemiah', *JSOT* 32: 501-20.
2008b 'Archaeology and the List of Returnees in the Books of Ezra and Nehemiah', *PEQ* 140: 7-16.
2009 'Persian Period Jerusalem and Yehud: A Rejoinder', *JHS* 9: Article 24.
2010 'The Territorial Extent and Demography of Yehud/Judea in the Persian and Early Hellenistic Periods', *RB* 117: 39-54.
2011 'Tell el-Fûl Revisited: The Assyrian and Hellenistic Periods (with a New Identification)', *PEQ* 143: 106-18.

Finkelstein, Israel, and Yitzhak Magen
1993 *Archaeological Survey of the Hill Country of Benjamin* (Pirsume Rashut ha-atikot; Jerusalem: Israel Antiquities Authority).

Finkelstein, Israel, and Lily Singer-Avitz
2009 'Reevaluating Bethel', *ZDPV* 125: 33-48.

Finley, Moses I.
1955 'Marriage, Sale and Gift in the Homeric World', *Revue international des droits de l'antiquité* 2: 167-94.

First, Mitchell
1997 *Jewish History in Conflict: A Study of the Major Discrepancy between Rabbinic and Conventional Chronology* (Northvale, NJ: Jason Aronson).

Fishbane, Michael
1985 *Biblical Interpretation in Ancient Israel* (Oxford: Clarendon Press).
1990 'From Scribalism to Rabbinism: Perspectives on the Emergence of Classical Judaism', in *The Sage in Israel and the Ancient Near East* (ed. John C. Gammie and Leo G. Perdue; Winona Lake, IN: Eisenbrauns): 439-56.

Fitzmyer, Joseph A.
1997 *The Semitic Background of the New Testament and a Wandering Aramean: Collected Aramaic Essays* (The Biblical Resource Series; Grand Rapids, MI: Eerdmans).
2003 *Tobit* (Commentaries on Early Jewish Literature; Berlin: Walter de Gruyter).
Fleishman, Joseph
1992 'The Age of Legal Maturity in Biblical Law', *JANES* 21: 35-48.
1995 'The Investigating Commission of Tattenai: The Purpose of the Investigation and its Results', *HUCA* 66: 81-102.
Fleming, Daniel
2004 *Democracy's Ancient Ancestors: Mari and Early Collective Governance* (Cambridge: Cambridge University Press).
Fletcher-Louis, Crispin
1997 'The High Priest as Divine Mediator in the Hebrew Bible: Dan 7:13 as a Test Case', in *1997 Seminar Papers* (Atlanta, GA: Scholars Press): 161-93.
Folmer, M. L.
1995 *The Aramaic Language in the Achaemenid Period: A Study in Linguistic Variation* (Orientalia lovaniensia analecta, 68; Leuven: Peeters Press and Department of Oriental Studies).
Fornara, Charles W.
1983 'The Theoretical Foundations of Greco-Roman Historiography and their Application', in *The Nature of History in Ancient Greece and Rome* (ed. C.W. Fornara; EIDOS—Studies in Classical Kinds; Berkeley, CA: University of California Press): 91-141.
Freedman, David Noel
1961 'The Chronicler's Purpose', *CBQ* 23: 436-42.
Frei, Peter
1996 'Zentralgewalt und Localautonomie im Achämenidenreich', in *Reichsidee und Reichsorganisation im Perserreich* (ed. Peter Frei and Klaus Koch; Fribourg: Univeritätsverlag): 8-131.
2001 'Persian Imperial Authorization: A Summary', in *Persia and Torah: The Theory of Imperial Authorization of the Pentateuch* (ed. James W. Watts; SBL Symposium Series, 17; Atlanta, GA: Society of Biblical Literature): 5-40.
Fried, Lisbeth S.
2001 '"You Shall Appoint Judges": Ezra's Mission and the Rescript of Artaxerxes', in *Persia and Torah: The Theory of Imperial Authorization of the Pentateuch* (ed. James W. Watts; SBL Symposium Series, 17, Atlanta, GA: Society of Biblical Literature): 63-89.
2002a 'The High Places (*Bamôt*) and the Reforms of Hezekiah and Josiah: An Archaeological Investigation', *JOAS* 122: 437-65.
2002b 'Cyrus the Messiah? The Historical Background of Isaiah 45:1', *HTR* 95: 373-93.
2002c 'The Political Struggle of Fifth-Century Judah', *Transeuphratène* 24: 9-21.
2003a 'A Silver Coin of Yohanan Hakkôhen', *Transeuphratène* 26: 65-85, pls. II-V.
2003b 'The Land Lay Desolate: Conquest and Restoration in the Ancient Near East', in *Judah and the Judeans in the Neo-Babylonian Period* (ed. Oded Lipschits and Joseph Blenkinsopp; Winona Lake, IN: Eisenbrauns): 21-54.
2003c 'A Governor of Byblos from Sippar', *NABU* 36.
2004 *The Priest and the Great King: Temple–Palace Relations in the Persian Empire* (BJSUCSD, 10; Winona Lake, IN: Eisenbrauns).

2005 'A Greek Religious Association in Second Temple Judah? A Comment on Nehemiah 10', *Transeuphratène* 30: 75-93.

2006 'The 'Am Ha'aretz in Ezra 4:4 and Persian Imperial Administration', in *Judah and the Judeans in the Persian Period* (ed. Oded Lipschits and Manfred Oeming; Winona Lake, IN: Eisenbrauns): 123-45.

2007a 'From Xeno-Philia to -Phobia—Jewish Encounters with the Other', in *A Time of Change: Judah and its Neighbours in the Persian and Early Hellenistic Periods* (ed. Yigal Levin; London: T. & T. Clark): 179-204.

2007b 'Shaving Joseph: The Historical Background of Genesis 41:14', *BAR* 33.4: 36-41,74.

2007c 'Did Second Temple High Priests Possess the *Urim* and *Thummim*?' *JHS* 7, Article 3.

2008 'Who Wrote Ezra–Nehemiah — and Why Did They?', in *Unity and Disunity in Ezra–Nehemiah: Redaction, Rhetoric, and Reader* (ed. Mark J. Boda and Paul L. Redditt; Hebrew Bible Monographs, 17; Sheffield: Sheffield Phoenix Press): 75-97.

2009 'The Concept of "Impure Birth" in Fifth Century Athens and Judea', in *In the Wake of Tikva Frymer-Kensky: Tikva Frymer-Kensky Memorial Volume* (ed. R.H. Beal, S. Holloway and J. Scurlock; Piscataway, NJ: Gorgias Press).

2010a 'Temple Building in Ezra–Nehemiah', in *From the Foundations to the Crenellations: Essays on Temple Building in the Ancient Near East and Hebrew Bible* (ed. Mark J. Boda and James R. Novotny; AOAT: Münster: Ugarit-Verlag): 319-38.

2010b 'Because of the Dread upon Them—Fear and Uncertainty in the Persian Empire', in *The World of Achaemenid Persia: History, Art and Society in Iran and the Ancient Near East (Proceedings of a Conference at the British Museum 29th September–1st October 2005)* (ed. John Curtis and St John Simpson; London: IB Tauris): 457-69.

2012a 'Ezra's Use of Documents in the Context of Hellenistic Rules of Rhetoric', in *New Perspectives on Ezra–Nehemiah: History and Historiography, Text, Literature and Interpretation* (ed. Isaac Kalimi; Winona Lake, IN: Eisenbrauns): 11-26.

2012b 'The Artaxerxes Correspondence of Ezra 4, Nehemiah's Wall, and Persian Provincial Administration', in *'Go Out and Study the Land' (Judges 18:2): Archaeological, Historical and Textual Studies in Honor of Hanan Eshel* (ed. A.M. Maeir, J. Magness and L.H. Schiffman; Supplement to the Journal for the Study of Judaism, 148; Leiden: Brill): 35-58.

2013a '*Deus ex machina* and Plot Construction in Ezra 1–6', in *Prophets, Prophecy, and Ancient Israelite Historiography* (ed. Mark J. Boda and Lissa M. Wray Beal; Winona Lake, IN: Eisenbrauns): 189-207.

2013b 'The Torah of God as God: The Exaltation of the Written Law Code in Ezra–Nehemiah', in *Reflecting upon Divine Presence and Absence in the Exile and Persian Period* (ed. Nathan MacDonald and Izaak de Hulster; FAT; Tübingen: Mohr Siebeck): 283-300.

2013c 'Implications of 5th and 4th Century Documents for Understanding the Role of the Governor in Persian Imperial Administration', in *In the Shadow of Bezalel: Aramaic, Biblical, and Ancient Near Eastern Studies in Honor of*

Bezalel Porten (ed. A.F. Botta; Culture and History of the Ancient Near East; Leiden: Brill): 319-31.

2014 *Ezra and the Law in History and Tradition* (Studies on Personalities of the Old Testament; Columbia, SC: University of South Carolina Press).

2015a 'No King in Judah? Mass Divorce in Judah and in Athens', in *Political Memory in and after the Persian Period* (ed. Carolina Waerzeggers and Jason Silverman; Ancient Near Eastern Monographs; Atlanta, GA: Society of Biblical Literature): 381-402.

2015b 'Did Ezra Create Judaism?', in *Marbeh Hochma: FS Victor (Avigdor) Hurowitz* (ed. Mayer Gruber *et al.*; Winona Lake, IN: Eisenbrauns): 171-84.

2015c 'The Exploitation of Depopulated Land in Achaemenid Judah', in *The Economy of Ancient Judah in its Historical Context* (ed. Marvin L. Miller, Ehud Ben Zvi and Gary N. Knoppers; Winona Lake, IN: Eisenbrauns): 149-62.

in press a 'What the Aramaic Documents Tell Us about the Achaemenid Administration of Empire', in *Arshama's Peoples* (ed. John Ma and Christopher Tuplin; Oxford: Centre for the Study of Ancient Documents; Oxford University Press).

in press b 'Artaxerxes' Letter and the Mission of Ezra—*noch einmal*', in *Festschrift for Charles Krahmolkov* (ed. Philip Schmitz, David Howard and Robert Miller II; AOAT; Münster: Ugarit-Verlag).

Fried, Lisbeth S. (ed.)

2011 *Was 1 Esdras First? An Investigation into the Priority and Nature of 1 Esdras* (Ancient Israel and its Literature, 7; Atlanta, GA: Scholars Press).

Fulton, Deirdre N., and Gary N. Knoppers

2011 'Lower Criticism and Higher Criticism: The Case of 1 Esdras', in Fried (ed.), 2011: 11-29.

Funk, Robert W.

1993 'Beth-Zur', in *The New Encyclopedia of Archaeological Excavations in the Holy Land* (ed. Ephraim Stern; Jerusalem: The Israel Exploration Society and Carta): 259-61.

Galil, G.

1996 *The Chronology of the Last Kings of Israel and Judah* (Studies in the History of the Ancient Near East, 9; Leiden: Brill).

Galling, Kurt

1951 'The "Gola-List" according to Ezra 2/Nehemiah 7', *JBL* 70: 149-58.

1961 'Serubbabel und der Wiederaufbau des Tempels in Jerusalem', in *Verbannung und Heimkehr: Beiträge zur Geschichte und Theologie Israels im 6. und 5. Jahrhundert v. Chr.—FS Wilhelm Rudolph* (ed. A. Kuschke; Tübingen: Mohr-Siebeck): 67-96.

1964 'Die Proklamation des Kyros in Esra 1', in *Studien zur Geschichte Israels im persischen Zeitalter* (Tübingen: Mohr Siebeck): 61-77.

Gammie, John G., and Leo G. Perdue (eds.)

1990 *The Sage in Israel and the Ancient Near East* (Winona Lake, IN: Eisenbrauns).

Gasquet, Francis Aidan (ed.)

1926–87 *Ezrae, tobiae, iudith* (ed. Aidan Gasquet, S.R.E., *et al.*; Biblia sacra iuxta latinam vulgatam versionem ad codicum fidem, iussu Pii PP. XI, 8; Rome: Libreria Editrice Vaticana).

Gehman, Henry Snyder

1972 ‘Ἐπισκεπομαι, επισκεψις, επισκοπος, and επισκοπή in the Septuagint in Relation to פקד and Other Hebrew Roots: A Case of Semantic Development Similar to That of Hebrew’, *VT* 22: 197-207.

Ginsberg, H. Louis

1960 ‘Ezra 1:4’, *JBL* 79: 167-69.

1982 *The Israelian Heritage of Judaism* (New York: The Jewish Theological Seminary of America).

Goldstein, Jonathan A.

1983 *II Maccabees* (AB, 41A; New York: Doubleday).

Goodman, Martin

1990 ‘Sacred Scripture and “Defiling the Hands”’, *JTS* NS 41: 99-107.

Gordon, Cyrus H.

1965 *Ugaritic Textbook* (Analecta orientalia, 38; Rome: Pontificium Institutum Biblicum).

Grabbe, Lester L.

1992 ‘Who Was the Bagoses of Josephus (Ant. 11.7.1, §297-301)?’, *Transeuphratène* 5: 49-61.

1998 *Ezra–Nehemiah* (Old Testament Readings; London: Routledge).

2004 *A History of the Jews and Judaism in the Second Temple Period* (London: T. & T. Clark International).

2006 ‘The “Persian Documents” in the Book of Ezra: Are They Authentic?’, in *Judah and the Judeans in the Persian Period* (ed. Oded Lipschits and Manfred Oeming; Winona Lake, IN: Eisenbrauns): 531-70.

2008 ‘Review of Jill Middlemas’ The Templeless Age: An Introduction to the History, Literature, and Theology of the Exile’, *Review of Biblical Literature*.

Graf, D.F.

1990 ‘Arabia during Achaemenid Times’, in *Achaemenid History.* IV. *Centre and Periphery* (ed. H. Sancisi-Weerdenburg and A. Kuhrt; Leiden: Nederlands Instituut voor het Nabije Oosten): 131-48.

Grant, E., and G.E. Wright

1939 *Ain Shems Excavations, Part V, Palestine* (Haverford, PA: Haverford College).

Grätz, Sebastian

2006 ‘Die aramäische Chronik des Esrabuches und die Rolle der Ältesten in Esr 5–6’, *ZAW* 118: 405-22.

2009 ‘Gottesgesetz und Königsgesetz: Esr 7 und die Autorisierung der Tora’, *Zeitschrift für Theologie und Kirche* 106: 1-19.

Gray, J.

1965 *The Legacy of Canaan: The Ras Shamra Texts and their Relevance to the Old Testament* (Leiden: Brill).

Grayson, A. Kirk

2000 *Assyrian and Babylonian Chronicles* (Winona Lake, IN: Eisenbrauns, orig., 1975).

Greenberg, Raphael

1993 ‘Beit-Mirsim, Tell’, in *NEAEHL* 1: 180.

Griffith, F. L.

1909 ‘The Petition of Peteesi’, in *Catalogue of the Demotic Papyri, III* (ed. F.L. Griffith; John Rylands Library, 9; London: Manchester University Press): 37-112.

Grimal, Nicolas
1993 *A History of Ancient Egypt* (Oxford: Blackwell).

Groot, Alon de
2001 'Jerusalem during the Persian Period (Hebrew)', in *New Studies on Jerusalem: Proceedings of Seventh Conference December 6th, 2001* (ed. A. Faust and E. Baruch; Ramat-Gan: Ingeborg Rennert Center for Jerusalem Studies): 77-81.

Gropp, Douglas M.
1990 'The Language of the Samaria Papyri: A Preliminary Study', *Maarav* 5-6: 169-87.

Gunneweg, Antonius H.J.
1982 'Die aramäische und die hebräisch Erzählung über die nachexilische Restauration—ein Vergleich', *ZAW* 94: 292-302.
1983 ''AM HA'ARES: A Semantic Revolution', *ZAW* 95: 437-40.
1985 *Esra* (Kommentar zum Alten Testament; Gütersloh: Gütersloher Verlagshaus Mohn).
1987 *Nehemia* (Kommentar zum Alten Testament, 19.2; Gütersloh: Gütersloher Verlagshaus Mohn).

Gurney, Oliver R.
1990 *The Hittites* (London: Penguin Books).

Guthe, H., and A. Erman
1906 'Ein Siegelstein mit hebräischer Unterschrift vom Tell el-Mutsellim', *MNDPV*, 5: 33-35, Fig. 32.

Habicht, C.
1961 'Falsche Urkunden zur Geschichte Athens im Zeitalter der Perserkreige', *Hermes*, 89: 1-35.

Hagedorn, Anselm C.
2007 'Local Law in an Imperial Context: The Role of Torah in the (Imagined) Persian Period', in *The Pentateuch as Torah: New Models for Understanding its Promulgation and Acceptance* (ed. Gary N. Knoppers and Bernard M. Levinson; Winona Lake, IN: Eisenbrauns): 57-76.

Hallock, R.T.
1969 *Persepolis Fortification Tablets* (University of Chicago Oriental Institute Publications, 92; Chicago: University of Chicago Press).
1985 'The Evidence of the Persepolis Tablets', in *The Median and Achaemenian Periods* (ed. Ilya Gershevitch; Cambridge History of Iran, 2; Cambridge: Cambridge University Press): 588-609.

Halpern, Baruch
1990 'A Historiographic Commentary on Ezra 1–6: A Chronological Narrative and Dual Chronology in Israelite Historiography', in *The Hebrew Bible and its Interpreters* (ed. William H. Propp, B. Halpern and D.N. Freedman; Biblical and Judaic Studies from the University of California, San Diego, 1;Winona Lake, IN: Eisenbrauns): 81-142.

Hanhart, Robert (ed.)
1974 *Esdrae Liber I* (Septuaginta: Vetus Testamentum Graecum auctoritate Academiae Scientiarum Gottingensis editum, 8.1; Göttingen: Vandenhoeck & Ruprecht).
1993 *Esdrae Liber II* (Septuaginta: Vetus Testamentum Graecum auctoritate Academiae Scientiarum Gottingensis editum, 8.2; Göttingen: Vandenhoeck & Ruprecht).

Hanson, Paul D.
1979 *The Dawn of Apocalytic: The Historical and Sociological Roots of Jewish Apocalyptic Eschatology* (Philadelphia, PA: Fortress Press).
Haran, Menahem
1961 'The Gibeonites, the Nethinim and the Sons of Solomon's Servants', *VT* 11: 159-69.
1985 *Temples and Temple-Service in Ancient Israel* (Winona Lake, IN: Eisenbrauns [reprint of Oxford: Clarendon Press, 1978]).
1986 'Explaining the Identical Lines at the End of Chronicles and the Beginning of Ezra', *Bible Review*, 2.3: 18-20.
Hartman, Louis F., and Alexander A. Di Lella
1978 *The Book of Daniel: A New Translation with Introduction and Commentary* (AB, 23; New York: Doubleday).
Harvey, Paul B.
2011 'Darius' Court and the Guardsmen's Debate: Hellenistic Greek Elements in 1 Esdras', in *Was 1 Esdras First? An Investigation into the Priority and Nature of 1 Esdras* (ed. L.S. Fried; Atlanta: Society of Biblical Literature): 179-90.
Hawkins, J.D.
1972–75 'Hamath', *RLA* 4: 69-70.
Hawley, Charles Arthur
1922 *A Critical Examination of the Peshitta Version of the Book of Ezra* (Contributions to Oriental History and Philology, 7; New York: Columbia University Press).
Hayes, Christine E.
2002 *Gentile Impurities and Jewish Identities: Intermarriage and Conversion from the Bible to the Talmud* (Oxford: Oxford University Press).
Head, B.V.
1963 *Historia numorum: A Manual of Greek Numismatics* (London: Spink & Son, new and enl. edn).
Heger, Paul
1999 *The Three Biblical Altar Laws* (Berlin: de Gruyter).
Heltzer, Michael
1992 'A Recently Published Babylonian Tablet and the Province of Judah after 516 B.C.E.', *Transeuphratène* 5: 57-61.
1995–96 'The Flogging and Plucking of Beards in the Achaemenid Empire and the Chronology of Nehemiah', *AMI* 28: 305-307.
Herodotus
1982 *Histories* (trans. A.D. Godley; Loeb Classical Library, 118; Cambridge: Harvard University Press).
Herr, L.
1993 'What Ever Happened to the Ammonites?', *BAR* 19.6: 27-35, 68.
1999 'The Ammonites in the Late Iron Age and Persian Period', in *Ancient Ammon* (ed. B. MacDonald and R.W. Younker; Leiden: Brill): 219-37.
Hirsch, S.W.
1985 *The Friendship of the Barbarians: Xenophon and the Persian Empire* (London: Published for Tufts University by University Press of New England).
Hizmi, Hanania
1993 'Khirbet El-Beiyudat', in *Abila-Elusa, NEAEHL* 1: 181-82.

Hjelm, Ingrid
2000 *The Samaritans and Early Judaism: A Literary Analysis* (JSOTSup, 303; Sheffield: Sheffield Academic Press).
Hoftijzer, J., and K. Jongeling
1995 *Dictionary of the North-West Semitic Inscriptions* (Leiden: Brill).
Hoglund, Kenneth G.
1992 *Achaemenid Imperial Administration in Syria-Palestine and the Missions of Ezra and Nehemiah* (SBL Dissertation Series, 125; Atlanta, GA: Scholars Press).
Holloway, S.W.
1992 *The Case for Assyrian Religious Influence in Israel and Judah: Inference and Evidence* (PhD diss., University of Chicago, The Divinity School).
Holmgren, Fredrick C.
1987 *Israel Alive Again: A Commentary on the Books of Ezra and Nehemiah* (Grand Rapids, MI: Eerdmans).
Honigman, Sylvie
2003 *The Septuagint and Homeric Scholarship in Alexandria: A Study in the Narrative of the Letter of Aristeas* (London: Routledge).
Hoonacker, A. Van
1890 'Néhémie et Esdras, une nouvelle hypothèse sur la chronologie de l'époque de la restauration', *Muséon* 9: 151-84, 317-51, 389-400.
Hornblower, S.
1982 *Mausolus* (Oxford: Clarendon).
Hout, M. van den
1949 'Studies in Early Greek Letter-Writing', *Mnemosyne* 4: 19-41.
Hughes, J.
1990 *Secrets of the Times: Myth and History in Biblical Chronology* (JSOTSup, 66; Sheffield: Sheffield Academic Press).
Humphreys, Sarah C.
1974 'The Nothoi of Kynosarges', *Journal of Hellenic Studies* 94: 88-95.
Hunt, Alice
2006 *Missing Priests: The Zadokites in Tradition and History* (Library of Hebrew Bible/Old Testament Studies, 452; London: T. & T. Clark).
Hurowitz, Victor (Avigdor)
1985 'The Priestly Account of Building the Tabernacle', *JAOS* 105: 21-30.
1992 *I Have Built You an Exalted House: Temple Building in the Bible in Light of Mesopotamian and Northwest Semitic Writings* (JSOTSup, 115; Sheffield: Sheffield Academic Press).
1993 'Temporary Temples', in *Kinattutu ša Darâti: Raphael Kutscher Memorial Volume* (ed. A.F. Rainey; Tel Aviv: Tel Aviv University, Institute of Archaeology): 35-50.
2003 'Tablet of the Sun-Disk of Nabubaladan King of Babylon (BBSt 36) (Hebrew)', in *Sefer Hayim and Miriyam Tadmor* (ed. Y. Epha'al, A. BenTor and P. Machinist; Eretz Yisrael, 27, Jerusalem: Israel Exploration Society): 91-109.
2006 'The Vessels of Yhwh and the Debate over the Divine Presence in the Second Temple—Downgrading a Divine Symbol', lecture, SBL Annual Meeting.

Jacobsen, T.
1940 'Review of *Lamentation over the Destruction of Ur* by S. N. Kramer', *American Journal of Semitic Languages and Literature* 58: 219-24.
Jacoby, Felix
1923 *Die Fragmente der griechischen Historiker* (Berlin: Weidmann).
Jameson, M.H.
1960 'A Decree of Themistocles from Troizen', *Hesperia* 29: 198-223.
Janssen, C.
1991 'Samsu-Iluna and the Hungry Naditums', in *Northern Akkad Project Reports* 5: 3-40.
Janzen, David
2000 'The "Mission" of Ezra and the Persian-Period Temple Community', *JBL* 119: 619-43.
2002 *Witch-hunts, Purity and Social Boundaries: The Expulsion of the Foreign Women in Ezra 9–10.* (JSOTSup, 350; Sheffield: Sheffield Academic Press).
Japhet, Sara
1968 'The Supposed Common Authorship of Chronicles and Ezra–Nehemiah Investigated Anew', *VT* 18: 330-71.
1982 'Sheshbazzar and Zerubbabel—Against the Background of the Historical and Religious Tendencies of Ezra–Nehemiah', *ZAW* 94: 66-98.
1983 'Sheshbazzar and Zerubbabel against the Background of the Historical Religious Tendencies of Ezra–Nehemiah', *ZAW* 95 218-30.
1993 *I and II Chronicles* (Louisville, KY: Westminster/John Knox Press).
2003 'Theodicy in Ezra–Nehemiah and Chronicles', in *Theodicy in the World of the Bible* (ed. Antti Morr Laato and Johannes de Cornelis; Leiden: Brill): 429-69.
2006 '"History" and "Literature" in the Persian Period: The Restoration of the Temple', in *From the Rivers of Babylon to the Highlands of Judah: Collected Studies on the Restoration Period* (ed Sara Japhet; Winona Lake, IN: Eisenbrauns): 152-68.
2007 'The Expulsion of the Foreign Women (Ezra 9–10): The Legal Basis, Precedents, and Consequences for the Definition of Jewish Identity', in *"Sieben Augen auf einem Stein" (Sach 3,9), Studien zur Literatur des Zweiten Tempels: Festschrift für Ina Willi-Plein zum 65. Geburtstag* (ed. Friedhelm Hartenstein and Michael Pietsch; Neukirchen-Vluyn: Neukirchener Verlag): 141-61.
Jerusalmi, Isaac
1982 *The Aramaic Sections of Ezra and Daniel* (Auxiliary Materials for the Study of Semitic Languages, 7; Cincinnati, OH: Hebrew Union College–Jewish Institute of Religion).
Joannès, Francis
1990 'Pouvoirs locaux et organisations du territoire en Babylonie achéménide', *Transeuphratène* 3: 173-89.
2004 *The Age of Empires: Mesopotamia in the First Millennium BC* (Edinburgh: Edinburgh University Press).
Joannès, Francis, and André Lemaire
1999 'Trois tablettes cunéiformes à onomastique ouest-sémitique (collection Sh. Moussaïeff)', *Transeuphratène* 17: 17-34, Pls. 1-2.
Jones, Ivor H.
1992 'Musical Instruments', in *ABD* IV (*K–N*), 934-39.

Joong, Ho Chong

1996 'Were There Yahwistic Sanctuaries in Babylonia', *Asia Journal of Theology* 10: 198-217.

Kalimi, Isaac

2005 *An Ancient Israelite Historian: Studies in the Chronicler, his Time, Place and Writing* (Studia semitica neerlandica, 46; Assen: Van Gorcum).

Kapelrud, Arvid S.

1944 *The Question of Authorship in the Ezra-Narrative: A Lexical Investigation* (Oslo: J. Dybwad).

Kasher, Aryeh

1990 *Jews and Hellenistic Cities in Eretz-Israel: Relations of the Jews in Eretz-Israel with the Hellenistic Cities during the Second Temple Period (332 BCE–70 CE)* (Texte und Studien zum antiken Judentum, 21; Tübingen: Mohr Siebeck).

Katzenstein, H.J.

1989 'Gaza in the Persian Period', *Transeuphratène* 1: 67-86.

Kellermann, U.

1967 *Nehemia: Quellen, Überlieferung, und Geschichte* (Berlin: Töpelmann).

Kelso, James L., and William F. Albright

1968 *The Excavation of Bethel (1934–1960)* (Cambridge, MA: American Schools of Oriental Research).

Kent, Roland G.

1953 *Old Persian: Grammar, Texts, Lexicon* (New Haven, CT: American Oriental Society).

Kenyon, K.M.

1993 'Jericho', in *NEAEHL* 2: 674-81.

Kidner, Derek

1979 *Ezra and Nehemiah: An Introduction and Commentary* (Tyndale Old Testament Commentary; Leicester: InterVarsity Press).

King, P.J., and Stager, L.E.

2001 *Life in Biblical Israel* (Louisville, KY: Westminster John Knox).

Klawans, Jonathan

1995 'Notions of Gentile Impurity in Ancient Judaism', *AJS Review* 20: 285-312.

2000 *Impurity and Sin in Ancient Judaism* (Oxford: Oxford University Press).

Klein, Ralph W.

2012 *2 Chronicles* (Hermeneia; Minneapolis, MN: Fortress Press).

Kloner, Amos, and Ian Stern

2007 'Idumea in the Late Persian Period (Fourth Century B.C.E.)', in *Judah and the Judeans in the Fourth Century B.C.E.* (ed. Oded Lipschits, Gary N. Knoppers and Rainer Albertz; Winona Lake, IN: Eisenbrauns): 139-44.

Knoppers, Gary N.

2003a *I Chronicles 1–9* (AB, 12; New York: Doubleday).

2003b 'The Relationship of the Priestly Genealogies to the History of the High Priesthood in Jerusalem', in *Judah and the Judeans in the Neo-Babylonian Period* (ed. Oded Lipschits and Joseph Blenkinsopp; Winona Lake, IN: Eisenbrauns): 109-33.

2004 *I Chronicles 10–29* (AB, 12A; New York: Doubleday).

2009 'Ethnicity, Genealogy, Geography, and Change: The Judean Communities of Babylon and Jerusalem in the Story of Ezra', in *Community Identity in*

Judean Historiography: Biblical and Comparative Perspectives (ed. Gary N. Knoppers and Kenneth A. Ristau; Winona Lake, IN: Eisenbrauns): 147-71.

2013 *Jews and Samaritans: The Origins and History of their Early Relations* (Oxford: Oxford University Press).

Knowles, Melody D.

2006 *Centrality Practiced: Jerusalem in the Religious Practice of Yehud and the Diaspora in the Persian Period* (Atlanta, GA: Society of Biblical Literature).

Koch, Heidemarie

1988 'Zur Religion der Achämeniden', *ZAW* 100: 393-405.

Koenen, Klaus

2003 *Bethel Geschichte, Kult und Theologie* (Orbis biblicus et orientalis; Göttingen: Vandenhoeck & Ruprecht).

Köhlmoos, Melanie

2006 *Bet-El—Erinnerungen an eine Stadt: Perspektiven der alttestamentlichen Bet-El-Überlieferung* (Tübingen: Mohr Siebeck).

Konkel, M.

2001 *Architektonik des Heiligen: Studien zur zweiten Tempelvision Ezechiels (Ez 40–48)* (Berlin: Philo).

Kornfeld, W.

1978 'Onomastica aramaica aus Ägypten', *Akademie der Wissenschaften philosophisch-historische Klasse Sitzungsberichte* 333: 1-144.

Kottsieper, Ingo

2008 'The Aramaic Tradition: Aḥiqar', in *Scribes, Sages, and Seers: The Sage in the Eastern Mediterranean World* (ed. L.G. Perdue; FRLANT, 219; Göttingen: Vandenhoeck & Ruprecht): 109-24.

Kraemer, David

1993 'On the Relationship of the Books of Ezra and Nehemiah', *JSOT* 59.18: 73-92.

Kratz, Reinhard G.

2005 *The Composition of the Narrative Books of the Old Testament* (trans. John Bowden; London: T. & T. Clark).

Kuhrt, Amélie

1983 'The Cyrus Cylinder and Achaemenid Imperial Policy', *JSOT* 25: 83-97.

1988 'Babylonia from Cyrus to Xerxes', in *Persia, Greece and the Western Mediterranean c.525–479* (Cambridge Ancient History, 4; Cambridge: Cambridge University Press): 112-38.

2007 *The Persian Empire: A Corpus of Sources from the Achaemenid Period,* II (London: Routledge).

Kuhrt, Amélie, and Susan Sherwin-White

1987 'Xerxes' Destruction of Babylonian Temples', in *The Greek Sources* (ed. Heleen Sancisi-Weerdenburg and Amélie Kuhrt; Achaemenid History, 2; Leiden: Nederlands Instituut voor het Nabije Oosten): 69-78.

Kümmel, H.M.

1979 *Familie, Beruf und Amt im spätbabylonischen Uruk: Prosopographische Untersuchungen zu Berufsgruppen des 6. Jahrhunderts v. Chr. in Uruk* (Abhandlungen der deutschen Orient-Gesellshaft, 20; Berlin: Mann).

Kushner, Harold S.

1981 *When Bad Things Happen to Good People* (New York: Schocken Books).

Kutsko, John F.

2000 *Between Heaven and Earth: Divine Presence and Absence in the Book of Ezekiel* (BJSUCSD, 7; Winona Lake, IN: Eisenbrauns).

Lafont, Sophie
1994 'Ancient Near Eastern Laws: Continuity and Pluralism', in *Theory and Method in Biblical and Cuneiform Law: Revisions, Interpolation, and Development* (ed. Bernard M. Levinson; Sheffield: Sheffield Academic Press): 91-118.
Landsberger, Benno
1939 'Die babylonischen Termini für Gezetz und Recht', in *Symbolae ad iura orientis antiqui* (ed. T. Folkers *et al.*; Leiden: Brill): 219-34.
Lapp, Paul W.
1965 'Tell el-Fûl', *BA* 28: 2-10.
Lapp, Nancy L.
1981 *The Third Campaign at Tel el-Fûl: The Excavations of 1964* (Annual of the American Schools of Oriental Research; Cambridge, MA: American Schools of Oriental Research).
1993 'Tell El-Fûl', in *NEAEHL* 2: 445-48.
1997 'Fûl, Tell El-', in *OEANE* 2: 346-47.
Lateiner, Donald
1989 *The Historical Method of Herodotus* (Phoenix: Journal of the Classical Association of Canada, Supplementary Volume, 23; Toronto: University of Toronto Press).
Lebram, Jürgen C.H.
1987 'Die Traditionsgeschichte der Esragestalt und die Frage nach dem historischen Esra', in *Achaemenid History.* 1. *Sources, Structures and Synthesis* (ed. H. Sancisi-Weerdenburg; Achaemenid History, 1; Leiden: Nederlands Instituut voor het Nabije Oosten): 103-38.
Lefkovits, Etgar
2008 'Seal of King Zedekiah's Minister Found in J'lem Dig', in *Jerusalem Post,* July 31.
Leithart, Peter J.
1999 'Attendants of Yahweh's House: Priesthood in the Old Testament', *JSOT* 85: 3-24.
Lemaire, André
1971 'L'ostracon de Mesad Hashavyahu replacé dans son contexte', *Semitica* 21: 57-79.
1990 'Populations et territoires de Palestine à l'époque Perse', *Transeuphratène* 3: 31-74.
1994 'Les transformations politiques et culturelles de la Transjordanie au VIe siècle av. J.-C.', *Transeuphratène* 8: 9-27.
1995 'La fin de la première periode perse en Égypt et la chronologie judéenne vers 400 av. J.-C.', *Transeuphratène* 9: 51-61.
2001 'Les religions du sud de la Palestine au IVe siècle av. J.-C. d'après les ostraca araméens d'Idumée', *CRAIBL* 145: 1141-58.
2004 'Another Temple to the Israelite God: Aramaic Hoard Documents Life in Fourth Century B.C.', *BAR* 30.4: 38-44, 60.
2006 'New Aramaic Ostraca from Idumea and their Historical Interpretation', in *Judah and the Judeans in the Persian Period* (ed. Oded Lipschits and Manfred Oeming; Winona Lake: IN: Eisenbrauns): 413-56.
2007 'Administration in Fourth-Century BCE Judah in Light of Epigraphy and Numismatics', in *Judah and the Judeans in the Fourth Century B.C.E.* (ed. Oded Lipschits, Gary N. Knoppers and Rainer Albertz; Winona Lake, IN: Eisenbrauns): 53-74.

Lemaire, André, and Hélène Lozachmeur
1987 'Birah/Birta' en araméen', *Syria*, 64: 261-66.
1994 'Histoire et administration de la Palestine à l'époque Perse', in *La Palestine à l'époque Perse* (ed. E.-M. Laperrousaz and A. Lemaire; Paris: Les éditions du Cerf): 12-53.
1995 'La Birta en Méditerranée orientale', *Semitica* 43-44: 75-78.
Lemos, T.M.
2010 *Marriage Gifts and Social Change in Ancient Palestine 1200 BCE to 200 CE* (Cambridge: Cambridge University Press).
Leuchter, Mark
2009 'Ezra's Mission and the Levites of Casiphia', in *Community Identity in Judean Historiography: Biblical and Comparative Perspectives* (ed. Gary N. Knoppers and Kenneth A. Ristau; Winona Lake, IN: Eisenbrauns): 173-95.
Levick, Barbara
2012 'Women and Law', in *A Companion to Women in the Ancient World* (ed. Sharon James and Sheila Dillon; Blackwell Companions to the Ancient World; West Sussex: Blackwell): 96-106.
Levine, Baruch A.
1963 'The Netinim', *JBL* 82: 207-12.
1969 'Notes on a Hebrew Ostracon from Arad', *IEJ* 19: 49-51.
1993 *Numbers 1–20* (AB, 4; New York: Doubleday).
2000 *Numbers 21–36* (AB, 4A; New York: Doubleday).
Levinson, Jon D.
1976 *Theology of the Program of Restoration of Ezekiel 40–48* (Harvard Semitic Monographs, 10; Missoula, MT: Scholars Press).
Lewis, Naphtali
1983 *Life in Egypt under Roman Rule* (Oxford: Clarendon Press).
Lichtheim, M.
1980 'Statue Inscription of Udjahorrensne', in *AEL* 3: 36-41.
Lim, Timothy H.
2010 'The Defilement of the Hands as a Principle Determining the Holiness of Scriptures', *JTS* NS 61: 501-15.
Lindberg, J.C.
1828 *De inscriptione Melitensi phoenicio-graeco* (apud G.I. Davies *et al.*, *Ancient Hebrew Inscriptions: Volume 1: Corpus and Concordance* (Cambridge: University of Cambridge Press, 1991).
Lipiński, Edward
1975 *Studies in Aramaic Inscriptions and Onomastics* (Orientalia lovaniensia analecta, 1; Leuven: Leuven University Press).
2000 *The Aramaeans: Their Ancient History, Culture, Religion* (Orientalia lovaniensia analecta, 100; Leuven: Peeters).
Lipschits, Oded
1998 'Nebuchadrezzar's Policy in "Hattu-Land" and the Fate of the Kingdom of Judah', *UF* 30: 467-87.
1999 'The History of the Benjaminite Region under Babylonian Rule', *Tel Aviv* 26: 155-90.
2001a 'Judah, Jerusalem and the Temple (586–539 B.C.)', *Transeuphratène* 22: 129-42.
2001b 'The Policy of the Persian Empire and the Meager Architectonic Finds in the Province of "Yehud" (Hebrew)', *New Studies on Jerusalem* 7: 45-76.

2003 'Demographic Changes in Judah between the Seventh and the Fifth Centuries B.C.E.', in *Judah and the Judeans in the Neo-Babylonian Period* (ed. Oded Lipschits; Winona Lake, IN: Eisenbrauns): 323-76.

2004 'Ammon in Transition from Vassal Kingdom to Babylonian Province', *BASOR* 335: 37-52.

2005 *The Fall and Rise of Jerusalem* (Winona Lake, IN: Eisenbrauns).

2006 'Achaemenid Imperial Policy, Settlement Processes in Palestine, and the Status of Jerusalem in the Middle of the Fifth Century B.C.E.', in *Judah and the Judeans in the Persian Period* (ed. Oded Lipschits and Manfred Oeming; Winona Lake, IN: Eisenbrauns): 19-52.

2011 'Shedding New Light on the Dark Years of the "Exilic Period": New Studies, Further Elucidation, and Some Questions Regarding the Archaeology of Judah as an "Empty Land"', in *Interpreting Exile* (ed. Brad Kelle, Frank R. Ames and Jacob L. Wright; Atlanta, GA: Society of Biblical Literature): 57-79.

Lipschits, Oded, and David S. Vanderhooft

2011 *The Yehud Stamp Impressions: A Corpus of Inscribed Impressions from the Persian and Hellenistic Periods in Judah* (Winona Lake, IN: Eisenbrauns).

Lipschits, Oded, Yuval Gadot, Benjamin Arubas and Manfred Oeming

2011 'Palace and Village, Paradise and Oblivion: Unraveling the Riddles of Ramat Rahel', *Near Eastern Archaeology* 74: 2-49.

Lozachmeur, H.

1998 'Un nouveau grafito araméen provenant de Saqqâra', *Semitica* 48: 147-49.

Luckenbill, D.D.

1925 'The Black Stone of Esarhaddon', *American Journal of Semitic Languages and Literatures* 41: 165-73.

Magen, Yitzhak

2000 'Mt Gerizim—A Temple City (Hebrew)', *Qadmoniot* 33: 74-118.

2007 'The Dating of the First Phase of the Samaritan Temple on Mount Gerizim in Light of the Archaeological Evidence', in *Judah and the Judeans in the Fourth Century B.C.E.* (ed. Oded Lipschits, Gary N. Knoppers and R. Albertz; Winona Lake, IN: Eisenbrauns): 157-211.

Magen, Yitzhak, and Israel Finkelstein (eds.)

1993 *Archaeological Survey of the Hill Country of Benjamin* (Jerusalem: Israel Antiquities Authority).

Malamat, Abraham

1950 'The Last Wars of the Kingdom of Judah', *JNES* 9: 218-27.

Manville, Philip B.

1997 *The Origins of Citizenship in Ancient Athens* (Princeton, NJ: Princeton University Press).

Marcus, David

2006 *Ezra and Nehemiah* (BHQ, 20; Stuttgart: Deutsche Bibelgesellschaft).

Margueron, Jean-Claude

1997 'Mesopotamian Temples', in *OEANE* 5: 165-69.

Martínez, Florentino García, and Eibert J.C. Tigchelaar

1997 *The Dead Sea Scrolls Study Edition* (Leiden: Brill).

Mazar, Amichai

1999 'The 1997–1998 Excavations at Tel Rehov: Preliminary Report', *IEJ* 49: 1-42.

Mazar, Amihai, and George E. Kelm

1993 'Batash, Tel', in *NEAEHL* 1: 152-57.

Mazar, Benjamin
1957 'The Tobiads', *IEJ* 7: 137-45, 229-38.
1993 'En-Gedi', in *NEAEHL* (ed. Ephraim Stern; Jerusalem: Israel Exploration Society and Carta): 399-405.
McCown, Chester C., Joseph Wampler, and William F. Badè
1947 *Tell en-Nasbeh Excavated under the Direction of the Late William Frederic Badè* (Berkeley, CA: The Palestine Institute of Pacific School of Religion and the American Schools of Oriental Research).
Merendino, Rosario Pius
1981 *Der Erste und der Letzte: Eine Untersuchung von Jes 40–48* (VTSup, 31; Leiden: Brill).
Merton, R.K.
1941 'Intermarriage and the Social Structure: Fact and Theory', *Psychiatry* 9: 361-74.
Meshel, Ze'ev
1979 'Did Yhwh Have a Consort? The New Religious Inscriptions from Sinai', *BAR* 5.2.
Meyer, Eduard
1965 *Die Entstehung des Judentums* (Hildesheims: Olms [orig., 1896]).
Meyers, Carol L., and Eric M. Meyers
1987 *Haggai, Zechariah 1–8: A New Translation with Introduction and Commentary* (AB; Garden City, NY: Doubleday).
Migne, J.-P. (Jacques-Paul)
1892 *Collection intégrale et universelle des orateurs sacrés du premier et du second ordre* (Paris: Gaume).
Milgrom, Jacob
1991 *Leviticus 1–16* (AB, 3A; New York: Doubleday).
Millard, Alan R.
1976 'Assyrian Royal Names in Biblical Hebrew', *JSS* 21: 1-14.
Miller, Patrick D.
1994 *They Cried to the Lord: The Form and Theology of Biblical Prayer* (Minneapolis, MN: Fortress Press).
Min, Kyung-Jin
2004 *The Levitical Authorship of Ezra–Nehemiah* (JSOTSup; London: T. & T. Clark International).
Monson, John
2000 'The New 'Ain Dara Temple: Closest Solomonic Parallel', *BAR* 26.3: 20-35, 67.
Moore, Carey A.
1971 *Esther* (AB, 7B; New York: Doubleday).
1996 *Tobit* (AB, 40A; New York: Doubleday).
Morgan, Teresa
1998 *Literate Education in the Hellenistic and Roman Worlds* (Cambridge: Cambridge University Press).
Mowinckel, Sigmund
1964a 'Ezr. 5:3, 9', *Studia Theologica* 19: 130-35.
1964b *Die Nehemia-Denkschrift* (Studien zu dem Buche Ezra–Nehemia, 2; Oslo: Universitetsforlaget).
1965 *Die Ezrageschichte und das Gesetz Moses* (Studien zu dem Buche Ezra–Nehemiah, 3; Oslo: Universitetsforlaget).

Muraoka, T., and B. Porten
1998 *A Grammar of Egyptian Aramaic* (New York: Brill).
Murphy-O'Connor, Jerome
1992 *The Holy Land: An Archaeological Guide from Earliest Times to 1700* (New York: Oxford University Press).
Myers, Jacob M.
1965 *Ezra–Nehemiah* (AB, 14; New York: Doubleday).
Na'aman, Nadav
1999 'No Anthropomorphic Graven Image: Notes on the Assumed Anthropomorphic Cult Statues in the Temples of Yhwh in the Pre-Exilic Period', *UF* 31: 391-415.
Nadelman, Yonaton
1994 'The Identification of Anathoth and the Soundings at Khirbet Deir es-Sidd', *IEJ* 44: 6-74.
Naveh, Joseph
1960 'A Hebrew Letter from the Seventh Century B.C.', *IEJ* 10: 130-36, Pl. 17.
1964 'Some Notes on the Reading of the Mesad Hashavyahu Letter', *IEJ* 14: 158ff.
1970 *The Development of the Aramaic Script* (Jerusalem: Israel Academy of Sciences and Humanities).
Naveh, Joseph, and Shaul Shaked
2012 *Aramaic Documents from Ancient Bactria (Fourth Century BCE)* (London: Khalili Family Trust).
Newsome, James D.
1975 'Toward a New Understanding of the Chronicler and his Purposes', *JBL* 94: 201-17.
Niditch, Susan
1996 *Oral World and Written Word* (Ancient Israelite Literature; Louisville, KY: Westminster John Knox Press).
Nims, Charles
1948 'The Term Hp "Law", "Right", in Demotic', *JNES* 7: 243-60.
North, Christopher R.
1964 *The Second Isaiah : Introduction, Translation, and Commentary to Chapters XL–LV* (Oxford: Clarendon Press).
Noth, Martin
1928 *Die israelitischen Personennamen im Rahmen der gemeinsemitischen Namengebung* (Stuttgart: Georg Olms).
1987 *The Chronicler's History* (trans. Hugh G.M. Williamson; Sheffield: Sheffield Academic Press [orig., 1943]).
Oded, Bustenay
1979 *Mass Deportations and Deportees in the Neo-Assyrian Empire* (Wiesbaden: Reichert).
1995 'Observations on the Israelite/Judaean Exiles in Mesopotamia during the Eighth-Sixth Centuries', in *Immigration and Emigration within the Ancient Near East: FS E. Lipiński* (ed. K. van Lerberghe and A. Schoors; Leuven: Peeters Publishers): 205-12.
Olmstead, Albert Ten Eyck
1948 *History of the Persian Empire* (Chicago: University of Chicago Press).
Olyan, Saul M.
2000 *Rites and Rank: Hierarchy in Biblical Representations of Cult* (Princeton, NJ: Princeton University Press).

2004 'Purity Ideology in Ezra–Nehemiah as a Tool to Reconstitute the Community', *Journal for the Study of Judaism in the Persian, Hellenistic and Roman Period* 35: 1-16.

Oppenheim, A. Leo
1977 *Ancient Mesopotamia: Portrait of a Dead Civilization* (Chicago: University of Chicago Press, orig., 1964).

Osborne, Robin
1997 'Law, the Democratic Citizen and the Representation of Women in Classical Athens', *Past and Present* 155: 3-33.

Oswald, Wolfgang
2012 'Foreign Marriages and Citizenship in Persian Period Judah', *JHS* 12: Article 6.

Pakkala, Juha
2004 *Ezra the Scribe: The Development of Ezra 7–10 and Nehemiah 8* (BZAW, 347; Berlin: de Gruyter).
2006 'The Original Independence of the Ezra Story in Ezra 7–10 and Nehemiah 8', *BN* 129: 17-24.

Parker, Richard A., and Waldo H. Dubberstein
1956 *Babylonian Chronology 626 B.C.–A.D. 75* (Brown University Studies, 19; Providence, RI: Brown University Press).

Pearce, Laurie E.
2006 'New Evidence for Judeans in Babylonia', in *Judah and the Judeans in the Persian Period* (ed. Oded Lipschits and Manfred Oeming; Winona Lake, IN: Eisenbrauns): 399-411.
2011 '"Judean": A Special Status in Neo-Babylonian and Achemenid Babylonia?', in *Judah and the Judeans in the Achaemenid Period: Negotiating Identity in an International Context* (ed. O. Lipschits, G.N. Knoppers, and M. Oeming; Winona Lake, IN: Eisenbrauns): 267-77.

Pearce, Laurie E., and Cornelia Wunsch
2014 *Documents of Judean Exiles and West Semites in Babylonia in the Collection of David Sofer* (Cornell University Studies in Assyriology and Sumerology (CUSAS), 28; Bethesda, MD: CDL Press).

Perdue, Leo G. (ed.)
2008 *Scribes, Sages, and Seers: The Sage in the Eastern Mediterranean World* (Göttingen: Vandenhoeck & Ruprecht).

Petersen, D.L.
1984 'Zechariah's Visions: A Theological Perspective', *VT* 34: 195-206.

Peterson, John L.
1992 'Anathoth', in *Anchor Bible Dictionary* (ed. David Noel Freedman; New York: Doubleday): 1:227-28.

Pilgrim, C. von
1999 'Der Tempel des Jahwe', *MDAIK* 55: 142-45.

Polaski, Donald C.
2004 '*Mene, Mene, Tekel, Parsin*: Writing and Resistance in Daniel 5 and 6', *JBL* 123: 649-69.

Poo, Mu-chou
2005 *Enemies of Civilization: Attitudes toward Foreigners in Ancient Mesopotamia, Egypt, and China* (SUNY Series in Chinese Philosophy and Culture; Albany, NY: State University of New York Press).

Porten, Bezalel

1968 *Archives from Elephantine: The Life of an Ancient Jewish Military Colony* (Berkeley, CA: University of California Press).

1978–79 'The Documents in the Book of Ezra and the Mission of Ezra (Hebrew)', *Shnaton* 3: 174-96.

1996 *The Elephantine Papyri in English: Three Millennia of Cross-Cultural Continuity and Change* (Documenta et monumenta orientis antiqui, 22; Leiden: Brill).

Porten, Bezalel, and Jerome A. Lund

2002 *Aramaic Documents from Egypt: A Key-Word-in-Context Concordance* (Winona Lake, IN: Eisenbrauns).

Porten, Bezalel, and Ada Yardeni

2006 'Social, Economic, and Onomastic Issues in the Aramaic Ostraca of the Fourth Century BCE', in *Judah and the Judeans in the Persian Period* (ed. Oded Lipschits and Manfred Oeming; Winona Lake, IN: Eisenbrauns): 457-88.

Posener, G.

1936 *La première domination perse en Égypt* (Cairo: Institut français d'archéologie orientale).

Pritchard, James Bennett

1962 *Gibeon, Where the Sun Stood Still: The Discovery of the Biblical City* (Princeton, NJ: Princeton University Press).

1993 'Gibeon', in *NEAEHL* 2: 511-14.

Propp, William H.C.

1998 *Exodus 1–18* (AB, 2; New York: Doubleday).

Rabinowitz, Yosef

1984 *The Book of Ezra* (The Art Scroll Tanach Series; Brooklyn, NY: Mesorah Publications).

Rainey, Anson F.

1970 'The Order of Sacrifices in Old Testament Rituals', *Biblica* 51: 485-98.

Redditt, Paul L.

2008 'The Dependence of Ezra–Nehemiah on 1 and 2 Chronicles', in *Unity and Disunity in Ezra–Nehemiah: Redaction, Rhetoric, and Reader* (ed. Mark J. Boda and Paul L. Redditt; Sheffield: Sheffield Phoenix Press): 216-40.

Redford, Donald B.

2001 'The So-Called "Codification" of Egyptian Law under Darius I', in *Persia and Torah: The Theory of Imperial Authorization of the Pentateuch* (ed. James W, Watts; Atlanta, GA: Society of Biblical Literature): 135-59.

Rehm, Rush

1992 *Greek Tragic Theatre* (London: Routledge).

Reich, R.

1993 'The Cemetery in the Mamilla Area of Jerusalem (Hebrew)', *Qadmoniot* 103-104: 103-109.

Reifenberg, A.

1950 *Ancient Hebrew Seals* (London : East and West Library).

Rendtorff, Rolf

1984 'Esra und das "Gesetz"', *ZAW* 96: 165-84.

1999 'Noch einmal: Esra und das "Gesetz"', *ZAW* 111: 89-91.

Richter, Sandra L.

2002 *The Deuteronomistic History and the Name Theology: lešakken šemô šam in the Bible and the Ancient Near East* (BZAW, 318; Berlin: de Gruyter).

Rofé, Alexander
1990 'An Inquiry into the Betrothal of Rebekah', in *Die hebräische Bibel und ihre zweifache Nachgeschichte: FS für Rolf Rendtorff* (ed. E. Blum, C. Macholz and E.W. Stegemann; Neukirchen-Vluyn: Neukirchener Verlag): 27-39.
Röllig, Wolfgang
1999 'Baal-Shamem', in *Dictionary of Deities and Demons in the Bible* (ed. K. van der Toorn, B. Becking and P. van der Horst; Grand Rapids, MI: Eerdmans, 2nd edn): 149-51.
Rooke, Deborah W.
2000 *Zadok's Heirs :The Role and Development of the High Priesthood in Ancient Israel* (Oxford Theological Monographs; Oxford: Oxford University Press).
Root, Margaret Cool
1979 *The King and Kingship in Achaemenid Art: Essays on the Creation of an Iconography of Empire* (Leiden: Brill).
Rosenmeyer, Patricia A.
2001 *Ancient Epistolary Fictions: The Letter in Greek Literature* (Cambridge: Cambridge University Press).
Rosenthal, Franz
1995 *A Grammar of Biblical Aramaic* (Porta linguarum orientalium, 5; Wiesbaden: Harrassowitz Verlag, 6th rev. edn).
Roth, Martha T.
1997 *Law Collections from Mesopotamia and Asia Minor* (Atlanta, GA: Scholars Press [orig., 1995]).
Rothenbusch, Ralf
2012 *'. . . abgesondert zur Tora Gottes hin': Ethnisch-religiöse Identitäten im Esra/Nehemiabuch* (Herder's Biblical Studies, 70; Freiburg: Herder).
Rowley, H.H.
1963 'Nehemiah's Mission and its Background', in *Man of God: Studies in Old Testament History and Prophecy* (ed. H.H. Rowley; London: Nelson): 211-45.
Rudolph, Wilhelm
1949 *Esra und Nehemia, samt 3.Esra* (Tübingen: Mohr).
Ruzicka, S.
1992 *Politics of a Persian Dynasty: The Hecatomnids in the Fourth Century* B.C. (Norman, OK: University of Oklahoma Press).
Samons, Loren J., II
2007 'Introduction: Athenian History and Society in the Age of Pericles', in *The Cambridge Companion to the Age of Pericles* (ed. Loren J. Samons II; Cambridge: Cambridge University Press): 1-24.
Sanders, Jack T.
2001 'When Sacred Canopies Collide: The Reception of the Torah of Moses in the Wisdom Literature of the Second-Temple Period', *Journal for the Study of Judaism in the Persian, Hellenistic and Roman Period* 32: 121-26.
Schaper, Joachim
2000 *Priester und Leviten im achämenidischen Juda: Studien zur Kult- und Sozialgeschichte Israels in persischer Zeit* (FAT, 31; Tübingen: Mohr Siebeck).
Schaps, D.M.
2004 *The Invention of Coinage and the Monetization of Ancient Greece* (Ann Arbor, MI: University of Michigan Press).

Schaudig, Hanspeter
2001 *Die Inschriften Nabonids von Babylon und Kyros'des Großen samt den in ihrem Umfeld entstandenen Tendenzschriften* (AOAT, 256; Münster: Ugarit-Verlag).

Schloen, J.D.
2001 *The House of the Father as Fact and Symbol: Patrimonialism in Ugarit and the Ancient Near East* (Winona Lake, IN: Eisenbrauns).

Schmid, Konrad
2007a 'The Late Persian Formation of the Torah: Observations on Deuteronomy 34', in *Judah and the Judeans in the Fourth Century* B.C.E. (ed. Oded Lipschits Gary N. Knoppers, and Rainer Albertz; Winona Lake, IN: Eisenbrauns): 237-51.
2007b 'The Persian Imperial Authorization as a Historical Problem and as a Biblical Construct: A Plea for Distinctions in the Current Debate', in *The Pentateuch as Torah: New Models for Understanding its Promulgation and Acceptance* (ed. Gary N. Knoppers and Bernard M. Levinson; Winona Lake, IN: Eisenbrauns): 23-38.

Schneider, Heinrich
1959 *Die Bücher Esra und Nehemia* (Die heilige Schrift des Altens Testamentes, 4; Bonn: Peter Hanstein Verlag).

Schröder, P.
1914 'Vier Siegelsteine mit semitischen Legenden', *ZDPV* 37: 174-76, #2, Fig. 9.

Schwiderski, Dirk
2000 *Handbuch des nordwestsemitischen Briefformulars: Ein Beitrag zur Echtheitsfrage der aramäischen Briefe des Esrabuches* (BZAW, 295; Berlin: de Gruyter).

Shaked, Shaul
2003 'De Khulmi a Nikhšapaya: Les données des nouveaux documents araméens de Bactres sur la toponymie de la région (IVe siècle av. n. è.)', *CRAIBL* 1517-35.
2004 *Le satrape de Bactriane et son gouverneur: Documents araméens du IVe s. avant notre ère provenant de Bactriane* (Paris: de Boccard).

Shallit, A.
1975 'The End of the Hasmonian Dynasty and the Rise of Herod', *World History of the Jewish People,* 7 (New Brunswick, NJ: Rutgers University Press): 44-70

Shiloh, Y.
1986 'A Group of Hebrew Bullae from the City of David', *IEJ* 36: 16-38.

Shupak, N.
1992 'A New Source for the Study of the Judiciary and Law of Ancient Egypt: The Case of the Eloquent Peasant', *JNES* 51: 1-18.

Slotsky, Alice Louise
1997 *The Bourse of Babylon: Market Quotations in the Astronomical Diaries of Babylonia* (Bethesda, MD: CDL).

Smith, Sidney
1945 '"Foundations". Ezra iv, 12; v, 16; vi 3', in *Essays in Honour of the Very Rev. Dr. J.H. Hertz, Chief Rabbi of the United Hebrew Congregations of the British Empire on the Occasion of his Seventieth Birthday, September 25, 1942 (5703)* (ed. I. Epstein, E. Levine and C. Roth; London: Edward Goldston): 385-96.

Smith-Christopher, Daniel L.

1994 'The Mixed Marriage Crisis in Ezra 9–10 and Nehemiah 13: A Study of the Sociology of Post-Exilic Judean Community', in *Second Temple Studies. 2. Temple and Community in the Persian Period* (ed. Tamara C. Eskenazi, and Kent Richards; JSOTSup, 175, Sheffield: JSOT Press): 243-65.

2002 *A Biblical Theology of Exile* (Overtures to Biblical Theology; Minneapolis, MN: Fortress Press).

Smitten, Wilhelm T. in der

1973 *Esra: Quellen, Überlieferung und Geschichte* (Assen: Van Gorcum).

Soden, W.

1970 'Zur Stellung des "Geweihten" (*qdš*) in Ugarit', *UF* 2: 329-30.

Spiegelberg, W.

1914 *Die sogenannte demotische Chronik des Pap. 215 der Bibliothéque Nationale de Paris* (Leipzig: Hinrichs).

Steiner, Richard C.

2001 'The *mbqr* at Qumran, the *episkopos* in the Athenian Empire, and the Meaning of *lbqr'* in Ezra 7:14: On the Relation of Ezra's Mission to the Persian Legal Project', *JBL* 120: 623-46.

2006 'Bishlam's Archival Search Report in Nehemiah's Archive: Multiple Introductions and Reverse Chronological Order as Clues to the Origin of the Aramaic Letters in Ezra 4–6', *JBL* 125: 641-85.

2007 'Why Bishlam (Ezra 4:7) Cannot Rest "In Peace": On the Aramaic and Hebrew Sound Changes that Conspired to Blot Out the Remembrance of Bel-Shalam the Archivist', *JBL* 126: 392-401.

Stern, Ephraim

1982 *Material Culture of the Land of the Bible in the Persian Period, 538–332 B.C.* (Jerusalem: Aris & Phillips/Israel Exploration Society).

2001 *Archaeology of the Land of the Bible* (Anchor Bible Reference Library, 2; New York: Doubleday).

2007 *Ein Gedi Excavations: Final Report,* 1 (Jerusalem: Israel Exploration Society).

Stern, Ephraim, and Yitzhak Magen

2000 'The First Level of the Samaritan Temple on Mt Gerizim: New Archaological Evidence (Hebrew)', *Qadmoniot* 33: 119-24.

2002 'Archaeological Evidence for the First Stage of the Samaritan Temple on Mount Gerizim', *IEJ* 52: 49-57.

Stolper, Matthew W.

1984 'The Neo-Babylonian Text from the Persepolis Fortification', *JNES* 43: 299-310.

1985 *Entrepreneurs and Empire: The Murašû Archive, the Murašû Firm, and Persian Rule in Babylonia* (Leiden: Nederlands Instituut voor het Nabije Oosten).

1989a 'The Governor of Babylon and Across-the-River in 486 B.C.', *JNES* 48: 283-305.

1989b 'Registration and Taxation of Slave Sales in Achaemenid Babylonia', *ZA* 79: 80-101.

2000 'Ganzabara', in *Encyclopaedia Iranica* (New York: Columbia University Center for Iranian Studies): 10:286-89.

Stronach, David

1978 *Pasargadae: A Report on the Excavations* (Oxford: Clarendon Press).

1997 'Anshan and Parsa: Early Achaemenid History, Art and Architecture on the Iranian Plateau', in *Mesopotamia and Iran in the Persian Period: Conquest and Imperialism 539–331* (ed. John Curtis; London: British Museum Press): 35-53.

Sukenik, Eleazar Lipa

1945 'Museum of Jewish Antiquities: Vol. 2', *Kedem* 2: #2.

Tallqvist, K.L.

1914 *Assyrian Personal Names* (Acta societatis scientiarum fennicae, 43; Helsinki: Helsingfors).

Talshir, David

1988 'A Reinvestigation of the Linguistic Relationship between Chronicles and Ezra–Nehemiah', *VT* 38: 165-93.

Talshir, Zipora

1986 'The Chronicler and the Composition of 1 Esdras', *CBQ* 48: 39-61.

1999 *1 Esdras: From Origin to Translation* (Atlanta, GA: Society of Biblical Literature).

2001 *1 Esdras: A Text Critical Commentary* (Atlanta, GA: Society of Biblical Literature).

2003 'Fragments of the Book of Ezra at Qumran' (Hebrew), *Megillot* 1: 213-18.

Tarragon, J.-M., de

1980 *Le culte à Ugarit: d'après les textes de la pratique en cunéiformes alphabétiques* (Paris: Gabalda).

Tavernier, Jan

2007 *Iranica in the Achaemenid Period (ca 550–330* B.C.*): Linguistic Study of Old Iranian Proper Names and Loanwords Attested in Non-Iranian Texts* (Orientalia lovaniensia analecta, 158; Leuven: Peeters).

Thiering, Barbara E.

1981 '*Mebaqqer* and *Episkopos* in the Light of the Temple Scroll', *JBL* 100: 59-74.

Thomson, H.C.

1960 'A Row of Cedar Beams', *PEQ*: 57-63.

Thureau-Dangin, F.

1921 *Rituels accadiens* (Paris: Leroux).

Tigay, Jeffrey H.

2013 'The Torah Scroll and God's Presence', in *Built by Wisdom, Established by Understanding: Essays on Biblical and Near Eastern Literature in Honor of Adele Berlin* (ed. M.L. Grossman; Bethesda, MD: University Press of Maryland): 323-40.

Toorn, Karel van der

1997 'The Iconic Book Analogies between the Babylonian Cult of Images and the Veneration of the Torah', in *The Image and the Book; Iconic Cults, Aniconism, and the Rise of Book Religion in Israel and the Ancient Near East* (ed. Karel van der Toorn; Leuven: Peeters): 229-48.

Torrey, Charles C.

1896 *The Composition and Historical Value of Ezra–Nehemiah* (BZAW, 2; Giessen: J. Ricker).

1970 *Ezra Studies* (New York: Ktav [orig., 1910]).

Tuell, Steven S.

1992 *The Law of the Temple in Ezekiel 40–48* (Harvard Semitic Monographs, 49; Atlanta, GA: Scholars Press).

Tufnell, Olga

1953 *The Iron Age* (Lachish [Tell ed Duweir], 3; London: Oxford University Press).

Tuplin, Christopher

1987a 'The Administration of the Achaemenid Empire', in *Coinage and Administration in the Athenian and Persian Empires* (ed. I. Carradice; British Archaeological Reports International Series, 343, Oxford: British Archaeological Reports): 109-66.

1987b 'Xenophon and the Garrisons of the Achaemenid Empire', *Archäologische Mitteilungen aus Iran* 20: 167-245.

Tur-Sinai, Naphtali H.

1938 *Lachish Letters* (Lachish [Tell ed Duweir], 1; London: Oxford University Press).

1987 *The Lachish Ostraca: Letters from the Time of Jeremiah* (Hebrew) (introduced and annotated by Shmuel Ahituv; Jerusalem: The Bialik Institute and the Israel Exploration Society).

Ulrich, Eugene

1992 '4QEzra–4Q117', in *Qumran Cave 4: XI, Psalms to Chronicles* (DJD, 16; Oxford: Clarendon Press): 291-93.

Ungnad, A.

1941 'Keilinschriftliche Beiträge zum Buch Esra und Ester', *ZAW* 57: 240-44.

Urie, D.M.L.

1948 'Officials of the Cult at Ugarit', *PEQ*, 80: 42-47.

1949 'Sacrifice among the West Semites', *PEQ*, 81: 67-82.

Ussishkin, David

1982 *The Conquest of Lachish by Sennacherib* (Tel Aviv: Tel Aviv University).

1993 'Lachish', in *NEAEHL* 3: 897-911.

1994 'Gate 1567 at Megiddo and the Seal of Shema, Servant of Jeroboam', in *Scripture and Other Artifacts: Essays on the Bible and Archaeology in Honor of Philip J. King* (ed. M.D. Coogan, J.C. Exum and L.E. Stager; Louisville, KY: John Knox Press): 410-28.

2004 *The Renewed Archaeological Excavations at Lachish (1973–1994)* (Emery and Claire Yass Publications in Archaeology; Tel Aviv: Tel Aviv University, Institute of Archaeology).

2006 'The Borders and *de facto* Size of Jerusalem in the Persian Period', in *Judah and the Judeans in the Persian Period* (ed. Oded Lipschits and Manfred Oeming; Winona Lake, IN: Eisenbrauns): 147-66.

Van Dam, Cornelis

1997 *The Urim and Thummim: A Means of Revelation in Ancient Israel* (Winona Lake: IN: Eisenbrauns).

Van de Mieroop, Marc

1997 *The Ancient Mesopotamian City* (Oxford: Clarendon Press).

1999 'The Government of an Ancient Mesopotamian City: What We Know and Why We Know So Little', in *Priests and Officials in the Ancient Near East* (ed. Kazuko Watanabe; Heidelberg: Universitatsverlag C. Winter): 139-61.

Van Seters, John

1972 'The Terms "Amorite" and "Hittite" in the Old Testament', *VT* 22: 64-81.

2003 'Review of S. Richter's *The Deuteronomic History and the Name Theology*', *JAOS* 123: 871-72.

Vanderhooft, David Stephen

1999 *The Neo-Babylonian Empire and Babylon in the Latter Prophets* (Harvard Semitic Museum Monographs, 59; Atlanta, GA: Scholars Press).

Vanderhooft, David S., and Wayne Horowitz
2002 'The Cuneiform Inscription from Tell en Nasbeh: The Demise of an Unknown King', *TA* 29: 318-27.
VanderKam, James C.
1991 'Jewish High Priests of the Persian Period: Is the List Complete?', in *Priesthood and Cult in Ancient Israel* (ed. G.A. Anderson and S.M. Olyan; JSOTSup, 125; Sheffield: Sheffield Academic Press): 67-91.
1992 'Ezra–Nehemiah or Ezra and Nehemiah?', in *Priests, Prophets and Scribes: Essays on the Formation and Heritage of Second Temple Judaism in Honour of Joseph Blenkinsopp* (ed. E. Ulrich, J.W. Wright and R.P. Carroll; JSOTSup; Sheffield: Sheffield Academic Press): 55-75.
2004 *From Joshua to Caiaphas: High Priests after the Exile* (Minneapolis, MN: Fortress Press).
Van Hoonacker, A.
1890 'Néhémie et Esdras, une nouvelle hypothèse sur la chronologie de l'époque de la restauration', *Muséon* 9: 151-84, 317-51, 389-400.
Vaux, Roland de
1937 'Les décrets de Cyrus et de Darius sur la reconstruction du temple', *RB* 46: 29-57.
Vittmann, Günter
1994 'Eine misslungene Dokumentenfalschung: Die "Stelen" des Peteese I (P. Ryl. 9, XXI-XXIII)', *EVO*, 17: 301-15.
1998 'Der demotische Papyrus Rylands 9, Teil 1 und 2', *Ägypten und Altes Testament* 38.
Waterman, Leroy
1954 'The Camouflaged Purge of Three Messianic Conspirators', *JNES* 13: 73-78.
Waters, Matt
2004 'Cyrus and the Achaemenids', *Iran* 42: 91-102.
Weinberg, Joel
1992 *The Citizen–Temple Community* (trans. D. Smith-Christopher; JSOTSup; Sheffield: JSOT Press).
Weisberg, David
1967 *Guild Structure and Political Allegiance in Early Achaemenid Mesopotamia* (New Haven, CT: Yale University Press).
Weiskopf, Michael
1989 'The So-Called "Great Satraps' Revolt" 366–360', *Historia: Einzelschriften* 63: 1-112.
Wellhausen, Julius
1957 *Prolegomena to the History of Ancient Israel* (New York: Meridian Books [orig., 1878]).
Wente, Edward F.
1995 'The Scribes of Ancient Egypt', in *Civilizations of the Ancient Near East* (ed. J.M. Sasson *et al.*; Peabody, MA: Hendrickson Publishers): 2211-21.
West, Stephanie
1985 'Herodotus' Epigraphical Interests', *Classical Quarterly* 35: 278-305.
Westbrook, Raymond
1985 'Biblical and Cuneiform Law Codes', *RB* 92: 247-64.
Westermann, Claus
1969 *Isaiah 40–66: A Commentary* (trans. David M.G. Stalker; Philadelphia, PA: Westminster Press).

Whitley, C.F.
1954 'The Term Seventy Years Captivity', *VT* 4: 60-72.
Wiesehöfer, Josef
2013 'Law and Religion in Achaemenid Iran', in *Law and Religion in the Eastern Mediterranean: From Antiquity to Early Islam* (ed. Anselm Hagedorn and Reinhard G. Kratz; Oxford: Oxford University Press): 41-57.
Williamson Hugh G.M.
1977 *Israel in the Books of Chronicles* (Cambridge: Cambridge University Press).
1983 'The Composition of Ezra i–vi', *JTS* NS 34: 1-30.
1985 *Ezra, Nehemiah* (Word Biblical Commentary, 16; Waco, TX: Word Books).
1987 'Clutching at Catchlines: Did the Author of Chronicles Also Write the Books of Ezra and Nehemiah?', *BR* 3: 56-59.
1994 *The Book Called Isaiah: Deutero-Isaiah's Role in Composition and Redaction* (Oxford: Oxford University Press).
2000 'The Family in Persian Period Judah: Some Textual Reflections', in *Symbiosis, Symbolism, and the Power of the Past: Canaan, Ancient Israel, and their Neighbors from the Late Bronze Age through Roman Palaestina* (ed. W.G. Dever and S. Gitin; Winona Lake, IN: Eisenbrauns): 469-85.
2004 *Studies in Persian Period History and Historiography* (Tübingen: Mohr Siebeck).
2008 'The Aramaic Documents in Ezra Revisited', *JTS* 59: 41-62.
Wilson, R.D.
1917 'The Title "King of Persia" in the Scriptures', *Princeton Theological Review* 15: 90-145.
Wisse, Jakob
1989 *Ethos and Pathos from Aristotle to Cicero* (Amsterdam: Hakkert).
Wright, C.J.H.
1992 'Family', in *Anchor Bible Dictionary: D–G* (ed. David Noel Freedman; ABD, 2; New York: Doubleday): 761-69.
Wright, Jacob L.
2004 *Rebuilding Identity: The Nehemiah-Memoir and its Earliest Readers* (BZAW, 348; Berlin: de Gruyter).
Wunsch, Cornelia, and Laurie Pearce
forthcoming *Judeans by the Waters of Babylon: New Historical Evidence in Cuneiform Sources from Rural Babylonia in the Schoyen Collection* (Babylonische Archive, 6; Dresden: ISLET).
Würthwein, E.
1936 *Der 'am ha'aretz im Alten Testament* (BWANT, 17; Stuttgart: Kohlhammer).
Wuttmann, M., *et al.*
1996 'Première rapport préliminaire des travaux sure le site de 'Ayn Manawir (oasis de Kharga)', *BIFAO* 96: 385-451.
1998 ''Ayn Manawir (oasis de Kharga)', *BIFAO* 98: 367-462.
2000 'The Qanats of 'Ayn-Manawir (Kharga Oasis, Egypt)', *JASR* 1: www.achemenet.com.
Yadin, Y., *et al.*
1961 *Hazor III–IV: An Account of the Third and Fourth Seasons of Excavations, 1957-1958: Plates* (Jerusalem: Hebrew University).
Yeivin, S.
1941 'Families and Parties in the Kingdom of Judah [Hebrew]', *Tarbiz* 12: 241-67.

1971 'The Benjamin Settlement in the Western Part of their Territory', *IEJ* 21: 141-54.

Younger, K. Lawson

1990 *Ancient Conquest Accounts: A Study in Ancient Near Eastern and Biblical History Writing* (JSOTSup, 98; Sheffield: Sheffield Academic Press).

2003 '"Give Us our Daily Bread": Everyday Life for the Israelite Deportees', in *Life and Culture in the Ancient Near East* (ed. Richard E. Averbeck, Mark W. Chavalas and David B. Weisberg; Bethesda, MD: CDL Press): 269-88.

Zadok, Ran

1979 *The Jews of Babylonia during the Chaldean and Achaemenian Periods according to the Babylonian Sources* (Haifa: University of Haifa Press).

1980 'Notes on the Biblical and Extra-Biblical Onomastica', *JQR* 71: 107-17.

1988 *The Pre-Hellenistic Israelite Anthroponomy and Prosopography* (Leuven: Uitgerverij Peeters).

2007 'Two Terms in Ezra', *Aramaic Studies* 5: 255-61.

Zertal, Adam

1990 'The Pahwah of Samaria (Northern Israel) during the Persian Period: Types of Settlement, Economy, History and New Discoveries', *Transeuphratène* 3: 9-30.

Zimmerli, Walther

1979 *Ezekiel I: A Commentary on the Book of the Prophet Ezekiel* (trans. Ronald Clements; Hermeneia; Philadelphia, PA: Fortress Press).

1983 *Ezekiel II: A Commentary on the Book of the Prophet Ezekiel* (trans. James Martin; Hermeneia; Philadelphia: Fortress Press).

Zorn, J.R., J. Yellin, and J. Hayes

1994 'The M(W)SH Stamp Impressions and the Neo-Babylonian Period', *IEJ* 44: 161-83.

Zunz, Leopold

1832 '*Dibre hajamim* oder die Bücher der Chronik', in *Die gottesdienstliche Vorträge der Juden: historisch entwickelt* (ed. Leopold Zunz; Berlin: N. Brüll, rev. edn, 1892): 13-36.

Index of References

Index of Authors

CPSIA information can be obtained
at www.ICGtesting.com
Printed in the USA
BVHW04s0008140818
524344BV00002B/5/P

9 781910 928264